AI Game Programming
Wisdom 4

Edited by
Steve Rabin

Charles River Media

A part of Course Technology, Cengage Learning

COURSE TECHNOLOGY
CENGAGE Learning™

Australia • Brazil • Japan • Korea • Mexico • Singapore • Spain • United Kingdom • United States

COURSE TECHNOLOGY
CENGAGE Learning™

Publisher and General Manager, Course Technology PTR: Stacy L. Hiquet

Associate Director of Marketing: Sarah Panella

Manager of Editorial Services: Heather Talbot

Marketing Manager: Jordan Casey

Acquisitions Editor: Heather Hurley

Project Editor: Dan Foster, Scribe Tribe

CRM Editorial Services Coordinator: Jennifer Blaney

Copy Editor: Julie McNamee

Interior Layout Tech: Judith Littlefield

Cover Designer: Mike Tanamachi

CD-ROM Producer: Brandon Penticuff

Indexer: Broccoli Information Management

Proofreader: Mike Beady

For product information and technology assistance, contact us at
Cengage Learning Customer & Sales Support, 1-800-354-9706

For permission to use material from this text or product,
submit all requests online at **cengage.com/permissions**
Further permissions questions can be emailed to
permissionrequest@cengage.com

Library of Congress Control Number: 2007939369
ISBN-13: 978-1-58450-523-5
ISBN-10: 1-58450-523-0

Course Technology
25 Thomson Place
Boston, MA 02210
USA

Cengage Learning is a leading provider of customized learning solutions with office locations around the globe, including Singapore, the United Kingdom, Australia, Mexico, Brazil, and Japan. Locate your local office at: **international.cengage.com/region**

Cengage Learning products are represented in Canada by Nelson Education, Ltd.

For your lifelong learning solutions, visit **courseptr.com**
Visit our corporate website at **cengage.com**

Printed in the United States of America
1 2 3 4 5 6 7 11 10 09 08

Contents

Preface

Welcome to the fourth, all-new volume of *AI Game Programming Wisdom*! Innovation in the field of game AI continues to impress as this volume presents more than 50 new articles describing techniques, algorithms, and architectures for use in commercial game development.

When I started this series over six years ago, I felt there was a strong need for AI game programmers to share their advances and expertise with each other. What I didn't anticipate is how successful this series would be. At nearly 250 articles across all four volumes, I'm extremely impressed with the generosity of these authors in sharing their valuable ideas, innovative algorithms, and source code with others. When each person contributes a little, we all benefit greatly.

This volume is indebted to the hard work of the five section editors who managed the authors and directed the content of each section. The section editors were instrumental in the creation of this book, offering tremendous help and guidance to each author. This provided specialized expertise for each section and introduced diverse viewpoints during article selection. The following is a list of the section editors and the areas that they managed:

Neil Kirby: Section 1: *General Wisdom*, and Section 6: *Scripting and Dialogue*
Steven Woodcock: Section 2: *Movement and Pathfinding*
Ryan Houlette: Section 3: *Architecture*
Kevin Dill: Section 4: *Tactics and Planning*, and Section 5: *Genre Specific*
John Manslow: Section 7: *Learning and Adaptation*

Refining the Basics

An important trend in game AI over the last couple years has been to hone and deepen the core elements that define game AI, such as movement and agent architecture. In retrospect, this is to be expected as core technologies are the ones that get the real work done and pay the bills. They are concrete in terms of observation, in the case of movement, and measurable in terms of agent flexibility and developer productivity, in the case of architecture. While not as sexy as learning algorithms, improvements in movement and architecture have tangible payoffs that contribute greatly to the perceived intelligence of agents. As a result, over half of the articles in this volume relate to movement and architecture.

In the area of movement, two very interesting advances have taken place. The first is realistic agent, squad, and vehicle movement, as exemplified by *Company of Heroes* with their coordinated squad movement and vehicles that are capable of making three-point turns. The second advance is the ability of agents to deal with dynamically changing terrain, which is a very hot topic at the moment since many games now feature destructible terrain. Several of the articles in this volume address the issue of changing terrain.

In the area of architecture, we're seeing further exploration of planning as a core architecture with four articles in this book, which is more than in any previous volume. Other interesting refinements of architectures include goal-based, subsumption, and, of course, finite state machines.

What Happened to Learning?

For the past six years, learning algorithms have consistently been on the cutting-edge, ready to leap out and make a big impact on game AI. Unfortunately, it hasn't quite materialized. In order to explain this, I'll make a few observations. First, agents in most games usually don't live long enough to ever benefit from learning, so for many games learning isn't that useful. Second, since learning is something that happens over time, it's difficult for players to perceive that agents or opponents are learning, so the benefits are extremely subjective and unclear. Third, learning requires a great deal of trial and error and tuning, so if the benefits are difficult to quantify, then the risk and time investment is consequently more difficult to justify.

This is not to say that learning isn't vastly interesting and could be instrumental to certain games, but for the majority of games it isn't on the radar and might not make an impact. That said, I think there are many games that could benefit from simple statistical learning in the form of player modeling. Player modeling is the simple concept in which a model of the player's behavior is constructed from observations over time. As the statistical observations start showing player preferences and idiosyncrasies, the AI can exploit this information to make the game either easier or harder. Player modeling is simple, easy to implement, and can be leveraged by many games. If learning is to make a real and meaningful impact on games, I believe it will come from player modeling.

Looking Forward

In our desire to look forward toward the future, many interesting topics arise that are explored in this volume. Subjects include multi-processor architectures, planning architectures, Bayesian networks, conversational AI, reinforcement learning, and player modeling. Each of these show great promise and offer the possibility of new game AI experiences. It's certainly very exciting to imagine how planning, reasoning about uncertainty, adapting to the player, and communicating more conversationally can take games to the next level.

Contributing to Future Volumes

If you would like to contribute an article for the next volume of *AI Game Programming Wisdom*, send an e-mail to steve.rabin@gmail.com. We are always on the lookout for great ideas and unique material that can appear in future volumes. It is my sincere hope that you can participate in this series and share your wisdom with the game AI community.

AIWisdom.com and IntroGameDev.com

For over five years, aiwisdom.com has been an important resource for locating AI articles that appeared in the *AI Game Programming Wisdom* series, the *Game Programming Gems* series, and other resources. The Web site aiwisdom.com indexes over 300 game AI articles and lets you quickly find articles on any game AI topic.

Over the last couple of years, *introgamedev.com* has been the equivalent of aiwisdom. com, but covering all of game development. The Web site *introgamedev.com* indexes over 1300 articles that appeared in compilation books, such as the *Game Programming Gems* series, covering areas such as general programming, mathematics, AI, graphics, physics, networking, production, game design, and the business of games. Take a look around and find out what you may have been missing!

About the Cover Images

The four images on the cover are from the award-winning game *Company of Heroes*. Chris Jurney, who worked as an AI programmer on *Company of Heroes*, has contributed two wonderful articles on squad formations and vehicle movement to this volume.

Real-time strategy (RTS) games, like *Company of Heroes*, are some of the most challenging to build in terms of AI, exemplifying what this book is about. RTS games feature individual AI agents, squad-level AI managers, and grand-scale strategy AI. Even more impressive are the extreme conditions in which the game AI must run, such as large maps, destructible terrain, hundreds or thousands of units, and many types of units (individuals, vehicles, aircraft, and watercraft). The AI must plan, build and manage resources, and coordinate strategy and attacks. All in all, architecting RTS AI is extremely challenging and offers many opportunities to innovate.

Acknowledgments

I would like to thank the nearly 70 authors who contributed to this book, helping make this series one of the most influential in the field of game AI. Each author's generosity in sharing their knowledge, wisdom, and hard work will surely have a profound impact on the game development community.

In addition to the authors, there were five section editors who were responsible for selecting articles, guiding their composition, and honing each article to deliver reliable and trustworthy information. Their contributions were critical in raising the bar and maintaining the quality of this series. I'd like to thank Kevin Dill, Ryan Houlette, Neil Kirby, John Manslow, and Steven Woodcock.

Turning these articles into a book wouldn't be possible without the expertise of the publisher, Charles River Media, a part of Cengage Learning. I would like to thank Emi Smith, Heather Hurley, and Jennifer Blaney at Charles River Media for their continued guidance and support of this series, as well as the entire team for helping deliver such a high- quality book.

Finally, I want to thank my family for their continued support—my wife Leslie and my children Aaron and Allison; my parents, Diane Rabin and Barry Rabin; and my in-laws, James and Shirley Stirling.

About the Contributors

Bradley G. Anderegg
bradanderegg@gmail.com

Bradley is an engineer at Alion Science and Technology and has been working closely with the open source Delta3D game and simulation engine for more than two years now. Brad was the AI programmer for the critically acclaimed Source mod "Eclipse," which was a runner-up for the IGF Source Mod of the Year in 2006. He earned a masters certificate in digital game design from the Guildhall at Southern Methodist University in 2005 and earned a B.S. in computer science from the University of Oregon in 2002.

Ramon Axelrod
mushroomramon@yahoo.com

As a cofounder of the Majorem studio, Ramon led the development of *Ballerium*, one of the first MMORTS titles. In this role, he dealt extensively with the problems raised by distributed AI, including planning with partial information, effective use of the processing power of client machines, and the constraints imposed by limited bandwidth. Prior to Majorem, he worked for several years in the field of military operations research. He holds a B.S. in mathematics and physics and is today the CTO of AIseek, a company specializing in AI acceleration.

Sander Bakkes
s.bakkes@micc.unimaas.nl

Sander Bakkes received his bachelor's degree in computer science in 2001 and his master's degree in computer science in 2003. In his master thesis, he discussed a novel approach to team AI for video games. To the present day, he continues to work on research in game AI as a Ph.D. student. His current research concerns adaptive AI for RTS games.

Jessica D. Bayliss
jdb@it.rit.edu

Jessica Bayliss is an assistant professor in the Information Technology department at the Rochester Institute of Technology where she is actively involved in both a B.S. and M.S. degree in game design and development. Jessica maintains a keen interest in artificial intelligence for computer game development. She co-led the "Art of Munging AI" roundtable at GDC in 2006. Whereas Jessica's dissertation developed a brain-computer interface that used virtual reality to demonstrate online control of a simple

3D apartment, Jessica has since become involved in the scholarship of teaching. She is the founder of the Reality and Programming Together (RAPT) program, which serves to attract students to computing by teaching games as an application area overlaid onto traditional introductory programming course curricula.

Igor Borovikov
igor.borovikov@gmail.com

Igor Borovikov graduated from the Moscow Institute for Physics and Technology (MIPT) with an M.S. in physics and a Ph.D. in mathematics. After graduation, Igor worked as a senior researcher on a space telecommunication project at the Institute of Microelectronics in Zelenograd, Moscow. In 1993, Igor joined AnimaTek Intl. and became one of the leads of World Builder, an innovative 3D modeling and rendering application for creating photorealistic natural environments. In 2001, Igor changed careers to work on PS2 games and joined the company 3DO. In 2002, he started at SCEA in Foster City. As a senior programmer at SCEA, he contributed to several game systems on *Rise to Honor*. Currently, he holds the position of lead scientist and works on advanced graphics and AI applications at FrameFree Technologies.

Vadim Bulitko
bulitko@ualberta.ca

Vadim Bulitko received his Ph.D. in computer science from the University of Illinois at Urbana-Champaign in 1999 and is presently a faculty member at the University of Alberta. He has been working on real-time heuristic search and decision making under uncertainty since 1996. Some of his academic interests include real-time heuristic search, online and supervised machine learning, and player modeling in real-time computer games. You can visit his Web site at *www.cs.ualberta.ca/~bulitko/*.

Michael Buro
mburo@cs.ualberta.ca

Michael Buro is an associate professor for computing science at the University of Alberta in Edmonton, Canada. He earned his Ph.D. in 1994 from the University of Paderborn in Germany where he studied selective search and machine learning techniques for improving AI systems for two-player games. The result was an Othello-playing program that defeated the human world champion 6-0 in 1997. He is currently conducting research in real-time AI applied to RTS games and sampling-based search for imperfect information games. Professor Buro also organizes the annual RTS game AI competition, which is based on his free RTS game engine ORTS.

Roberta Catizone
R.Catizone@dcs.shef.ac.uk

Roberta Catizone is a research fellow at the University Sheffield where she has worked with the Natural Language Processing Group in the Computer Science department since 1994, following research positions at the Computing Research Lab in New Mexico, the University of Pittsburgh Learning Research and Development Center, and the Institut Dalle Molle in Geneva, Switzerland, where she did research on Natural Language Tutorial systems, a multilingual concordance system, and a content-based text alignment system. She has worked on four European Union Fourth, Fifth, and Sixth framework projects funded by the Information Society and Technology (IST) sector, including the ECRAN Information Extraction (IE) project (1995–1998) and the NAMIC IE and authoring project (1998–2001). Her most recent work in building dialog systems includes being the Sheffield team leader of the multimodal dialog project COMIC (2002–2005) and the Sheffield research team leader of the Companions project, which is a large-scale multimodal dialog project focusing on intelligent personalized multimodal interfaces to the Internet. She also played a key part in the development of the CONVERSE program, which won the Loebner competition judged for being the most realistic conversationalist in 1997.

David Hernández Cerpa
david.hernandez.cerpa@gmail.com

David is currently a senior AI Programmer at Pyro Studios where he is working in an unannounced next-gen project. Previously, he was a senior AI programmer at Enigma Software Productions for almost two years where he implemented several AI systems for the game *War Leaders: Clash of Nations*. Before joining the game industry, he was an AI researcher at the University of Las Palmas de Gran Canaria, where he worked on his Ph.D., which is focused on artificial emotional systems. His paper *BDIE: A BDI-Like Architecture with Emotional Capabilities* was published in the proceedings of the AAAI 2004 spring symposium held at Stanford University. His main research interest focuses on new AI architectures and their applications to games while taking into account performance and engineering restrictions.

Alex J. Champandard
alexjc@AiGameDev.com

Alex J. Champandard has worked in the entertainment industry as an AI programmer for many years, most recently for Rockstar Games. With a strong academic background in artificial intelligence, he also authored the book *AI Game Development: Synthetic Creatures with Learning and Reactive Behaviors* and often speaks about his research—most notably at the Game Developers Conference. Currently, Alex is a freelance consultant for games companies in central Europe, helping developers integrate state-of-the-art techniques into commercial games. He maintains open source AI engines at *http://AiGameDev.com*, where he also publishes tutorials for game programmers.

Christian J. Darken
cjdarken@nps.edu

Christian is currently an associate professor of computer science at the Naval Postgraduate School in Monterey, California, where he collaborates intensively with the MOVES Institute. He was previously a project manager at Siemens Corporate Research in Princeton, New Jersey, and was on the programming team of what was perhaps the first 3D massively multiplayer online game, *Meridian 59*. He received his Ph.D. in electrical engineering from Yale University in 1993.

Doug Demyen
doug.demyen@gmail.com

Doug Demyen is a programmer for BioWare/Pandemic Studios at BioWare's Edmonton location where he works on both tools and game code for next-generation titles. He earned a B.S. High Honors in computer science from the University of Regina in Regina, Saskatchewan, and an M.S. in computing science from the University of Alberta in Edmonton, Alberta, for the research on which this article was based.

Kevin Dill
kdill4@gmail.com

Kevin graduated from Carleton College with a B.A. in computer science in 1992. After some soul searching (and some job searching, neither of which went horribly well), he decided to join the Army. He spent the next four years in the infantry—first toting a machine gun and later flipping PowerPoint slides and correcting grammatical errors for his superiors in military headquarters (where life was considerably less exciting but also considerably less muddy).

Upon his release, he decided that he was going to pursue his dream of making computer games for a living... but first, he went back to school. He attended the University of Pittsburgh, where he studied subjects such as real-time systems, networking, simulations, and AI. He quickly fell in love with AI, so he transferred to Northwestern University where he could concentrate on his primary interests: believable agents and computer games. Two years later, after completing his master's degree, he finally did what his mother had hoped for all along and got a real job.

That was in 2001. In the subsequent six years, Kevin has worked for three companies on five published titles, ranging from strategy games to animal simulations. He is currently working for Blue Fang Games, helping to develop the next-generation AI for its highly successful *Zoo* games.

In his copious free time, Kevin teaches classes at Harvard Extension School, serves on the organizational committee for the AI and Interactive Digital Entertainment conference (*www.aiide.org*), and is a section editor for the book you now hold in your hands, *AI Game Programming Wisdom 4*.

Darren Doherty

darren.doherty@nuigalway.ie

Darren Doherty is a Ph.D. research candidate in NUI, Galway. He is currently researching techniques for the evolution of team behaviors. He has published papers on his work in the national AI conference, international genetic and evolutionary computation conference (GECCO), and international computer games conference (C-GAMES) where he was awarded a best-paper prize. He holds a first-class honors degree in IT. His research interests include evolutionary computation, artificial intelligence, and computer game development.

Alistair Doulin

alistair@doolwind.com

Alistair Doulin is a senior programmer at Auran Games where he creates games for Xbox 360 and PC. His second game, *Battlestar Galactica,* has just been released on Xbox Live Arcade and PC. Before Auran, Alistair worked as a business applications programmer while at the university. He works primarily as a gameplay programmer with a special interest in AI and graphics. When not at work, he spends most of his time working on his personal project *Combat Information Centre* and writing articles for his game development blog (*doolwind.com*). Alistair earned a Bachelor of Information Technology (Software Engineering) degree with distinction from the Queensland University of Technology.

Benjamin Ellinger

benjamin.ellinger@microsoft.com

Benjamin Ellinger is a Program Manager at Microsoft, working with Carbonated Games. He writes game development kits, helps creates casual games, and writes some AI code every now and then. He also teaches the Junior game project class at the DigiPen Institute of Technology. Before Microsoft, Benjamin was a programmer and game designer working on titles such as *This Means War!, Dawn of War, Ultima Online, Ashen Empires, The Matrix Online,* and *Bicycle® Texas Hold'em.* Long ago, he broke in to the game industry at Steve Jackson Games, working on board games such as *Car Wars* and role-playing games such as *GURPS.* Strangely enough, Benjamin has a B.S. in Kinesiology (specializing in weight training) from the University of Texas. He also claims to be the strongest game designer in the world.

Julien Hamaide

julien.hamaide@gmail.com

Julien started programming a text game on his Commodore 64 at the age of 8. His first assembly programs would follow soon after. He has always been self-taught, reading all of the books his parents were able to buy. He graduated 4 years ago as a multimedia electrical engineer at the Faculté Polytechnique de Mons (Belgium) at the age of 21.

After two years working on speech and image processing at TCTS/Multitel, he is now working on next-generation consoles at 10Tacle Studios Belgium/Elsewhere Entertainment as lead programmer. Julien has contributed several articles to the *Game Programming Gems* series.

David Hamm
trianglegamer@gmail.com

David Hamm is a senior software engineer at Red Storm Entertainment, where he has contributed to PC and console releases for 10 years. His recent work has focused on extensible AI systems, including character pathfinding, tactical planning, and remote debugging. David has also developed four generations of scripting systems for Red Storm games. Since 2000, he has focused on the *Tom Clancy's Ghost Recon* line of tactical shooters. In addition to AI and scripting, David has extensive experience and interest in game engine architecture and tools. He holds a B.S. in computer science from Harvey Mudd College.

Chad Hinkle
hinks85@gmail.com

Chad graduated from DigiPen Institute of Technology, majoring in real-time interactive simulation and minoring in mathematics. Using a background in both customer service and software development, Chad is always trying to improve games to help the players have a more enjoyable experience. He is currently working at Nintendo of America.

Ryan Houlette
houlette@gmail.com

Ryan is a senior engineer at Stottler Henke, an AI software consulting firm, where he has spent the past 10 years working on a variety of commercial and government AI applications ranging from automated planning to data mining to intelligent tutoring systems. He is the architect of Stottler Henke's SimBionic® game AI middleware product. His research interests include AI engines for games and simulations, visual authoring environments, and interactive narrative systems. He holds an M.S. in AI from Stanford. In his free time, he enjoys performing and recording music, hiking, reading, and also playing board games and computer games.

Devin Hyde
devinhyde@gmail.com

Devin Hyde completed his B.S. in computer science (Honors) in 2006 at the University of Saskatchewan. His undergraduate thesis involved researching Bayesian networks, fuzzy logic, and the Dempster-Schafer theory to reason about uncertainty in video games. He is currently employed as a systems analyst for the Western Canada Lottery Corporation.

Chris Jurney
jurney@gmail.com

Chris Jurney is a senior programmer at Kaos Studios, where he works on AI for console and PC games. Before Kaos, Chris worked on real-time strategy games at Relic, and on weapon simulators, slot machines, and online worlds at various companies in Atlanta. He has spoken at the Game Developer's Conference, GDC China, and local IGDA chapter meetings. Chris has a B.S. in computer science from the Georgia Institute of Technology where he specialized in AI.

Aleksey Kadukin
akadukin@gmail.com

Aleksey Kadukin is a software engineer at The Sims Division of Electronic Arts Inc., where he designs and develops tools and technologies for *The Sims* game projects. Before joining Electronic Arts, Aleksey worked as a software engineer at Sony Computer Entertainment America, Press Start, and AnimaTek. He contributed to titles such as *The Sims 2 Pets*, *The Sims 2 Glamour Life Stuff*, *The Sims 2 Sampler: Create-A-Sim* for PC, and *Jet Li: Rise to Honor* for PS2. Aleksey earned an M.S. in computer science from Moscow State University.

John D. Kelly
wackonian@aol.com

John is a Lieutenant in the U.S. Navy and a recent recipient of a master's degree in modeling and simulation from the MOVES Institute of the Naval Postgraduate School in Monterey, California.

Neil Kirby
nak@alcatel-lucent.com

Neil Kirby is a member of the technical staff at Bell Laboratories, the R&D arm of Alcatel-Lucent. His assignments have included architecture consulting, tool development for CMMI certification, and the development of speech recognition systems. He has contributed articles to *The Bell Labs Technical Journal* and to the *AI Game Programming Wisdom* series of books. He has spoken at the Game Developers Conference and has numerous papers published in the conference proceedings. He cohosts the AI Roundtables at GDC as well as the AI Programmers Dinners. Neil is the chapter coordinator of the IGDA Columbus, Ohio, chapter and a member of the IGDA Foundation board of directors. Neil earned a B.S. in electrical engineering and an M.S. in computer science from Ohio State University. He is a guest speaker for the OSU Fundamentals of Engineering Honors program and a judge for their annual robot competition.

Philipp Kolhoff
pkolhoff@kingart.de

Philipp Kolhoff graduated in 2007 from the Media Informatics study program of Hochschule Bremen, University of Applied Sciences. Philipp is a software developer at the game studio KING Art based in Bremen, Germany. Currently, he is working on a turn-based strategy game called *Battle Worlds: Kronos*, which will be released this summer, and he is also contributing to two upcoming titles. Philipp presented a short paper at Eurographics 2005 and a full paper at SIBGRAPI 2006.

Dr. Brett Laming
brett@tilda.plus.com

Dr. Brett Laming is now a programmer for Rockstar Leeds, where he continues to search for the beauty inherent in simple AI. A B.S. in cognitive science and Ph.D. in computational neuroscience now seem a distant memory, as do many of the earlier tribulations of AI programming. He has now had the pleasure of working on *Independence War 2, Powerdrome, Burnout: Revenge,* and *GTA: Vice City Stories,* and in doing so has worked alongside some of the UK's best talent.

He continues to reside in Sheffield where he frustrates his partner, Katherine, by having the same hobby as his work. He has, at least for the moment, given up on the idea of a Web site, as it has been in construction so long, the URL has lapsed.

Marc Lanctot
lanctot@cs.ualberta.ca

Marc Lanctot is a Ph.D. candidate in the Computing Science department at the University of Alberta. He earned both a B.S. (Honors) with a minor degree in mathematics and an M.S. in computer science at McGill University in Montreal, Quebec. His previous work has focused on locally adaptive virtual environments, behavior learning, and dynamic waypoint repositioning from collected player data in persistent-state multiplayer games.

Nachi Lau
nachilau@hotmail.com

Nachi Lau has been in the video game industry since 2002. He obtained a B.S. in computer science from Simon Fraser University, Canada. Presently, he is a senior AI software engineer with LucasArts. Some of his past video game projects include *Shrek 3, X-Men 3, True Crime 2, Iron Man,* and *SoccerZ*. He started his game development adventure after winning the international Online Game Open Source Code Design Competition in Taiwan for re-implementing an MMO title. His favorite video game genre is role-playing games, which is also the main focus of his career.

Stephen M. Lee-Urban
sml3@Lehigh.edu

Mr. Stephen Lee-Urban is currently a fourth-year computer science Ph.D. student at Lehigh University studying artificial intelligence under his advisor, Dr. Muñoz-Avila. His research on AI in games includes the use of plan generation and repair, reinforcement learning, transfer learning, and ontology-based case retrieval.

Habib Loew
habibloew@gmail.com

Habib Loew has worked as a system administrator, security engineer, and Web developer, but the best job he's ever had is as a game programmer. Habib is a graduate of DigiPen Institute of Technology, where he earned a B.S. in real-time interactive simulation. He has spoken at the Pacific Northwest Numerical Analysis Seminar, the University of Washington, and to just about anybody else who will listen about the intersection of mathematics and game development. He currently works at ArenaNet.

Jörn Loviscach
jlovisca@informatik.hs-bremen.de

Jörn Loviscach has been a professor of computer graphics, animation, and simulation at Hochschule Bremen, University of Applied Sciences since 2000. A physicist by education, he turned to journalism after finishing his doctoral degree. He covered media-related software at several computer magazines, ending up as deputy editor-in-chief of *c't* computer magazine, Hanover, Germany. Since his return to academia, Jörn has contributed to *GPU Gems, Shader X3, Shader X5,* and *Game Programming Gems 6.* In addition, he is the author and coauthor of numerous academic works on computer graphics and on techniques for human-computer interaction presented at international conferences, such as Eurographics and SIGGRAPH.

John Manslow
john@jmanslow.fsnet.co.uk

John Manslow has a Ph.D. in AI from one of the UK's top-ranked research universities and has spent nearly 15 years applying his expertise in fields as diverse as credit and fraud risk analytics, commodity trading systems, and computer games. He occasionally lectures in game AI and is a regular contributor to, and section editor of, the *AI Game Programming Wisdom* series of books. His primary interest lies in real-time learning and the ways in which it can be applied in games.

Paul Marden
pmarden@digipen.edu

Paul Marden is currently a junior at the DigiPen Institute of Technology in his third year in the real-time interactive simulation program. He recently finished an internship at 3M in St. Paul, MN.

Dave Mark
dave@IntrinsicAlgorithm.com

Dave Mark is the president and lead designer of Intrinsic Algorithm, LLC, an independent game development studio and AI consulting company in Omaha, Nebraska. He has been programming since 1984 when he was in high school. Much to the dismay of his teacher, he wrote his first text adventure on the school's DEC PDP-11/44. After a brief detour in the music business as a composer/arranger, keyboard player, and recording engineer during the early 1990s, he reentered the technology arena in 1995. He worked in a variety of capacities, including network design and rollout, Web design, and world-wide e-mail systems, before turning to business database application design and programming for Fortune 500 companies. After being in the IT consulting and development world for eight years, Dave left to start Intrinsic Algorithm, LLC, with his wife, Laurie. As a side project, he also combined a passion for football (the one with touchdowns) and an addiction to statistics by designing an NFL statistical analysis and prediction system that was released as a subscription service on the Internet from 2002 through 2004.

Colt "MainRoach" McAnlis
duhroach@gmail.com

Colt "MainRoach" McAnlis is a graphics programmer at Microsoft Ensemble Studios where he researches new rendering techniques and algorithms. Before Ensemble, Colt worked as a graphics programmer at TKO Software and a programming intern at Petroglyph Games. He is also an adjunct professor at SMU's Guildhall school of game development where he teaches advanced rendering and mathematics courses. After receiving an advanced degree from the Advanced Technologies Academy in Las Vegas Nevada, Colt earned his B.S. in computer science from Texas Christian University.

Michelle McPartland
michelle@itee.uq.edu.au

Michelle is undertaking a Ph.D. at the University of Queensland and concurrently working for Bohemia Interactive Australia (BIA) as a programmer. Her research is focused on learning techniques in FPSs. Prior to commencing her Ph.D., Michelle completed a Bachelor of Information Technology (Honors) where she specialized in genetic algorithms and neural networks.

Manish Mehta
mehtama1@cc.gatech.edu

Manish Mehta is a Ph.D. student at the College of Computing at the Georgia Institute of Technology. He worked full time on a project aiming to demonstrate universal natural interactive access (in particular for children and adolescents) by developing natural, fun, and experientially rich communication between humans and embodied historical and literary characters from the fairy tale universe of Hans Christian Andersen. He has also been involved in developing an augmented reality version of a desktop-based game called *Façade*. *Façade* is an AI-based art/research experiment that is attempting to create a fully realized one-act interactive drama. *Augmented Reality Façade* moves this interactive narrative from the screen into the physical world. The player wears a video see-through display allowing the virtual characters, Trip and Grace, to inhabit the physical room with them. More details about his work can be obtained at *www.cc.gatech.edu/~mehtama1*.

Héctor Muñoz-Avila
hem4@Lehigh.edu

Dr. Héctor Muñoz-Avila is an assistant professor at the Department of Computer Science and Engineering at Lehigh University. Prior to joining Lehigh, Dr. Muñoz-Avila did post-doctoral studies at the Naval Research Laboratory and the University of Maryland at College Park. He received his Ph.D. from the University of Kaiserslautern (Germany). Dr. Muñoz-Avila has done extensive research on case-based reasoning, planning, and machine learning, having written more than 10 journal papers and more than 30 refereed conference/workshop papers on the subject. Two of these papers received awards. He is also interested in advancing game AI with AI techniques. He has been chair, program committee member, and a reviewer for various international scientific meetings. He will be program co-chair of the Sixth International Conference on Case-Based Reasoning (ICCBR-05) to be held in Chicago, Illinois.

Colm O'Riordan
colm.oriordan@nuigalway.ie

Colm O'Riordan lectures in the IT department in NUI, Galway. His main research interests are in the domain of AI (including evolutionary computation, artificial life, evolutionary game theory, and multi-agent systems). He has authored more than 80 papers in peer-reviewed conferences and journals.

Julio Obelleiro
julio.obelleiro@gmail.com

Julio Obelleiro has been a senior AI programmer at Pyro Studios and Enigma Software Productions where he has designed and developed several AI architectures for a next-gen unannounced title and the strategy game *War Leaders: Clash of Nations*.

Before moving to the games industry, Julio was professor and researcher at different labs, including Human Computer Technology Lab and Computational Neuroscience Institute, both at Autonoma University in Madrid; and Interactive Technology Group at Pompeu Fabra University in Barcelona. He is interested in the research of new AI techniques, new ways of human-computer interaction, and computer vision techniques applied to games and interactive digital art installations. He has run computer vision workshops at MediaLabMadrid, where he collaborated in the development of projects such as Play the Magic Torch (*www.playthemagic.com*).

Per-Magnus Olsson
perol@ida.liu.se

Per-Magnus Olsson is a Ph.D. student at the Division of Artificial Intelligence and Integrated Computer Systems, Department of Computer Science, Linköping University, Sweden. Before becoming a Ph.D. student, he was an artificial intelligence programmer at Massive Entertainment where he worked on the real-time strategy game *Ground Control 2* released in 2004, as well as on concepts for future games. After that, he did consulting in the defense industry, mostly working with decision support for fighter aircraft. Currently, he is involved in applied artificial intelligence in several areas, including unmanned aerial vehicles as well as simulators and games. He encourages comments and discussion about the article and artificial intelligence in general. Per-Magnus earned a B.S. in computer engineering from the University of California Irvine and an M.S. in computer science and engineering from Linköping University.

Santi Ontanon
santi@cc.gatech.edu

Santi Ontanon is a post-doctorate researcher at the College of Computing in the Georgia Institute of Technology. His Ph.D. thesis focused on case-based reasoning techniques applied to multi-agent systems. His main research goal is to enhance the case-based reasoning paradigm so that it can deal with real tasks, such as computer games. His current research involves the application of case-based reasoning techniques to computer games, in particular strategy games and interactive adventures, in order to provide computer games AI with adaptive capabilities. More details about his work can be obtained at *www.cc.gatech.edu/~santi*.

Curtis Onuczko
onuczko@cs.ualberta.ca

Curtis Onuczko has an M.S. from the Department of Computing Science at the University of Alberta. His research interests are in plot generation using generative design patterns in computer role-playing games. He works for BioWare.

Ferns Paanakker
ferns.paanakker@gmail.com

Ferns Paanakker is lead programmer at Wishbone Games B.V. Previous to founding the company, he worked in logistical optimization for more than a decade where he designed and implemented systems such as large-scale planning, user interfaces, and GIS. Most of his implementations are heavily influenced by AI techniques such as evolutionary algorithms, expert systems, and pathfinding.

Wishbone Games B.V. creates computer games for both PC and consoles and additionally performs game AI consultancy services. Ferns earned his M.S. in artificial intelligence from the University of Amsterdam. He is now pursuing his Ph.D., creating innovative AI techniques to solve difficult optimization problems.

Borut Pfeifer
borut_p@yahoo.com

Borut Pfeifer is an AI engineer at Electronic Arts Los Angeles. He has worked on AI and gameplay for games such as *Scarface: The World Is Yours* (PS2, Xbox, PC) and *Untold Legends: Dark Kingdom* (PS3). He has also taught in the game design program at the Vancouver Film School and has published various articles on game development in the *Game Programming Gems* series, Gamasutra, and elsewhere. Borut graduated from Georgia Tech in 1998 with a B.S. in computer science. His blog, The Plush Apocalypse (*www.plushapocalypse.com/borut*), discusses the development of games that combine entertainment with deeper social themes.

Hugo Pinto
hugo@hugopinto.net

Hugo Pinto is an artificial intelligence engineer specializing in computational linguistics and interactive entertainment. Currently he works as a research associate at the University of Sheffield (UK), where he investigates dialog in the context of artificial human companions and computer games. He acts as a developer lead and architect to his team.

His research and work has spanned natural language processing and text mining (financial, military, and biomedical domains), cognitive architectures (Webmind and Novamente), computer games, multi-agent systems, and machine learning. He developed commercial AI applications in diverse international teams, associated to companies such as Webmind, Vetta Tech, and Novamente LLC. He also worked for a brief time on the integration of legacy systems in the public sector.

Parallel to his research and consulting jobs, he pursues a Ph.D. at the University of Sheffield, where he researches the application of dialog technologies to games. He received his M.S. in computer science from Universidade Federal do Rio Grande do Sul in 2005, defending a thesis on real-time planning, personality modeling, and computer games. In 2001, he received a B.S. in computer science from Universidade Federal de Minas Gerais, with a monograph on cognitive architectures.

David Pittman
david.pittman@gmail.com

David Pittman is currently a programmer at Stormfront Studios, working on an unannounced project. He previously developed AI tools at Gearbox Software for *Brothers in Arms: Hell's Highway*. His lifelong passion for game development began at the age of 6, when he learned to write games in BASIC on his parent' computer. He received a B.S. in computer science from the University of Nebraska-Lincoln and subsequently attended The Guildhall at Southern Methodist University in Dallas, Texas. There, David nurtured a growing interest in game AI programming and helped make history by being among the first 24 students to receive a master's degree in video game development. When he is not working, David enjoys playing games, researching new technologies, and entertaining delusions of rock stardom.

Frank Puig Placeres
fpuig@fpuig.cjb.net

Frank Puig Placeres is the leader of the Virtual Reality Project at the University of Informatics Sciences, located in Cuba. He developed the CAOSS Engine and CAOSS Studio, which have been used to create games such as *Knowledge Land* and *Turning Points*. He has been a contributor to *Game Programming Gems 5*, *Game Programming Gems 6*, and *ShaderX5*. He has also spoken at the GameOn 2006 conference as well as at the Cuban Virtual Reality Congress. Frank has also worked as a software engineer at SolStar Games, where he researched modern engine architectures, graphic rendering, and artificial intelligence simulations.

Marc Ponsen
m.ponsen@micc.unimaas.nl

Marc Ponsen is a Ph.D. student at the computer science department of Maastricht University, The Netherlands. His research interests include machine learning and, in particular, reinforcement learning. Current research focuses on scaling reinforcement learning algorithms to complex environments, such as computer games. He coauthored several refereed conference papers, workshop papers, and international journal papers on these subjects.

Steve Rabin
steve.rabin@gmail.com

Steve is a principal software engineer at Nintendo of America, where he researches new techniques for Nintendo's next-generation systems, develops tools, and supports Nintendo developers. Before Nintendo, Steve worked primarily as an AI engineer at several Seattle startups, including Gas Powered Games, WizBang Software Productions, and Surreal Software. He managed and edited the *AI Game Programming Wisdom* series of books and the book *Introduction to Game Development*, and has over a dozen articles published in the *Game Programming Gems* series. He's spoken at the Game Developers Conference and moderates the AI roundtables. Steve teaches artificial intelligence at both the University of Washington Extension and at the DigiPen Institute of Technology. He earned a B.S. in computer engineering and an M.S. in computer science, both from the University of Washington. Finally, Steve maintains a Web site that catalogs more than 1,000 game development articles at *www.introgamedev.com*.

Ashwin Ram
ashwin@cc.gatech.edu

Professor Ashwin Ram is a recognized leader in introspective learning and case-based reasoning, two of the key aspects of this proposal. In his earlier work, he developed a novel approach to self-adaptation in which introspective analysis of reasoning traces was used to determine learning goals (similar to behavior modification goals in this proposal), and planning was used to carry out the modifications. This work was well received and published in major journals (including *Artificial Intelligence* and *Cognitive Science*) in addition to serving as a framework for an MIT Press book *Goal-Driven Learning*. More details about his publications can be obtained at *www.cc.gatech.edu/faculty/ashwin*.

John W. Ratcliff
jratcliff@infiniplex.net

John W. Ratcliff is a long-time game industry veteran, starting with Electronic Arts in the mid-1980s where he worked as an independent artist. John's Electronic Arts titles include the original *688 Attack Sub*, *SSN-21 Seawolf*, and *S.C.A.R.A.B.* John also contributed technology to many other Electronic Arts titles. After leaving Electronic Arts, John was the lead client programmer for *Cyberstrike 2*, published by 989 Studios, when he worked for Simutronics Corporation. In 2000, John established the St. Louis office of Sony Online Entertainment (then Verant Interactive) and built a team to create the world's first massively multiplayer online shooter called *Planetside*. After *Planetside*, John went on to work for Ageia Technologies to assist in the development of tools, technology, and demos for physics middleware. Recently, in 2007, John rejoined Simutronics Corporation to work on their MMO game engine *Hero Engine*. In addition to John's professional work, he has been active in releasing source code into the public domain as well as publishing magazine articles and book chapters.

Adam Russell
chronotopia@gmail.com

Adam recently returned from the front lines of commercial game development to take a position as lecturer in computer game programming at the University of Derby. This move follows two years as a senior programmer at Eurocom Entertainment, one of Europe's largest independent developers, where Adam led AI development for an unannounced next-generation project. Prior to that, he spent three years working at Lionhead Studios, where he played a pivotal role in the AI design for Microsoft's XBox RPG *Fable*. Adam holds a master's degree in evolutionary and adaptive systems from the University of Sussex, but his first education was studying philosophy and psychology at Oxford University.

Frantisek Sailer
sailer@cs.ualberta.ca

Frantisek Sailer is an M.S. student in the computing science department at the University of Alberta. He earned his B.S. (Honors) in computer science at the University of Manitoba. Before he entered the graduate program, he worked as lead AI programmer for Complex Games in Winnipeg, Canada, concentrating on automated pathfinding in 3D worlds without the use of manual waypoint placement. Currently he works on real-time strategy game AI. His thesis work on real-time planning in RTS games—on which this article is based—was presented at CIG 2007.

Raúl Sampedro
rghoul@gmail.com

Raúl Sampedro started as AI and gameplay programmer in July 2005 for previous Enigma Software Productions projects, and joined *War Leaders: Clash of Nations* game a few months later, working with gameplay, AI, and tools. He has been working as senior AI programmer for Silicon Garage Arts' *The Shadow of Aten* project and has recently joined Pyro Studios to work on a new exciting project. He is also researching AI learning techniques applied to turn-based strategy games as the final project for his master's degree.

Jonathan Schaeffer
jonathan@cs.ualberta.ca

Jonathan Schaeffer is a professor in the Department of Computing Science at the University of Alberta. His research interests are in artificial intelligence and parallel and distributed computing. He is best known for his work on computer games, and he created the checkers program *Chinook*, which was the first program to win a human world championship in any game. He has a Ph.D. in computing science from the University of Waterloo.

Andrew Slasinski
ExtraStanlo@gmail.com

Andrew Slasinski is currently an intern working at Microsoft Robotics Initiative, where he works on a 3D simulation environment used as a test bed for robotics. He earned a B.S. in real-time interactive simulation from DigiPen Institute of Technology, and specializes in 3D graphics.

Forrest Smith
fsmith@gaspowered.com

Forrest Smith graduated with a bachelor's in real-time interactive simulation from the DigiPen Institute of Technology in the Spring of 2007. He is currently working as a software engineer at Gas Powered Games.

Megan Smith
mev2@Lehigh.edu

Mrs. Megan Smith completed work on *RETALIATE* as part of her master's thesis, which coincided with her employment as a developer at Travel Impressions. She received her B.S. in computer science in 2005 and her M.S. in computer science in 2007 from Lehigh University, working with Dr. Héctor Muñoz-Avila on various projects involving computer games and reinforcement learning. She continues to work as a developer at Travel Impressions.

Marcia Spetch
mspetch@ualberta.ca

Marcia Spetch is a researcher and faculty member in the Department of Psychology at the University of Alberta. Focusing on comparative cognition, Marcia investigates the cognitive aspects of fundamentally important human and animal behaviors, such as locating and remembering important places, and recognizing important objects. Some of her research interests include comparative studies of learning, memory and cognition, including spatial memory and navigation, avian visual cognition, and object recognition. Visit her Web site at *www.psych.ualberta.ca/~mspetch/spetchm.htm*.

Pieter Spronck
p.spronck@micc.unimaas.nl

Pieter Spronck received his Ph.D. in computer science in May 2005. His thesis was titled "Adaptive Game AI." It discusses how machine-learning techniques can be used to allow game opponents to adapt to gameplay experiences. One of the major requirements of the techniques he researched was that they should be applicable by game developers in state-of-the-art games. He coauthored about 50 scientific articles for international conferences and journals, half of which are on machine learning and game AI. He is currently employed as assistant professor at the computer science department of Maastricht University, The Netherlands.

James Stewart
jms@jmstewart.net

James's first exposure to the games industry was an internship at Gearbox Software, where he worked on *Brothers-In-Arms: Hell's Highway*. In March 2007, he received a master's degree in interactive technology from the Guildhall at Southern Methodist

University. James is currently an associate programmer at Stormfront Studios in San Rafael, California. His home page can be found at *http://jmstewart.net.*

Nathan Sturtevant
nathanst@gmail.com

Nathan Sturtevant is a postdoctoral researcher for the University of Alberta in Edmonton, Alberta, where he does research on search algorithms for single-player, two-player, and multiplayer games. He has authored more than a dozen scientific articles in these areas and has taught courses on similar topics. Nathan received his B.S. in electrical engineering and computer science from UC Berkeley and his master's and Ph.D. in computer science from UCLA. Nathan spent his college years writing the popular Macintosh shareware game *Dome Wars.*

Duane Szafron
duane@cs.ualberta.ca

Duane Szafron is a professor in the Department of Computing Science at the University of Alberta. His research interests are in using programming languages, tools, and environments to integrate artificial intelligence in computer games. He has a Ph.D. in applied mathematics from the University of Waterloo.

David Thue
davidthue@gmail.com

David Thue is currently a second year master's student in computing science at the University of Alberta, and received his B.S. in computer science with High Honors from the University of Regina in 2005. He created the PaSSAGE project in the Summer of 2006 to serve as a basis for his M.S. thesis. His primary research interests include interactive storytelling, player modeling, dynamic gameplay alteration, and level-of-detail AI. Secondary interests include natural language generation, graphics, animation, and audio. Visit his Web site at *www.cs.ualberta.ca/~dthue/.*

Erik van der Pluijm
erik.van.der.pluijm@gmail.com

Erik van der Pluijm works for a large game company in The Netherlands. The past four years, he has worked on several projects for both PC and consoles. He is currently completing his B.S. in artificial intelligence at the University of Amsterdam in The Netherlands.

Terry Wellmann
terry.wellmann@high-voltage.com

Terry Wellmann has been programming computers since 1983 and has been developing games professionally for over 10 years at High-Voltage Software, Inc. He was responsible for architecting and writing the AI as well as leading the overall development effort for Microsoft's *NBA Inside Drive* franchise on the PC and Xbox. In addition to his work on basketball, Terry was the lead programmer on *All-Star Baseball 2001* for the N64 and *Charlie and the Chocolate Factory* for the Xbox, PS2, and GameCube. He holds a computer science degree from Purdue University. In the summer, you can find him playing baseball in a Chicago-area amateur league and working in his garden. In the fall, you will find him lurking around the marshes of Minnesota hunting ducks or helping out on the family farm, and in the winter, you can try to catch him on one of Wisconsin's vast network of snowmobile trails.

Baylor Wetzel
baylorw@yahoo.com

Baylor Wetzel is an instructor at Brown College's Game Design and Development program, where he is the lead instructor for artificial intelligence. For the two decades prior to Brown, Baylor held almost every computer job imaginable, from help desk to architect to entrepreneur. He occasionally speaks at conferences, has been a member of the International Game Developer Association's Artificial Intelligence Interface Standards Committee, and runs the Web site *PracticalGameAI.com*.

Daniel Wilhelm
dan@dkwilhelm.net

Daniel Wilhelm is a Ph.D. student in computation and neural systems at the California Institute of Technology. He has interdisciplinary interests in AI, neurobiology, psychology, and computer science. A self-taught programmer, Daniel's passion for computer game development has continually motivated him to learn and extend his programming knowledge. He holds a B.S. in computer engineering from Purdue University, and he is a contributor to the open source Fast Artificial Neural Network (FANN) library.

Steven Woodcock
ferretman@gameai.com

Steven Woodcock's background in game AI comes from over 20 years of ballistic missile defense work building massive real-time war games and simulators. He has worked on a variety of arcade- and PC-based games and irregularly maintains a Web page dedicated to the subject of game AI at *www.gameai.com*. He is also the author of various papers and magazine articles on the subject and has been proud to have both contributed to and been technical editor for several books in the field, including the *Game Programming Gems* and *AI Game Programming Wisdom* series. Steve lives in the mountains of Colorado with the lovely Colleen, an indeterminate number of pet ferrets, and a basenji that hates squirrels with a passion.

Fabio Zambetta
fabio@cs.rmit.edu.au

Fabio Zambetta is a lecturer at the School of Computer Science and Information Technology (RMIT University) where he teaches games programming, games modding, and computer graphics. His research interests revolve around interactive storytelling, online virtual worlds, and game AI, and he is particularly keen on multi-disciplinary projects involving diverse areas of computer science and art. Fabio has published some 30 papers in conference proceedings, journals, and book chapters on topics such as facial animation, intelligent agents, embodied conversational agents, and interactive storytelling in games. He devotes his little spare time to programming and modding games, and he is currently busy with his *Neverwinter Nights 2* module project, *The Two Families*. Fabio earned an M.S. and a Ph.D. in computer science, both from the University of Bari (Italy).

GENERAL WISDOM

1.1

Situationist Game AI

Adam Russell

chronotopia@gmail.com

This article examines the tension in game content production between the systematic reduction of specific cases to general rules and the deliberate construction of unique player experiences. Market and design trends are pushing games toward hybrid styles that combine these two approaches. However, most work in contemporary game AI is committed to strongly autonomous game agents and, as such, remains too closely tied to the reduction of specific cases to general rules. A quick review of related themes in sociology and psychology sets up the last part of the article, exploring the notion of what we call a *situationist* game AI that is capable of meeting this hybrid challenge.

Reductionism Versus Constructivism in Game Content

During the production of game content, one section of a game level might require a highly custom set piece interaction with a group of NPCs (non-player characters). Most likely, a level designer has authored this content for the purposes of advancing the game's story, rather than being created directly by an AI programmer. The authoring might be achieved by describing this scene to the general AI within its universal representations—for example, by increasing alertness levels, enabling stealth mode, or applying a faction change so that the player will become perceived as an enemy. Alternatively, the level designer might choose to temporarily disable and replace the NPCs' autonomous AI. The NPCs could be forced into playing back a scripted sequence of specific animations. However, neither of these approaches is completely satisfactory— we are forced to choose between a loss of either a unique story moment on the one hand or a loss of consistent game mechanics on the other.

The example choice described previously is symptomatic of a recurring design question in engineering the behavior of game agents. Time and again, game AI developers are faced with this kind of choice. In this article, we refer to this as a choice between the *reductionist* approach and the *constructivist* approach, as summarized in Table 1.1.1.

Table 1.1.1   Key Characteristics of Reductionist and Constructivist Approaches

	Reductionist	Constructivist
Types	Few types of entity	Lots of types of entity
Instances	Many repeated instances	Few occurrences of each type
Rules	General rules	Specific rules
Control	Local control	Global control

In a reductionist approach, the game world is populated by many repeated instances of a small set of types, for example, unit types in an RTS, building zones in a tycoon sim, or soldier types in a squad-based shooter. These types are governed by rules with very general application, which form a great part of what is normally called "the game mechanics," such as general rules about unit movement rates, supply requirements, health and armor, damage and ammo, and so on. However, although these rules have great generality and often dictate behavior across the entire game, the *locus of control* required to apply the rules is extremely local. The system does not need to know the current state of other units or the player's progress through the current story mission in order to apply attrition damage to a building under siege. The rule can be applied by looking at a very small part of the whole simulation, often just the unit in question, its immediate location, and perhaps one other unit that it is paired up with in a local interaction.

By contrast, a constructivist approach to the production of game content results in a game world that is populated by lots of different types of entities, with few occurrences of each type. Many of the types will be tailored to a particular section of the game. There might even only be one instance of a certain type in the game, for example, a boss monster with unique combat AI and a custom animation rig playing hand-animated motion sequences that are only seen in that one encounter. The rules governing these numerous types of entity are likely to be highly specific because they were defined for the particular scenario where that particular custom-made type appears and performs its specific function. These entities are rarely completely bound by the general rules that determine the behavior of units in a reductionist approach. Finally, note that although the rules applying to these constructed entities and scenarios are extremely specific to those contexts, the *locus of control* required to apply the rules is typically highly global. The choreography of the particular scene where our hypothetical boss monster appears is a carefully scripted interplay between every aspect of the game, from camera, sound, and music, to the behavior and incidental speech of every member of the player's squad, everything must be tightly coordinated together to achieve the desired dramatic effect.

Strengths and Weaknesses of the Two Approaches

Of course, the opposing approaches outlined previously are rarely pursued in isolation. There will almost always be a little of both styles in any game project. The question is how much of each, and how do they interact? Can we say that one is better for games than the other? Unsurprisingly, in practice, both approaches have strengths and weaknesses and must be assessed relative to the context of a particular game project, as summarized in Table 1.1.2.

Table 1.1.2 Strengths and Weaknesses of Reductionist and Constructivist Approaches

	Reductionist	Constructivist
Strengths	Good scalability	Supports narrative
	Supports player creativity	Allows cinematic presentation
	Suggests open-endedness	Promotes richness
Weaknesses	Tends to homogenize	Poor scalability
	Hard to control	Limits replayability

A reductionist approach has various powerful strengths that make it very attractive. First and foremost is that it scales extremely well. After a small number of types are working, and the rules that control them are ticking away, it is pretty easy to manufacture large amounts of content. To take an extreme example, when David Braben and Ian Bell presented an early version of the legendary space sim *Elite* to their publisher Acornsoft, they boasted that the game could deliver nearly *three hundred thousand billion* different galaxies for the player to explore, thanks to each one being entirely procedurally generated from a single 48-bit seed! Wisely, Acornsoft insisted that the game limit itself to only eight hand-picked galaxies from the billions available to make them feel more deliberately constructed [Spufford03]. A rather more pertinent strength in today's game design climate is that reductionist approaches are good at supporting player creativity. As Harvey Smith so persuasively argued after his experiences designing on Ion Storm's *Deus Ex*, the application of consistent general rules creates the prospect of players inventing strategies the designers had not envisaged, and the exploration of the large and consistent space of possibilities created by the rules is empowering for players [Smith02]. Also, this quality of emergent gameplay creates a strong suggestion of open-endedness to players, a sense that they could keep playing around in the sandbox almost indefinitely and still come up with new ideas.

Despite that, the dreams of bottom-up emergence associated with reductionist approaches are typically disappointing in practice. After a while, playing around with the same pieces subject to the same rules, the game can start to feel a bit repetitive. There is a general tendency among heavily reductionist games toward homogeneity of content. Although each land in Peter Molyneux's seminal god-game *Populous* was a unique terrain configuration and a unique starting point for the player and his opponent, at the end of the day, every land presented the same elements in different arrangements. Once developed, the same optimal strategies could be used again and again with the same success. Much less visible to the players but of great concern to the developers is that reductionist approaches can be hard for the designers to control.

Generally this issue arises when a heavily reductionist game needs to include an element of constructivism, which, as you will see shortly, is very likely to occur.

The constructivist approach has contrasting strengths and weaknesses. Its greatest advantage over simulation is that it supports the delivery of narrative. As argued passionately by members of Joseph Bates' now-defunct Oz project at Carnegie Mellon University, both engaging drama and believable characters can only be achieved through construction of unique variations and highly specific traits [Mateas97]. Character-driven dramas do not *explicitly* strive toward the communication of universal rules and the reduction of all circumstances to instances of generic types, even though they might well employ such techniques in their development. On a related and more specific theme, the constructivist approach supports the developer in achieving a cinematic presentation of game content. To plan out the camerawork in a scene, the cinematics specialists on a development team need to know that the scene is likely to take place, what happens in the scene, where the player will arrive in the space, the positions and behavior of other protagonists/antagonists in the scene, and so on. This goes hand in hand with the earlier example of the boss monster encounter, a classic case where even heavily reductionist action games will resort to constructivism. Overall, the constructivist approach promotes richness in game content because individual areas or characters can have highly tailored work done on them to make them unique and memorable.

The downsides of constructivism should be well known to any game developer. The need to hand craft all this unique content results in very poor scalability. For example, who has not heard someone say, "if you want another 8 hours of gameplay, we are going to need another 30 content creators on the team or another 9 months of development." This is a clear sign of a heavily constructivist game. An additional 9 months of development on a reductionist title might give the rule set that extra depth and balance providing 50% greater longevity to the existing world content. This might lead players to stick with the *same* content for another 8 hours of nonlinear interaction. But on a strongly constructivist title, a linear model of content production is usually allied to a linear narrative and an overall player experience of "working through" the various different bits of content the developers have set up for them. Intimately related to this issue is that constructivist approaches tend to limit the replayability of game content. Although reductionist approaches tend to homogenize the elements encountered, they also promote variation on repeated playthroughs of the same content. Constructivist game content, on the other hand, promotes the delivery of unique experiences across different sections of a single playthrough but tends to limit variation across repeated playthroughs of the same section because each unique experience is always the same.

The Drive Toward a Hybrid Approach

If every game could focus on one of these approaches to the exclusion of the other, life would be a lot simpler for the development team. Each design could play to the strengths of the content style, playing down the accompanying weaknesses by a wise choice of subject matter. However, there are many indications that this kind of project is no longer a viable economic proposition in today's marketplace. Certainly this is true for triple-A titles on the latest generation of consoles.

The first indication of a general trend toward hybrid approaches that mix strong reductionism with strong constructivism is an overall erosion of extremes at both ends of the spectrum. Even previous extremely reductionist simulation games are now trying to provide more authored structures for their players to work through. For example, consider the addition of "wants and fears" to *The Sims 2*, which help the player work their Sims through little micro-narratives that are built on top of the general rules of basic desire satisfaction. At the other extreme, there seems little room in today's marketplace for almost exclusively constructivist game content such as found in the traditional point-and-click adventure genre. Those adventure games that survive have had to make concessions to a reductionist style of content, for example, the addition of "stealth" mechanics to sections of Revolution's *Broken Sword 3*.

Another fairly recent force behind this trend is the huge influence of the *Grand Theft Auto* franchise, also known as "the GTA bandwagon." The massive success in 2001 of Rockstar North's third title in the series cast a five-year long shadow over the rest of triple-A game development. This sometimes produced the feeling that every other title under the sun, whatever its fundamental genre, was trying to offer a *sandbox gameworld* combined with *nonlinear mission-based narratives*. This has pushed both players and developers toward a jack-of-all-trades attitude, where individual titles are expected to cover a broad range of gameplay styles in one package. Developers are then forced to employ a mixture of both reductionism and constructivism to produce the content.

Last but not least, and this goes hand in hand with the GTA bandwagon, is the trend in marketing and PR blurbs that make statements such as "become the hero in a cinematic action adventure" *alongside* statements such as "immerse yourself in a fully interactive world." These statements sound great, but what do they really mean for developers? Making players feel like a movie hero requires a heavy dose of constructivism, but helping players to immerse themselves in a world of interactivity requires a significant degree of reductionism. Only reductionist simulations can give players that sense of a complete world, a closed loop, and a lack of artificial boundaries. The result is that many of today's front-of-house blockbuster games have settled on what we might almost call a new game genre, the *cinematic action-adventure RPG*. Games of this type cross many previously well-defined genre boundaries and fuse disparate elements together in a new blend of design styles that demand an impressive mixture of constructivism and reductionism from the developers.

The Failure of Reductionism in Game AI

As touched on at the beginning of this article, most of the work that is viewed as "progressive" by the game AI community (and most of the material collected in this volume) involves increasing the individual self-sufficiency of game agents in one way or another. Whether it be by adding a search-based planner to action selection, enforcing sensory honesty in game world representation, or catering for dynamic physics objects in the pathfinding system, the general interest amongst AI developers tends to be toward models with greater depth, realism, and cognitive sophistication *in themselves*, without reference to the rest of the game content. In the simplest instance of this view of game AI, imagine that you just had one type of entity (a game NPC) that had sufficiently deep and complex general rules (a cognitive model), and then the designers could just drop a bunch of these NPCs into the game world and they would be interesting to interact with. This emphasis on strong autonomy in game AI is a particularly advanced and complex form of reductionism.

However, as was argued in the previous section, a purely reductionist style cannot be the answer to the challenges of today's hybrid game styles. Players expect more and more realism, interactivity, and consistency in game agents, but they also expect more and more tightly authored dramatic experiences at the same time. This puts game AI developers in a very difficult position. Of course, all games that include some degree of autonomous AI behavior along with some amount of narrative content (i.e., most games in today's market) are already confronting this issue and coming up with some kind of solution. The problem is that most of these solutions are actually avoiding the issue.

The most common response is simply to keep the two aspects as far apart as possible, with heavily reductionist gameplay leading to carefully constructed but entirely noninteractive cutscenes, followed by more reductionist gameplay. This is often better disguised by using a successive alternation in styles of game space, where some contain heavy emphasis on reductionism, and others contain a heavy emphasis on constructivism, with each type of space very light on the other approach to content. This solution was used to great effect in the original *Half Life 2*, where combat zones would be interrupted by story sections that involved carefully choreographed character interactions but no combat, such as the checkpoints on the train out of City 17.

The biggest problem with this kind of simple separation is that if the designers ever want the *same characters* to appear in the reductionist environments and in the constructivist environments, it becomes very difficult to ensure consistency between whatever state the "reduced" characters might be in and the state they are shown to be in during the constructed content. *Grand Theft Auto 3* solved this issue by allowing cutscenes to take place in the game world as long as they only involve simple visual changes such as the vehicle driven, weapons held, and so on, and by keeping all of the mission-delivering story characters confined to cutscenes that take place outside the game world, such as Donald Love's rooftop apartment. The only exception is in-game appearances in missions that concluded with the story character's death.

The Need for a Situationist Perspective

If developers are to meet the challenge of hybrid game content head-on, rather than just coming up with various ways of working around it, they must reconsider commitments to both strongly autonomous agents and to tightly preconceived narrative experiences. Game AI developers helping to deliver hybrid content should *not* be asking "Is this agent interesting if I play with it in an empty test level?" but rather "Can we make seamless transitions between scripted and unscripted behavior? Can we choreograph richly interactive scenes? Can the AI coordinate its actions with those of other agents?"

This change of emphasis calls into question much of the application of work in the academic AI field to our own work in game AI. Academic theories and techniques had no connection to choreography and story-level orchestration of behavior, so why should their cognitive models be relevant to generating that kind of behavior? In fact, the whole program of cognitive science that underpins most work in academic AI is founded on a reductionist approach. To meet the challenge, we must search for perspectives on behavior that are different from those found in the academic AI field. We need to find new ways of thinking about our game characters so that they are reconceived from the ground up, not primarily to function as autonomous individuals. Instead, they should function under an organizing principle that can potentially span the entire game world at any given state in the narrative. Somehow, we must allow for both the creative player expression and the sense of open-endedness that reductionism supports, and for the accompanying scalability, consistency, and potential for reuse that reductionist content can provide.

Through a quick cross-disciplinary review covering related themes in sociology and psychology, you will see how these other fields have encountered similar problems with reductionist ways of thinking and how certain thinkers in those fields have already laid paths toward an admission of constructivist elements into the theoretical framework. This review will help frame the concluding discussion of examples of hybrid approaches to building agent behaviors in current game AI.

Situationism in Sociology

As it turns out, sociologists have been wrestling with a very similar problem to this reductionist/constructivist dilemma for almost as long as their field has existed. One of the fundamental debates in sociological theory regards whether the structure of society should be viewed as the voluntary creation of a collaboration of free-willed individual subjects, or whether the apparently free choices made by each individual member of society should be viewed as primarily determined by the existing structures of the society in which they exist. This is known as the "agency/structure" debate, and it has several parallels with our own. It is also sometimes known among sociologists as the "individualism/holism" debate, highlighting the parallels with our tension between global and local control.

Sociologists who see agency as the primary force in society argue that the individual's wants precede the society that he helps to create. Each individual is viewed as freely making the same choice every day to keep maintaining his society. As such, all subjects are essentially the same wherever in the world and even whenever in history they happen to find themselves. The subjects could always potentially choose to reconstruct their society along different lines that might be found in another time or place. This is analogous to the reductionist approach with its homogenizing tendency to reduce all characters to some general model and its highly local locus of control.

Those in the opposing camp see structure as the primary force in society. They argue that the existing social structure precedes the individual subjects who are constructed within it. Thus society is maintained because the hopes and fears of each subject *implicitly conform* to the overall values of the society at large. As a result, every individual is a unique product of the time and place in which they were brought up. This is analogous to a constructivist approach with its profusion of different types with small numbers of instances of each, its support for truly unique content, its promotion of richness and diversity, and its highly global locus of control.

Bourdieu's Habitus

The French sociologist Pierre Bourdieu built a "middle way" in the agency/structure debate by arguing that society constructs individual agents to the extent that they inhabit a system of dispositions toward certain forms of practice. He employed the term *habitus* to refer to this system, emphasizing the many wordless and everyday aspects of human social behavior that in many cases elude conscious awareness, such as styles of dress, patterns of speech, accents, posture, and so on. We might say to an extent that the *habitus* is the agent's "way of being" or "way of seeing" in the social world. Crucially, the fundamental role played by this *habitus* in structuring the minutiae of everyday behavior is not meant to imply that social agents are subjected to any kind of closed *rule* that limits their capacity for free creative action. Instead, Bourdieu insisted that the system of dispositions forms a *generative framework* within which agents are free to act.

Situationism in Psychology

The young field of psychology was dominated for a time in the 1940s by B.F. Skinner's radical behaviorism, which rejected the existence of internal mental states. However, this was an almost contradictory position for a field whose aim was to study minds, and it could not last. The solution to this tension was found through analogy with the very new field of computer science in the 1950s, which had developed its vocabulary beyond the study of mere circuitry, valves, and logic gates and now spoke confidently of the existence of *data* and *programs* inside the machine. These that had no physical substance but all agreed were entirely proper subjects of scientific enquiry. The information processing analogy viewed the brain as the hardware, mental processes as the software, sensory stimulation as the inputs, and observable human behavior as the outputs. This gave psychologists an escape route from radical behaviorism and made it possible to admit internal mental states back into experimental science.

However, although it legitimized the experimental study of internal mental processes, the information processing view only did so under several crucial assumptions. The first assumption was that mental processes could be broken up into independent modular components (programs) and that these modules interacted by passing information. This information was assumed to be separable into constituent tokens that could be stored independently of the processes that manipulated them (data). As a result of these assumptions, the sensory processes (inputs) were conceived as being only very indirectly related to the separate motor control processes (outputs) of the system. The function of sensory processes was confined to the construction of internal mental representations of the external environment, so that these tokenized representations could then be stored and manipulated by the independent mental processes. These assumptions can be summarized philosophically as *cognitivism*.

These assumptions in both cognitive psychology and in its sister discipline of classical AI have come under increasing assault over the past 20 years. Game AI has flirted in recent years with certain aspects of the *nouvelle* AI that resulted from this debate. However, there has been little awareness or acceptance in that field of the general failure of cognitivism as a principled approach to the generation of character behavior. If anything, the arrival of another console generation with further increased levels of visual fidelity in character models and the accompanying vogue for realistic game settings has given game AI a renewed appetite for old-fashioned cognitivism in our attempts to control these complex physical simulations of characters, despite the ever-growing emphasis on constructivism in level design.

Varela's Enactivism

The 1980s saw a growing alternative to cognitivism led by the Chilean biologist and philosopher Francisco Varela in what he called the *enactivist* perspective. This approach, also sometimes referred to as *embodied cognitive science*, takes particular issue with the cognitivists' assumed independence of sensory and motor tasks. Varela and others were aware of a growing body of evidence demonstrating the essential role of motor control in the development of perceptual skills and in the resolution of sensory ambiguities. This led to the fundamental claim that both sensory and motor processes could only be understood in the light of closed-loop *sensory-motor coordinations*. Putting it another way, these theorists claimed that there was no such thing as perception or action in themselves, but only *enactions*, which are fully embodied coordination tasks such as walking or grasping.

Situationism in Game AI

Looking back over key responses to the strongly reductionist views in both psychology and sociology, we can recognize a few overall themes. Sensory processes are not task-neutral. Bodily motion is highly contextual. Local behavior is subject to multiple simultaneous organizing principles that are not intrinsic to the agent in question.

These principles are what we call *situations*. An approach that takes all of these themes seriously is called a *situationist* game AI.

Contextual Animation

The situationist theme with the most immediate relevance to the challenges of controlling characters on the latest generation of consoles is the demand that all bodily actions be fully situated in the context that they take place. This means going beyond the traditional approach to interactive character animation, which is only "contextual" to the extent of attempting to choose the right time at which to play the appropriate predefined or canned movement. In the animation of a strongly situated character, there should be no such thing as "the walk cycle," "the lever pull," or "the ladder climb," but instead only "this walk here," "pulling this lever," and "climbing this ladder," with every unique action motion being situated in a unique combination of dynamic features, such as the exact position of the interaction object, the entry speed and posture of the agent, the emotional and physical state of the character, and so on.

One of the most readily achievable forms of contextual animation is Rose's verb-adverb approach [Rose98], in which a set of prototypical examples of one particular motion verb (e.g., waving) are scored offline against multiple adverbial parameters (e.g., energy and height of the waving), and then unique instances of the verb motion are generated at runtime by weighted blending of the example motion clips (e.g., a low energetic wave). This verb-adverb motion model was the basis of the highly influential c4 architecture presented by MIT's synthetic characters group at the GDC in 2001 [Burke01, Downie01].

Useful though they are, adverbial models remain tied to a library of offline motion clips, which severely limits their potential to deliver strongly situated character motions. Far more ambitious are approaches that attempt true motion generation, such as Ken Perlin's Improv [Perlin96] and more recently the solutions provided by Torsten Reil's company NaturalMotion. It remains to be seen how far these techniques can take us, and worth noting that each motion generator has to be painstakingly constructed/trained for the performance of a specific preconceived motor task (e.g., putting hands out to break a fall). The key feature of these methods for this discussion is that although the task is preconceived, the particular implementation of the motion is highly situational.

Ecological Perception

The next promising area for our proposed shift toward a situationist model is one that has already seen a lot of interest in recent years under various different banners, which we refer to collectively as *ecological perception* in honor of its theoretical heritage in the work of J. J. Gibson [Gibson79]. These approaches are of particular interest in this discussion because they transcend two of the most basic reductionist assumptions. The first assumption is that agents' sensory representations are task-neutral descriptions of their objective physical environment, which could potentially be passed between any number of independent internal processes. The second assumption is that agents carry around their own self-contained behaviors (e.g., patrolling, searching, attacking, idling), which they attempt to apply to whatever world they find themselves in.

Any method of constructing task-dependent spatial representations at runtime can be described as a form of *dynamic terrain analysis*. The most common instance of this in current game AI is on-the-fly identification of spatial locations for the application of combat tactics, for example, by selecting from a list of potential positions using a task-dependent evaluation function [vanderSterren01] or by iterating some kind of finite-element domain model to a steady state to identify semantically significant features, such as zero-point crossings, a technique better known as influence mapping [Tozour01, Woodcock02].

Another increasingly common form of ecological perception found in today's game AI is the movement of specific task knowledge out of the agents and into entities found in the environment, also known as the *smart objects* or *smart terrain* approach. Will Wright's monumentally successful franchise *The Sims* is by far the best-known example of this strategy, although it has roots in earlier academic models of synthetic characters [Kallmann99]. A slight generalization of smart object approach is the general use of semantic annotations in the game environment, such as social ownership relations [Orkin04], task-specific grouping of positions [Butcher02], or embedded narrative [Doyle98].

For a much more in-depth discussion of the conceptual motivations and practical applications of ecological perception in game AI, refer to the article "Turning Spaces into Places" in this same volume [Russell08].

Situation Layering

Perhaps the greatest technical challenge in our proposed shift toward situationist game AI is the demand to stop separating behaviors into mutually exclusive agent states and instead provide support for layering and parallelism of action. Being *able* to play multiple simultaneous animations on one skeleton, such as running and aiming at the same time, is only the beginning of answering this challenge. The real complexity comes when the AI must consider *what* multiple animations to play and *when* to play them. Most implementations of parallel action in games to date have depended on assumptions of orthogonality between the separate tasks, but this is not enough. What is really needed are better models of adaptive coordination between *conflicting* situations, such as aiming a gun while opening a door, or performing full-body conversation animations while navigating through an environment.

This problem becomes even more acute when considering situations that span multiple agents. How do we coordinate all the interdependent body motions in a sophisticated performance of a multicharacter conversation while each agent might simultaneously be involved in any number of parallel situations, such as controlling a vehicle or moving to catch a projectile? Although most games tackle these problems to some extent, there is surprisingly little published discussion of formal models of action layering and concurrency in game AI.

Turning to academic models, a number of useful precedents might be fruitfully employed in constructing a situationist game AI. As is becoming common in game AI, Cremer's HCSM framework employed hierarchical finite state machines, but it also supported concurrent state activation and competition over conflicting demands for limited resources [Cremer95]. Possibly the most sophisticated example of parallel action sequencing on a single character model has been Lamarche and Donikian's HPTS framework, which includes a priority system and resource annotations on the nodes of concurrent state machines to enable intelligent adaptation of parallel tasks. This was demonstrated in their example of an agent drinking coffee and smoking a cigarette while reading a newspaper [Lamarche01]. If this formalism could be extended to multiagent coordination, then it would be an incredibly powerful general framework for authoring game situations, allowing designers to script specific scenes while still providing a space for the enforcement of general rules about character behavior.

Conclusion

Contemporary game AI needs to relax its commitment to autonomous game agents. The notion of a "situationist" game AI can help to organize the behavior of agents in collaboration with their narrative environment. Through recognizing situationism as a distinct design style in game AI architectures, we can learn to distinguish it from simple scripting approaches and build on its strengths.

References

[Burke01] Burke, Robert, et al., "Creature-Smarts: The Art and Architecture of a Virtual Brain." *Proceedings of the Game Developers Conference*, (2001): pp. 147–166.

[Butcher02] Butcher, Chris and Jaime Griesemer, "The Illusion of Intelligence." *Proceedings of the Game Developers Conference*, (2002), available online at http://halo.bungie.org/misc/gdc.2002.haloai/talk.html?page=1.

[Cremer95] Cremer, James, Joseph Kearney, and Yiannis Papelis, "HCSM: A Framework for Behavior and Scenario Control in Virtual Environments." *ACM Transactions on Modeling and Computer Simulation*, Vol. 5, no.3, (July 1995): pp. 242–267.

[Downie01] Downie, Marc, "Behavior, Animation and Music: The Music and Movement of Synthetic Characters." MSc Thesis, January 2001.

[Doyle98] Doyle, Patrick, and Barbara Hayes-Roth, "Agents in Annotated Worlds." *Proceedings of the Second International Conference on Autonomous Agents*, (1998): pp. 173–180.

[Gibson79] Gibson, James J., *The Ecological Approach to Visual Perception*, Houghton Mifflin, 1979.

[Kallmann99] Kallmann, Marcelo, and Daniel Thalmann, "A Behavioral Interface to Simulate Agent-Object Interactions in Real Time." *Proceedings of Computer Animation*, (1999): pp138–146.

[Lamarche01] Lamarche, F. et al., "The Orchestration of Behaviours Using Resources and Priority Levels." *Computer Animation and Simulation*, (Sep 2001): pp. 171–182.

[Mateas97] Mateas, Michael, "An Oz-Centric Review of Interactive Drama and Believable Agents." Technical Report CMU-CS-97-156, School of Computer Science, Carnegie Mellon University, Pittsburgh, PA. June 1997.

[Mateas00] Mateas, Michael, "Towards Integrating Plot and Character for Interactive Drama." Working notes of the Social Intelligent Agents: The Human in the Loop Symposium, AAAI Fall Symposium Series, 2000.

[Orkin04] Orkin, Jeff, "Constraining Autonomous Character Behaviour with Human Concepts." *AI Game Programming Wisdom 2*. Charles River Media, 2004.

[Perlin96] Perlin, Ken and Athomas Goldberg, "Improv: A System for Scripting Interactive Actors in Virtual Worlds." *Computer Graphics* (SIGGRAPH 1996): pp. 205–216

[Rose98] Rose, Charles et al., "Verbs and Adverbs: Multidimensional Motion Interpolation Using Radial Basis Functions." *IEEE Computer Graphics and Applications*, Vol. 18, No.5, (Sep/Oct 1998): pp. 32–41

[Russell08] Russell, Adam, "Turning Spaces into Places." *AI Game Programming Wisdom 4*. Charles River Media, 2008.

[Smith02] Smith, Harvey, "Systemic Level Design for Emergent Gameplay." *Game Developers Conference Europe*, (2002), available online at *http://www.planetdeusex.com/witchboy/systemic_ld.zip*.

[Spufford03] Spufford, Francis, "Masters of Their Universe." Available online at *http://www.guardian.co.uk/weekend/story/0,,1064107,00.html*, October 2003.

[Tozour01] Tozour, Paul, "Influence Mapping." *Game Programming Gems 2*. Charles River Media, 2001.

[vanderSterren01] van der Sterren, William, "Terrain Reasoning for 3D Action Games." Available online at *http://www.gamasutra.com/features/20010912/sterren_01.htm*, 2001.

[Woodcock02] Woodcock, Steve, "Recognizing Strategic Dispositions: Engaging the Enemy." *AI Game Programming Wisdom*. Charles River Media, 2002.

Artificial Personality:
A Personal Approach to AI

Benjamin Ellinger—Microsoft

benjamin.ellinger@microsoft.com

Much of the discussion about AI for games revolves around algorithms. Algorithms such as pathfinding, threat maps, flocking, neural networks, and so on are all important. Implementing, optimizing, and applying these algorithms is the primary work that we do. But what is the ultimate purpose of these algorithms? How do we ensure that these algorithms not only work correctly and efficiently but also engage and delight the player?

The primary goal when writing game AI is to pull players into the game so that they stop thinking about it as a game. Just like good animation and good physics, good game AI should make the virtual reality of the game seem deeper, richer, and more engaging (in terms of the game's reality, not the real world). This can be achieved by shifting focus away from creating AI and moving it toward creating artificial personality.

After defining what artificial personality actually is and how it is created through the use of personality archetypes, this article will go over some sample archetypes that can be applied to many types of characters. This is followed by a case study of a *Texas Hold'em* game that used the artificial personality approach and a discussion of how other possible approaches either supplement or conflict with this one.

What Is Artificial Personality?

Artificial personality emerges when AI algorithms are presented in a way that allows the behavior of virtual characters to be easily interpreted as expressing personality archetypes. People are accustomed to interacting and engaging with personalities, not with abstract "intelligences." When presented with a personality (even an artificial one), the player will project motivations, desires, and emotions onto any game behaviors. This encourages a style of play that revolves around understanding and exploiting the personalities in the game.

For most players, this is a much more satisfying and immersive experience than mastery of game mechanics and tactics alone. Defeating an efficient optimization algorithm is not what most players are interested in. Players do not think, "Fascinating—it appears that applying reactive armor to a heavy tank results in a 4.52% increase in survivability for only a 2.36% increase in production costs." Most would much rather engage with a human-like personality; "Rommel is brilliant, but he can never resist the opportunity for a bold, preemptive strike—which will be his downfall!"

Artificial personality is not an algorithm and is not created by discarding traditional AI algorithms. Any combination of traditional AI algorithms can be used as tools in the process of creating artificial personality. When those tools are used to create a set of clean, clear, and appropriate personality archetypes for a game, then that game will have artificial personality.

Personality Archetypes

A *personality archetype* is a clear, bold, and consistent set of behaviors that a player can easily identify with a single word. Archetypes are painted in bold strokes, not in subtle details. Personalities such as "the coward," "the defender," and "the psycho" are archetypes. Finer distinctions, such as "the lonely coward," "the jovial defender," and "the playful psycho" are not really archetypes and should be avoided for purposes of game behavior. These finer distinctions are best left for areas such as character backgrounds, storytelling, and dialogue.

Broad and Bold

The most important but easy-to-forget aspect of personality archetypes is *that they must be painted with broad, bold strokes!* It is usually a mistake to add lots of clever, subtle nuances. The player will fill in subtle behaviors, even if they are not actually there. Each character's primary behaviors must be very easy to identify so that the player can recognize the character's archetype.

It is almost impossible to overdo this. In fact, the game should usually just directly tell the player what the archetype of each character is. Even when a game is this direct, many players will be slow to realize that each character's behaviors are actually tied directly to their archetypes. This is because many players expect the characters to behave like a computer, not like a person. Because most players are not looking for these behaviors, the game must shout to be heard.

The only way to tell if a game's archetypes are easy enough to identify (even if the game is directly telling the player) is to observe completely new players who are given no help or clues of any kind. If they can see what is going on, then the game is being direct enough. But anyone who has any knowledge that there are multiple AI types in the game is not a valid subject for this test.

It is tempting to believe that figuring out a character's archetype is part of the fun of the game. Usually, this will only be true if figuring out archetypes is the primary thing the game is about. If this is attempted, this aspect of the game must be tested with brand-new testers throughout the game's development. The game will also need to make it very clear that figuring out the personality type of each character is something the player needs to do to be successful in the game.

Minimize Random Behaviors

Although many games make good use of randomness, random (or even apparently random) behaviors should be minimized as much as possible. Random behaviors make it difficult to identify archetypes and predict how a character will behave. Randomness is often used to make an AI more difficult to predict (and therefore more difficult to defeat), but this is rarely enjoyable for the average player.

A better approach is to have a given archetype behave in a clever but predictable way. After the player has figured out what a character is doing, winning is just a matter of figuring out how to counter the character's behavior. If the character switches tactics, especially if it does so at random, the average player will often become frustrated. The player's carefully planned counter-tactics are now pointless. Players want to win and want to feel that they won through skill or planning, not just through luck or persistence.

For example, a game might have an archetype that runs away half the time and fights the other half of the time when attacked. Or the odds could be based on a morale statistic or some other data. But all the average player knows is that sometimes it runs, and sometimes it does not. Because players cannot predict how the character will behave, the character's behavior cannot really be used to defeat it. But if the same character always runs away when outnumbered and always fights otherwise, that is something players can see and develop tactics around.

Randomly switching between personality archetypes for a single character is another common mistake. This will quickly convince players that these characters just behave randomly and have no archetypes at all. Players will not be able to tell that a character switched archetypes unless the game makes it incredibly obvious, with both visual and audio reinforcement, and does it in a way that makes sense in the context of the game (a mind control spell, a berserker potion, etc.).

This does not mean that randomness should never be used in a game's AI, of course. An aggressive AI might always build attack units first but randomly select among air, ground, or sea units. Just make sure any randomness does not obscure the AI's personality.

Reinforce the Archetypes

Be sure to make the archetypes in the game clearly different. Subtle differences between archetypes will be perceived as random behavior by players and will dilute the power of both archetypes. If each archetype is made as unique as possible, this will reinforce each one in the player's mind. This becomes difficult with more than 8 to 10 archetypes. Staying well under this limit meshes nicely with the number of archetypes players can keep track of.

Most players will have difficulty keeping more than 4 to 6 different archetypes in mind at the same time. More than 6 should only be considered if it really adds a lot to the game. More than a dozen is pointless—it would be better to keep the best 12 and discard the rest. The quality of a game's archetypes is always more important than the quantity, so do not keep weak archetypes in a game just to "fill out" a number of slots.

Archetypes should also be reinforced at every opportunity by the art style, animation, audio, dialogue, story, and so on. If all of these elements for a given character are specifically designed to match the character's archetype, it will be almost impossible for the player to forget which character has which personality. This will also bring the characters, story, and entire game to life in a way that behavior alone cannot.

It is especially important to have an audio cue when a character makes an important decision based on its archetype. When the coward decides to run away, it should yell: "Run away!" When the defender decides to rejoin his comrades, it should yell: "Regroup!" Directly tell the player what characters are thinking or doing—that is how the player will figure out when and how to use their personalities against them.

Sample Archetypes

There are an infinite variety of archetypes and names for archetypes, but there are some moderately generic core types that can be applied to many games. The following list and descriptions are not meant to be exhaustive. They are just a starting point—a small sample of basic archetypes. Of course, a given archetype can be applied to an individual unit in a strategy game, a "bot" in an action game, the commander of an entire military, a player at a card table, or a more traditional character in a role-playing game.

The Coward

This archetype is way too cautious. It always runs away when outnumbered and only fights when the odds are very favorable or when cornered. It never takes chances or bluffs and is very predictable. The coward will surrender in bad situations, if possible, and might even switch sides.

The Defender

This archetype is not aggressive but will always fight back when attacked. The defender prefers to stick with other characters as much as possible, so they can protect each other (even when this is not the best tactical choice). The defender will retreat if necessary but will never surrender or leave anyone behind. In a strategy game, it will build too many defensive units and not enough offensive units.

The Psycho

This archetype is always aggressive and will fight at any time, even against impossible odds. The psycho will act alone and unprotected, often not waiting for reinforcements or backup. It takes crazy chances and make foolish bluffs. The psycho will never retreat, never surrender, and might even destroy itself to take out a few more enemies. In a strategy game, it will build too many offensive units and not enough defensive units.

The Champion

This archetype does things by the book. It reacts to what the opponent does in solid tactical fashion but does not do anything clever. Generally, the champion does not take chances but will occasionally bluff just to keep opponents off balance. The champion retreats when necessary but attacks aggressively when the opportunity is there. *For most games, this is the "smartest" archetype needed.*

The Idiot

This archetype makes all the mistakes a raw beginner would. It builds the wrong types of units, does not react to nearby units being destroyed, bets foolish amounts, and is easily bluffed or tricked. It might not even know the layout of a level or the victory conditions. The idiot's actions are all based on short-term thinking—it does not really have a strategy at all.

The Genius

This archetype never makes a basic mistake and always fights efficiently. It lays traps for other players. The genius performs elaborate maneuvers and feints designed to confuse opponents. It anticipates the opponent's reaction to what it is doing and plans accordingly. The genius knows everything about every level, unit, and so on that a player could possibly know. This archetype is as smart as the AI can possibly be (within practical limits).

The Builder

This archetype is generally only found in strategy games (or some board games). It builds and manages resources very efficiently but focuses on building and resource production to the detriment of military readiness. The builder will only attack when it can no longer continue to grow.

The General

This archetype is the opposite of the builder. It creates military units as quickly as possible, at the expense of long-term growth. It manages unit upgrades and repairs very efficiently. The general scouts enemy positions aggressively and attacks at the first opportunity.

The Comedian

This archetype does things for humorous effect, such as building only one type of unit for the whole game, stopping to dance after every fight, betting everything on every hand in poker, and so on. The comedian is an AI designed to simulate a silly, nonserious player, or someone who is completely insane.

Texas Hold'em Case Study

It is fairly easy to see how to apply the artificial personality approach to a first-person shooter or a real-time strategy game. However, this approach can be applied to almost any type of game and was applied to *Bicycle® Texas Hold'em* developed by Carbonated Games in 2006 for MSN Games. The AI for the game was designed around the four classic poker personality types: the novice, the rock, the maniac, and the shark. Unlike what is seen in many other poker games, there are no fine gradations between these types. Every novice behaves exactly like every other novice, and every maniac behaves exactly like every other maniac.

Styles of Play in Poker

As a quick review of poker strategy, there are two basic axes of behavior in poker: tight versus loose and aggressive versus passive. A tight player is one who bets only with good hands that are likely to win. A loose player is one who bets with any hand that could possibly win, even if the odds are unlikely that it will. An aggressive player is one who usually bets large amounts, forcing other players to fold or pay a lot of money to challenge him. A passive player is one who usually bets small amounts, never forcing other players to fold, and will fold when challenged by other players.

The novice is a loose-passive player, which is the worst possible way to play. Novices do not win a lot of money when they do manage to win a hand, they play lots of hands that are not likely to win, and they can easily be bluffed into folding. Novices can easily be beaten just by playing normal poker and betting big if they seem to have a better hand (they will usually fold). The novice is effectively the idiot archetype from the list of sample archetypes.

The rock is a tight-passive player. Rocks are better than novices because rocks only play good hands, but because they do not bet aggressively, their winning hands do not get them a lot of money. Rocks can be defeated by just waiting them out. Just fold when they bet (because they must have a good hand) and wait for the blinds and/or ante to whittle away their chip stack. The rock is effectively the defender archetype from the archetype list.

The maniac is a loose-aggressive player. Maniacs are fairly dangerous because they play a lot of hands and bet them aggressively. They win a lot of money but lose a lot too. Maniacs will also bluff with hands they know will not win. It is very difficult to know whether a maniac actually has a good hand or not, so the way to defeat them is to wait for a really good hand, let them bet first until the final card, and then keep raising until they fold or call. The maniac is effectively the psycho archetype.

The last type of player is the shark, a tight-aggressive player. This is what all poker players try to be (and most think they are, even when they are really rocks or maniacs). This is the perfect balance—sharks do not play a lot of hands, but when they do, they play them aggressively. Sharks also bluff occasionally, which usually works because they almost never play weak hands, and it costs a lot to call their bluff. The only way to beat a shark is to get lucky or to be a better shark. The shark is effectively the champion archetype.

Discovering the Archetypes

In *Bicycle® Texas Hold'em*, each AI player is represented by a simple, cartoon-like face. All novice players have a happy face. All rocks have a frowning face. All maniacs have a tilted smile and crazy eyes. All sharks have a completely flat, expressionless face. This means that a player does not have to watch how a character plays to determine that character's archetype—the game just directly tells the player.

However, although this might seem fairly obvious, the majority of players do not figure out that this game has different personalities for different players unless they are told by another person who has figured it out. This is because the game does not tell players that there are different personality types! If we were to do it over again, we would, at the very least, have the names of the AI players be "Rock1," "Novice3," "Shark2," and so on instead of "Player1" or "Player3." In addition, we would have the game tell players when they selected an AI game that they were playing against "three novices, one rock, two maniacs, and a shark."

Another possibility with a little more flavor would be to name the AI players "Rick the Rock," "Sam the Shark," "Mike the Maniac," or "Ned the Novice." However, this can easily be taken too far. Names like "Rick Rockford," "Sammy Sharkskin," "Mike Mann," and "Ned Newman" might seem better, but if a game does this, it will be a little bit harder for the average player to figure out what's going on. This could be okay but will require plenty of testing with average players.

So the overall result was that although we knew we needed to tell the players the exact archetype of each opponent, we did not take a strong enough approach. Remember, it is almost impossible to overdo this.

Playing Against the AI

Although the archetypes are not as clearly named as they could be, after a player knows about them, the game is quite fun (for a novice poker player). Because each of the four archetypes is very different and behaves in a way that makes sense to any poker player, all a player has to do is pay attention to the archetype of each opponent and make bets based on the known behavior of those archetypes. Barring a run of bad luck, this almost guarantees success.

The overall result is that the best strategy in this game is for players to pay attention to the personality of their opponents and use the flaws in those personalities to defeat them. Go after the novices early and aggressively to get an early lead. Leave the rocks alone and do not challenge them. Wait for the right moment to take out the maniacs in a single hand. Leave the sharks until the end and then just try to play better than them. This is exactly how to win at real poker, so it leaves the player feeling like a real pro.

Ironically, the shark AI was not very good by poker AI standards, but it was still a success. Any good poker player could crush the shark easily even though it didn't make any stupid mistakes and played by the book (we did not have time to implement the genius). But this made little difference to most players, who are generally not that good and would rather play against other humans if they were available.

An additional factor is that the shark appears to be smarter than it actually is to most players. This is because players are also facing a lot of novices, rocks, and maniacs, so the shark seems pretty good by comparison. This effect should not be underestimated—it is much easier to make an archetype feel smart by contrast with lesser archetypes than it is to create a truly smart AI.

Difficulty Levels

When playing against the AI in *Bicycle® Texas Hold'em*, there are three difficulty levels: easy, normal, and hard. The behaviors of each archetype are not changed at all based on the difficulty level—a given archetype always behaves the same way. Instead, the easy level puts players up against mainly novices, a rock or two, and sometimes a single maniac. The normal level puts players up against an even mix of all types. The hard level puts players up against mainly sharks and maniacs, with occasionally a rock.

This method of setting the difficulty of a game just by changing the mix of archetypes the players will face works well for many games. Especially when players are working their way up through the difficulty levels, the effect when they reach the hard level is excellent. The players know very directly what they are up against because they know what maniacs and sharks are like from the normal level—and now here is a table full of them!

Note that players never face a large number of rocks (there are never more than two at any table), no matter what the difficulty level is. This is because playing against a lot of rocks is as exciting as it sounds—it takes forever because few hands are played and nobody bets much when a hand is played. This is an important point—some archetypes are only fun in small doses. Do not think that a game needs to use all of them equally.

Making It Better

The biggest improvement would be to make the archetypes of the AI players clearer, but there are some other obvious possible improvements. Adding a "genius" AI would have been a lot of fun to write and would have given even experienced poker players a challenging game. However, this would have taken at least 10 times longer to write and was not necessary for most of our players. It is important to remember that players generally want to win when they play—our job is just to make winning enjoyable.

So what about adding more AI types? We could add a coward or a comedian pretty easily if we wanted. Although these additions might be good for the game, always be cautious about adding more archetypes just because it is easy. Having only a few archetypes makes it easier for a player to understand each type. If we added a coward, it might be difficult for players to distinguish that archetype from the novice (i.e., the idiot) in a poker game. The best number of archetypes will depend on the exact game and the intended audience, but most games need fewer archetypes, not more.

Although it would have taken a good amount of additional work, we could also have added a lot of archetype reinforcement to the game. The AI players could have chatted about the other players, pointing out their weaknesses, and complaining whenever someone challenges any rock at the table. The maniac could have gotten a really angry-looking face after any hand that it lost a lot of money on, indicating that it is "on tilt" and will not fold on the next hand no matter what kind of hand it has. The novice could have occasionally asked whether or not a straight beats a flush. The shark could have made comments about how it won a national tournament with the same hand. The possibilities are endless, but the point is always to reinforce the archetypes.

Other Approaches

AI in games can be approached in a variety of different ways, of course. Different approaches can certainly work to some degree, but in most cases, focusing on personality first and foremost will get better results for a game that needs to simulate human behavior.

The Sophisticated Algorithm Approach

AI can be written by focusing on the creation of the most sophisticated and advanced algorithms possible. It is easy to fall into this approach on occasion, becoming enamored of a complex but beautiful algorithm that really does not fit the game being created. Classic examples are using a neural network when there is no way to get good training data, or using a genetic algorithm when there is no good fitness function (or when it is difficult to have enough generations for the algorithm to produce good results).

The limitations of this approach are obvious: lots of complicated code that does not result in behaviors that the player understands or is interested in. Although this approach can be useful for research purposes (discovering new algorithms, for example), making it the primary way a game's AI is developed will get mediocre results at best.

The Pure Intelligence Approach

Another approach is to write AI that is just as smart as possible. The AI can then be "dumbed down" dynamically to account for different levels of player skill. This might seem like a good idea, but it rarely gives satisfying results in a game. This approach is much better suited to real-world AIs (robots, vehicles, and so on) or to game AIs whose purpose is to defeat the best humans in the world (*Deep Blue*, for example).

The problem is that for most players, an AI written to just be as intelligent as possible is not much fun to play. Even when the AI has been adjusted to match the player's skill level, the player wins by avoiding mistakes and being more efficient than the AI-controlled characters. This is almost never as fun as knowing the personality of an opponent and using the flaws in that personality against it.

Most game AI just needs to be smart enough that it does not make stupid mistakes that only a computer would make. As long as the mistakes that are made would be made by human players as well, the AI is smart enough for the vast majority of players. Spending huge amounts of time and energy making the "perfect" AI is usually not worthwhile when that is not what most players want.

Worries that a game's AI will not be challenging enough without a pure intelligence approach are usually unfounded. Remember that the best challenge for most players will be multiplayer games. But even for single-player games, things such as asymmetric starting positions, limited resources, and challenging victory conditions can easily be used to adjust the difficulty in a satisfying way.

The Make-It-Fun Approach

This is the approach that most veteran AI developers take. It has a lot going for it—it is difficult to go wrong when you are just focusing on making the AI fun. Any successful game AI will make good use of this approach. The problem is that this approach only identifies the goal, not how to get there, which often results in a lot of false starts and wasted effort that a more focused approach could avoid.

The other problem with this approach is that it is very easy for a game developer to write AI that is fun for a game developer to play against, but this usually does not work as well for average players. Because we already know how the AI is supposed to behave, we can see things that a normal player cannot. Even having many different people play the game while it is being developed is not adequate because they will rarely be good proxies for average players. Moreover, by the time broad play-testing is started, it might be too late to rewrite the game's AI.

A personality-based approach that uses strong archetypes will help avoid creating AI that is only interesting to game developers. By immediately focusing on how the player will interact with the archetypes in the game, the developer is put in the player's mind right away, instead of waiting until it is too late. In the best case, each archetype mimics a specific type of player personality, so the developer is forced to really understand how different players think.

Conclusion

Artificial personality can be used on small projects or large ones, regardless of whether there is limited AI with a few characters or highly advanced AI with an enormous cast of characters. It is a powerful conceptual framework that gives direction and focus to the underlying algorithms that make up all AI. The designer should always remember that although an intelligent opponent can be challenging, an opponent with a personality will be fun!

To give artificial personality a try, just follow these steps:

1. Identify all the personality archetypes of actual people who play the game.
2. Eliminate all archetypes that are uninteresting or too similar.
3. Identify the particular behaviors/tactics/strategies that the remaining archetypes use.
4. Identify and implement the traditional AI techniques needed for those behaviors.
5. Reinforce the archetypes with visuals, audio, and dialogue.

1.3

Creating Designer Tunable AI

Borut Pfeifer—Electronic Arts

borut_p@yahoo.com

Designers and AI programmers have very different skill sets, yet this interaction is a crucial part of game development [Reynolds04]. AI programmers are responsible for building the systems designers will use to create interesting player encounters with the AI. The easier it is for designers to use these AI systems, the better the AI will look, and the better the game will be in the end.

Sometimes even experienced AI programmers create compelling gameplay features that go unused or misused simply because the designers are not able to control them properly. Spending the time to create the best interfaces for designers to manipulate the AI avoids those problems and helps to create more compelling gameplay.

This article covers tips, techniques, and pitfalls to avoid when implementing the interfaces and tools that give designers access to the AI. Although there are numerous articles on AI algorithms in this and other volumes, this article instead deals with the tools and interfaces needed to manipulate those algorithms.

The important factors that drive the definition of designer-AI interfaces are authorability, workflow, and communication. *Authorability* denotes where and how much control the designers have over the AI, whereas *workflow* involves the process they have to go through to do so. Whether the game uses data-driven or scripted methods to expose functionality to designers, these two concepts drive the creation of good interfaces. *Communication* among team members about how underlying AI systems work via training sessions, debugging tools, reference documentation, or even just casual e-mail, is the glue that unites great AI with great gameplay. Better tools and processes in AI development naturally make for better games.

Authorability

When working with designers, keep in mind the range of control they will want over the AI. The authorability of an AI system is defined by how easily the designers can use it to create the gameplay they want. Understanding designers' needs and desires is key in effectively building the AI.

Even with games that have a great deal of autonomous AI, designers will typically want very fine control during certain moments. For an action game, this can be scripted sequences that convey a plot point or an important mission detail. By default, assume the worst case: any action the AI can perform by itself is something that the designers might want to have direct control over at some point. This is why experienced game AI programmers tend to avoid black box solutions, such as genetic algorithms or neural networks, whose internals are not easily accessible for those exceptional cases. The important question becomes, "*How often* will designers need that level of control?" Frequent tasks should be very easy to accomplish, whereas it is acceptable for infrequent tasks to be more difficult.

An Example of Authorability—Pathfinding Data

A good example of the spectrum of authorability can be seen in pathfinding data. To save designers from manually creating path node graphs for levels, many games automatically generate navigation graphs. Whatever type of navigation graph is automatically generated needs to be edited to handle these problems:

False positives: Perhaps there is some detailed geometry in the level that is needed for collision or other purposes. If this geometry is picked up by the graph generation algorithm, it can cause lots of strange pathfinding anomalies, such as NPCs walking on banisters. These areas will need to be manually disabled from being considered by the graph generation.

False negatives: There might be a small piece of a level that the designers want to place enemies on that is not recognized by the algorithm (such as a ledge that is not wide enough). Designers should be able to mark seed points for the graph generation to make sure it is included in the final graph.

Although these examples are specific to pathfinding, the same is generally true of any algorithm that procedurally generates data to solve an AI problem in a game. Sometimes these problems can be handled by improvements in the algorithm but rarely can they be completely solved that way. After it is clear where the designers will need to input their intent into the system, how often will these situations occur? If there are false negatives and positives on every level, take the time to add functionality to the interfaces in the level-editing tools to quickly handle those cases. If they only happen a handful of times, it can be acceptable to leave the editing cumbersome (such as editing a text file) to spend more time simplifying the commonly edited aspects of the AI.

Workflow

After considering what AI functionality will need designer input, the next step is to consider the workflow for getting that input into the game. There are a number of different constraints to keep in mind.

Existing Tools

If there are existing tools within the game engine, it is usually best to work within that framework. If designers are accustomed to loading data files in a certain manner in a certain format, then creating a new pipeline for getting that data into the game makes them spend their time using and debugging two data pipelines instead of tuning that data. If existing data uses XML files that the designers are familiar with, then it might be best to stick with that format. If there is a custom game data format that meets most needs, it's better to make minor extensions instead of creating a new pipeline and the tools to use it.

Multiple Users

If any single data file or asset needs to be edited by multiple designers frequently, this can pose problems. Designers can become blocked from working while they wait on someone else who has the file locked, or in the case of text files, there can be frequent problems merging files. Try to piece out the data inside the file into separate component files. It helps if the components are logically tied to different designers' roles (such as a level designer editing a file containing only general prop locations, and a mission scripter editing mission-specific level data).

Iteration Speed

Whatever methods designers have to manipulate the AI, being able to load and evaluate their changes without restarting the game will have a profound impact on the quality of their work. The ability for designers to quickly iterate on their AI tuning will help them find what is fun and compelling much faster than if they have to reload the game every time they want to change AI settings. This could be as simple as reloading an XML file to read in new gameplay parameters or as complex as compiling and reloading a script file at runtime, but it is usually worth the effort.

Analyzing Technical Strengths

In the game industry today, designers often have computer science degrees. Alternately, they might have come by scripting experience while working on previous games. To a designer who has not had either type of experience, scripting can be fairly daunting. Some solutions to AI problems are easier for a nontechnical design team but might take more implementation; other solutions might require technical expertise to use but allow for flexibility and can take less time to create. Assessing the strengths of the design team can be just as big a factor in the search for solutions as the requirements of the game itself. Here the lead designer can help in making that initial assessment, but the key is to balance chosen AI solutions with the skills of the team.

Data-Driven Methods

Data-driven design has become a very common approach used in game development, due to its many benefits during the production process [Rabin00]. There are a number of good practices when it comes to getting the most out of data-driven design. Making it easy to add parameters without invalidating existing data, fully supporting data versioning when it does get invalidated, and being able to reload data at runtime, all make data-driven design that much more effective. But there are a number of other guidelines to consider when organizing how designers input data into the game.

Tuning Behavior

Working closely with designers is necessary to clarify what parameters they will care about for any individual behavior. Exposing a few relevant parameters can give design-ers a great deal of flexibility and allows reuse of existing behaviors [Tapper03]. This is especially the case if the game design calls for autonomous NPCs who are aware of their surroundings and must deal with a wide range of player behavior. Driving behavior through small, well-defined sets of parameters is a good way to allow designers to author the player interactions with the AI they want, without sacrificing the AI's ability to autonomously handle dynamic situations.

Designers can then customize NPCs via these parameters and by assigning them different behaviors. One type of NPC might use melee weapons, use shields, and find nearby cover, whereas another type of NPC might use cover, fire long-range weapons, and dodge. A third, more aggressive NPC might have both long-range and melee weapons but does not have any defensive behaviors. Creating these behaviors as assign-able modules, with minor variations allowed through data assigned to NPCs, allows the AI programmer to determine the right circumstances to start and stop those behaviors. Meanwhile, the designers can focus on defining what kind of strategies the player must use against an AI.

Take care to implement the behavior parameters that the designers actually want control over. A very complex aiming accuracy model specified with more than 10 dif-ferent parameters for a gun-toting NPC might simply not get used if all the designers really wanted was to specify an NPC's accuracy as high, medium, or low.

Spatial Markup

One of the most common types of data a designer enters during game production is *spatial markup*. This could be manually entering nodes for a navigation graph, adding patrol or cover points for enemy NPCs, adding other tactical information about a space, such as good sniping spots, or adding objects NPCs can interact with in a level. Because it is a common task, make sure adding the AI data associated with these points or objects is also trivial. Use of indirection (detailed next) is especially useful for classifying different points with data categories defined elsewhere.

Data Indirection

If there are exposed parameters for tuning behaviors, the designers might need the abil-ity to define these parameters for each NPC. However, this might also be a rare case, so forcing designers to add this data to each NPC creates a lot of work to just add one NPC to a level. Separating out these types of parameters into a data set that is then assigned to an NPC simplifies these matters. Designers create lists of these data sets (combat parameters for aggressive enemies, weak enemies, and so on), and then assign a data set to an NPC when it is created.

This indirection allows designers to change all the parameters associated with that set without having to actually edit any of the NPCs. If a designer needs to create an NPC with a unique set of parameters, he must create a new data set that is only used by that NPC. This is a little more work to define custom parameters on an NPC, but this task is done much less frequently, so there is a large benefit from being able to reuse data by assigning it indirectly.

Data Orthogonality

When defining these data sets, keep in mind the orthogonality of that data. Are there different chunks of parameters within the data set that serve separate purposes? Will it simplify the designer's workflow to break up this data into separate sets? For example, if an NPC's combat parameters can be broken up into attack parameters and defense parameters, it can be easier to create unique types of NPCs.

For example, the designers might want five different types of aggressiveness in NPCs (involving combat speed, attack rate, accuracy, and so on) and four types of defensive behavior (varying dodge ability, blocking percentage, and so on). If designers had to create each combined type as a unique data set, there would be 20 data sets. If they could simply mix and match, assigning an attack data set and a defensive data set to each NPC, they would only have to create 9 sets of data. If there were 10 attacking NPC classifications and 10 defensive NPC classifications, without splitting up the data sets orthogonally, designers would have to create and maintain 100 different data sets! Care must be taken to not overdo it as well; if designers do not actually use the data orthogonally (i.e., every NPC attack data set always corresponds to the same defensive data set), this might just be more work for them.

Keeping Names and Units Consistent and Intuitive

As different programmers write AI or gameplay functionality that gets exposed, keeping consistent names and units for similar parameters can occasionally be a problem. Two separate programmers might expose the same type of parameter with very different names or units. This leaves the design team perpetually trying to remember which one is appropriate in each case. With inconsistent units, it is easy to make mistakes that result in wasted time modifying and retesting parameters. When adding additional parameters, take care to verify their consistency with any existing code.

In addition, stick to the most intuitive units. For values of time, this typically means seconds instead of milliseconds. For angles, *never* expose a value in radians—most people naturally think of orientations in angles. When designers have to enter data regarding varying degrees of chance (e.g., how often an NPC uses a particular behavior or what type of NPCs to spawn), stick with weights or odds instead of percentages or probabilities. Percentages and probabilities require the numbers to sum to a specific value, so they are more complex to enter and do not allow for easy adding and removing of elements. Exposing the data as odds greatly simplifies entering that kind of data (i.e., for three options A, B, and C, values of 3, 1, and 1 mean A would be selected 3 times as often as B or C).

Values should always be displayed in more intuitive types for designers' debugging, even if internally, the information is stored as the less intuitive unit (removing any unnecessary calculation on the designers' part from the process). Any minor performance offset is made up for in readability and ease of use many times over. When forced to choose between keeping unit consistency over intuitive units, lean toward consistency. If the existing code is reasonable enough to refactor to a more intuitive unit, refactoring is the better choice—the designers will no doubt appreciate the effort.

Scripting Systems

Data-driven design solves a lot of designer interface problems, but there are still times the designers will need to customize game logic or behavior via a scripting language. Besides trying to make the language more usable (with case insensitivity, simple keywords, weak typing, and so on [Poiker02]), it is very beneficial to determine ahead of time just how much direct control over game functionality will need to be exposed. In some cases, more is not always better. There are few guidelines to follow, allowing for variance on the technical strengths of the design team and the requirements of the game itself.

Provide a Simple Framework

A programming language, just like a regular language, often provides many ways of accomplishing the same task. To anybody who has not received formal programming training, it can be a daunting task to figure out how to implement something correctly when there are many means of achieving it. Provide a simple framework for designers to accomplish important or frequent tasks:

- Expose straightforward callback functions that designers can override per NPC in script, such as OnDamage, OnDeath, OnArriveAtDestination, and so on.
- Keep consistent API declarations. Similar to data-driven methods, try to ensure consistent units as well as consistent function naming conventions, function parameter declarations, and so on.
- Expose only one level of an API unless absolutely necessary (typically the highest level). For example, designers might want to set behaviors on an NPC, such as Attack, Defend, Follow, or Flee. If they also have access to the lower level APIs, they might inadvertently recreate the same behavior if they do not notice it in the higher level script interface.

Streamline Common Scripting Tasks

The most common tasks a designer performs via a scripting language need to be as simple as possible. The following are good examples of tasks that should be trivial to do in a game's scripting language (allowing some variance for different game types):

- Creating, querying, setting, and resetting flags or other variables on objects. Designers will need to easily add flags to objects to perform tasks such as mission or quest scripting. Besides setting and querying the values, there might need to be a quick way to reset to a known good state (e.g., if a mission fails and the original premission state needs to be restored).
- Querying whether or not an object belongs to a set of objects (such as if it is a targetable enemy), and selecting objects from a set.
- Waiting for a specified amount of time. This should be as simple as a wait command that pauses script execution for a number of seconds.
- Giving simple commands to NPCs: patrol, attack a target, defend a position, or use an ability or animation.

Visual Scripting Languages

Visual scripting systems, including finite state machine editors, are typically much easier for people without a lot of technical experience to learn. However, they have a number of limitations as well. A nontechnical designer can easily learn to script a sequence of actions by an NPC, but it typically becomes difficult to reuse those visual scripts (such as passing parameters between invocations). When a visually scripted system or sequence becomes reasonably complex or interconnected, it becomes much more difficult to maintain than the same functionality implemented in a text programming language. The benefits of such a system are more apparent when there are small scripting requirements and a team of nontechnical designers.

Behavior Scripting

When the designers have the ability to write AI behavior in script, it can be compelling to let them define all aspects of a behavior. This can work well for behaviors only used in one specific context in a game (e.g., a behavior one NPC might display when it reaches a certain point in a level). When the behavior is to be used in multiple contexts, however, getting it to work in those contexts, handling errors, and returning to the appropriate behavior is a complex engineering task that is not reasonable for designers to handle.

Designer control of behavior is most effective when they can easily swap between sets of the individual behaviors implemented by the AI programmer, or if they have the ability to queue existing behaviors as commands in a straightforward fire-and-forget manner. Even if AI is going on behind the scenes to determine when to switch to the next command, it is an effective mechanism for designers to script their desired behavior. Ideally, NPC agents retain enough autonomy that designers can simply place them in the level and assign their initial behavior set, and the NPCs can function well without additional scripting.

Failure Cases

Because of the flexibility of scripting languages, it is easy to expose different functionality with them, but not all functionality is well suited for it. Be very careful when exposing the entry of data via script—try to remove it and apply the guidelines in the previous section. For example, NPC paths and cutscene scripting are visual tasks best left in level-building tools, rather than entered as sequences of path points and events in a text file. NPC behavior parameters are best stored in separate data files, which allow instantaneous reloading without having to recompile scripts.

Avoid forcing designers to implement any sort of solution to a systemic problem in script. For example, if working on a multiplayer cooperative action game where players can act together to solve simple puzzles, the designers will want to script the logic and behavior used in the puzzles. If designers have to deal with complex multiplayer problems, such as race conditions, in their puzzle scripting, that functionality will need to be moved into code, while existing script API functionality is disabled and replaced with a more encapsulated system.

Debugging Tools

Designers who author gameplay with AI systems must be able to debug their own work. With complex systems, often it is not clear why an AI is failing to perform as expected. Debugging tools save time when trying to find errors or track down problems in a script or data file. Additionally, it also saves programmer time because designers are empowered to find the problems themselves.

Visual Overlays

Most games feature debug visualization using spheres, lines, and such. If this information is well organized and easy to toggle on and off, designers will be able to narrow down the point of failure for any particular problem. When visual debugging tools are properly implemented, they make it exceptionally easy to spot NPC errors in behavior. Without visual debugging tools, a designer will have to sift through huge logs of frame-by-frame data, which is less efficient because it takes much longer to understand the problem within the context it occurs.

Similar debug data should be combined into overlays that can be toggled on and off (either via a console command, key presses, or a simple onscreen menu). A good organization of overlays allows designers to quickly find the reason why an NPC is not performing as expected. Consider the following separate overlays:

General NPC information: Position, velocity, name, ID, and class.
Animation state: Current animation names, length, and animation state.

AI intent: The NPC's target location, its current attack target, its current state or the action it wants to perform, and any associated data.

AI perception: Currently or recently seen enemies and objects that factor into its decision making.

AI state: Current and past states, especially if the AI uses any sort of pushdown automata that stores states or commands that are queued to execute.

Path information: The NPC's overall navigation graph and its current path along the graph.

Designers should be able to see an NPC in a failure state, such as an NPC that should be attacking, and go through the overlays to narrow down the problem. The animation state overlay can determine if the NPC is trying to play the animation but failing (such as in the case of a missing asset). The AI perception overlay will show if the NPC correctly perceives an available attack target, and the AI intent overlay will show if the NPC is actually attempting to attack but is being prevented for other reasons. If a designer comes across a bug that requires detailed research by a programmer, try to find a way to make this problem immediately diagnosable via overlay information. The small amount of time to add the additional information is greatly offset by the debugging time it will save.

Ideally, the debug information in the overlays should be instantly understandable. Use different colors to denote different states. A line drawn to the NPC's target location is useful, but a line that is green, yellow, or red based on its pathfinding status (valid, pending, or failed) is much more useful. Depending on the number of NPCs active at one time, additional commands might be needed to restrict the debug display to the currently selected NPC and to toggle which NPC is selected to display.

Data Validation

Wherever possible, validate designer data and handle error cases appropriately:

- Give visible onscreen notification (which can be optionally turned on/off). An error message in a log with thousands of lines of text is difficult to find. The easier it is for the designer to find his own error, the less help he will need from an AI programmer.
- Write clear messages that point to the problem data. Programmers often use technical language that designers are not familiar with, so it always helps to review an error message for plain English immediately after writing it. If someone asks what an error message means, immediately rewrite it for clarity.
- Fail gracefully. The game should handle as many error cases of bad data as possible. The game might not behave correctly, but it should run. If necessary, revert to default data options in these cases. One designer's data error should not prevent others from working.

Script Debugging

If designers will be writing scripts, they must have the tools to debug them (and when things go wrong, the AI programmers must have good tools to debug the script, too). An existing, mature scripting language solution has many, many advantages over a custom built solution. Lightweight languages such as Pawn (a simple C-style language [Riemersma06]) and Lua ([Celes07, Lake07]) that have existing debug APIs and debug tools will greatly simplify the development of a useful game scripting environment.

Communication

Communication between AI programmers and designers is critical to making AI that designers can use effectively. Good communication between AI programmers and designers involves written specifications of systems to be implemented and reference documentation. Upfront outlines of systems can allow designers to verify that the system will meet their needs and allows the AI programmer to manage expectations by exposing any limitations.

Even after designers have been given intuitive tools, a key part of the process is offering training on each tool's features and limitations. Training should be an ongoing process as systems are changed and as new designers join the team. Because people have different communication styles, this information should be offered in different forms. Additionally, reference documentation is a good resource during production and helps train new designers.

System Design Goals and Limitations

Early on in the development process, it is common for programmers to get designers' feedback on the code systems that are planned for implementation. Emphasize this part of the process to make sure it is clear what the designers want and that the technical design will meet their goals. Just as important, and subtly different, is to cover system limitations—what the system will *not* do. Designers need to know the limits of AI systems just as much as they need to know what functionality is implemented.

For example, there might be some script functions exposed that a designer can use to create friendly NPCs that rudimentarily follow the player. A designer might see that basic interface and plan for a level where an NPC is meant to act as a robust squad mate, following the player while also attacking nearby enemies. Experienced AI programmers are well aware that delivering that level of functionality is an order of magnitude more difficult. It can be time consuming to implement all the behaviors necessary: behavior to keep the ally out of the player's way during combat, to follow the player's combat behavior, and to provide support behaviors such as covering fire or healing magic. However, this distinction might not be clear unless explicitly communicated to the designers (that the AI will *not* do that).

Reference Documentation

Good reference documentation can save time in communicating minor details of functionality. During their work, designers will have questions about small details around the implemented functionality. They can either ask an AI programmer, experiment with the system, or they can look it up in the documentation (which saves everyone time). Here are a few guidelines for good reference documentation:

- Make it easy to access via a well-organized team wiki page or even an HTML link button directly in the game tools.
- Describe how the system works in exceptional and common cases. Make sure to cover both special and default values for parameters in data-driven systems.
- Try to keep the language plain and nontechnical, even when describing very technical concepts.
- Ensure that it is searchable.

Training

Good reference documentation can never take the place of good training. Training gives designers solid examples for common cases they will encounter using these systems. Whereas some designers might learn by poring over reference documentation, others will learn better through visual representations, listening to the information, or by being taken through examples. There are several things to keep in mind for presenting this information for training:

- Keep any presentation slides as visual as possible. Use screenshots of tools or the game with annotations to convey the same information found in the reference documentation.
- Use concrete examples. Go through step-by-step how designers would accomplish common tasks using the software. Explain the steps the designer should take to look into possible error causes if the task fails.
- Try to give designers an understanding of how the underlying system works. While at their desks working/scripting, the underlying mechanics might not be apparent to them even through reference documentation, so they might come to different conclusions about what the system is actually doing behind the scenes.
- Keep points of information short so as to not overwhelm anybody's memory or attention during the training session. Break up training into multiple sessions if necessary.
- Keep any training presentation notes around, update them, and present them again when enough new designers come onboard.

Keep It Up to Date!

Naturally, as systems change, the documentation will need to be kept up to date. As new designers join the team, or as other designers who were previously tasked on other things start to use the software, it greatly reduces confusion if they can start with documentation that is up to date and get the same training as well. Finally, try to make sure new designers are aware of the system's original design goals and limitations to avoid problems with improperly implemented script functionality (because new designers might also make assumptions about the underlying capacity of existing technology, like the earlier squad-mate example).

Conclusion

Taking the time to find the right interfaces for different team members with different skill sets is well worth the effort. Empowering designers to work with the AI adds more to the overall value of the game and allows AI programmers to work more effectively. It is the AI programmer's job to optimally expose the AI to designers in a simple manner that streamlines workflow. Giving them the tools to understand and debug the AI will allow them to use the AI systems to the fullest.

References

[Celes07] Celes, Waldemar, et al., "The Programming Language Lua." Available online at *http://www.lua.org*, May 28, 2007.

[Lake07] Lake, Rici, "ldb – A Lua Debugger." Available online at *http://www.dzone.com/links/ldb_a_lua_debugger.html*, April 19, 2007.

[Poiker02] Poiker, Falko, "Creating Scripting Languages for Nonprogrammers." *AI Game Programming Wisdom*, Charles River Media, 2002.

[Rabin00] Rabin, Steve, "The Magic of Data-Driven Design." *Game Programming Gems*, Charles River Media, 2000.

[Reynolds04] Reynolds, Brian, "AI and Design: How AI Enables Designers." Game Developers Conference, 2004.

[Riemersma06] Riemersma, Thiadmer, "The Pawn Language." Available online at *http://www.compuphase.com/pawn/pawn.htm*, November 14, 2006.

[Tapper03] Tapper, Paul, "Personality Parameters: Flexibly and Extensibly Providing a Variety of AI Opponents' Behaviors." Available online at Gamasutra, *http://www.gamasutra.com/features/20031203/tapper_01.shtml*, December 3, 2003.

1.4

AI as a Gameplay Analysis Tool

Neil Kirby—Bell Laboratories

nak@alcatel-lucent.com

Do game designers really know how people play their games? If the only way to know something is to measure it, then AI can be an effective gameplay analysis tool. This article uses case studies of two popular casual games, *Minesweeper* and *Sudoku*, to show how small amounts of AI can illuminate what core gameplay actually is. There is no claim that the AI measures what is fun, but it can measure what players actually do. The numbers may tell a different story than expected. Although AI can most easily be applied to casual games, the results indicate value to more complex games as well. Writing such AI leads to new gameplay concepts. A potential two-player *Minesweeper* game from that case study is shown. Demonstration software for both games is included on the CD-ROM.

ON THE CD

Methodology

Both games have been analyzed elsewhere [Wikipedia07, Delahaye06], and solver programs exist as well [Collet05, Kopp01]. Two factors are novel in the case studies presented here. First is the slanting of the AI to play as people do, even when superior software solutions exist. Second is the instrumentation giving hard numbers and an accurate basis for comparisons.

Both games use a rules-based AI. The rules are ranked in complexity order, and the simplest rules are attempted first. "Simple" means that the test to see if the rule applies is easy to understand, and the code to execute the rule is easy to understand. Because it is simulating a human player, the AI always tries the easy stuff first. All rules are deterministic. If the current rule cannot make a move that it knows is good, the next rule is tried in succession. If any rule finds a move, the AI drops back to the simplest rule first when looking for the next move. The AI runs until it can make no more moves.

The games are implemented as fully playable games and require some human interaction. The AI can be adjusted from being turned off, to using only the simplest rule, on up in complexity order to having all rules available. If the AI is enabled, it runs after every human move and after every AI move until it can make no more moves. If the game is not solved, the human player can take the next move. The AI does not guess—it only takes known good moves. In the *SmartMines* version of *Minesweeper*, the human player always makes the first move. In the *SmartNumbers* implementation of *Sudoku*, the human has to either load a saved game or enter the board clues to begin a game.

There is no "undo" in *Minesweeper,* but there is in *Sudoku* because there is no hidden information. The *Sudoku* game logic will not allow the player or the AI to solve one tile that removes the last possible solution from any other unsolved tile. If the AI is prevented from making a move for this reason, the AI stops looking for moves, and the program beeps. Because the AI does not make mistakes, such a board must come from human mistakes. The human player can also use the undo feature. In *Minesweeper,* if the human player makes a mistake, then the AI is very likely to make a fatal move based on that bad information.

All moves are counted. The counts are displayed in the menu bar. The moves made by the human player are tagged with H. "Free" moves in *Minesweeper,* the result of clearing the neighbors to a tile with zero surrounding mines, are tagged with F. Free moves in *Sudoku* are the solved tiles at the start of a game loaded from a file. The moves made by the AI are tagged by which rule made them. AI0 is the simplest rule, then AI1, and, finally, AI2 is the most sophisticated.

SmartMines

The *SmartMines* game plays the same as the version of *Minesweeper* that comes with Microsoft Windows 2000. The Beginner, Intermediate, and Expert boards have the same number of tiles and the same number of mines as their Windows counterparts. As expected, the first move is always safe.

Rules

The rules for the AI in *SmartMines* will only examine tiles that have been clicked and that have unmarked neighbors. The tile being examined shows the number of mines present among its neighbors. In order to capture the first three figures shown next, the human player made moves that would have been made by the AI.

The rule for AI0 is based on what can be deduced by looking at a single tile and its immediate neighbors (usually eight of them). In human terms, the question asked is, "What does this one tile tell me about the unsolved tiles around it?" The rule first looks to see if the flagged neighboring tiles can account for all of the mines indicated. If so, then all unmarked neighboring tiles are safe to clear, and the AI will make a move by clicking one of them. Such a move was made on the left side of the second board in Figure 1.4.1. If there are more mines than flags, the AI will see if the number of unaccounted for mines is equal to the number of unmarked neighboring tiles. If so, all of them must be mines and the AI will move to flag one of them. Such a move was made to get the third board of Figure 1.4.1.

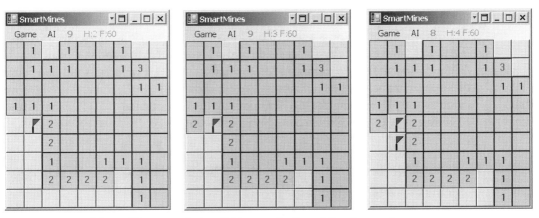

FIGURE 1.4.1   Moves AI0 can make by clicking a safe tile and flagging a mine.

The rule for AI1 uses a clicked tile that has both another clicked tile and at least one unknown tile among the surrounding tiles (usually eight). In human terms, "How does a neighboring clicked tile help me with the unsolved neighbors of this clicked tile?" If either tile had enough information to generate a move by itself, AI0 would have fired. The other neighbors to the two clicked tiles can be categorized as "mine," "yours," or "ours," depending on whether one, the other, or both clicked tiles are adjacent. Each tile of the pair can provide the other with a min and a max on the number of mines in the shared tiles. This min and max information may be enough for either tile of the pair to make a deterministic move. AI1 will only take a single move, even when multiple moves are known. Figure 1.4.2 shows AI1 making a move leading to other moves by AI0.

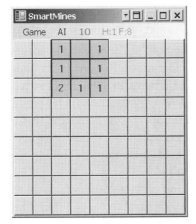

FIGURE 1.4.2   The algorithm for AI1 finds a safe tile to click.

The rule for AI2 uses the same algorithm as AI1 but not with an adjacent cleared tile. Instead, the other tile is a cleared tile from the next outer ring of tiles (usually 16). If AI2 finds moves, it will make a single move. Figure 1.4.3 first shows a board where AI1 and AI0 can find no moves. AI2 is not enabled, but if it were, it would find 5 safe tiles beside and below the singleton clicked tile showing 1 nearby mine. A single move made by the player using the algorithm of AI2 causes a cascade of 20 free moves and 11 moves by AI0, giving the second board of Figure 1.4.3.

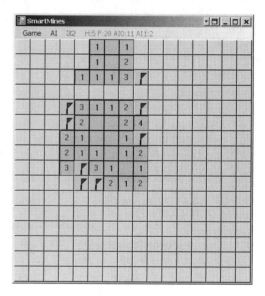

FIGURE 1.4.3   AI0 makes great progress after an AI2 move.

Results

The results are surprising. AI0 does the bulk of the work. AI0 makes 10 times more moves than AI1. AI1 makes 10 times more moves than AI2. The finished expert-level game played with all AI rules available (shown in Figure 1.4.4) recorded 4 human moves, 155 free moves, 280 moves by AI0, 39 moves by AI1, and 2 moves by AI2. Most players were surprised by these numbers. They thought that *Minesweeper* was harder than it is. In simple terms, the gameplay for *Minesweeper* is, "Don't make any mistakes doing the simplest stuff, do a modest amount of thinking now and then, and do a small amount of more considered thinking."

On the beginner level, there are 81 moves, 40 to 50 of which are usually free. Here, AI0 typically provides 30 moves. Many such games have only 1 or 2 human moves and often do not need AI1 at all. On the intermediate level, it is much the same with more than half of the 256 moves being free. Here AI1 provides 1 or 2 moves to keep things going. It is rare for AI2 to fire on an intermediate or beginner board.

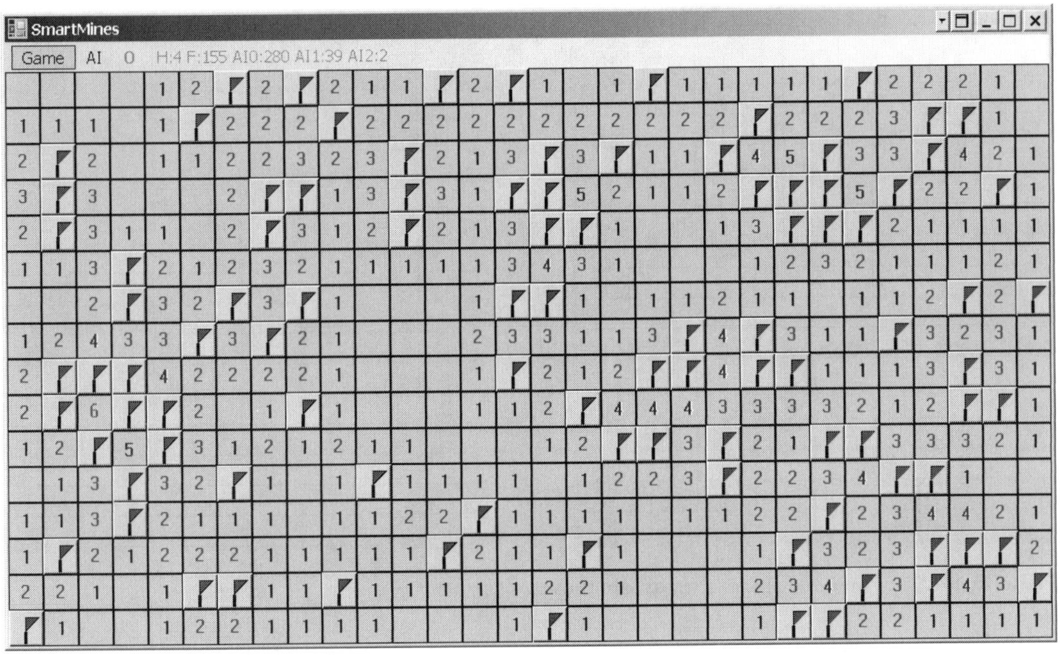

FIGURE 1.4.4 An expert-level board solved with four human moves.

Further Results

No other rules were implemented because expert-level games had been reduced from more than 300 player moves to typically less than 20 and often less than 10. The board has 480 tiles, but the number of free moves reduces the number of tiles the player has to mark or click. The moves that the more sophisticated rules would make were the most interesting moves of the game, and human players liked making them. Other rules were considered for their utility and for their ability to play as human players do.

In some games, three-tile analysis can sometimes yield deterministic moves (see Figure 1.4.5). Although such analysis is not beyond the capabilities of human players, such a rule was not implemented due to the success of the one- and two-tile rules and the desire to explore different basic concepts. Extending the concept to long-chain perimeter analysis of arbitrary length might yield deterministic moves, but most human players lack the concentration or the patience to play that way, so it was not implemented. Human players are more likely to memorize specific long patterns rather than analyze borders of arbitrary lengths and mine counts. Particular patterns of up to five tiles can be seen online at *http://www.planet-minesweeper.com* [Duffez06].

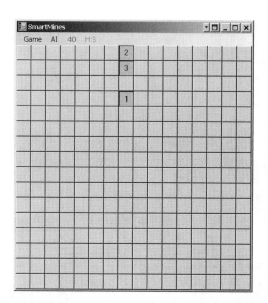 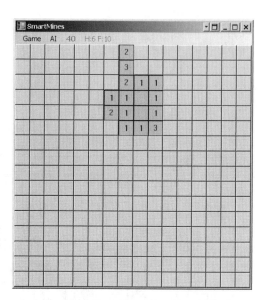

FIGURE 1.4.5   Three-tile analysis yields safe moves.

Statistical analysis provided candidates for further rules. In the end game, when the number of mines is more manageable, careful counts may be able to prove that all the remaining mines are on the perimeter. This in turn implies that all the tiles not on the perimeter are safe, yielding deterministic moves. In some cases, two- and three-tile analysis will place all of the mines. Because this analysis is reasonably easy for a human player to do, this would have been the next rule to be implemented. In the first board of Figure 1.4.6, there are three mines left. It can easily be shown that they all are on the perimeter of the cleared areas. The six tiles on the lower-right corner and one tile in the upper-left corner could be safely cleared as interior tiles. Likewise, the two mines in the upper left and the single mine on the lower right can be deterministically placed. After three such moves, the regular AI finishes the board.

Statistics offers guidance for the inevitable nondeterministic moves. Expert *Minesweeper* places 99 mines on a 480-tile board of 16 × 30 tiles averaging 0.20625 mines per tile, a bit more than 1 mine per 5 tiles. (Beginner and intermediate levels have a value of 0.1235 and 0.15625, respectively.) For first-order analysis, assume this ratio is reasonably constant for most of the game. A human player is unlikely to bother recomputing it until the end game. Complete accuracy would involve computing interior tiles and mines separately from perimeter tiles and mines. This is not always possible because the number of mines in perimeter tiles cannot always be narrowed to a single number. Although the number of perimeter mines cannot always be determined, the probability of a mine in a perimeter tile is usually exactly known or nearly so. Whether they are computing it numerically or not, the human player is asking, "Is it better to pick on the edge or some new place in the middle?"

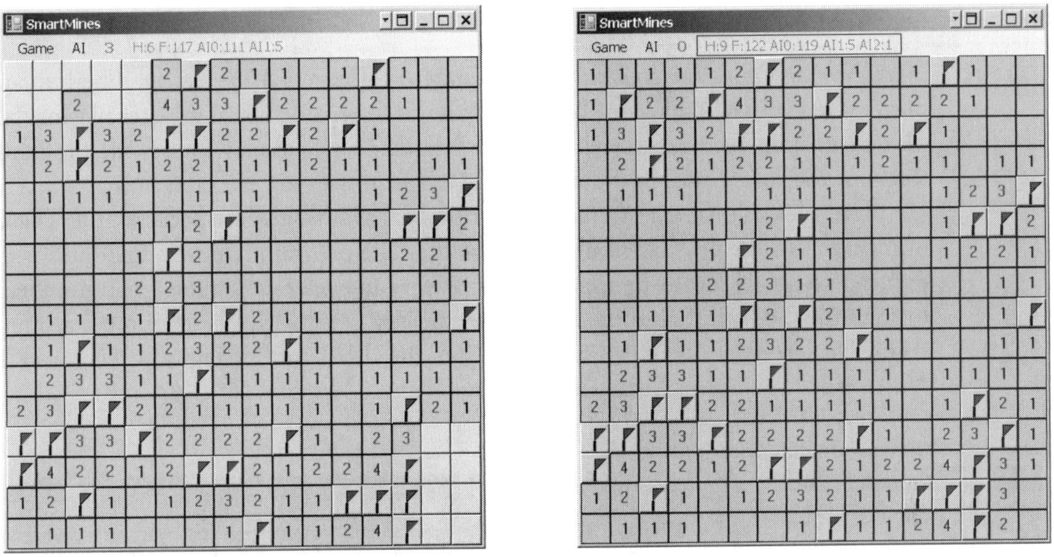

FIGURE 1.4.6 Perimeter analysis yields final moves.

When there is no deterministic move, a perimeter move with a risk value of one mine among two to four tiles is more risky than the average risk presumed to be at 0.20625. A risk value of one mine in five tiles is even, and one mine in six to eight tiles is less risky than the presumed average. If interior tiles prove less risky, the player must decide, "Which interior tile do I click?"

Because all interior tiles have identical risk, the player is best off picking the one with the best reward. Interior tiles one tile away from the perimeter tiles have higher reward than tiles farther away from a known tile. These tiles are within the range of AI2 and may yield a deterministic move! The first board in Figure 1.4.3 showed such a move, and the second board showed the rewards.

Even when picking on the perimeter of the minefield, the player should compare risk and reward. Tiles on the edge of the board are more constrained, and picking one of them may yield deterministic moves.

Risk and reward considerations gave rise to a potential two-player version of *Minesweeper*. The second player would be allowed to move mines around as long as this movement did not change any of the numbers shown to the regular player. The first player can no longer assume that all tiles in the interior have identical risks. Although this might be considered fun only by die-hard *Minesweeper* aficionados, most people do not regard *Minesweeper* as having any two-player potential at all. The rule for AI2 and statistical considerations were the inspiration for two-player *Minesweeper*. The important point here is that writing an AI can inspire new gameplay ideas.

SmartNumbers

SmartNumbers does for *Sudoku* what *SmartMines* does for *Minesweeper*. The human player starts with a blank game board and can create a game board for later play or the player can simply proceed. Saving a game board and reloading it causes the program to count the solved tiles in the saved game as free moves instead of as human moves. Unsolved tiles will have up to nine small numbers against a white background. These numbers show the possible solutions to the tile. The program removes small numbers that can no longer legally be selected. The player can click one of these small numbers to solve the tile with that number. A solved tile is marked with a large number against a gray background. All of this can be seen in the first board of Figure 1.4.7. *Smart-Numbers* has two rules, AI0 and AI1.

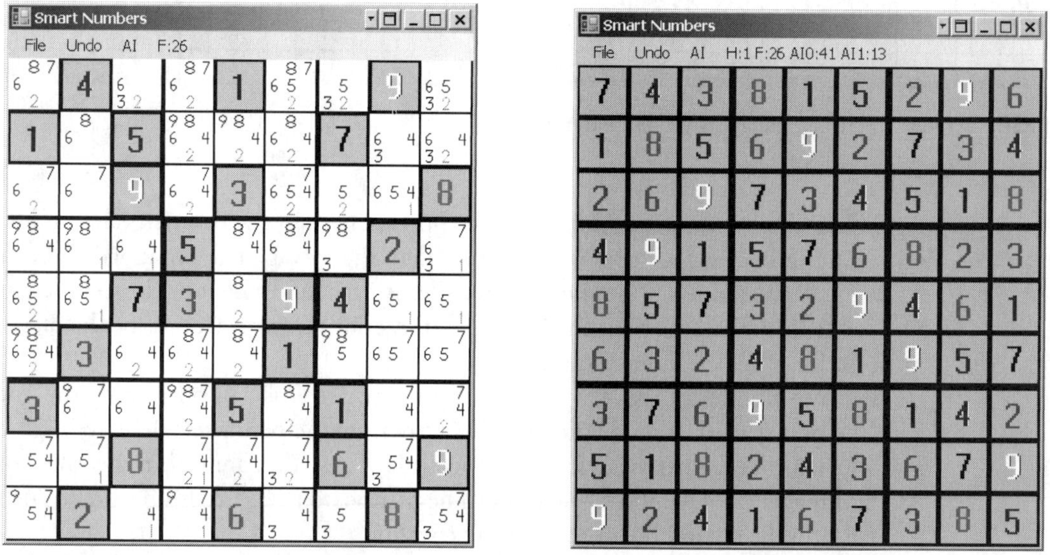

FIGURE 1.4.7   A board of 26 clues solved with 1 carefully selected human move.

Rules

The rules run on unsolved tiles. The rules compare the possible solutions for a tile to the constraints imposed by the game.

AI0 notices that when a tile has only one possible number remaining, that remaining number must be the solution. This is the simplest possible rule.

AI1 checks the possible numbers of a tile against tiles in the same row, column, and square. If that number is the only one of its value remaining in the row or column or square, it must be the solution. It codifies the statement, "All numbers must be present in each row, column, and square."

Results

For any difficulty level lower than "evil," these two rules suffice to solve the puzzle. At the evil difficulty, the human player is usually needed for two or three moves, and the AI can do all of the rest. Even with the AI turned off, the *SmartNumbers* game board is much easier to play than the same board in a newspaper. The program shows how part of the challenge of the game is to keep track of the impact of solved tiles on unsolved tiles. Many human players pencil in the nine small numbers on the unsolved squares and mark them off when playing with pencil and paper for this very reason.

The numeric results again show that the simplest rules do most of the work. An evil difficulty game scored 26 tiles free, 1 human move, 41 moves by AI0, and 13 moves by AI1. With *SmartNumbers,* the ratios vary more widely than *SmartMines,* but in general, AI0 fires more often than AI1 by a factor of two.

The numeric results also suggest that more complex rules would have very little utility. What is more, they would again be taking the most interesting moves away from the human player. The two rules already reduce the most complex boards from more than 50 moves to fewer than 5. *Sudoku* can be solved exactly with backtracking algorithms, but human players do not play it that way. Other rules within the reach of human players can be found in [Delahaye06] and more extensively at [Gupta05].

Conclusions

Both case studies show that a little bit of AI goes a long way with these two casual games. They also show that using AI to analyze games need not be overly difficult. The instrumentation shows that both games provide a number of easy challenges, a modest amount of medium challenges, and a few hard challenges. Another way of stating this is that the games give constant rewards of varying sizes, a typical marker of fun games. With an instrumented AI, it is easy to get numbers to show how the reward levels are balanced. The most surprising result is that nearly all of the game designers who were shown *SmartMines* at GDC 2006 and 2007 thought that *Minesweeper* was much harder than *SmartMines* proved it actually was. There was a disconnect between what the designers thought players did and what the players actually did. Perhaps of greater value to game designers is that the process of adding an instrumented AI to a game fosters new gameplay ideas.

Future Work

The obvious additions to these case studies are to implement more of the deterministic rules that human players use. It would be particularly interesting to see the usage ratios between the existing rules and these new, more sophisticated rules. *SmartMines* shows a 10:1 ratio, and *SmartNumbers* shows approximately a 2:1 ratio between the utility of the simple rules to the more complex rules. *SmartMines* clearly could use a display of the number of unmarked tiles or even the average risk value of the unmarked tiles.

References

[Collet05] Collet, Raphaël, "Playing the *Minesweeper* with Constraints." Multiparadigm Programming in Mozart/OZ, Second International Conference MOZ 2004. Lecture Notes in Computer Science, Vol. 3389, Springer, 2005. Paper and software available online at *http://www.info.ucl.ac.be/~raph/minesweeper/*, October 18, 2004.

[Delahaye06] Delahaye, Jean-Paul, "The Science Behind *Sudoku*." *Scientific American* (June 2006).

[Duffez06] Duffez, Grégoire, "Planet Minesweeper." Available online at *http://www.planet-minesweeper.com/schemas.php*, August 6, 2006.

[Gupta05] Gupta, Sourendu, "*Sudoku* Tips: How to Solve *Sudoku*: The Mathematics of Su Doku." Available online at *http://theory.tifr.res.in/~sgupta/sudoku/algo.html*, October 13, 2005.

[Kopp01] Kopp, Hans, "Truffle-Swine Keeper." Available online at *http://freenet-homepage.de/hskopp/swinekeeper.html*, April 4, 2001.

[Wikipedia07] Author unknown. Available online at *http://en.wikipedia.org/wiki/Minesweeper_(game)*, June 18, 2007.

1.5

Ecological Balance in AI Design

Adam Russell

chronotopia@gmail.com

This article considers the ways in which entrenched methods of game design can lead to unproductive tensions with advances in game AI technology. This issue encompasses not only methods of thinking about game design but also styles of design documentation and working relationships between designers and AI coders when iterating on game features. The result is not only a failure to produce useful increases in gameplay complexity. In some cases, the result is actually a reduction in complexity due to the inability of outdated design approaches to effectively control a more complex AI system.

The dream of emergence often seduces both designers and publishers. Advances in AI features can provide the publisher with marketing-friendly unique selling points, typically accompanied by great hopes among the designers of "limitless replayability" and "unique experiences." However, all too often a powerful new AI technology is brought in and just bolted on to existing approaches without corresponding changes in game design methodologies. In many cases, design approaches to behavior remain stuck in a simple state machine mindset even though the AI architecture has become considerably more complex. For example, whereas the design documents for a game are likely to specify precise actions in response to specific events, an agent architecture that uses search-based planning might consider a variety of responses to a given event depending on its longer-term goals.

The Principle of Ecological Balance

The field of situated robotics emerged in the late 1980s out of frustrations in the academic AI community with the general failure of Newell and Simon's *physical symbol systems* model of intelligence [Newell76]. Rodney Brooks' famous attack on symbols and search was motivated by his dramatic success in constructing a series of autonomous robots at MIT that were able to robustly perform physical tasks (such as Coke can collecting) in extremely noisy and dynamic environments without the use of any kind of internal knowledge representation either of those environments or of the task that they were performing [Brooks90]. After a half-decade of rapidly growing interest in this perspective, Swiss researcher Rolf Pfeifer laid out a set of design principles to summarize insights to date and to help guide further work in the field [Pfeifer96]. The sixth of these was his *principle of ecological balance*, which argued that increases in the supply of complex information from an autonomous agent's sensory systems are pointless unless balanced by an increase in demand from their motor coordination tasks, and that the overall sensory-motor complexity of the agent must be balanced to the needs of the ecological niche it inhabits.

In our version of the principle, increased complexity in game AI technology must be accompanied by a corresponding increase in design complexity if it is to deliver a significant change in gameplay. Game AI techniques and design methodologies must reach a balance within the overall gameplay niche. Unfortunately, there is very little observation of this principle in today's large-scale game development. Every development discipline has ambitions for increasing the sophistication of its contributions to the overall game, whether in applying cloth physics to plant models or adding search-based planning to the AI characters. In many cases (such as environment art), these complications can be made without concern for their interaction with other disciplines. However, game AI is intimately bound up with game design, and an increase in AI sophistication is pointless unless accompanied by a design mechanic that makes good use of it. The following sections explore several different sources of ecological imbalance in AI design, from defensive design attitudes and problematic working relationships, to counterproductive level design and different models of AI processes.

Defensive Design

Sadly, one major contributor to design imbalance in game AI is not technological, conceptual, or organizational, but a purely psychological problem. Generally speaking, the designers on a project are seen as being chiefly responsible for guiding the work of the other creative disciplines, for example, dictating the animation move set for playable characters, detailing how the HUD (Heads-Up Display) should operate, and specifying the required AI features. This responsibility requires that designers understand enough about the type of work involved in each of these areas that they are capable of making sound strategic decisions and capable of effectively communicating these decisions to the area specialists.

When it comes to modern game AI technology, there are so many factors for the designers to consider that the challenge of directing work on AI features is likely to result in more than a little insecurity. So many mechanics are at work in contemporary game AI solutions that designers often feel lost when attempting to conceive and execute specific designs using the AI systems.

Unfortunately, a common reaction is for the designers to tighten their grip on the AI to ensure it does not run away from them. Instead of increased feature complexity enabling a greater range of design expression, in practice, the increased complexity can result in a highly defensive design posture and a more limited range of design applications of AI features in the gameplay.

Problematic Working Relationships

The structure of working relationships between game designers and AI programmers is often a source of ecological imbalance between the two disciplines. Like most programmers, AI developers are generally concerned with fitting specific design concepts for the game into consistent overall software architectures, following logical patterns, and building systematic relationships between subsystems. This process means that at any given time in a typical working day, an AI programmer's attention is often deeply buried in some architectural issue, whether it is sketching out a new subcomponent and putting together some skeleton code for numerous new classes, or taking a long hard look at whether some particular design suggestion should necessitate a major refactoring of some existing system to accommodate this new variation.

By contrast, a designer's day is often spent reviewing and tweaking a particular functional area of the game, whether it is a specific level or perhaps a specific aspect of the game mechanics across all levels. This process tends to involve a brainstorm of notes in response to playthrough, capturing lots of little individual thoughts for improvements or tweaks to the design. As a result, the designer's attention is often very broadly connected to a great variety of surface gameplay phenomena, some imagined and some already present in the game.

The problem arises when these two mental states collide. If the designers are considering a bunch of small gameplay tweaks, it is very likely that they have a long list of accompanying questions for the AI programmers regarding these tweaks, such as "can we already do this?," "what exactly does that parameter do again?," "can you add a flag for us to turn that feature on and off?" Further, the desire to make progress in their design work that day often creates a pressure to have answers to these questions as and when they arise. Whether face-to-face or by some electronic means, it's most likely that these questions will produce a steady stream of brief communications between designers and AI programmers throughout any given day.

In an ideal world, this kind of working relationship produces a good level of mutual understanding between the two disciplines and helps to keep them up to date with each other's differing goals and objectives. However, in practice, it can often devolve into a constant stream of minutiae from the design team, which breaks up the AI programmers' attention throughout the day and makes it extremely difficult for them to stay focused on the overall technical architecture. As pressure builds toward a major project milestone, this problem is likely to worsen, and the design communications with AI can come to seem like nothing more than constant nitpicking.

This difference in working styles between the AI programmers and the designers is more than just a source of friction and reduced efficiency. Sustained over a long period, this problem has the potential to systematically undermine the engineering quality of the AI code. More and more time is spent satisfying short-term design changes, and less and less time is given to maintaining a coherent technical architecture. Of course, it is part of the AI programmer's job to help bring the designers' specifications in line with a consistent engineering framework, and a great part of this task is to continually educate and inform the designers so that they can understand how to design "with the grain" and not against it.

However, as the AI framework gradually becomes more complicated as a result of the design tweaking described previously, it becomes more difficult for the programmers to summarize and explain the system to the designers. Hence, it becomes ever more difficult for the designers to understand how any single concept they might come up with either fits into or contradicts the engineering picture that the AI programmers are trying to maintain. In a worst-case scenario, the result is ill-fitting concepts and excessive special-case complications to the AI framework. In this way, the whole working relationship becomes trapped in a vicious cycle to the detriment of the overall game.

Counterproductive Level Design

Nearly every game will have some equivalent to the concept of *levels*, where a level is a specific arrangement of game content with its own unique challenges and experiences. Also, nearly every game team is going to have people whose job it is to mastermind the design and implementation of these levels, whatever name is given to the discipline. For the sake of argument, we will call them level designers. At the end of the day, game AI features have no purpose except within the levels delivered in the final version of the game. If the level designers are working against the AI features instead of with them, the results are counterproductive.

The relationship between level design and game AI is rather like that between painting and brushes. The specific effect produced when the AI is employed by a level designer is not something intrinsic to the AI itself but rather something that the level designer achieves through the AI. The various general game mechanics and AI features will be brought together to create the effect. In theory, the available features are perfectly suited to achieving the desired effect. In practice, tension often exists between the generality of game features and the needs of a specific area of a level. We can identify several typical categories here, namely the perceived need in level design for specific event orders, precise timings, predictable movements, and predefined animations. Let's take a look at each of these categories.

Specific Event Order

Game AI architectures these days are increasingly capable of producing novel sequences of events on repeated play of the same area, for example, due to the use of dynamic terrain analysis or search-based planning. In many cases, this is great for the level designers. However, on many occasions, this can be a big problem because the level design requires that a certain sequence of events occurs in a consistent order at a specific point in the flow of the level. The repeated need for level designers to control the sequence of events at many points in the game can seriously undermine the drive toward more generative game AI.

Precise Timing

Even with level design taking very tight control of the order of behavioral events, the sheer complexity of the conditions on AI execution of behavior means that the timing of specific actions is not fully predictable in advance. For example, consider an action-adventure game where the level designers specify that at a certain point in the level, a conversation must take place between several characters, consisting of a series of lines of prerecorded dialogue that must be delivered in the correct order. This is a straightforward requirement and is easily met if the audio is simply played over the top of whatever the characters were doing at the time. However, contemporary character AI systems might well be waiting for other dialogue to finish, waiting until a speaker stops and turns to face the listener, or perhaps even waiting for some of the characters to navigate into each other's vicinity before starting to play the next line of audio. Variations in the time taken to achieve these conditions cause variations in the pacing and feel of the conversation. If the level designers do not come to accept this variable pacing and design their levels with it in mind, then they are likely to make a series of feature requests to the AI programmers that allow them to enforce timing of events. Unfortunately, all too often, the only way to ensure this precise timing is to make the behaviors unresponsive to their environment. This makes for extremely brittle and error-prone AI and also limits player interaction.

Predictable Movement

Just as the order and position of AI actions in time is a source of tension between level designers and AI developers, the same is also true of the spatial aspects of behavior. Search-based path planning is a vital feature of most contemporary game AI across a broad range of genres. Automated generation of navigation graphs is increasingly common, and this is very unlikely to support the exact patterns of spatial motion that the level designers envisage for an area. Further, even where the level designers are responsible for setting up some of the search metadata themselves, it is often difficult for them to predict the effects of such a change on the final movements of game agents. Anyone who has tried to control the results produced by a heuristic search algorithm would agree that it is very hard to predict all the consequences of a particular cost function. Unfortunately, in many cases, this complexity can be interpreted as a threat to the level design and again results in requests being made to enforce strict constraints on the AI behavior, such as "the NPCs must always enter the zone at this point and then travel through this waypoint."

Predefined Animations

Today's game character AI is likely to have very complex animation control systems capable of interleaving multiple simultaneous animation states such as locomotion, body posture, weapon aim, head tracking, facial mood, and lip synchronization. To drive these many concurrent channels of expression, many independent subsystems will be driving the animation state in parallel. For example, the aiming and head tracking code might be targeting the current primary threat, while the locomotion controller is following the current navigation path, the lip sync is blending in an appropriate phoneme shape based on the current audio state, and the body posture and facial mood are displaying extreme fatigue because the character is seriously injured. In principle this sounds great, but despite all that, the level designers are likely going to request direct control of the character's animation at certain points, for example, having the system play a custom animation interacting with the environment while delivering some accompanying dialogue.

This request can be served by having the level designers place some kind of map triggers that play specified animations on characters. However, problems start to arise when these triggers interact with the autonomous AI animation. If the designers have predetermined that a particular animation must play, but at runtime that animation might be preceded or followed by a variety of possible character animations, then it becomes very difficult to maintain consistency and believability. Even worse, there might be layers that are still running autonomously on top of the specified animation, such as facial mood, which can create highly inappropriate combinations.

With the level designers finding a contradiction in expression between the autonomous animation state and their triggered animation, their natural response is to ask for the ability to force the autonomous state to certain values. But then what began as a single specific animation gradually creeps out into general constraints on AI-driven animation throughout an entire area of the level, and before long, the repeated use of specific animations in levels can systematically undermine any attempts by the AI programmers to maintain a consistent relationship between external animation and internal AI state. Finally, this inconsistency can lead the design team to question the very purpose of having such internal state variables because it is proving difficult to clearly represent them to the player, and so aspects of the internal state model are dramatically simplified or just cut altogether.

Different Process Models

A model is never equivalent to the real system that it models, especially in software engineering. Just as the dominant representations at work in a field change over time, so the models employed vary across disciplines within a single project. The description of AI processes used in the work of artists and animators are likely to be massively simplified relative to the code architecture but good enough to appropriately structure their work on the art assets that will be connected to the processes. The descriptions used among programmers will vary depending on which area of the code is being focused on, but the descriptions can always be made more sophisticated as necessary by referring to the actual code under discussion. However, in design, we find a rather more difficult and hazardous relationship between description and implementation. The game designers are driving the engineering of AI features through the representational models they employ to describe AI processes. Any deep structural difference between the process models used by designers and those at work within the AI team is going to be a source of problems.

There have been many developments over the years in the approaches used to describe and implement game agent processes. The simplest way of thinking is what we might call a *stateless reactive* model, with a single update routine and a single handler routine for all event callbacks. This description is then made more powerful by allowing variables to persist across updates and different event handlers. For example, the enemy ships in *Space Invaders* can be described easily using a reactive model with some simple persistent variables. The ships always reverse their direction and drop down a level when reaching the screen boundary, they drop bombs every time a timer expires if there is no Invader below them, and they always die when struck by a player missile.

Even among nontechnical team members, most description of game agents goes beyond this simple reactive model and assumes the more systematic finite state machine metaphor. Here we describe agents as always being in exactly one state from a predefined list and view the event handling logic as being separate for each state, accompanied by a specialized update routine during which the current state can pursue whatever spontaneous action is appropriate. We might also very likely presume persistent variables that are local to the current state. To take another simple example, *Pac-Man*'s ghosts are most conveniently described as always being in one of two states, either chasing the player or fleeing from the player, with this division determining everything about their movement, animation, sound effects, and what happens when they touch the player [Lammers90].

Note that how these descriptions are implemented in code is to a great extent irrelevant—the important point here is the model used to represent the agent's behavior. A finite state machine description can always be translated into a stateless reactive model with persistent variables and vice versa. However, there will always be certain features which fit comfortably under one representation that become awkward to describe in another. For example, a reactive model can translate into a poorly defined state machine because there are variables that need to span states, and, by contrast, a state machine can translate into a messy reactive model because there are persistent variables whose values only have meaning at certain times.

As mentioned, the game designers are driving the engineering of AI features through the representational models they employ to describe AI processes. These models constrain the AI design in two senses. On one hand, the designers use their own models as a framework for themselves within which they are able to picture new AI features. On the other hand, they use these models as a language through which to express their designs back to the AI programmers. Of course, there will always be a difference in representation between the designers and the programmers they are working with. In an ideal world, this difference is only one of details, and the overall structure remains the same whichever discipline is describing it. Unfortunately, in practice, this is becoming less and less true as the technical architectures for AI become more and more sophisticated. If we take a look at the typical models used for game AI today within the design and the programming disciplines, we find a number of deep structural differences.

Game AI programmers are increasingly dealing with multiple simultaneous states, for example, agents might be looking at an interesting object while moving to operate a switch and simultaneously delivering lines in an ongoing conversation. More and more frequently, they are building goal-driven agents whose responses to stimuli vary depending on their current agenda, for example, deciding not to immediately attack on sighting an opponent because ammo is low [Orkin06]. Architectures are now relying extensively on subsystem encapsulation to remain robust and scalable in the face of today's increasingly complex game worlds, for example, decoupling the precise animation state of a character from higher-level decision making and imposing intervening abstractions such as pose requests [Burke01]. As a result of all these factors, surface behavior is more and more likely to vary on each play through a given section.

By contrast, design approaches to AI processes still tend to assume a single overall state, for example, "attacking," "searching," "idling," and so on. They typically apply a strongly reactive model of action-selection, for example, "every time the player executes that command, the character should immediately shout this response." Even where concurrency is considered, little concession is made to the need for encapsulation between subsystems, for example, "when they are navigating to a scripted position at which point they are going to start a conversation, they should look at the characters they are about to talking to." Also, despite marketing spin to the contrary, design will often still expect a surprisingly high degree of consistency in surface behavior in a particular encounter, for example, "when they come around this corner, they should always be aiming to the right." This overall disconnect between today's advanced AI process models and the established approaches to designing AI content has, in many cases, reached dangerous levels.

Conclusion

As we have seen, there are a number of different sources of ecological imbalance between game design and AI programming. Some of these are social issues, as seen with defensive design attitudes and tensions in the structure of working relationships. Others are technical issues, as seen with counterproductive approaches to level design and differences in conceptual models of AI processes. Either way, greater balance is needed in AI design between the different needs and concepts of designers and of programmers.

Two and a half thousand years ago, in his great utopian vision of the ideal city, Plato argued that political strife would not end until the philosophers came to rule the state, or at least until the rulers of the state became philosophers [Plato55]. In game AI, it is the design kings who make the executive decisions and the AI philosophers who ponder how to make sense of these decisions. Let's hope that more game designers can emulate Alexander the Great, a king who studied at the feet of Aristotle before riding out to conquer the known world.

References

[Brooks90] Brooks, Rodney, "Elephants Don't Play Chess." *Robotics and Autonomous Systems*, Vol 6 (1990): pp. 3–15.

[Burke01] Burke, Robert, et al., "CreatureSmarts: The Art and Architecture of a Virtual Brain." Proceedings of the Game Developers Conference (2001): pp. 147–166.

[Lammers90] Lammers, Susan (ed.), *Programmers at Work*. Tempus Books, 1989. Interview with Iwatani is also available at *http://www.geocities.com/SiliconValley/Heights/5874/iwatani.htm*.

[Newell76] Newell, Albert, and Herbert A. Simon, "Computer Science as Empirical Inquiry: Symbols and Search." *Communications of the ACM*, Vol 19, no.3 (March 1976): pp. 113–126.

[Orkin06] Orkin, Jeff, "3 States and a Plan: The AI of F.E.A.R." *Game Developers Conference*, (2006), available online at *http://web.media.mit.edu/~jorkin/*.

[Pfeifer96] Pfeifer, Rolf, "Building Fungus Eaters: Design Principles of Autonomous Agents." *Proceedings of the Fourth International Conference on Simulation of Adaptive Behavior* (1996): pp. 3–12.

[Plato55] Plato, *Republic*. Trans. H. D. P. Lee. Penguin, 1955.

MOVEMENT AND PATHFINDING

2.1

Company of Heroes Squad Formations Explained

Chris Jurney—Kaos Studios

jurney@gmail.com

The squad formations in *Company of Heroes* are designed to provide very complex and believable motion for groups of soldiers moving through a highly destructible environment. This article explains how this was accomplished in enough detail that you can implement a similar system or just steal a few of the tricks for your next game. The techniques primarily apply to games with an overhead view where the positioning and tactical movement of units is of high importance.

Squad Makeup

In *Company of Heroes*, infantry units are grouped together in squads. Players are only able to issue orders to squads, so it is up to the squad AI to make the units look smart while executing orders. Squads are broken up into three elements: core, left flank, and right flank. Each element has a leader, and the leader of the core element is the leader of the squad. These roles are assigned to soldiers and updated whenever one is killed or the squad is reinforced. The assignments are made based on an extensive set of game-specific rules, for example:

- Put squad leaders in the core.
- Allies put heavy weapons in the flanks; Axis put heavy weapons in the core.
- Put an even number of soldiers in the left and right flanks.

These assignment changes are "stable," meaning that the system does the minimum number of swaps necessary to obey the assignment rules. Extra swaps are avoided because it looks awkward when a soldier randomly runs from the left side of a squad to the right when a reinforcement arrives. The hierarchical structure of the squads is shown in Figure 2.1.1.

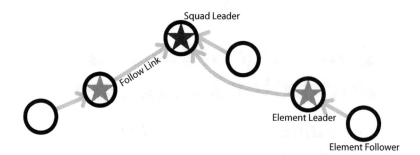

FIGURE 2.1.1   The formation layout is hierarchal. At the top of the hierarchy is the squad leader who has an immediate follower represented by the hollow circle and two element leader followers that are represented by the circles filled with gray stars. Each element leader has a single element follower, which is represented by a hollow circle.

Move Out

Now, let's move on to the basics of movement. When a move order is issued to a squad, its leader receives an order to move all the way to the move order's goal. He immediately computes a path and starts moving. To generate goals for other squad members, we predict the future position of the leader along his path roughly two seconds ahead. We then take an offset from the leader's future position and orient it using the leader's future heading to generate goals for element leaders. The formation is hierarchal, so element followers make predictions for their element leaders' positions and move to offsets from there, as shown in Figure 2.1.2.

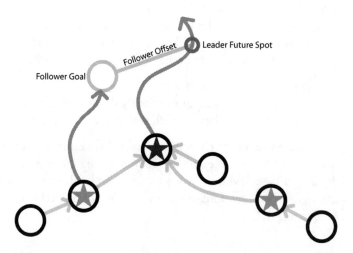

FIGURE 2.1.2   Followers move to an offset from a point in the leader's future. The goal for the left-hand element leader is computed using the predicted future position of the squad leader and the offset between the element leader and the squad leader rotated according to the predicted heading of the squad leader.

Now the units are moving, but there is a problem. Without some control of the units' speeds, the formation will quickly lose its shape as some units fall behind and others pull ahead. To overcome this problem, we introduce a speed modifier that is used to adjust the speed of movement of individual units. To get the speed modifier, we take the same formation offset we used to calculate the follower's goal, rotate it according to the leader's current heading, and apply it relative to the leader's current position instead of his future position.

If the follower is ahead of the offset position in the axis of the leader's motion, we slow him down proportional to the distance he's ahead; if the follower is behind, we speed him up proportional to the distance he's behind (see Figure 2.1.3). We don't really care if he gets out of place in the axis perpendicular to the direction of motion of the leader because the follower's goal will bring him back in line eventually.

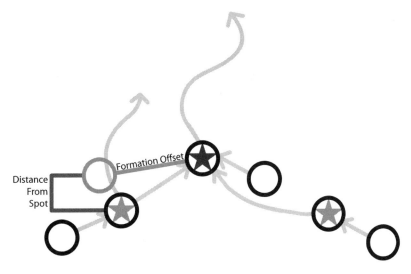

FIGURE 2.1.3 The distance of a squad member from his current offset position in the current direction of motion of the squad leader is used to adjust his speed.

Softening the Shape

Now the units are moving out, but they will occasionally run into problems. Sometimes when using fixed offsets, the followers' goals will be inside or on the far side of obstacles, which is particularly problematic when the pathfinding distances to those goals are significantly larger than the straight-line distances.

To resolve this, the system never uses offsets directly. Instead, for the goal offset points described previously, a cheap A* pathfind with a search step limit of around 50–100 nodes is run from the leader's future position to the follower's ideal future offset position. Whether or not the search succeeds, the offset that will actually be used by the follower will be the point touched by the search that was nearest to the ideal offset position. The net effect of this approach is to make the formation squeeze in organically at chokepoints and route around small obstacles that don't divert too much from the leader's path. The behavior of this technique is shown in two different scenarios in Figures 2.1.4 and 2.1.5.

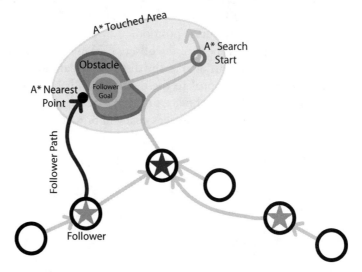

FIGURE 2.1.4   The actual follower offset goal is picked by pathing from the leader's future spot to the ideal offset position. The nearest point found by the pathfinding algorithm to the ideal offset position is used as the actual offset position.

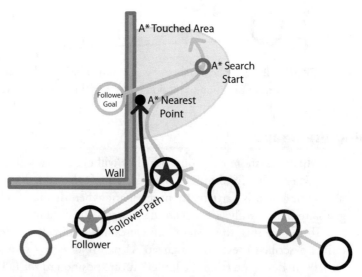

FIGURE 2.1.5   Using a search to choose a follower's goal produces good results in nearly every scenario.

The formation is now handling movement amid obstacles and chokepoints, but it will look a bit robotic because the combination of the fixed offsets, speed control, and obstacle avoidance code is too good at keeping units in their formation-mandated spots. To counteract this, we have each unit store a personal drift variable that is added to its formation offset for all the formation calculations. Each tick of the simulation this drift value floats around via a random offset within a maximum radius.

All the systems that have been described for controlling the movements of individual units in formation have one major drawback: performance. The cost of the pathfind searches that are used to calculate goal positions are inexpensive because they can be accomplished with a very low search step limit, however, pathfinding from the followers' current positions to the followers' goals is slightly less constrained. Because we are giving slightly different move orders to each unit each tick, we are asking each unit to repath each tick.

Even though the pathfinding is only performed over relatively short distances, it does add up. To counteract this, when the system calculates the final goal position and speed modifier for a unit, it compares these to the unit's current movement. If the difference is within a small delta, then the new order is not given because it would have little impact. By tuning this delta, we can have our follower units repath only every half-second to three-quarters second during formation movement, which is enough to keep their pathfinding from showing up significantly in the profile stats for the game.

Formation Context

Not all formations are appropriate for all situations. When in a wide-open field, for example, a broad wedge shape looks very natural, but when navigating along cramped city streets, the same shape seems unnatural. To fix this, we decide which of a set of formations to use based on the terrain the squad leader is passing over. Specifically, we used a wide wedge for open areas, a tight wedge for confined areas, and a staggered column for roads.

Leapfrogging

Now that the soldiers are moving in formation, it would be nice if they could leave the formation occasionally to leapfrog to cover or some other interesting feature of the game world. Specifically, *leapfrogging* means that one of the elements is going to leave his normal place in the formation, run to some interesting spot in the world, hold for some amount of time, and then resume moving in formation. Such interesting spots are selected by searching for points of interest in the area of a follower's goal. When we find something interesting, we change the mode of movement of the element to have it follow the leapfrogging pattern. Only element leaders perform this behavior, and element followers are simply along for the ride. Occasionally, a leapfrog is performed even when there is no interesting feature, just to keep the squads looking interesting. The leapfrogging pattern is shown in Figures 2.1.6 and 2.1.7.

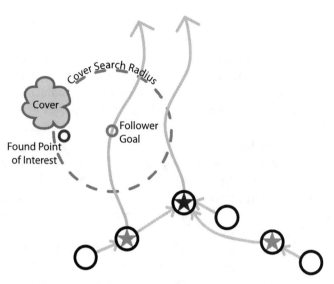

FIGURE 2.1.6   Followers search for points of interest by leapfrogging in the area of their goal.

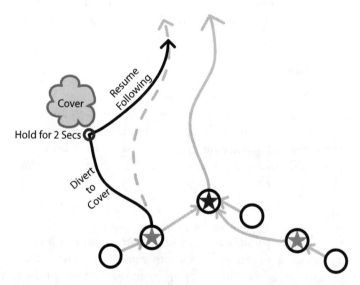

FIGURE 2.1.7   Leapfrogging units move to the point of interest, stop, and then resume following.

This system works, but in some cases, putting a hard stop in the middle of a leapfrog looks wrong, especially when the squad is in a hurry, such as when it is retreating. To fix this, we add a second type of leapfrogging called a "soft" leapfrog. In the case of a soft leapfrog, we calculate both the normal formation move order for the element leader and the leapfrog order. We then send the element leader to a point on the line between the two orders, about 80% on the side of the leapfrog order. This results in the character veering out of formation obviously toward cover and slowing a bit but never stopping. The effect is a very intelligent-looking unit who is in a hurry, but not so much as to totally ignore his own safety and his environment, as shown in Figure 2.1.8.

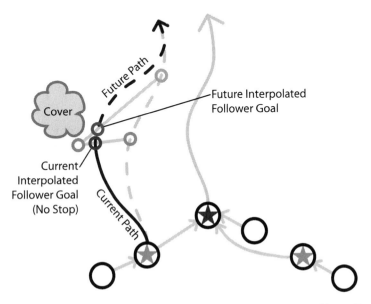

FIGURE 2.1.8 Soft leapfrogging modifies the follower's goal by pulling it in the direction of the point of interest.

Virtual Leader

Adding leapfrogging into the formation system creates a new problem. When the leader of the squad and of the core element stops heading for the goal and heads for some cover in a leapfrog, the entire squad will veer off to follow him. To fix this problem, we add the idea of a virtual leader that the formation will follow instead of the real one. Most of the time, the virtual leader is snapped to the position of the real leader, but when the squad leader leapfrogs, the virtual leader continues on the original path to the goal. When the real leader finishes leapfrogging and resumes heading to the goal, the virtual leader interpolates back and eventually snaps to the real leader. The interpolation helps prevent jerks in the motion of the units that would be caused by sudden changes in goal positions. The effect of the virtual leader is shown in Figure 2.1.9.

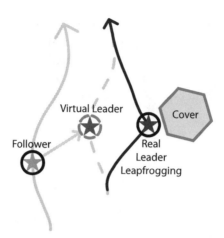

FIGURE 2.1.9   While the real leader is leapfrogging, followers use a virtual leader that continues on the real leader's previous path.

The reason for not using a virtual leader all the time is that the virtual leader is not a real unit dealing with all the obstacles of the dynamically changing world and can therefore get significantly ahead of, or behind, the actual units. When the leader is a significant distance from the followers, follower behavior will become less intelligent because their goals and any leapfrogging behavior will be based on objects too far in their future to appear relevant. Initially, the formations implemented for *Homeworld* had issues with this, so we avoided the problem in *Company of Heroes* by keeping the virtual leader as nonvirtual as possible.

Destination Formation

A separate formation system is used when a squad gets near its destination. This formation has the same shape and uses the same drift values as the moving formation to avoid any jarring shifts. In the separate system, each soldier marks his destination spot with a reservation to make sure that no one else is standing there when he arrives, and no one else is allowed to use that spot as a destination until he gives it up.

The user can set the facing of the formation in *Company of Heroes* by right-dragging the mouse instead of right-clicking. If he doesn't do that, we try to help him out by making the formation face any enemies in the area; if there aren't any, units simply face the average direction for the move order, defined by the vector from the squad leader's start position to the position the user clicked.

Each individual soldier in the formation does a search in the area surrounding his formation spot looking for cover to protect him from enemies that lie in the direction of the formation heading. If he finds cover, he'll go there instead of his formation spot. Just like in the moving formation, we find a spot for the leader first, then we use cheap pathfinds to validate any spot chosen by the destination formation, and we use the closest available if it isn't reachable. This keeps squad members from ending up on the wrong side of a long wall or building at the end of a move but allows them to go to the other side of small obstacles.

Handling Destruction

Fortunately, no additional code is required for this system to handle a highly dynamic and destructible environment. Because everyone but the leader is recalculating their paths every four to six ticks, any changes to the environment are immediately reflected in units' routes. As long as the leader also periodically recalculates his route to the goal, he will also react to any changes. In practice, having the leader repath every time he leapfrogged was sufficient.

The performance impact of all the repaths required by this formation system is mitigated for the followers by the fact that their paths are all very short distances and almost always direct due to the fact that their goal positions are close to a future position of the leader and hence almost always directly reachable. Color Plate 1 shows a formation from *Company of Heroes* with examples of these short paths. The performance impact of the leader repaths is mitigated by the relatively smaller number of leaders and by using hierarchal pathfinding.

Conclusion

The motion produced by the system that is described in this article played a significant part in making the soldiers in *Company of Heroes* into believable characters. Using the system, you can achieve tactically and visually interesting motion. Even if you can't use the entire system, you should be able to use the individual pieces to improve the quality of your own group movement. The parts described can be developed iteratively to build up advanced behavior gradually. After you apply them all, you will have squads that will impress your players with their incredibly tactical and life-like motion.

2.2

Turning Spaces into Places

Adam Russell

chronotopia@gmail.com

This article explores the complex relationship between the forms of spatial representation employed by game agents and the forms of behavior that are easily supported by them. You will see how most game agents typically reduce space to little more than a list of individual entities with objective spatial features existing in a task-neutral navigational representation of the global environment, and you will see how this is likely to severely limit their behavioral sophistication. This observation leads us into an extended discussion of the much richer notions of place found in the philosophical literature, before returning to practical themes with a review of place-based models in game AI. We will discuss affordance theory, smart object models, terrain analysis, influence mapping, and informed environments, relating these specific approaches back to the general philosophical notions of place identified in the middle section of the article.

The Impoverished Umwelt of Game Agents

Jakob von Uexkull was an Estonian biologist who studied the way in which different organisms are adapted to their environments. He argued that it is misleading to talk of organisms responding to a subset of the objective features of a physical environment and to view these environmental features as something separate from the organisms that respond to them. Instead, he pointed out that the only environmental features that exist as far as the organism is concerned are those formed by sensory-motor response mechanisms specific to the organism in question. Von Uexkull employed the German word *Umwelt* or "about-world" to refer to this notion of the environment as seen from the organism's point of view, what we might call its "subjective environment" [von Uexkull57].

Applying this notion to game AI, we find a huge difference between the *Umwelts* of the player and of the game agents. Whereas a human player experiences the game world as a rich tapestry of meanings, the game agents' subjective environment typically consists of just two types of information: a list of entities recently observed in local space and some form of navigation graph representing the global spatial structure.

Local Entities

Any game agent is likely to have some sort of list of handles to other entities in the game database, such as "current target," "nearest cover point," and so on. In the simplest case, these handles are nothing more than pointers to the entities themselves, and the agent will pull state data directly off the entities as necessary, for example, to determine their current position or velocity. In more complex setups, there will be some kind of data structures referring to the entities, with various fields whose values are unique to the agent in question [Orkin05], for example, "last observed position" or "last observed time," along with a pointer to the entity so that the agent can still cheat when it needs to. In a very sophisticated setup [Evans00, Burke01], the entities themselves will be completely hidden from the sensory representation, and there will be an extensible and modular data structure within which to capture observed features of sensory stimuli, such as "hot" or "making a noise."

Whatever the complexity of the data, certain general traits can be identified. First, whether the description is made directly ("this entity") or indirectly ("an entity like this"), it is still a static description. It might describe changing spatial features of the entity, such as its position, but at any given time, the description is typically a single frozen snapshot of the entity's state (or perceived state). These representations are almost completely *atemporal*, with generally only a very limited sense of time, often no more than a simple timestamp and "is still valid" query that depends on how old the description is. It is extremely rare for such sensory data to include a history of previous states or any kind of prediction of future state, such as an estimated trajectory [Isla02].

Second, the description typically consists entirely of *objective features*, which is to say it conveys facts about the entity that are observer-independent, such as its height or location. The furthest that these descriptions might venture into observer-dependent features is to use an egocentric spatial measure such as "current distance." However, these kinds of egocentric measures are simply derived from the objective features of two entities, which in the case of distance are, of course, the position of the observed entity and the position of the agent itself. These kinds of variables are egocentric but still represent objective relations between entities and could be determined from any point of view that wanted to consider them. It is exceedingly rare in game agents to find truly subjective descriptions of observed entities, that is, descriptions that are task-dependent and possibly meaningless to any other observer, although this approach can be found in work on situated robotics [Brooks90].

Finally, these descriptions don't just attach a list of observed features to an entity. Almost certainly the descriptions are also classifications of the entity under some type, probably within a hierarchy of types, such as "pickup" or "door." Much like the descriptive features discussed previously, these types are usually an *objective classification* of the entity, which means they apply a shared typology that any other observer would apply in the same way and arrive at the same classification. Most likely the types employed are the actual entity classes from the game database, and thus correspond directly to the nature of the entity. "Call a spade a spade" could almost be a motto for these kinds of sensory representations.

Global Structure

In addition to awareness of certain game objects, agents will almost certainly have access to some kind of navigational representation of the overall structure of the game space. Navigation graphs provide agents with a considerably simpler environment model than that of an environment's collision geometry, which is likely to be much simpler than its render meshes. By reducing space to a set of nodes on a graph and a set of connections between them, agents are able to use graph-based search algorithms to plan paths through the game environment [Stout00]. Under this representation, following a reduction of the agent's physical volume to a single point, the positions of both the agent and its goal are reduced to single nodes based on proximity, in the case of waypoint graphs, or based on containment, in the case of space-filling graphs.

Although many games now incorporate some form of dynamic navigation representation, the runtime data changes are normally just annotations on top of an underlying structure that is static—the positioning of waypoints, or the identification of navigation polygons is extremely difficult to automate and, even when automated, will almost certainly remain an expensive offline task [Tozour02]. This means that the spatial structure upon which dynamic annotations can be made at runtime is precomputed and thus fixed for all agents at all times during the course of the game.

Objective Space

From the preceding review, it seems at first that spatial information appears under two contrasting extremes. On one hand, we have instantaneous spatial measurements regarding nearby entities, and on the other, we have a permanent navigational structure regarding the whole of the current game space; we have one local and one global form of information, one temporary and one permanent. However, despite this contrast, both representations are united by a general *objectification* of spatial information in two related senses of the word. First, these representations objectify space because they capture spatial information that is observer-independent. Second, these representations objectify space because they reduce space to the locations of entities (i.e., objects) at specific points in space.

In Search of a Sense of Place

At the inaugural AIIDE conference in 2005, Damian Isla discussed in considerable depth the many varieties of spatial representation at work in Bungie's *Halo 2* [Isla05a]. Despite demonstrating a state-of-the-art variety of spatial representations in the game, Isla admitted that even *Halo* still lacked much representation of spatial semantics, such as recognition of rooms and their doorways, distinguishing between inside and outside, and capturing the mission-dependent sense of forward and backward through a game level. At the same conference, Doug Church explored his concerns that the game AI discipline is endlessly refining a narrow set of agent competencies and not addressing broader issues, such as the interaction between level design and autonomous behavior, and the lack of tools for pulling narrative out of cutscenes and putting it into the game [Church05].

The basic motivation behind this article is that an increase in the complexity of representations of spatial semantics will have a direct positive impact on the broader issues that Church was discussing. We need better representations of *place* within our AI frameworks to support more believable character interactions. The impoverished *Umwelt* of game agents is intimately bound up with the general lack of development in nonadversarial social interactions such as conversation models, opinion systems, and interactive drama. In this search for more complex notions of place, we need to broaden our discussion beyond the established terminology of game AI and draw on related literature from other fields, such as philosophy, psychology, and sociology.

Places Are Observer-Dependent

No discussion of place is complete without mention of the French thinker Henri Lefebvre. His work on place has been a massive influence on a whole generation of thinkers across a multitude of fields. Much of the "spatial turn" in social sciences over the past 15 years can be attributed to the publication in English of Lefebvre's master-work *The Production of Space* [Lefebvre91]. In this book, Lefebvre identifies three interrelated perspectives on space: spatial practice, by which he means the physical construction of spatial patterns by our culture; represented space, by which he means the ways in which we conceive of space in our culture; and *representational* space, which he uses to refer to the dynamic interplay between our spatial practice and our represented space.

This approach of taking two opposing notions of space and then introducing a third notion that mediates between them is typical of concepts of place. In fact, it is directly analogous to the points made earlier regarding the gap between local entities and global structure in game AI and the suggested need for spatial representations that lie between the levels of individual objects and the global environment. As mentioned previously, game agents need far more sophisticated representations of spatial semantics, such as doorway, inside, outside, forward, and backward. These semantics are not objective features of the physical environment (even though they might be consistently perceived by all observers), and in many cases, they are task-dependant and highly temporary. However, they are also often shared between agents, and agreement on their application is required for spatial coordination of groups. Similarly, Lefebvre's representational space refers to the interactions in society between our physical environment (spatial practice) and our private mental concepts of that environment (represented space).

Places Are Integrated with Behavior

The phenomenologist Maurice Merleau-Ponty is unusual among his trade for being sincerely interested in the work of empirical scientists. In his book *The Structure of Behaviour,* he draws attention to the body as an active center that integrates the mental and physical domains [Merleau-Ponty65]. As James Gibson would discuss 30 years later, our perception of the spatial environment is structured by the sorts of actions it affords our body [Gibson79]. We see things for grasping, pushing, pulling, and sitting on. We do not see distance, volume, angles, and so on. This is what Merleau-Ponty means when he talks of the "functional body."

As it happens, one of Merleau-Ponty's most well-known examples of his notion of perception is that of the player of a game, namely American football. The football player does not see the field as an object with objective features, such as evenly mown grass and regularly spaced painted white lines. Instead, he sees the field in terms of what Gibson would call *affordances for action*, such as blocks and openings; potential passes; and ultimately the goal itself, which in Merleau-Ponty's view is again not an object but a powerful sense of direction that pervades the entire field. This work again speaks of the need for a sense of place in game agents, for what Damien Isla called spatial semantics, and as we shall discuss later, is directly mirrored in the current state of the art approaches to dynamic tactics in combat AI.

Places Are Hierarchical and Concurrent

The basic thrust of Lefebvre's work is that our sense of place is neither simply objective nor simply subjective but socially constructed. It should also be noted that each individual belongs to many social groups and as such is likely to experience many different senses of place at once in the same space. But space is also layered with places by the existence of multiple individuals representing separate social groups. Lefebvre discusses this point in the light of the appropriation by teenagers of spaces constructed for the purposes of adult capitalist society, and the imposition of their own sense of place on these spaces. For example, Lefebvre is fascinated by the teenage appropriation of a fountain in a mall and how this might represent a rupture in capitalist place due to the presence of individuals uninterested in consumption.

At first sight, these observations seem quite remote from the issues of game spaces and their habitation by game agents, but it is important to consider the ways in which simultaneous representations of place can overlap and conflict with one another in games. For example, it's all very well for a pair of NPCs to designate a place where they are "having a conversation," but this can look pretty stupid if they ignore the fact that other NPCs keep walking through the middle of their conversation or that they are standing in the middle of a fight between the town guards and some criminal.

Places Are Associative Structures

We have seen how places are socially constructed; how they are structured by and, in turn, structure our actions; and how multiple places can coexist simultaneously in a space. But places can be more than just direct inscriptions of action into the environment, such as "hide here" or "snipe from here" or "hang out here." Places can also provide a typology or a categorization with which to plan and reason about behavior or with which to associate patterns between different spaces. In some cases, places can even be said to form a vocabulary for a language of space.

The sociologist Erving Goffman developed what he called the dramaturgical perspective on everyday life [Goffman59]. He drew an analogy with the requirement in stage theater that an actor remain "in character" while performing in front of the audience. According to Goffman, many everyday social situations can be characterized as providing roles for actors to perform, and people will go to great lengths to preserve the role they are playing, even if the actions they take to do so contradict actions that they take at other times and places in other roles. For example, the serving staff in a hotel will always endeavor to maintain their roles of humility and disinterest toward the private lives of the guests, even when in fact they take great interest in the guests' affairs and often consider themselves superior to the guests.

The most interesting aspect about Goffman's application of the dramaturgical perspective is that it brings with it a spatial vocabulary involving terms such as "front stage" and "back stage," which Goffman argues are critical notions of place that we apply throughout our social lives. He pointed out that it is very common for service environments, such as hotels or cafes, or even workshops, to be physically arranged in such a way as to support these notions. They might have a small "front stage" area (such as behind the counter of a store) within which the performers appear and maintain strict adherence to the role, along with a generally hidden back stage area, such as the kitchen, within which the performers can discuss their performances of the roles and express quite different opinions of the audience outside. Throughout our everyday life, Goffman argues, we are constantly framing our spatial environment with respect to whatever roles we might currently be performing, and this continual process structures every detail of our paths through the environment, our body language, and our facial expression.

Models of Place

We've now described various concepts of place from a largely philosophical point of view. You have seen how a sense of place differs from a simple awareness of objective space in a number of ways. Places are socially constructed notions; they are action-oriented structures; they are layered on top of one another in the spatial environment, both concurrently and hierarchically; and finally they can provide us with what you might call a vocabulary for reasoning about space. Let's now take a look at how elements of these abstract philosophical themes are embodied in some concrete models of place.

Affordance Theory and Action-Oriented Perception

As mentioned previously in our discussion of Merleau-Ponty, the psychologist James Gibson argued that our perceptions of the environment are primarily structured around possibilities for action. He coined the term *affordance* to refer to this kind of perception and suggested that we don't principally experience objects in our local environment, but rather we experience affordances that are presented to us by objects [Gibson79]. It is important to note that the affordance is not an intrinsic feature of the object in itself but depends on the interaction between the object and our sensory-motor activities. This takes us back to the points made earlier about the *Umwelt*. The things that we see in the environment are intimately connected with the things that we do in that environment. Whereas a human sees a world of containers for filling, handles for turning, text for reading, and so on, a cat sees a world of surfaces for marking, corners for hiding in, and items for pouncing on.

Many games are already exploiting the affordance theory to structure the interactions between game agents and their environment, most famously Will Wright's *The Sims* with its "smart object" model. We could say this approach was already implicit in our earlier discussion of game agents' awarenesses of local entities, when we mentioned the ascription of types to entities such as "pickup" or "door." In many cases, the entity types employed by the AI map directly to actions, such as "activate," "open," "shoot at," and so on. Although it is true that the types ascribed are typically observer-independent and as such do not seem to arise from an interaction with the agent, the object type hierarchies created for the game database are in fact often designed around the sorts of actions that both the player and the game agents are capable of performing, and so these object types already represent a system of affordances for the AI.

However, as stressed in earlier sections, having a sense of place requires being able to see the same space in many different ways depending on our engagement in different social activities. The same should apply to the ascription of affordances to game objects, and it might be that the direct use of a single type of hierarchy by all game agents, even if this hierarchy represents a system of affordances, is largely responsible for the lack of variety in game behavior. If everything is either a resource for picking up or an enemy for shooting at, then it's difficult to persuade your game agents to do much more than pick stuff up and shoot stuff. This is why *The Sims* is so clever—although it does reduce all objects to a predetermined set of affordances in an abstract sense (things that make agents less tired, more happy, less stressed, and so on). At a more concrete level, there is no limit to the actions that can be afforded to agents by the addition of new types of object to the simulation because the concrete actions (drink coffee, cook at gas stove, dance in front of stereo, and so on) are determined by scripts, animations, and sound effects that are all provided by the object. However, even *The Sims* is limited in its representation of place because both the drives satisfied and the actions afforded by an object are fixed. A book in the game is only ever an educational device; it is never alternately a doorstop or a shelf support or a ramp for a toy car track.

Direct Identification of Affordances Through Terrain Analysis

So far, we have been associating affordances with existing game entities, such as "a chair is for sitting on." But implicit in such discussions is the assumption that the entities are already identifiable objects in the environment and that their existences precede any attachment of affordances to them. It is very common practice in combat AI to require level designers to place helper entities, such as cover point markers, into maps, but normally, each helper entity has to be identified and placed manually by the designers. These entity-based approaches can support a dynamic sense of place by the runtime selection of a subset of "currently valid" positions taken from the complete set of existing helper entities. However, the runtime selection of an active subset is only very effective if a large number of such locations is available to choose from in the first place, and this is not a very scalable approach when each entity has to be manually placed by a level designer.

Here we shall use the term *terrain analysis* to refer to any kind of spatial search either offline or online that identifies the existence of affordances at locations in space without requiring the existence of an intervening entity [van der Sterren02]. We'll use "static" terrain analysis to refer to offline searches, with "dynamic" terrain analysis being reserved for online searches that identify affordances at runtime. The offline approach is still useful in supporting a dynamic sense of place because it lacks the scale limitations of human-authored approaches and can be used to generate very large numbers of potential affordances, such as cover locations in advance, giving the runtime AI a large set from which to select currently valid affordances. However, an online approach will always be superior if it is computationally feasible because it saves on the space that is required to store potentially enormous quantities of predefined affordances, it avoids the search costs of iterating through these very large sets when most of the members are invalid most of the time, and it also supports the identification of affordances that depend heavily upon dynamic situational features, such as ambush locations.

Constructing Regional Affordances with Influence Maps

Affordance theory is a good way of thinking about closer integration between action and perception, but it doesn't necessarily help us bridge the gap between individual affordances (e.g., "hide here") and a broader sense of place (e.g., "this area makes us alert and tense"). Whether we consider local entities that present affordances for action rather than objective physical features or perhaps identify affordances at spatial positions using terrain analysis, both of these approaches still tend to conjure an image of point-like affordances hanging in a neutral space through which we navigate to reach the point where the affordance is available. We are still left with a "go here, do this" model of spatial behavior, with the "do this" at the end not telling us very much about the "go here" that precedes it. This intervening space remains physical, observer-independent, and without any of the qualities of place that we explored earlier. Let's take a look now at influence mapping, which is able to construct entire spatial regions that have observer-dependent and action-oriented meanings.

Influence mapping is a well-known technique in strategy game AI that takes a list of unit types held at known positions by different factions (traditionally by two opponents) and uses this information to construct spatial representations, such as areas of principal control or border lines. It does this by using some kind of iterative propagation of scalar influence values from the units across an existing discrete spatial representation, such as a grid or a hexmap [Tozour01]. The interesting point about influence mapping in our discussion is that it supports the identification of action-oriented spatial features (e.g., border, no man's land, front, flank, rear) that are local to an observer's point of view, local to a particular moment in the game when the units happen to be in the configuration being analyzed, and are not simply point-like affordances but actually define spatial regions with contextual meaning [Woodcock02]. In the light of our earlier conceptual discussion, these characteristics clearly qualify influence mapping as a model of place.

Supporting Narrative Through the Construction of Unique Places

You've now seen how semantic maps can take us beyond a "go here, do this" model of place and attach a sense of place to spatial regions and how the influence mapping technique is an example of a place representation that is completely integrated into the AI architecture. However, one of the great strengths of influence mapping is also its main limitation, namely that it operates by reducing particular units to a generalized model of value and by reducing these values to generalized types of places. When using an influence map to determine the location of the current front line between two opposing forces, all units on both sides will be reduced to one measure. The values assigned to each unit can vary of course, but nevertheless in substituting some general influence for each unit, we lose everything that was specific about that unit type. It doesn't matter that castles take years to build, are good at withstanding sieges, and can produce militia units, or that arable lands can be quickly created, are impossible to defend, and can produce grain resource; instead, all we can say is that "one castle is worth five arable lands." Having obtained these value reductions, the generalized types of places then identified by the influence map (e.g., front, flank, rear) will feed into some kind of generalized heuristics for action selection, such as "defend the front; attack the flanks" [Woodcock02].

These limitations are both the blessing and the curse of the influence mapping approach. The ability to recognize strategic dispositions in dynamic environments is great for creating a robust and reusable AI, but it makes it very difficult for level designers to produce unique encounters and to support preconceived dramatic narratives. Although there is never going to be a single overall "best representation" because these matters are highly application-dependent, in many ways, the most powerful form of place representation identifies observer-dependent spatial regions that can have unique content associated with them. This is like a combination of the strengths of point-like affordances as seen with domestic objects in *The Sims*, along with those of the space-filling sense of place as found in sophisticated strategy games.

The concepts of orders, areas, and styles in *Halo 2* go some way toward this kind of representation [Isla05b]. *Areas* are predefined groupings of designer-placed firing positions, and *orders* instruct a squad to operate within a particular area while using a particular style. *Styles* do not directly select actions on the squad but apply predefined subsets of the complete behavior tree, such as "aggressive," "defensive," or "noncombatant." These representations give the designer control over the squad without preventing autonomous action-selection, and instead of "go precisely here, do this action," it gives us a "go roughly there, behave like this" model of spatial behavior.

Conclusion

In this article, we have criticized the tendency of contemporary game AI architectures to rely on objective spatial representations, both through the reduction of the spatial environment to a list of objects at specific points and through the use of observer and task-independent features to describe those objects. A brief detour among the philosophical literature contrasted this approach to space with the notion of *place*. Places are socially constructed, action-oriented, layered both concurrently and hierarchically, and can provide a vocabulary for reasoning about space. Finally, we showed how a variety of approaches in contemporary game AI are already applying practical models of place, albeit to a limited extent. In conclusion, there is still a long way to go before game spaces are as richly filled with meaning for game agents as they are for human players and before the complexity of agent behavior has a chance of matching that of human players.

References

[Brooks90] Brooks, Rodney, "Elephants Don't Play Chess." *Robotics and Autonomous Systems,* Vol. 6, (1990): pp. 3–15.

[Burke01] Burke, Robert, et al., "CreatureSmarts: The Art and Architecture of a Virtual Brain." *Proceedings of the Game Developers Conference,* (2001): pp. 147–166.

[Church05] Church, Doug, "AI Challenges in Entertainment and Player Expression." Artificial Intelligence and Interactive Digital Entertainment Conference, 2005. Available online at *http://www.aiide.org/aiide2005/talks/church.ppt,* December 21, 2007.

[Evans00] Evans, Richard, "AI in Games: From Black & White to Infinity and Beyond." Available online at *http://www.gameai.com/blackandwhite.html,* December 21, 2007.

[Gibson79] Gibson, James J., *The Ecological Approach to Visual Perception.* Houghton Mifflin, 1979.

[Goffman59] Goffman, Erving, *The Presentation of Self in Everyday Life,* 1959. Reprint Penguin Books, 1990.

[Isla02] Isla, Damian, and Blumberg, Bruce, "Object Persistence for Synthetic Creatures." *Proceedings of the 1st International Conference on Autonomous Agents and Multiagent Systems* (AAMAS), (2002): pp. 1356–1363.

[Isla05a] Isla, Damian, "Dude: Where's My Warthog? From Pathfinding to General Spatial Competence." Artificial Intelligence and Interactive Digital Entertainment

Conference, 2005. Available online at *http://www.aiide.org/aiide2005/talks/isla.ppt*, December 21, 2007.

[Isla05b] Isla, Damian, "Handling Complexity in the Halo 2 AI." Available online at *http://www.gamasutra.com/gdc2005/features/20050311/isla_01.shtml*, December 21, 2007.

[Lefebvre91] Lefebvre, Henri, *The Production of Space*. First pub. 1974, trans. Nicholson-Smith. Blackwell, 1991.

[Merleau-Ponty65] Merleau-Ponty, Maurice, *The Structure of Behaviour*. Trans. Fischer. Metheun, 1965.

[Orkin05] Orkin, Jeff, "Agent Architecture Considerations for Real-Time Planning in Games." *Proceedings of the Artificial Intelligence and Interactive Digital Entertainment*, 2005. Available online at *http://www.media.mit.edu/~jorkin/aiide05OrkinJ.pdf*, December 21, 2007.

[Stout00] Stout, Brian, "The Basics of A* for Path Planning." *Game Programming Gems*, Charles River Media, 2000: pp. 254–262.

[Tozour01] Tozour, Paul, "Influence Mapping." *Game Programming Gems 2*, Charles River Media, 2001.

[Tozour02] Tozour, Paul, "Building a Near-Optimal Navigation Mesh." *AI Game Programming Wisdom*, Charles River Media, 2002: pp. 171–185.

[van der Sterren 02] "Terrain Reasoning for 3D Action Games." Available online at *http://www.gamasutra.com/features/20010912/sterren_01.htm*, 2001.

[von Uexkull57] von Uexküll, Jakob, "A Stroll Through the Worlds of Animals and Men: A Picture Book of Invisible Worlds." *Instinctive Behavior: The Develepment of a Modern Concept*, International Universities Press, 1957: pp. 5–80.

[Woodcock02] Woodcock, Steve, "Recognizing Strategic Dispositions: Engaging the Enemy," *AI Game Programming Wisdom*, Charles River Media, 2002.

2.3

Dynamically Updating a Navigation Mesh via Efficient Polygon Subdivision

Paul Marden—DigiPen Institute of Technology

pmarden@digipen.edu

Forrest Smith—Gas Powered Games

fsmith@gaspowered.com

In recent years, graphics and physics advancements have allowed for the creation of wildly more complex and dynamically changing environments, but pathfinding systems are often not able to adapt. Navigation meshes are commonly used but often in a precomputed form that can't be updated during runtime.

This article proposes a method for creating and storing navigation mesh (navmesh) information in a manner that allows for both rapid creation and updating of pathfinding nodes. It is made possible through a clever series of clipping techniques that allow for a complete navmesh to be created and updated without the need for any recursive operations. The final navmesh allows for the creation of a graph that can be used with a classic A* algorithm.

Definitions and Rules

Before diving into the algorithm, some definitions need to be given.

node: A strictly convex 2D polygon built from dynamic geometry that represents a walkable surface and its associated A* cost. AI or players may freely move from any point to any point within the convex region.

edge: Polygon edge used by, at most, two nodes. Stores front and back pointer to the nodes by which it is used.

base cell: An unchanging, strictly convex 2D polygon built from static geometry that contains a collection of nodes. "Base cell" is interchangeable with "cell."

navmesh: A collection of base cells and their contained nodes and edges.

overlapping geometry: Any dynamic geometry used to create unwalkable regions is said to be overlapping the navmesh.

There are some subtleties to note in these definitions. Nodes are strictly convex because this guarantees freedom of movement within the node. Concave polygons would allow for potentially uncrossable intrusions. Our pathfinding solution moves from edge to edge—rather than moving from the center of one node to the center of another—which requires edges to be used by, at most, two nodes.

Overview

The entire process, from starting in a full 3D world taken all the way down to a series of line segments used as a path, can be broken down into four sections. The basic premise is that first, static geometry is used to generate a static base state, and then, at runtime, dynamic geometry is used to continually create and update the mesh that will be used for pathfinding. Before going into the details of the process, the following summarizes each section:

Static Representation: A base state of the world is built from static geometry and stored in base cells that are never forgotten. Dynamic geometry overlapping the mesh is projected into the base cells.

Creating Mesh: The projections of overlapping geometry are used to subdivide the base cells into walkable and unwalkable nodes by clipping the base cells against the edges of the projection. This is the most complicated step.

Updating Mesh: When dynamic geometry moves, the cell it was in and the cell it's now in are both reset to their base states and resubdivided based on all overlapping geometry. The majority of the mesh remains unchanged. The subdivision process is fast and, by clearing the affected cells and recalculating their contents, a minimum number of nodes are created, which allows for a faster A*.

Pathfinding: To run the classic A*, we need a way to represent the navmesh as a graph. We can make this by treating the center of every navmesh edge as a graph-vertex that is connected to all other edges in the two nodes that share the original edge. This method allows for efficient paths that are highly optimizable. Figures in a later section will more clearly demonstrate this concept.

Static Representation

The first step is to create the base cells of the navmesh from the static geometry of our world. We refer to all base cells as the base state of the navmesh. There are a few rules relating to base cells:

Cells store nodes: Nodes are the actual geometry representing walkable regions. Every node is contained by one, and only one, cell.

Cells track overlapping geometry: When geometry overlaps the navmesh, the base cells store what geometry they are overlapped by.

Cells cover all walkable surfaces: Any region that could be walkable, provided no overlapping dynamic geometry, must be covered by cells.

Edges used by cells are marked as *outside*: Edges used by nodes but not the cell are termed "inside." This distinction is used when resetting a cell because inside edges can be discarded.

There are a few implications from these rules. A cell with no intersecting geometry contains a single node that fits the cell dimensions exactly. Cells should cover all ground that can possibly be walked on, as any ground not covered by a cell will never be contained by our navmesh. Cells never overlap. Furthermore, an ideal base state is actually a grid, as the uniformity allows for several optimizations later on. In the case of a multifloored world, multiple grids are needed.

When creating the base state, a careful balance must be struck between having too many or too few cells. Imagine a massive open field with no static geometry and a thousand dynamic objects. This field can be covered with either a single base cell or a large grid of cells, but which is better? Having a single cell will lead to fewer nodes after dynamic geometry is accounted for, which will mean a smaller search space and thus faster A*. Recall that when dynamic geometry moves, only the cell (or cells) that contained the geometry needs to be updated. So for a world with only a single base cell, anytime one of a thousand objects moves, the entire mesh needs to be recalculated. With a grid of cells, when one object moves, only one or two cells need to be updated—the rest of the grid remains unchanged. How this balance is struck is entirely dependent on the game.

For simplicity's sake, the rest of this article assumes a base state of coplanar cells forming a grid in a right-handed coordinate system where the y-axis is up.

Overlapping Geometry

After the base state of the navmesh has been created, the next step is to detect overlapping geometry. We will define two planes, one at the level of the navmesh and one at some height y above the mesh, and all vertices between these two planes will be defined as overlapping. The top plane is chosen so that geometry over an actor's head does not affect the potentially walkable surface. This allows for pieces of an object high above the ground, such as the top of an arch, to not interfere with the mesh. A series of steps are needed to extract useful information.

Create a bounding volume. A complex object may contain thousands of vertices, so a simplified bounding volume will be needed. Any convex polyhedron is acceptable, however, complex objects may require multiple convex volumes to produce a tight fit.

Intersect volume with planes. We need to form a set of all points in the bounding volume that exist between the two planes. This includes all points actually between the planes, as well as the intersection of all line segments in the volume with each plane. The intersection of segments and planes is not covered by this article.

Projection of points to navmesh plane. With all of the intermediate points in hand, they need to be orthogonally projected to the navmesh plane. Simply setting the y value of each vertex to zero can do this, assuming the navmesh is at 0 height.

Build a convex hull around projected points. With the arbitrary points projected to the surface, we need to form a new 2D convex hull. An algorithm to do so is described in the next section.

In our final product, we want actors to have the ability to walk not directly beside geometry but rather some radius away to prevent models from clipping. This can be accomplished with expanding bounding volumes by that radial distance. This will later insure that not only is the surface walkable, but that it can also be done safely without character models intersecting halfway through a wall or box.

Quick Hull Algorithm

Given an arbitrary set of coplanar points, a single bounding convex hull can be created. This hull can be visualized as filling a board full of nails and then taking a rubber band, stretching it around all of the nails, and letting it snap into place. Many of the nails, or vertices, will be inside this new convex hull and can be ignored—we only care about the ones along the edges. The process is as follows and is shown in Figure 2.3.1:

1. Find two extreme points (the leftmost and rightmost can be used) to form a chord (AB). These two points will be part of the hull.
2. Divide all other points into two sets (S0 and S1), for those points above the chord and those below.
3. For each set of points, find the farthest point from the chord, and call it C. This point will be part of the final convex hull because it cannot be encapsulated. It should be inserted between points AB in a list of vertices we maintain to define our convex hull.
4. Form a triangle ABC from the two chord points and the point farthest from the chord.
5. All points in triangle ABC are already inside our convex hull and can be discarded.
6. Form new sets S0 and S1 for those points outside chord AC and BC.
7. Recursively perform steps 3 to 6 until no points remain and a hull is formed.

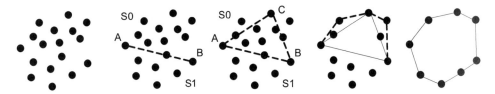

FIGURE 2.3.1 Quick hull algorithm.

Creating the Mesh

Assuming we have a navmesh that is in its base state and the projected 2D convex hull of an object, we can now begin the process of splitting the mesh cells based on the hull. There are several parts to this process.

Clipping the Hull to the Base Cells

A large amount of clipping is about to be performed inside each cell, so we first clip our hull against the base navmesh cells and form lists of line segments that are wholly interior to each cell. If our cell structure is grid-based, this can be easily and quickly performed through a digital differential analyzer (DDA) grid-traversal algorithm. With a line segment's start and end points in a normalized grid—where each cell is 1×1—the DDA algorithm can iterate along the segment returning the intersected cells by checking at each step whether the segment will next enter a cell in the x-direction or in the y-direction and incrementing accordingly. The following code shows the algorithm.

```
// DDA Algorithm
Vec2 startPoint, endPoint; //Points of line segment

int curRow = floor(startPoint.y); //Grid starting point
int curCol = floor(startPoint.x);

Vec2 dir = endPoint - startPoint;
//If dir.x = 0 or dir.y = 0 then early out
//If dir.x = 0 intersected cells are from
//grid[curRow][curCol] to grid[curRow][floor(endpoint.x)]
//Similar for dir.y = 0

Vec2 curPoint = startPoint; //Incremented value

while( distanceTraveled < Mag( endPoint-startPoint ) )
{
    //Segment is in grid[curRow][curCol]

    float xDist = dir.x > 0 ? floor(curPoint.x+1) -
    curPoint.x : curPoint.x - ceil( curPoint.x - 1 );
    float timeX = fabs( xDist / dir.x );
```

```
      float yDist = dir.y > 0 ? floor(curPoint.y+1) -
      curPoint.y : curPoint.y — ceil( curPoint.y — 1 );
      float timeY = fabs( yDist / dir.y );

      if( timeX < timeY )
          curCol += dir.y > 0 ? 1 : -1;
      else
          curRow += dir.y > 0 ? 1 : -1;
  }
```

This code snippet assumes a space normalized so that each cell is 1 × 1 in dimension, which means the test segment should be transformed accordingly. It calculates how far it is to the next cell along the x-axis and z-axis, and then how long it will take to reach that point. Whichever time is less determines whether the next intersected cell is in the x or z direction. When the distance traveled exceeds the distance between endPoint and startPoint, the algorithm should terminate.

Clipping the convex hull against the cells allows us to then clip the cells against only those edges we know intersect, which may be far fewer than the number of edges that are part of the convex hull.

Clipping Cells Against Intersecting Edges

This part is perhaps the most complex part of the algorithm, so each step will be described in detail. Before getting started, here's a list of a few things that we are going to accomplish:

- Each cell will be split into multiple nodes based on intersecting edges.
- Nodes will be strictly convex in form.
- No single edge will be used by more than two nodes.
- Nodes will properly share edges.
- Adjacency between nodes will be complete with no missing connections.

For each interior edge (interior to the cell) in the hull:

1. For each node that the edge overlaps:
    a. Create two new nodes, designating one as front and one as back.
    b. Extend the edge to form a line.
    c. For each edge in the current node:
        i. If the edge is in front of the line, add it to the front node.
        ii. If the edge is in back of the line, add it to the back node.
        iii. If the edge straddles the line:
            1. Create three new edges.
            2. Two of these edges correspond to the splitting of the current edge of the node.
                a. Make sure to set the front and back pointers appropriately for each line fragment.

     b. Update the node's neighbor (across the edge that is being split) so that it incorporates the new fragments.

3. The third edge is the edge that will be shared by the splitting of the current node. This splitting edge is comprised of the two intersection points where the node crosses the line.

     iv. If one of the edge's endpoints lies on the line, then the splitting edge must be updated with the intersection point, but there is no fragmentation of any edge here.

Things to watch out for when clipping:

- Never assume clockwise or counterclockwise ordering of vertices along an edge. It can be different for each node using the edge.
- When an outside edge is split, its fragments need to be marked as *outside*. The corresponding edge in the parent cell's list of outside edges needs to be replaced with the two new fragments.
- Make sure that orphaned edges are removed from the edge pool.

Because this is a tricky concept to understand, the visual example in Figure 2.3.2 will help greatly. On the left side is a depiction of a single cell being split into nodes by a square. The right side shows the underlying nodes and their connections at the completion of each step.

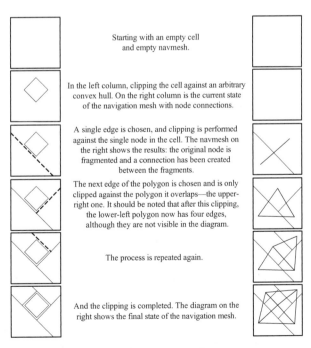

FIGURE 2.3.2 Cell clipping example.

Updating the Mesh

Any time an object inside a cell moves or a new object intersects a cell, that cell should be invalidated, which means that the cell should be reset to its base state so that it can be split again based on the new internal edge positions.

Resetting a Cell

As mentioned earlier, resetting a cell isn't a trivial matter. The issue is that the border from one cell to the next may be comprised of a single large edge, but previous splitting may have cut that edge up into smaller pieces. Due to the reset, it now needs to be checked to see if it can be "welded" back into its former state. The process is as follows:

1. Restore the cell to its original state.
2. Iterate through all outside edges.
3. For each pair of edges, they may be welded (fused to form a single edge) if they are adjacent, are collinear, and have identical front/back nodes.
4. If they can be welded, weld them, setting front/back pointers properly, and update the polygons in the adjacent cell so that they use the welded edge.
5. Delete old nodes.

Pathfinding with the Mesh

By this point, we should have a fully updated mesh ready to be used, but right now, there isn't a data set on which we can operate directly. To run A*, the mesh needs to be converted into a graph by treating the center of every edge as a vertex. This edge is part of, at most, two nodes in the navmesh, so our graph vertex will be connected to all other edges in those two nodes. This concept is difficult to explain but easy to visualize in Figure 2.3.3.

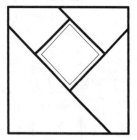 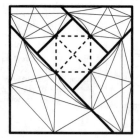 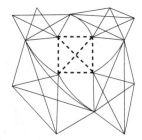

FIGURE 2.3.3   Graph formed from navmesh.

This first frame of Figure 2.3.3 is a single cell that is split into four nodes, plus the overlapping object in the middle. The second frame shows the connections between all of the edges with connections inside the object represented by dotted lines. The final frame shows just the graph that an A* algorithm needs to operate on. This graph should resemble a fairly standard search space.

Notice that the graph includes edges inside the overlapped region (dotted lines), which might seem odd at first. This is because weights can be attached to nodes making an area not necessarily unwalkable but simply more expensive to pass through. Imagine a hallway with a pool of acid in the middle. The acid could be added dynamically, and an AI could go through the acid, but it would be more expensive as far as pathfinding is concerned. If a route around the acid exists, that's wonderful, but wading through it is still an option. Additionally, a node can be set as completely unwalkable, which would cause those edges to not be added to the graph at all.

Optimizing the Path

With the graph, we can generate a path that will get us to a target properly, but it won't look pretty. Edges in our navmesh are not equally sized and not evenly spaced, which causes a zigzag path. The more nodes the world has, the more jagged the path becomes. It is likely that the path will go somewhat further than it actually needs to due to the pathfinder going through the middle of edges when a sharp turn occurs. Luckily, there are things that we can do to create a satisfying path.

Removing Path Points

For a given path, there may be a series of points where a straight path exists between the first and last, making any points in between, but potentially not on the line, unnecessary. Finding and removing these unnecessary points along our path will make straight lines. The process to do this isn't complex.

1. Take three consecutive points, and build a segment between the first and the third.
2. If this segment passes through no unwalkable nodes, then remove the second point.

Of course, finding which arbitrary nodes a segment passes through isn't trivial. With our setup, however, there is enough information to avoid most unnecessary checks. Based on the direction we are going, we can say that points 1 and 3 lie in a single node. We also know that point 2 lies on an edge shared by two nodes, which are the two nodes that contain points 1 and 3. With this in mind, we can do the following:

1. Find the intersection with the segment and all edges in the first point's node. There is one, and only one, intersection.
2. If the intersection edge uses the same node as point 3, then we can say there is a safe, straight line from point 1 to point 3, and we can throw away point 2.
3. If the intersection edge does not use the same node as point 3, then repeat steps 1 to 3 with the new node.

Figure 2.3.4 demonstrates these concepts. The first frame shows an arbitrary cell where solid lines are uncrossable, and dotted lines are crossable node boundaries. A path is built through these edges, but it's not very smooth. A new line is draw from point 1 to point 3, and it undergoes the operation described previously.

After performing the segment test, we will find that the second point could be removed, which is shown in the second frame of Figure 2.3.4. This test is repeated down the path, removing points where possible. The final frame shows a path with much straighter lines and only five points compared to the original eight.

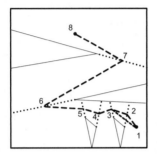 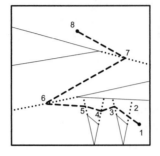 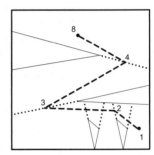

FIGURE 2.3.4   Path point removal demonstration.

Rubber-Banding

To help with the zigzag issue, a *rubber-banding* technique was developed, which is a variation on the *string-pulling* method [Johnson06]. If you recall, our path vertices lie in the middle of node edges. The convexity of the nodes allows us to freely move the point along its edge. The algorithm for this is given here:

For each set of three adjacent path-points:

1. Find the intersection of the line between the first and last points and the edge on which the middle point lies.
2. If that point lies on the middle point's edge, then replace the middle point with the intersection point.
3. Otherwise, replace the middle point with the closest endpoint on the middle point's edge.

Figure 2.3.5 demonstrates this concept. The first frame starts with our path from the previous section with a new line added between points 1 and 3. Following the previous algorithm, point 2 slides down its edge creating point 2b as shown in the second frame.

The same operation is then performed on the 2b-3-4 points triplet. The resulting point 3b is shown in the third frame as well as the line for the 3b-4-5 points triplet. The final frame shows the resulting path after a single pass. In many situations, a single pass is not enough to satisfactorily smooth the path. For our purposes, three passes produced the desired result.

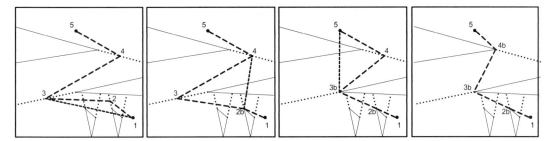

FIGURE 2.3.5   Rubber-banding demonstration.

Point removal cannot occur before rubber-banding. A simple example, as shown in Figure 2.3.6, demonstrates why. For the given geometry, an initial path consisting of five points is created. After point removal, the new path is through points 1, 3, and 5. Running rubber-banding next would create the path through points 1, 3b, and 5. This is a clearly unacceptable path. Running point removal strictly after rubber-banding prevents such situations from occurring.

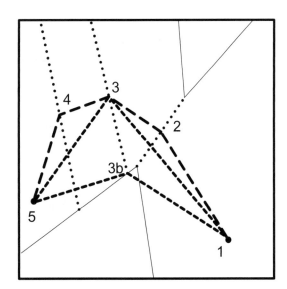

FIGURE 2.3.6   Example showing why point removal before rubber-banding is wrong.

Dealing with a Dynamic Mesh

When a portion of the mesh is modified, any paths that are using nodes in that portion must be recomputed to some degree, if not completely. Any path that uses a node that changes must be updated either by recalculating the entire path or by trying to repair only the broken section.

Paths are broken frequently in a dynamic world. The simplest solution is to avoid updating the mesh whenever possible. Updating only when an object starts and stops moving can work in some simulations. Objects in motion tend to stay in motion, which makes updating the mesh every frame useless because the data will just become invalid the next frame. When forming a bounding volume, you can also take into account an object's velocity so that the volume encompasses not only where the object is but also where it's going to be. Updating only every few seconds is wildly more efficient than having to update every single frame. Another option is to use local steering techniques to avoid objects that are in motion.

Conclusion

Navigation meshes are a common part of many AI systems, but not all of them adapt to the complexities brought by other systems such as physics. This article presents a new approach to a navmesh system that successfully reached its goal of dynamically updating at runtime. It is a modular system with several subalgorithms that stand by themselves and can thus be highly optimized for both speed and memory consumption.

This technique is flexible enough to be custom-tailored to most any situation. For example, information from an overlapping object can be retained. Sometimes, an object in the way is simply meant to slow the path of an actor rather than stop it completely. Nodes can store a weight that allows the AI to go through the cells, potentially kicking the object out of the way, rather than walking around. It is even possible to embed world information, such as an area being marked as a cover spot, into the bounding polyhedron so that even more information can be stored in the navmesh.

The concepts discussed in this article are simple enough that they can be worked into an existing framework in only a few weeks but still powerful enough to support a dynamic and immersive world.

Resources

[Johnson06] Johnson, Geraint, "Smoothing a Navigation Mesh Path." *AI Game Programming Wisdom 3*, Charles River Media, 2006: pp.134–135.

2.4

Intrinsic Detail in Navigation Mesh Generation

Colt "MainRoach" McAnlis—Ensemble Studios

duhroach@gmail.com

James Stewart—Stormfront Studios

jms@jmstewart.net

In the years since Greg Snook's seminal article in the first *Game Programming Gems* [Snook00], navigation meshes have become the search space representation of choice for pathfinding in games. Compared to the waypoint approach of the previous generation, navigation meshes are more amenable to automatic offline generation, produce better (in many cases, optimal) paths, and provide more useful information to entities that must negotiate dynamic obstacles. These benefits come at the cost of increased memory usage and slower search performance, problems of increasing severity given the content demands of next-gen titles—open-world games in particular.

In this article, we present a mesh simplification scheme that reduces the size of the search space while maintaining details necessary for optimal paths. This approach can be used to generate high-fidelity paths over very large terrains and is ideal for incremental refinement via streaming or progressive transmission over a network. Due to the regularity of the triangulation, it also allows fast lookup into the search space.

The key to our approach is a modified version of Restricted Quadtree Triangulation (RQT), which provides the minimal representation of a regular grid given a world-space error metric. RQT is well suited to navigation meshes because it preserves detail in high-frequency regions where pathfinding must be more precise while representing low-frequency terrain (flat plains, for example) with fewer vertices. Throughout this article, we use a 2D regular grid as our example world, but this is only to simplify the explanation. In subsequent sections, we suggest how this technique can be applied to arbitrary and irregular world geometry.

Overview

The navigation mesh structure is ideal for movement over 2D surfaces in 3D space. The core of this scheme is to treat a series of connected faces of a mesh as a search space for pathfinding algorithms such as A*. In Snook's original description, each node of the search space corresponds to a single face of the navigation mesh and contains the three indices needed to represent the face. Each node references a maximum of three neighbors (one for each edge of the triangle). The navigation mesh must also enforce two constraints. First, it must be composed entirely of triangles to ensure that each node occupies exactly one plane. Second, adjacent triangles must share only a single edge (and therefore two vertices). These two constraints are easy to satisfy given a world representation that conforms to a regular grid, such as height field terrain.

Navigation meshes don't always scale to large environments. Suppose you are developing an RTS that takes place on the surface of an entire planet. This world is massive, perhaps a $2^{15} \times 2^{15}$ regular grid of heights, for a total of 1,073,741,824 vertices. Because it is an open world, it is impossible to use portal-based segmentation to divide the space. In fact, the rendering team has to stream portions of the terrain model and use a variety of level-of-detail and culling techniques to update the player's view in real time. As the AI engineer for this project, you must develop a pathfinding solution and choose, among other things, a search space representation for this massive environment.

Simply reusing the visual representation will be difficult. Although it might be possible to share vertex and index buffers between the rendering and pathfinding modules, it is unlikely that the rendering pipeline has the bus bandwidth to spare. Even then the search space will have to be streamed; a billion vertices, even with the best compression, will be far too large to fit into system memory all at once. Even with unlimited memory, path generation will be quite expensive given the size of the map. Regardless, the cost of streaming the search space for a single path will likely be amortized over many frames, and there will likely be many entities requesting paths—this is a world-spanning war, after all. In the end, you are faced with a choice of two evils: Don't move an entity until the path query is complete, or do a quick "best guess" for initial movement and hope there's no need to backtrack.

Under these circumstances, you might consider the most reliable trick in the AI programmer's handbook: cheating. Generate high-fidelity paths for all entities in the same chunk as the player, prioritizing those that are visible in the frustum. More distant entities will follow greatly simplified paths. Although this approach certainly solves the problem, it limits development in a number of ways. First, you will need a variety of restrictions on the simplified paths so that they remain reasonably plausible. What if two opposing platoons—both flying through the sky like F-16s because realistic paths were too expensive—meet over an island that would be impossible to reach on the ground? More special cases will have to be generated for dynamic obstacles—the player who blockades the Suez Canal won't appreciate it if enemy battleships somehow teleport from the Mediterranean to the Indian Ocean. These rules will become even more complex if we introduce multiple human players or allow random access views into the world (the armchair generals playing your game, having invested heavily in the satellite technology upgrade, perhaps, might want a minimap to watch troop movements on the neighboring continent).

How much better would it be to have a more economical search space representation that maintains the beneficial qualities of a navmesh—namely a high-fidelity representation of the game environment?

To solve the problems presented in this scenario, we turn to a solution from the world of real-time rendering: mesh simplification. Although a huge number of simplification schemes exist, we have chosen the Restricted Quadtree Triangulation (RQT) for two reasons. First, it preserves intrinsic details of the mesh that are needed for generating paths (more on this in a minute). Second, the algorithm produces a triangulation that maintains quadtree boundaries. Regular decimation—subdivision of the mesh along regular boundaries—offers a number of advantages as a search space representation, chief among them incremental refinement and fast lookup when performing local searches. This becomes very important when avoiding dynamic obstacles or updating the navigation mesh to account for terrain deformation.

Intrinsic Detail

Any surface can be said to contain some degree of intrinsic detail. Although numerical methods exist to quantify detail exactly—the compression and frequency analysis domains are rife with examples—the concept is simple enough to describe. Imagine two meshes that represent perfectly flat planes. One mesh is a simple quad, that is, two large triangles. The second mesh represents the same plane in a network of 1,024 triangles. The second mesh, although represented with more polygons, contains no more intrinsic detail than the two-polygon version: Both are just (sections of) planes.

In this example, it is clear that the second mesh is over-tessellated (i.e., divided into more triangles than necessary). But when dealing with more complex models, the difference isn't so easy to detect. Despite the difficulty of the problem, intrinsic detail is a crucial concept when looking for ways to reduce the size of our search spaces because naive simplifications will likely omit path possibilities that would be obvious to a player when viewing the high-fidelity visual representation of the world.

Consider a naive level of detail (LOD) implementation for heightmap terrain. At each level of detail, we double the sample rate of the heights in exchange for exponential reduction in the number of heights. If the terrain has a low frequency (picture the "lumpy soup" produced by basic procedural terrain algorithms), we might even be able to get away with naive sampling in this manner. This approach will likely produce artifacts, however, when applied to high-frequency regions. Imagine a terrain in which a narrow valley passes through an otherwise impassable mountain range. These vertices might coincidentally be retained in a naive simplification if they happen to be indexed near powers of two, but it is more likely that they will be skipped by exponential sampling. The naive simplification would likely retain the mountain range but not represent the narrow valley—not particularly useful, as search spaces go.

RQT solves exactly this problem. It allocates polygon budget where it matters most—to regions of the mesh that contain the most detail. When generating our navigation meshes, we can use RQT to reduce the size of the search space without sacrificing the details needed to generate realistic paths. We define a world-space error metric to test which vertices are needed for a given refinement. The issue becomes a matter of data tolerance—how exact a representation does the application need to produce convincing paths?

Next we describe the RQT algorithm and suggest some of the various ways RQT can be leveraged when generating navigation meshes.

Restricted Quadtree Triangulation (RQT)

Traditionally, terrain is viewed as a regular grid of heights. Although thorough in its representation, this approach incurs a large memory footprint, even with the latest image-based compression technologies. But the process of generating an efficient lower polygon mesh representation for a massive terrain data set is far from a trivial task. Refinement algorithms must balance memory footprint and visual quality, often falling on their faces near the edge cases of either. Many polygonal refinement algorithms focus largely on the use of view-space metrics to eliminate unneeded polygons [Duchaineau97, Hoppe94-07]. The terrain is stored at its highest resolution representation, and lower resolution versions of the mesh are used at runtime.

Lower resolution representations, such as triangulated irregular networks (TINs), are desirable for their smaller memory footprint and the capability to closely represent the original data. TINs suffer from one crucial flaw, however: They are not easily integrated with the natural runtime representation of terrain. Height field terrain easily represents its data structure in a form that is ideal to be contained in a 2D hierarchal data structure. By breaking the terrain into small MxN groups of vertices called "chunks," the 2D organizational system speeds up culling and offers an efficient memory layout. TIN representations rely on combinations of low-frequency polygons spanning larger areas to achieve greater memory representations, but this does not lend itself an efficient management representation as its regular grid counterpart. To fit a sparse TIN representation into a similar 2D data structure, we often run into the problem of large sparse polygons spanning multiple nodes at a single time. To represent this efficiently, these large polygons can be split against the chunk boundaries to create new polygon sets that fit well into the representation. Because of its geometric nature, this is not a desirable task—the computations can be heavy-handed and prone to problems such as T-junctions and holes in the output representation that require a complicated fix-up. Instead, we seek a representation of the terrain that combines the efficient memory footprint of a TIN with the efficient bounding data structure of a regular grid.

RQT provides the best of both worlds. RQT takes in a regular grid of input data and outputs a triangulated regular network (TRN) that adheres to the layout requirements of a given 2D data structure, such as a quadtree or octree.

Prior research presented bits and pieces of the RQT algorithm, but Pajarola was the first to present RQT in a practical manner [Pajarola98]. Szofran defines a usage system for runtime RQT generation and validates some of the prior research but does not delve too deep into any implementation details [Szofran06]. We present a simplified explanation of the RQT algorithm described by Pajarola as well as a minimization of the dependency marking and mesh generation processes specifically for terrain.

Features of RQT include the following:

RQT is segmented. With proper tessellation, you are guaranteed that no polygon crosses chunk boundaries. This is a major problem with TINs—even in streaming media, you are never guaranteed that a chunk will holistically contain a given polygon.

RQT is "water-tight." RQT is free of T-junction intersections and fits perfectly into terrain chunks without the need for polygon splitting or a second fix-up pass to repair these problems.

RQT's control parameter is singular. All that's needed as input is a single world-space error metric value. This is simple enough to use in art tools for content designers.

RQT Refinement

Our implementation of the RQT algorithm has two stages: the rejection phase and the mesh generation phase. The first generates a grid of Boolean values corresponding to the vertices that pass our refinement test and will be included in the output mesh. The second phase uses this data as an acceleration structure to quickly generate a polygon list.

ON THE CD

Despite the length of the explanation that follows, the actual amount of code involved in small. Both phases of the algorithm are clearly marked in the source code that accompanies this book. It may be helpful to reference the code when reading this section.

For this article, we define a *patch* as a 3 × 3 grouping of points in our regular grid representation of the terrain. As shown in Figure 2.4.1, these points can be spaced at any regular interval. Patch A is a patch with a stride of one—that is, the neighbor vertices are all one mark away. Patch B is also a patch but with a stride of three, so that all neighbor vertices are two marks away.

Rejection Phase

The first phase of RQT scans the terrain for points to be included in the final mesh, marking these values in a Boolean grid (or *mark grid*) of the same dimensions as the input terrain. At the beginning of this phase, the mark grid is completely false. When a vertex is chosen to be inclusion, we mark the grid position as true.

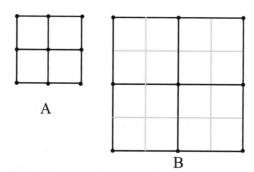

FIGURE 2.4.1   A) A patch with a stride of one.
B) A patch with a stride of three.

The first step of this phase is to manually mark points of significance to provide anchor points for specific generation types. For terrain, we mark all the corners of our primary chunks. This is a required step because it signifies that the lowest tessellation that the terrain can decimate to is at the chunk level. These manual markings must by no means be static, as designer input may indicate that other areas be marked as well. It is useful to provide users with tessellation override brushes, allowing them to specifically override the marking rules for distance and directly affect the tessellation level of specific regions. It is important to note that the chunk size chosen for the automatic markings is considered the maximum size that a patch can span, as differing values can cause problems with dependency information crossing chunk boundaries.

Next, we define a single world-space distance tolerance to use as an error metric when choosing points to mark. A point-line distance test between the vertex in question (the *pivot* point) and its two neighbors in the current patch determine whether the pivot should be marked (see Figure 2.4.2 for an example). If the distance from the point to the line is greater than the error metric, the vertex is considered to have enough displacement to provide a visual difference to the final mesh. If the distance is less than the error metric, the point is considered noise in the image; it is assumed that removal will not cause a great loss in visual quality. By definition, this test requires three sources of input data: a vertex V and neighbor points A, B.

To test all the points in our grid, we scan the entire input terrain in steps of increasing patch size. That is, we walk the entire terrain in patch sizes of 3 × 3, and then we walk the entire terrain in patches of 5 × 5, then 9 × 9, and so forth. This process continues by doubling the size of each patch on subsequent passes: 3, 5, 9, 17, 31, 63 … K, where $K = 2^N + 1$, and N is the maximum size of a patch (for terrain, this should be the size of a chunk). This method requires that K be an odd number, so that there will always be a center vertex to pivot over to perform the distance test. Even intervals of K cause a loss of the pivot vertex and degeneration of the algorithm.

To demonstrate the marking process, consider the 1D example depicted in Figure 2.4.2. Given a line with nine points, we test a vertex V against the line constructed between two neighbor points A, B, which are located at half the patch size away from the pivot on the line. Starting with a patch size of 3 at location 0, our patch center (and thus pivot V) is point 1 along the line, with neighbor points A, B as point 0 and point 2. To determine if V should be included in the final mesh, we test the distance from V to line AB. We then move along to the next patch that starts at a nonoverlapping interval with our current patch. This next patch would be points 2, 3, 4, with [A, B] = [point 2, point 4] and V = point 3. We continue in this manner until we've tested all the patches of this stride.

The next scan of the terrain defines a stride of 5. This scan starts at point 0 (A) again, but the pivot point (V) is now point 2 (which was the corner point of the prior patch size) with the other corner being point 4 (B). Each point will be tested in the grid due to the fact that at each successive level, corner vertices become pivot vertices and must be tested as well. In Figure 2.4.2, vertices passing the distance test at each level are highlighted.

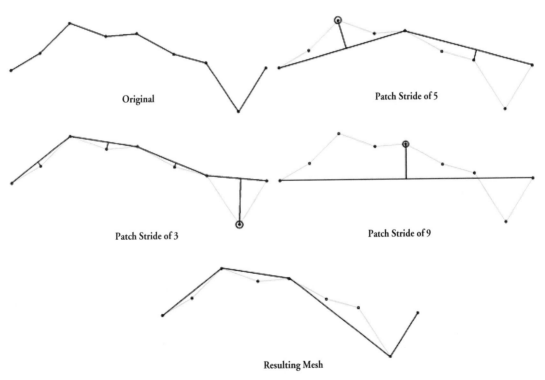

FIGURE 2.4.2 The point-line distance test between neighboring vertices at different strides. Vertices passing the distance test at the current stride are marked. The resulting mesh layout is the accumulation of all the passing verts at all encompassed substrides.

As defined previously, a patch—a 3 × 3 set of vertices—gives us enough information to compute the distance test for all noncorner vertices in the given patch. For cardinal vertices that lie on the edges of the patch, we define points A, B as the given corner points of the edge that it lies on. For the center vertex of a patch, we allow A, B to be the cardinal verts that span the center vertex.

For a given patch, we need to test only five points. We identify the center point C of the patch, located at [I, J] in our mark grid, where I and J are multiples of half the patch stride (HPS = patch stride >> 1 and I % HPS = 0). Our top, bottom, left, and right points are the vertices that lie on the edges of the patch, obtained by adding HPS C in the cardinal directions: [0,HPS], [0,–HPS], [HPS,0], [–HPS,0]. To test these noncenter verts (top, bottom, left, right), we construct our line for distance from the two corner points of the edge that our target point lies on. For example, to test our top vertex, we would use the top-left corner and top-right corner to construct the line AB. Figure 2.4.3C, shown in the next section, indicates the corner and center vertices of a 3 × 3 patch.

The center vertex is tested for validity by testing distances from both sets of noncenter points. That is, we test the distance from C to the line formed by [top, bottom], and also the distance from the line formed by [left, right]. If C passes the distance test for either line, it is marked as true. Figure 2.4.2, shown earlier, provides a representation of this test at several different patch strides.

As an additional test, if any edge point of a patch has been marked for inclusion into our mark grid, we also mark C to be included as well. This sort of dependence marking ensures that no patches with valid edge points lack a center for proper tessellation. This concept is the cornerstone of the RQT algorithm, as marking dependent points along with the target point ensures that the triangulations are free of polygonal artifacts.

Dependency Marking

When marking a point as valid, vertices "dependent" upon this vertex must also be marked to generate valid polygons in the next phase of the algorithm. This allows us to generate the polygon list very quickly later on. Not only that, but these dependencies create an output mesh that is free of T-junctions without requiring a separate fix-up pass.

If the vertex under inspection is on a vertical edge (X % HPS = 0), we must mark the neighbor vertices of half stride horizontally. These verts are the center points of the patches that share the vertical edge that the point is on (see Figure 2.4.3A).

If the vertex is on a horizontal edge (Y % HPS = 0), we must mark the neighbor verts of half stride vertically. These verts are the center points of the patches that share the horizontal edge that the point is on (see Figure 2.4.3B).

If the vertex is a center point, all four corners of the current patch stride need to be marked (see Figure 2.4.3C).

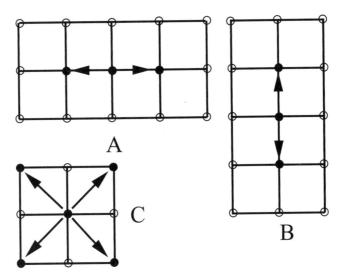

FIGURE 2.4.3 Dependency examples. A & B: Edge dependencies mark the centers of the neighboring patches. C: A center point in the current patch marks the edges of this patch.

While marking vertices, it is important to consider that a point might have already been marked as a dependent vertex prior to this test. If this is the case, we assume that this vertex is needed and mark its dependents as though it passed the distance test.

Mesh Generation Phase

The reason for the extra dependency marking of the rejection phase is to create an easily accelerated system for generating our triangle lists. By ensuring any given vertex has a valid relationship with neighboring vertices to construct a triangle, we can rely on the fact that our output mesh omits any incorrect layouts. This constraint allows us to chart out a set of potential 3 × 3 patches emitted from the dependency marking phase, resulting in a discrete set of triangle layouts. Specifically, our dependencies allow us to define 7 archetypal triangle layouts for a given patch, resulting in 17 possibilities after transforming each archetype. The 6 archetypal layouts are shown in Figure 2.4.4, along with their resulting valid transformations.

Three of the archetypes, A, B, E, are unique in that their transformations result in the same orientation as the input (we call these the *identity* archetypes). Types C and D have unique transformation representations that are labeled with a numeric identifier to distinguish them. Two of our archetypes, F and G, serve a dual purpose: They actually exist as hybrid tessellations between two patch levels spanning the same area. They contain valid patches at lower levels as well as a valid partial triangulation at upper levels. We do not consider the fully tessellated patch to be a hybrid patch, even

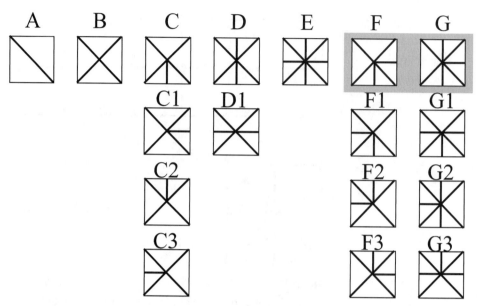

FIGURE 2.4.4 All 17 possible patch combinations. The 7 key archetypes are in the top row. Possible transformations are listed vertically. Hybrid archetypes are listed at the far right with a different selection.

though it could be considered to contain four valid children. Rather, we consider this orientation a member of the identity set and consider it a leaf node (a node with no children).

For each archetype, we define a simple set of indices to represent a polygonal layout representing that type. When generating our triangle lists, we add the current offset of the patch to the archetype layout indices and append the resulting triangles to the running list. This tessellation process is much faster than other algorithms that require geometric equations to calculate polygon splits and triangle areas. We can forgo that entire process by relying on our dependencies to define preset patterns for our patches. Because of this, the mesh generation process for RQT is exceptionally fast, allowing it to be done even at runtime.

Archetype Hash Keys

To output our final triangle list, we scan the marked grid as input and test each patch—at each stride—against the archetypes to find a valid match. To accelerate this process, we generate a unique hash key for each archetype layout, giving us a precompiled lexicon to compare against during this search process. A given target patch in the mark grid generates a hash key on the fly. The comparison to find the valid archetype layout becomes a fast switch statement block.

To generate a unique hash key for each archetype, we opt to use information contained in its polygonal layout, as that information is unique to each type. We represent each point in our 3 × 3 patch as a Boolean value—true if a vertex exists there, false otherwise. Starting at the upper-left corner of a patch, we move to the right and down, packing each binary test result into a 16-bit variable via bit shifting. Figure 2.4.5 demonstrates this process. While walking the marked grid, we generate a similar hash key for each 3 × 3 patch that we encounter and test it against the lexicon.

Using this representation allows us to represent both unique layouts and encompassing transformations in the same span. In other words, the result contains an identifier that uniquely represents a given archetype and its rotation. Another advantage is that the approach uses only the nine lower bits of the variable, which allows more data to potentially be stored in the upper bits for other data you may want to add (such as marking passability or storing slope data).

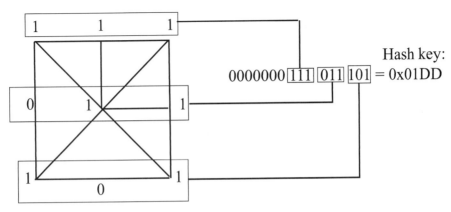

FIGURE 2.4.5   Hash key generation for a given patch.

Patch Layout Identification

To generate a valid triangle list for the refined terrain, we visit each patch in our grid, starting at the largest patch (size N). For each patch, we grab the 3 × 3 Boolean values from our mark grid and generate a hash key. If the given key is found in the lexicon (the set of archetype hash keys), we have encountered a leaf node, and add the vertices to the list. If the given patch does not have a valid match in the lexicon, the patch is invalid, so we recurse to the next lowest patch level; that is, we continue on to the four children of this patch. Recall that the two hybrid types terminate one node earlier than the leaves because not all of their children are valid. To test for this, the parent first tests its child patches against the lexicon before moving to them. If all four children have valid matches, the parent node contains leaf nodes. If one, two, or three of the children are valid, we must test against one of the hybrid types for this level. This process continues until all leaf nodes for a patch have valid matching archetypes. Listing 2.4.1 provides pseudocode for this process.

Listing 2.4.1 Pseudocode for Polygon List Building Algorithm

```
int giveTriListForPatch(patch)
{
  if( patch.areCornersMarkedTrue() )
  {
    if( !patch.isCenterMarkedTrue() )
    {
      GivePolyList( blockType0 );
      return 1;
    }
    else
    {
      C0 = giveTriListForPatch(children0);
      C1 = giveTriListForPatch(children1);
      C2 = giveTriListForPatch(children2);
      C3 = giveTriListForPatch(children3);

      if(c0 + c1 + c2 + c3 == 0) //no children
      {
        GivePolyList( GenHashKey(patch));
      }
      else if(c0 + c1 + c2 + c3 != 4) //hybrid patch
      {
        GivePolyListHybrid( GenHashKey(patch) );
      }
      return 1;
    }
  }
  return 0;
}
```

Navigation Mesh Refinement

Using RQT-reduced navigation meshes requires a 2D or 3D regular grid of vertices for the world representation. If the world for your project is already constructed on a regular grid (such as height field terrain), you're in luck. Otherwise, you'll need to regularize the representation. This is a massive topic beyond the scope of this article, but research on the quantization of irregular meshes is abundant. In particular, Hugues Hoppe has a variety of papers on this subject [Hoppe94-07]. Relief-based reconstruction and other approaches are also possible [Szymczak02]. Depending on the needs of your application it will probably suffice to quantize the search space and keep the visual representation irregular. Imprecision with regularization will not win you any friends among the artists on the project.

After you have a regular world representation (all vertices are situated on a regular grid of two or three dimensions), there are numerous ways to use an RQT refinement, depending on how deeply you want to incorporate it into your project.

At the simplest level, RQT can be used to reduce the size of existing navigation meshes. Reducing the memory footprint for the pathfinding data reduces the time spent to search the space, reduces read time when paging from storage, and requires no decompression step. This modest incorporation of RQT requires no changes to pathfinding algorithms that already use navigation meshes and is easy to incorporate into an existing tools chain—expose a world-space error metric to the designers (as a slider perhaps) in the navmesh generation tool and add an RQT post-processing step that uses this metric at export time.

But compression just scratches the surface of what can be done with RQT. Where this simplification really shines is as a method of incremental refinement when streaming pathfinding data from storage, such as optical media, a hard drive, or a network.

Starting with a "good enough" path and then refining it during subsequent game loops is a well-known strategy. Given how well RQT represents intrinsic detail, we can apply this idea to a pathfinding solution that scales to large terrains.

Two sets of navigation meshes are generated in an offline tool. The first is the summary mesh, or the high-tolerance model, that represents the entire world using an in-core memory model. The summary mesh should be small enough to reside wholly within system memory. The second set of meshes is the set of low-tolerance models, each representing a different chunk of the world. Together they would be far too large to fit into memory but provide higher-fidelity representation of regions of the world.

When an entity requests a path, one is generated on the summary mesh. In subsequent frames, low-fidelity meshes that fall along this preliminary path are paged in and used to refine the entity's course over the world. The query to the summary mesh will return a list of path nodes. As part of the refinement process, we mark transitions between chunks by inserting transition nodes into this list. These nodes provide the index of the next chunk to page during refinement but are not actually used to move the entity.

Because the RQT-refined navigation mesh maintains boundaries between nodes at all levels of detail, we could examine the preliminary path nodes in order and insert transition nodes when the path moves to a different leaf. This will work but isn't amenable to parallel processing. A better way to mark these transitions is to project the path into 2D and examine the line segments connecting each set of nodes. In *Game Programming Gems 2*, Matt Pritchard describes a fast test to determine whether a line spans a quadtree boundary [Pritchard01]. In each dimension, XOR the integral portions of both ends of the line segment. Because quadtrees are subdivided along powers of two, the position of the highest set bit indicates the level of the quadtree where the spanning occurs. Because all chunks in this implementation are leaf nodes at the same level of the quadtree (i.e., no leaves are contained at other levels of the structure), this test can be used to quickly mark transitions.

The relative speeds of the paging strategy and the entity's movement determine how much time the entity will path along the preliminary path versus the refined path.

In practice, ground-based entities moving at slow speeds spend only a few frames moving along the preliminary (low-tolerance) path. Although the seek times of storage media are a crucial concern when streaming, this approach minimizes the impact of slow seeks because entities can travel along the preliminary path, whereas higher fidelity navigation meshes are paged from storage. In the worst case, in which so many entities are requesting paths that it overwhelms the paging mechanism, the preliminary path is still convincing.

This approach allows you to apply generic A* to an RQT-reduced navigation mesh, but other solutions are possible. The Internet abounds with hierarchical approaches to pathfinding; the regular, hierarchical characteristics of RQT meshes are well suited to these approaches.

These last few points are highly dependent on the particular needs of your game but are worth noting:

First, there is huge potential for parallel processing here. Because both high- and low-tolerance navigation meshes feature regular decimation, locking can be highly localized when updating the meshes to account for dynamic obstacles. Likewise, when refining the preliminary path, it is trivial to divide and conquer both when marking transitions between chunks and when refining the path. When marking chunk transitions, each thread examines a subset of the preliminary path. After the transitions have been marked, each path segment can be refined in a separate thread without the need for a stitch-up step when all refinements are complete.

Second, RQT reduction can be used alongside other navigation mesh optimizations, many of which are described in previous volumes of this series. For games that exclusively use ground-based entities, faces above a certain steepness threshold can be removed from the exported mesh. Preprocessed paths can certainly still be used and modified at runtime to account for dynamic obstacles—in fact, RQT can be used to speed up the offline generation of these paths. As always it can be dangerous to optimize too early because one of the motivations for this search space representation is that it copes well with dynamic changes to the world. One safe optimization is run-length encoding of the search space, which outperforms wavelet compression in the case of RQT that has already in a sense been compressed using frequency information.

Finally, it is certainly possible to imagine a scenario in which the terrain is so large that it is impossible to fit it entirely into memory while maintaining a meaningful error metric. In lieu of paging the summary mesh outright, it might be more fruitful to discard the summary mesh concept and look instead to incremental refinement [Pajarola98]. As with almost all data structures available, memory is the ultimate limitation, but RQT extends the dimensions of the worst-case scenario to truly gigantic proportions.

Search Space Comparisons

In the second volume of *AI Game Programming Wisdom*, Paul Tozour outlined criteria for evaluating search space representations [Tozour04]. Borrowing his metrics, let's see how RQT-reduced navigation meshes stack up.

Memory Usage/Performance

When devising a search space, developers often trade path optimality for simplicity of the graph. RQT provides a solution for creating high-fidelity paths while reducing the memory footprint of the search space representation. This is the primary motivation for application of RQT to the world of pathfinding. Navigation meshes exhibit poor performance and increased memory usage when compared to waypoints. RQT reduction addresses this weakness specifically by representing the search space in a more concise format. The actual compression ratio varies with the frequency of the terrain and the aggressiveness of the error metric. Given the paltry RAM available on modern consoles and the exploding content demands for next-gen titles (both in terms of world size and the number of pathfinding entities), this is perhaps the most important metric of all. Although waypoints still provide a more concise representation, RQT reduction is a vast improvement over unsimplified navigation meshes.

Path Optimality

In addition to the path optimality of unsimplified navmeshes, RQT-reduced navmeshes guarantee the minimal representation of the search space for a given error metric. It is important to note, however, that an infinite error metric would reduce a terrain to four vertices and two triangles (a flat plane with dimensions equal to the original world). Such aggressive reduction would obviously not be conducive to optimal paths. The previous section discussed a path-refinement scheme with a streaming navigation mesh, and one of the optimizations proposed was that the first path node in any chunk be retained from the preliminary path generated on the summary mesh, which could not be said to be truly optimal. Once again, this devolves to an issue of data tolerance—how optimal do the paths need to be for your application? In the case of games and even military simulations, the highly detailed paths over arbitrarily large regions produced by this approach are a vast improvement in path fidelity at the cost of "near" optimality. In practice, RQT minimizes the tradeoff between path optimality and memory usage that AI programmers are often faced with.

Suitability for Offline Generation

RQT reduction is ideal in this regard. Any world representation that allows regular decimation can be reduced via the algorithm described in this article. When working with networks of irregular points (i.e., almost all meshes in current 3D applications), it is possible to quantize the world representation to a regular 3D grid for the purposes of generating the navigation mesh. The navmesh generation tool can contain a slider that allows designers to set an error metric—preferably along with a preliminary visualization of the reduction—for use at export time. The drawback of RQT reduction is the trial and error of selecting a suitable error metric, which must be evaluated by the designers via inspection of the mesh emitted by the navmesh generation tool. This drawback is minimized by the fact that it is controlled by a single variable and that impressive compression ratios are achieved even with a conservative error metric. As a final option, Pajarola describes an objective method to derive an optimal error metric for a given mesh [Pajarola 98].

Suitability for Dynamic Environments

As Tozour describes, this is the major advantage of navigation meshes—triangular (as opposed to polygonal) navigation meshes in particular. This feature is enhanced by the fact that RQT-reduced meshes feature regular decimation. If leaf nodes are of uniform dimensions and stored contiguously in memory, random access is possible. If leaf nodes can be contained in different levels of the tree, neighbors can be found either through backtracking to a least common ancestor, a process with logarithmic complexity that in practice rarely requires examination of more than four nodes [Samet84]. This inexpensive access allows fast examination of the local space to avoid dynamic obstacles, rapid update of the search space representation to reflect recent terrain deformations, and so forth. In addition, the frequency analysis inherent in the algorithm allows for some interesting possibilities—if a certain unit can leap long distances, for example, it's possible to flag high-frequency regions as good search candidates for jumping over dynamically created ravines and so forth. The unused bits in the patch strings for the mesh generation stage of RQT are an ideal place to tag such data.

Suitability for Hierarchical Solutions

Although portal-based segmentation was a great solution for the previous generation of games, in practice, it is expensive to segment procedurally and often requires direct intervention on the part of an environment artist. Likewise, portal segmentation often limits game design in the sense that the world must converge at discrete chokepoints. In terms of pathfinding, RQT reduction allows the representation of truly open worlds. It does so in a way that is explicitly hierarchical; much of Pajarola's original work concerned incremental progression over a network (although we've glossed over this point, the vertices at each level of the quadtree represent a valid triangulation, meaning that it is possible to stream vertices first from the root of the tree, and then from children nodes as bandwidth allows, without ever pushing the same vertex twice). Finally, as described in the previous section, we can keep a summary navigation mesh of the entire terrain in memory to produce preliminary paths, and then refine these paths as higher-fidelity chunk navigation meshes that can be streamed from storage. In addition to being hierarchical, this approach scales well regardless of terrain size or number of pathing entities because the preliminary path already accounts for the intrinsic detail of the world representation.

Orthogonality to Visual Representation

Although Tozour omits this metric, we submit that it is a useful consideration when choosing a search space representation. In fact, it is one of the implicit advantages of using navigation meshes in the first place. Because RQT was originally developed to simplify rendering of large terrains, it is possible that some code can be shared between the rendering and pathfinding systems, both in terms of offline generation (in particular, visualization tools) as well as for online problems such as streaming, network transmission, culling, and so forth.

Source Code

ON THE CD

A visualization tool on the CD-ROM accompanying this book allows you to step through various levels of reduction of a 2D terrain. The demo provides source code for both the dependency marking and mesh generation stages of the algorithm in a concise and readable format. The reduction code has no dependencies and can be dropped into an existing project with little to no hassle. However, the code deals only with refinement of a single chunk. Multichunk environments are left as an exercise to the reader, as this depends highly on the spatial organization structure of your project.

Conclusion and Future Work

Using the refinement described in this article, you have two additional tools at your disposal when dealing with search-space representations: a method to compress existing triangular navigation meshes while preserving important details (with little or no change to your existing pathfinding solution) and a method to generate navigation meshes for very large worlds in a format amenable to streaming and fast dynamic update. Determination of a useful world-space error metric is the drawback of this approach—an overly aggressive error can omit crucial details.

We've given you a whirlwind tour of a topic that could be a book full of the different ways to incorporate regularity, reduction, and incremental refinement into your search spaces. From the kernel provided in this article, there are many paths to take.

Although the presented RQT algorithm is an offline, world-space error metric, the core technique behind it allows it to be an exceptionally fast runtime technique as well. The rejection/marking phase can be tailored to a generic marking system that can allow other types of triangulation processes to exist besides RQT.

The marking grid of RQT can also serve as a great data structure for efficient streaming of tessellation data. For example, every vertex streamed into the system comes in the form of its XZ location in the Boolean grid. When a point is added to a chunk, we can evaluate whether that added point will change the tessellation of the edges of this chunk (a simple &= operation with what the edges were prior). If the edges of this chunk have changed with the addition of this point, we then recalculate the polygon list for this chunk and the neighboring chunks on the edges that have been modified. If not, then we just recalculate the polygon list for ourselves.

This shows that the Boolean grid serves an even more powerful purpose: an abstraction from the polygon snapping/splitting process, which is usually the brain-bending part of up/down tessellation. Using other methods to fill the Boolean grid structure, we can achieve the same complex tessellation processes of more traditional algorithms in a faster, more stable process.

In addition, although the error metric presented here, based on slope information, is a good general-purpose solution, more advanced metrics are certainly possible. If impassable regions have been marked in raster data, for example, a texture lookup could be used to scale the metric at each vertex.

Finally, we hope that this article has demonstrated that there are opportunities to improve the navigation mesh concept by adapting algorithms from the rendering domain. Mesh simplification is a vast playground—the devil is in the details.

Acknowledgements

James wishes to thank Dr. Anton Ephanov and Dr. Wouter Van Oortmerssen, both faculties at the Guildhall at Southern Methodist University. Thanks for your feedback and encouragement.

References

[Duchaineau97] Duchaineau, Mark, et al., "ROAMing Terrain: Real-time Optimally Adapting Meshes." *Proceedings IEEE Visualization '97,* (October 1997): pp. 81–88.

[Hoppe94-07] Hoppe, Hugues, "Hugues Hoppe's Home Page." Available online at *http://research.microsoft.com/~hoppe/#mra,* June 15, 2007.

[Pajarola98] Pajarola, Renato, "Large-Scale Terrain Visualization Using the Restricted Quadtree Triangulation." *Proceedings IEEE Visualization '98* (October 1998): pp. 19–26.

[Pritchard01] Pritchard, Matt, "Direct Access Quadtree Lookup." *Game Programming Gems 2,* Charles River Media, 2001: pp. 394–401.

[Samet84] Samet, Hanan, "The Quadtree and Related Hierarchical Data Structures." *ACM Computing Surveys* (June 1984): pp. 187–260.

[Snook00] Snook, Greg, "Simplified 3D Movement and Pathfinding Using Navigation Meshes." *Game Programming Gems,* Charles River Media, 2000: pp. 288–204.

[Szofran06] Szofran, Adam, "Global Terrain Technology for Flight Simulation." Game Developers Conference, 2006, available online at *http://download. microsoft.com/download/5/6/f/56f5fa07-51a4-4c0d-8a9a-2e8539214f2e/ GDC2006_Szofran_Adam_Terrain_v1.doc.*

[Szymczak02] Szymczak, Andrzej, et al., "Piecewise Regular Meshes: Construction and Compression." *Graphical Models, Special Issue on Processing of Large Polygonal Meshes,* 2002, pp. 183-198.

[Tozour04] Tozour, Paul, "Search Space Representations." *AI Game Programming Wisdom 2,* Charles River Media, 2004: pp. 85–102.

2.5

Navigation Mesh Generation: An Empirical Approach

David Hamm—Red Storm Entertainment

trianglegamer@gmail.com

Many games rely on navigation meshes as inputs for AI pathfinding. Automatically generating these meshes can be a big win for development because it eliminates both a major art task in the content pipeline and a corresponding class of bugs. A computational approach to navigation mesh generation has previously been presented [Tozour02] and extended in the *AI Game Programming Wisdom* series [Farnstrom06].

This article proposes an alternative, empirical approach to navigation mesh (navmesh) generation being developed for the *Tom Clancy's Ghost Recon* series of games. This technique scales very well with increasing world detail, including outdoor or natural environments. The output is a surprisingly uniform triangle mesh especially well suited for pathfinding use. Secondary advantages include the avoidance of floating point precision issues and localized customization of the algorithm when desired.

Algorithm Overview

Five steps are involved in empirical navmesh generation:

1. Simulate moving a character shape around the map, essentially flood-filling regions with breadcrumbs everywhere characters can reach.
2. Process the resulting grid of points, throwing out points in tight areas that could complicate navigation.
3. Identify boundary points, and optimize their connections to form simplified impassable walls.
4. Select a balanced distribution of interior points to promote to navmesh vertices.
5. Connect the interior vertices with the impassable walls to form a triangle mesh.

Various heuristics and optimizations are applied at each step, as well as possible extensions for representing additional information in the navmesh valuable to pathfinding. Each of these steps is further developed in the following sections.

Step 1: Sampling the World

Empirical navmesh generation begins with extensive sampling of the world via collision tests. This process generates a database of navigability information that drives the construction of the final mesh. It is this basis on experimental evidence that suggests the term "empirical."

World sampling must be seeded by inputting a single known navigable point in the world for each disjoint navmesh to be generated. A basic implementation might assume valid traversable terrain at the world origin. A more sophisticated system should allow multiple seed points to be graphically specified throughout the rendered world geometry. Disjoint meshes, and thus multiple seeds, can come into play for maps with NPCs placed on isolated terrain that is inaccessible to players, such as sniper nests.

Outward from each seed point, collision tests are performed on an axis-aligned grid to determine the navigability of the terrain. A ray cast fired relative to the closest resolved sample is used to find the height of the terrain. Then, a capsule corresponding to the approximate volume of a game character is positioned just above the terrain to check for world collisions. If these tests find a valid place for a character to stand, the slope of the path between this point and the previous location is checked for navigability. If the slope traversed between the points is too great, the new point is rejected as unreachable. A visualization of the resulting point collection is shown in Figure 2.5.1.

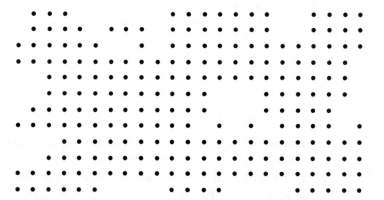

FIGURE 2.5.1   Navigable points are collected by performing collision tests and checking for reachable neighbors.

The distance between points on the grid must be carefully selected. It should be sufficiently shorter than the collision radius of the game's characters to avoid blindly stepping past obstacles when sampling the world. However, a shorter increment along the grid will increase the precision of the navmesh at the cost of added mesh complexity and overall computational cost. That is, better results will increase the runtime of both the algorithm and operations on the resulting mesh. Typical characters in the *Ghost Recon* series have a collision radius of 35 centimeters (about a foot). A sample grid of 25-centimeter increments produces a nice balance between mesh precision and complexity.

The collision tests in this first stage of the algorithm can be extended to describe additional attributes of the terrain relevant to the characters that will be navigating it. For example, *Ghost Recon* navmeshes track water-covered areas and stance-restricted regions, such as low ceilings that force crouched or prone movement. These situations can be identified and recorded by extracting additional information from ray casts and by testing additional collision volumes to represent different character stances.

The grid of breadcrumbs resulting from world sampling highlights both strengths and weaknesses of the empirical algorithm. Working on an axis-aligned grid simplifies data management and avoids floating-point precision issues arising from arbitrarily close positions but fundamentally limits the degree to which the generated mesh can match actual world geometry. Note that because the "grid" is generated by a breadth-first search of queued neighbors, regions of terrain are free to overlap. As long as a minimal clearance is maintained, the algorithm generates a valid navmesh for a stacked navigable terrain.

Step 2: Cleaning the Navigable Space

The initial network of navigable points is based on direct tests of the world geometry, and thus inherently reliable within the tolerance of the sampling rate. Because this data is still just an approximation of continuous terrain, some cleanup will be required before using it as the basis for an actual navmesh. In general, we want to smooth the point network to eliminate unnecessary complexity and potentially dangerous areas of marginal navigability.

At this point, it's useful to move from considering the samples as a collection of points to thinking of them as navigable regions with actual geometric area. To do this, the point grid is searched for "cycles" of navigability. Any point that can trace a North–East–South–West cycle through neighboring points is considered to anchor a "cell" of navigable space bound by those navigable connections. This cell search is again performed with a breadth-first search of queued points, thus intentionally missing undesirable regions that cannot be reached cleanly via navigable cells. The result can be visualized as a tiled landscape of navigable area.

To generate navmeshes that allow multiple agents to cleanly navigate the world, it might be desirable to further restrict the acceptance of navigable cells. For example, we can require that all valid cells be connected to other neighboring cells, so that blocks of 2 × 2 or 3 × 3 meta-cells are present. In cases where such a block cannot be identified, the cells are no longer considered part of the navigable space. This additional cleanup will eliminate narrow corridors from the resultant navmesh, which can ease the burden on pathfinding and path following.

After navigable cells are noted, boundary points can be identified. These are important because they will ultimately define the shape of the navmesh. A boundary point is a valid (navigable) point not contributing to navigable cells on all four corners. Typically, a boundary point will have two other boundary points as neighbors (such as when they're along a wall or cliff). It is an important simplification that we avoid cases of boundary points connecting to more than two boundary point neighbors. This is an indication of multiple tiny obstacles breaking up navigability. The solution is to merge the obstacles by removing connections between boundary points, effectively filling tight areas with impassable space.

FIGURE 2.5.2   The point network is processed to eliminate excess complexity and areas of marginal navigability.

This cleanup process of finding navigable cells, removing corridors, marking boundaries, and filling tight areas is repeated until no new tight areas are found. Although this seems like a lengthy and time-consuming process, in practice, this condition is met in just a few iterations. The result, as represented in Figure 2.5.2, is a polished description of the navigable space ready to serve as input to mesh construction.

Step 3: Refining Boundaries

Now that the point network is optimized, we will reexamine the boundary points with an eye toward choosing the impassable vertices and edges in the final navmesh. Simply promoting all boundary points to vertices and connecting them with impassable edges would result in a very dense navmesh. The goal will instead be to generate a simplified series of edges that still represents most of the precision stored in the boundary point network.

Each boundary point is examined until an unvisited chain of boundary points is found. A trace operation is then executed. As each neighboring boundary point is iterated over, a record is constructed noting the compass direction traced to continue the chain. For example, a simple obstacle might result in a closed cycle of boundary points that traces out the pattern North–East–South–West. Similarly, a diagonal wall segment might generate a stair step pattern such as North–East–North–East, and so on.

Theses recorded trace sequences are then compared to a set of patterns targeted for simplification. Instead of creating eight individual navmesh edges from a sequence of eight collinear, neighboring boundary points, a single edge will be created to span the entire length represented by the points. Likewise, a stair-step sequence will be identified as a common pattern and approximated with a single diagonal edge near the boundary points. Ultimately, this is likely to result in a four-fold decrease in boundary complexity compared with directly promoting all boundary points to impassable navmesh vertices. In some cases, such as the stair-step patterns, it is also likely that the smoothed boundary edge is a closer match to the actual obstacle geometry.

This process of tracing boundaries to produce optimized impassable navmesh vertices and edges can be extended to also generate internal mesh regions representing other navigation properties. For example, water or stance restriction information stored with navigable points can be embedded in the final mesh if navmesh polygons are generated so that each polygon has consistent traits throughout. In this case, rather than tracing obstacles via chained boundary points, the algorithm is modified to build edges around different terrain regions by tracing through points with mismatched neighboring cell traits.

After navigation boundaries have been simplified to produce the impassable vertices and edges of the navmesh, some of the most important work is done. Figure 2.5.3 shows a representation of the algorithm at this stage. All that remains is to round out the mesh into a complete data structure ready for pathfinding.

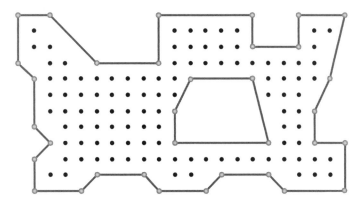

FIGURE 2.5.3 Impassable navmesh edges are generated by tracing through boundary point chains and looking for easily simplified patterns.

Step 4: Selecting Interior Vertices

Although the impassable edges represent key information in a navmesh, interior vertices and edges are also needed to complete the mesh and provide connectivity across passable regions. The first two steps of the empirical algorithm have provided a multitude of interior navigable points for inclusion in the navmesh. How should we choose among these points to construct a desirable mesh?

Game-specific considerations might come into play here. In general, a relatively uniform navmesh density is helpful if additional data is to be attached to the mesh vertices or polygons. For example, tactical pathfinding information, such as line-of-sight considerations, can be embedded with navigation data [Straatman06]. A relatively uniform density makes storage and application of this additional data more consistent across a map.

Gameplay might also dictate that the majority of character movement happens near obstacles and other areas of good cover. In this case, it can be valuable to encourage greater navmesh density around obstacles, giving pathfinding agents more tactical options in these areas of special interest. In any case, it is wise to have sufficient internal vertices near the navmesh edges to avoid a proliferation of "sliver" triangles joining the internal vertices with the impassable edges.

These goals can be met by first flood-filling to find and record the closest distances to boundaries for each interior point. Then, for those interior points, a few heuristics can be applied when considering which to promote to vertices. First, we enforce a minimum distance from other vertices and boundaries and reject points that are too close. Second, we promote any points exceeding a maximum distance from both existing vertices and boundaries. Finally, we also promote points closer to an obstacle than an existing vertex.

These rules will select a well-distributed collection of vertices for the navmesh, as shown in Figure 2.5.4. Combined with the boundary vertices selected earlier, they will complete the vertex list for the final navmesh.

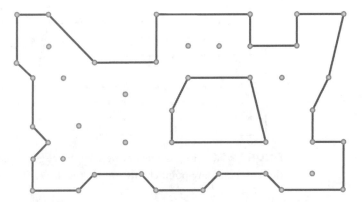

FIGURE 2.5.4   A few simple heuristics will help select a set of internal vertices that give a relatively uniform density to the final navmesh.

Step 5: Constructing the Triangle Mesh

We are now left with the task of constructing interior edges from the vertices and ultimately linking the edges into a triangle mesh. The original navigable point grid will continue to serve as a source of connectivity information for validating possible navmesh edges. Tracing candidate connections along the point grid will, for example, avoid incorrectly linking stacked navmeshes with vertical edges.

We begin by identifying edge candidates up to a maximum length, which is chosen to support the length needed to connect interior points as dictated by the specific heuristics used in interior vertex promotion. Furthermore, edge candidates are ignored if they are already linked boundary edges, do not match up with a passable route through the point grid, or pass outside (or are collinear with) boundary edges.

Candidate edges that pass these tests are then sorted by length and considered shortest edge first. We reject any edges that intersect second-degree neighbor edges. All other edges are accepted and added to the mesh. Choosing the edges in this fashion avoids all intersecting or otherwise invalid edges.

The navmesh structure can now be finalized by building triangles from the set of edges. For each edge, the associated triangles must be identified. In the case of impassable edges, there will be only a single associated triangle. Care should be taken to avoid selecting triangles that enclose smaller triangles. Also, impassable obstacle triangles should not be included in the mesh. Keeping these caveats in mind, the triangles can be identified efficiently just by examining neighboring edges.

The empirical navmesh generation algorithm results in a collection of vertices connected into edges and, in turn, connected into triangles as seen in Figure 2.5.5. The final representation of the navmesh will depend on the needs of pathfinding or any other optimized algorithms that operate on the data structure. Subject to tuning parameters and precision/complexity tradeoffs, the navmesh should be a viable approximation of the navigable terrain.

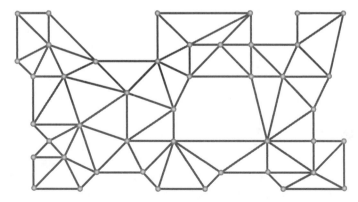

FIGURE 2.5.5   The generated navmesh in its final state with vertices connected into edges and triangles.

Optimizations

As the preceding description suggests, empirical navmesh generation is both computationally intensive and memory intensive. The traditional advice of getting the code correct and then making it efficient is not entirely applicable here because any naïve approach to implementation will quickly exhaust memory while only very slowly converging on a solution. However, with careful data structure choices and extensive refinement, the *Ghost Recon* implementation is capable of generating 20,000 triangle meshes for highly detailed maps roughly 300 meters in each dimension, taking roughly 45 seconds on a single core 3 GHz PC.

The first step of the algorithm, performing the millions of physics queries required to produce the initial grid of navigable points, is difficult to optimize for most detailed environments. After all viable performance tuning is complete, it is likely to remain the dominant resource drain. With this in mind, it is important to verify that the ray casts and collision tests are done as efficiently as the game's physics technology allows. It is also crucial that no extra tests are performed during terrain traversal. Results should be cached at each point and reused when the breadth-first search encounters previously tested regions to minimize overall processing.

Memory optimizations should begin with an examination of the data stored with each navigable point. The grid-like nature of the point samples can be leveraged to compress the representation of a location. It is likely that 16-bit indices will suffice for distinguishing unique coordinates on the navigable terrain. Attention should also be given to compressing additional data fields stored with each of the potentially millions of navigable points. The *Ghost Recon* point implementation includes a set of some 16 flags toggled at various stages of the algorithm. These are represented as a single compacted bit field to avoid wasted memory.

Consideration should also be given to the containers used to store and access data as the algorithm runs. The *Ghost Recon* implementation includes a custom three-level grid hierarchy for storing the initially sampled points. This representation allows large regions of data storage to be pre-allocated and quickly referenced without tying up a lot of excess, wasted memory for nonnavigable regions. Later in the algorithm, an optimized spatial hash table might also be valuable for efficient edge candidate lookup [Farnstrom06]. Such measures are necessary to produce an implementation that will scale to large, complex environments. Furthermore, every memory optimization has the potential to double as a speed improvement due to reduced cache misses.

Tuning the Results

This algorithm can generate production-quality navmeshes for a wide variety of terrains just by using a common set of heuristics. However, problems will inevitably arise when special circumstances break the basic assumptions of navigability. For example, an unusually steep staircase intended to be climbable or a low-rising ridge intended to be impassable can be misrepresented by the generated navmesh. Happily, tuning parameters can be easily added to the algorithm both at a per-mesh and per-region granularity.

Listing 2.5.1 shows a GUI-generated configuration file that can be used to specify a variety of custom inputs to the navmesh generation process. Such a file will be necessary for holding the SeedPointList, which provides the required starting points for navigable terrain sampling. Other useful global settings include GridStepXY, which controls the granularity of the point field used to build the navmesh; VertexSpacingMin and VertexSpacingMax, which control the density of interior vertices in the navmesh; and a StanceList, which defines different character representations to test for navigability.

Listing 2.5.1 Using a Configuration File to Tune Navmesh Generation for a Particular Environment

```
<NavGenConfig>
    <PointLimit>1000000</PointLimit>
    <GridStepXY>0.25</GridStepXY>
    <CollisionRadius>0.35</CollisionRadius>
    <VertexSpacingMin>1.5</VertexSpacingMin>
    <VertexSpacingMax>4</VertexSpacingMax>
    <MeshTerrainOffset>0.7</MeshTerrainOffset>
    <StanceList>
        <Stance Name = "Prone" Height = "0.7"
            MaxDepth = "0"/>
        <Stance Name = "Crouch" Height = "1.1"
            MaxDepth = "0.5"/>
        <Stance Name = "Upright" Height = "1.9"
            MaxDepth = "1"/>
    </StanceList>
    <SeedPointList>
        <SeedPoint>-14.72;22.03;13.80;</SeedPoint>
    </SeedPointList>
    <TerrainTypeList>
        <TT Name = "Natural" Clearance = "0.2"
            Slope = "1"/>
        <TT Name = "Urban" Clearance = "0.4"
            Slope = "2"/>
        <TT Name = "Blocked" Clearance = "-0.1"
            Slope = "-1"/>
    </TerrainTypeList>
    <ZoneList>
        <Zone Terrain = "Urban" Default = "1"/>
        <Zone Terrain = "Blocked">
            <Point>149.21;67.02;0.00;</Point>
            <Point>149.11;61.43;0.00;</Point>
            <Point>153.07;66.98;0.00;</Point>
        </Zone>
    </ZoneList>
</NavGenConfig>
```

Finer control of navmesh generation can be achieved by also specifying custom slope limits and ground clearance tolerances for specific regions of a map. Such exceptions can be nicely managed by the concept of terrain types, which are defined and then referenced by specific zones across the map. A default terrain type can be used to describe the most widely prevalent conditions of an environment. These terrain "hints" allow a correct interpretation of unusual cases in the geometry each time the navmesh is regenerated without requiring the source art to be modified.

Implementation Advice

Before diving into empirical navmesh generation coding, there are a few implementation guidelines to consider. Thinking about these issues early on will yield savings in the long run and avoid some frustration. The *Ghost Recon* implementation reached a proof of concept state in about three weeks of development. The first version suitable for production testing was ready after three months. This investment was minimal compared to the expected payoff, but closer attention to these lessons might have provided an even larger win.

First, consider investing in debugging capability from the start. The algorithm lends itself well to visualization at most stages of generation. Yet a decision must be made to put in a little extra work up front to expose the navigability data as it is processed. Even in the rare cases when portions are coded bug-free the first time, visualization aids will help build confidence in the algorithm.

Second, provide profiling support to log timing information as the implementation progresses. There are many optimizations to consider when coding navmesh generation. Having concrete feedback about where time and memory are going will allow informed decisions about which optimizations to prioritize. It can also serve as encouragement to see the algorithm using fewer resources over time.

Finally, plan on having a convenient method of comparing generated navmeshes with assets created under any previous workflow. It is very useful to see side by side how well the generated navmeshes are measuring up against a legacy approach on the same environments. This can suggest areas of the implementation that need further tuning.

Future Work

The automated process presented in this article addresses a pressing problem shared by many content pipelines. However, different games will have different needs, and, in general, those needs are getting more elaborate. For example, game environments are becoming much more dynamic and interactive. This limits the usefulness of precomputed data in many contexts, including AI and navigation. More research will be needed to explore whether empirical navmesh generation can be adapted to produce a runtime solution for highly dynamic or destructible worlds.

Any runtime version of navmesh generation is likely to involve rebuilding and merging localized sections of mesh. This ability would also be of great value for tool-time editing where tweaks to the world terrain and static objects could update the associated navmesh incrementally instead of relying on a slower regeneration of the whole mesh. Further optimizations of the algorithm could also be explored, including opportunities for parallelization.

Conclusion

Navmeshes are a widely implemented basis for AI pathfinding and tactical reasoning. The algorithm presented here seeks to automate the generation of navmeshes with a scalable, tunable approach. Furthermore, the relatively uniform density of the resulting meshes provides reliable navigation options and well-distributed anchor points for additional metadata. The *Ghost Recon* series is leveraging this technology to improve pipeline efficiency and AI performance.

Acknowledgements

This navmesh generation research was supported by the Red Storm AI group, including John O'Brien, Deirdre Toomey, Christopher Port, and Dmitriy Buluchevskiy. The author is grateful for their assistance.

References

[Farnstrom06] Farnstrom, Fredrik, "Improving on Near-Optimality: More Techniques for Building Navigation Meshes." *AI Game Programming Wisdom 3*, Charles River Media, 2006: pp. 113–128.

[Straatman06] Straatman, Remco, Beij, Arjen, and van der Sterren, William, "Dynamic Tactical Position Evaluation." *AI Game Programming Wisdom 3*, Charles River Media, 2006: pp. 389–403.

[Tozour02] Tozour, Paul, "Building a Near-Optimal Navigation Mesh." *AI Game Programming Wisdom*, Charles River Media, 2002: pp. 171–185.

2.6

Navigation Graph Generation in Highly Dynamic Worlds

Ramon Axelrod—Alseek

mushroomramon@yahoo.com

The game world of today is rapidly becoming more complex and dynamic through the use of physics engines. A major bottleneck for achieving the true potential of in-game physics is the creation of an AI subsystem capable of handling a fully dynamic world. Although some techniques exist for dealing with movement and pathfinding in dynamic worlds, these are limited in two aspects. First, such techniques have problems with fast or large-scale changes because they depend on maintaining a great deal of pre-processed information (e.g., a navigation graph generated offline from raw 3D data). Second, they do not take into account that the game's agents can change the world.

This article describes a new approach for generating and updating navigation graphs directly from raw 3D data in real time. The method proposed supports extremely dynamic worlds and accounts for all agents. Moreover, this technique can be extended to handle situations where the agents themselves can affect the environment.

Background

One of the most basic requirements of AI modules in games is to move the game agents through the 3D environment in a way that looks natural, that is, to plan a route for the agent (pathfinding) and then to execute that route with small local corrections when changes or obstacles are encountered. Presently, the standard practice for pathfinding is based on searching for an optimal path on a prebuilt navigation graph and then applying some postprocessing (e.g., string pulling, smoothing) to the result. The navigation graph itself is prepared "manually" by a game developer or generated automatically by a graph-generation process. Typically, such automatic graph generators produce the graph and the navigation data from raw geometrical data and the collision/movement model.

Processing of full maps with current generation techniques requires considerable time—on the order of many minutes to hours. For simple scenarios, it is possible to adapt these techniques to support real-time updates by generating the graph only around a small number of moving objects. However, such adaptations prove inadequate for highly dynamic worlds that can undergo large-scale physical changes affecting dozens to hundreds of characters (e.g., collapsing buildings with significant debris dispersing over a wide area). At peak times, such *scenes* can include many thousands of moving objects. Nevertheless, the navigation graph must be updated within a few seconds. It is also important that the graph, and the graph updates, account for the various movement abilities of the characters (e.g., the simple walking ability of a character may have been blocked by fallen debris, but that character might still be able to jump over the newly created obstacle or crawl underneath it). Lastly, the graph-generation method should take into account that objects that form obstacles can also be part of walkable surfaces.

Before describing the new method, we will first review several common techniques for generating the navigation graph. In particular, we will clarify the challenges that existing techniques face in highly dynamic scenes (see Figure 2.6.1). This review also lays the groundwork for understanding our new technique, which draws on certain aspects of existing methods.

FIGURE 2.6.1   Examples of simple but highly dynamic scenes.

Movement-Based Expansion

Movement-based expansion generates the graph by moving the agent systematically through the virtual world space and checking for collisions using a collision/movement model (usually the same one used by the game itself). Specifically, this algorithm starts with one or more seed points and tries to move an agent in all directions for a small distance (see Figure 2.6.2). Each point the agents visits is also expanded in the same fashion, until the entire space is exhausted. Usually, after the graph is built, a graph size-reduction phase is applied (e.g., consolidating nodes to form triangles for navmeshes, or rectangles by means similar to [Miles06]).

The main benefit of this algorithm is that it does not depend directly on the actual geometry but instead calls the engine to provide collision and movement results. In addition to requiring only a simple interface to the engine and facilitating portability between engines, this independence allows movement-based expansion to cope with highly irregular and complex character shapes (assuming that the engine code itself

FIGURE 2.6.2 Graph generation using movement-based expansion.

does so). Similarly, the costs of movement between adjacent positions can be extracted from the engine regardless of their dependency on geometry and shape.

Another important aspect of this method, and one that is harder to address by other methods, is easy support for multiple character actions (e.g., jumping, crawling, or even supernatural powers). Such actions can be included simply by trying all of them at each point in each direction. At a sufficiently high resolution, the graph created is the most complete and accurate one possible because it reflects the actual capabilities of the character in the game, including any loopholes the developer put in the code.

However, these benefits come at a great cost: It can take hours to build a full graph, even with highly optimized collision code. Therefore, where real-time updates are required, this method can only be used to update a very small area of the game world (some maps require over a million movement checks, which will not be affordable even with the CPU budget of the near future).

Another problem with this approach is that it depends on seeds. In highly dynamic terrains, certain regions that were disconnected at the beginning might become connected later and vice versa (and the AI characters can affect this). Essentially every part of the graph might be accessible at any one moment, not just the regions connected to the seeds.

3D Rasterization (Voxelization)

Another technique for graph generation is 3D *rasterization* (also known as voxelization or volume filling). This method tries to place the character's bounding box (or cylinder) iteratively at all positions of the virtual world (see Figure 2.6.3). If the character can occupy two adjacent positions, and a predefined set of rules regarding their difference in height or in slope is satisfied, the objects are deemed connected. The movement cost for a given character is determined by a set of rules and functions describing the character's capabilities (e.g., how high it can jump, how high it can step, the cost as a function of slope). Although some of these rules resemble their movement code counterparts, others can be complicated and must be designed specifically (e.g., checking for open space above, instead of fully simulating a long jump), especially if a more accurate graph is required.

To cope with multiple character types and multiple actions, this method usually tries several box sizes. Each box test comes with its own set of rules for deciding which positions are connected and the corresponding costs. With proper design of the order in which the boxes are checked, the overall performance hit from checking multiple boxes can be kept to a minimum (by using earlier boxes to cull tests for later boxes), even with multiple characters and multiple actions. However, the number and complexity of rules can increase considerably, depending on the level of accuracy required. Although not a critical drawback at runtime, this can be problematic during development because ongoing changes in the movement code have to be accompanied by corresponding changes in the graph-generation code (usually writing different code, unlike movement-based expansion).

FIGURE 2.6.3 Graph generation using 3D rasterization (voxelization).

This method usually works better and faster when given a height map of the terrain because in that case, it is possible to limit the collision tests to the terrain surface only rather than the entire world space. *Terrain* here is used in the broad sense: Floors in buildings should also have a height map, and the corresponding graph generated is a connected set of multiple 2.5D maps.

Typically, the 3D rasterization method generates the graph faster than the movement-based expansion approach, albeit at the cost of accuracy, especially in tight places where the approximation of a character by an axis-aligned bounding box is too coarse, and the actual shape of the character becomes important. In certain cases, good results can require a nonaligned box or even a simplified mesh for the character and another nonaligned box for the weapon. When using height maps instead of full 3D rasterization, this method can also miss places where the displacement of physical objects produces new walkable surfaces (e.g., a beam connecting two roofs).

Other Generation Methods

Another class of graph generation methods do not rely on collision checks because they tend to be slow. For example, the *points of visibility* technique builds a navigation graph by placing nodes at all the corners of the orthonormal projection of objects and connecting only nodes that are visible to each other (see Figure 2.6.4). Put differently, this method connects nodes between which an agent can move in a straight line.

To account for the character's size (width and height), the entire scene geometry is usually extruded: Half the agent width is added to all walls, and, optionally, half the agent's height is added to all floors and roofs. For more information, see the "References" section [Young01].

FIGURE 2.6.4   Extrusion and graph generation using points of visibility.

The time it takes to generate a graph using this method depends on the number of objects in a volume rather than the size of the volume. This results in greatly improved performance for sparse open scenes when compared with the earlier methods. However, such sparse scenes do not usually contain many physical objects. In fact, in highly dynamic scenes (meaning a lot of objects with a lot of vertices), this can lead to a combinatorial explosion [Tozour02] and considerably worse runtimes than previous algorithms. To some extent, this is also true for other algorithms in this class, such as creating a navmesh directly from the polygons.

Like the 3D rasterization algorithm, this method also relies heavily on data describing the character's movement capabilities (cost as a function of slope and steps). However, it is more difficult and time-consuming to deal with the related issues (e.g., jumps, cost dependency on terrain type) because the method is based on visibility and not on local decisions.

For completeness, it should be noted that the graph produced in this way does not require further size-reduction steps and that the paths found on it do not require string pulling.

Real-Time Graph Generation

A basic intuition for a new algorithm can be gained by studying the results of previous methods. By comparing movement-based expansion and 3D rasterization, you'll find that the latter provides better performance but fails in tight places or near obstacles (where movement tests with the actual character shape are required). Therefore, it might be useful to perform true collision and movement checks only in these situations, and use capsule or box rasterization (it does not even matter which) with simple rules to approximate the character for all other normal situations.

By using a few different box sizes, you can rule out a position or decide that the character can indeed stand there. Internally, some physics engines use bounding boxes to rule out collisions early on, but usually they do not test a small (bounded) box to determine that a collision is certain to occur. Moreover, the systematic collision testing of adjacent places allows for optimizations that cannot be done using standard movement code (which performs a single test each time):

- Many checks are shared in adjacent places.
- Testing larger boxes makes it possible to classify entire regions in advance, thereby avoiding collision tests per point (at least when the ground height is uniform).

The main point of the previous discussion is that in all cases, it is possible to determine whether actual movement checks are required using 3D rasterization. The implication is that by using a variant of 3D rasterization, together with judiciously applied movement checks, we can achieve great speed without sacrificing the accuracy associated with movement-based expansion.

A second point to note is the resemblance between a graph generated for a terrain and the rendering of the terrain in the 3D graphics sense. Specifically, we find that the graph (in grid form) resembles the height maps that can be produced by rendering. You can think about 3D rasterization based on height maps as an algorithm for "blocking" pixels in the height map or replacing them with costs. Based on this similarity, it seems plausible that a variation on a rendering technique can be used to speed up all the steps required to build the graph.

System Overview

Next we describe a graph-generation system that builds a navigation graph from raw 3D meshes for very large areas in real time with minimal "rules" from the user.

Basically, the system uses rendering-like techniques to find "floors," "roofs," and obstacles, and, for each floor position, decides between three options: (1) a character is sure to collide there, (2) a character can definitely stand there, or (3) the answer is undecided. In the last case, the node is added to a list of nodes for which actual movement tests will be performed.

The system is based on four components:

Main generation algorithm. This component performs several "rendering" passes of the geometrical meshes, using the results to produce the graph and fill the movement costs for most of the game area. This portion may be further accelerated using the GPU (see "Using the GPU" later in this article).

Movement-based expansion variant. This component fills all the "undecided" holes left by the main phase.

Self-building dictionary. An algorithm for automatically learning movement capabilities and characteristics of the agents from the results of movement-based expansion. Like 3D rasterization and the points of visibility method for graph generation, our rendering-like algorithm depends on a lot of knowledge about the agents' movement abilities. These can be extracted using movement-based expansion in a limited manner, which we will discuss later.

World segmentation. This step divides the world into bins that are used to keep track of the parts of the world that have changed, for which the graph needs to be updated.

To make the discussion more tractable, we'll next describe building a graph for a single NPC with a single action and touch on the more general problem later. We'll also simplify the explanation and refrain from describing the world segmentation component that is common to many other subsystems in a game engine.

In this discussion, we assume that you have a basic understanding of 3D rendering techniques and shader programmability.

Main Generation Algorithm (Render-Generate)

Using several passes, this rendering-like algorithm (we will refer to it as *render-generate*) builds the graph and populates it with cost data. Notice that most of the rendering passes that will be described output either depth or other calculated data instead of actual color. Again, it is important to stress that if the render-generate algorithm is unable to resolve particular positions, these positions are marked for actual movement tests.

The algorithm detailed starts by finding the heights of all floors, roofs, and obstacles and later uses this information to decide where characters can stand and decide where to build the graph. As in the 3D rasterization case, the floors and roofs are more generic height maps: They can be true floors in a building, the terrain outside, and the sky, or even a cave floor and its roof. Despite this generality of the algorithm, a good intuition can be gained by imagining a normal building with several apartments that have floors, ceilings, and furniture acting as obstacles.

Using the building scene as an example, the first two rendering passes produce the floor of the top apartment and its ceiling as height maps. Inside the apartment, we then take into account all obstacles (furniture) and render them to figure out how high they are. We then set the maximum height for the rendering to be the next floor and go over the same steps again (see Figure 2.6.5).

The algorithm renders the meshes and objects of the collision model used for actual collisions tests and not the graphics meshes. Only polygons with which the game engine actually interacts are taken into consideration, and polygons used for visual effects only are ignored.

The algorithm, of course, has to deal with situations that are much more complex than our building example. However, it is designed to be conservative, so that any mistakes or problems in the rendering phases will not risk the correctness of the final graph but simply cause more movement tests. Put differently, rendering problems result in performance hits (more movement tests) rather than graph mistakes.

The following describes each algorithm pass.

Floor Height Map Passes

As stated before, the purpose of this stage is to find the "floor," including all walkable areas but ignoring small obstacles. For example, in the apartment situation, we want to take into account the floor and maybe a large table but ignore a support column or a stack of books. These will be taken into account later. The results of this stage are *floor height manifolds*: a collection of height maps for all the outside terrain, floors, and so on.

To produce the top-floor manifold, we render the nonsmall objects in the scene (objects where any axis of the bounding box is above 1 m) from above using ortho-normal projection. For each pixel, we output its depth, which is actually the height at that point. We cull back-facing polygons to "see" through roofs, and, for each pixel, we output the height and slopes of the mesh at each pixel instead of the color.

Unlike traditional rendering, we render our pathfinding pixels even if the center of the pixel is not occupied to ensure that we render at least one pixel per scan line, so that thin objects or objects perpendicular to the viewing directions (e.g., walls and wires) will still be seen. To produce the next floor, we render the entire scene again, but this time, we cull pixels that are above the last floor. This process is repeated several times to produce most of the floors and terrain. It is not important to retrieve all height maps this way because the movement-based expansion stage will investigate and find all the missing graph nodes.

Following are some notes to consider:

- Slopes are calculated from the original polygon (by calculating its derivatives along x and along y) per pixel.
- Back-facing polygons means (for those not familiar with 3D rendering jargon) polygons with a normal away from the camera, that is, facing away from the camera.
- Stitching of different floors together will occur automatically thanks to later movement tests.

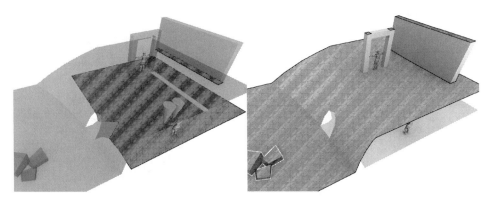

FIGURE 2.6.5   3D rendering passes to extract the topmost floor (right) and the next floor (left).

Roof Height Map Passes

To turn the apartment in our example from a floor plan to a room, we need a ceiling. Therefore we create *roof height manifolds*: a collection of height maps for the roofs above the floors, where roofs are defined as the lowest point above each floor point, as shown in Figure 2.6.6.

To produce the roofs, we render all the objects in the scene using orthonormal projection and back-face culling, but this time from below (i.e., we look up from the floor to "see" the ceiling). We cull any pixel that is below or equal to the current floor height or above the last floor height. In other words, we render only objects (or part of them) that lie above the current floor and below the previous floor. In practice, we cull everything below the current floor plus a small threshold height so that the bottom of objects that lie on the ground will not count as a roof (which would lead to unnecessary movement checks but not to an error, as will be explained later). Again, we render pixels even if the center is not occupied to capture lamps, wires, and other thin objects.

Walkable Ground and Obstruction Passes

Now we need to deal with the obstructions and all the objects we ignored before. We do this by rendering all objects (big or small) from above that are between the floor and roof, including the floor, outputting the height (actual walkable height), slopes (in both x and y directions), and object material (the cost of moving on different terrain types might vary).

Some clarifications are in order here. The obstacle height map is also potentially a walkable surface height map (you might not be able to step from the floor onto a high closet, but you can walk on it if you are there and have enough room below the roof). Of course, if the "big object" size threshold was a bit smaller, the top of the closet would be rendered as "floor," and the side of the closet would appear as a wall. As you will see, this does not really affect the actual graph produced, only the amount of collision checks required.

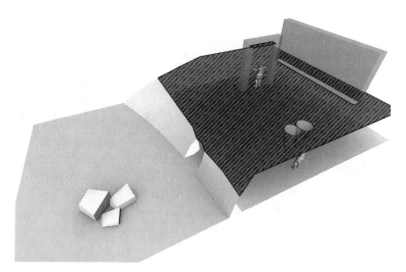

FIGURE 2.6.6   3D rendering passes to extract the roofs of the floors in
Figure 2.6.5.

In some games with complex 3D models, finding the correct floors can be a deli-
cate matter. For example, consider two rooms located one above the other. In the top
room, we have a table. The previous process will result in three levels: (1) the top floor
and top of the table, (2) the bottom floor and top floor beneath the table, and (3) the
bottom floor beneath the table. As you will see, all these vast changes in floor height
will be marked for collision checks (including the bottom floor), and the bottom floor
parts will be linked. The movement checks can be reduced by dividing the floor-
generation part in two: the first (ignoring objects smaller than, say, 5 m) to find the
floor of the room, and the second (ignoring only very small objects) to find walkable
areas.

Another example might be two buildings with a wooden beam connecting them.
The beam will not be seen as part of the floor but will appear as an obstacle. Therefore, the beam will be considered in the rendering as if it were a large wall causing
later stages to perform actual movement tests on it, thereby getting correct results
with only a minor performance hit.

Building the Graph

Using the information about floors, roofs, and obstacles, we are now ready to create the
graph. We do this in two stages: First we find out which pixels can actually be nodes in
our graph (where a character can stand without colliding with the scene), and later we
connect these nodes, marking the resultant edges with appropriate movement costs.
Places that cannot be decided are sent to actual collision or movement tests.

Extrusion and Finding the Graph Nodes

For each roof manifold, we define the *extruded roof map* as follows: For each pixel, we take the minimum height of the roof manifold in a radius of half a character width (rounded up). Similarly, we define the *extruded obstruction map* by computing for each pixel the maximum height of the walkable manifold in a radius of half a character width (rounded up).

Extrusion maps have the property that a character can stand at every place where the difference between the *extruded roof map* and the *extruded obstruction map* is greater than the height of the character's bounding box height. Together with the idea that a character cannot stand at a place if his height is more than the difference between the floor and the roof, we have everything we need to make a decision or send it for a collision test.

Following is pseudocode for the entire decision:

```
for each pixel v in the floor map:
    diff[v] = roof[v] - walkable[v]
    ext_diff[v] = Extrude_Roof[v] - Extrude_walk[v]
    if (diff[v] < character height)
        the character CANNOT stand there
    else if (ext_diff[v] > character height)
        the character can stand there
    else Undetermined - send to actual movement test
end loop
```

Consider a character with bounding cylinder radius r and a floor of area A. In theory, the extrusion map can be calculated very quickly in time $O(A \cdot r)$ because a lot of data is shared between adjacent pixels. For large radiuses, there is really no need to calculate minimum roof and maximum floor heights according to the exact radius— any bigger radius or bigger rectangle will do. Bigger shapes do not change the resulting graph but simply send more points to actual movement tests. Nevertheless, these approximations are still worthwhile because they can be computed in $O(A \cdot \log 2r)$. To accomplish this, you build a map at half resolution, where each pixel holds the minimum (maximum) of the appropriate four pixels in the original map. This mipmap-like process is repeated several times until the resolution is low enough to include the radius.

When dealing with multiple characters, there are several radiuses and heights associated with them. By using all the lower resolution maps and searching higher radiuses and heights first, you can find the actual characters that can stand at a point in sublinear time. No extra rendering passes are required. Similarly, multiple actions also require different opening sizes (e.g., crawling can be done at a lower height) and can also be done at once. The end result is a graph with data associated with each edge, as shown in Figure 2.6.7.

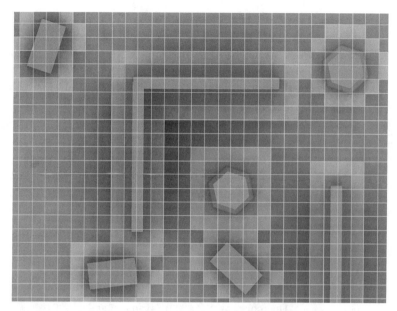

FIGURE 2.6.7   The extrusion of the walkable ground manifold of the scene in Figures 2.6.2 through 2.6.4.

Finally, it is worth noting a few additional considerations:

- Basically, the reason the entire method works fast enough (even when you do not use a GPU, as discussed later) is that instead of simple box collision tests for many points, we are doing an even simpler point test.
- Walls get at least 1 pixel, which means they are much higher than the floors around them, and, therefore, nodes near them are sent to movement tests automatically.
- In scenes created by art designers, there can be many interpenetrating objects, and the algorithm described might create nodes on floors inside objects. Strictly speaking, these nodes do not produce pathfinding problems because the generation ensures that there are no edges connecting the nodes outside to those inside. Still, for aesthetic reasons, we rule out the nodes inside objects by counting the number of front-facing and back-facing polygons above a floor pixel while rendering. This is a known technique: For pixels outside an object, the numbers should be equal.

Connectivity and Cost Filling

For each two adjacent nodes in the same floor manifold where a character can stand, we use a set of rules to determine whether the edge between them should be blocked based on the difference in height, slope, material, action, and so on. If the edge is unblocked, and all but one of the geometrical characteristics are negligible (i.e., either a step or a large slope), we fill it from a dictionary cost function that was learned automatically (and the cost can also be infinite). If there is more than one abnormality, we send the edge for actual movement tests.

The following is a reduced version of the corresponding pseudocode (note that if there is a large height difference, the nodes are sent to movement tests, e.g., near all walls):

```
for each adjacent pixels src, dst:
    diff = walkable [dst] - walkable[src]
    if (diff < max step height)
        if (slope > max_slope)
            cost = blocked
        else if (slope < slope threshold)
            cost = slope_cost_dictionary(slope,material)
        else if (diff < diff threshold)
            cost = step_cost_dictionary(diff,material)
        else complex place - send to movement test
    else Undetermined - send to movement test
end loop
```

When dealing with multiple actions, the algorithm looks up the cost for all allowed actions (as given by the extrusion phase) and takes the minimal cost.

Movement-Based Expansion Variant Used to Fill Gaps

An implementation of the movement-based expansion method is used to resolve undecided points. The implementation starts with an open list of seeds equal to all the edges marked as undecided by the render-generate part. The algorithm retrieves an edge from the open list and tries to move the character along that direction using all allowed actions, deciding the movement cost in tight places and adding nodes and edges if it finds new unvisited places. During the expansions, it also connects between different floor levels (different manifolds) and provides a complete graph. We let the algorithm run until there are no more edges in the open list.

Self-Building Dictionary

During graph building, the edges' costs are filled from several *dictionary cost functions*. These functions give the cost for a character to traverse one particular geometrical characteristic using a particular action. These functions are per agent type.

At design time, we run movement-based expansion on a sufficiently complex scene to learn these functions by sampling the cost at particular values (depending on the actual scene) and linearly interpolating between them later. The dictionary continues to be updated at runtime: If for a given characteristic, there are too few samples, or if they are too far apart, the dictionary will be updated when new points are found in the scene with the corresponding characteristic.

During the first pass, the self-building dictionary also learns the sizes of the characters. These sizes are not necessarily the static bounding boxes of the animations but might depend on the actual implementation in the engine (e.g., some engines allow swords carried by the characters to intersect the walls briefly, and some characters have clothes).

Using the GPU

Although the algorithm works very fast in software running on the CPU, it can be accelerated significantly using programmable GPUs. This includes all the rendering passes and the extrusion pass using *2D passes* (where the GPU is simply acting as a massive floating-point computation engine).

Because the GPU does not allow full control over the rendering pipeline, certain modifications must be made to overcome these limitations:

Ensuring at least one rendered pixel. For perpendicular polygons to be apparent, we need to render at least 1 pixel per scan line, even if the center of the pixel is not occupied. On the GPU, we render the object a second time in wireframe mode.

Rendering target type. Certain render targets and inputs need to be of type float and not RGBA (which only have 8 bits each). To save memory and bandwidth, it is possible to encode the extrusion and obstruction maps in RGBA channels by storing the values relative to the floor and roof (thus, 8 bits are enough)

Using vPos. Use vPos to get the current pixel without computation.

Using ddx(), ddy(). Use these operators for computing the slopes.

Rendering at high resolution. GPUs can handle this easily, and it leads to much better results in tight places. The results can be turned into a navmesh faster and more accurately.

Multitasking the GPU. Assuming the GPU runs the game's graphics in parallel, the rendering passes and extrusion passes should not be done consecutively to avoid hiccups in the graphics.

In the near future, it should be possible to render the extruded floor and roof directly from the geometry using the geometry shader in DX10, providing a useful shortcut [MS07].

Results

We will compare the results and runtime for full graph generation in movement-based expansion (being the most accurate but also the most time consuming) with the render-generate algorithm running in software and on the GPU. We tested two scenes:

The ruined temple. A 250 m × 250 m scene with two floor levels in most of the terrain (see Figure 2.6.1 on the right). The scene contains 1,000 objects with a total of ~100,000 triangles (these are the number of polygons in the collision model, not the graphics!).

The valley of Shaharit. A 1,000 m × 1,000 m scene that contains outdoor terrain, caves (with a large tunnel below the terrain), and 2 cities with several floors (~5,000 objects with ~500,000 triangles). The characters of the scene have several actions per NPC.

The graph generation is linked to a third-party engine to run actual movement tests and runs on a dual core X86 CPU running at 2.5 GHz capable of making ~3,000 movement tests per second on a single core allocated for the task (including early checks of whether a simplified character bounding box can stand at the origin of the movement at all). Table 2.6.1 shows graph generation timings for two example environments.

Table 2.6.1 Amount of Time Needed for Generating the Graph (Net)

	Ruined temple (250 m × 250 m)	Shaharit (1 km × 1 km)
Movement-Based	5 minutes	>1 hour
Software Render-Generate (SSE optimized)	3 sec. rendering 4 sec. exact move tests	30 sec. rendering 2 min. exact move tests
GPU Render-Generate (including transfer to main memory)	0.5 sec. rendering (by scene design), under 3 sec. for exact move tests	~5 sec. rendering 1 min. exact move tests

The results for render-generate running on the GPU show total graph generation times (rendering plus movement tests) of 2–3 seconds per each 200 m × 200 m region. When dealing with more frequent updates of smaller regions (say, 50 m × 50 m), the algorithm runs in a fraction of a second. Thus, the algorithm meets our original goal of updating large portions of the graph in real time.

Besides the difference in runtime, there is also a slight difference in the generated graphs. The movement-based algorithm was initialized with four seeds, but the scenes contain several parts that are not connected to them (but can be if certain walls will be knocked down or objects moved). The render-generate algorithm finds about 25% more traversable area in the ruined temple than the movement-based algorithm, without the need for any seeds. Also, because the intermediate rendering algorithm is at a higher resolution than the resolution at which the movement-based algorithm is run, it also produces slightly better results at tight spots.

An interesting fact to note is that in highly dynamic worlds, the density of objects is high (and gets higher as the game progresses), and there are hardly any large obstructed convex areas. This calls in question the usefulness of navmeshes and similar approaches: An 8-way grid of 250 × 250 with 8-bit traversal cost between nodes (this suffices because the distances between nodes are small) consumes 0.5 MB, regardless of obstructions. A navmesh of the same scene starts at ~100 KB (2,000 triangles, 3 indexes each, vertices of floats, and so on) and can reach 1 MB when most of the scene becomes messy. The actual library implementation contains an option to convert the extended grid into a navmesh by means similar to [Miles06] using a modified version of the FIST triangulation library [Held07]. The conversion increases the runtime by 10% to 20%.

Future Directions: Incorporating Changes Due to Agents

In highly dynamic environments, the agents themselves can alter the scene—they can move objects, build walls, and so on. It is possible to alter the graph-generation process to take such possibilities into account by adding *physics influence maps*—a type of influence map similar to [Tozour01] that contains physics information.

Like all influence maps, a physics influence map changes the weight of edges (movement costs) to prefer a path or deter a character from moving there. However, this influence map incorporates certain aspects of agents affecting the terrain without simulation. The basic idea is to build or alter the influence maps during graph generation. Following are two examples:

Avoiding physically problematic places. The idea is to find paths that avoid areas where collapse can occur and cause a lot of collateral damage. To achieve this, we add an influence map made from the potential energy of objects above the ground (so taller walls or structures with a lot of beams will be avoided).

Pathfinding that considers "opening a path" (e.g., shooting a hole in a wall). The idea is to replace the default "blocked" weight of obstacles with a high weight.

This work, while still experimental, shows great promise.

Conclusion

When combined with a system for keeping track of changed areas, the *render-generate* algorithm allows real-time graph updates for very large areas with minimal compromises on graph quality. It can also be useful during development to speed up graph generation of large scenes. Moreover, this algorithm enables a robust solution for destructible worlds: If a falling beam connects two floors, the pathfinding will use it.

The algorithm translates well to GPUs. Today's GPUs are programmable and widely available. They should be used when a large amount of floating-point processing is needed. More processing power makes great AI possible.

References

[Held07] Held, Martin, "FIST: Fast Industrial-Strength Triangulation of Polygons." Available online at *http://www.cosy.sbg.ac.at/~held/projects/triang/triang.html*, 2007.

[Miles06] Miles, David, "Crowds in a Polygon Soup: Next-Gen Path Planning." Available online at *http://www.babelflux.com/gdc2006_miles_david_pathplanning.ppt*, GDC06.

[MS07] Microsoft, *DirectX 10 SDK*. Available online at *http://msdn.microsoft.com/directx/*.

[Smith02] Smith, Patrick, "Polygon Soup for the Programmer's Soul: 3D Pathfinding." Available online at *http://www.gamasutra.com/features/20020405/smith_01.htm*, GDC02.

[Tozour01] Tozour, Paul, "Influence Mapping." *Game Programming Gems 2*, Charles River Media, 2001.

[Tozour02] Tozour, Paul, "Building a Near-Optimal Navigation Mesh." *AI Game Programming Wisdom*, Charles River Media, 2002.

[Young01] Young, Thomas, "Expanded Geometry for Points-of-Visibility Pathfinding." *Game Programming Gems 2*, Charles River Media, 2001.

2.7

Fast Pathfinding Based on Triangulation Abstractions

Doug Demyen—BioWare Corp.

doug.demyen@gmail.com

Michael Buro—University of Alberta

mburo@cs.ualberta.ca

Pathfinding is arguably the most fundamental AI task in current video games. No matter the technique used for the decision making of in-game characters, they lose the desired illusion of intelligence if they cannot navigate about their surroundings effectively. Despite its importance and that it is a well-studied problem, pathfinding is often performed using techniques that do not provide or take advantage of information on the structure of the environment.

In this article, we present an approach to pathfinding that addresses many of the challenges faced in games today. The approach is fast, uses resources efficiently, works with complex polygonal environments, accounts for the size of the object (for example, character or vehicle), provides results given varying computational time, and allows for extension to dynamic pathfinding, finding safe paths, and more. At the heart of this approach is an abstraction technique that removes all information from the environment that is extraneous to the pathfinding task.

Motivating Example

As an example, imagine a man planning a route between two houses in a city. If the originating house is in a bay, for example, the man can assume that as long as the destination house is not in that same bay, the start of the route will be to leave the bay. After that, he won't consider turning off onto side streets from which there is no exit unless they contain the destination because they would be dead ends. When the route reaches main roads, the man needs only consider at which intersections to turn; he ignores making decisions partway between intersections because the only possible options are to proceed or turn back, which would be nonsensical.

Each intersection represents a decision point in planning the route—they are where the man will decide to travel on the north or south side of the stadium for instance. After a series of these decisions, the route will reach the destination, and although the man ignored dead-end streets and going partway between intersections to this point, he can still plan a route to a house in a cul-de-sac or in between intersections on a street. You will also notice that the path is formed at the high level of streets, and after it is formed, particulars such as lanes can be determined. After all, it would make no sense to consider using each possible lane if after forming the complete path, it becomes obvious that the left lane is preferred or perhaps necessary. Our algorithm follows a similar high-level human-like decision-making process.

Outline

We will start by introducing triangulations, our environment representation, and in particular Dynamic Constrained Delaunay Triangulations (DCDTs), which provide many advantages for this work. We will cover some considerations for pathfinding with this representation and some for the extension to nonpoint objects (specifically circular objects with nonzero radius). From there, we describe the abstraction method used to achieve the simplified representation of the environment and how the search uses this information. Finally, we provide some experimental results, draw conclusions, and suggest possible extensions to the work.

Pathfinding in Triangulations

Here we will introduce some different triangulations as well as how they are constructed and considerations for their use as an environment representation and for pathfinding.

Types of Triangulations

A fundamental aspect of the methods represented here is the use of triangulations to represent the environment. Here we will briefly cover the different types of triangulations and how they relate to pathfinding.

Given a collection of vertices in two dimensions, a triangulation (see Figure 2.7.1a) is formed by joining pairs of these vertices by edges so that no two edges cross. When no further edges can be added, all faces in the convex hull of the vertices are triangular.

A special case is a Delaunay Triangulation (DT) (see Figure 2.7.1b) that specifies that the minimum interior angle of the triangles in the triangulation must be maximized. This avoids thin triangles wherever possible, which is a useful property that we will explore later. DTs can be constructed from triangulations by taking (convex) quadrilaterals in the triangulation formed by two triangles sharing an edge, and replacing that shared edge with one joining the other two vertices in the quadrilateral, whenever this results in a shorter diagonal.

Another version of a triangulation is a Constrained Triangulation (CT), which specifies that certain edges must be included in the final triangulation. We now make the distinction between these predetermined edges (called constrained edges) and those added during the triangulation process (called unconstrained edges). CTs are constructed in the same way as regular triangulations but with the constrained edges added first to ensure they are included. Constrained edges that cross are broken up at the intersection points. When used as an environment representation, a CT uses constrained edges to indicate barriers between traversable and obstructed areas.

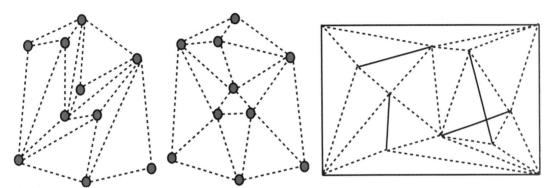

FIGURE 2.7.1 (a, b, c) Examples of (from left to right) regular, Delaunay, and Constrained (Delaunay) Triangulations.

A CT can also carry the Delaunay property, forming a Constrained Delaunay Triangulation (CDT) (see Figure 2.7.1c). CDTs are formed from CTs using the same edge-flipping technique for creating DTs, with the added proviso that constrained edges cannot be flipped. CDTs maximize the minimum interior angle of the triangles as much as possible while maintaining constrained edges. This is the representation used by the techniques described in this article but with one more technique that makes it ideal for use in games.

A technique presented by Marcelo Kallmann [Kallmann03] allows for the creation of DCDTs. This algorithm handles the online addition and removal of vertices or constrained edges in an existing CDT with minimal performance cost. Constraints are added to or removed from those already present, affected unconstrained edges are removed, and the surrounding area is retriangulated, and then the Delaunay property is propagated out to areas that have since lost it. This update requires minimal resources and can be done in real time.

Triangulations offer many advantages for pathfinding over other environment representations, such as the ability to handle edges that are not axis-aligned. Specifically, triangulations can represent environments with straight barriers perfectly and can represent curved barriers using a number of short segments, providing an approximation that is superior to axis-aligned methods.

When stored, triangulations often require fewer cells than grid-based methods. This not only presents an advantage for pathfinding but also provides more information about the environment. For example, the traversibility of a tile contains no information on the surrounding area, whereas assuming all vertices and constrained edges in a triangulation represent obstacles (otherwise, they just add unnecessary complexity to the representation), a triangle indicates the distances to obstacles in each direction. This makes triangulations a perfect candidate for working with different-sized objects; you can determine if an object can pass through a section of the triangulation with relative ease using a technique introduced later.

Considerations for Pathfinding

The basis of triangulation-based pathfinding is the idea that paths are formed by moving from triangle to adjacent triangle across unconstrained edges, much like moving between traversable adjacent cells in tile-based environments. However, when using tiles, the exact motion of the object is known to go through the centers of the tiles (at least before smoothing) as the path is being formed. If you assume during the search that the path goes through the center of the triangles it traverses, the approximation of the path's length can be very poor because triangles are typically much larger than tiles. This can lead to suboptimal paths that can spoil the illusion of intelligence by moving an object to its destination by a longer than necessary path. Here we present requirements for finding optimal paths on a triangulation, which together form the first search algorithm presented, Triangulation A* (TA*).

Pathfinding (and, in fact, all heuristic search) uses a pair of values to guide its search: the distance traveled to the current point in the search, or g-value, and an estimate of the distance remaining, or h-value. To find an optimal path, the h-value must be no more than the actual distance remaining to the goal because overestimates could make the search abandon a branch leading to an optimal solution. The g-value is assumed to be exact, so when the search reaches somewhere that was reached by a shorter path, the current path is abandoned because taking the other path must be shorter.

However, for triangulations, a path being searched may enter a triangle through one edge and then leave through one of the two others. The full path between the start and goal points as a result of this decision (and likely subsequent ones) produces different paths leading to this triangle, and so the distance covered to reach it cannot be known exactly during the search. Therefore, to produce an optimal solution, we must introduce two constraints. The first is that the g-value must not be larger than the true distance between the start of the search and the current triangle as it is reached in the final path to the goal. This follows the same logic in preventing the search from abandoning a potentially optimal path. The other constraint is that we cannot eliminate a node in the search simply because it was reached with a potentially shorter path because we do not know which path was shorter.

These requirements fit well with an *anytime algorithm*, that is one that finds a solution and improves it as long as it is given more resources. As with any other point in the search, when the goal is reached, the shortest path is not immediately known. Therefore, even after the goal is found, the search continues, accepting paths to the goal shorter than the best one currently known. Search is determined to have found an optimal path when the length of the shortest path found is less than the sum of the g- and h-values of the paths yet to be searched. This follows from these being underestimates of the path length, so any paths remaining in the search must be longer than the best one found.

Other Enhancements

To find the triangle that contains the start (and goal) point, you must perform a task called *point localization*. An inefficient approach, such as performing a greedy walk along adjacent triangles, would mask any benefits the triangulation could afford.

There is a simple but improved way to handle this task. First, the environment is divided into rectangular cells (for our experiments, a modest 10×10 grid was used). When the triangulation is constructed, triangles are tested as to whether they lie on the center point of any cells. If so, the triangle is recorded for that cell. When locating a point, its containing cell is determined easily, and the process of moving progressively closer to it is started from the triangle covering the midpoint of that cell. This results in shorter point localization times, allowing the full advantage of the triangulation-based methods.

In some cases, the possibility of the search visiting a triangle multiple times could mean the search converges more slowly on the goal. However, for maximum flexibility, we want to find the first path quickly in case the pathfinding task is not given much time. Therefore, we modified the search algorithm to only expand each triangle once until the first path has been found, after which they can be expanded again. This makes the first path available earlier without affecting the algorithm's ability to converge on an optimal path.

Triangle Width

One of the main challenges of pathfinding is dealing with objects larger than points. Incorporating this constraint is necessary to achieve paths that do not bring objects into collision with obstacles in the environment. A popular method for achieving this result is to enlarge the obstacles in the environment by the radius of the object and then perform pathfinding as if for a point object. This technique has the drawback that a separate representation of the environment must be calculated and stored for each size of object, resulting in compounded time and memory costs. An advantage to the use of triangulations for pathfinding is their aptitude in handling this kind of problem.

We have developed a method for measuring the "width" of all triangles in a CDT, which is, for any two (unconstrained) edges of the triangle, the largest circular object that can pass between those two edges. We use circular objects because they require no consideration for orientation, and, in most cases, the pathfinding footprint of game objects can be fairly well approximated by a circle of some radius.

After this is calculated for all triangles in the triangulation, pathfinding for an object of any size can be done as if for a point object except that paths which traverse between two edges of a triangle with a width less than the object's diameter are excluded. The calculation does not require much processing and memory and is done once only. This allows for objects of any size, eliminating the restrictive need to create game objects of discrete sizes for the sole purpose of pathfinding.

Finding the width for the traversal between two edges of a particular triangle is equivalent to finding the closest obstacle (a vertex or point on a constrained edge) to the vertex joining those two edges, in the area between them. If one of the other vertices of the triangle represents a right or obtuse angle, the closest obstacle is the vertex representing that angle, and the width of the triangle is the length of the edge joining this vertex to the one where the two edges meet.

Otherwise, if the edge opposite the vertex in question is constrained, the closest obstacle is the closest point to the vertex on that edge, and the width is the distance between them. Finally, if the edge opposite the vertex being considered is unconstrained, a search across that edge will determine the closest obstacle to that vertex. This search is bounded by the shorter of the distances to the other two vertices in the triangle because they are potential obstacles. It considers vertices in the region formed by the extension of the edges of the original triangle for which the calculation is being done and constrained edges in this region that would form acute triangles if their endpoints were connected to the base vertex.

Note that because the search is always bounded by the distance to the closest obstacle found so far and that Delaunay triangulations make it impossible for the search to traverse any triangle multiple times, this operation can be performed on a triangulation very quickly.

Modified Funnel Algorithm

The result of pathfinding in a triangulation is a sequence of adjacent triangles connecting the start to the goal called a *channel*. However, because triangles are larger than tiles, it does not translate directly into an efficient path through them. Luckily, you can find the shortest path through a channel quickly using a *funnel algorithm* (see Figure 2.7.2a). This algorithm has the effect of conceptually pulling a rubber band through the channel between the start and the goal, producing a sequence of line segments touching the vertices of the channel and forming the shortest path.

However, this operation is meant for point objects, and our generalized solution seeks to find shortest paths for circular objects of nonzero radius. Therefore, we developed a modified version of this algorithm (see Figure 2.7.2b) that basically consists of adding a circle with the same radius as the object centered around each vertex in the channel except the start and goal vertices. The shortest path is found by a similar method but now consists of arcs along these circles and line segments between and tangent to them to avoid collision with the obstacles.

Some considerations to keep in mind are that this algorithm assumes that the channel is wide enough to accommodate the object in question. Although this technique produces the optimal path for the object through the channel, it assumes the object is capable of traveling in a curve. If this is not the case, the object can approximately follow the arcs produced by this algorithm by traveling in several short straight segments, turning in between.

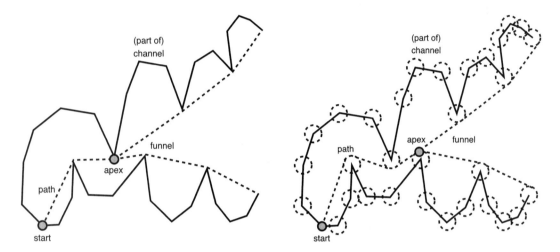

FIGURE 2.7.2   (a, b) The funnel algorithm (left) determines paths for point objects, and the modified version (right) produces paths for circular objects of some radius.

Triangulation Abstraction

The most important part of the process we use to reduce the pathfinding graph produced by the triangulation (see Figure 2.7.3a) is a simple classification of each triangle as a node in the abstract graph by *level*. We do this by assigning each triangle an integer value between 0 and 3 inclusive, indicating the number of adjacent graph structures. The graph resulting from this procedure (see Figure 2.7.3b) carries additional information about the structure of the environment.

Level-0 nodes, or *islands,* are simply triangles with three constrained edges. These are easily identified when the algorithm passes over the triangles in the triangulation.

Level-1 nodes form *trees* in the graph and represent dead ends in the environment. There are two kinds of level-1 trees in a reduced graph: *rooted* and *unrooted.* The root of a rooted tree is where the tree connects to the rest of the graph (via a level-2 node). Unrooted trees have no such connection; they are formed in areas of the graph that do not encompass other obstacles.

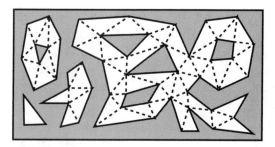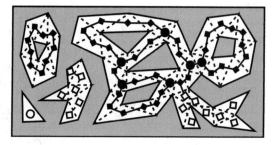

FIGURE 2.7.3   (a, b) A triangulation (left) is reduced to an abstract graph (right) where circles, squares, filled squares, and filled circles represent level-0, -1, -2, and -3 nodes, respectively.

Level-1 nodes are identified as triangles containing two or fewer constrained edges and containing, at most, one unconstrained edge across which is a level-2 node. Level-1 nodes with two constrained edges are easily found in a first pass over the triangulation, and for each of these found, the triangle across the unconstrained edge is put in a queue for processing as a possible level-1 node. Each triangle on the queue is evaluated if it now fits the description of a level-1 node, and if so, is classified as one; the unclassified triangle adjacent to it across an unconstrained edge (if one exists) is put on the queue for processing. This process will propagate through a rooted tree until the root is reached, or for an unrooted tree, throughout the whole connected component.

Level-2 nodes represent *corridors* in the environment and are adjacent (across unconstrained edges) to two nodes that are either level-2 or level-3. A connected group of level-2 nodes can form a corridor between two distinct level-3 nodes, a loop beginning and ending at the same level-3 node, or a ring with no level-3 beginning or end. All triangles remaining after the level-0, -1, and -3 nodes are identified and classified as level-2.

Level-3 nodes are the most important in the pathfinding search because they identify *decision points*. Search from a level-3 node can move directly to level-3 nodes adjacent across either unconstrained edges or level-2 corridors and represent choices as to which direction to pass around an obstacle. After level-0 and level-1 nodes are identified, level-3 nodes are those triangles with neither constrained edges nor adjacent level-1 nodes.

Abstraction Information

In addition to each triangle's level, the abstraction stores other information about each node in the environment for use in pathfinding. The adjoining node is recorded for each direction depending on its type. For level-1 nodes in rooted trees, the root of the tree is recorded for the edge through which it is reached. For level-2 nodes not in rings, they are the level-3 nodes reached by following the corridor through the edges for which they are recorded. For level-3 nodes, they are the level-3 nodes adjacent directly or across level-2 corridors in each direction.

The abstraction is also where a triangle's widths (between each pair of edges) are held. It also stores the minimum width between the current triangle and each adjoining node so the search can tell instantly if the object can reach that node.

We also included an underestimate of the distance between the current triangle and each adjoining node to be used in the search to improve the accuracy of this value and make the search more efficient.

Abstraction Search

Finding a path on the reduced triangulation graph requires more steps than performing the search on the base triangulation. First, a number of special cases are examined to determine if a search of the level-3 nodes needs to be done at all, then the start and goal points need to be connected to level-3 nodes on the most abstract graph, and finally, a search between level-3 nodes is run. This is the basis for Triangulation Reduction A* (TRA*), described later. As before, at each step, the width of the triangles being traversed is checked against the diameter of the object for which pathfinding is being performed, and paths that are too narrow for it are not considered.

The simplest check performed is to see if the endpoints are on the same connected component in the environment—that is, they are not in separate areas divided by constrained edges. Because identifying the different components requires no more processing on top of the reduction step, we can instantly see if there are any possible paths between them. If they are on different connected components, no path can exist between them. If they are on the same one, there is a path between them, and the only question is whether it's wide enough to accommodate the object. You can then check whether the endpoints are in the same triangle; if so, the path between them is trivial. This covers when the endpoints are in the same island triangle.

Next we check whether the endpoints are in an unrooted tree or in a rooted tree with the same root. In these cases, we can search the tree for the single path between the start and the goal. Because trees are acyclic (no two triangles can be joined by multiple paths that do not visit other triangles more than once), we can eliminate aspects of the search meant for finding the shortest path because only one exists (other than those containing cycles that needlessly lengthen the path). The result is a simplified search where the midpoints of the triangles are considered as exact points on the path, the Euclidean distances between them are used as distance measures, and no triangle needs to be considered twice. Also, in the case of rooted trees, the search need not venture outside the tree. Note that these searches are so localized and simple that they are almost trivial in nature (see Figure 2.7.4a).

Then for search endpoints in level-1 nodes, we search moves to the root of the tree. In some cases, the other endpoint will be at the root of this tree. This can be determined instantly and the optimal path constructed easily by simply moving along the one (acyclic) path to the root of the tree (see Figure 2.7.4b). Otherwise, the search next examines patterns with level-2 nodes.

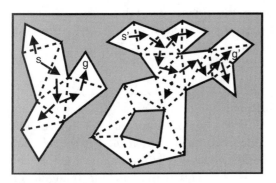
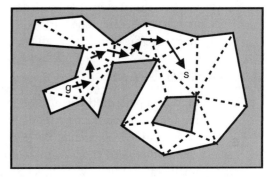

FIGURE 2.7.4   (a, b) Cases where the endpoints are in the same tree and a path is easily found.

If both endpoints are on level-2 nodes (or in level-1 trees rooted at level-2 nodes) on a ring or the same loop (see Figure 2.7.5a), there are two possible paths between them—going clockwise or counterclockwise around the ring or loop. Both of these paths are fully constructed, and the shorter of the two is taken as the optimal path.

If the level-2 nodes associated with the endpoints are on the same corridor (see Figure 2.7.5b), we form one path along that corridor and determine its length, and then the level-3 nodes found by going the opposite directions are considered the start and goal nodes for the level-3 search, respectively. The level-3 node search is performed as usual from here, except that the search now has an upper bound: the length of the path already found.

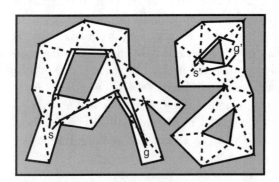
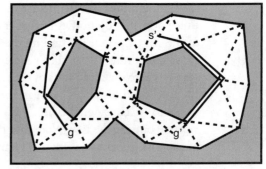

FIGURE 2.7.5   (a, b) The start and goal can also be on the same level-2 corridor, loop, or ring.

If none of these cases applies, the search travels from the level-2 nodes associated with the start to the level-3 nodes on either end of that corridor. These are the starting points for the level-3 node search. If the starting point is on a level-3 node, there is only one starting point for this search. The same procedure is performed for the goal point—potential goals are the level-3 nodes at either end of the corridor if the goal point is on a level-2 node, and if it was on a level-1 node, from the corridor on which the goal node's tree is rooted. If the goal point is on a level-3 node, that is one goal for the level-3 search.

The search from here is performed similarly to TA*, except instead of moving across unconstrained edges to adjacent triangles, it moves across corridors of level-2 nodes to other level-3 nodes. A few additional techniques are available for estimating distances on the abstract graph. The same tests for g- and h-values, the anytime algorithm, and the revisiting of nodes are performed as before.

Discussion

The criteria that decide about the adoption of new algorithms in video games are their space and time requirements, quality of the results, versatility, and simplicity. Usually at least one of these conditions is violated—in our case, it's simplicity.

The implementation of TA* and TRA* relies on efficient code for point localization and maintaining Delaunay triangulations dynamically. For this, we use Marcelo Kallmann's DCDT library [Kallmann03] whose point localization procedure we improved. Dealing with arbitrarily located points usually complicates computational geometry algorithms due to limitations of integer or floating point–based computations. The DCDT library we used is general and complex. However, for new game applications, it's conceivable that all line segment endpoints are located on a grid, and segments only intersect in grid points. This constraint greatly simplifies the DCDT algorithm. In addition, the TA* and TRA* abstraction and search mechanisms are not exactly easy to implement, although the software provided at *http://www.cs.ualberta.ca/~mburo/aiw4* can help AI programmers get familiar with the technique and test it in their settings.

The space requirement of TRA* is only slightly larger than the original polygonal map description because the size of the abstraction is linear in the number of islands in the world, which is usually orders of magnitudes smaller than the total number of triangles. Moreover, compared with grid-based representations, the space savings when using triangulations at the lowest level can be substantial if there are big unobstructed areas (see Figure 2.7.6a). In the experiments we touch on here [Demyen-Buro06, Demyen06], we used 120 maps taken from *Baldur's Gate* and *Warcraft 3* scaled up to 512 × 512 tiles, and the total memory requirement for TRA* was, at most, 3.3 MB. We did not try to optimize memory consumption, and with 184 bytes per triangle allocated by the DCDT library, there is certainly room for improvement.

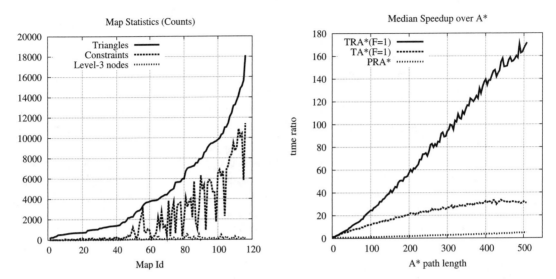

FIGURE 2.7.6   (a, b) Environments have few triangles and level-3 nodes, giving TA* and TRA* greater speedup over A* than even enhanced grid-based methods such as PRA*.

TRA*'s runtime can be broken down into two components: map preprocessing time (triangulation, reduction, sector computation) and actual pathfinding time. The most complex maps could be preprocessed within 400 milliseconds (ms) on an Athlon 64 3200+ computer, which were split roughly in half between triangulation and reduction. The median preprocessing time was 75 ms. In this set of experiments, we focused on static environments. However, you can repair triangulations and the reduced graph efficiently if changes are local. TA* and TRA* are considerably faster than grid-based A*. We observed 170× median speedups over A* for TRA* and 30× for TA*, for finding the first approximation of optimal paths of length 512 (see Figure 2.7.6b). The absolute times for TA* (see Figure 2.7.7a) and TRA* (see Figure 2.7.7b) show they work well for real-time applications.

In over 95% of the considered cases, the length of the path first reported by TA* is shorter than the grid-A* path. We know that A* computes the shortest paths, so this statement doesn't seem correct. However, the object motion in grid-A* is restricted to eight directions, whereas in triangulation-based pathfinding, objects can move freely. The TRA* path quality reaches that of grid-A* if after finding the initial path, we continue to search for better paths for the time it took to find the first. Thus, equating path quality, TRA* is about 85 times faster than grid-A* when finding long paths in the maps we considered. Note this is an abridged version of a more complete experimental analysis provided in the accompanying thesis [Demyen06].

Triangulation-based pathfinding as we described it is not only fast but also versatile. TA* and TRA* can be regarded as anytime algorithms: The more time we invest after the initial search phase, the shorter paths become. These algorithms also find

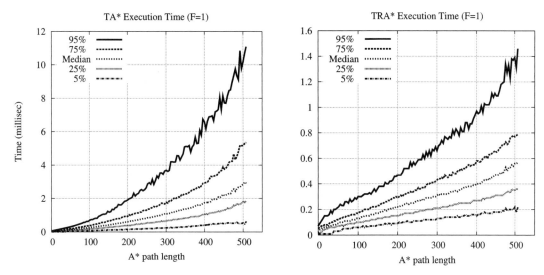

FIGURE 2.7.7   (a, b) TA* and TRA* find a path within a couple milliseconds.

optimal paths for moving circles of varying size, which is useful for group pathfinding when we use bounding circles. Triangulations are also very suited for detecting strategic terrain features, such as chokepoints.

Conclusion

We have shown the usefulness of triangulations for environment representations, both in efficiency and for the benefits it affords to pathfinding. We have also shown enhancements to pathfinding on the triangulation itself, providing an anytime algorithm for finding better paths when given more resources and converging on the optimal path.

The main contribution of this work, however, is the reduction step performed on the triangulation. On top of identifying useful structures in the environment, it allows for much faster pathfinding. Coupled with the many opportunities for extending this work for different needs and situations outlined next, we hope the efficiency and flexibility of these techniques will find application in the games industry.

Future Work

One of the most exciting aspects of these techniques is their suitability to further extension. Among these is the ability to deal with dynamic environments. For example, if mobile obstacles block an object's path, it could possibly steer around the object within its channel to avoid running the pathfinding search again. If pathfinding is being done for a group of objects, one search could yield a channel for all objects to use. In the case of a narrow path and many or large objects, more paths could be found, and the objects split between them to meet up at the goal. If paths are being found for multiple objects going in different directions, you could avoid collisions by recording at which times each object will be going through a triangle when its path is found. How crowded a triangle is at any time could be calculated based on the size of the triangle and the size and number of objects going through it at that time. When finding paths for subsequent objects, those going through crowded triangles could be avoided, and some steering should be adequate to avoid collisions.

There are also several possible extensions if more precomputation is a desired tradeoff for more speed. For example, precalculating the best paths between level-3 nodes would require a fraction of the memory required by most navigation mesh approaches. The pathfinding task would only require moving from the start and goal to adjoining level-3 nodes and fetching the rest from a table. The level-3 node graph could be abstracted even further by collapsing any doubly connected components of this graph into single nodes in a higher-level graph. This graph would then consist of a group of trees, and because paths in trees are trivial, only pathfinding between the entry points of the doubly connected components would be necessary. If some suboptimality is acceptable, you could even precalculate and cache paths between these entry points for lightning-fast pathfinding with minimal memory cost.

If pathfinding needs to be done for only a few sizes of objects, separate environment representations could be constructed for each. The exchange for the increased memory would be instant knowledge of a path existing for a particular object and not having to test paths for minimum width requirements.

You could also use these techniques in more complex cases. Pathfinding on the surface of 3D environments could be done by triangulating the passable surfaces. Overlapping areas, such as bridges, could be handled by forming separate triangulations and creating virtual links between the edges. These links could also be given costs to simulate additional time or effort for moving between meshes by jumping or climbing ladders, for example.

If objects need to take paths with certain properties, such as being clear of enemies or containing enemies whose total power is less than the object, then other information, such as the "threat" of an enemy, can be localized to a triangle and propagated through the abstract graph in the same way as triangle widths. The pathfinding search could then avoid returning paths that traverse corridors where the total enemy power is greater than a certain threshold.

Source Code and Demo

The software at *http://www.cs.ualberta.ca/~mburo/aiw4* contains Marcelo Kallmann's DCDT implementation, with the work shown here built on top. Functions of interest are `SearchPathBaseFast`, `SearchPathFast`, and `Abstract`, which implement TA*, TRA*, and the reduction process, respectively. The executables are found in the se/bin directory—setut.exe will run a GUI for visualizing pathfinding in a reduced triangulation. Press "6" when the program opens to see the DCDT, noting the red constrained edges, gray unconstrained edges, yellow level-1 trees, green level-2 corridors, cyan level-0 islands, and magenta level-3 decision points. Click two points to find a path between them; the black lines are the channel, and the blue lines are the path. You can also drag the obstacles around and see the triangulation, abstraction, and path change. The information contained in the abstraction for the triangle over which the mouse is currently positioned is printed in the console window.

Acknowledgments

We thank Marcelo Kallmann for making his DCDT software available to us, allowing us to get so far so quickly. Financial support was provided by NSERC and iCore.

References

[DemyenBuro06] Demyen, D. and Buro, M., "Efficient Triangulation-Based Pathfinding." *Proceedings of the AAAI Conference*, Boston (2006): pp. 942–947.

[Demyen06] Demyen, D., "Efficient Triangulation-Based Pathfinding." Master Thesis, Computing Science Department, University of Alberta, Edmonton, Canada. Available online at *http://www.cs.ualberta.ca/~mburo/ps/thesis_demyen_2006.pdf*, 2006.

[Kallmann03] Kallmann, M. et al., "Fully Dynamic Constraint Delaunay Triangulations." *Geometric Modeling for Scientific Visualization*, Springer Verlag, 2003: pp. 241–257.

2.8

Automatic Path Node Generation for Arbitrary 3D Environments

John W. Ratcliff—Simutronics Corporation

jratcliff@infiniplex.net

This article presents a general-purpose algorithm to produce high-quality navigation meshes for arbitrarily complex static 3D environments. The navigation mesh (navmesh) is ideally suited to perform high-speed path planning for AI. This spatial data structure can serve innumerable other purposes because it comprises a meaningful way to describe the world. It can be used by game designers to associate metadata with the environment and by programmers to implement additional algorithms. The navmesh produced is both compact and highly efficient, yet it can also describe every relevant nook, cranny, and corner of a game level.

The algorithm we will be presenting has been proven to work in several commercial games. It was originally developed for the first-person shooter *S.C.A.R.A.B.*, published by Electronic Arts in 1997. It was later adapted for the game *Cyberstrike 2*, published by 989 Studios and developed at Simutronics Corporation. More recently, it was integrated into the *Planetside* game engine for Sony Online Entertainment. Today, Simutronics Corporation is using it in the MMO (massively multiplayer online) game development environment *Hero Engine*.

In addition to presenting the algorithm, this article is accompanied by public domain source code as well as a detailed demo application. To fully build and run the demo requires the use of the AGEIA PhysX SDK, which is provided on the CD-ROM courtesy of Ageia Technologies.

ON THE CD

Requirements and Assumptions

There are a few important assumptions to consider before using this algorithm. Although these restrictions match most game designs, it may not accommodate a number of situations. The most critical assumptions are as follows:

- The game has a definitive constant orientation or up-vector.
- The game models gravity so that characters fall relative to the up-vector.

- Characters may only walk up surfaces of a specific steepness (no crawling on walls or ceilings).
- The class of character that is to use the navmesh is of a consistent size and behavior (although you can produce separate navmeshes for different classes of characters).
- The game level is largely a static environment and can be described as a set of triangles.
- The algorithm requires the ability to process navmeshes offline as part of the level building step. Depending on the complexity of the environment, this tool can take a substantial amount of time to run.

Although these assumptions may not match every game design, it does fit the standard model of most first person shooters (FPSs) or other games that have a carefully crafted prebuilt static environment. The algorithm could be relatively easily adapted to remove the assumption that characters only walk along a single predefined up-vector by running it in multiple passes for each distinct surface orientation.

Algorithm Overview

The starting point for this algorithm is to identify which surfaces in the game level qualify as valid for a character to stand on. Next, all of these surfaces are voxelized into a giant data set that represents every point in 3-space where it might be possible for a character to stand. From this giant source data set, a modest number of pathfinding nodes are produced. The designer can tune the detail level applied at each stage of the algorithm to best match the characteristics of their own game.

The final step is to run the actual in-game character controller to compute the node connectivity graph.

Because the algorithm is independent of any specific game engine, the game needs to supply the answer to four questions:

1. Is a particular point in 3-space a valid location for a character to stand?
2. Is a particular point in 3-space embedded in world geometry?
3. Can a character walk from point A to point B?
4. What is the exact altitude of the nearest walking surface relative to an existing location?

In the sample application provided, the interface that answers these questions uses the PhysX SDK from Ageia Technologies. A character controller is a complex piece of software and can be a major part of a game engine. The PhysX SDK provides a programmable character controller implemented by Pierre Terdiman, the author of OPCODE [Terdiman03]. A character controller encompasses all of the collision-detection code and logic to move a simulated character around a 3D environment while taking into account sliding along walls, walking up stairs, or bumping the head against a ceiling. In addition to a character controller, the game engine also provides a general-purpose collision detection and ray-casting system.

Assuming the algorithm computes a navigable space mesh using the same character controller as the game engine itself, it is guaranteed that connectivity between all nodes is entirely valid.

A general overview of the steps employed by the algorithm is as follows:

1. Represent the game level as a collection of triangles in world space.
2. Clean up the input mesh to remove degenerate triangles and duplicate triangles, and to extrude double-sided triangles into solid geometry.
3. Create the thread-safe instance of the `AIPathSystem` class and send it the world geometry.
4. Classify all triangles in the world that are to be considered walkable surfaces based on the up-vector and slope limit provided by the user.
5. Tessellate all walking surfaces down to a specific detail resolution.
6. Convert each triangle into a "candidate" point.
7. Eliminate candidate points that the application rejects as an invalid location for a player to occupy.
8. Consolidate (or merge) nodes by expanding rectangles built against the large data set of candidate points. Keep doing this until all input points have been examined.
9. Validate each node by asking the application if it is possibly embedded within the world geometry.
10. Compute connectivity between each node and every other neighbor node storing the results.

The World Geometry

ON THE CD

Before the `AIPathSystem` can begin processing, it needs access to the entire game-level geometry. The algorithm expects triangles, so if your input level contains geometric primitives or other parametric shapes, they should be triangulated first. We often find that game artists introduce physically incorrect geometry into a scene. The most common example is when an artist creates a double-sided polygon to represent a wall. Because the wall has no thickness, it is impossible to tell which side of the wall you are on. Double-sided triangles also cause problems for some physics engines.

Another problem with using raw graphics content as game-level geometry is occasionally encountering duplicate or degenerate triangles. A utility called `MeshCleanup` is provided that will remove duplicate and degenerate triangles as well as extrude double-sided triangles to form closed convex shapes. You can avoid this cleanup step if you know that your game-level geometry is already in a good state.

Finally, your input game level should be in metric units. Although it is certainly possible to run the algorithm with any set of physical units, it is generally not desirable. If your game level is not represented in metric units, you might consider converting it into metric before submitting it to the `AIPathSystem`. You can then return the results transformed back into your own coordinate space.

Potential Walking Surfaces

In real life, you can only walk up a surface that is not too steep. With this consideration in mind, it is reasonable to pick a particular slope limit for your characters. Even if your game engine has a mechanism that allows characters to climb walls, this particular algorithm does not deal with that case. It focuses primarily on the portion of game environment that players can walk upon.

Having been given a particular slope limit, the AIPathSystem will compute the plane equation of each triangle. It will then consider only those with a vector normal in the direction of the up-vector and within the slope limit specified by the user. In a typical game level, this will generally comprise roughly 30% of the original input data set. During this computation, the surface area of all potentially walkable surfaces will be calculated and returned (see Figure 2.8.1).

Note that potentially walkable surfaces can include surfaces inside objects, and surfaces without enough room for the character to stand, which the next steps will eliminate.

FIGURE 2.8.1   All potential walkable surfaces have been identified and highlighted.

Tessellation of Walking Surfaces

Because the input triangles can be of all different sizes, we need to tessellate the geometry to reach a sufficient detail resolution. Generally, that detail level will be some fraction of the distance a character will cover while standing. A detail level of 20 or 30 centimeters generally works well, but you might want to use a coarser resolution for larger characters, such as monsters.

To tessellate the input mesh, we simply measure the longest edge of each triangle. If the longest edge exceeds the detail level, we then bisect that edge and recursively call the routine with the two triangle fragments. Wash, rinse, and repeat until the input mesh has reached a sufficient level of detail (see Figure 2.8.2).

FIGURE 2.8.2   All walkable surfaces have been tessellated down to a fine resolution.

Generating Candidate Data Points

For each fragment triangle, we compute its center location. Next, we convert the ground plane components into integer values. For example, if the detail level is set to 20 cm (0.2 meters), we multiply each of the source points by 5.0 and then add 0.5 for rounding before converting it to an integer value. This is critical because the next phase of the algorithm, node generation, operates in a fixed grid space of integer components.

As we convert multiple candidate points into integer space, we often find that more than one point maps to a single grid location. When this happens, the mean vertical component should be computed to produce a representative sampling of the altitude at this specific location. However, you should only merge candidate points if the difference in the mean altitude is below the "step height" threshold specified by the application.

In virtually all character controllers, logic is in place to take into account how high a character may "step up" as it moves through the game environment. If a particular point is at a vertical height that is beyond the step height of a preexisting node, then it is considered unique. This produces a sort of 2D grid where each hash location contains a list of all points at various altitudes in the game level.

For large game levels, this can produce a massive number of data points. Imagine that the input game level is simply two triangles, each covering 1 km on a side. With a detail level of 20 cm, this would produce a grid of points 5,000 on a side for a total of 25 million seed points (see Figure 2.8.3).

FIGURE 2.8.3   Candidate-walkable data points have been derived from the tessellated surfaces and placed into a fixed-resolution grid.

Removing Data Points That Cannot Be Occupied

After the set of candidate data points is complete, we must validate each one. Validation is performed via a callback to the application. The application is expected to answer the yes/no question, "Is it ok for a character to be here?" we posed previously. There are a couple of different ways to determine this. The easiest method is simply to generate an axis-aligned bounding box (AABB) that roughly encompasses the extents of a character but is raised above its step height. Next, query the collision system for all triangles that intersect this AABB (usually a very high-speed process in most game engines). If no triangles intersect, then clearly this is a valid place for a player to stand. Otherwise, examine the vector normal of any of the other intersecting triangles to determine if they comprise a wall, ceiling, or some other property that might restrict a player from standing at this location. This method may be called millions of times, so it must be a very fast operation.

Another approach might be to simply create a character at this location, and see if the controller will accept it as a valid position. This is an ideal solution, but it can be much more time consuming to perform this operation. It's likely best to perform the AABB triangle query as an early accept and reject test before examining the location in greater detail.

Remember that this determination is not made by the `AIPathSystem` class but is supplied by your own application via a pure virtual interface. Even though a sample implementation is provided using the PhysX SDK for collision services, you will most likely provide your own validation routine relative to your specific application.

Merging into Potential Pathfinding Nodes

Initially, we claimed that this algorithm would produce a compact and efficient description of navigable space. Now that we have generated hundreds of thousands, if not millions, of candidate data points, you might be feeling a little bit skeptical of that claim.

In the previous example of a single flat surface with a kilometer on a side comprising millions of candidate data points, it could still be represented as simply one very large pathfinding node (indicating that a character can walk unobstructed anywhere within its range). In practice, however, we would never do this. Nevertheless, we can use fairly large nodes to describe big empty spaces and thus, from the millions of candidate points, easily produce a solution set of several thousand pathfinding nodes.

Each pathfinding node is represented as an AABB and a surface altitude. To build these nodes, perform the following steps (see Figure 2.8.4):

1. Copy all of the candidate points into a single vector container.
2. Allocate an array to track the points that have been "consumed" and that still need to be processed.
3. Optionally, create a lookup table to access the input data randomly.
4. Candidate seed points may be selected either sequentially or at random because each produces a different type of node distribution. We prefer the results from a more random distribution, but this is a user-selectable option.
5. For each of the original source points, first check to see if it has already been "consumed," "merged," or neither.
6. If it has not been consumed, then attempt to merge this node with others by expanding its size, pushing outward in a clockwise direction on each axis.
7. Imagine starting with the original point and then drawing a 1-pixel border around it.
8. At each iteration, draw the border exactly one unit thicker than the last time. When there are missing points on any side, stop expanding that particular edge.

9. If there are matching points, but they are higher than the user-provided step height, stop expanding those sides as well.

10. Continue to expand the edges in each of the four cardinal directions until all four have stopped or the maximum user-specified node size has been reached.

11. After the seed point has been grown to form a contiguous rectangular surface of all neighbor points, next evaluate whether you want to keep it or not. If the node produced is below the minimum size specified by the user, then throw it away; otherwise, add it to the list of potential pathfinding nodes. At this time, every point that was included in the node is marked as consumed and is no longer used.

12. If you decided to keep the node, next compute the best-fit plane equation through the set of data points. This allows each node to record an approximate plane for each node. This data item is often important during the pathfind phase to change weighting values based on the steepness of a surface.

13. A call is performed back into the application to resolve the exact altitude at this node location. Because the original points were snapped relative to a grid, the computed altitude is only an approximation based on the mean altitude of all points that matched a particular grid entry. On steep surfaces, the error introduced can cause the connections step to fail if you do not use the precise value.

14. This process continues until all seed points have been considered.

Because each completed node consumes a large number of candidate points, this process can actually be surprisingly fast to complete.

FIGURE 2.8.4 Potential pathing nodes are created by growing seed points.

Removing Pathfinding Nodes Inside Objects

Now that we have a set of pathfinding nodes that roughly describes all navigable space in the game level, we must run a validation pass to see which ones we can keep. Due to how art for game levels is built and the way objects are placed with game editors, many seemingly valid walking surfaces are actually embedded within other objects.

A simple example is a large rock that someone has sunken down into a piece of terrain. The terrain itself is usually not cut out, so it simply continues right on through the rock. If you were to fly a camera inside the rock, you might find plenty of space to stand and walk around, but, clearly, this is not a valid location for a character to be. Another common case is when an artist places a pillar inside of a building. Usually a hole is not cut out of the floor geometry for the pillar to fit neatly inside; rather, it is simply placed on top of the floor. In our previous pass to find potential nodes, we might have considered the inside of the pillar as a perfectly valid place for a character to stand.

In this cleanup phase, the centroid of each pathfinding node is sent back to the application for validation. The default validation technique provided performs an operation called `DeathBlossom`, which sends ray casts in 45-degree increments from the center of the node in all possible directions. We called it `DeathBlossom` because it uses the same strategy that Alex Rogan employed during the climatic battle sequence in the film *The Last Starfighter*. If any of these rays hits a back-facing triangle (indicating that the node is embedded inside another object), then the node is rejected.

This process could have been performed when generating the candidate points in the first place but would have substantially slowed down the process. By performing this cleanup check based on the nodes produced, we end up calling `DeathBlossom` about 1/200th as many times.

Nodes that pass this test are placed into a vector container as the final solution set. Because we earlier rejected nodes that were considered too small, this data set will have many gaps in it and will not cover every square inch of the world. This is absolutely normal and by design.

The goal is to produce as absolutely few nodes as possible while also making sure we have all that we need. As long as there are enough options that an AI can navigate every place the game design calls for, there is generally no need to cover every square inch of the surface. When performing pathfinding, it is nearly always reasonable to accept the closest node to our destination, even if that destination is located in the small gap between two adjacent nodes.

How many nodes you need and at what resolution is ultimately a design choice. The more nodes that are available, the more choices the AI has to navigate the environment. On the other hand, if you have too many nodes, you are over-describing the environment, and the extra nodes are just consuming memory and CPU during the search phase. Observation of the AI's choices will ultimately guide the designer here.

Computing Node Connectivity

The final step is to compute the connectivity between each node and all of its neighbors. To speed this process up, we first insert the index for each node into a Kd-Tree. A Kd-Tree is an ideal data structure for performing high-speed range searching against a static set of 3D objects. It is important to remember to insert the nodes into the Kd-Tree in random order to ensure a balanced tree [Sedgwick84].

Next, for each of the original nodes, we find the nearest neighbors within a reasonable distance. A value of 16 to 32 meters will generally provide plenty of candidates to review. To avoid data duplication, we eliminate any node where the connectivity would intersect a previously connected node. To prevent this culling process from cutting too many possible connections, the intersection test can be relaxed so it accepts connections even if they cut corners on neighboring nodes. The next step involves calling a pure virtual method canWalk back into to the application. The callback receives both the starting point of the source node and the ending point of the neighbor.

In the default implementation provided, this invokes the character controller built into the PhysX SDK. However, we cannot simply move the character from point A to point B and see whether or not the controller gets there. This might work fine on a flat surface, but it would allow connectivity between nodes even if there were a chasm in-between them. Rather than simply warping the character, we instead substep the movement and, at each step, apply a simulated force of gravity as would happen in a real game. In the example of a chasm between two nodes, the character controller would fall and fail to reach the destination. On the flip side, this will also create connections where falling would allow the character to reach the destination node, which is often desirable.

Pierre Terdiman implemented the character controller that comes with the PhysX SDK. Pierre is the author of the popular collision-detection library OPCODE as well as many other excellent open source tools [Terdiman03]. This character controller is shockingly fast, and computing connectivity even for thousands of nodes in a complex game level can be done very quickly.

If you insert a callback to your own game engine, you can make this logic as simple or complex as you wish.

As we check each neighbor and retrieve success results from the canWalk callback, we simply add the child node index to a parent node's connections list.

The final step is yet another cleanup pass. When we performed the initial generation, we pruned many potential connections due to the fact that we culled for a maximum number of candidates and tested for overlapping connections. Because these are applied relative to each individual node, it will often produce unidirectional connections. The final cleanup pass traverses each connection in each node and tests to see if it is unidirectional. If it is, then we test to see if the connection could in fact be bidirectional. An important optimization is to remember which connections had already been tested to avoid performing the same test again.

With node connectivity complete, the final data set has now been produced. We have gone from an arbitrarily complex 3D game environment to potentially millions of seed points placed on a grid so we can finally end up with just a few thousands nodes with an average of four to six connections apiece. Although we are only connecting to the middle of nodes, the data set is guaranteed to allow the in-game character controller to traverse all connected paths and can be searched extremely quickly. The graph is so sparse that often simply searching 15- to 20-ply deep will get an AI a massive distance across the world (see Figure 2.8.5).

FIGURE 2.8.5 The final solution set is created by computing connectivity between neighboring pathfinding nodes.

Jumping and Other Forms of Locomotion

The implementation provided here does not support jumping or other forms of character motion beyond simply walking along a surface. Adding a callback canJump and creating new connections if the jump succeeds can easily implement this feature. In the *Cyberstrike 2* implementation, which supported jumping, we simply placed the character at the center of the source node and jumped in the direction of the destination. This test was only performed against nodes that had failed the previous walk test. A successful jump was recorded if the character ended up anywhere inside the destination node.

This operation found hundreds of successful jump connections, even though it missed what seemed like many other possible jump opportunities. Often, these connections would show up in places that few people would have thought they could get to. Watching the AI robots navigate the entire 3D environment, jumping from ledge to ledge while hunting the player down was always one of the most impressive features of the game.

For other types of connectivity, such as elevators or doors, a layered mechanism would be needed to create and remove these forms of dynamic connections on the fly.

Dynamic Environments

Even if the basic game level itself is static, modern games are beginning to incorporate a much greater use of highly dynamic objects. Fortunately, the navmesh produced by this algorithm is ideally suited to handle this.

Because each pathfinding node is described as an AABB, the entire data set can be inserted into an axis-aligned bounding volume hierarchy (AABVH). An AABVH can be searched very quickly and can easily be updated to reflect the status of numerous dynamic objects. As dynamic objects move throughout the environment, they can be attached and removed relative to individual pathfinding nodes and marked as potential obstructers.

Other aspects of dynamic environments include doors, drawbridges, and changes in the environment that should effectively turn on and off intersecting path nodes. The path-searching system also must account for dynamic connections such as those created by elevators or other automatic transport systems. Once again, the static data set will have to be annotated in real time to reflect these changes and the links taken into account by the pathfinding algorithm.

Other Uses for the Navigable Space Mesh

The navigable space mesh provides a powerful data set to associate game metadata with. The nodes can be marked for all kinds of purposes, such as spawn points, hunting grounds, or tied to game scripts. It is often a much more meaningful way to ask questions about the world in terms of "where players can be" as opposed to a large collection of raw triangles.

Source Code and Demo

The source code for the AIPathSystem is almost entirely contained in a single file AIPathSystem.cpp. It has a few additional dependencies on some math routines, but the total source needed is modest. A small console application is provided to show the minimal implementation of the tool. The source is not intentionally operating system specific and should compile on any platform with relatively few changes. It does make heavy use of the standard template library for container classes.

In addition to the algorithm itself, a complete functioning demo is provided that allows you to import an arbitrary mesh as a *Wavefront* OBJ file. All of the steps of the algorithm are illustrated and every tunable parameter is exposed. The demo requires DirectX and the Ageia PhysX drivers to run. To build the complete demo, the source code requires the DirectX SDK and the Ageia PhysX SDK.

All of the source code provided is in the public domain and is updated at the Code Suppository Repository website from time to time [Ratcliff07]. Documentation is included as well.

Future Work

We were surprised to see how fast this version of the algorithm runs. It was originally written in 1995 when our fastest machine had a bare fraction of the CPU available on modern processors. The fact that we switched to using an integer approach to grow the nodes is another major speed improvement. Additionally, the collision-detection systems provided by the PhysX SDK are extraordinarily fast. In a previous implementation, we used to have to run the utility to generate a navigable mesh overnight, even when the entire game level was relatively simplistic geometry. This implementation now operates in either seconds or the low minutes even with huge game levels.

For this reason, we believe it is quite likely that the algorithm could be adapted to run in a background thread and continuously provide updated navmeshes on the fly, even as the game environment changes. It could easily generate data on demand rather than processing every square inch of the entire game level.

Conclusion

This article has presented a reliable method to produce a compact and efficient navigable space mesh for an arbitrary static 3D environment. It has been used successfully in several commercial games and is still being incorporated into new products today.

The data set can be searched at extremely high speeds to satisfy pathfinding for a massive number of NPCs as well as to maintain a representation of dynamic objects and occluders in the world. Although it does not necessarily support all of the requirements for all game environments, especially those that are highly dynamic, it may be an excellent starting point for a number of projects.

One of the major advantages of a heavily precomputed solution is that it serves as an expert system for the AI, giving it the same highly detailed knowledge of a game level that an experienced human player has. So, not only is it not cheating, but also it can hunt a player down to the depths of hell, if necessary, assuming your game level actually has a hell to path to.

References

[Ratcliff07] Ratcliff, John W., "Code Suppository Repository." Available online at *http://www.amillionpixels.us/sourcecode.htm*, 2007.

[Sedgwick84] Sedgwick, Robert, *Algorithms*. Addison Wesley Publishing, 1984.

[Terdiman03] Terdiman, Pierre, "OPCODE." Available online at *http://www.coder-corner.com/Opcode.htm*, June 3, 2003.

2.9

Risk-Adverse Pathfinding Using Influence Maps

Ferns Paanakker—Wishbone Games B.V.

ferns.paanakker@gmail.com

In this article, we describe a pathfinding algorithm that allows the use of *influence maps* to mark hostile and friendly regions on a terrain. This algorithm allows us to find the optimal path from point A to point B very quickly, while taking into consideration the different threat and safety regions in the environment. We demonstrate this algorithm in a basic real-time strategy (RTS) setting where we plan a number of paths. Some units are allowed to take more risk than others while traversing their paths, which allows for more gameplay depth.

We'll first discuss the representation of our game world and then explain how influence maps can provide valuable information when evaluating a path, which allows us to include risk in the paths. We allow both static and dynamic influences to be active simultaneously. With risk-adverse costs represented in the search space, the impact on search speed will be discussed. Finally, we include an example program with full source code so you can test different situations.

Overview

When navigating game worlds, we use pathfinding algorithms to assist the human player or the computer player. Most games use a point-and-click device to mark where this unit needs to go and rely on the pathfinding algorithm to take a unit to its destination. When the unit walks the path we just created, it will probably pass through a number of friendly and hostile territories, which can substantially increase or decrease the risk to the unit.

If we create a pathfinding algorithm that allows us to include risk-awareness for our units, we can create more intuitive paths and prevent the player from performing mundane tasks, such as manually clicking temporary targets (waypoints) to make sure the unit follows a low-risk path. High-risk areas can be created and changed based on the observations of units, for example, the visual confirmation of an enemy or the death of a unit that marks the place of death as a high-risk area.

Integrating risk sensitivity into the pathfinding search space is not a trivial task, especially when the threat and safety regions can change frequently. By making a few alterations to the basic pathfinding algorithm, we can create a new algorithm that is both fast and flexible, allowing us to create paths that take into consideration properties such as terrain type; terrain risk; unit properties, including size, weight, and emotional state; and so on.

To illustrate this pathfinding solution, we will use a simple RTS game world that consists of a basic terrain with land and water. The game objects are a single unit, an enemy tower, and the goal location of our unit. The layout of our simple world is shown in Figure 2.9.1. In our example, the unit is not allowed to move across the water, so if the unit wants to get to the target location, it must pass the enemy tower's attack range. The tower has an attack range that covers a wide area, and it is impossible get to the destination without passing through the attack range of the tower.

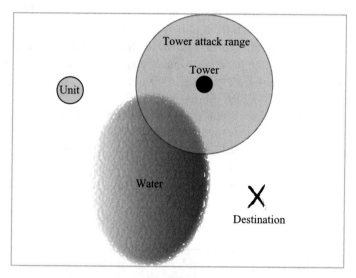

FIGURE 2.9.1   An RTS situation in which a unit must pass hostile territory to get to its destination.

Influence Maps

An *influence map* (IM) is a location-based system that contains data about game objects and ties it to a specific world position [Tozour01]. Many implementations use a 2D grid overlaid on the world, but other representations can be used just as easily. For our representation, we will use an IM that is integrated into the pathfinding graph so that every connection in the pathfinding graph has an influence property. This is done because in our pathfinding algorithm, we use information from both the terrain and the IM. If these representations are the same, we will not have to perform additional conversions. The influence of the individual game objects is stored in the IM and allows us to retrieve information about the risks involved in traversing an edge. The influences we use can come from a number of sources such as the units or the terrain, or the user can specify the influences (such as specifying that a specific region should be avoided or prioritized).

For example, an enemy guard tower can attack every enemy unit within a specific range around the tower, whereas the edge of a forest might similarly provide cover for units. Note that the influences can be different for every player: An enemy guard tower provides safety for the units of your opponent because the tower can provide cover fire, but it provides risk for you. Furthermore, a guard tower does not have unlimited range where it can attack units, but it has a specific influence zone. We model this ranged influence for simplicity as a circle, thus defining an *influence disc*. In our case, the influence discs have the same risk value across the disc, but it is, of course, possible to use linear, exponential, or square risk fall off. We use this disc representation of the influences in the world and convert it to our IM, which is designed to be exactly the same as our pathfinding graph. When updating the IM, we intersect every edge of the graph with the influence discs to calculate the risk involved with traversing that edge.

We indicate safe terrain with negative values and risky terrain with positive values. The sum of all the influences is the total risk for traversing the edge. However, we do not allow negative values because of the nonnegative edge cost restriction required by search algorithms. We therefore offset the value so the safest terrain still has a nonnegative edge weight.

You can calculate the intersection of an edge with an influence disc in a number of ways. One way is to solve the geometric problem and calculate the exact intersection points between the circle and the line segment [Bourke92]. We can then use the length of this line segment to calculate the precise risk in traversing the edge. Because finding this intersection is relatively expensive, we will for our purposes assume the edges in our graph are relatively small compared to the size of the influence disc. Therefore many edges will be either completely inside or outside the influence disc, and we can speed up our check considerably by only checking the start point and endpoint of the edge. If only one of the points is inside the influence disc, we use half the risk. It would be a game-specific issue to handle cases where both points lie outside the influence disc, but the edge passes through it.

In an RTS setting, every unit and building has an influence disc, resulting in possibly hundreds of discs. The execution time of mapping the influence discs depends heavily on the number and the size of the discs. You can speed up the mapping by using spatial hashing, such as a grid or quadtree, to find the edges that are influenced by a certain disc. You can also group the discs based on their update frequency. Static structures, such as buildings, are located at a fixed position in the game world and do not move. The buildings can be erected or destroyed, but they do not change position and therefore have a static mapping to the pathfinding graph. We can also have dynamic influence discs. These are dynamic because they can move and therefore change the mapping to the pathfinding graph. Another possible speedup is to group units and influences into a single unified influence, thereby reducing the total number of discs.

For an RTS setting, we have found that using three layers in an IM works well: one layer for the static influence, one for the stationary influence, and one for the moving influence. *Static influences* are updated only when buildings are erected or destroyed, which only happens sporadically. *Stationary influences* are updated when units start or stop moving, which in RTS games happens infrequently. The *moving influence* is updated every pathfinding frame and has therefore the highest frequency. A pathfinding frame is related to the frequency at which the pathfinding is performed, which might be different from the graphics or AI frame rate.

In our example situation, the IM has a risk area around the tower, as shown earlier in Figure 2.9.1. If we were to plan the shortest path, only based on distance, our unit would follow the shoreline and be under attack from the tower for a long period of time. This is exactly the behavior seen in many RTS games. Many human players work around this problem by using waypoints to carefully direct the units around the threat. However, using our modified pathfinding algorithm, we can create the same behavior fairly easily by incorporating risk into the pathfinding algorithm.

Different Paths Depending on Unit Risk Tolerance

Having both the roadmap and the influence map now gives us two major sources of information about the game world. When we calculate the path from point A to point B, we indicate how much weight we put on each map. If we ignore the IM, we only use speed and distance to guide us, which might expose the unit to high risk as shown in Figure 2.9.2A. On the other hand, if we ignore the roadmap data, we only use the risk analysis, possibly creating a longer path as shown in Figure 2.9.2B. Mathematically, this can be represented by the following formula:

$$\alpha_1 * edge_{time} + \alpha_2 * edge_{risk} \quad \alpha_1, \alpha_2 \geq 0$$

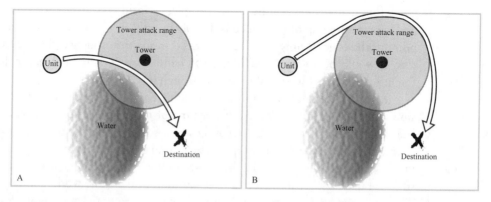

FIGURE 2.9.2   Different paths taken for different tolerance risk parameters (left is high-risk tolerance; right is low-risk tolerance).

You can use α_1 to specify the weight of the roadmap and α_2 for the weight of the IM. This provides the tools to create different paths for different players.

For example, let's say we have two different units: a scout and an soldier. Both units have a different allowed risk: the scout wants to be as inconspicuous as possible with minimal risk. The soldier has more confidence and allows for more risk in its path. This kind of pathfinding is sometimes called tactical pathfinding and allows for many game-play elements. For example, when a unit dies, we can place a high-risk IM at this location on the presumption that something nasty killed it. All calculated paths that cross this IM can be recalculated, which helps in the identification of chokepoints and ambushes not only for the AI player but also for the human player.

Search Speed Considerations

Unfortunately, risk-adverse pathfinding can undermine the ability of A* to quickly find a path. This occurs because an admissible heuristic must account for both cheap terrain and areas of extremely low risk (in the case of influence discs that are protective of the unit). When risk is weighed several times higher than terrain cost, the directed A* search reverts to Dijkstra because the heuristic value, $h(x)$, becomes insignificant compared with the given cost, $g(x)$. This can be seen in that the cost calculation of A*, $f(x) = g(x) + h(x)$, is equivalent to the cost calculation of Dijkstra, $f(x) = g(x)$, as the influence of $h(x)$ approaches zero. This has interesting implications for whether A* is the best search algorithm in such an environment.

If an optimal path is required, and the heuristic is not overestimated, then the CPU cost of calculating the heuristic (typically the Euclidean distance scaled by the most optimistic terrain/risk) is wasted computation. Therefore, it would be considerably faster to simply execute a Dijkstra search and not calculate the heuristic because A* will not result in fewer searched nodes. Another reason to prefer Dijkstra is its ability to be used in tactical decisions by calculating one-to-many paths to multiple enemy targets. With many paths/targets to choose from, the unit can prefer the cheapest one, thus leveraging a single Dijkstra search for both tactical information and a planned path.

If fast pathfinding is required, then path quality must be compromised. By over-estimating the heuristic, search speed can be restored at the cost of forgoing an optimal path. In this scenario, the heuristicmust estimate the cost to the goal, $h(x)$, using the average risk instead of the lowest risk. Although this speeds up the search, the resulting path might unnecessarily stray into dangerous territory. However, the quality of the path can be flexible (varying between Dijkstra and an inadmissible heuristic-tuned A*) based on the needs of the unit and the current CPU load.

Source Code and Demo

ON THE CD

Included on the CD-ROM is the source code of a demonstration program that allows you to experiment with risk-aware pathfinding and the effect of Dijkstra versus A* searches. The code is strictly for demonstrational purposes and moderately optimized, but it might serve as a good starting point for your own implementation. The program uses influence discs and allows the user to place both the start and goal positions of the unit. By altering the risk parameter, different paths can be achieved. A screenshot from the demo is shown in Color Plate 2.

Conclusion

In this article, we have shown how we can perform risk-aware pathfinding.

Using influence maps to model the risk and safety regions in the search space allows for interesting behavior, which in turn allows for additional gameplay elements. By allowing a custom cost function, we can specify the amount of risk a unit is allowed to take and how this results in completely different paths.

References

[Bourke92] Bourke, Paul, "Intersection of a Line and a Sphere (or Circle)." Available online at *http://local.wasp.uwa.edu.au/~pbourke/geometry/sphereline/*, November 1992.

[Tozour01] Tozour, Paul, "Influence Mapping." *Game Programming Gems 2*, Charles River Media, 2001.

2.10

Practical Pathfinding in Dynamic Environments

Per-Magnus Olsson—Linköping University

perol@ida.liu.se

As games are set in increasingly dynamic worlds, player demands for a more dynamic and realistic world will continue to increase. Game developers must try to live up to these expectations. One of the areas receiving more attention is to make the world more dynamic through the addition of destructible objects, such as buildings. However, if you only change the visual representation of a damaged or destroyed object, without changing the actual traversability and visibility of the area in and around the object, it will quickly spoil the illusion of a believable world. Moreover, as more games are featuring AI companions for the player, it is important that these agents can also understand the environment and act in a way that seems intelligent and believable to the player. The area of search algorithms for dynamic environments has been quite thoroughly researched, so this article will focus on maintaining the underlying pathfinding graph. It describes how to handle situations involved in updating the underlying pathfinding graph when adding, removing, or partially demolishing objects.

Using Edges to Store Information

Many pathfinding algorithms only use nodes to store information when computing a path. It can be beneficial in dynamic environments to also use edges to store information. An example will serve to show why this is advantageous.

In Figure 2.10.1, there are four nodes numbered 1 through 4, together with a bridge crossing a chasm or stream. The nodes are connected by edges, where the edge between nodes 2 and 4 lies across the bridge.

If the bridge is destroyed and can no longer be used, we have two different ways to represent this. We can either disallow nodes 2 and 4 because these are the endpoints of the edge that crosses the destroyed bridge, or we can disallow the edge that goes through the area (connecting nodes 2 and 4). If the nodes are disallowed, it will be impossible to move from node 1 to node 3 using node 2 even though node 2 is not located on top of the bridge. Clearly this is not the intended effect. Using the other method, it is still possible to move from node 1 to node 3 using node 2, but it is impossible to use the edge

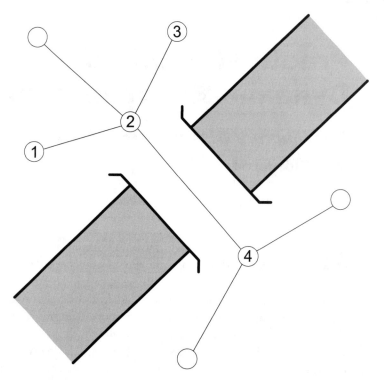

FIGURE 2.10.1   A simple pathfinding graph showing why it is beneficial to use edges to store information. A bridge has an edge on top of it. If the bridge is removed, the edge will be disallowed, making it impossible to use.

going across the bridge itself. This achieves the effect we are looking for without the adverse side effects.

Nodes and Edges

A pathfinding graph consists of *nodes*, which represent positions, and *edges*, which represent the nominal path that a unit can travel between the nodes. For most games, the graph is calculated in an offline tool, such as a level editor. Because nodes and edges are the only components in the pathfinding graph, we will examine them in some detail.

```
class Node
{
    /* EXTRANEOUS DETAIL OMITTED */

    //General information
    Vector3d m_position;
    std::vector<Edge*> m_neighbors;
    unsigned int m_id;
    unsigned int m_graphId;
```

```
    //Information used in A* search.
    float m_g;
    float m_h;
    Node* m_predecessor;
};

class Edge
{
    /* EXTRANEOUS DETAIL OMITTED */

    Node* m_left;
    Node* m_right;
    bool m_allowedFlag;
    float m_length;
};
```

Let's go through these attributes in order; starting with the Node class:

- m_position is Node's location in the world.
- m_neighbors is the set of Edges that this Node is connected to.
- m_id is the ID number of the Node, which should be unique for each instance.
- m_graphId is the ID of the graph to which the Node belongs. This attribute will be covered in greater detail later.
- m_g is the total cost so far in the search, from the start position to this Node.
- m_h is the estimated cost from this Node to the goal position.
- m_predecessor is a pointer to the Node prior to this one in the path.

The last three attributes are used with an A* search; if another search algorithm is used they will need to be modified accordingly. For an overview of the A* search algorithm, refer to [Stout00].

The Edge class has the following attributes:

- m_left and m_right are the Nodes at each end of the Edge, which the Edge connects.
- m_allowedFlag is used to signify if the Edge is allowed to be used in a path. This variable allows you to set the use of an Edge because it must be set to true for all Edges used in a particular path and for a given Edge to be valid.
- m_length is the length of the Edge. It is precalculated and stored to be used as a cost in pathfinding searches.

Storing additional data within node entries has been suggested as a way to make it easier for the AI to understand and exploit the terrain [Straatman05].

m_id and m_graphId

The attributes m_id and m_graphId in the Node class deserve some extra attention. As stated earlier, m_id is a unique ID for each instance of the Node class and is used to quickly separate two or more nodes from each other. If the class holding the nodes is using an array/vector to store them, the nodes can be stored with the m_id used an index. It can then be used to quickly access the specific instance:

```
//will return the Node with m_id value bestNodeIndex.
Node* bestNode = m_Nodes[bestNodeIndex];
```

m_graphId is a more interesting attribute because it is not unique for each node but for each graph in the world. At creation, after all nodes are created and connected by edges, the m_graphId is propagated from a randomly chosen start node. A simple recursive algorithm can be used to propagate the value of m_graphId to each node that is part of this graph. The m_graphId tag provides a quick way to separate the different graphs in the world from each other and to prevent the pathfinder from making unnecessary calculations. The most expensive call to a pathfinder is the one that returns no path because it requires all possible paths from the start to the goal to be searched. Some of these calls can be predicted and avoided by using the information stored in m_graphId. It is used in the following way, before a call to the pathfinder is made:

```
Node* startNode;
Node* goalNode;
...
if(startNode->m_graphId == goalNode->m_graphId)
{
    //Path possibly exists, call pathfinder.
    ...
}
/* else startNode and goalNode are in different graphs, no path can
exist. */
```

Not all unnecessary calls to the pathfinder can be avoided in this way. If a player has placed limitations on the traversability of edges, a more elaborate scheme must be used.

Removal of Objects

As shown by the destruction of a bridge in the introduction, some objects can be removed from a map and cause an area to become disallowed for movement. An area can be disallowed either by the server or a player. An area disallowed by the server applies to all the movement of all players, whereas an area disallowed by a player only affects that player's movement (perhaps a player is disallowed an area due to the amount of enemies there). If an area is disallowed, all edges that fully or partially intersect that area should be disallowed.

As discussed earlier, we don't explicitly store whether a node is allowed or not; in our design, this information is stored in the edges. As a consequence, whether a unit is allowed to travel through a given node is not explicit. If all of a given node's edges are disallowed, the node itself becomes implicitly disallowed because it is not possible to get to or from that node in the current situation. This can happen if a unit builds structures in such a way that it is blocking its own path out of an area. It is important to try to detect this situation before it happens by predetermining the position that the building unit will have at the end of the build phase. If the unit at the final position can reach a valid node, then it can continue to move from that node; otherwise, the unit must be moved during the build phase so that it ends up at a position that allows it to reach a valid node.

Not all objects affect the pathfinding in the manner just described. For example, a building can cover an area and provide a part of the pathfinding graph for that area, but if the building is demolished enough that it can be removed, we will need to update the pathfinding data to allow pathfinding through it again. This can be done in several ways with perhaps the most obvious being to place new nodes (using the same methods used in the preprocessing stage) and then create a new subgraph that is then connected to the existing graph. This ensures that the area has a pathfinding graph that connects with the rest of the world. Another option that can work in certain situations is to simply keep the old pathfinding graph unchanged. This is computationally cheap but will not give the same level of traversability and accuracy as generating a new subgraph and can look very bad if the destroyed object covered a large area.

Updating m_graphId **When Removing Objects**

When an object such as a bridge has been removed, the object might have edges that acted as a connection between two different graphs. If the edges on the newly removed object were the only links between the different graphs, the graphs are now disconnected, and their m_graphId should now be different. Determining if the object was the last connection between graphs can pose some difficulties, especially if we consider indirect transitive connections (which most pathfinding algorithms do). One method that works well is to perform a search between the parts of the graph that are suspected of being separated, after the object has been removed and the affected edges disallowed. This can be done fairly quickly because normally just a few parts of the graph are involved. In the bridge example in the introduction, there are two possible graphs, one at each end of the bridge. If a valid path between the parts is found, then the graph has not been separated, and no update of m_graphId is necessary. If no path is found, the start and the goal nodes are now in different graphs. In this case, one of the graphs must have its m_graphId updated to reflect the change. Simply use the next unused m_graphId and propagate it in one of the graphs. As before, any valid node in the graph can be used as start node.

Addition of Objects

Similar problems are encountered when an object is added to the world. Examples of this might be a building or wall created in an RTS game.

When an object is added, modifying the pathfinding graph to accommodate the change is very important. Exactly how this is done depends on how the pathfinding graph was generated in the first place. For an overview of different graph generation and node placement algorithms, see [Tozour03].

You can handle the addition of new nodes in several different ways. Some games use an extra reserved area around the object, larger than the bounding box, where pathfinding nodes are placed at precalculated positions as soon as the object is placed. The positions are calculated offline when the asset is created, and nodes placed at these positions are known to connect to each other. Because the object can only be placed if there are no objects that intersect with the reserved area, connecting the new nodes to the existing pathfinding graph becomes a simple matter of using the same algorithm as used in the level editor when creating the pathfinding graph to begin with.

Even if there is no reserved area around the object, there can still be precalculated positions for the nodes (which can also be calculated offline). However, if there is no reserved area around the object, we must test for each attempt to insert a new node to determine if the precalculated position is valid. If not, another position close by must be found to place the node to ensure traversability around the object. This does allow the object to be placed arbitrarily as long as no intersecting objects are under the object's footprint. But this flexibility comes with the risk of decreased traversability because there might not be enough room to place nodes around the new object.

Whether or not a reserved area is used, the new nodes must eventually be connected to the existing graph. The connection is done in exactly the same way as the basic pathfinding graph was originally generated. Because the creation of the basic pathfinding graph is normally done offline in the level editor and can be computationally expensive, it pays to time slice the connection phase if possible. However, this means that the graph will not be complete until the connection phase is finished.

Handling Doors and Other Connections into Objects

To add objects that units in the game can enter and move around inside, there must be nodes close to the doors and other possible entrance points. These nodes must then be connected to the existing pathfinding graph in the same manner as the nodes surrounding the object on the outside. The inside of the object must also have a pathfinding graph that is connected to the nodes by its entrance points, which in turn are connected to the existing graph. A simple example of this can be seen in Figure 2.10.2, in which an object with a reserved area around, including pathfinding nodes, is added to an existing pathfinding graph. Nodes 1–8 are part of the existing pathfinding graph, and nodes 9–14 are part of the graph in and around the building that is added during the game. The building comes with a reserved area around it, including nodes in a precalculated pathfinding graph. This ensures that it is possible to move around the building after it has been placed, as the building cannot be placed if the reserved area intersects any object in the world.

In the reserved area, there are four pathfinding nodes in the corners of the building. These are connected to each other, as well as to another pathfinding node by the door, which is connected to a node inside the building. When the building is placed, it intersects some pathfinding nodes and edges in the existing pathfinding graph.

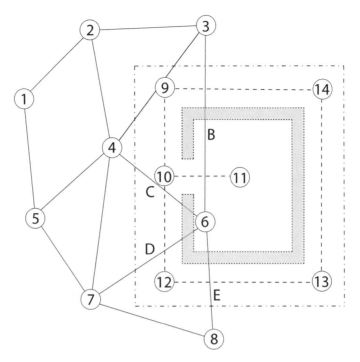

FIGURE 2.10.2 An example of a building with a reserved area around it.

When the building is placed, the edges B through E are disallowed because they intersect the building. Node 6 is implicitly disallowed because all edges leading to it are disallowed. Edge A is interesting because it does not intersect the building itself, or connect to a node that does, but only intersect the reserved area. Either it could be left allowed if desired and no harm is done leaving it this way, or it could be disallowed in the interest of completeness. Both methods are certainly possible and will yield the same result. If the building is later removed completely, any edges and nodes that were disallowed due to the addition of the building can be allowed again, and the pathfinding graph can be restored to the state it was in before the building was added. This can be achieved by saving the current state of the edges when the object is added, and then when it is removed, the graph is restored to its old state. Edge A was removed to make the figure clearer.

Figure 2.10.3 shows the new graph after disallowing edges and connecting the graphs internal to and external to the building. Only allowed edges and nodes are shown, so the disallowed edges B–E and the implicitly disallowed node 6 have been removed. New edges connecting nodes 2 and 9, 3 and 9, 4 and 9, 4 and 10, 7 and 12, and 8 and 12 are shown. The new edges are found by connecting nodes that are within a certain distance from each other. Node 10 makes it possible to enter the building through the door, and because that node was already part of the graph for the building, giving units access to the building becomes a simple matter of connecting the pathfinding graph for the building to the existing graph in the world, in the same way nodes are normally connected.

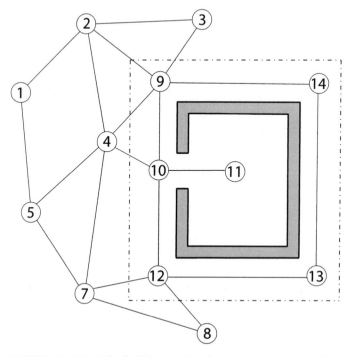

FIGURE 2.10.3   The building is placed and new edges are added to connect the building's graph to the existing graph.

Updating `m_graphId` When Adding Objects

After all new nodes have been connected to the existing graph, `m_graphId` must be propagated to the new nodes. If the object has been placed in an area where all nodes have the same `m_graphId`, propagation should be no problem. If the new object's nodes act as a bridge between two separate pathfinding graphs, one of the graphs must have its `m_graphId` updated for all nodes to show that the graphs are now connected.

Partially Demolishing an Object

An interesting situation occurs when an object is partially demolished, perhaps as a result of an explosion or a collision with a vehicle. If the object's mesh is changed for a completely new mesh, this can be handled in the same manner as adding a completely new object. If the existing mesh is modified extensively (for example, using geometry shaders), the pathfinding graph likely must be modified in the vicinity of the object.

For example, if a hole has been created in a wall large enough to allow a unit to pass through, the parts of the graphs on both sides of the hole should be connected.

Example of Partially Demolishing an Object

Let's walk through an example of how to handle a partially destroyed building and modification of the surrounding pathfinding nodes. On the left in Figure 2.10.4, nodes 1 and 2 are located outside the building and are connected by edge A. Inside the building, nodes 3 and 4 are connected by edge B. Because the wall is partially demolished, a potential new path is created. When this happens, tests should be performed to determine if the resulting hole is large enough to allow a unit to travel through it. If so, a new node, labeled 5, is placed directly outside the hole on top of edge A. The same procedure is used inside the building to create a new node 6, placed between 3 and 4, close to the hole and placed so that edge B passes through it. How positions for the nodes can be found is described in the next section "Placement of New Nodes." In this case, edges A and B are found, and the new nodes are placed on top of them. New node 5 divides old edge A into two new edges, A' and A", where A' connects 1 and 5, and A" connects 2 and 5. In the same way, edge B is split into B' and B", where B' is connecting 3 and 6, and B" is connecting 4 and 6. New nodes 5 and 6 are then connected using another new edge C. Finally, the attributes for nodes 1, 2, 3, 4, 5, and 6, as well as edges A', A", B', B", and C, are updated. In the update, a comparison is done to see if the "old" nodes inside the building, 3 and 4, have the same m_graphId as the nodes on the outside of the building, 1 and 2. If m_graphId differs, the two different graphs must be reconciled by forcing the nodes inside the building to match the m_graphId of nodes outside the building. The resulting new graph is depicted on the right side of Figure 2.10.4. It is now possible to travel from outside the building to the inside of the building, using new nodes 5 and 6 and the new interconnecting edge C.

Placement of New Nodes

When an object has been modified sufficiently to allow for new venues of movement, new nodes should be placed to allow the use of them. The nodes should be placed on positions along existing edges if possible, as such positions are guaranteed to be free of obstacles, and this will make the incorporation of the new nodes into the pathfinding graph easier. In Figure 2.10.4, approximate positions for nodes 5 and 6 can be found by first locating the hole in the object and then expanding the building geometry by a factor equivalent of a unit's collision radius. This is to decrease the risk that the unit gets stuck when trying to move too close to the wall. A line is then traced from the middle of the hole, perpendicular to the wall, and traversability is checked from the hole along the way. As soon as an allowed edge is found, the node can be placed on top of that edge. If no edge is found, the exact position for the node must be found using the normal node placement algorithm, which should check if the position is valid. If it is, then the node must be connected to the pathfinding graph. If no edge is found, and no valid node position exists, then no legal node can be placed. Of course,

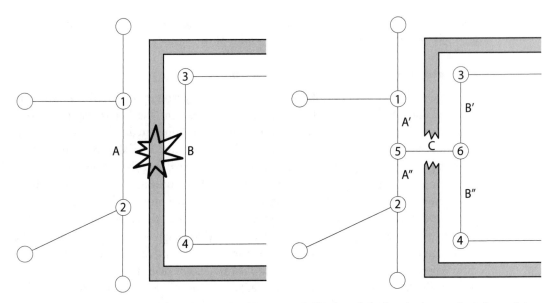

FIGURE 2.10.4   The situation before the building is partially demolished is shown on the left, resulting in a hole in the wall. The right figure shows the same area after modification of the pathfinding graph to allow passage into the building.

it would be possible to ignore the restrictions and add a node anyway, but this comes with the risk of units getting stuck when trying to traverse edges leading to it.

If an object is changed more than marginally, the new nodes can be placed on either side of the original object instead of where the change occurred, in the manner described previously. An example of this can be seen in Figure 2.10.5, where nodes 5–7 have been added. Nodes 5 and 6 are sufficient to ensure traversability through the hole in the wall. Thus node 7 is superfluous because it only allows for travel between nodes 5 and 6 through edges C and D. Even if node 7 had not been created, traversability would still exist through the hole, and thus node 7 could be removed without any decreased traversability. An exception might be if it is important to accurately determine when a unit has entered a room or building; in this case, it can be beneficial to have a node in the opening as a way of solving that problem.

When handling modifications of existing objects, it is important to think about some situations that can arise. Suppose the hole created by an explosion is large enough for a unit to use as an entrance point into a building, but only if the unit is crawling. Should that be considered a valid entrance and thus included into the pathfinding graph, or should it be ignored? Perhaps it can be included with a certain cost or restriction that the pathfinding algorithm will have to consider. If included in the pathfinding graph, it is likely the developer will want to store information on the edge related to travel through the hole, perhaps to play a certain animation (such as crawling) as described in [Reed03].

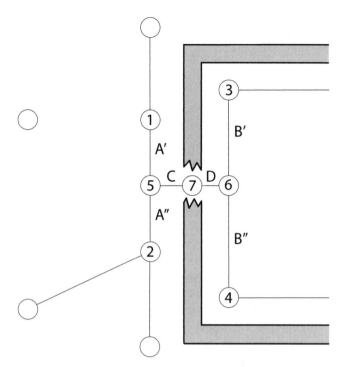

FIGURE 2.10.5   Node 7 can be used to determine if a unit has entered or left the building.

Updating m_graphId When Partially Demolishing Objects

There are two possibilities when objects have been demolished: either new nodes have been added or not. If a destroyed object requires no new nodes to be added, it might still be necessary to modify the surrounding pathfinding graph. In this case, a simple comparison can be made among the involved nodes to see if they all have the same m_graphId. If they do, then nothing more needs to be done. If the m_graphId for the nodes are different, they will need to be reconciled because the nodes were part of different graphs.

If new nodes have been added, they will be added in the pathfinding graph in the normal manner. The m_graphId must be propagated to all new nodes. If two or more graphs were joined by the new nodes, the m_graphId of the graphs must be changed to reflect this.

Verifying Existing Paths

What happens if a valid path has been found, but then the environment has changed while a unit is en route, for example, by the addition or removal of some object that could possibly affect the path? This happens often in games set in dynamic environments. One possibility is to simply perform a new search when the unit reaches the blockage, from that position to the goal position. Another option is to use the variables m_graphId and m_allowedFlag to determine path validity. The m_graphId for the next node in the path is compared to the m_graphId of the goal node, in the same way as described in the earlier section "Updating m_graphId When Removing Objects." If the m_graphId of the two nodes are the same, the nodes are in the same graph. Even if the nodes are in the same graph, it is not certain that the path between them is valid. The edges could have become disallowed for some other reason, such as a building collapsing into the street or a vehicle wreck. Whether the edges are allowed or not is investigated in the following step, when all remaining edges in the path are checked using the edges' m_allowedFlag. If all edges are allowed, then the path should be valid. If any of these tests fail, the path is invalid, and a new path must be calculated.

Conclusion

In this article, methods for handling the addition, removal, and in-game modification of objects such as buildings have been presented. By using not only nodes but also edges to store information to be used in the pathfinding, it is easy to turn on and off traversability in various areas without adverse side effects. By storing extra information in the edges, we can detect unnecessary calls to the pathfinder and verify existing paths even after a unit has started to traverse them.

As the games require more and more interaction, more demands will be put on AI as well as on the pathfinder. More interaction means more possibilities and more things that the AI has to be aware of. By maintaining a correct pathfinding graph, it is easier for the AI to understand the environment as well as how to use it to create a competent and entertaining enemy and buddy.

References

[Reed03] Reed, Christopher, and Geisler, Benjamin, "Jumping, Climbing, and Tactical Reasoning: How to Get More Out of a Navigation System." *AI Game Programming Wisdom 2,* Charles River Media, 2003.

[Stout00] Stout, Brian, "The Basics of A* Path Planning." *Game Programming Gems,* Charles River Media, 2000.

[Straatman05] Straatman, Remco, Beij, Arjen, and van der Sterren, William, "Killzone's AI: Dynamic Procedural Combat Tactics." Available online at *http://www.cgf-ai.com/products.html,* Game Developers Conference, 2005.

[Tozour03] Tozour, Paul, "Search Space Representations." *AI Game Programming Wisdom 2,* Charles River Media, 2003.

2.11

Postprocessing for High-Quality Turns

Chris Jurney—Kaos Studios

jurney@gmail.com

Units with limited turning ability, such as Jeeps and motorcycles, present problems for pathfinding and movement systems. Calculating turns for these units during the search multiplies the time required for an already expensive step (described in [Pinter01]). This same article describes a way to modify an A*-generated path by converting corners in a smoothed path into turns. In this article, we will refine this technique by defining a broad set of turn types, and then we will explain a method for selecting the most optimal turn at each corner.

This technique is directly applicable to strategy games but can be used in any game with units that have limited turning capability and must generate their movement path in advance (as opposed to those using steering behavior). The system described is used for all the moving units in *Company of Heroes,* including humans, motorcycles, Jeeps, halftracks, and tanks.

Background

To help explain the turning technique, we'll first give some context for where it fits into the overall system. The input paths this system works on are generated by standard A* and then smoothed by cutting pairs of segments down to a single segment where possible. This results in a valid but linear path, as shown in Figure 2.11.1.

The path is defined as a series of waypoints. Each waypoint has a position, a heading, and some additional data used by units when following the path. The waypoint headings are initially set to the direction traveled by the previous segment because units must first pivot to match the heading of the next waypoint before starting to move. After they have achieved the next waypoint's heading via pivoting, units simply slide along the line to the next waypoint.

Because path following is so simple in *Company of Heroes,* using these paths directly would result in jagged and unrealistic movement. For wheeled vehicles such as Jeeps, we want as few hard corners as possible in the path to avoid pivoting in place (the fallback behavior). We do this by adding turns.

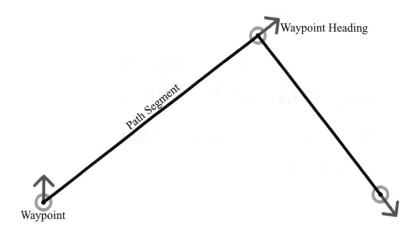

FIGURE 2.11.1   This is a basic smoothed A* path, the starting point for the system.

Basic Turning

To get from a path of line segments to a path of turns, we walk through the existing path and try to replace each segment with a curve. This technique is extensively described in two articles by Marco Pinter [Pinter01, Pinter02]. The model for the curved path is for the vehicle to make a fixed radius turn to either the left or right, follow a straight segment, and then make another fixed segment turn to either the left or right. We'll call this shape a "curve turn" as shown in Figure 2.11.2.

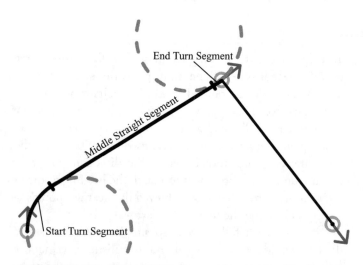

FIGURE 2.11.2   This is the curve turn described in "Realistic Turning between Waypoints" from the first volume of *AI Game Programming Wisdom* [Pinter02].

The turn radius can be tuned to get variations on this turn. Because different radii result in different paths, it can be desirable to try more than one. Tighter turns are more likely to succeed in practice because they more closely match the original, already-proven path. Units in *Company of Heroes* use a fixed rotation speed, so the turn radius they can manage without slowing down is

$$fastTurnsRadius = speed_{max}/rotationRate$$

Rotation rate is in radians per second. Turns with radii larger than this can be taken at full speed. Turns with radii smaller than this require that the unit slow to a speed defined by the following equation:

$$turnSpeed = speed_{max}(turnRadius/fastTurnRadius)$$

Usually all four combinations of left and right turns (see Figure 2.11.3) result in a valid path, but some of them are longer and take more time to follow. When applying this turn to the path, we attempt to use only the shortest of the four variants. This means we need to calculate the distance for all four types before picking the one to use.

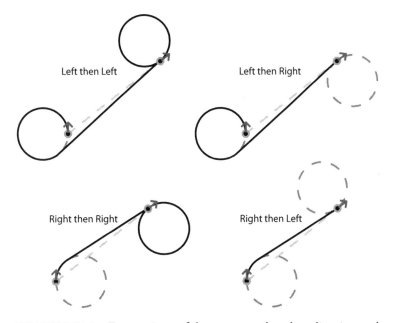

FIGURE 2.11.3   Four variants of the curve turn based on direction at the start and end.

After we've picked the shortest turn, we compare the path to the environment using our game's collision routines to see if the unit is able to successfully follow the path. If the unit can follow the new path without hitting any obstacles, we replace the original segment with the curved turn. We use this validation step for all turn types described in the next section.

In an early iteration of the *Company of Heroes* path system, only straight-line segments were supported in paths. To get the new curved path into the system, we tessellated the curve into line segments. As long as you tessellate enough that the line segment length is shorter than the unit can move in a single tick, there is no visible quality difference between using line segments and actual curves. For *Company of Heroes*, the simulation rate is 8 Hz, so the tessellation was not so detailed as to cause a problem by wasting memory on lots of subdivisions.

There is one last wrinkle in the creation of the replacement path. The original system required the vehicle to pivot in place to match the next heading before starting to roll. We'll fix this for the new curved path by setting a flag in the waypoint that tells the unit to interpolate from its previous heading to the waypoint's heading over the course of the path. This gives us the nice smooth interpolation for rotation that we want when driving around turns.

A Palette of Turns

The basic curve turn works, but in many situations, the motion it produces does not look natural. To remedy this, we define a palette of turns to use in different scenarios. A simple implementation can use a heuristic based on the direction to the next waypoint and the distance to decide which of these turns to use, but we'll look at a search-based refinement to this later on.

Smoothed Curve Turn

The basic curved turn works well, but when rounding corners, it tends to overshoot them by a significant amount because it doesn't modify the existing path's direction at each waypoint. To avoid this, we can use the exact same code we used for the curve turn, but first modify the heading of the path at the destination before calling the function.

To pick a good heading, we use the circle described by the three points: the start of the current segment, the end of the current segment, and the point after the end of the current segment (as shown in Figure 2.11.4). The new heading is the tangent of the circle at the point it touches the end waypoint of the current segment. Because this uses a point beyond the current segment, it doesn't work for the final leg of the path, but this is okay because we don't need it for the final segment.

When the curve turn is applied with the modified heading, the effect is to cut the corner tightly like a race driver (see Figure 2.11.5). Using the modified heading for the start of the next turn gives a nice sweep out, cut in, sweep back out pattern on all your corner turns.

Constant Radius Turn

The turns described so far work well in tight areas, but they run into problems in open areas. The effect of the curve turn is as if the driver yanked the wheel to one side

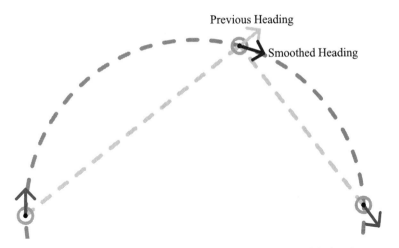

FIGURE 2.11.4   For a smoothed turn, the normal is modified to be tangent to this circle.

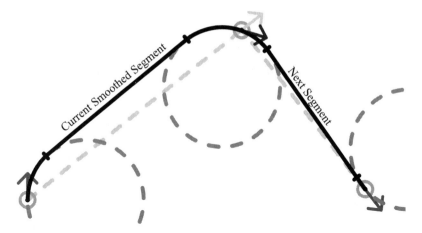

FIGURE 2.11.5   When a smoothed turn is used, the heading is modified to round the corner.

for the initial turn segment, yanked it back straight for the middle segment, and then yanked the wheel hard for the final turn segment. In an open field, this looks disturbing. To combat this effect, we introduce a new turn called the *constant radius turn*.

The constant radius turn is defined as the path along the unique circle described by the start point, the start direction, and the destination point, as shown in Figure 2.11.6. Because we don't consider the direction at the destination, this turn requires that we modify the destination. This may exclude its use on the final line segment of a raw path in cases where we care about the final heading, but we'll get into that situation a bit later.

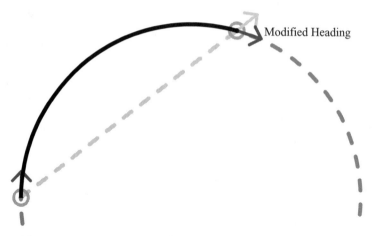

FIGURE 2.11.6   Constant radius turns use the circle shown and modify the goal waypoint heading.

Three-Point Turn

The turns so far all handle most scenarios that come up when processing a path, but when used on wheeled vehicles with a nontrivial turning radius, there is a problem. If you use the curve turn to reach the destination, the vehicle makes a full loop. If you use the constant radius turn, the turn is extremely tight and unnatural. To solve this problem, we use a three-point turn.

A three-point turn is broken into two parts, as shown in Figure 2.11.7. The first part is a reverse while rotating to face the goal point of the turn. This initial backup segment ends when the vehicle is facing the midpoint of the original path segment. In practice, this amount of backing up seems to produce visually acceptable results, although any system that avoids backing up to face past the goal is likely acceptable.

The second part of the turn simply reuses the curve turn logic to get the unit to the goal. This finishes the turn, and it means that three-point turns are able to match a final destination heading without modifying it. This will become important when we bring all of these turns together.

Reverse

So far we've only dealt with forward vehicle motion, but many times it is better for a unit to go backward to get to his destination. If the unit loops around to reach the goal in these instances, it will look awkward to the user. To resolve this, we can add a simple reverse turn to our palette.

Fortunately, this is the easiest case to implement. To get a reverse, simply use the curve turn code as is, but before calling it, reverse the heading of the start points and endpoints. If the curve turn is successful, then walk the replacement points, and invert each heading.

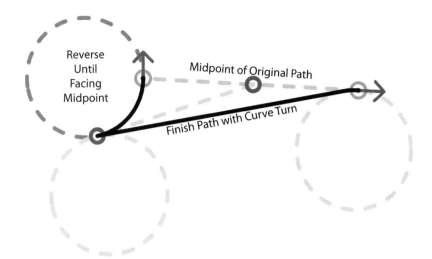

FIGURE 2.11.7   Three-point turns reverse until facing the midpoint and then use the curve turn code.

Turn Search

You can apply the previously defined turns using a heuristic. The system can walk through each turn segment, and based on the direction change, select the one best turn to try. This works in practice, but there are problems. First, defining a heuristic that selects the best turn in all cases is difficult. Second, if the turn selected isn't possible due to obstacles in the environment, it doesn't offer a fallback.

To address this, we have to search to find the optimal turn for each segment. To define which of the available turns is best, we use the time it takes to complete as a metric. The turn that gets the unit to the goal in the least amount of time is the most desirable.

The list of turns to consider will likely need to be defined differently for each unit type in the game. The palette of turns used by a tank is very different from the palette of turns used by a motorcycle or a Jeep (pivots are more acceptable for tanks). Although a pivot is normally considered to be the last resort, it is important to include it in the turn palette and score it along with the other turns because often some turns take longer than the pivot they are replacing.

The exact method of estimating how long it takes to follow a given path will vary depending on how your path following works, but the following method works for many games. As an estimate, assume infinite acceleration, so the unit is always at the top speed possible based on the turn radius. For curved sections of the path with a turn radius greater than the vehicle can achieve at top speed, assume the vehicle is moving at top speed. For curved sections of the path with a turn radius smaller than the vehicle can achieve at top speed, multiply the vehicle's top speed by the ratio of the turn's radius to the top speed turn radius and use that. When you have a speed for a turn section, just divide by the length to get the time, and add up the time for all segments.

Entries in the turn palette need a number of properties. The first property is the type of turn (curve turn, constant radius, and so on). The second property, for some turn types, is a radius multiplier. This is multiplied with the unit's normal full-speed turn radius to get the turn radius to try for this palette entry. It is useful to tune using a multiplier instead of a fixed distance because this lets you tweak your unit speeds and rotation rates without having to go back and modify your turn palettes. The third property is a tunable value in seconds that is added to the calculated time for the turn. This value lets us slightly prefer some turns over others. As an example, we are including the pivot in the list of possible turns, but it looks terrible when Jeeps pivot in place; we can fix this by adding five seconds to the estimated time for that palette entry.

Finally, we add a tunable maximum path distance to the entry so that it is not considered for paths that exceed this maximum. This is primarily used on reverse entries to prevent units from backing up over long distances. Color Plate 3 shows an example of a Jeep's turn palette applied to a path around a number of obstacles (also see Table 2.11.1).

Table 2.11.1   Example Turn Palette for a Jeep

Turn Type	Radius Multiplier	Tuning Time Modifier	Max Valid Path Length
Constant Radius	N/A	−0.40	N/A
Curve Turn Smoothed	1.00	−0.35	N/A
Curve Turn Smoothed	0.50	−0.35	N/A
Reverse	0.75	−0.20	30 meters
Curve Turn	5.00	−0.20	N/A
Curve Turn	1.00	−0.15	N/A
Curve Turn	0.50	−0.15	N/A
Three-Point Turn	0.50	−0.10	N/A
Curve Turn	0.15	+0.50	N/A
Curve Turn	0.10	+1.00	N/A
Pivot	N/A	+5.00	N/A

Matching a Destination Heading

Depending on your game, it may be important for the unit to end its movement with a specific heading unrelated to the path it used to move there. This is the case in *Company of Heroes* because users are allowed to specify the final heading independent of the move itself (see Figure 2.11.8). In our case, it is highly desirable that the unit arrives at the destination already facing the correct direction instead of having to pivot in place after arrival. We can add turns to our palette for the final segment in the path to help achieve this.

When processing the final segment, we duplicate all entries of the original palette; however, for the duplicate entries, we require that the final output direction match the user's order. These entries also have a large bonus time subtracted from their estimation to put them at the top of the sorted pile.

For the turns that are always able to match the existing destination heading (curve turn, reverse, three-point turn), we modify the path's final heading to be the user's specified direction before processing the copied entries. For turns that do not allow matching an existing heading (constant radius), we add a requirement to the verification step that the copied palette entry does in fact match the user's heading. We ignore the smoothed curve turn for the final segment. The result of these extra entries and their bonus tuning time is that turns matching the goal are almost always valued over turns that do not, unless they are extremely slow to perform.

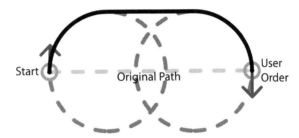

FIGURE 2.11.8   Matching a final direction specified by the user to avoid pivoting at the goal.

Optimization

One major performance issue with doing the search in this form is validating each turn against the environment. Because any of the available turns might be the best for the current segment, we must test collision for all of them to find the cheapest. To optimize the process of selecting a turn for each segment, we can split the process into two sections. The first piece is to calculate the shape of the turn and find its estimated time cost. The second piece is to validate the turn by testing collision. The first is done for all turns, and then the turns are sorted based on their estimated time.

Now, with the turns sorted, you can try the collision validation in order from shortest to longest. The first turn that is validated is accepted, and you can stop testing. If you find the pivot in this sorted list, it means that all the turns below it were more expensive, even with the tuning value applied, so just leave the segment unmodified and move on.

Discontinuity and Stopping

After implementing this system, we found one major remaining problem with individual vehicle motion. When a unit already in motion receives a move order, it immediately gets a new path and throws away the old one, so there can be a discontinuity in speed from the unit stopping on a dime or shooting off in a new direction. To resolve this, whenever a moving unit receives a new order, we do a continuity test comparing his current motion to the start of the new path.

If the new path starts in a direction different from the current motion of the unit (see Figure 2.11.9), we create a halting path out of the path the unit was previously following. The unit slows to a stop along the original planned route. The distance traveled along the original path is based on the current speed and deceleration rate for the vehicle:

$$dist_{stop} = speed^2 / deceleration$$

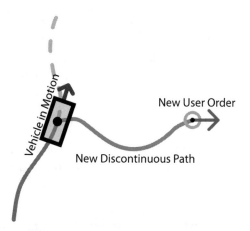

FIGURE 2.11.9   Changing paths on new orders can result in a sudden stop.

After generating this halting path, we *repath* to the unit's new goal from the end of the halting path (see Figure 2.11.10). We then merge these two paths together. The result is that the unit comes to a stop slowly before pivoting to follow his new order.

Additionally, if the halting path and the repath to the goal happen to be continuous, then we don't have to stop at the end of the halting path. The result is that the unit just extends his current motion a bit before turning to reach his new goal (see Figure 2.11.11).

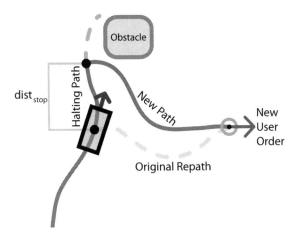

FIGURE 2.11.10 A stop path and a new path from the stop endpoint replace the original path.

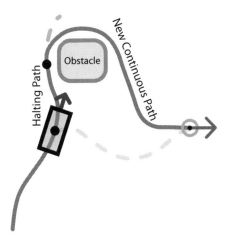

FIGURE 2.11.11 After repathing from the stop path's endpoint, the new path is continuous, so the unit never has to stop.

Conclusion

The techniques described in this article were used to control all the vehicles in *Company of Heroes*. They resulted in units that move in the expected direction and along the expected route when an order is issued. They also behave predictably when a user specifies the final direction for the unit. The system provides for easy tunability and executes with only slightly more execution overhead than a basic smoother.

References

[Pinter01] Pinter, Marco, "Toward More Realistic Pathfinding." Available online at *http://www.gamasutra.com/features/20010314/pinter_01.htm*, March 14, 2001.

[Pinter02] Pinter, Marco, "Realistic Turning Between Waypoints." *AI Game Programming Wisdom*, Charles River Media, 2002.

2.12

Memory-Efficient Pathfinding Abstractions

Nathan Sturtevant—University of Alberta

nathanst@gmail.com

In the fall of 2006, BioWare Corp approached us about pathfinding research that we were doing at the University of Alberta, in particular to see if our work could be adapted for use in their latest game, *Dragon Age*. Most of the memory budget allocated to pathfinding was already taken by the map representation, and so we were challenged to build a pathfinding abstraction that would minimize memory usage and still provide a performance boost.

We describe the results of this collaboration in this article. In addition to the representation itself, we also describe how to use the representation for pathfinding, as well as a number of techniques that improve the performance and quality of resulting paths. We have implemented the methods described here as the core pathfinding module in *Dragon Age*.

Building a Memory-Efficient Abstraction

The key to building a memory-efficient abstraction is the representation used to store the abstraction. The choice of the underlying representation depends on the game being built and the types of maps used in the game. In a game where players traverse large, mostly unoccupied areas of terrain, an explicitly represented grid is likely quite wasteful. A game with tightly packed areas might be more amenable to a grid-based representation. In this article, we will assume an underlying grid-based representation as this is the representation that BioWare Corp chose to use in its title *Dragon Age*.

We take an approach that is common in games that contain both static and dynamic data. As much planning is done as possible on the static game data before dynamic data is taken into account. This is the basic approach used, for example, in *Saboteur* [Dunki07]. We limit our discussion here to static planning only.

In this section, we describe the process of building an efficient graph representation of a low-level, grid-based map. We will refer to the original map as the low-level map and locations in the low-level map as coordinates. The abstract structure is based upon dividing the low-level map into fixed-sized sectors. These sectors are further divided into regions. When referring to the abstraction, we will usually refer to abstract regions, which correspond to a node in the abstract graph.

Sectors and Regions

We begin by overlaying a large grid over the low-level world. This grid defines the sectors in the world. Given an x/y location in the low-level map, the sector can be implicitly determined from the sector size and map width. We limit sector sizes to 16×16 (256 grid cells) so that any point within a sector can be represented by a single byte. Smaller sector sizes can be used, but we will show later that larger sector sizes are more efficient.

Sectors are laid down without regard for the underlying topology of the world. This means that the topology of the map will be divided by sector boundaries. Unlike the abstraction representation of navigation meshes [Snook00] or quadtrees [Tozour04], it might not be possible to visit every location in an abstract sector without leaving the sector. To address this, we further divide sectors into regions, one region for each contiguous area within a sector. Regions can be determined by performing a breadth-first search on the low-level grid within each sector. Regions are not guaranteed to be convex. A single x/y coordinate is chosen as a representative location for each region, and this becomes a node in the abstract graph.

After sectors and regions are determined, we must find the edges between different regions. This can be done by tracing the edges of each sector and comparing the sectors on each side of the boundary. An edge is added to the abstract graph for each pair of regions that share a sector border.

We demonstrate the initial layout in the left portion of Figure 2.12.1. The map shown here is 32×32 and divided into four 16×16 sectors. Black walls cannot be crossed. Sector 0 has only a single region, *a*, but Sector 1 has three regions *a*, *b*, and *c*. We will refer to a region in the map as *sector:region*, (e.g., region 1:c). Region centers can be chosen arbitrarily, although the choice of a region center can have a large impact on the amount of work required for path planning using the abstraction. Initially region, centers are placed at grid cells close to the weighted center of a region, as in the left portion of Figure 2.12.1. Locations are later optimized, as in the right portion of Figure 2.12.1, which shows the full graph. The optimization process is described later in the article. The original 32×32 world has been reduced to a graph with seven nodes (region centers) and eight edges.

Storing the Abstraction

The memory used to store the abstraction is divided into two parts. The first portion is fixed sized and stores basic sector information, whereas the second portion is variable sized, storing region and edge information.

In the sector data, we need to store the number of regions in the sector as well as an index into the second portion of memory indicating where the region and edge

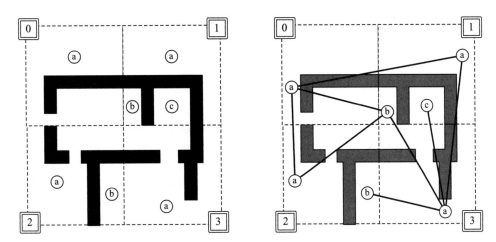

FIGURE 2.12.1 Sectors and regions (left) and the resulting graph after region optimization (right).

information is stored. A simple implementation uses 32 bits to store this information, although it is possible to reduce this to 16 bits if necessary. The data layout is shown in the left of Table 2.12.1.

Table 2.12.1 Memory Used to Store the Abstraction

Sector Data		Region Data		Sample Region Data
Num. Regions	(8 bits)	Center	(8 bits)	14
Region Index	(16 bits)	Edge Index	(8 bits)	2
		Center		243
Unused	(8 bits)	Edge Index	(8 bits)	3
		Edge Data		N : 1
		Edge Data		NW : 0
		Edge Data		S : 1

The region data for each sector is broken into two parts, a fixed-sized portion for region information and a variable-sized portion for edge data. The region data contains the center of that region as well as an index into the edge data. This is shown in the right portion of Table 2.12.1. The edge index stores the index of the first outgoing edge of the next region. By computing the difference between the edge indices in successive regions, the total number of edges in a region can be computed.

The example shows sample data for a sector with two regions. The first region's edges begin at offset zero in the edge data, and there are a total of two outgoing edges. The second region's edges begin at offset two, and there is one $(3 - 2 = 1)$ outgoing edge from this region. This method means that only two memory accesses are needed to find the total number of edges in a region as well as their offset in memory. If we just stored the number of edges in a region, we might have to look at all regions to find the offset of the edges in memory.

Eight bits are used to store each edge. Three bits are reserved for the edge direction, and five bits are reserved for the region that is connected by the edge. The target sector can be computed from the current sector and the direction.

Besides the 32-bit sectors, there are two noticeable inefficiencies in memory usage. First, we are storing every edge twice as an outgoing edge from every sector. We could further reduce memory usage by only storing each edge once, however, this makes the process of generating moves more expensive because we would have to look at all neighboring regions to check for potential edges, which also detracts from cache locality. Second, on open areas of a map, there can be many sectors that are essentially identical; they have a single region with eight edges, one to each neighbor. Instead of storing these regions, we can just mark them and generate the default data when needed.

We show the total memory required to store the abstraction averaged over a set of 120 512 × 512 maps in Figure 2.12.2. The top (dotted) line is the memory required using exactly the methods described here. Our experiments suggest that an additional 25% or more memory could be saved using 16 bits for the sectors instead of 32 bits. Using a sector size of 16, less than 10 Kb is needed to store the entire abstraction. We also consider the possible gains from not storing sectors that match the default profile (one region and eight edges). This compression is valuable for small sector sizes but less so on larger sectors, although this depends on the types of maps being compressed.

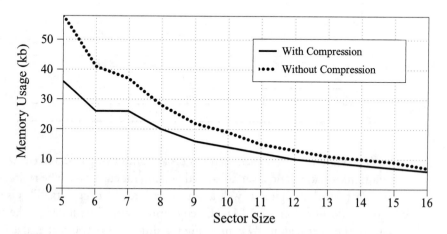

FIGURE 2.12.2   Memory usage as the sector size increases.

Using the Abstraction

Now that we have described how to build and store a memory-efficient abstraction, we will next describe the methods needed to use the abstraction for pathfinding. We first describe the basic process of building a complete path from the start to goal and then consider ways to optimize the process in the next section.

Three stages are required to build a complete path using the abstraction. First, given a location in the real map, we must find the corresponding nodes in the abstraction. Second, a path must be found through the abstraction. Finally, the abstract path must be refined into a low-level path.

Finding Abstract Nodes

Given x/y coordinates in the map, we can compute the corresponding sector using just the sector and map size. The only difficult task is to compute the region. When a sector has only one region, we must be in that region, so this case is easy. If a sector has more than one region, we can use one of two methods to find the current region.

The first method is to perform a breadth-first search (BFS) from the low-level x/y coordinate until one of the region centers is found. This search is limited to passable points within the current sector and so is not too expensive, although this depends on the relative locations of the region center and the given coordinates.

An alternative approach is to use an A* search from the region centers [Grimani05]. If we put each of the region centers onto the A* open list and use the low-level x/y coordinates as the goal, we will find a path from the region center that is reachable from the low-level location. The A* approach can look at less nodes because it uses heuristic information to help find the closest region, but a BFS does not need to maintain a priority queue so the overhead of a BFS search is lower. In practice, we use a BFS, but in other domains an A* search might work better. We will describe further optimizations for finding abstract nodes at the end of the article.

Finding Abstract Paths

Finding paths through the abstract space is fairly straightforward. An A* search can be used after the start and goal locations have been found within the abstraction. Instead of storing precomputed edge weights inside the abstraction, we use the octile-distance between region centers as abstract edge weights. (Given the x and y offset between two locations, the octile-distance is $x + 0.5y$ if x is greater than y, and $y + 0.5x$ otherwise, assuming that diagonals have a cost of 1.5.) We also use the octile-distance as the heuristic cost between regions that are not directly connected.

Path Refinement

Paths can be refined from abstract paths into low-level paths via many methods. The simplest way to do this is to first compute a path from the start location to the region center for the start location. We can then compute paths to successive region centers of the abstract path. Finally, we can compute a path from the last region center to the goal.

We demonstrate this process, as well as how it can go wrong, in Figure 2.12.3. In this case, the start is in region 0:a, and the goal is in region 1:a; however, the start and goal are actually next to each other. Refining paths as described will lead to the path shown in the figure, first going to region 0:a and then to region 1:a before going to the goal. This can be easily fixed with a simple special case that covers the start and the goal. Higher-quality paths are produced if, from the start location, we skip the current region center and plan directly to the next region center on the abstract path. Additionally, we can skip the final region center and find a path directly to the goal from the next-to-last region center. In this case both rules would apply, and we would search directly for a path between the start and goal.

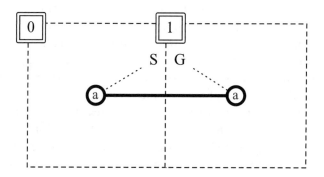

FIGURE 2.12.3   Refining an abstract path into a low-level path.

This idea can be extended to the full refinement process by skipping region centers when refining other portions of the path. For example, we might choose to skip every other region center. This will result in higher-quality paths at the cost of extra work. Weighted A* can also be used to perform this step, as it is often cheaper than A*, although we will discuss how the refinement cost can be minimized in the next section.

Another approach for limiting the refinement cost is to restrict the planning process to the regions along the path being refined. We know that the regions along the abstract path are connected in the low-level space, so this will avoid spending time searching in areas that might not be relevant for the current path. The drawback of this approach is that it is not flexible in situations where dynamic obstacles might block paths.

To measure the effectiveness of these approaches, we took a set of 120 maps and computed 93,000 paths, evenly divided in length from 1 to 512. We used the simplest approach of refining only a single edge at a time, except in the case of the start and goal where we skipped the first/last region center. Region centers were dynamically adjusted, as described in the next section. We compare the total work required to build a complete path in Figure 2.12.4. Note that Nodes Expanded is a logarithmic scale.

A* must expand nearly 100,000 nodes in the worst case. Using our abstraction method requires just over 1,000 nodes in the worst case. For paths of length 512, this means that, at worst, we are only expanding 2 nodes for each node in the final path. Additionally, unlike A*, the computation required using the abstraction can easily be spread over multiple frames of computation with no substantial memory overhead. When comparing the curves for various sector sizes (not shown), we found that we did the least overall work using the largest sector size, as long as we optimized region centers. Without optimizing region centers, the least work was done with 14 × 14 sectors.

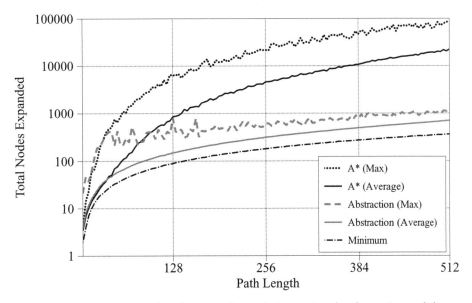

FIGURE 2.12.4   A comparison between the work done using the abstraction and the work done by A*.

Optimizing Performance

In this section, we consider a variety of methods that can be used to improve the quality or the cost of the paths produced using this abstraction.

Optimizing Region Centers

The work done during refinement depends on the location of region centers. Navigation meshes and quadtrees guarantee a straight-line path between adjacent parts of the abstraction. There is no guarantee that a straight path will exist between adjacent regions in the abstraction. In the worst case, it can actually be very difficult to find a path between adjacent region centers. One solution is to just cache each of these paths and reuse them as needed. But, besides being memory intensive, the cached data would not account for dynamic obstacles in the world or dynamic adjustments to the abstraction.

An alternative approach is to optimize the placement of the region centers to minimize the work needed at runtime. The idea behind this approach is to first use a simple method for placing region centers. An optimization phase then looks for adjacent regions with high pathfinding costs. These regions are then optimized individually. The pseudocode for this process follows. This code simply tries all possible locations for the region center and chooses the region center that minimizes the maximum cost. Besides optimizing planning costs, it is also possible to optimize region locations based on other metrics. For example, we can try to avoid putting region centers near walls or on top of other placeable objects in the world.

```
void OptimizeRegionCenter(Region &r)
{
    maxCost = ∞;
    bestCell = null;
    for (each cell c in r)
    {
        cost = ComputeMaxCostToAndFromNeighbors(cell);
        if (cost < maxCost)
        {
            maxCost = cost;
            bestCell = &c;
        }
    }
    r.SetCenter(bestCell);
}
```

This computation can be expensive, but it can also be performed at export time. There are a number of ways the cost can be reduced, such as by not considering all possible region centers or by using other reasoning to bound the cost incurred when computing the cost to the neighbors. Returning to Figure 2.12.1, this is the process by which the default region centers in the left half of the figure can be converted to optimized region centers shown in the right portion of the figure.

To measure the effectiveness of optimizing region centers, we measured the maximum work done in a single edge-refinement while computing the paths in Figure 2.12.4. Over all paths, we then looked at the 95th percentile of the work done, which we plot in Figure 2.12.5. The top curve is the work done with static region centers, whereas the bottom curve is the work done with dynamic region centers. For small sector sizes, the dynamic adjustment isn't important. With larger sector sizes, there is almost a factor of three reduction in nodes expanded.

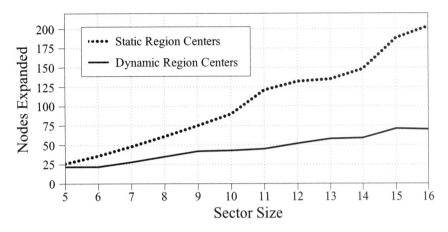

FIGURE 2.12.5   Savings in work by dynamically adjusting region centers.

Dynamically Modifying the Abstraction for Abstract Planning

We discussed special cases for computing the low-level paths from the abstract path. One disadvantage to this approach is that the low-level path is constrained to follow the abstract path. This means that inaccuracies in the abstract path will be reflected in the low-level path. We demonstrate one particular example in Figure 2.12.6.

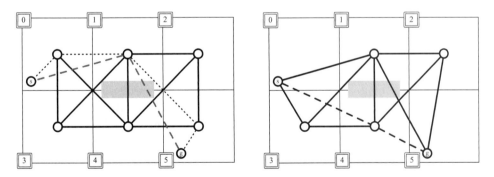

FIGURE 2.12.6   Temporarily moving region centers improves the quality of abstract paths.

In the left portion of this figure, we show a simple map with six sectors and a small barrier in the middle of the map. There are two possible optimal abstract paths between sector 0 and sector 5, [0:a, 1:a, 5:a] and [0:a, 4:a, 5:a]. This same abstract path will be followed no matter where the start is in 0:a and the goal is in 5:a. Suppose that the abstract path is [0:a, 1:a, 5:a], then the resulting abstract path is shown in the left portion of Figure 2.12.5. This path is improved by skipping the first and last region center, but it is still quite poor.

Fortunately, there is an easy fix for this problem. The problem is that the region centers in the abstraction do not accurately reflect the current problem being solved. We address this by simply moving the abstract region centers to the start and goal locations before computing the abstract path and then moving them back afterward. This results in the graph on the right portion of Figure 2.12.6, and the path indicated by the dotted line.

Selecting Sector Size

We have discussed the parameters that influence our decision regarding how large to build our sectors in several locations. Larger sectors are better as long as it is still easy to refine a single abstract edge. We maintain this property with larger sector sizes by optimizing the location of our region centers. Although we could use sectors larger than 16×16, this is a natural limit due to the underlying representation of the abstraction. One thing we did not show is the effect of sector size on optimality. It ends up that larger sector sizes result in fewer suboptimal paths because the optimal paths between region centers are longer. When using smaller sector sizes, we are forced to travel through more region centers along any path, which increases suboptimality.

Smoothing

The paths returned using the abstraction as described thus far averaged about 10% suboptimality. Note that these paths are restricted to a grid and are also restricted to travel through region centers. In practice, we can take the grid-based paths and smooth them. Approaches described before include Bézier splines [Johnson06], Cat-mull-Rom smoothing [Rabin00], and many other nuanced techniques [Pinter01]. Many of these techniques assume that you already have a high-quality path that just needs to be smoothed, but we want to remove some of the suboptimality with our smoothing.

One approach to improving the optimality of paths generated by a hierarchical abstraction is to trim the paths, either to room openings [Rabin00] or by some other method. We investigated trimming our refined paths, and this did decrease suboptimality, but it also increased the cost of planning. So in addition to a minimal amount of trimming, we also implemented a smoothing procedure that shrinks the paths.

In practice, we always do a straight-line check before computing any path. If this fails, we fall back to a two-step process for smoothing. The first step is to look for segments of the path that are optimal on the underlying grid (e.g., a straight line segment followed by a diagonal line segment). We then check to see if these segments can be replaced with a straight line. If this process fails on a particular segment, we recursively divide the segment in half and try again on each half. This smoothing step occurs as early as possible in the planning process so that we can begin executing paths while they are still being computed.

The second step in the smoothing process is to look at adjacent line segments along the path to see if we can smooth them by adding a new segment between the midpoint of the original segments. We demonstrate this in Figure 2.12.7. In part (a) we show a path has been formed around a large obstacle. To smooth this path, we check two adjacent path segments to see if their centers can be connected by a straight line. If they can, we connect their centers and remove the extra portion of the path, resulting in the path in (b). We then continue the process as time allows. If the length of a line segment is below some minimum constant, we do not consider splitting the line segment, but instead try to replace the entire segment with a smoother component. The final path after smoothing everything is shown in part (c). The straight-line check prevents us from smoothing too close to a barrier. If needed, the smoothing can be focused on adjacent line segments that form a sharp angle. Long segments can also be split to facilitate smoothing.

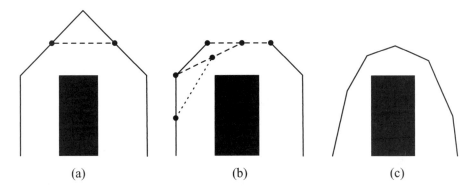

(a)   (b)   (c)

FIGURE 2.12.7   Splitting segments to smooth a path.

This is an iterative process that can be applied as many times as necessary or as many times as there are CPU cycles available. In practice, we iterate between planning and smoothing as paths are executed in the world. We describe this process in the next section. Delaying the smoothing step not only helps to spread the computation across as many frames as possible, but it also allows us to remove segments that might have been planned around a dynamic obstacle that is no longer in the way when we reach that portion of our path.

High-Level Control

We have described many different pieces of a pathfinding framework centered around an abstraction that attempts to optimize memory usage. To conclude the major content of this article, we describe how each of these components can be combined to form a complete pathfinding framework.

The first step is to find a complete abstract path. Then, the following steps are performed in order of their priority: planning the immediate path, smoothing the immediate path, and planning the long-term path.

Each time a unit is given time in the current frame to do pathfinding, it looks at its current needs. If an immediate path is not available, it is computed. If the path is available but not smoothed, a smoothing pass is applied as described in the preceding section. If there is an immediate path ready to follow, and the path has already been smoothed, then the next segment of the abstract path is computed.

During the planning process, agents can be given priority based on how much of their immediate path has been planned, their importance in the world, and whether they are visible to the user or not.

The pseudocode for the process follows:

```
void DoIncrementalPathfinding(Unit &u)
{
    if (!u.HasAbstractPath())
    {
        u.PlanAbstractPath();
        return;
    }
    if (!u.ImmediatePathSmoothed())
    {
        u.SmoothImmediatePath();
        return;
    }
    RefinePath();
}
```

The only information retained between pathfinding calls is the abstract path, the current low-level path, and a few state variables. We do not need to maintain the open list from an A* search, which can be expensive. This process allows units to begin moving with only a few hundred microseconds of computation; the rest of the pathfinding computation is delayed until needed. A final advantage of this approach is that if the user changes his mind while the unit is still traversing the path, we will not have wasted the extra computation planning the rest of the path that will never be followed. These cycles can instead be given to other units.

Additional Optimizations

A number of additional optimizations can be applied to optimize different steps of the pathfinding process. The best approach depends on the memory and CPU available in any particular game.

Finding the Abstract Sector/Region

If there are extra bits available in the low-level grid, we can use them to store region information. When no bits are allocated, we can only know the current region if a sector has only a single region. If there is one bit of storage, we can use it to mark the largest region in a sector, although we will still need to search in other unmarked regions. If more bits are available, they can be used to mark additional regions within a sector.

If more memory is available outside of the low-level grid, multiple locations can also be stored in each region. This will reduce the time required to find a marked region location because there is more likely to be a region center nearby.

Finally, units can cache their current region and update it as they traverse the environment. This eliminates the need to find the abstract region for a given start location. If the goal region is selected by an arbitrary mouse click, however, this will have to be computed using one of the methods described here.

Caching Paths and Costs

If more memory is available, we can refine any number of edges ahead of time so that they do not need to be computed at runtime. Instead of storing all possible refinements, we can also just store the ones that are most expensive to compute at runtime.

Similarly, we can annotate abstract edges with their underlying cost. This can improve the quality of the abstract paths computed, especially in maps that are more constrained. Again, we can just annotate the edges for which the abstract cost is much higher than the heuristic estimate.

Dynamic World Optimizations

Most of what we have described here is optimized for static maps; however, there are also several optimizations that help with nonstatic maps. First, if we know how the maps will change in advance, we can precompute how the sectors/regions will change and store this information in the abstraction. Then when the map changes take place, we can just point the sector to the updated information, and the abstraction will immediately be updated.

Additionally, we can annotate regions and/or sectors with occupancy information and increase the pathfinding costs through crowded areas. Similarly, if a region center is blocked, we can increase the cost of traveling through that region center, which will direct the abstract path around temporarily blocked areas of the map.

Other Optimizations

We have attempted to minimize the memory used by the abstraction here. But much more memory is being used by the underlying map representation than by the abstraction. This data can be streamed in and out at runtime, just leaving the abstraction in memory. In this case, refinement only occur when the map is available in memory.

Besides storing just the abstract graph, we can also annotate connected components in the abstract graph. This information can be used to quickly answer queries about whether or not their exists a path between any two regions in the world. This avoids having to perform a complete search at even the abstract level to verify that there is no path between two locations in the world.

Source Code and Demo

ON THE CD

Included on the CD-ROM with this book is sample source code for building and using the abstraction described here. The program compiles under Unix-based systems using makefiles, and project files are included for Visual Studio 8 as well as XCode 2.4. OpenGL and GLUT are required. A few sample maps are included, which will load when passed on the command line. Otherwise, a map will be generated from random line segments. More details on visualizing the abstraction optimization and testing various paths on both optimized and unoptimized abstractions are found in a Readme file included with the source code.

Future Work

In this article, we have not described in detail the methods used for dynamic obstacle avoidance. We implemented the basis for some of these techniques in the pathfinding engine, but other programmers are still implementing some of these details. Still, it would be worthwhile to perform a detailed study of the techniques suggested by the game development community and their effectiveness in practice.

These abstraction techniques are also built around a simple grid-based map. Although we have an understanding of how these ideas could be used with more complex map representations, we have yet to fully describe how this is possible.

Conclusion

This article has described a hierarchical abstraction technique that works to minimize the memory overhead of the abstraction, as well as the details needed to use the abstraction in practice. A number of optimizations are considered and their usefulness is measured in practice. We have implemented these ideas in the game *Dragon Age* by BioWare Corp.

References

[Dunki07] Dunki, Quinn, "Streaming, Open-World Pathfinding." Invited talk, Third Annual Artificial Intelligence and Interactive Digital Entertainment Conference, June 6, 2007.

[Grimani05] Grimani, Mario, and Titelbaum, Matthew, "Beyond A*." *Game Programming Gems 5*, Charles River Media, 2005: pp. 367–382.

[Johnson06] Johnson, Geraint, "Smoothing a Navigation Mesh Path." *AI Game Programming Wisdom 3*, Charles River Media, 2006: pp. 129–139.

[Pinter01] Pinter, Marco. "Toward More Realistic Pathfinding." *Gamasutra*. Available online at *www.gamasutra.com/features/20010314/pinter_01.htm*, March 14, 2001.

[Rabin00] Rabin, Steve, "A* Aesthetic Optimizations." *Game Programming Gems*, Charles River Media, 2000: pp. 264–271.

[Snook00] Snook, Greg, "Simplified 3D Movement and Pathfinding Using Navigation Meshes." *Game Programming Gems*, Charles River Media, 2000: pp. 288–304.

[Tozour04] Tozour, Paul, "Search Space Representations." *AI Game Programming Wisdom 2*, Charles River Media, 2004: pp. 85–102.

ARCHITECTURE

3.1

A Flexible AI Architecture for Production and Prototyping of Games

Terry Wellmann—High Voltage Software, Inc.

terry.wellmann@high-voltage.com

This article presents an AI architecture that was developed for a game where the player encountered many different AI enemies, each with its own personality and abilities. We determined early in the development of the game that we wanted an AI system that was flexible enough to support a wide variety of enemies as well as easy to maintain and tune by the design team. One of our goals for the AI was to give each enemy a unique and recognizable personality, which we accomplished through the use of models, animations, and the decision-making system discussed here.

Although the architecture presented here was designed to accomplish our specific goals, it is applicable to a wide variety of games. With the help of this article, you will gain a better understanding of the factors to consider when building an AI architecture, and you will have all of the tools necessary to successfully design a system that is easy to understand, build, maintain, and extend.

The Architecture

One of the first tasks in designing any AI system is to identify the high-level decisions that the agents are going to have to make. One important thing to keep in mind while doing this is to keep the list short and think of things in generic terms: the details of the decisions will come later. If you try to be specific with every decision, you will quickly end up with an overwhelming list.

In our game, the user is bombarded with enemies that he must battle and defeat. Many of the decisions an enemy can make are common across all enemies, whereas others are unique to particular enemies. Examples of decisions that all enemies make include moving forward, moving backward, moving to the sides, and standing, as well as staying idle or occasional behaviors, such as taunting. Attacks or specialty moves are examples of decisions that are generally unique for each enemy.

For our game, we chose to represent each AI decision using a 32-bit mask. This limited us to 32 unique decisions for each AI agent, but this was more than sufficient for our needs. We could have also represented the decision list with an enumerated type, but there are a few drawbacks to this that we will discuss in the "Decision Chaining" section.

For the purposes of this article, we will use the following decisions and their assigned bit values:

```
D_NONE          0x00
D_FORWARD       0x01
D_BACK          0x02
D_LEFT          0x04
D_RIGHT         0x08
D_LIGHT_ATK     0x10
D_HEAVY_ATK     0x20
```

We also need to define a structure to store the critical data for each decision. The following code shows what the basic structure will look like:

```
struct TDecision
{
    int mDecision;
    float fProbability;
    int mChainedDecisions;
    int mFlags;
}
```

The mDecision variable indicates the decision represented by this structure. This variable is intended to hold a single decision; they are never bitwise ORed together. The fProbability variable represents the overall probability of choosing this decision over any other decision. The mChainedDecisions variable is used to build more complex decisions; we will discuss the use of this variable further in the "Decision Chaining" section. The mFlags variable is a generic bit mask variable that can be used for a variety of things, such as coordinating an attack with several other independent AI agents. We will discuss this in the "Agent Communication and Coordination" section.

Each AI agent has an array of TDecision structures that are initialized whenever a decision is to be considered. The code for setting and maintaining the array can be handled with basic STL (Standard Template Library) operations or your own custom handling.

The Decision-Making Process

Now that we have established the underlying representation that is shared by all AI agents, we can discuss the decision-making process that is performed whenever one decision completes and a new one needs to be made. To simplify the architecture for this article, we will make the assumption that all actions that result from an AI decision are performed in their entirety and execute quickly enough that they never need to be aborted.

The first step in making a new decision is to clear the array of TDecision structures. After that is done, we can build a new list. When building the decision array, we consider each decision to determine if it is currently valid and should be considered for execution. If it is valid, we add it to the decision array. At the same time, we determine how likely the decision is to be chosen relative to all other valid decisions. In addition, we can specify which decisions, if any, need to be considered as follow-up or chained decisions as well as any other data that we may want to accompany the decision. We will discuss both decision chaining and accompanying data extensions to the decision-making process later in the article.

When assigning a probability value to a decision, we can take a couple of different approaches. The first is simply to assign a predetermined or hard-coded value. For example, if we want the AI agent to always consider performing an idle action, such as a taunt, we can assign a small value, such as 0.05. Another method for assigning a probability value is to dynamically compute it based on runtime or situational data. For example, if our agent has been hurt and has a low health value, we might want him to be more cautious and have an increased likelihood of moving away from a dangerous situation. By adjusting the move-backward probability value relative to his health, not only are we making the AI more dynamic, but we are also defining a personality trait that will vary based on the events of the game and will most likely be noticed by the player.

After all of the valid decisions have been added to the decision list, we can select one for execution. This process is straightforward. First, we sum the probability values for all of the valid decisions, which we can do as we add the decisions to the array. Next, we compute a random value between zero and this sum. We then simply find the decision in the list that corresponds to the randomly generated value.

Let's now consider an example where we want our agent to consider the following choices:

- Move forward with a 20% relative chance.
- Move backward with a 10% relative chance.
- Perform a heavy attack with a 15% relative chance.

The pseudocode for setting up the decision-making system for this would look as follows:

```
ClearDecisionList();

// add the decisions that we want to consider
AddDecision(D_FORWARD, 0.2);
AddDecision(D_BACK, 0.1);
AddDecision(D_HEAVY_ATK, 0.15);

// pick and execute the decision
PickDecision();
ExecuteDecision();
```

In this example, we added three decisions to our agent's list. The sum of the probability values for all three decisions is 0.45, so to make a decision, we will randomly generate a value between 0.0 and 0.45. Table 3.1.1 shows how the probability values of each decision map to the total range of 0.0 to 0.45.

Table 3.1.1   Decision Chance Value Ranges

Decision	Chance Value Range
D_FORWARD	0.0 to 0.2
D_BACK	0.2 to 0.3
D_HEAVY_ATK	0.3 to 0.45

The final step in the process is to execute the chosen decision. While executing the decision, there is one important aspect to take into consideration. The primary responsibility of the execution process is to manage the animations and visual effects and to apply any physical changes, such as damage to the environment and other characters. When developing a system to pair an AI decision to these assets and attributes we want to keep them as decoupled as possible. By decoupling our physical game assets from our AI system, we make our life easier when we want to reuse the AI system for another game or if we need to port it to another engine.

Decision Weighting

The previous section touched on the concept of assigning probability values, or decision weight values, to each decision as it is added to the decision list. In the simplest form, the probability values are static, but with a little additional effort and thought, we can introduce a very dynamic element to the AI system that will help our agents react to runtime changes to themselves or their environment.

Decision weighting is a technique that can give the agents a lot of personality and provides hooks that will allow us to easily create unique personalities for each. There are many ways in which you can implement a dynamic decision-weighting scheme, so you will want to find the one that works best for your particular application. However, one approach is to give each decision a base value so that there is always some chance that the decision will be made, and then add in a modifier computed at runtime to make it dynamic.

For example, if we want to increase the likelihood that our agent will back away from a threat as his health is lowered, we could do the following:

```
// fHealthPct is defined and set elsewhere
// and it holds the agent's health as a value from
// 0.0 to 1.0, where 1.0 is full health
```

```
// set the base chance for this decision
float fMoveBackChance = 0.1;

// factor in the health of the agent by adding up to
// an additional 0.25 chance based on the health
fMoveBackChance += (1.0 - fHealthPct) * 0.25;

// add the decision to the list for consideration
AddDecision(D_BACK, fMoveBackChance);
```

Decision Chaining

In some cases, single decisions are not sufficient, and we need to string multiple decisions together, which can be accomplished by decision chaining. Recall the mChained-Decisions variable in the TDecision structure declaration. This variable is intended to hold one or more decisions that are ORed together. Upon completion of the primary decision, one of the decisions listed in this variable will be chosen and executed.

If we add a third parameter to the AddDecision function to accommodate chained decisions, and we properly set the mChainedDecisions variable of the TDecision structure, we can now specify more complex behaviors.

Let's now look at an example of what decision chaining offers. Consider the case where we have two enemy agents, each very similar in functionality and personality. Agent A has basic capabilities to move forward, backward, and side to side, and offers two different attack types, a quick, light attack and a slower heavy-damage attack. Agent B has the same capabilities but also has the ability to move forward followed by a quick, light attack. Instead of defining a totally new and unique decision for this combined behavior, we can simply chain the quick, light attack to the move-forward decision.

The following specifies agent B's decisions. Notice the D_FORWARD decision with the chained D_LIGHT_ADK.

```
AddDecision(D_FORWARD,   0.25, D_NONE);
AddDecision(D_FORWARD,   0.25, D_LIGHT_ATK);
AddDecision(D_BACK,      0.10, D_NONE);
AddDecision(D_LEFT,      0.15, D_NONE);
AddDecision(D_RIGHT,     0.15, D_NONE);
AddDecision(D_LIGHT_ATK, 0.20, D_NONE);
AddDecision(D_HEAVY_ATK, 0.15, D_NONE);
```

In some cases, we may want to specify multiple possible chained decision options. For example, a primary decision to move forward followed up with either a backward movement or an attack. The following describes this decision:

```
AddDecision(D_FORWARD, 0.20, D_BACK | D_LIGHT_ATK);
```

The specific needs for controlling and specifying how chained decisions are weighted and chosen can vary, but a straightforward implementation is to assume all chained decisions have an equal probability. In the preceding example, the chained decision to move backward or perform a light attack would thus have an equal chance of being chosen as the follow-up decision. In many cases, this method will be sufficient. If you need more control, you can instead specify the primary decision multiple times, each time with a different chained decision. If we have chosen to represent the decisions as an enumerated type instead of a bit mask, we are restricted to this decision-chaining technique.

Using this technique, our decision would appear as:

```
AddDecision(D_FORWARD, 0.10, D_LIGHT_ATK);
AddDecision(D_FORWARD, 0.10, D_HEAVY_ATK);
```

Note that whenever we choose to split decisions up in this way, we must distribute the probability values accordingly. If not, we can easily end up with a set of decisions that occur more frequently than intended.

Agent Communication and Coordination

Inevitably, situations will arise that require agents to function and make decisions in a coordinated manner. One easy way to accomplish this is to expand the parameter list of AddDecision to also specify the mFlags variable that exists in the TDecision structure declaration.

For example, if we want a mob of enemies to all attack within a few moments of each other and then back off to regroup or to give the player an opportunity to recover from the attack before being bombarded again, we would use this technique. An easy way to achieve this is to define a mob-attack flag in the mFlags bit mask. Whenever a decision is chosen that includes this flag, a message is broadcast to all other enemies to prefer an attack decision if possible. The code would look like this:

```
// define flags to modify decision behavior
F_NONE          0x00
F_MOB_ATK       0x01

// add the attack decision with mob coordination
AddDecision(D_HEAVY_ATK, 0.15, D_NONE, F_MOB_ATK);
```

When the D_HEAVY_ATK decision is selected, and the mob attack event has been sent to all other agents, it is the responsibility of each agent to receive and handle the event appropriately. Using the decision-weighting techniques that we have already discussed, this can be easily accomplished by adding a large bias to all attack decisions upon receiving the event. With a little tweaking and balancing with respect to other possible decisions, we can still maintain our other key personality behaviors, such as retreating if the AI agent is severely injured.

Handling Special Cases

Inevitably, we will encounter situations where some AI agents just do not fit the standard template. They might have special logic needs or decision execution that is unique and cannot be handled in a generic manner. One way to handle these cases is to define a set of custom decisions in our overall list so that they can be weighted relative to the agent's other decisions. Whenever one of these custom decisions is selected for execution, it is up to the agent to handle it appropriately. This is shown in the following example:

```
D_NONE          0x00
D_FORWARD       0x01
D_BACK          0x02
D_LEFT          0x04
D_RIGHT         0x08
D_LIGHT_ATK     0x10
D_HEAVY_ATK     0x20
D_CUSTOM1       0x40
D_CUSTOM2       0x80
```

Another technique is simply to overload the bit values on an agent-by-agent basis. If you choose to do this, take care to ensure that you never mix and match the decision definitions among agents.

Conclusion

The concepts we have discussed here can be applied (possibly with some extensions) to satisfy the AI requirements of a wide variety of games. The architecture is simple yet powerful and is well suited for iteration and game balancing. This architecture can also serve as a prototyping tool when you need to rapidly develop a proof of concept or gameplay examples.

Remember, AI development is all about good planning and trial and error. All experienced AI programmers will tell you that they did not get it right the first time and that they are always learning and discovering better ways to do things.

3.2

Embracing Declarative AI with a Goal-Based Approach

Kevin Dill—Blue Fang Games

kdill4@gmail.com

We are on the brink of a new age of video game AI. The previous generation of AI might excel at the mechanical aspects of play (micromanaging worker allocation or taking head shots, for example), but it still falls short in the areas of strategy and tactics. More importantly, previous-generation AI is not compelling enough to allow for true suspension of disbelief. It feels scripted and artificial. All too often, it doesn't feel intelligent at all.

Here are a few of the things we can hope to see in the future:

Cunning opponents: Opponents who have the ability to outmaneuver and ambush you, cut your lines of supply, and attack with decisive force where you are weak or vulnerable. Opponents who play without unfair economic or military advantages, who need to be "dumbed down" on the easier levels of difficulty to give the player a fighting chance.

Intelligent, responsive allies: Allies who understand the rules of the game, who can operate independently, who know where and when to offer aid (and where and when to ask for it).

Compelling, emotionally appealing characters: Characters you care about. Characters you love or hate. Characters that feel alive.

To achieve these goals, we need to change the way we think about our AIs. The vast majority of AI engineers seem to still be using finite state machines (FSMs) or scripted AI in their games. It is our contention that these techniques, although useful in many cases, are not sufficient for the sort of emergent behavior we want to see from our characters in the future.

In software engineering, we make a distinction between *procedural programming*, in which we describe what to do, and *declarative programming*, in which we describe what that thing is like [Wikipedia07]. A similar distinction could be made for game AI. Most of what exists today is *procedural AI*. The role of the developer is to tell the AI what to do in every conceivable situation. As we learn to write *declarative AI*, we will instead tell the AI what things are possible to do and how it should evaluate its situation to select the best action available.

The choice between procedural and declarative programming is made by selecting the programming language to use, which enforces a particular problem-solving approach. Similarly, the choice between procedural and declarative AI is largely a result of the architecture we use, coupled with a particular way of thinking about character behavior. Any number of architectures could be classified as declarative programming available in the academic AI community. This article concentrates on *goal-based AI*, which is an approach that has been used successfully in a number of games across multiple genres in the past.

The remainder of this article briefly discusses the most common procedural AI architectures and then presents goal-based AI. Finally, we will discuss hybrid approaches that capture some of the best of both worlds. This article will leave you with a feel for how and when to use declarative AI and perhaps also the inclination to apply goal-based AI to your own games.

Procedural AI

When building procedural AI, we attempt to enumerate the possible situations and tell the AI what to do in each one. One strong advantage of this approach is that it is easy to test: Simply place an NPC in each enumerated situation, and observe whether or not it takes the expected action. In addition, every game contains numerous situations in which the correct action is obvious. In an FPS, for example, if an NPC is low on health and being attacked, then it clearly makes sense to run away and look for health packs. There is an elegant simplicity to being able to tell the AI exactly what to do when those situations pertain. Of course, the tricky part is determining whether or not the situation truly pertains—in our previous example, for instance, if the player were nearly dead, then standing and fighting might be a better option—but we will leave that for the next section.

The disadvantage of procedural AI is that, as researchers have discovered in creating AI for a game as deceptively simple as chess, there is a limit to the complexity of AI that can be written in this way. Beyond that point, increasing the complexity of the AI causes the size (and fragility) of the code to grow at an alarming rate. The result tends to be either relatively simple characters (such as those found in a game such as *World of Warcraft* or *Neverwinter Nights*) or relatively few distinct characters (such as in your average FPS).

Scripted AI

In many ways, scripted AI represents the ultimate in procedural AI. A well-designed scripting language gives the developers the tools they need to have straightforward, explicit control over the AI. Scripts are comparatively easy to write, easy to balance, and easy to test. As a result, this architecture is extremely popular, particularly in games where AI needs to be created for a large number of individual characters in a short period of time (e.g., RPGs such as *Neverwinter Nights*).

The primary weakness of scripted AI is that it can easily result in characters whose behaviors are highly repetitive and predictable. Although modern scripting languages do support branching scripts and random selection, the use of these tends, by necessity, to be fairly simplistic. Worse, if a branching script results in expected behavior being unavailable for a reason that is not apparent to the player (e.g., the NPC will not give the player a quest), the result is often frustration rather than fun.

Finite State Machines (FSMs)

As we all know, an FSM is a collection of *states* and *transitions* between those states. The states typically represent actions that the AI can take (e.g., attack, retreat, search for health) or situations the AI can be in (e.g., going to the station, riding the sky tram, exiting the sky tram), and the transitions tell us when it is appropriate to shift from one state to another.

At first blush, FSMs appear to be an example of declarative AI. After all, they describe what the world is like (in terms of possible states that can pertain in that world). The difference is in what they do with that description. Rather than having the AI reason about the state it is in, the transitions provide a simple set of procedural rules for choosing a state, and further procedural code is written for each AI to tell the AI precisely what to do while in that state. In essence, an FSM can be summed up as a list of procedural rules that take the form, "When in state X, if condition A applies, then transition to state Y."

Like scripted AI, FSMs have some powerful advantages that help to explain their popularity. The division of the possibility space into states is a natural way for many people to think, making FSMs easy to understand. In addition, FSMs are dead simple to implement because at their core, they are just glorified switch statements. Finally, a fair number of middleware products have adopted this architecture, making it a natural choice for integrating with your tools.

Unfortunately, if we want to solve the sorts of problems alluded to in the introduction, FSMs have some distinct problems. First, they scale poorly because the number of transitions is exponential on the number of states. It's easy to think that we can avoid this problem by keeping the number of transitions per state small, but the problem is that the intelligence is in the transitions. If there is no transition between two states, then there is no way to take the actions represented by one when the AI is in the other. For example, if an FPS AI is in a state without a transition to the "attack" state, and it encounters the player, it won't be able to engage him. Furthermore, the duplication of logic between transitions leading into a single state can result in rampant duplication of code. Finally, FSMs can only be in one state at a time, which means that they produce AI that can only do one thing at a time. If you need to be able to control multiple resources in a coordinated fashion (in a squad-based FPS, sports, or strategy game, for example), then this limitation can make things difficult.

In fairness to state machines, a number of extensions are available that can help to solve these problems, some of which might even be classified as declarative AI. The key thing to look for is an architecture that allows you to define the parameters used to make a decision in a general way, rather than forcing you to enumerate every situation the AI can react to and the action it should take in each case.

Goal-Based AI

Goal-based AI is an example of a declarative AI architecture that has been used in a number of successful games over the years (*Zoo Tycoon 2*, *The Sims*, and *Empire Earth 2* and *3*, to name just a few). We will discuss the architecture briefly and then look at ways to overcome the most commonly mentioned challenges in its creation.

Architecture

Numerous other sources (e.g., [Millington06]) discuss the details of goal-based AI, so we will keep our description brief.

Like an FSM, goal-based AI begins by defining a list of possible actions we can take. We call them *goals* rather than *states* but use them in similar ways. For example, an RTS game might have goals to attack, defend, and explore. In a game such as *Zoo Tycoon 2*, an animal might have a goal to satisfy its hunger or to play with other animals in its exhibit. Note that our goals, and particularly the ways we reason about them, are somewhat different from a deliberative planning architecture, such as Orkin's goal-oriented action planning [Orkin05].

The difference between this architecture and an FSM is the way that goals are selected. Whereas an FSM uses Boolean logic, goal-based AI instead assigns a priority (sometimes called an "insistence") to each goal and then selects the goal with the highest priority. If we have sufficient resources, we might even pursue multiple goals simultaneously (e.g., attack with one set of units while exploring with another), but we will always pursue the highest-priority goals that are available.

One significant advantage of goal-based AI is that it uses a float value for arbitrating between competing choices, rather than a simple Boolean. This might seem like a minor difference, but the additional expressiveness means that it can consider a much wider variety of complex factors when choosing from a large selection of options.

Although a Boolean expression can be arbitrarily complex internally, it is, at best, an awkward format for expressing subtle weightings of various factors. To illustrate this point, let's return to our FPS example where we had an NPC that was low on health and under attack, trying to decide what to do.

The priority of a "retreat" goal would presumably be based on the NPC's tactical situation (i.e., his health, whether he is under attack, what weapon he is using, what weapon the player is using, how much ammo he has, etc.), so it is going to be fairly high in this situation.

Similarly, one of the factors that contributes to the priority of the "attack" goal might be the player's current health. This priority consideration might be fairly low under normal conditions but increase exponentially when the player's health is very low. Thus, the NPC might decide to "go for it" and stay to fight (that is, the "attack" goal's priority might win out).

Now imagine writing the Boolean expression for this relatively simple decision. We can't simply say "fight if the player's health is below 25%" because then the NPC would stay even if it was at 5% while the player was at 25%. On the other hand, we can't say "run if your health is lower than the player's" because then the NPC will run away immediately if the player gets the first shot off. Certainly this logic could be condensed into a Boolean expression if we worked at it long enough—but then we would be back to exactly the sort of convoluted, case-specific logic that we are trying to escape!

Using float-based logic also allows us to optimize the allocation of resources (such as units or money) in a simple way. If we build a prioritized list of all active goals, we can simply work down the list and arbitrarily assign enough available resources to satisfy as many of the highest-priority goals as possible. This is not likely to generate the best possible resource allocation, however. For example, sometimes it is better to accomplish two lower priority goals than one higher priority one. Similarly, it is usually better to assign units that are already located in the area where the goal will take place. Thus, we can make one or more optimization passes where we consider moving resources between goals, trying to maximize the total priority in the system. This technique has been used to good effect in RTS games in the past [Dill05].

Another advantage of goal-based AI is that the selection logic is placed on the goal (or, more specifically, the priority calculation for the goal) rather than on the transition between a specific pair of goals. As a result, every possible action can be considered on every update. We do not have to worry that a missing transition will prevent the NPC from taking appropriate action in an unusual situation because a transition is always implicit in the priority of the goal (although if you want to explicitly prevent a particular transition, you can certainly do so by setting the priority to zero in that case).

This placement of the selection logic also means that the complexity of goal-based AI scales in a much more reasonable fashion as the size of the AI grows. It would be an exaggeration to say that it scales linearly because we do have to worry about the interactions between goals when balancing the priorities, but it is much closer to linear than we get with FSMs. In addition, there is no duplication of transitions, which means that the resulting code duplication is eliminated as well. Finally, because all of the intelligence is in the priority calculations, it is trivial to move that information into a data file and allow designers or even play testers to balance the AI.

The main disadvantage of goal-based AI is a side effect of its greatest strength. Thinking about AI decisions as a "bucket of floats" is significantly less intuitive than thinking about them as a set of discrete decisions, each of which can be implemented with custom code. Overcoming this challenge is the subject of the next section.

Balancing Priorities

Goal-based AI derives its strength from the ability of its priority functions to combine a large variety of factors into a single value, which can then be compared to other values in order to decide what to do. The challenge is to balance those factors in a way that yields behavior that appears intelligent rather than random or demented.

Other sources (e.g., [Dill06]) discuss at some length how to generate the numbers that go into priority calculations. Here we will focus instead on tools and techniques that can be used to manage the complexity of balancing the priorities for different goals.

Shared Conventions

It is helpful to have explicit conventions about the values that are reasonable. For example, in an RTS, we might say that exploration should generally have a priority of roughly 250, whereas attack goals will have priorities ranging from 0 to 800, and defend goals will have priorities ranging from 100 to 1000. Further, we might decide that the value of an attack goal is doubled after the enemy is engaged, making it easier to decide whether to break off an attack to rush to defend your own cities. These shared conventions help you to design the expected behavior of your AI before you delve into the specifics of writing priority calculations. They also make it easy to look at the values actually being generated and recognize situations where priorities are too high or low. Finally, shared conventions simplify coordination between multiple AI developers.

Bonuses, Multipliers, and Exponents

Getting balance right requires the ability to tweak the relative value of all the factors that feed in to priority calculations. One trick is to allow developers to apply an additive bonus, a multiplier, and/or an exponent to every value that goes into the priority calculation, including the final priority for each goal. This results in a powerful, easy way to balance the importance of each consideration.

Big Numbers for Big Decisions

One common complaint about goal-based AI is that it is difficult to debug because every priority has to be considered in the context of every other priority. There are two answers to this. First, we often have goals that use completely different resources (e.g., building a mine uses engineers, whereas defending that mine uses military units) and hence do not interfere with one another. Second, even goals that use the same resources can usually be divided into sets of goals that are essentially disjoint. For example, a puppy game might have one set of goals for peeing (e.g., pee on the carpet, scratch to be let out) and another for playing (e.g., play with the ball, take the ball to the player to throw, chase my tail). If we use big numbers for big decisions (e.g., whether to pee or play) and small numbers for small decisions (e.g., whether to play with the ball or chase my tail), then we can balance them in isolation.

Debugging Tools

The value of good debugging tools cannot be overemphasized. For example:

Graphical Debugging Tools: If a decision is based on the position, rotation, or movement of objects in the game, then find a way to display that graphically. For example, a sports game might only pass to a receiver if no nearby opposing players are in front of him, and the nearest player behind him is at least 3 feet away. We can display arrows on the players to indicate their linear velocity, and circles around the receivers to show the area that needs to be clear of opponents.

Statistical Analysis: It is useful to run the game for a while and then do a statistical analysis of the priorities generated. What were the minimum, maximum, and average priorities for each type of goal? What was the standard deviation? This information can be used to validate your shared conventions and to provide insight into the use of bonuses, multipliers, and exponents.

Priority Spam: Sometimes you just have to dig into the raw numbers. To this end, there needs to be a way to see the overall priority of each goal, so that you can see explicitly what was considered and what was selected. There also needs to be a way to see the calculations that go into each of those priorities, so that you can see why the decision went the way it did. This can result in a huge amount of data, so be careful how much of it you store and ensure that you have the ability to turn it off when it is not needed.

Replay: If at all possible, find a way to replay the game, generating the same player inputs automatically and using the same random number seeds. This will allow you to revisit a buggy situation and drill down on it over and over until you can find the problem and fix it. Then you can replay that same situation with the new logic and make sure that the fix worked. This same technology can be used to give players a "film" of the game, which they can replay to their heart's content.

Data-Driven Design

To achieve rapid iteration, it is critical that the AI be data driven, so that it can be balanced without recompiling the code. This also allows the values to be edited by designers or even modified by players to create custom AI. The *Kohan* games, created by TimeGate studios, are examples of games using a goal-based architecture that have had particularly good success with player-created AI.

Hybrid Architectures

Goal-based AI does very well in dynamic situations where it needs to be able to interpret the game state and react appropriately. There are some cases, however, where there is a clear "Right Thing" to do. In those cases, it can make sense to combine this architecture with more procedural architectures.

Hierarchical Implementations

The most obvious way to combine architectures is to implement them hierarchically. For example, in *Zoo Tycoon 2*, if a guest chooses to ride on a sky tram, then he will run a mini-FSM that has the guest go to the tram station, board the sky tram, ride to the destination, and then exit from the sky tram.

Similarly, you can imagine a strategy game in which the high-level actions (whether to attack, defend, or explore, for example) are selected using an FSM, and then goal-based AI is used to select a target (or targets) for those actions. At Blue Fang, we have found a technique similar to this to be useful in our next generation of animal AI.

We have also considered (but not implemented) the use of similar techniques with scripts. Possibilities here include the following:

- Letting a goal execute a script.
- Letting a script set a variable that can be used to influence the priority of a goal.
- Letting the priority evaluation on a goal call a script and use that script to calculate its value.

Overwhelming Bonuses

Another way to apply procedural logic to goal-based AI is to use an overwhelmingly high (or low) priority. For example, if your shared convention is that the AI will only assign priorities between 0 and 1000, then you can set the priority of a goal to 10,000 if you want to force it to happen. In *Kohan 2*, there are certain buildings that should always be built together in a certain order as early as possible. This was enforced by using *build templates* [Dill06]. After the AI decided to apply a build template in a particular situation, the template would set the priority for building the corresponding buildings to be overwhelmingly high.

There are also times when you want to prevent the AI from taking actions that will look stupid (whether they are really stupid or not). For example, it almost always looks like a mistake to withdraw undamaged units from combat—even if they are on their way to satisfy a high-priority goal. To prevent this from happening, you can simply set the priority for any goal (other than a retreat) that would use an engaged unit to zero.

The values used for overwhelming bonuses should be part of your shared conventions. You might even use multiple different overwhelming bonuses to create a hierarchy of forced goals.

Related Work

Goal-based AI is not the only way to approach declarative game AI. The following are a few other areas of research that seem to be producing good results.

Planning

Goal-oriented action planning [Orkin05] has caused something of a stir in the game AI community in the past few years. It is similar to goal-based AI except that it uses a planning architecture rather than priorities to select goals. A similar approach is *hierarchical task network planning* [Gorniak07].

Intelligent Scripting

Scripting remains a powerful and useful technique for generating AI, particularly if you need to generate AI for a lot of characters in a short amount of time. Approaches that seek to improve the intelligence and utility of scripting include *ScriptEase* [Cutumisu06] and *dynamic scripting* [Spronck06].

Terrain Analysis

Terrain analysis is not an architecture in its own right but rather a collection of techniques for generating useful information and decisions about the game map. Although not the topic of this article, good terrain analysis is essential to achieve the cunning opponents and responsive allies alluded to in the introduction to this article. Many publications discuss terrain analysis as it relates to computer games [Pottinger00, Forbus02, Higgins02, Dill04, Jurney07].

Conclusion

The intent of this article is to inspire you to reconsider the ways that you think about game AI. Instead of writing AI that explicitly tells the AI what to do, write AI that tells the AI about the factors it should weigh, and let it do the thinking. Instead of writing AI that behaves predictably, write AI that can behave in emergent, unpredicted ways—but in ways that are both intelligent and appropriate to the situation at hand.

We have discussed two of the most common procedural AI architectures in use today and one popular declarative AI architecture. Many other declarative architectures exist in the academic AI community, and you are encouraged to do further research to find the techniques that are most appropriate for their particular game.

References

[Cutumisu06] Cutumisu, Maria, et al., "Generating Ambient Behaviors in Computer Role-Playing Games." *IEEE Journal of Intelligent Systems*, Vol. 21, no. 5 (Sep/Oct 2006): pp. 19–27.

[Dill04] Dill, Kevin, et al., "Performing Qualitative Terrain Analysis in *Master of Orion 3*" *AI Game Programming Wisdom 2*, Charles River Media, 2004: pp 391–397.

[Dill05] Dill, Kevin, "A Goal-Based Architecture for Opposing Player AI." *Proceedings of the First Artificial Intelligence and Interactive Digital Entertainment Conference*, (June 2005): pp 33–38.

[Dill06] Dill, Kevin, "Prioritizing Actions in a Goal-Based RTS AI." *AI Game Programming Wisdom 3*, Charles River Media, 2006: pp. 321–330.

[Forbus02] Forbus, Kenneth D., Mahoney, James V., and Dill, Kevin, "How Qualitative Spatial Reasoning Can Improve Strategy Game AIs." *IEEE Journal of Intelligent Systems*, Vol. 17, no. 4 (July/August 2002): pp. 25–31.

[Gorniak07] Gorniak, Peter, and Davis, Ian, "SquadSmart: Hierarchical Planning and Coordinated Plan Execution for Squads of Characters." *Proceedings of the Third Artificial Intelligence and Interactive Digital Entertainment Conference*, (June 2007): pp. 14–19.

[Higgins02] Higgins, Daniel, "Terrain Analysis in an RTS—The Hidden Giant." *Game Programming Gems 3*, Charles River Media, 2002: pp. 268–284.

[Jurney07] Jurney, Chris, and Hubick, Shelby, "Dealing with Destruction: AI from the Trenches of *Company of Heroes*." *Proceedings of the Game Developers Conference*, 2007.

[Millington06] Millington, Ian, *Artificial Intelligence for Games*. Morgan Kaufmann Publishers, 2006: pp. 376–402.

[Orkin05] Orkin, Jeff, "Agent Architecture: Considerations for Real-Time Planning in Games." *Proceedings of the First Artificial Intelligence and Interactive Digital Entertainment Conference*, (June 2005): pp. 105–110.

[Pottinger00] Pottinger, Dave C., "Terrain Analysis in Real-Time Strategy Games." *Proceedings of the Game Developers Conference*, 2000.

[Spronck06] Spronck, Pieter, et al., "Adaptive Game AI with Dynamic Scripting." *Machine Learning*, Vol. 63, no. 3 (2006): pp. 217–248.

[Wikipedia07] Wikipedia, "Declarative Programming." Available online at *http://en.wikipedia.org/wiki/Declarative_programming*, August 21, 2007.

3.3

The MARPO Methodology: Planning and Orders

Brett Laming—Rockstar Leeds

brett@tilda.plus.com

This article and associated demo elaborate on a previously outlined AI design paradigm [Laming03] nicknamed MARPO (Movement, Avoidance, Routing, Planning, and Orders). Resting on the premise that AI architectures, regardless of genre, tend to include certain key building blocks and interfaces, MARPO abstracts these genre-independent concepts to create a design framework that produces flexible and manageable AI from first principles.

This article introduces the planning side of MARPO and its foundational principles. By imposing various design restrictions, it shows how to create a clean goal-based hierarchical state machine that embraces some aspects of academic rule-based reasoning systems. It also addresses common pitfalls at this behavioral level, showing how maintaining strong MARPO discipline maximizes efficiency, flexibility, manageability, and successfulness of the end result. The associated demo on the CD-ROM demonstrates this technique and its modular approach.

ON THE CD

A Brief Introduction to MARPO

MARPO was originally formed as a design strategy for maximizing the chances of producing solid AI from first principles. It aims to generalize, mostly from experience, the best practice of writing AI across different genres, titles, and platforms. It consists of a number of core observations and principles, some of which have been detailed previously [Laming03].

The MARPO Mantra

AI implementations are notoriously difficult to generalize. Genres exhibit different approaches and trends, titles require different game data, and platforms have different limitations. In addition, to make for a better title, even the most generic AI architecture needs to be tailored to the specific needs of the game in question.

Thankfully, ideas, as opposed to implementation specifics, generalize more easily, and it is these ideas that underlie MARPO. The entire MARPO methodology is based on four important observations:

- If implemented with a degree of discipline, AI lends itself nicely to compartmentalization resulting in a series of self-contained black boxes, or *components*, from which we build an AI *circuit*. Although the internals can be quite complex and different, the inputs and outputs, if kept properly self-contained, should form neat finite interfaces that are inherently understandable.

- Within AI systems, the flow of information, per frame or iteration, is predominantly one way. Information about the *game state* flows downward through the AI circuit, being sequentially digested by the black boxes into increasingly manageable data. The end result of this digestion is a subsequent change back to the game state. This lends itself to a multitiered hierarchical approach to AI, which promotes increased manageability via techniques such as individual tier diagnostics.

- AI is almost always applied to an individual—a sentient thing in the game world. Although group behavior is common in AI, it is almost always modeled as communication between a set of individuals. For the purpose of this article, we will call these entities *actors*. As with most systems, an *actor* applies its AI independently on each frame.

- Across genres, games, and platforms, a number of key interfaces can be identified that respect unidirectional information flow. MARPO identifies five of these interfaces as being important, Movement, Avoidance, Routing, Planning, and Orders. At these points, the flow of information is so well defined that it can be seen to generalize across titles regardless of genre.

The MARPO Interfaces

The MARPO interfaces are described here:

Orders: At its highest level, the AI is ordered to perform some task. These orders might come from the player ("cover me"), from a script ("attack the player"), or from the game itself ("perform ambient behavior"). The AI doesn't need to know where the order came from—just what it is trying to do so that it can plan. At this level, scripting languages exert their influence, with designers giving the highest-level orders to produce custom AI for their circumstances.

Planning: This tier takes input in the form of an order and plans how to realize it. This is one of the least easy tiers to generalize. The planning tier, and the amount of emphasis it receives, will be highly dependent on both title and genre. One factor we can generalize is movement. With few exceptions, planning is going to tell the actor to move to a particular *target position*.

Routing: Given that we need to move to a target position, we need to work out how to get there while navigating any static environment. This is the level of the A* algorithm [Matthews02] or other navigation solutions. Although it is also highly genre-specific, its output is well defined. It breaks down the journey into one or more *waypoints*. These are given to the actor in sequence, the combined effect being to take us to our desired destination.

Avoidance: Given a waypoint to head for, we now need to navigate the dynamic environment. This is the realm of *object avoidance* and, if there is any deviation off our path, further *static avoidance* of the environment. The output of this tier is an adjusted target position that steers us away from trouble.

Movement: Given a desired target position, we now need to calculate the inputs to the simulation and physics that cause our actor to head for that position. This involves finding an inverse kinematics (IK) solution for the physics, usually via some type of control system. These inputs might come from a simple heuristic or a PID controller [Forrester03]. Its ultimate output is a collection of *control inputs* that drive the simulation to produce the desired effect.

MARPO Good Practice

In addition to these key interfaces, various common sense principles have evolved within MARPO to help produce and maintain reliable AI.

Game AI quickly grows beyond easy human diagnosis; this is part of its beauty. Much has been made of this "emergent behavior" in recent years, and it is an integral part of pleasing AI. But at some stage, someone is going to ask, "What is the AI doing?" and expect an answer that you cannot provide. At times like this, it is important that the AI can justify its behavior to you, so having a good debugging system in place [Laming03] is essential.

As AI grows in complexity, it becomes hard to establish what is behavioral nuance and what is implementation error. As the title grows, it is increasingly important that the foundational building blocks work as expected. Using a modular approach allows us to test a component independently, by variation of its inputs. An assert system is used to protect input and output at our interfaces.

The relationship between AI and gameplay is extremely symbiotic. To be efficient, direct communication between the AI and game engine is essential. Expecting to keep a working copy of game state for the AI is both unrealistic and inefficient. But AI that is too entwined with gameplay is difficult to debug and hard to encapsulate. As such, we compromise and say that AI can query the game state arbitrarily but cannot modify it. The rest of the simulation can alter the game state, but only using output from the AI, not by inspection of the AI itself.

A consequence of this is that a strict divide is formed between AI and simulation. If we consign simulation control input solely to the output of the AI delivered through the movement interface, we maintain a clear simulation divide. By clever use of constrained public interfaces and const keywords, we limit the AI to read-only access.

The Basic Architecture

At this stage, we are in a position to define two of the most important components of the AI: the virtual yoke and the target class.

The Virtual Yoke

The primary role of the *virtual yoke* is to deliver control inputs to the simulation, fulfilling the need for a movement interface. Its secondary role is to provide *direction* for the other game subsystems. The yoke's design comes from similarities observed between the AI and player control of an actor.

Table 3.3.1   Per-Frame Processing of the Human Player and AI Actors

Human Player	AI Actor
The player takes audiovisual input that provides insight into the current game state.	The AI queries the current game state to access information.
The player processes this input and prepares to act.	The AI digests this information through the MARPO interfaces and prepares its control inputs.
The player acts through a human interface device, providing control inputs to the simulation.	The AI provides the control inputs to the simulation through the movement interface.
The simulation executes without accessing the player's brain.	The simulation executes without inspection of the AI's internal state.

Following MARPO, Table 3.3.1 shows that our AI directly mimics the per-frame input, output, and restrictions of the player. Taking this concept further provides the following:

- AI control output, being no different from player output, should drive simulation through the same device, essentially a virtual controller or *yoke* for the AI. AI and player control are then directly interchangeable: the AI setting the yoke through its tiered processing, the player setting the yoke directly from the physical pad mapping.
- The simulation cannot access the player's brain. Good design also prohibits it from inspecting the AI's internals. Hence, it is driven solely by control input. Except for optimizations, then, gameplay logic should remain totally independent of the nature of our actor. In an ideal world, there would be no player-specific behavior.
- Forcing both player and AI to drive the simulation through the virtual yoke has a number of advantages. The virtual yoke probably exists already. Most games have some notion of a physical input device mapping onto a virtual controller to facilitate multiple control schemes. It allows the player and AI to seamlessly take control of any actor, which is great for autopilots, in-game cutscenes, or AI possession mechanics.
- Provided we maintain actor independence, the AI will perform actions just like the player. This is great for believability and immersion, a holy grail in today's AI world.

- Keeping the simulation code independent of AI and player means we only need to create one code path, and we can get rid of many traditional `IsPlayer()`-style conditionals.
- Finally, although initially harder to adjust to and implement, thinking about AI in terms of pad input changes how we write AI, leading to a much more "human" approach.

The simple virtual yoke of our demo looks as follows:

```
struct sVirtualYoke
{
    sVirtualYoke() : mGas(0), mSteer(0), mbCraft(0),
            mbUse(0) {}
    tFloat mGas;
    tFloat mSteer;

    tBool mbCraft : 1;
    tBool mbUse : 1;
};
```

The yoke provides a combined interface shared by both AI and player. Both parties will impart their own properties to the structure as the game grows. For example, mGas and mSteer were added immediately to store the player's directional pad input (which the AI needs to replicate). By contrast, mbCraft was added later to allow our AI to attempt to craft objects in our demo, but there is no reason why the player could not map a control to this input and have the same functionality.

We mentioned previously that the yoke is responsible for *directing* other components of the game engine such as the camera, animation, and sound subsystems. This is necessary to produce the complex realism demanded by today's games and maintain strong timing control over AI actions and audiovisual output. Intended to grow rapidly, without need for storage over the frame, the yoke transmits any information needed to achieve this role even down to individual timing or animation blends. In essence, we are answering questions such as "where should my animations be now?" before they need to be asked.

The Target Class

The notion of target position or waypoint has been referred to many times, and many interfaces use it as part of their input and output. As a location to move to, it is often viewed as a position in the world, but there are many times when we want our AI to go to another entity, follow a path node, or get within a certain radius. Unfortunately, it is still too common to find these cases handled separately, even though they represent the same thing—an arbitrary position in the world, albeit one that can change each frame.

Target needs, regardless of genre, usually fall into a set pattern. We start with a base of reference. Common bases include world positions, an entity, or a path node, giving us our initial position. We apply any local vector offset to the target (e.g., 3 meters to its left). We then apply any *approach radius* (e.g., get within 10 meters) backward along the vector to our reference entity to give us a final position to aim for.

The demo target class, cTarget, is designed to encompass these requirements. The class is self-contained, takes a limited amount of input (a reference entity), provides finite output (a world position), and can reason about what it is doing by use of a debug function—a classic MARPO component. Its primary purpose is to allow us to combine similar AI instructions so that "go to position" is now no different than "go to entity."

```
class cTarget
{
public:
    // Initial setup
    void Set( const sVec &position );
    void Set( const cEntity &entity );
    // ...

    // True if the given entity completes this frame -
    // should take into account velocity etc...
    bool IsCompleting( const cEntity &entity ) const;

    // The world position [output] to head for.
    sVec WorldPos( const cEntity &entity ) const;

    // Debug function - what we are currently doing.
    void Debug( const cEntity &entity,
                sRGBA baseColour,
                sRGBA aimColour ) const;

private:
    enum eComponents
    {
        C_Entity            = 0x01,
        C_WorldPosition     = 0x02,
        F_Radius            = 0x04,
        F_LocalOffset       = 0x08
    };

    // Various parameters - can union to save space.

    sVec            mOffset;
    const cEntity *mpEntity;
    tFloat          mRadius;

    // Component flags
    tNat8           mComponents;
};
```

In addition to its initial parameters, cTarget also maintains a *completion radius*. Although not responsible for the target position itself, it defines a radius from the final computed point, inside which we are said to have obtained our target. Although this could go in client code, we justify its storage here on the grounds that most uses of cTarget will involve entities arriving close to the target.

The Think/Act Loop

Having explored the advantages of separating AI and simulation and having decided on the virtual yoke to communicate between the two, we can now define the update loop for our actors. As the AI drives the simulation, and the flow is unidirectional inside our once-per-frame Update() method, dubbed the Think()/Act() loop, the loop is extremely simple:

```
sVirtualYoke yoke;
Think(yoke, dt);  // Yoke passed by reference
Act(yoke, dt);    // Yoke passed by const reference
```

For any given frame time dt, a fresh yoke input is filled in by the Think function, which queries the AI or the player, and is then enacted in the Act function, which contains the rest of the simulation.

Debugging and Testing

Even in this simple demo, some notion of debugging and modular integrity is necessary. We will handle this in two ways. First, we put in place assert and debugging facilities. The debugging facility in this demo (cDebug) is, in essence, a large display list that allows for delayed direct rendering. This means we can debug intermediary calculations at their point of instantiation, without having to explicitly record them for the render loop. For further ideas, see [Laming03].

Second, we test each component as it is built. In our case, we use the debugging facilities to test the target class, using both a world position and an entity-based target. By directly plugging player input into the virtual yoke, we also test the Think()/Act() loop. You can play with the targets in Example1.cpp on the CD-ROM.

ON THE CD

The Movement, Avoidance, and Routing Tiers

Having verified the simulation with player input, the remaining AI components are built using a bottom-up approach allowing each component and tier to be tested piecewise. However, as planning is the primary focus of this article, we will limit the discussion to the remaining tiers.

The first three tiers in the demo are represented by the following functions:

```
// Routing
tBool GetCurrentWaypoint( const cTarget &in,
                const cEntity &entity,
                cTarget &out );
```

```
// Avoidance
tBool ApplyDynamicAvoidance( const cTarget &in,
                 cTarget &out);
tBool ApplyStaticAvoidance( const cTarget &in,
                 cTarget &out);

// Movement
void SolveIKTo( const cTarget &target,
        const cEntity &entity,
        tFloat dt,
        const sPropertySheet &propSheet,
        sVirtualYoke &yoke );
```

Routing and avoidance are not implemented. Routing in our demo environment is not particularly complicated—the world is mostly empty—and a full discussion of dynamic avoidance is outside the scope of this article. However, as information flow is unidirectional, we keep the method stubs so that they can be easily added later. Currently, each takes and passes back the same target.

The movement tier always needs implementation, however. Its purpose is to resolve, for any given `entity` and entity property sheet (`propSheet`), a target position (`target`) into movement control inputs for the virtual yoke (`yoke`) over the given frame time (`dt`). In the case of the demo, this means determining the correct `mGas` and `mSteer` values.

Solving this tier can often be complicated and, as with a lot of IK problems, usually results in an approximated solution that mostly holds. For our simple demo, where the actors can turn quite quickly, this problem can be solved with a near perfect solution by making use of equations of motion. However, because it's not the main focus of this demo, the rationale behind its derivation will be left for another time. Its methods can be found in `AIIK.cpp`.

Now that we have our IK in place, it is time to test the new components. By supplying a temporary dummy target position to the `SolveIKTo` and leaving debugging on the target, we can observe the AI on the move.

The Task System

With the MAR tiers of MARPO handled, debugging in place, and our components tried and tested, we can now move onto the planning tier, the main focus of this article. Similar architectural solutions have been derived before [Gilgenbach06, Johnson06] and provide a useful comparison.

Our planning system consists of a goal-based, hierarchical finite state machine designed to combine the simplicity, understandability, and elegance of the finite state machine (FSM) with the power of more academic rule-based reasoning. In doing so, we will build an efficient modular planning system, flexible enough to accommodate different AI approaches while remaining easily comprehensible.

The Finite State Machine (FSM)

The FSM is unarguably still the bedrock of AI components. Although other alternatives have gained favor recently [Orkin06, Isla05], the expression of AI output in terms of finite actions will ensure, at some level, that FSMs remain a key component of AI systems. Easy to understand and modular in design, the FSM is a natural representation of control flow. Many critically acclaimed titles have been built around the FSM, and the approach is well documented through game literature [Fu03]. Like it or not, ask any designer and chances are that the notion of finite control flow, regardless of implementation specifics, will be the preferred way of describing the behavior the designer wants.

It would be foolish to ignore this fact. Having designers onboard and being able to meet their specific requirements ensures that everybody is happy. They are, after all, the principle clients of your AI toolbox. That said, a multitude of post-mortems on even the best-intentioned FSM systems reveals that common mistakes are being alarmingly repeated.

An example that illustrates most of the problem points is *Grand Theft Auto's (GTA)* paramedic. Death happens a lot in the predominantly FSM-driven *GTA* world. Actors can, and generally are, run over or killed by vehicles at the most inopportune times. Regardless of what it was doing, the actor is told it is dead—so whatever myriad of states an actor is in, it needs to handle this case.

Suppose we have a state DEAD that we immediately transition to when death occurs. Could this sudden change leave our previous state in a bad internal state? For example, if death happens when we are getting in a car, whose responsibility is it to unbook the seat? If the paramedic resurrects us, what state do we return to? If we had been attacking someone, for example, we don't want to just wander off.

A clever approach to solving this problem is to maintain a stack of previous states. The DEAD state is pushed onto the stack and popped off again, should we be resurrected. This sounds like a neat solution, but what about the storage required? It is, after all, not just the state that needs to be stored but also any target we might have had at the time and any other properties that customized it—and to make matter worse, we need such a stack for each actor in the world.

We could of course offload some parameterization to individual states, KILL_ALLOWING_FLEE, for example. But won't this lead to state proliferation and confusion? How can we share the same code across multiple states, without littering the code with unwieldy State() == KILL_ALLOWING_FLEE style conditionals?

Another alternative is to have each state handle the fact that we are dead, indicated by a member property of the actor. This might be great for understanding the event coverage of a state, but are all those extra IsDead() checks going to cramp efficiency and readability? Is adding each global state as a property going to bloat our actor?

In general then, if we are to follow the FSM approach so favored by designers, we need a system that can handle the previous cases. This gives us a chance to define some new design principles.

- The planning system needs the ability to react to critical events that can temporarily take control away from the current state at any time.
- It needs to be able to safely return to its previous state and resume processing following any immediate reactions to these events.
- Minimizing code repetition is highly desirable, especially where it involves conditional logic. Later addition of a missing conditional on instances of duplicated code generates some of the worst problems to track down.
- As a direct result, conditional logic should be kept encapsulated and minimal to improve code readability, maximize performance, and minimize potential problems later.
- State parameterization is generally more desirable than state proliferation. Having fewer states minimizes confusion and maximizes code reuse.
- To be memory efficient and easily comprehensible, only information pertinent to existing states should be kept around.

Goal-Based Reasoning

What do we mean by goal-based reasoning? The simplest definition is the achievement of a high-level *goal* by repeated decomposition into smaller and smaller *subgoals* until each can be seen to represent a finite sequence of *actions*.

One technique that has had great success solving problems of this ilk in academic circles is goal-based reasoning, a subset of rule-based reasoning [Bratko90, Hopgood00]. We will briefly describe the traditional academic approach here before discussing its strengths and weaknesses.

A traditional academic rule-based reasoning system consists of three main parts: working memory, a rule base, and an inference engine. The working memory consists of our actor's knowledge about the world and a list of goals it is trying to achieve.

The rule base defines a collection of rules, each responsible for solving a particular goal and each with various preconditions. Should the preconditions *match* and a rule *fire*, it will generate a series of actions and possibly some additional subgoals. Rules can use wildcards and pattern matching for more general applicability (essentially a form of parameterization).

An example rule for driving to a location might read as follows:

(goal) actor drive to location and
(precondition) actor has vehicle then
(action) remove goal actor drive to location and
(action) vehicle at location.

A second rule might be the following:

(goal) actor drive to location and
(precondition) not actor has vehicle then
(subgoal) add goal actor get vehicle.

An inference engine works by choosing rules that match their preconditions to facts in the world. Firing a rule then creates actions that modify the working memory, changing facts about the world, and possibly producing new subgoals. On the next pass, these changes will probably match other rules, and this will continue until either the goal is solved, or we cannot find a rule that matches.

Often, more than one rule will match at any one time. Traditionally, academic inference engines, freed of tight real-time constraints, have used recursion to explore each possibility. If this type of inference engine ever reaches a state where it cannot fire any more rules but still has goals, it will backtrack (a handy byproduct of the recursive approach) and try another possibility. In essence, then, most academic inference engines take a brute force approach to reasoning, trying various rules in sequence until they find a solution that solves the given goal.

There are historically a number of problems with applying this academic technique to commercial games. First, it makes heavy use of recursion. This might be appropriate to the toy domain, but with a vast array of problems to solve and many potential rules to solve them, other techniques, such as time-slicing or A*-directed searching [Orkin06], are generally required. On top of this, the amount of memory required to store the game state during recursion grows exponentially.

Having said that, this approach does have a number of nice properties that we can exploit. First, each rule is self-contained. It needs little information about the bigger picture, just what is required by its preconditions and what is changed by its actions. By using subgoals, it allows someone else to take care of lower-level details. In terms of AI understandability, this is an extremely appealing trait because it allows us to define how to solve the task at hand without micromanagement. For example, if we have a goal to *get in a car,* and we *are not in a car*, we can generate the subgoals *find a car* and *enter the car.* That being done, we leave it to an inference engine to work out exactly how to *enter the car.*

In addition, we can get around the need for expensive search techniques because actions and their sequencing are often well defined. The *get in a car* goal makes no sense, for example, if we try *enter the car* before *find a car.* Because we know the order of actions and subgoals, we have already pruned our search tree without the need for an automated planner. As subgoals are, for the most part, executed sequentially, each goal only needs to act upon one subgoal at a particular time with our goal tree essentially becoming a goal queue.

In this example, our *get in a car* goal knows to put on *find a car* before *enter the car.* This is sensible knowledge to embed. By making use of an internal FSM whose states are directly linked to subgoals, *get in a car* can control the subgoal sequencing itself. Should we already have found a car, *get in a car* will realize this and immediately transition itself to the *enter car* state, putting on the *enter car* subgoal.

This notion of a task embodying a single rule is quite powerful, and one we will adopt. Conveniently, it follows the MARPO principles of self-containment with limited input—the working memory (our game state)—and limited output—actions (virtual yoke output), and subgoals (our child). If we restrict a task to only knowing about its children, as is implicit in most recursive rule-based reasoning systems, then we also maintain the desired one-way flow of information.

The only question remaining is what happens if we start exploring a solution that does not achieve the requested goal. In recursive rule-based reasoning systems, we simply backtrack to the original state before we made the decision. Unfortunately, we do not have that luxury, and to make matters worse, our current goal stack might become invalidated by factors outside our control—that car we were getting into just blew up, for example. The solution then is to start replanning again from the original goal. However, if we are to do this, we need to minimize the time required to get back to the state we were previously planning from. We will see shortly how this fits in neatly with our approach.

This results in the following ideas:

A task is a self-contained code component that replaces the traditional production system rule. As we lay no restrictions on it, a task could be a neural network, simple *if-then* rules, Bayesian reasoning, or a callback to script. As it is executed procedurally, the need to store an ongoing working memory is redundant—decisions are now made directly on the current game state. Although this may produce suboptimal results compared to other search-based planning systems, some argue that the player will often not notice. By allowing random choices of subgoals wherever possible and similar sequencing tricks [Isla05], it is possible to generate believable results. Considering that suboptimal plan generation often introduces more movement, a key output in making the AI look busy, we argue that the wins in terms of memory and searching overhead have so far outweighed the restrictions.

At any one time, a task is allowed to use a single subtask to help achieve its goal. The active subtask is determined by an internal FSM. Note that it is quite possible for a goal to require multiple subtasks and quite possible to keep around more than one subtask at a time, but in terms of processing, only one is active at a time. As a search-based inference engine considers each solution in sequence anyway, this has not yet caused a problem.

The previous role of pattern matching is now replaced with parameterization on construction. The notion of wildcard "binding" is replaced with task-specific storage, allowing generic parameterization within the scope of the task.

Because rules fire only if their preconditions are valid, our task will have a notion of validity. A task must monitor this over time, as events can happen that invalidate it. If a task becomes invalid, it will be removed. A similar action will occur on success.

The planning system needs to be able to wind itself forward to match the best task overview for any given game state. By returning the topmost task to an initial state and, from here, sequencing and continuously processing subtasks atomically in their respective orders until we succeed, fail, or are forced to wait (e.g., by a subtask waiting for arrival at a target), it is possible to return a task to its most relevant current state.

The Task Class

The core component of our planning system is the *task*. A task seeks to solve a particular goal by making use of subtasks and sending instructions to the simulation via the virtual yoke. The sequencing of subtasks is managed via an internal FSM. A direct correlation between the internal state and the currently running subtask has the handy side-effect of providing runtime type identification (RTTI) for our subtask pointer.

We can now see our cTask class starting to take shape.

```
virtual tBool IsValid(const sTaskIn &in) = 0;
virtual tBool HasCompleted( const sTaskIn &in ) = 0;
```

These are our validity checks. At any time, IsValid indicates whether we have failed, and HasCompleted indicates whether we have succeeded. The sTaskIn argument is just a wrapper for task-specific input and will be discussed shortly.

```
... Process(const sTaskIn &in, sTaskOut &out ) = 0;
```

This is the main process function that needs to be written for each task. The sTaskOut argument is simply the output equivalent of sTaskIn and will also be introduced shortly.

```
cTask *mpSubTask;

tNat mCurrentState;
tNat mNextState;
```

These hold our current subtask and corresponding internal FSM state. By explicitly keeping track of the next state to transition to, we can delay state change until safely outside each call to Process(). By knowing mCurrentState, we can also resolve mpSubTask to an appropriate concrete task.

```
eTaskStatus Update(const sTaskIn &in, sTaskOut &out);
```

This is the main update method, responsible for getting the given task up to date with the current game state. Its processing is shown in Figure 3.3.1.

A few things are worth noting.

- The Update() method forms an infinite loop (atomic processing), with termination only occurring because of success, failure, or the task requesting a wait. As touched on before, this gives us our immediate winding property to match the current game state.

- While we have a subtask, we will recurse on its Update() function, although we can still monitor the subtask, should we need to, using ProcessOverWatch(). This ensures subgoals are processed first and has the neat property that Process() is only called on a task in the absence of subtasks.
- We always get the opportunity to handle any subtask success or failure in OnSubTaskReturn() before it is destroyed, giving us a way to query subtask information before it disappears.

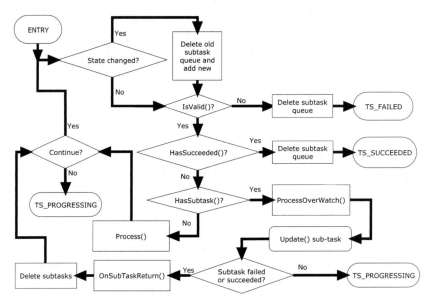

FIGURE 3.3.1   Flowchart showing the processing of cTask::Update().

Task Input and Output

Each task takes as input sTaskIn and gives as output sTaskOut. These are really just wrappers to allow future expansion. In the demo, sTaskOut simply wraps the virtual yoke, and sTaskIn identifies our actual actor.

Task Queues and the Task Hub

As mentioned before, tasks and their subtasks form a task queue, a simplified version of a goal tree. As tasks are linked in a queue anyway, our task queue cTaskQueue is simply a container for the root task and any subtask we might have pending.

Now if we draw an analogy between tasks and the notion of a traditional FSM state, we see a direct correlation with hierarchical FSMs. The state queue is a hierarchical representation of states, each of which is controlled by its own state machine. With such a strong correlation, it is important to ensure that we can address all the previously discussed problems with FSMs.

If we declare that tasks and subtasks will be added by dynamic allocation of instances of cTask-derived objects, then they can both be parameterized by member properties. When they are deleted again, this information no longer needs to be kept around. The winding property of Update() recognizes subtask sharing, and the ability to create arbitrary queues from subtasks leads as well to subtask sharing. This leaves us with the need to handle unexpected events that temporarily disrupt our processing. This is the responsibility of cTaskHub.

Consider a gang member running a *long-term goal* to get to a meeting point. While doing so, he comes under fire from an enemy that he decides to kill, giving himself a *reactive goal* to do so. In the process, he nearly gets run over by a car, yielding an *immediate goal* to roll out of the way. After he has rolled out of the way, he can go back to killing his enemy, before continuing to the meeting point.

We have three key goals here, each layered on top of and suppressing the behavior of another. We can implement this behavior as a series of prioritized task queues, with higher-priority queues suppressing lower-priority queues. In this example, we could have a long-term goal queue, a reactive queue, and an immediate action queue as shown in Figure 3.3.2.

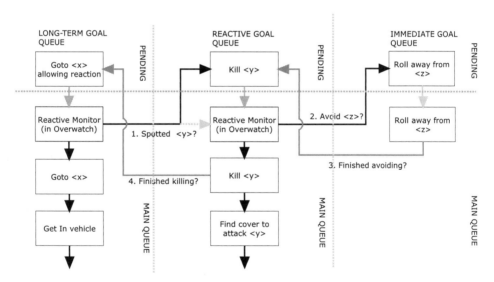

FIGURE 3.3.2   An illustration of temporary goal queue suppression.

The immediate queue would suppress the reactive queue, which would suppress any long-term queue. Similar task priority rerouting can be seen in other approaches [Isla05]. In this case, the task hub manages these queues.

It works by scanning an array of task queues in priority order until it finds a queue that is already running a root task or has one pending. If a pending task is found, then if it is on the same queue, it replaces the existing goal. If the task is on a different queue, we suppress the previous queue. This processing flow is summarized in Figure 3.3.3.

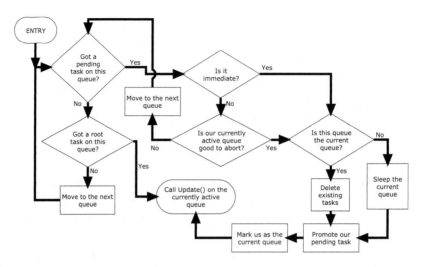

FIGURE 3.3.3   Flow chart for the task hub's management of the task queues.

At this point, we have defined the skeleton for our planning system. To flesh it out, we need to put it into context.

The Demo

ON THE CD

Hopefully you have already tried out examples 1 and 2 from the demo on the CD-ROM. The rest of the demo will show how it is possible to build a procedural planner using the techniques explored in the article to solve a simple alchemy problem. Consider a role-playing game scenario where we are interested in creating the material "white." In our simple world, we have a number of materials: yellow, red, blue, and green. Some of these are raw materials, others need to be created at a forge, and some just need our skills to craft them together. Let's assume that our actor has studied the tomes and already understands how to create the various components, as summarized in Table 3.3.2.

Table 3.3.2   Alchemy Rules Used in the Demo

End Product	Component 1	Component 2	Creation
Blue	-	-	Blue Mine
Green	-	-	Green Mine
Red	Green	Blue	Forged
Yellow	Red	Blue	Crafted
White	Yellow	Green	Forged

Given that our actor lives in a world consisting of blue mines, green mines, and forges, our end goal is to get him to create "white."

The journey begins at example 3 and will show how it is possible to sequence a series of `cTask`-derived classes into a `cTaskQueue` that, under the control of a `cTaskHub`, will solve the problem. It will illustrate how the solution is directed by sequential actions, random choice, and appropriate light recursion to grow a piecemeal solution in the absence of overall knowledge. In addition, it will justify its current action through debugging its current task queue.

The description for each example is in its source file, and you can enable the examples by following the instructions in `ExampleSwitch.h`.

Conclusion

This article summarized MARPO, a collection of common sense rules for maximizing the chances of creating good, maintainable AI from first principles. A byproduct of nine years of front-line AI experience, MARPO hopefully highlights the inherent beauty found in AI systems. The article also introduces a goal-based reasoning system, including the concept of goal queues, and shows how the common problems of multiple goals and prioritization can be solved simply and effectively using multiple queues.

References

[Bratko90] Bratko, Ivan, "*PROLOG: Programming for Artificial Intelligence.*" Addison-Wesley Publishers Ltd., 1990.

[Forrester03] Forrester, Euan, "Intelligent Steering Using PID Controllers." *AI Game Programming Wisdom 2*, Charles River Media, 2003.

[Fu03] Fu, Dan, and Houlette, Ryan, "The Ultimate Guide to FSMs in Games." *AI Game Programming Wisdom 2*, Charles River Media, 2003.

[Gilgenbach06] Gilgenbach, Matt, and McIntosh, Travis, "A Flexible AI System Through Behavior Compositing." *AI Game Programming Wisdom 3*, Charles River Media, 2006.

[Hopgood00] Hopgood, Adrian A., "*Intelligent Systems for Engineers and Scientists.*" CRC Press LLC, 2000.

[Isla05] Isla, Damian, "Managing Complexity in the *Halo 2* AI System." *Proceedings of the Game Developers Conference*, 2005.

[Johnson06] Johnson, Geraint, "Goal Trees." *AI Game Programming Wisdom 3*, Charles River Media, 2006.

[Laming03] Laming, Brett, "The Art of Surviving a Simulation Title." *AI Game Programming Wisdom 2*, Charles River Media, 2003.

[Matthews02] Matthews, James, "Generic A* Pathfinding." *AI Game Programming Wisdom*, Charles River Media, 2002.

[Orkin06] Orkin, Jeff, "Three States and a Plan: The A.I. of F.E.A.R.." *Proceedings of the Game Developers Conference*, 2006.

3.4

Getting Started with Decision Making and Control Systems

Alex J. Champandard—AiGameDev.com

alexjc@AiGameDev.com

Game developers have been using hierarchical finite state machines (HFSMs) to manage low-level conditions and actions for years [Fu03, Isla05]. Such systems are built from traditional state machines nested within each other, which mainly provide generalized transitions (i.e., transitions that apply to whole groups of states).

More recently, the industry has seen increasing adoption of behavior trees (BTs). Instead of using an FSM at every level of the hierarchy, BTs rely on simpler primitives, such as sequences and selectors, which improve scalability thanks to task-specific memory and depth-first search mechanisms.

Ultimately, however, what gives such systems their power is the ability to handle special cases by building hierarchies of custom tasks. This type of architecture is popular because it is a superset of both HFSMs and the original BTs, and, as such, is a good place to start for most games.

This article summarizes some of the best techniques for implementing such a decision-making and control system, including the following:

- Support for modular tasks with latent execution
- A framework for managing them concurrently
- Primitives for assembling hierarchies easily

The ideas presented here will prevent you from succumbing to common pitfalls when implementing BTs and help your implementation scale to better handle large data sets.

Building Blocks

No matter what features you build into your BT, getting the basics right will make a big difference in terms of extensibility and robustness. This section establishes the low-level primitives that can be used to assemble all types of behaviors.

Modular Tasks

When implementing AI, it is best to think in terms of control flow and computation rather than abstract terms such as "behaviors." The *task* primitive is a chunk of code that can be used in combination with other tasks to implement a behavior.

More specifically, think of a task as a *closure*: a function with its own execution context. In practice, these can be implemented as member functions of C++ object instances. Because tasks provide a modular way to manage computation, using tasks exclusively at the base of your AI engine enables the rest of the code to be much simpler and more flexible.

All other concepts in your decision-making and control system can be expressed as combinations of tasks. For example, a *condition* is a task without memory that gathers information from the game engine and usually returns immediately. An *action* is a task that makes changes to the world representation and executes for a short amount of time.

Latent Execution

A key feature for tasks in game engines is allowing them to run over multiple frames, known as *latent execution*. Technically speaking, this is called a *coroutine*; like a closure, a coroutine has its own execution environment, but it can interrupt itself during execution and temporarily return control to its owner. The next time the owner runs the coroutine, it resumes where it left off with the execution context intact.

C++ doesn't support this directly, so typically game developers end up with a compromise: an object with a single entry point that can be called multiple times, as shown in the following Task class. This is the simplest solution for providing lightweight coroutines because it delegates to the implementer of custom tasks the job of deciding which block of code to jump to from the single entry point.

```
class Task
{
public:
    virtual Status execute() = 0;
    virtual ~Task() {}
};
```

The Status object is used to specify whether the task has finished or is still running. It is also used as a way to signal the result of the computation to other behaviors.

Termination Status

Reasoning about the success and failure of current or hypothetical scenarios is the main purpose of any decision-making or control system. A *termination status* is a standard code that each task returns after it has completed to indicate its success or failure.

To determine what termination status codes are necessary, it helps to understand the three well-defined ways a behavior can terminate:

Completed successfully: The behavior accomplished its purpose and terminated without any problems. The world representation was modified as intended.

Failed cleanly: The behavior did *not* accomplish its purpose but still terminated cleanly. All problems were anticipated by the programmer, and all of the assumptions that were true before the behavior's execution still hold. This typically means that there were no side effects on the world representation.

Unexpected error: The behavior could not accomplish its purpose and broke the starting assumptions while trying to do so. There were side effects on the world representation; higher-level logic should take this into account.

For your system to make accurate decisions about tasks, it somehow needs information about these three different situations. There are three ways to implement this:

- Establish a convention that all tasks must fail cleanly if they encounter problems.
- Separate the process of deciding whether to run (which always fails cleanly) from the actual running (which may result in an error).
- Keep one entry point, and provide a return status for both kinds of failure.

The third approach is the most flexible and generic solution. It is also the simplest, so code using this API is less cluttered.

Support Framework

Having some robust principles at the core of an AI engine is a great start, but making sure they are used optimally is also important. To do this, it helps to centralize the most commonly used functionality.

Scheduler

The *scheduler* is responsible for managing tasks. It stores a list of active tasks and calls them one after another during its update. Owners of tasks can request them to be executed via the scheduler's API and no longer need to worry about managing them locally. As such, all the tasks are called by the scheduler, and the call stack remains constant regardless of the number of tasks.

This has many advantages:

- A variable C++ call stack is no longer required to update large trees of tasks. Overflow problems can be dealt with gracefully.
- The update can easily be suspended at any point or split across multiple frames.
- Using tasks is much easier. Client code becomes as simple as calling a run() function in the scheduler. Because the scheduler is the only class responsible for respecting the intricacies of the task API, the code also tends to be more reliable.
- Tasks can be monitored centrally, which is useful for debugging and metabehaviors.

A basic scheduler is simple to implement, although it can quickly grow in complexity with the addition of features, such as allowing new tasks to be executed during an update or supporting task priorities. The basic definition looks like this:

```
class Scheduler
{
public:
    bool run(Task&);
    bool halt(Task&);

    void update();

protected:
    struct Entry
    {
        Task* task;
        Status status;
        // Other data for execution.
    };
    std::vector<Entry> m_ActiveTasks;
};
```

The run() function adds the task to the list of active tasks, whereas the halt() function removes it. The Boolean return value indicates whether the scheduler managed to process the request or an error occurred (e.g., maximum number of running tasks exceeded). The value returned is not the return value of the task itself, as tasks are only executed when the scheduler is asked to update. The status of the task can be queried later from the scheduler.

As for the update() function, it runs through the list of active tasks and executes them one by one. When a task completes, it is removed from the list after the next update.

Global Observers

An *observer* is a design pattern that allows external code to be notified about specific events that occur during the execution of an algorithm. In the case of the scheduler, the implementation of update() dispatches global observers when any task terminates. The interface of this observer is defined along with the scheduler:

```
class SchedulerObserver
{
public:
    virtual void onTaskFinished(Task&) = 0;
    virtual ~SchedulerObserver();
};
```

The advantage of the observer is that new scheduling features can be implemented without affecting the core algorithm. Additional functionality, such as debugging, logging, recycling memory, or metabehaviors, is implemented by deriving from the base

`SchedulerObserver` class. Instances are then registered in the scheduler with the `Scheduler::addObserver()` function.

Support for multiple observers can be achieved by implementing composite observers (one big observer that notifies all its children) or by making a simple linked list within the scheduler itself.

Task Observers

Having a way to monitor every task globally in a scheduler is particularly useful from a software architecture perspective. However, behaviors most often are only interested in specific tasks. For example, tasks that delegate responsibility need to observe these other tasks to deal with the outcome.

This is implemented in a very similar way to the global scheduler observer, using a virtual base class called `TaskObserver`. Any task interested in monitoring another task should derive from this class and implement a pure virtual `onFinished()` function, which takes the final return status as its argument.

Typically, to use an observer, you should provide it to the scheduler when a task is run. The main scheduling algorithm is responsible for notifying the observer when that specific task is done. To accommodate this, the scheduler's `run()` function must change to have an extra optional parameter for the observer.

```
// class Scheduler
bool run(Task&, TaskObserver* = 0);
```

Using this mechanism, behaviors can be notified of the final return status of any task, allowing them to take action based on the outcome. Not only is dealing with return status codes very important for the robustness of the AI logic, but it also provides the basis for hierarchical logic.

Hierarchical AI

Given modular tasks as building blocks and a scheduler framework that makes tasks easy to manage in the AI engine, it is time to think about creating more interesting behaviors for your actors. The best way to approach this is to use hierarchies for your logic.

One popular approach to building hierarchies is to use standard script functions, formulated in a language such as Lua, as tasks in the tree. For example, an `Attack` function could contain script code to determine what specific behavior to perform in the current context (e.g., `AttackFromCover` or `Assault`) and then execute it. There are a number of drawbacks to this method, however:

- Reusing these scripts is difficult because they are often very situation-specific.
- Writing the scripts to deal with all failures and errors is tedious.
- Supporting concurrent behaviors is hard because scripts are very linear.

An alternative approach is to create some parameterized building blocks that can be frequently reused as branches in the BT, simply with different inputs provided by the designers. These are called *composite tasks*, as they use the composite pattern to manage multiple child tasks. The most common composite tasks are *sequences, selectors*, and *parallels*, all of which use the scheduler and task observers to define control flow.

Think of these composites as a domain-specific language suitable for expressing behaviors. Instead of using the low-level features of C++ or Lua to create behaviors, you can assemble them much more quickly from higher-level concepts.

Sequences

Sequences provide a mechanism for expressing linear control flow in BTs. They essentially execute their child tasks one after the other. This can be implemented easily by following these steps:

1. Use the scheduler to manage the execution of the current task.
2. Rely on a task observer for notification when it is done.
3. Process the return status.
4. Continue with the next task in the sequence.

Sequences can be further customized by a set of parameters. For example:

- Keep looping, or run through the sequence just once.
- Ignore tasks that fail and keep going as normal, or terminate the whole sequence when a task fails.
- Allow sequences to be modified dynamically at runtime, behaving as queues for runtime orders.

Sequences are very commonly used to string multiple behaviors together because they provide a good means for control and monitoring.

Selectors

Selectors, by contrast, express conditional logic and hence are very useful for decision making. Based on the current context, selectors decide which child task to run and then execute it. If a child fails, the selector falls back to a lower-priority task.

There are many possible ways to customize selectors, including the following:

- How they order the child tasks: using probabilities, priorities, or any other custom rank
- If they make the decision once (static), or if they keep monitoring the decision (dynamic)

Selectors, together with sequences, make up the bulk of any BT. Most of the logic that is typically implemented as a state machine can be expressed with these two composites instead.

Parallels

Parallels allow you to introduce concurrency into your hierarchies by forking control to different subtrees. All the child tasks of a parallel composite are executed together by the scheduler.

Instances of parallel composites also can be customized by common parameters:

- The number of child tasks that should succeed before the parallel succeeds
- The number of tasks that should fail before the parallel itself fails

The process of creating parallel BTs is certainly not trivial, but it can be used very safely in a localized fashion specifically by using one action in combination with multiple preconditions to be monitored. For example, a `CrouchInCover` action can be combined into a parallel with a condition `IsBeingShotAt` so that the behavior does not terminate until it is safe to stand up.

Decorators

Technically, a *decorator* is a composite node with only one child. They are used to extend the functionality of individual behaviors. For example:

- Filters to prevent behaviors from running in certain situations (e.g., limit the number of executions, or prevent overly frequent execution using a timer)
- Control modifiers to force a certain return status (e.g., ignore failures, or keep running instead of terminating)

Many features in a BT can be implemented as decorators, and it is often wise to do so because it allows you to recombine modular features easily in a data-driven way. Most of all, it is a great way to keep the other composites simple by putting additional features into decorators instead.

Applications

Most BTs are built primarily from the composites described previously. Thanks to the logic within the selectors, updating the tree effectively performs a depth-first search of the possible tasks, always falling back to a valid alternative. This is an extremely powerful concept for a decision-making architecture.

To control the main behavior of in-game actors, you can create a single tree rooted in a "Behave" task. This top-level task decomposes into more specific tasks that achieve objectives inside the game. At this level of the tree, selectors are very common, particularly the dynamic ones that recheck conditions in the world (like a state machine).

For example, in an action game, the top-level task selects among self-preservation, attacking the enemy, or idle patrol (in order of priority). Each of these child behaviors is defined as a sequence with a conditional check first (e.g., is there an enemy around), and then the corresponding behavior. On a regular basis, a higher-priority behavior is attempted to check if the situation has changed.

All tasks in the tree are designed to decompose recursively into simpler behaviors, until an atomic behavior is reached. Sequence composites are much more common in the lower levels of the tree, defining specific behaviors such as patrol routes.

As for reactions to events that are not part of the main behavior, another task called "React" is defined and executed in the scheduler in parallel with the main tree. The challenge of having two trees running concurrently is dealt with automatically by the search. If two actions require the same resources at the same time (e.g., playing a full-body reaction animation), then the second action fails, and the tree search continues looking for an alternative task that can achieve a similar purpose (e.g., making a shouting sound).

Conclusion

A robust decision-making and control system is the best place to start with any AI engine. The BT described in this article covers the major elements: implementing low-level tasks with latent execution, building a framework for managing them concurrently, assembling them into hierarchies using standard composites, and designing the system for depth-first search.

Probably the most useful aspect of the system is its extensibility: each task in the tree is modular and can override the search and modify the behavior of the rest of the system. Using standard composite tasks, such as sequences and selectors, BTs prove to be very intuitive and easier to manage than traditional HFSMs because subsequent tasks are not encoded explicitly as transitions in the states but specified by higher-level tasks instead. These concepts provide a logical structure for designers to reason about AI without having to worry about scripting syntax.

References

[Fu03] Fu, Dan, and Houlette, Ryan, "The Ultimate Guide to FSMs in Games." *AI Game Programming Wisdom 2*, Charles River Media, 2003.

[Isla05] Isla, Damian, "Handling Complexity in the Halo 2 AI." *GDC 2005 Proceedings*. Available online at *http://www.gamasutra.com/gdc2005/features/20050311/isla_01.shtml*, 2005.

3.5

Knowledge-Based Behavior System—A Decision Tree/Finite State Machine Hybrid

Nachi Lau—LucasArts

nachilau@hotmail.com

In the modern game-development environment, designing and implementing a behavior system that meets the diverse needs of designers and programmers can be a challenge. From the perspective of game designers, a declarative behavior system that can be easily understood by nontechnical users facilitates the incorporation of designer suggestions, enabling faster development iterations. Because designers rely on trial and error for design refinements, a system that simplifies the addition or removal of NPC logic and offers a tight feedback loop allows effective testing of the fun factor. Furthermore, a behavior editing tool with multiple customized user interfaces enables the intuitive manipulation of AI behaviors by different users. For example, a script interface for detailed NPC logic allows low-level adjustments by experienced designers, whereas a simple interface for tuning variables permits high-level behavior editing by novice designers.

From the perspective of programmers, on the other hand, a clear debugging interface is crucial because it allows the straightforward assessment of NPC behaviors. Also, because users often want to create new AI behaviors by modifying existing ones, a system with an architecture designed to enable behaviors to inherit from one another can accelerate the prototyping process. Furthermore, as programmers often have to hack the system to accomplish quick fixes, a certain level of built-in "hackability" in the system allows for such fixes without violating the system architecture.

In an attempt to satisfy the diverse needs of designers and programmers, we have developed the *knowledge-based behavior* (KBB) system, which we describe in this article.

The Knowledge-Based Behavior System

The KBB system is a variant rule-based system that attempts to encompass the advantages of both the decision tree and the finite state machine (FSM) architectures while minimizing their respective disadvantages. The main components of the system are as follows.

Knowledge Elements

The *knowledge unit* is the basic building block of the system. A knowledge unit can be thought of as a simple if-then statement, which can easily be understood by any nontechnical person. The following knowledge unit describes an NPC who attacks targets when they come within range.

```
If (TargetInRange(3.0)) then (MeleeAttack())
```

The assessment function that appears in the "if" portion of a knowledge unit is known as a *cause entity*. A cause entity can perform arbitrary computations as long as it returns a Boolean value. In the previous example, TargetIsInRange() is a cause entity. When we want to modify an existing NPC behavior, we might simply change the input parameter to the cause entity for a particular knowledge unit. If the desired modification is more complicated, we can create a new knowledge unit with a different cause entity. The freedom to associate different cause entities with a knowledge unit allows us to build custom behaviors easily.

The construct that appears in the "then" portion of a knowledge unit is called a *result entity*, and its purpose is to execute a specified AI behavior. In the previous example, MeleeAttack() is a result entity that instructs the NPC to chase after its target. When the cause entity returns true during evaluation of a knowledge unit, the associated result entity is triggered and queued up in the knowledge controller to wait for execution.

In the knowledge-based approach, an NPC behavior is described by arranging one or more knowledge units into a *knowledge tree*. The following is an example of a simple knowledge tree for an NPC who will chase and attack targets depending on their current range.

```
If (TargetInRange(3.0)) then (MeleeAttack())
If (TargetInRange(5.0)) then (ChaseTarget())
```

We will discuss more complex knowledge tree structures later in this article.

The Knowledge Controller

The *knowledge controller* is the central control component for the KBB, responsible for managing the process flow of the system. It executes three main phases in each frame update, as shown in Figure 3.5.1.

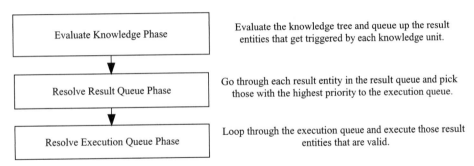

FIGURE 3.5.1   Process flow in the KBB system.

First, in the "evaluate knowledge" phase, the controller evaluates the knowledge tree structure and queues up any triggered result entities. Second, in the "resolve result queue" phase, the knowledge controller selects result entities from the result queue based on priority and puts them into an execution queue. More than one result entity can be selected for execution during this phase to simulate simultaneous behaviors. Third, in the "resolve execution queue" phase, the result entities in the execution queue are executed.

Result Entity Execution Cycle

The knowledge controller is also responsible for maintaining the execution cycle of any currently running result entities. On every frame, the knowledge controller selects result entities from the result entity queue to be placed in the execution queue. These result entities are then executed on every frame until they either decide to stop or get interrupted by other result entities. Each result entity contains logic to keep track of the current game state and detect when it is no longer valid and should be terminated by the knowledge controller.

Result entities that are already in the execution queue and have the same priority as the newly selected result entities continue executing. Result entities with lower priorities are interrupted, causing them to be removed from the execution queue and cease execution.

Result Entity Priorities

A result entity's *priority* is a numeric index used to determine the execution order of result entities. All result entities with the highest priority are executed, which means that more than one result entity can be executed at each update. All other result entities in the queue that do not have the highest priority are ignored. Consider this example:

```
If (TargetInRange(5.0)) then (RangeAttack())    P5
If (OutOfAmmo())        then (ReloadWeapon())   P6
If (GetHit())           then (HitReaction())    P10
```

The knowledge units in the preceding example specify that whenever the target is in range, the NPC should perform its ranged attack. When the ranged weapon is out of ammo, the NPC should reload the weapon instead. If the NPC gets hit by someone, however, it should react to the hit. Because we specified a higher priority for the HitReaction() result entity, the NPC will respond to a hit even if the RangeAttack() and ReloadAmmo() result entities are also in the result entity queue.

Two special priorities are used in the system. The first special priority causes the associated result entity to be executed regardless of other result entities' priorities (as long as its knowledge unit has been triggered). This is useful for defining result entities that are independent of other result entities. For example:

```
If (TargetInRange(2.0)) then (MeleeAttack())     P5
If (GetHit())           then (HitReaction())     P10
If (TargetInSight())    then (AcknowledgeAllies())P-1
```

The third knowledge unit in this example will always be executed as long as the target is in sight, regardless of whether the other result entities are executed or not.

The second special priority informs the system to execute the result entity immediately without putting it in the result queue. This allows us to define result entities that other knowledge units might be dependent on. For example:

```
If (TargetIsInTriggerVolume(1))   then
    (SetTargetIsReady())                 P(-2)
If (TargetIsInTriggerVolume(2))   then
    (SetTargetIsReady())                 P(-2)
If (IsTargetReady())              then
    (RangeAttack(MachineGun))            P(10)
```

The first two result entities in this example will be executed immediately as long as the associated cause entities return true. The third knowledge unit relies on the execution result of the first two knowledge units to determine whether its result entity should be queued up.

Advanced Knowledge Tree Structures

We describe here some extensions to the basic KBB architecture that provide increased power and flexibility.

Result Entity Containers

A result entity container is a special type of result entity that allows multiple result entities to be attached to it. A result entity container has an associated selection method that determines which of its child result entities should be executed. For example:

```
If (PlayerEnterVolume())
    then (RandomResultContainer())
        (Flee(), 50%)
        (RangeAttack(), 50%)
```

```
If (TargetIsClose())
    then (SequenceResultContainer())
            (MeleeAttack(Combo1))
            (MeleeAttack(Combo2))
```

When the random result container in the first knowledge unit is executed, either the `Flee()` or the `RangeAttack()` result entity will be selected. The second knowledge unit uses a sequence result container to define a series of melee attack actions that will be executed in order. Result entity containers are typically useful for describing random and sequential NPC behaviors.

Knowledge Groups

A *knowledge group* is a collection of knowledge units. A given knowledge group can be included in multiple NPCs' knowledge trees, enabling us to share common behavior across NPCs. For example:

```
Common Knowledge Group:
If (HealthIsZero())      then    (Death())
If (TargetIsVeryFar())   then    (Idle())
If (PlayerIsDead())      then    (Idle())
```

Including the previous knowledge group in each NPC's knowledge tree automatically ensures that all NPCs have default death and idle behaviors.

Knowledge States

Much like FSMs, the KBB system uses states to split knowledge into easily manageable chunks according to their required situational context. For example:

```
State Air
    If (TargetIsClose())   then (RangeAttack())
    If (TargetIsFar())     then (FlyTowardTarget())
    If (LoseFlyAbility())  then (ChangeState(Ground))
State Ground
    If (TargetIsClose())   then (MeleeAttack())
    If (TargetIsFar())     then (WalkTowardTarget())
```

The knowledge states in this example define an NPC that can perform attacks in the air and on the ground. When the NPC is in the "Air" state, the knowledge units in that section of the knowledge tree are evaluated, while those in the "Ground" section are ignored. If the NPC changes to the "Ground" state at some point during the game, the "Air" knowledge units become inactive, and the "Ground" knowledge units now apply. Through the use of states, we can thus better organize and maintain the knowledge tree.

Comparison with Other Architectures

In this section, we discuss the relative advantages and disadvantages of the KBB system compared to other common game AI architectures.

Finite State Machines

The FSM is a popular method used to describe NPC logic in terms of states and transition rules. FSMs are effective in representing simple logic with few states and transition rules to manage. However, as NPC logic gets complicated, the number of states and transitions explodes, making the state machine difficult to understand and maintain. Consider an NPC that can attack both in the air and on the ground. Figure 3.5.2 shows one possible way of representing this behavior using an FSM.

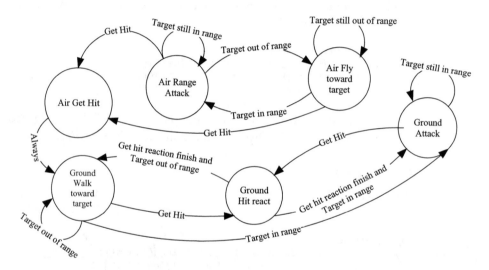

FIGURE 3.5.2   The FSM describes an NPC that can attack in the air and on the ground.

The FSM representation involves many states and transition rules even for such a simple NPC. Moreover, it is difficult to add logic to or remove logic from an existing FSM because the states are tightly coupled. For example, if the user wants to add a special hit reaction behavior to the NPC, it requires adding one more state and four more transition rules to the FSM. In addition, at least two existing transition rules need to be modified to adopt the change. Figure 3.5.3 shows the modified FSM.

Decision Trees

Decision trees are another commonly used game AI solution. Figure 3.5.4 shows a decision tree describing the same NPC behavior as Figure 3.5.2.

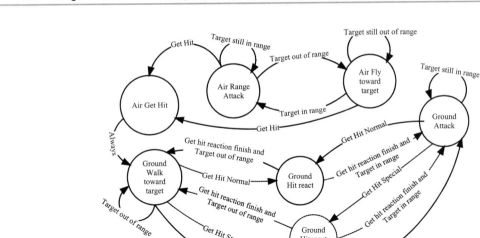

FIGURE 3.5.3   A modified FSM with special hit reaction behavior. (The dashed line indicates the change.)

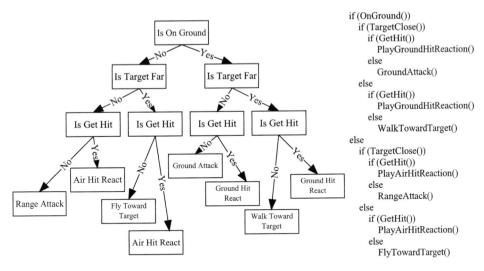

FIGURE 3.5.4   A decision tree describing the NPC from Figure 3.5.2.

The NPC behavior, as described by a decision tree, requires a three-level tree structure. Similar to the FSM approach, adding and removing logic to and from the existing decision tree can get complicated. Figure 3.5.5 shows the modified decision tree after adding a special hit reaction behavior to the NPC. Even though the behavior change to the NPC is relatively simple, the change requires restructuring parts of the decision tree. If the change to the NPC behavior is more complicated, a complete reconstructing of the whole decision tree might be necessary.

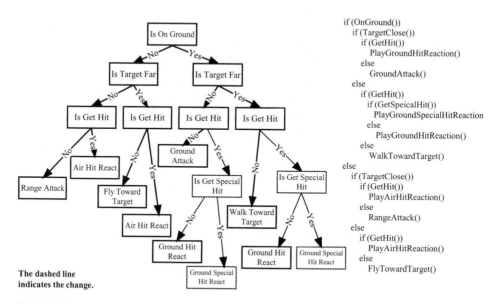

FIGURE 3.5.5   A modified decision tree with special hit reaction behavior. (The dashed line indicates the change.)

KBB System

The NPC example described previously can be implemented using the KBB approach as follows:

```
State Air
    If (TargetIsClose()) then (RangeAttack())     P5
    If (TargetIsFar())   then (FlyTowardTarget())P10
    If (GetHit())
        then (AirGetHitContainer())   P5
                GetHitReact()
                ChangeState(Ground)
State Ground
    If (TargetIsClose()) then (MeleeAttack())     P10
    If (TargetIsFar()) then (WalkTowardTarget())P10
    If (GetHit())        then (GroundHitReact())  P5
```

When we add the new special hit reaction behavior to the NPC, only one more knowledge unit needs to be added to the system:

```
If (GetHit()) then (GroundHitReact())                P5
If (GetHitSpecial()) then (GroundHitSpecialReact()) P4
```

The new knowledge unit is associated with a higher priority index. As a result, when the NPC reacts to the special attack, the special hit reaction automatically overrides the normal hit reaction. The KBB approach, therefore, allows user to easily add new behavior to the NPC while the existing knowledge remains intact.

Compared with the FSM approach, the KBB approach has fewer states and transitions to manage. Moreover, the KBB solution generates a flatter tree structure than the decision tree method. These advantages make the KBB solution easier to maintain and understand. Furthermore, the KBB approach is much more tolerant to frequent design changes due to its modular nature.

Implementation

ON THE CD

The implementation of the KBB system is straightforward. We describe the major classes here (these classes are included on the CD-ROM).

The Knowledge class implements the knowledge unit. The most important function of this class is the Evaluate() function, which is defined as follows:

```
void Knowledge::Evaluate() {
    if (pCause->Evaluate())
        pKnowledgeController->QueueResult(pResult);
}
```

Cause is the base class for all cause entities. It contains one pure virtual Evaluate() function that returns a Boolean value:

```
class Cause {
    public:
        virtual bool Evaluate() = 0;
}
```

Result is the base class for all result entities:

```
class Result {
    private:
        int m_priority;
    public:
        virtual void Execute();
        virtual void Interrupt();
        virtual bool IsValid();
        // ...
}
```

The class has a priority member variable to indicate the priority of this result entity instance. The Execute() function is called if the result entity gets selected for execution. The knowledge controller calls the Interrupt() function when a currently executing result entity gets interrupted by a higher-priority result entity. The IsValid() function is used to tell the knowledge controller to stop executing this result entity.

The KnowledgeController class implements the knowledge controller. The pseudocode for the ResolveResults() function is as follows:

```
for each result entity in result queue
{
    if (entity has highest priority in result queue)
    {
        if (entity is not in execution queue)
        {
            interrupt any result entities with lower
                priority in execution queue
            put result entity into execution queue
        }
    }
}
```

Here is the pseudocode for the ExecuteResults() function:

```
for each result entity in execution queue
{
    if (result entity is still valid)
        execute result entity
    else
        remove result entity from execution queue
}
```

Conclusion

The goals of the KBB system are to provide a simple solution for constructing NPC behaviors and to accelerate the iteration process during prototyping. Because each knowledge unit is an if-then statement, nontechnical users can easily understand the system.

Furthermore, the modular nature of knowledge units allows them to be readily adapted to modify NPC behaviors during the development process. The straightforward implementation of the system also reduces programming maintenance effort. In addition, users can easily extend the features of the system by implementing new types of cause and result entities.

3.6

The Emotion Component: Giving Characters Emotions

Ferns Paanakker—Wishbone Games B.V.

ferns.paanakker@gmail.com

Erik van der Pluijm

erik.van.der.pluijm@gmail.com

In this article, we discuss the *Emotion Component*, a software component that can be inserted in an AI engine to model complex emotions, enabling the implementation of more human-like behavior in game characters. This will in turn encourage the player to form a stronger connection with characters, resulting in a deeper gaming experience.

By using the Emotion Component, game characters can have emotions that influence their behavior and color their perception of the world. They internally maintain a condition that influences their behavior and reactions so that the human player is persuaded that the character is experiencing emotions such as fear, anger, ambition, or love. The Emotion Component is set up to function either as a separate unit or in conjunction with other AI processes. Furthermore, this component can model not only the emotions of a single character but also emotions for a group of characters.

We begin by defining what we mean by emotions and their relevance to video games. Next, we explain how present-day games typically model emotions. We then give a detailed description of the Emotion Component, including a discussion of how to integrate the Emotion Component with the game world.

The Role of Emotions in Games

In computer games, player immersion is becoming increasingly important to producing a successful game. One way to encourage immersion is to increase the player's connection to the game characters (NPCs, the player's avatar, buddies, and so on) by enhancing them with emotional cues. As a result, the player subconsciously ascribes emotions to the characters, making them seem more real and enabling deeper emotional attachment [Freeman03].

Traditionally, in games without an explicit Emotion Component, emotion is suggested through cutscenes with facial animation, gestures, scripting of emotional behavior, and the use of sounds, physics, and animations. In some cases, this might be sufficient.

However, this approach can easily break down because it often suffers from a lack of consistency. For example, there is presently a gap between full-motion video cutscenes and actual gameplay in terms of the level of emotional sophistication that can be achieved. When a character seems very emotional in the cutscene preceding a mission but not in the mission itself, the player will subconsciously discard the notion that the game character is an actual person, breaking the suspension of disbelief.

To counter this problem, we need a way to enhance the behavior of the characters in in-game situations so that emotions expressed in the storyline can be sustained to create a consistent experience throughout the game. We can do this by modeling the emotions in the game characters themselves.

Emotions

Emotions are an important part of everyday human life. They strongly influence our actions and our perception of reality and enable meaningful interaction with other human beings and the world around us. Human beings can experience a large number of different emotions, and the differences between them can be subtle. Psychologists still have not reached a consensus on exactly which different emotions exist [Minsky85, EmRec07]. In fact, there is not even a universally accepted definition of emotion [EmComp07]. For our purposes, we will define emotion as a mental state that is not the product of conscious effort but instead arises spontaneously and is usually accompanied by physiological changes.

Because an emotion is not a product of conscious effort, it seems reasonable to assume that there must be a separate subconscious mechanism that creates a mental state associated with that emotion. The physiological changes associated with an emotion can manifest themselves in a number of ways, such as changes in posture, skin tone, facial expression, and vocal timbre. An observer takes cues from these visible physiological changes of the subject to reason about their emotional state.

Besides producing changes in posture and facial expression, emotions can also influence larger-scale behavior selection. People who are very scared, for example, might instinctively choose to run away to a safe location and hide. It should be noted that the influence on behavior selection is often irrational. A fight or flight response can be triggered in situations where it is not effective, preventing the selection of a more intelligent course of action. An example of irrational behavior is attacking a unit that is obviously of superior strength.

In addition, a person's perception of the world is not objective because his emotional state constantly influences what he perceives. If a person is very angry, for example, he might feel less pain from physical damage than someone in a more relaxed state. The angry person effectively ignores the pain response, opting for an aggressive behavior instead. We will call this phenomenon the "coloring" of perception. In games, we can mimic this phenomenon by altering the amount of perceived damage based on the character's emotional state.

Emotions in Games

One way to model emotions in games is by using finite state machines (FSMs). We will quickly discuss the strengths and weaknesses of this approach, and then construct our own component to solve a number of the problems.

Traditional Implementation: Finite State Machines

FSMs are among the most popular architectures used in games ([FuHoulette04]), and they are a common way to model emotions. In an FSM, a graph describes all the possible states and the transitions between them. If we use an FSM to represent emotions, we can assign an overriding emotional response to each state. For example, states can represent anger or fear as shown in Figure 3.6.1. The FSM starts in the "neutral" state where the agent does not have an explicit emotion. Internal thoughts or external stimuli cause the agent to transition to a new state, with a corresponding change in emotional state. Such an FSM, where the transitions between behavioral states are directly linked to inputs, can be viewed as a naive stimulus-response model.

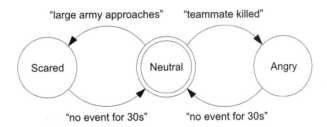

FIGURE 3.6.1 An FSM representing emotional state.

FSMs are easy to implement, efficient, and very easy to author, tune, and debug. They are also straightforward to interface with other systems, such as animation, physics, and sound, because it is easy to retrieve the current state of the character. When using this approach, however, we tend to model the behavior of the character (e.g., scared, angry) rather than the underlying emotion (e.g., fear, anger).

Additionally, in an FSM, only one discrete state can be active at a time. By contrast, emotions normally have a graduated activation level: you can be a little scared, quite scared, or scared witless. To capture this in an FSM would require many additional states. An alternative to the standard FSM is the *fuzzy-state machine* (FuSM), in which every state has a level of activation [Champandard04]. FuSMs are thus well suited to modeling the graduated nature of emotions, and they serve as a springboard for the design of our Emotion Component.

The Emotion Component

To represent emotions in games while avoiding the problems associated with FSMs, we use a system that is loosely based on an FuSM. The Emotion Component is positioned between the "sense" and "think" parts of the traditional AI loop, as shown in Figure 3.6.2. The feedback link from the "think" component to the Emotion Component indicates that the agent's thought processes can influence emotions.

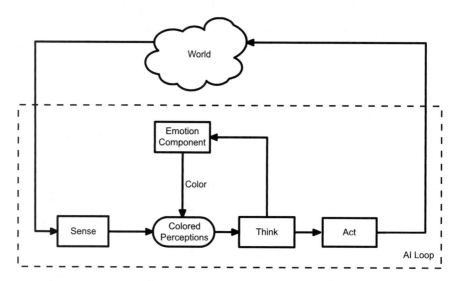

FIGURE 3.6.2   The placement of the Emotion Component in the AI architecture.

How the Emotion Component Influences Character Behavior

We will now discuss the typical Sense/Think/Act modules of the AI architecture and their relation to the Emotion Component.

The Sense Module: Coloring Perceptions with Emotions

The stimuli from the outside world are presented to the game character as perceptual events. For example, the character might spot an opponent or take damage from a weapon. The Emotion Component allows us to color this information based on the emotional state of the character, resulting in a change to the value and/or type of the event. This can be seen in Figure 3.6.3, where the actual damage taken by the character is scaled down by the anger level to determine the *perceived* damage.

The Think Module: Influencing Behavior Selection with Emotions

Emotions also influence behavior selection for the character. The occasional selection of irrational behavior can give the player a vivid indication of the intensity of a character's emotions. In addition, the contrast between the normal situation—in which a character behaves quite rationally—and the emotion-induced irrational state will make his rational actions seem all the more rational, thus making the character more

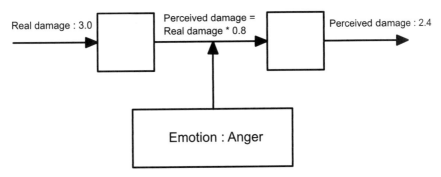

FIGURE 3.6.3   The coloring of perceptions.

believable. Of course, the injudicious use of irrational behavior can lead to the appearance of stupidity, which detracts from the believability of the character.

The Act Module: Influencing Behavior Execution with Emotions

In the Act module, specific physiological phenomena, such as posture and facial expression are overlaid on the selected behavior in accordance with the character's emotional state. For example, if the behavior is set to "run away," the posture might be "panicked" or "stealthy."

Implementation Issues

When implementing the Emotion Component, we first have to discuss how emotions are represented. We can distinguish between the case where only a single emotion influences the agent's behavior selection and situations where multiple emotions influence behavior selection simultaneously.

Representing a Single Emotion

The Emotion Component can model an arbitrary set of emotions, where each emotion has an activation level between 0.0 and 1.0 that represents its current strength. For mutually exclusive emotions (e.g., "confidence" and "fear"), we can use a range between -1.0 and 1.0. By using such a range, we can represent two emotions in a single activation level, although this can make naming emotions less intuitive.

Multiple events can influence a single emotion (e.g., every enemy within visual range might induce fear). Thus, instead of allowing the event to directly influence the activation level of the emotion, we have opted to include a mapping function that transforms an internal variable into the emotion's activation level. For example, every enemy within visual range might induce five fear "points." The accumulated score ("emotion points") is then used to calculate the activation level of the fear emotion.

Example activation functions that can be used for such transformations are shown in Figure 3.6.4. You can choose an activation function based on how well the activation function matches a particular emotion. For example, you might use 4E for impatience,

4C for excitement, and 4D for fear. There is no single best activation function to use. For example, what activation function would you choose for the emotion "love"? Some people might choose 4F for a love that grows over time, with every step of the floor-function being a special experience that deepens the feeling, but others might experience something like 4D or maybe 4B for love at first sight. This also gives the opportunity to create characters with a rich set of subtle differences.

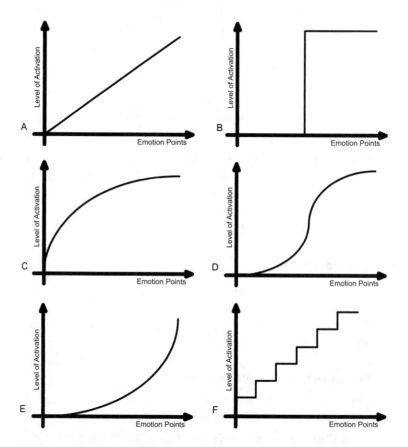

FIGURE 3.6.4   Different activation functions.

Handling Multiple Emotions

If we represent the emotional state of a game character as a set of emotions, we can no longer directly identify one single discrete emotion as being dominant. A character might be angry and confused at the same time. One solution is to order the different emotions by their level of activation, granting the emotion with the highest level of activation the title of dominant emotion (much like a single state in an FSM).

Another point concerns mutually exclusive emotions, such as fear and confidence. As we mentioned previously, these emotions can be seen as two endpoints of the same spectrum or alternatively as two separate emotions with their own activation levels. The main reason to use separate emotions is that they permit a clear and distinct name for each emotion. To simplify the implementation in this case, we could make the activation level of one of the emotions dependent on the other (so you could define "confidence" as 1.0 minus "fear").

We should be aware, however, when two emotions are simultaneously highly activated because any lack of hysteresis will cause problems. *Hysteresis* is a property of systems that do not instantly react to the forces applied to them but instead change slowly. The state of such a system depends on its immediate history. When a system contains a threshold between two alternative behaviors, and the reaction speed of the system is too fast, then the system might oscillate wildly around that threshold, giving rise to unwanted behavior. Translated to the realm of game AI, we might alternate between emotional states too quickly if their activation levels are very close together, but their associated behaviors are very different.

For example, suppose we have a character with a high level of activation for both fear and anger. At one moment, its fear activation level is highest, so it runs away. As it runs away, its fear level decreases, and its anger level becomes highest. The character now changes behavior to attack the opponent from which it was first fleeing. Moving toward the opponent and being hit increases the fear level, so after a few steps, the fear emotion becomes dominant. This cycle of events repeats, all other factors being equal, and makes the character seem very indecisive and artificial.

Is There a Silver Bullet?

After reading the previous paragraph, you should be aware that the Emotion Component as such does not provide a "silver bullet" against the difficulties and pitfalls of correct behavior selection. Defining descriptive behaviors that convey the agent's emotional state to the player and making sure they are selected at the right time is unfortunately still a task of long hours of testing and fine-tuning. The Emotion Component does provide a more flexible approach to this fine-tuning by adding the explicit internal emotional state. Because of this state, it becomes easier to decouple the agent's emotional response from the game world stimuli, making it possible to have greater subtlety and greater variation among the agent's expressed behaviors. This even holds true in the case of agents of the same type, which will express subtly different behaviors based on their own internal state. Unfortunately, it comes at the cost of greater complexity when modeling and fine-tuning the behavior.

Sustaining Emotions Over Time

We all know that our emotions fade. If we are scared, but there are no stimuli that keep us scared, our fear will gradually diminish. We can model this by using a decay function.

The simplest decay function decreases the activation level by a fixed amount over time, giving a linear decay rate. We can also use an exponential decay function that defines a relative amount by which the activation level changes—for example, 1% every second. The exponential decay function might be appropriate for a wide range of emotions, such as fear, anger, and ambition, where the absence of stimuli reduces the strength of the emotion. To make sure the Emotion Component has a sense of time even in the absence of stimuli, we send a time event to the Emotion Component in every AI update cycle so the Emotion Component can execute the decay.

Showing Emotions

The emotional state of the character must be portrayed in a way that provides appropriate cues to the player. This can be done by influencing animation, physics, sound selection, responsiveness to orders, or even direct visual markers, such as a red question mark above the character to indicate he is confused.

Consider the execution of a walk cycle of a game character. We create two candidate walk cycle animations: one where the character has a bent back and hanging shoulders and drags its feet (an insecure animation), and another where the character has a very straight back, with chest forward, shoulders back, vigorous arm and shoulder movement, and a springy step (a confident animation). By querying the Emotion Component for the activation level of "confidence," we can blend or select between the two animations to convey the appropriate level of emotion. The transition times between such emotions are incorporated directly in the Emotion Component as well via the activation levels and decay functions. Humans are highly attuned to such subtle visual clues, and a convincing implementation will help strengthen the connection between the player and the game world.

Group Psychology

Agents that are part of a group are not only driven by their own emotions. The emotions of other agents of the group are just as important.

We can achieve group-level emotional response using the Emotion Component by allowing members of a group to send messages to others nearby concerning their emotional state. The emotional state of the other members of the group thus becomes just another input to the agent's Sense/Think/Act cycle and can be used to influence the character's emotional state. With the correct settings, it should be possible to create "emotional flocking behaviors" that give rise to emergent behavior. Naturally, when implementing this for large groups, this calls for techniques to minimize the amount of communication.

Source Code

We have now set the stage for our Emotion Component. We invite you to take a look at the demo program and source code to gain a more detailed understanding of its function.

Included on the CD-ROM is the source code of a demonstration program that allows you to experiment with the Emotion Component. The code is strictly for demonstration purposes and not heavily optimized, but it serves as a good starting point for your own implementation. The program uses a number of different types of agents, each capable of their own set of emotions. By allowing the agent to interact with the environment and the other agents, the emotional state and the behavior of the agents can be changed.

Conclusion

In this article, we have shown how to create a component that can represent human-like emotions while supporting multiple active emotions at the same time. We have discussed how our representation of emotions can color both perception and actions and how to closely integrate with other modules, such as animation and AI.

Although the Emotion Component has by no means finished its evolution, we do have a number of guidelines that we can offer as a starting point for your own experiments with adding emotions:

- Make your behavior selection descriptive. When we used a simple difference in speed between "flee" and "wander" behavior, with "fleeing" agents moving twice as fast, the difference became immediately clear.
- Test to make sure behavior rules do not interfere with each other to end up in dead-lock or feedback loops. For example, it seems like a nice idea to have a "scared" agent run to the nearest friendly agent (which will boost its confidence), but this approach breaks down if that friendly agent is scared too, and there is no additional fallback behavior: both agents will run toward each other and then oscillate. Discriminating between scared and confident friendly units would help in that case.
- Make sure that during implementation, you don't add too many emotions and agents into the system at once. When the mix becomes complex, it is increasingly tricky to figure out what is going wrong. Making sure the system is first tested with one or two basic important emotions is the easiest way to go.
- Define a "pecking order" for how your emotions influence your behavior selection. So, for example, fear will overrule anger, and anger will overrule idle behavior. In that way, it is easier to avoid two emotions becoming gridlocked.

The Emotion Component provided in the accompanying source code is a good place to start experimenting with giving agents emotions. Even with a straightforward architecture, such as the Emotion Component, the possibilities are vast. Be aware, however, that making complex emotions that affect gameplay can greatly increase the time needed to play, test, and balance games. As always, try to balance the pros and cons.

References

[Champandard04] Champandard, Alex J., *AI Game Development*. New Riders Publishing, 2004.

[EmComp07] "Emotional Competency." Available online at *http://www.emotionalcompetency.com/emotion.htm*, August 14, 2007.

[EmRec07] "Emotional Competency." Available online at *http://www.emotionalcompetency.com/recognizing.htm*, August 14, 2007.

[Freeman03] Freeman, David, *Creating Emotion in Games*. New Riders Publishing, 2003.

[FuHoulette04] Fu, Dan, and Houlette, Ryan, "The Ultimate Guide to FSMs in Games." *AI Game Programming Wisdom 2*, Charles River Media, 2004: pp. 283–302.

[Minsky85] Minsky, Marvin, *The Society of Mind*. Simon and Schuster, 1985.

3.7

Generic Perception System

Frank Puig Placeres

fpuig@fpuig.cjb.net

Perception is one of the most important topics in game AI. Every game has to address perception in some way. This can be as simple as the NPC knowing the complete map, hearing all sounds, and always seeing the player. On the other hand, more sophisticated perception can also mimic the real-world limitations of the character types being modeled (e.g., humans or animals).

However, perception is much more than just seeing and hearing. It encompasses all of the ways that an NPC gathers data about the world, including environmental and tactical information such as hiding spots, ambush locations, and the positions of walls and obstacles.

This article presents a perception system that analyzes the environment to provide the AI agents with world data as well as static and dynamic events. The system also allows customization of most of its modules to match the space partitioning structures used to organize the visual and physical world. It was designed to allow integration of features such as time slicing, priority scanning, goal negotiation, movement prediction, and short- and long-term memory.

System Architecture

The cPerceptionSystem object (see Figure 3.7.1) is responsible for updating all of the cDataGatherer entities, which store the perceptual information about the world that can be sensed by agents. That information can be anything from tactical data (such as hints about best sniper locations and potential attack zones), to environmental data (such as the locations of walls, stairs, characters), to events that happen in the world (such as the sounds of gunfire or footsteps).

All of these types of information are implemented as subclasses of the abstract cDataGatherer class and are detailed in the following sections. Maintaining all the data gatherers as separate classes allows the inclusion of only the ones that are needed for a specific game. Thus, a football game might discard environmental and tactical classes, whereas a first-person shooter (FPS) would need them all.

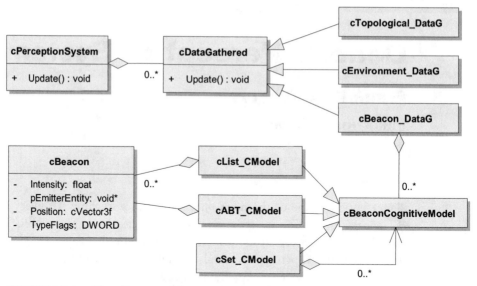

FIGURE 3.7.1   Class diagram of the perception system.

Environmental Data

When creating game levels, artists build graphical and geometric representations of the environment. You can automatically simplify these representations into basic shapes that help the NPCs understand their surroundings. In this way, a complex 3D world can be described as in Figure 3.7.2, with obstacles delimited by circles and walls represented by straight lines.

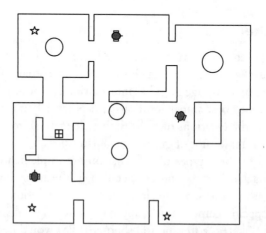

FIGURE 3.7.2   Environmental data composed of straight lines (walls) and circles (obstacles).

At any moment, the agent can query the environmental data gatherer to learn about the structure of its surroundings to make movement decisions. Because the returned shapes are very simple, well-documented algorithms, such as steering, behaviors can be used to determine how to move to a target location while avoiding collisions or where to hide from an enemy using the closest obstacles.

Tactical Data

For AI agents, perception is more than simply knowledge about the world's geometry. Information about the tactical characteristics of the surrounding environment is often important—for example, hiding spots, sniper locations, ways to enter a room, and places that can be ambushed, among others [vanderSterren01]. Figure 3.7.3 shows some of the tactical and environmental information that the data gatherers can provide about the world.

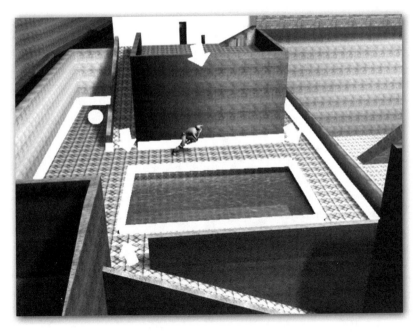

FIGURE 3.7.3   Tactical and environmental data. The arrows and circles represent tactical tips, such as possible hiding spots and room entries. The lines indicate the nearby walls used for collision avoidance.

Beacon Data

So far, the described data gatherers hold information about static locations and structures. However, most of the useful hints will come from dynamic objects or events that are created and modified at runtime. The third type of data gatherer deals with this type of information, which it encapsulates as a *beacon* [Orkin02].

Each beacon represents an event or situation that could interest the AI agents. Examples of beacons are visibility messages, smells, and sounds. Take for instance a situation where a player is moving across a level. When the player object is created, it registers a visibility beacon. When nearby agents are notified of this beacon by the data gatherer (as described in the next section), agents know that they can see the player. Similarly, every time the player moves, footstep beacons are created.

Figure 3.7.1 lists some of the properties that are stored on the beacons. For instance, beacons store the position and identity of the emitter entity as well as the emission intensity, which represents how loud the sound is or how visible/camouflaged the entity is. The beacon also stores a flag describing the type of perception, such as GUN_FIRE, FOOTSTEPS, or DEAD_BODY. This enables the AI agent to take appropriate action depending on whether the beacon represents a sight, sound, smell, or other perception.

Data Gatherer Internal Management

As presented in the UML diagram of Figure 3.7.1, the cBeacon_DataGatherer object is composed of one or more cognitive models that manage the various beacons. The simplest cognitive model is a list, but more specialized models, such as octrees, ABTs, BSPs, and grids, are also possible. This flexibility enables the world representation to match as closely as possible the structures used to handle visibility and collision, simplifying and optimizing the updating of cognitive models and the retrieval of nearby beacons.

The AI Agent

Now that the perception system has been introduced, let's see how the NPC makes use of it. Figure 3.7.4 depicts the AI agent's sensors and memory subsystems.

Sensors

As in the real world, the AI agent receives information from the environment by using sensors. These sensors constantly scan the surroundings in search of useful information and keep the agent updated. To do this, they connect to the various data gatherers in the perception system, which provide environmental, tactical, and beacon data about the world.

When an agent is created, it registers the sensors that it will need. For a dog character, it may not be necessary to register a tactical sensor because it does not need to receive information about where to set up an ambush. However, it does indeed need to register an environmental sensor to avoid collisions and know where to move next. Also, it will need a beacon sensor to spot the player.

Each of the sensors has a set of filter properties that determines the sensory capabilities of the associated agent. Those attributes are defined according to the type of data that the sensor is designed to search. For instance, the environmental and tactical

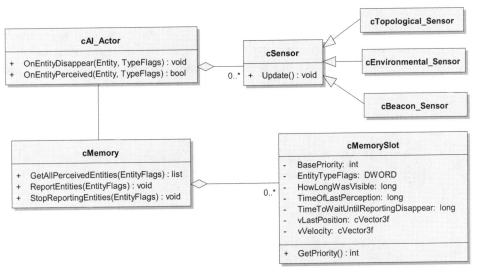

FIGURE 3.7.4 Class diagram presenting the components of the AI agent.

sensors define visibility attributes so that only the closest visible data is returned when the scanning is performed. Similarly, the beacon sensor provides attributes to specify the types of beacon that it will detect. For instance, a particular sensor might only detect gunfire beacons.

Every time an agent is updated, all of its sensors are also updated, causing them to perform a scan of the data gatherer to which they are connected. This scan is implemented in the data gatherers so that it can be optimized according to the constituent cognitive models, allowing fast searches via space-partitioning trees for large environments with lots of useful information or simple list searches when small environments are scanned. After the scan finds data that matches the sensor's filter properties, this data is placed in the agent's memory.

Agent Memory

Often, short- and long-term memory is not included as a fundamental system in the implementation of AI agents [Buckland05]. In the proposed architecture, however, this system plays a fundamental role, serving not only to improve the agents' capabilities but also to optimize retrieval of perceptual data requested by the decision-making algorithms.

As has been mentioned, after a piece of data matching a sensor's filters is found in the data gatherers, it is reported to the memory system of the agent that owns the sensor. The memory system holds a set of memory slots that stores information about all sensed data.

Each of the slots contains a description of the type of data that it holds as well as general information, such as the time and location where the emitter was last perceived. This enables the agent to know where to find that emitter in the environment.

One of the key aspects of the memory system is its capacity to prioritize data. When the agent requests information about the data reported by its sensors, the information that is returned is sorted by priority so that the agent can simplify its decision-making logic by only analyzing the most important data.

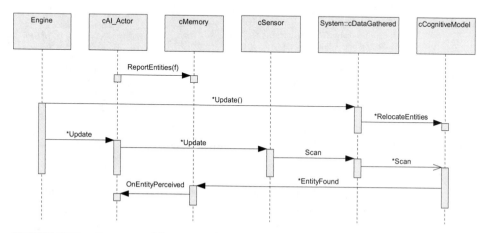

FIGURE 3.7.5   Sequence of function calls that happens when the perception system is updated.

Priorities are also used to manage which information should be kept and which should be forgotten and deleted. Whenever some information is not useful to the agent or its relevance is below a minimum threshold, it can be discarded by the memory system. When a sensor reports data, the agent computes the base priority as appropriate to its character in the game. Thus, a dog assigns a high priority to a bone that it could eat, whereas a person assigns the bone a lower priority because he does not consider it to be a useful object.

Priority also depends on the length of time that the data was perceived as well as how much time has elapsed since it was last perceived. The longer the period during which the data was perceived, the higher its priority, and the greater the elapsed time since it disappeared, the lower its priority. For instance, suppose an agent enters a room and sees a door. At first, the door has a low priority, so the agent does not immediately analyze it, but after a few seconds, its priority increases, causing the agent to notice it and decide to pass through. For a few more seconds, the agent will remember the door. After a while, though, the door's priority will be so low that the agent will forget about the door and release that memory slot.

Agent Requests

When implementing the agent's logic, sensor information can be retrieved from the memory system using either event-driven or polling approaches. In the event-driven approach, memory slots can be directed to report all objects of a certain type. This way, infrequent sensor data, such as dead bodies or footsteps, can be noticed by the agent as soon as the memory system receives data of that type, without requiring the agent to poll for them directly every frame. The implementation of the decision-making algorithms is thus simplified because they do not need to take into account infrequent events, only processing them when the callback functions OnEntityAppear and OnEntityDisappear are executed by the memory system.

The agent can also use poll requests to get information from its memory slots. The memory system provides a function that returns all current sensor data, sorted by priority so that the agent can focus its decision making on the most important sensor data.

Expanding the Perception System

The perception system discussed so far is capable of handling the basic perceptual needs of an AI agent. However, the implementation can also be expanded to include some optimizations and additional interesting capabilities.

Time Slicing

Huge game worlds have the disadvantage of increasing the sensor scanning time because many cognitive model subnodes have to be traversed, each of which may contain a large amount of relevant sensor data. Time slicing helps reduce the stalling that occurs every time a sensor scans the world. Basically, the system can be implemented to handle two types of time slicing: per-sensor and per-agent.

Per-sensor time slicing spreads the sensor's scanning process over several frames. This way, every time a sensor performs a scan, instead of waiting until the complete traversal of the cognitive models is finished, it just signals the data gatherers, which perform a fraction of the scan on each frame until the search gets completed. The number of frames into which the sensor scan is sliced can be adjusted to match current performance.

The second type of time slicing distributes agent sensor requests across multiple frames. Instead of each agent constantly scanning the world, it is possible to perform a scan for 20 agents on one frame, then for 20 more on the next, and so on until all agents get updated. This can be combined with a level-of-detail optimization so that agents far away from the player have lower scanning priorities, only scanning the world every few seconds, whereas characters near the player constantly scan their surroundings.

The drawback of using time slicing is that objects are not immediately perceived. It can be a few seconds before they are reported to the agent. However, this can also add a touch of reality to the perception system because in the real world, most people do not immediately have a full understanding of their surrounding but notice objects and events a few moments after they happen. The number of frames between sensor scans might thus be set to reflect the reaction time of a particular agent.

Priority Scanning

Coupled with the time-slicing feature, the system can also be implemented to handle priority scanning. The idea here is to mimic real-world behavior where important events are noticed first, and finer details are detected on later frames.

To implement priority scanning, the cognitive models that comprise the data gatherers can maintain their sensor data sorted by priority. When scanning is performed, the nodes with higher priority are traversed first. For example, a door might have a higher priority than a wall and a lower priority than a dead body. Of course, because the cognitive models are not agent-specific, only one priority ordering exists across all agents. In practice, however, this is not a major limitation.

Goal Negotiation

The proposed perception system is not limited to describing and understanding prebuilt environments. The system can also be extended to handle new events and manage knowledge acquisition.

Suppose, for example, that an artist creates an elevator that is called using a lever in the middle of the room. The elevator moves any agent standing on its platform to the higher floor. Integrating this new entity normally would require changing some of the agent's logic to handle the elevator behavior. However, using the perception system, a goal-negotiation approach can be implemented instead.

At the moment that the elevator is placed in the environment, it registers a beacon signaling that it can move agents. When an agent senses the beacon, if that agent needs to move to a higher level, it asks the beacon how to use it. The beacon returns a goal, a script, or some other description of how to correctly use the elevator, which in this case is "search for the lever, pull it, and then stand on the main platform until it reaches the next floor."

This procedure can be used to increase the artist's capabilities while simplifying the character's logic implementation. The environment itself will explain to the character how to use the entities that surround it.

Using the System

Next is presented an example of how agents can use the perception system to move and understand the environment. When implementing an FPS, the main loop constantly updates the perception system and all active characters. Artists create simplified representations of the world as in Figure 3.7.2 and add it to the environmental data gatherer using a space-partitioning technique to accelerate the search for nearby entities and obstacles. Similarly, tactical data is precomputed based on the world representation and stored in the appropriate data gatherer.

At the moment that each character enters the game, it registers visibility beacons, and every time the character moves, shoots, or picks up an item, a sound beacon is created for a few moments. The characters also create sensors to scan the world according to their perceptual limitations. This way, only trained soldiers access the tactical data, whereas zombies just scan the environmental data to avoid collisions.

To understand the AI implementation of the characters, consider this situation. An NPC is placed in the world. He has a weak gun, so he decides to search for a better one. He runs a pathfinding algorithm, which reports that a rocket launcher is in the next room. His environmental sensors provide him with knowledge of his surroundings, enabling him to use steering behaviors to move without collision to the door that leads to the next room.

The door is locked but has a beacon that signals that it can indeed lead the agent into the next room, so the character takes the script offered by the door. This script informs him that he needs to step on the switch on the floor to open the door.

In the next room, he spots the rocket launcher beacon and moves in that direction. After a few seconds, its time-sliced sensor scan informs him of a visibility beacon on his left side representing a dead agent. Immediately, the player increases its state of alertness by increasing the number of beacons to be reported and lowering the minimum priority that the scan uses for filtering data. The updated scan retrieves other beacons with very low priorities showing footprints on the floor.

The character decides to follow these footprints, but after analyzing and removing the footprint and dead body beacons from the sorted list of data, the beacon with the next-highest priority is the rocket launcher. The character thus moves to its location, picks it up, and then uses his sensors to follow the footprints and hunt the player.

Conclusion

The perception system described in this article simplifies decision-making logic and expands the capabilities of NPCs by providing prioritized information about the environment. It can also increase the realism of NPC behaviors by automatically handling short-term memory, movement predictions, and variable reaction times.

This system can be scaled to reduce the performance impact of a large number of agents interacting in the world. In addition, it can provide the ability to easily include new complex objects by associating goals and scripts with them, making it well suited to implementing complex character behaviors in next-generation games.

References

[Buckland05] Buckland, Mat, *Programming Game AI by Example*. Wordware Publishing, Inc., 2005.

[Orkin02] Orkin, Jeff, "A General-Purpose Trigger System." *AI Game Programming Wisdom*, Charles River Media, 2002.

[vanderSterren01] van der Sterren, William, "Terrain Reasoning for 3D Action Games." *Game Programming Gems 2*, Charles River Media, 2001.

3.8

Peer-To-Peer Distributed Agent Processing

Borut Pfeifer—Electronic Arts

borut_p@yahoo.com

This article covers methods to spread the processing requirements for agent-based AI across multiple machines in a peer-to-peer game architecture. As networked gameplay becomes more and more common across the range of gaming platforms [Isensee03], we have to consider network architecture as a fundamental aspect of the structure of our AI. Client-server and multitiered server architectures are often more secure and scalable, but peer-to-peer architectures do have clear benefits for small groups of players.

With a peer-to-peer architecture, any given player can leave without disrupting the game, and that player can rejoin later on. With the increasing popularity of handheld gaming systems with ad hoc wireless networking, these types of failure cases are becoming more common, such as when players temporarily go out of range of each other. A peer-to-peer architecture can improve the players' experience by handling these cases gracefully. Peer-to-peer architectures can also allow network messaging optimizations in certain circumstances, even for some aspects of massively multiplayer games (MMO) [Knutsson04]. To properly take advantage of the benefits of peer-to-peer architectures, we have to architect our AI systems around the concept of distributed agent processing.

Overall Architecture

To create peer-to-peer games, there is commonly a peering server, a separate, centralized machine that all players communicate with to get information about possible game matches. The peering server can also be used if a final arbitrator between the various peers is needed, for instance, to determine who should take ownership of agents controlled by a departing player. After the players successfully create or join a game, they communicate by each broadcasting messages to every other peer in that game.

In terms of the AI architecture, the more autonomous the agents are in their decision making, the easier it is to distribute their processing across machines. If a large

group "brain" is coordinating decision making for all the agents, it will be more difficult to distribute its workload. If there are smaller decision-making groups, such as
squads or teams of agents, it may still be more straightforward to keep the processing
for an entire team on the same machine. For this reason, you should keep decision
making simple and at the individual agent level, and keep interagent communication
over group decision making, thereby making it easier to distribute agent processing.

Agent Communication

To coordinate the actions of separate agents, we will need a simple conduit for controlling their communication. Such a concept already exists for agents controlled by just
one machine: a blackboard [Isla02, Orkin04]. With a few extensions, a blackboard can
solve many problems with coordinating multiple agents' actions across the network. To
achieve this, however, we have to lean ever so slightly away from peer-to-peer distribution of agent communication.

One machine, initially the player who started the game, controls the blackboard.
Every machine has its own version of the blackboard object, but only one is tagged as
the owner. The others are remote proxies to ensure that agents process blackboard
messages in the proper order. Given the nature of a peer-to-peer game, you can't guarantee receiving messages in order from peers. For example, if one player shoots at and
hits an agent owned by another player, a third player might not receive the "shoot"
message before the "hit" message due to lag. Because many entries on the blackboard
require synchronization of handshaking-type requests between agents (where two or
more agents need to each receive agreement from the others), a guaranteed ordering is
necessary and is achieved by having the blackboard owned by one machine.

Blackboard entries consist of a type, a source object (typically the posting agent),
and related data (such as a position, a target object, and a timestamp). One agent puts
an entry on the blackboard, and other agents can react to it. At the most basic level, a
blackboard has these interface functions:

AddRecord: Adds a data entry to the blackboard.
FindRecord: Searches for an entry on the blackboard matching a given description.
RemoveRecord: Removes an entry on the blackboard. There can also be a similar
convenience function that removes all records matching a certain description.

Finding a record works the same on any machine: it runs through the local machine's
list of entries to determine whether a record exists with a matching record type, source,
and so on. On the machine that owns the blackboard, the AddRecord and RemoveRecord
functions add or remove entries from the local list of data. They also broadcast the
request to add or remove the record to the other machines in the game. The other
machines' blackboards respond to the broadcast by performing the desired command on
their local list of records. On remote machines, when an agent invokes AddRecord or
RemoveRecord, this request is transmitted to the blackboard owner. The owner updates its
data and then broadcasts the change to all the peers.

Note that a remote agent that originally requests a blackboard change will wait for the owner to broadcast the change back to it. This communication could be optimized so that the original remote requester simply makes the change internally to its copy of the blackboard, and the blackboard owner only broadcasts the change to all the remaining peers. However, this would violate the requirement that the blackboard owner be the final authority on the ordering of blackboard additions and removals. On the remote machine that originated the request, if any agent queried the blackboard for that record, the agent might get a different result from an agent on another machine that would have to wait for notification from the blackboard owner.

Example of Networked Blackboard Coordination

One example of blackboard use for coordinating agent behavior is enabling two agents to flank a player. The desired behavior is that any two available agents of the same type will approach their target from opposite sides. Although this behavior could be explicitly scripted for two agents, if one agent dies, and the player moves toward a third flanking agent, the new agent would not continue the flanking attack.

The first agent initially searches for flanking requests that have been posted on the blackboard. Finding none, it adds its own request. The second agent finds the request and adds a flanking partner match record. The first agent, polling for flanking partner matches, picks the first one it finds. It then assigns this agent as its flanking partner and tells its partner of the match via another record on the blackboard. If the first agent also finds other matches that it does not choose, it can remove those records from the blackboard so that those agents will keep searching for a new match to their original request.

Now that the two agents have found each other via their handshaking messages on the blackboard, they can calculate approach vectors to reach their target on opposite sides (given their current positions relative to their target). If the agents are being processed on separate machines, the distributed blackboard has kept this fact hidden from each agent. Using the blackboard to coordinate tactics and decision making allows an agent to have a single unified way to interact with other agents, both local and remote.

A blackboard is a very efficient means of coordinating multiple agent behaviors. If flanking or other group tactical behaviors were made at another level (e.g., a squad-level "brain"), coordinating actions between agents across the network would become more difficult. If we restrict all squad members to be processed on the same machine, we will run into problems if we need to distribute agent processing by locality (where nearby agents are processed on the same machine) when agents in the squad get separated. Alternatively, each chunk of tactical decision-making code could perform all the network communication between its subordinate agents itself, but that could result in code duplication and inefficient communication. The code required to add network communication to the blackboard, on the other hand, is minimal and has the advantage of abstracting this functionality from any agent's decision making.

Arbitrating Blackboard Ownership

Because the blackboard is owned by one player's machine, it effectively acts as a small server for coordinating AI communication. This means that when the player who started the game and owns the blackboard leaves, the ownership of the blackboard must be shifted seamlessly to another player. The simplest way may often be to rely on the peering server to arbitrate ownership between the existing players. It receives notification that a player has left the game or determines that he has lost the connection (when no messages have been received for a certain period of time). It can pick the next player to own the blackboard (and potentially other singleton objects) and then notify all of the players of the new owner.

You can avoid the additional communication with the peering server by establishing a mechanism by which each remaining player's machine can deterministically select the new blackboard owner. This can be based on data assigned by the peering server when the players join the game (such as the order in which the peering server processed the players' join game requests). Because the blackboard is always kept up to date on each machine, whether the decision is made by the peering server or all peers in unison, the existing blackboard on the new owner's machine should not need any special updates to take ownership; it can assume that its state of the blackboard is valid.

Although add or remove messages can potentially be lost if they were sent to the blackboard owner after disconnect but before the new owner is decided, typically that error case is infrequent, and the results are minor. Agents may not be able to act on messages they are expecting momentarily until their state changes and they begin looking for new records accordingly. If this error case is critical, agents can keep resending their blackboard requests until the blackboard sends the acknowledgment that the record is to be added or removed. This does require tracking each add and remove request individually, to distinguish it from the case where an agent simply wants to add a duplicate record to the blackboard.

Agent Ownership

The two main goals behind load sharing of agent processing are better handling of streaming or spatial locality and performance improvements.

Streaming/Locality—Passive Load Distribution

If the game world is streamed, an agent may not be able to be simulated on a machine that does not have nearby geometry loaded. If all the agents are being processed on the first player's machine, and a second player wanders far from the first's location, the geometry around the second player might not be loaded on the first's machine. Agents simulating on the first player's machine near the second player's location would fall through the world without collision. That simple case might be handled by disabling gravity, but agents would still need to perform line-of-sight tests, avoid walls, and so on. Non-collision-related data, such as information about nearby props or other game objects, may also be needed for the AI to function properly. A passive load-sharing mechanism, one that transfers agent ownership as agents leave and enter players' controlled areas, will solve this problem. Three boundaries are considered in this decision making-process:

- The *update boundary* **around the player:** This boundary defines the region of the world around the player that is guaranteed to be valid for simulation because the level geometry is loaded and objects are under an active level of detail of simulation.
- The *ownership-acquiring minimum boundary* **for a player:** Objects within this boundary will come under the player's ownership if they are not actively owned by another player.
- The *ownership-leaving maximum boundary* **for a player:** If an object is inside this boundary of a player, it will not be considered for changing its ownership to other players.

For simplicity's sake, these boundaries can be simple circle radii, but some games might require more detailed boundary mechanisms (especially if they take place in more than 2½ dimensions). Every agent that is inside a player's update radius and is owned by that player is processed on that player's machine. As players and agents move through the world, when an agent exits a player's ownership-leaving boundary, it will begin to test other player's ownership-acquiring boundaries on a per-frame basis. If the agent ever enters the ownership-acquiring boundary of another player, it will request its ownership to be transferred to that player's machine.

This means agents outside of a player's ownership boundaries might still in fact be owned by that player, but they will be transferred as soon as they come within the ownership-acquiring boundary of another player. Because the update boundary is larger than both ownership boundaries, the agent is guaranteed to be in a valid simulated world position while under active processing. Whenever it leaves its owner's update boundary without being transferred to another player, it goes into a nonsimulated state so that the lack of valid level geometry and associated information won't cause problems (see Figure 3.8.1).

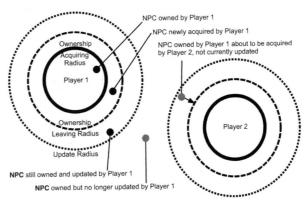

FIGURE 3.8.1   Visualization of update and ownership boundaries.

The ownership-leaving boundary must be larger than the ownership-acquiring boundary. The difference should be large enough to prevent thrashing problems with an agent leaving a player's ownership and being reacquired, as determined by the maximum agent movement speed. The update boundary should be larger than both ownership boundaries to ensure that all agents owned by a player or waiting to be transferred are still being processed. Also note that if the second player comes back in range of the first player, and their ownership boundaries overlap, agents owned by the first player will not be transferred until they explicitly leave the first player's ownership-leaving radius.

Performance—Active Load Distribution

The case where agent load must be transferred simply to balance processing performance across all machines is less common. If the game has a steady, deterministic number of agents per player, distributing their processing during regular gameplay would not be effective; it would be simpler to parcel out agents to each machine when a player joins the game. For many multiplayer games, this is the case because a comparable amount of AI is used for both single-player and multiplayer gameplay, so a single machine already must be able to handle all agent processing. However, if the nature of agent creation, due to gameplay, is more dynamic across all machines in the game, an active load-sharing mechanism can address the problem. This is best illustrated when two players, after playing the game for a period of time, come to play together, and one player is processing significantly more agents than the other.

Each machine keeps track of the agents it currently owns and the agents owned by each other machine. Instead of each agent individually testing whether or not it needs to transfer ownership, all the agents on one machine are considered at the same time. There are three thresholds each machine must consider when determining whether to request a transfer of ownership for an agent:

The *high processing boundary*: This number represents the limit on processing load that the machine must be *over*, relative to other machines, before requesting to transfer its agents.

The *low processing boundary*: This number represents the processing limit a machine must be *under*, relative to other machines, before an overloaded machine will request to transfer agents to it.

The *minimum agent count*: If a machine currently owns fewer agents than this number, it will not consider transferring its agents even if it has a higher load relative to the other machines.

The processing load of a machine is defined relative to the other machines. If one machine is processing 10 agents and all the others are processing 5, it would have a processing load of 2.0, and the others would be at 1.0. As agents are created and destroyed, when one machine goes past the high processing boundary relative to the other machines, it looks for a likely candidate to transfer agents to. If two machines pass the high processing boundary at the same time, only the machine most drastically over the boundary is allowed to request transfer of its agents.

This machine then checks to see if any of the other machines are under the low processing boundary. If the machine doesn't find any, it keeps all of its agents. Although this will result in suboptimal performance on the burdened machine, the other machines are already at reasonable capacity. Overburdening them instead would simply cause thrashing as agents are transferred back and forth between the most heavily burdened machines.

If the overburdened machine does find machines under the low processing boundary, it requests to transfer a number of agents, enough to take it below the high boundary, to those machines. Agent lifetime is used to determine which agents to transfer. The oldest agents are transferred first to reduce the chance that a single agent may get rapidly transferred between two or more machines before finding a more permanent home. The machines that respond first to the requests are acknowledged by the overburdened machine, and ownership is transferred.

This assumes agents have roughly similar processing requirements. In the case of disparate processing requirements per agent, a simple weighted score could suffice to adjust processing. For example, an agent that uses twice as many ray casts in its behavior code might be assigned a weighted score of 2 in the processing load calculation, assuming that ray casts are the bulk of the agent processing requirements. Using an abstract score to represent processing load, separate from a machine's actual processing power or network bandwidth, allows us to change the calculation of an agent's impact on both of those factors by simply adjusting the two boundaries and the weighting of any individual NPC.

Serializing AI State

After machines have coordinated the transfer of ownership of an agent, the agent must continue its current actions relatively seamlessly on the new machine. During normal processing, an agent frequently transmits a small amount of information about its current state. This typically includes position, velocity, and animation state changes. Unfortunately, this is not enough to properly transfer ownership when distributing an agent's processing or when a player disconnects. If an agent fails to continue the behavior it was executing, game-locking bugs can occur (if the actions the agent was performing were required to progress in the game). Additional information is also necessary for any player to save the game, even though he does not control all of the agents at that point.

When we decide to transfer ownership, we could simply send all pertinent information about an agent's state that is not transmitted on a regular update, but this amount of data could be prohibitive. It also does not solve the problem that arises when a player disconnects before there is an opportunity to send an agent's full state. Ideally, we want to keep this additional state information as small as possible by taking advantage of its more persistent nature.

Agents driven by basic FSMs can simply transfer information when they change states, specifying the new state and what caused the transition. More complex decision-making structures, such as stack-based state machines or hierarchical finite state machines (HFSMs), would require data about past states and the state of each level of the hierarchy. For instance, an agent with a high-level attack state might need to send the information that triggered the attack (such as the enemy it saw) as well as information about which substate it was in under the attack state (such as finding cover, retreating, melee attacking, or reloading).

We need to be careful as we serialize additional lower-level state information. Sending information about an agent's attack state might in turn require information, such as the agent's lower-level animation data. The key to keeping this data small is restricting it to the information that causes the agent to change state or perform new actions. Information that is relevant while in the middle of an action will be recreated when the agent's ownership is transferred or the saved game is loaded. In the previous example, it may not actually be necessary to send substate information for an agent in a hierarchical attack state because the agent will resume at the high-level attack state and redetermine the appropriate substate from there. Even if the AI is not implemented strictly as a state machine, the same guidelines apply to persistent information required by other decision-making mechanisms.

Other Issues

A number of other concerns arise when creating AI for a peer-to-peer game, which vary in importance depending on the type of gameplay.

Scripted Game Logic

Having AI behavior scripted by game designers is fairly common and often beneficial. This might include scripting gameplay logic, such as how much damage various attacks perform under different circumstances, or it might be scripting sequences of actions that agents must perform. In any case, only the machine that owns a particular agent should run scripts associated with that particular agent (such as an OnDamaged script function tied to a specific NPC). This allows the script to run on that machine, complete execution, and send any resulting messages to the other peers.

Some scripting languages allow for a particular script function to execute over more than one frame. That particular script state is saved between frames, and the script can determine how long it will pause or sleep between executions. Although this capability adds flexibility for designers, it makes it very difficult to serialize AI state. Each peer has to broadcast the script state for all currently executing script threads so that agents can continue functioning properly on other machines when their ownership is transferred. The overhead associated with this transfer is prohibitive compared to any small flexibility gained on the scripting side.

Cutscenes

Games that feature cutscenes—in-game noninteractive sequences where agents perform scripted actions for storytelling purposes—place additional requirements on distributed agent processing. Due to the nature of these sequences, timing is often crucial. Cutscenes do not have to be perfectly in sync across all players' machines, but on each machine, agents must perform their sequenced actions at exactly the right times to coordinate with camera movement and other scripted elements.

If the agents are trying to perform these commands while their processing is distributed on different machines, it will be very difficult to achieve this level of visual synchronization on a given machine. There are a number of solutions, but they all typically involve turning off each agent's normal processing. They can then receive commands directly from the "server" (an arbitrary player designated to run the cutscene and send it to the other players). Alternatively, every agent on each machine can execute a series of commands stored on disk for a particular cutscene, before they are returned to their normal processing.

Security and Cheating

Because there is no server that can validate game messages from clients, a peer-to-peer game does not normally allow for strong measures against player cheating and other security issues. However, each peer can perform validation checks on the messages and data it receives from other players and AI agents. This includes checks for valid movement rates (to detect messages that move a player or NPC faster than allowable by game logic), valid rates of fire for any attacks, damage amounts appropriate to an attack, and so on. This approach at least requires all players to cheat together if they want to cheat.

Message Ordering Between Peers

As noted in the case of the blackboard, the order of messages between peers may not be consistent. A player may receive notification that an NPC shot a weapon from one peer and notification that it hit something from another peer, out of order. With the blackboard, it is easiest to assign ownership to one machine to solve synchronization issues, but this is not always a valid or ideal solution for all message types. There are other solutions for message synchronization [Lu04]; the most straightforward is to discard messages outside a certain causality window. In the case of the shoot and hit messages, after a machine receives the hit message, it can ignore any messages with a game time predating the timestamp of the hit message (assuming all the peers have a synchronized game time). The shoot message is then ignored if received afterward, which is acceptable because we have already dealt with its effect upon receiving the hit message.

Conclusion

Creating AI that is distributed across a peer-to-peer game raises some very different issues than building AI for a client-server architecture. Although client-server architectures have certain benefits for larger-scale games, peer-to-peer architectures have their own benefits for players, such as graceful player disconnect handling. With a few straightforward architectural changes, we can distribute agent processing dynamically across multiple peers, allowing us to take full advantage of a peer-to-peer architecture.

References

[Isensee03] Isensee, Pete, and Ganem, Steve, "Developing Online Console Games." Gamasutra. Available online at *http://www.gamasutra.com/features/20030328/isensee_01.shtml*, March 28, 2003.

[Isla02] Isla, Damian, and Blumberg, Bruce, "Blackboard Architectures." *AI Game Programming Wisdom*, Charles River Media, 2002.

[Knutsson04] Knutsson, Björn, et al., "Peer-to-Peer Support for Massively Multi-player Games." Available online at *http://www.cis.upenn.edu/~hhl/Papers/infocom04.pdf*, 2004.

[Lu04] Lu, Honghui, et al., "The Design of Synchronization Mechanisms for Peer-to-Peer Massively Multiplayer Games." Available online at *http://www.cis.upenn.edu/~hhl/Papers/MS-CIS-04-xy.pdf*, 2004.

[Orkin04] Orkin, Jeff, "Simple Techniques for Coordinated Behavior." *AI Game Programming Wisdom 2*, Charles River Media, 2004.

3.9

AI Architectures for Multiprocessor Machines

Jessica D. Bayliss, Ph.D.—
Rochester Institute of Technology,
Information Technology Department

jdb@cs.rit.edu

Single-threaded games are still written, but such games do not take advantage of the full processing power of machines with multiple cores or processors. The proliferation of multicore consoles and PCs means that games must now be threaded to run on these architectures. This threading changes the overall architecture of a game and may change the way AI is done as well.

Because multiple characters in a game need to do the same fundamental actions, AI has traditionally been split into modules. The modularization of the AI influences how it can be threaded. A common modularization of AI within a game is shown in Figure 3.9.1. The AI receives sensory input from the environment, such as the locations of agents, sounds, or even smells. The pathfinder contains information about the game map and finds paths for entities. The strategic AI module decides on goals for the AI agents in the game. Goals may be as diverse as killing an enemy target or getting coffee from the next room.

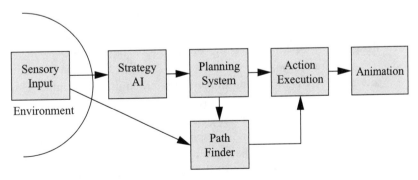

FIGURE 3.9.1 A common modularization of AI within games.

The planning module decides how to accomplish the goals for agents in the game. To obtain coffee, the game character may need to stand up, plan a path into the next room, go to the next room, take a cup out of the cupboard, and pour coffee into it. The action execution AI is the low-level physics and movement involved with the chosen action and may provide feedback to previous steps when an action has been fully executed. Animation is often closely linked with action execution and may be stopped, started, or blended depending on the action sequence. Time slicing is commonly used to control the flow of many agents through the AI modules.

Functional and Data Decomposition

Figure 3.9.1 breaks the game AI into different types of tasks. This approach is called *functional decomposition*, and it is the most commonly used decomposition in games. In this approach, each module is assigned to its own thread—for example, pathfinding in one thread and planning in another. Functional decomposition is more effective on architectures where the number of processing units does not exceed the number of functional modules in the game. As computing devices gain more and more processing units, it will become increasingly difficult for functional decomposition to make full use of available computing resources.

Functional decomposition can work well when the hardware contains homogenous cores. PCs contain one or two homogenous cores, with more cores being put on a chip every year, and there are enough functions in a game (e.g., physics, graphics, AI) to make functional decomposition worthwhile. The Xbox 360 contains three homogenous cores for running different game tasks, and functional decomposition is reasonable for this platform as well.

The non-homogenous architecture of the PlayStation 3 (PS3) is a different story, however. Each of the seven Synergistic Processing Elements (SPEs) contain 256 KB of local memory, and they are linked together by a high-speed bus. One of the SPEs is dedicated to the PS3 operating system ,and thus only six of them are usable by game code. These six SPEs lend themselves to Single Instruction Multiple Data (SIMD) parallelism. The PS3 also contains a PowerPC processor that runs two hardware threads that can be used for some functional decomposition. The bulk of the PS3 is thus not designed for functional decomposition but for *data decomposition*.

Data decomposition occurs when the data for a computational task is divided among different processing units. Massively multiplayer online (MMO) games make heavy use of data decomposition. MMOs commonly decompose the game environment onto different physical servers. Each server runs its own AI, physics, and so on, but on different data. MMOs often split their data up by physical game location to reduce the number of messages between physical server machines. This ordinarily works well, except when many players visit the same game location and overload that server.

When decomposing AI in terms of data, it is natural to decompose agents into different groups. An example architecture for this is shown in Figure 3.9.2. This type of architecture has been successfully implemented for schools of fish on the PS3 by

Craig Reynolds [Reynolds06]. This implementation consisted of a spatial hashing of fish according to their position. Fish that were close to each other were then parceled out to different SPEs for processing, and the fish calculated their own movements. Because the fish move by steering behaviors rather than path planning, this worked well. If computationally intense pathing were required, the approach would not work as well. In this case, path information could potentially be precalculated and then loaded into the appropriate SPE's memory, or the A* pathfinding algorithm could be parallelized and split across the SPEs.

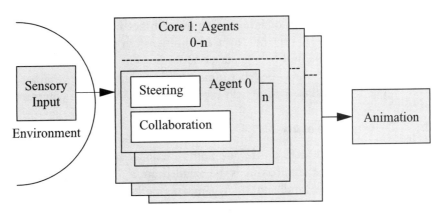

FIGURE 3.9.2 An example architecture for data parallel AI.

Alexander Repenning takes data decomposition further with the idea of *antiobjects* [Repenning06]. Repenning concentrates on putting AI into the environment as opposed to putting AI into the individual characters. He eschews the creation of a separate pathfinding module in his Pac-Man grid world and instead uses individual tiles as objects, embedding important information in the tiles. For example, at each step, the location of Pac-Man is mathematically diffused over the floor tiles. To reach Pac-Man, the ghosts follow his scent with a simple hill-climbing algorithm. The act of diffusion as well as the simple hill-climbing algorithm both lend themselves to parallel systems such as the PS3. Repenning has additionally created collaborative soccer players that operate on similar principles.

If a game has been architected to run on the PS3 through data decomposition, it will not run as well on the Xbox 360 because the 360 does not have as many processing units. Functional decomposition may yield better performance on a machine such as the Xbox 360, especially when different functional components can help each other by predicting the future state of the game. This may happen when a physics engine processes data fast enough to get ahead of rendering and thus can make predictions about the state of the game that can help the AI.

Demonstration Game

ON THE CD

A simple program that demonstrates threading accompanies this article on the CD-ROM. It is missing many components of a real game and is not optimized to keep the program simple for the demonstration of different architectures. The demo is best used in conjunction with a thread profiling tool (such as AMD's Code Analyst or Intel's Thread Profiler) to see the effects of checking the threading box and how the threads are split onto different machine cores. The AMD tool is free to download.

In this demo, the player is a zombie (green triangle) that chases after humans (yellow triangles) to gobble them up. The humans flee (purple triangles) when the player gets too close but sometimes gang up with neighboring humans to attack the player (red triangles). Both the player and humans can pick up food pellets (blue triangles) to help restore health. The player never dies, and the humans always respawn so that the simulation may be left running while techniques are compared. Examples from the demo will be used to help explain concepts in the following sections.

Hybrid Decomposition

Hybrid game architectures use both functional and data decomposition. One example of such an architecture is the parallelization of the *Half-Life 2* engine as shown in Figure 3.9.3 [Lindberg07]. A game engine loop runs in the main thread, and the sound thread is separated from the rest of the system. A task queue is created to organize tasks according to necessity. Tasks in this architecture are very high-level concepts and may consist either of sets of individual agents doing the same thing (data decomposition) or of different system functional tasks (functional decomposition).

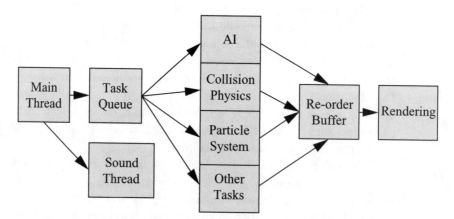

FIGURE 3.9.3   A hybrid game architecture where several parallel threads of execution run. The tasks shown are example tasks that could be run on such an architecture.

Rather than using processing power to create and delete threads as they are needed for tasks, a ready pool of threads is kept alive, and the individual threads in the pool can take on whatever tasks are required by the task queue. Tasks are independent from one another and may run on different processing units. The reorder buffer exists to make sure that the rendering obtains items in the correct rendering order. Both the task queue and the reorder buffer help to keep thread synchronization to a minimum so that thread synchronization issues, such as deadlock, are less likely to occur.

The simplest way to parallelize AI in this architecture is to enable the individual agents to submit tasks to the task queue for execution on different processing units. This is the technique used in the following finite state machine (FSM) example.

Finite State Machines

The demonstration program contains both a threaded and nonthreaded FSM implementation. The individuals are hashed according to their location and split among cores. Additionally, when an agent is close to the border of a processing unit's "region," it is given to the two closest processors, with one copy being read only. This allows agents to sense each other when not running on the same core. This kind of architecture may also be used for collision detection and avoidance (which the demo does not do). The FSM consists of the following rules for individual humans:

```
If DIE then
    State = BORN
Else if health <= 0 then
    State = DIE
Else if ( health < maximum health &&
    state == SEEK FOOD ) then
    State = SEEK FOOD
Else if ( those around player > 2 &&
    I'm around the player ) then
    State = SWARM
Else if ( State != SWARM &&
    health == maximum health &&
    I'm not around the player ) then
    State = WANDER
Else if ( State == FLEE && near player ) then
    State = FLEE
Else if ( health < maximum health / 2 ) then
    Look for the closest food and set as a target
    State = SEEK FOOD
Else if ( I'm around the player ) then
    State = FLEE
Else
    State = WANDER
```

Although different independent agents may be split onto different processing units according to location, it is possible for groups of cooperative agents to become split onto different processing units. This can greatly increase message passing between two different processing units. There are a couple of ways to deal with this case. Conditional code may be written to ensure that individuals in the same unit are never separated onto different processing units. Another method of splitting units consists of placing them in a hierarchical relationship with individuals. In this case, groups could be hashed onto different processing units rather than individuals. In games with both individuals and groups, it is possible to have a group of size one for consistency.

It is also possible to functionally decompose state machines. Because FSMs consist of states with connections representing state transitions, individuals that have the same state machine can simultaneously run code to check a given transition. If there are multiple possible transitions, each transition can be checked independently of the others and thus could run on a separate processing unit. The drawback is that all transition checks for a particular state are likely to use almost exactly the same data for the check, resulting in too many data transfers between processing units.

This is a common problem when trying to make several parallel threads, and it is helpful to make the sharing of data more explicit in the AI architecture. FSMs are known to have drawbacks. For one thing, it is not immediately obvious what data is being shared unless the state machine author has been very careful to document shared data. For another, there is coupling between planning and action execution. In the demo, for example, we could decide that there are two kinds of humans: those who flee and die, and more aggressive humans who will always attack and become zombies rather than dying. In the previous state machine, the addition of a new kind of NPC means that new states need to be added to implement the new character's behavior. Decoupling the planning and action execution can make this sort of change easier and can lead to a more functional type of parallelism with a more explicit model of shared data.

Planning Systems

An example planning AI system is shown in Figure 3.9.4 and is similar to the decision-making process from the game *F.E.A.R.*, which used a version of the STRIPS planning system [Orkin06]. This AI architecture is also similar to the game architecture used by the *Half-Life 2* engine in Figure 3.9.3.

The goal, planning, and action execution threads have been decoupled in this architecture and can run on different processing units. The goal and planning threads could potentially remain linked in the same thread depending on how much overlapping data they modify because data must be locked if both threads use it. Working memory serves to keep track of the environmental state of the game and allows the different decoupled parts of the AI to converse. Working memory represents the state of the game environment to the agent. A queue of changes to working memory, such as the task queue from Figure 3.9.3, can be used to prevent locking and unlocking between the threads. A queue can also allow prioritizing some changes over others.

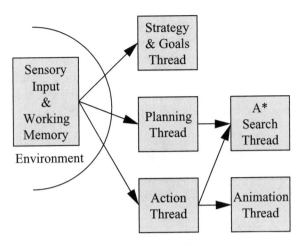

FIGURE 3.9.4   A planning AI architecture.

The goal thread picks a goal to achieve, and then the planning thread finds a plan of changes to working memory—that is, actions to be taken by an NPC—that achieve that goal. If some actions are better than others, then A* may be used as a search algorithm to find a plan. In the demo program, there are so few actions that it is not worth using A*.

Actions have a series of preconditions that determine when they fire. Preconditions can be methods or can evaluate the state of working memory. The planner for the example program is simple: it consists of looking at sensory data and deciding on STAY ALIVE, ATTACK, BORN, or BOUNCE goals. Several working memory variables take the place of states from the FSM implementation: near others (OTHERS_YES/OTHERS_NO), mood (FEARFUL/ANGRY/NEUTRAL), near the player (CLOSE/FAR), health (NONE/LOW/HIGH), and wall (HITTING/NOT_HITTING).

The goals are decided in the following manner:

```
If health == NONE then
    Next goal = BORN
Else if ( wall == HITTING) then
    Next 9 goals = BOUNCE
Else if ( near others == YES &&
    near player == YES &&
    health != NONE ) then
    Add goal of ATTACK to the queue
Else Add a goal of STAY_ALIVE to the queue
```

The preconditions and actions are shown in Table 3.9.1. The main benefit of this architecture is the decreased coupling between the different parts of the AI system when compared to the FSM implementation. As reported by the creators of *F.E.A.R.*, this architecture enabled them to easily add different characters via reusable actions and goal lists. The flexibility of this type of system does come at a price: the working memory for such a system is going to be larger than the working memory for an FSM because the goals and actions communicate through working memory. For the demo, it is possible to fit all states within an unsigned integer and use bit masks to tell which ones are applicable. In addition, the added infrastructure to support this system takes more time to program when compared with an FSM.

Table 3.9.1   The Actions, Necessary Preconditions for Firing the Actions, and Goals Satisfied for the Example Rule-Based System.

Actions	Preconditions	Satisfies Goal
Swarm	None	ATTACK
Flee	CLOSE && (FEARFUL || NEUTRAL) && Goal is STAY_ALIVE	STAY ALIVE
Seek Health	LOW && !ANGRY && Goal is Stay Alive	STAY ALIVE
Seek Screen Center	Goal is BOUNCE	BOUNCE
Born	Goal is BORN	BORN
Wander	FAR && !ANGRY && Goal is Stay Alive	STAY ALIVE

The working memory in this architecture is shared among the goals, planning, and actions, which may be a concern on processing units without physically shared memory. If this is the case, it may be better to use an architecture that makes shared memory explicit so that it can be split up.

Blackboard Systems

Blackboard systems are based on the metaphor of a group of individuals trying to solve a problem at a blackboard [Russell02]. The central idea is that only one individual has the chalk at a given time and may pass the chalk to another person for help in solving one or more problems on the blackboard. Each individual contributing to a solution is known as an "expert," and its domain is necessarily limited. Each expert operates independently of all other experts and uses the blackboard as a repository for shared data. An arbiter is used to make sure that only one expert acts on the shared data at any one time. The arbiter decides who has priority to access and modify data. *No One Lives Forever 2* used a blackboard for coordination among agents [Orkin02].

There can be multiple decision makers and tactical planners in such a system, each vying to dictate what should be done next. Individual experts possess arbitrary internal architectures, including FSMs, neural networks, or planning systems.

A potential blackboard for the demo might consist of experts for each of the main actions from the rule-based architecture discussed previously. There could be a health expert that determines when a character needs health, a movement expert that chooses the type of movement a character should make at any one time, and an attack expert that determines when attacking is appropriate.

These experts look at a portion of the world state that is of interest to them and decide what action they should propose, if any. The arbiter then decides which of the action-proposing experts had the highest priority and has that expert update the blackboard. Changing game-state information on the blackboard updates agents within the game. An example of this architecture is shown in Figure 3.9.5.

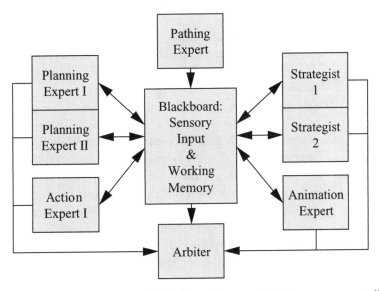

FIGURE 3.9.5   An example blackboard system. Each box may potentially be broken up into a separate thread.

The blackboard system makes working memory explicit, so that the shared data between components is well known. Different experts may only operate on a piece of the blackboard and thus do not need to be concerned with the operation of other experts. As an example, the health expert only accesses a character's health and does not care about its weapons or attack power.

The decomposition of AI into threads for a blackboard system is thus a hybrid decomposition, where some of the data is exclusive to individual experts, and some experts represent functional components of the game task.

The main benefit of the blackboard system is that it makes the shared memory among different pieces of the AI system explicit. Further, the hybrid decomposition suggests that a blackboard system is a scalable architecture as the number of processing units continues to grow. Compared with both FSMs and planning system architectures, blackboard systems require the most program infrastructure to create. Additionally, they can have a steep learning curve, and hence special tools may be needed to enable game designers to use the blackboard system effectively.

Conclusion

The ability to develop threaded games is becoming more and more important, and AI can benefit from the increasing number of cores on machines. To do this with the least amount of pain possible, it is helpful to look at AI architectures that can support the move to multiple threads. Architectures that decrease coupling among different pieces of the AI or that make shared data explicit will likely be more useful for long-term development needs.

Two primary types of decomposition exist: functional and data. Individual AI characters may be split onto different processing units and represent data decomposition. It is fairly easy to keep the traditional FSM implementation of agents with this type of architecture.

Several types of functional decomposition exist. The planning system described here decouples goal, planning, and action functionality for characters. This comes at a price: more memory is used. Still, games such as *F.E.A.R.* have successfully used this type of architecture, and it shows promise due to its flexibility. Much like a system based on a state machine, it enables designers to easily design goals and actions that can then be used to make plans that drive character behaviors.

The blackboard system represents a hybrid of functional and data decomposition. Because the blackboard makes shared memory explicit, it is easier to split it among different functional experts so that they can run on different processing units. Blackboard systems are less frequently used in commercial games but could potentially be the most scalable architecture due to the emphasis on data parallelism between different agents. Experts may be difficult to construct for people who are not programmers, and this is probably one of the main reasons that blackboard systems are not seen more often in commercial games. Infrastructure is needed to make the experts easy to construct for designers.

The three architectures discussed here are certainly not the only possible AI architectures for games. The AI architecture should be carefully considered within the constraints of the entire game system. Other needs, such as the ability to expose pieces of the AI to designers, integration with existing tools, and testing, may constrain the architecture. In the future, threading will necessitate a careful consideration of traditional AI architectures and will push the AI to be more decoupled, either functionally, in terms of data, or both.

References

[Lindberg07] Lindbereg, P., and Werth, B., "Threading Games for Performance: A One Day Hands-On Workshop by Intel." *Proceedings of the Game Developers Conference,* 2007.

[Orkin02] Orkin, J., "Simple Techniques for Coordinated Behavior." *AI Game Programming Wisdom 2,* Charles River Media, 2002.

[Orkin06] Orkin, J., "Three States and a Plan: the AI for F.E.A.R." *Proceedings of the Game Developers Conference,* 2006.

[Repenning06] Repenning, A., "Collaborative Diffusion: Programming Antiobjects." OOPSLA 2006, *Proceedings of ACM SIGPLAN International Conference on Object-Oriented Programming Systems, Languages, and Applications,* Portland, Ore., 2006.

[Reynolds06] Reynolds, C., "Big Fast Crowds on PS3." *Proceedings of Sandbox* (an ACM Video Games Symposium), Boston, Massachusetts, July 2006.

[Russell02] Russell, S. and Norvig, P., *Artificial Intelligence: A Modern Approach* (2nd Ed.). Prentice Hall, 2002.

3.10

Level Up for Finite State Machines: An Interpreter for Statecharts

Philipp Kolhoff—KING Art

pkolhoff@kingart.de

Jörn Loviscach—Hochschule Bremen

jlovisca@informatik.hs-bremen.de

Finite state machines (FSMs) have become commonplace in game programming [Fu04]. Their uses range from simple game logic to complex behavior of non-player characters (NPCs). However, FSMs have a tendency to confront the programmer with an explosion of states and to become heavily entangled with other parts of the game code. Harel's statecharts provide some much-needed improvements over FSMs that help to alleviate these problems [Harel87].

Many game programming scenarios that stretch FSMs to their limits can be formulated with statecharts in a tidy and intuitive fashion. For example, statecharts handle nested hierarchies of increasingly specific states as well as simultaneous actions. This article introduces the statechart formalism and its use in game development. We discuss how to create an efficient and flexible interpreter and provide both an implementation in C++ that allows minimally invasive integration with existing game code as well as a full-fledged implementation in C# with a graphical statechart editor/debugger.

Statecharts help to create and modify a game's behavior without writing code; they offer the visual approach and the simplicity of standard FSMs but surpass them in functionality. This benefits game designers working on tight schedules as well as those having little expertise in programming. It may also open up new avenues for complex user-generated game content.

Statecharts as an Extension to FSMs

In 1987, David Harel published his seminal work on statecharts, an extension of FSMs. In this section, we describe the major ideas that form the basis of this extension, illustrating their use in a hypothetical dungeon-crawler game. We use standard

UML (Unified Modeling Language) statechart notation [OMG07] as defined in Figure 3.10.1 for all of the statechart examples in this article.

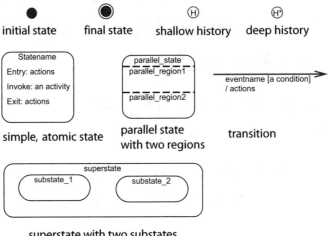

FIGURE 3.10.1   The elements of the UML statechart diagram.

Two basic elements of statecharts are on-entry and on-exit actions, which are invoked when a particular state is entered or exited. In addition, transitions between states may be guarded by conditions, which must be satisfied before the transition can be followed. This is especially useful for transitions without an associated event, which would otherwise be activated by any event. Consider the simple example in Figure 3.10.2. The current value of our hero's health is stored in a variable. Each time the character suffers a hit, his health is reduced until the condition this.Health <= 0 is satisfied and the game ends.

In addition to the simple states and the transitions mentioned before, the statechart in Figure 3.10.2 contains two additional elements, which are familiar from FSMs: a point from which to start the statechart and one to mark a possible end. These so-called initial and final states are nameless pseudostates. Initial states immediately yield to the first actual state to which they are connected.

Hierarchy Through Substates

The dungeon of our game consists of several levels. The player may only proceed to the next level after he has finished the previous one. At any level, the game will be over if the player dies. This is signaled by a die event and leads to a state called dead. To build this behavior with an FSM, you have to add a transition from every single level to a dead state, as in the left half of Figure 3.10.3. The die event triggers this transition. The resulting number of transitions can lead to a maintenance nightmare. Imagine, for example, that the game has a huge number of levels, and at some point late in

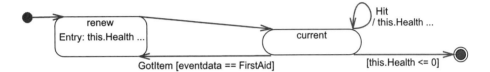

FIGURE 3.10.2   The current health is reduced with each hit but may be recovered with a first-aid kit.

development, the name of the die event needs to be altered or a condition needs to be added to the event.

To overcome this and related problems, Harel introduced a notion of hierarchy into his statecharts, enabling a collection of states to be aggregated into a superstate. Reconfiguring our original dungeon-levels FSM using this approach yields a new superstate called alive, as shown in the right half of Figure 3.10.3. All levels of the game will reside inside this state. A single transition from the alive state to the dead state takes care of every die event that occurs during the game. If the event has to be altered, changes now only have to be made once.

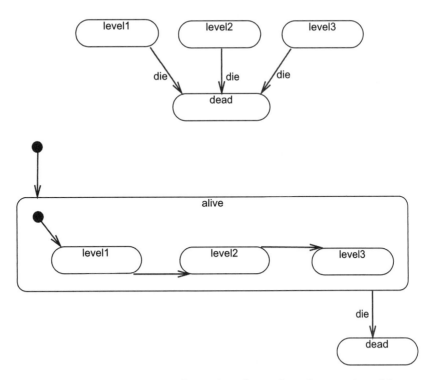

FIGURE 3.10.3   FSM (top) and statechart (bottom) implementation of the dungeon level example.

Upon entering a superstate, the statechart interpreter looks for an initial substate. This behavior is often seen in hierarchical compositions of FSMs, but hierarchy in statecharts can do more because it allows interlevel transitions. Consider the `alive` state that encompasses all the dungeon's levels. In level two, a nasty poisoned trap awaits the hero, killing him if he did not previously ingest an antidote. This trap can send a `poison` event to the statechart, activating an interlevel transition from `level2` to `dead`. This transition is guarded by the condition `AntidoteActive == false`. Such a complex transition across the borders of the hierarchy would not be possible with a composition of standard FSMs.

In addition, hierarchies of states facilitate specialization and generalization, similar to object-oriented programming languages. For example, one designer can lay out the whole dungeon game by deciding how many levels there are and where special transitions, such as secret doors from one level to another, are available. This rough layout is then handed over to a number of level designers. Each of them can implement his level as a collection of substates without touching the logic of the other levels.

Concurrency Through Parallel States

Standard FSMs can create a combinatorial explosion of states to deal with even basic logic. Suppose that to finish level one in our dungeon-crawler game, we have to find the red key and the blue key. The naive way of coding this would be to add four states with appropriate transitions: `no_key_possession`, `red_key_possession`, `blue_key_possession`, and `both_keys_possession`. Because the player can receive the two keys in any order, the event of receiving a particular key has to be considered in two transitions. Things get quickly worse with more keys: for n keys, you need 2^n states, as shown in Figure 3.10.4.

To counteract this exponential growth, Harel proposes to model concurrency with *parallel states*. Declaring a state to be parallel causes its direct substates to exist in independent contexts. Each of the substates are entered and exited simultaneously as the parallel superstate is entered and exited. Typically, these substates will contain nested states that define their actual logic. Using parallel states, the four-key example from Figure 3.10.4 can be simplified to the statechart in Figure 3.10.5, which has one parallel superstate that contains a substate for every key color. Every key-color substate itself contains an initial subsubstate, a subsubstate `not_found_yet`, and a final subsubstate to represent the possession of the key.

To put it differently, regular states are combined in a manner that can be compared to an `XOR`, with exactly one of them active at any time. By contrast, parallel states combine their substates in an `AND` fashion, with all of them active at the same time.

Memory Through History

On entering a state with nested substates, the statechart interpreter searches for the initial substate and then follow its transitions. If the nested substate is left and later reentered, execution restarts at the initial substate.

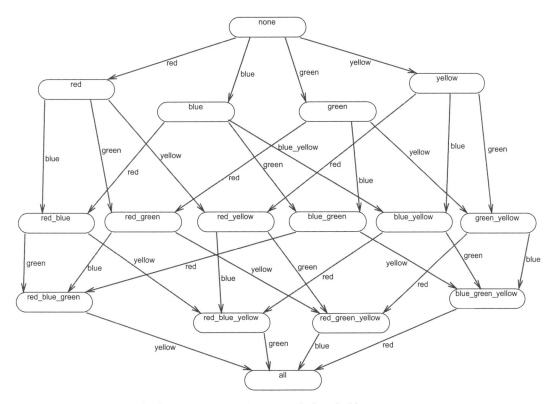

FIGURE 3.10.4   A standard FSM requires 16 states to deal with 4 keys.

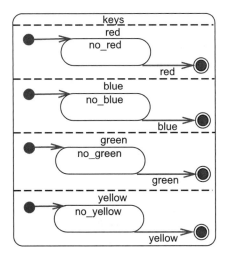

FIGURE 3.10.5   Thanks to the parallel states allowed in a statechart, the order in which the keys are retrieved is of no importance.

Suppose that in our dungeon-crawler game, the player wants to leave a level part of the way through and then return to it later without having to play through the entire level again. To offer this capability, Harel introduced the notion of *history states* (H states). H states resemble normal initial states, except that on reentry, they immediately switch the current state to the substate saved on the previous exit. Consider Figure 3.10.6. When the hero returns from the vault to the princess' bedroom, the H state restores the state that was active when the hero was last in the bedroom.

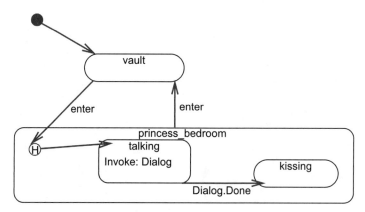

FIGURE 3.10.6   Example of the use of an H state.

H states come in two varieties: shallow and deep. A shallow H state only stores the active state of the same substate hierarchy level. Thus, if the `talking` state consisted of several substates that form a dialog, a shallow H state would not remember which of these substates was active when the superstate `princess_bedroom` was exited. Reactivating the shallow H state only would lead to the activation of `talking` at its initial substate. A deep H state, by contrast, stores the deepest active subsubstate(s). Note that there may be a multitude of these, due to parallel substates. If the H state of the statechart in Figure 3.10.6 were a deep H, reactivating it would also restore the active states inside the `talking` state, ignoring any initial states.

Temporally Extended Tasks Through Activities

Typically, FSMs employ "actions" to send messages to the rest of the game code. A specific action can be invoked for every transition from one state to another. Actions are generally short fragments of code that quickly return control to the FSM.

Suppose, however, that our dungeon-crawler game displays a text window to the player and requires the hero to engage in a dialog with the princess, trying to flatter her. He will either succeed, or the princess will lose her temper. Alternatively, the player may close the text window before a decisive outcome is reached. Managing such a dialog is a temporally extended process and as such is not suitable for an action. Although this can be implemented in traditional FSMs by either polling or sending status messages to the statechart as well as start and stop messages to the task, the statechart offers a far more convenient tool for this typical programming task: the activity.

An *activity* is a process that starts when a certain state is entered and ends when this state is exited. If the activity ends on its own (e.g., because the princess sent the hero away), the activity sends a corresponding event to the state, as shown in Figure 3.10.7.

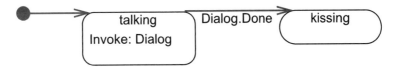

FIGURE 3.10.7   The state `talking` starts the activity `Dialog`. When this activity ends, it sends the `Dialog.Done` event.

Figure 3.10.8 shows the whole statechart of the dungeon-crawler game. The main part of the game is contained in the `alive` state. Two parallel substates handle the location and the health of the hero separately. The `location` state tracks the progress inside the dungeon through several substates. The first level is another parallel state that is done when its substates both reach a final state—in other words, the hero found the two keys. Levels two and three are displayed collapsed for better readability.

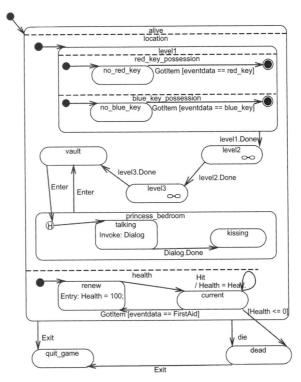

FIGURE 3.10.8   The statechart for the dungeon-crawler.

Interpreting a Statechart

In most cases, it is intuitively clear how a statechart should behave, even though it offers significant extensions over a classical FSM. However, developing an interpreter that can understand highly complex statecharts requires that certain rules be established regarding which transitions are to be taken under which circumstances.

Starting Up

Some kinds of FSMs allow marking several states as initial ones. In contrast to that, a Harel statechart requires exactly one initial state on the topmost level. If there are nested substates, every level should possess its own initial substate. This makes a statechart's startup phase easy to understand and debug.

Nonetheless, there is still a vital reason to allow starting from an arbitrary state: persistence. For example, you must be able to save the current state of the game to disk and continue it later. This saving and restoring could be handled with standard serialization mechanisms that ignore the statechart's behavior. Alternatively, integrating persistence with the statechart interpreter itself might also make sense: the interpreter would enter all states that were persisted as being active, invoking their on-entry actions and starting their activities.

Processing Events

A statechart is a reactive system, changing its states only when triggered by an event (either external or generated by actions and activities invoked by the statechart itself). In practice, it has proved useful to pass these events as a two-part data structure that contains a character string that identifies the event type and a pointer or reference to an eventdata object that identifies the concrete cause.

Using a character string offers several benefits. In a log file or the output of a debugger, the string is readily understandable. For testing, the developer can fire events by typing them into a console embedded into the game. In addition, character strings can be operated on with simple wildcards or even with sophisticated regular expressions. For example, a transition on the topmost level of states could listen for events called Error.* to catch all error events that are not caught otherwise. This can eliminate a huge number of transitions. Although such behavior could also be modeled with class inheritance, wildcards prove to be more flexible.

The statechart interpreter does not process the eventdata object, which simply stores data for use by the game engine. In some situations, the eventdata object may not be necessary—for example, if all interesting conditions are obtainable from global or static variables.

The statechart interpreter can run in a processing thread separate from the rest of the game code. Thus, events can occur while the statechart interpreter is still evaluating previous events. To avoid making the application code wait, the statechart interpreter requires a queue that accepts and stores incoming events in a first-in first-out manner. Only when one event is fully processed will the interpreter start to work on the next one.

To keep the AI behavior independent of the frame rate, it can be useful to implement two event queues: one handles events sent by the statechart, which are processed first, and the other handles regular external events, which are only accepted when the first queue is empty.

Sending events should be the only way to trigger state changes. It may be tempting to activate states directly, in particular through actions and activities, but this runs the risk of violating consistency, for example, by skipping over activation or deactivation code.

Choosing the Transition

Upon receiving an event, the statechart interpreter checks which transitions, if any, might apply. Because transitions can occur from and to different levels of nested states, this seemingly simple task requires more caution than with an FSM. The interpreter might find an appropriate transition on the top level of the hierarchy or deeply hidden in subsubstates. A policy is required to determine which of these transitions should be taken. In adherence to the idea that substates are specializations of superstates, the transition that starts at the deepest substate is favored. This policy defines the order in which all transitions of all active (sub)states are queried, regardless of whether or not they are applicable to the event at hand. Due to the hierarchy, a statechart requires a more extended search for transitions than a standard FSM. To model the same behavior, the FSM would, however, need many more states and transitions and thus require an equally expensive search.

For every transition that is checked, the interpreter has to determine if the event's type matches the transition and if all conditions on the transition are fulfilled. The event type check is performed by comparing two character strings, possibly with wildcards or regular expressions. The evaluation of transition conditions cannot be accomplished by the statechart interpreter alone because it requires access to external game data. A typical solution is to formulate the condition in a scripting language, attach this condition script as text to the transition, and send it to the game code for evaluation as true or false. Typically, the eventdata object passed along with the event will come into play here because it may contain data needed during condition evaluation—for example, which item the player clicked on or which NPC has cast a spell on the hero.

When to Activate and When to Deactivate

The order of activation and deactivation is another tricky point for statecharts. When a transition is taken in an FSM, the old state is deactivated, and the new state is activated at the same time. When on-entry/on-exit actions come into play, the old state should be deactivated first, which triggers its on-exit action, and then the new state should be activated, triggering its on-entry action.

Things get more complex when substates are present at one or both ends of the transition. The interpreter deactivates the deepest active substate first and continues with its active superstates. It stops the deactivation when it hits a superstate that encapsulates both the origin and the target of the transition. If such a superstate exists, it remains active. From this point, the activation proceeds downward. This rule ensures that all superstates of an active state are active, thus preserving the statechart's consistency.

Imagine State_1111 of the statechart in Figure 3.10.9 is active, and the transition to State_121 is activated. The interpreter has to ensure that first of all State_1111 is deactivated, followed by State_111 and State_11. The State_1 can remain active because the target of the transition also is a descendant of State_1, like the start state of the transition. After deactivating all necessary states, the activation starts in reverse order: State_12 is activated before State_121, its substate. This facilitates specialization through hierarchy because on-entry-actions of a substate succeed those of their superstates and so, for example, can override values.

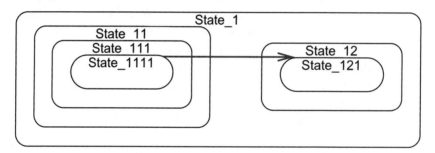

FIGURE 3.10.9   A statechart with a deeply nested hierarchy.

Parallel states require special caution. At all times, their substates must either all be activated or all be deactivated. In practice, however, this is not possible because actions attached to theses substates will not be invoked simultaneously but one after the other. To produce a deterministic interpreter, we need to define an ordering policy—for example, the order in which the substates were added to the state in the editor. The order of activation should be the reverse of the order of deactivation. Of course, the substates of these substates require recursive inside-out deactivation and outside-in activation.

The statechart interpreter automatically takes transitions for which no events are specified. This happens after all substates have been activated. Otherwise, an eventless transition on a higher level would short-circuit the states below. A more subtle case occurs when a condition guarding an eventless transition becomes true after some time without anything else happening. The interpreter won't notice the change because it only reacts to events; thus, such a condition change would go unnoticed until its next evaluation, triggered by the next event. One way to prevent this problem is to send an event with an empty type when something changes in the game. This may be expensive, and hence possibly one such event per frame suffices.

Building a Statechart Interpreter

The statechart interpreter can be created in a straightforward manner as a monolithic object. Depending on its use, this may be inefficient, however. A statechart may, for example, represent an NPC with thousands of instances in existence at the same time. In this case, it becomes reasonable to separate data that is unique to a single NPC instance from data that is the same for everyone using that statechart. Taking this approach, the interpreter needs to maintain a list of active states and an event queue for each NPC instance. The statechart template—that is, the collection of rules that make up the statechart logic—is shared by all NPCs.

This separation of the instance data from the statechart template saves memory, which may be important for games on mobile devices. A more prominent advantage is modularization: the interpreter can be exchanged, possibly even dynamically, without changing the template. This design is along the lines of the flyweight design pattern [Gamma95].

Modeling a Template

A statechart's template contains its structure and perhaps some functions to alter this structure or to step through it, but not the functions to interpret it. Given the hierarchical construction of a statechart, it is natural to create a tree structure, comparable to the scenegraph used to organize 3D worlds. Every state is represented by a node; substates that specialize a superstate become subnodes of its node. This structure allows us to add or delete entire subtrees. Furthermore, the interpreter can quickly walk through the hierarchy to search for relevant transitions.

Every node can be modeled as an instance of the class `BasicState`. From this class, we could derive separate classes for regular states and parallel states as well as for pseudostates, such as initial states and H states. However, it turns out that the different kinds of states require mostly the same data. Furthermore, a polymorphic approach would incur a lot of type checks and downcasts. To remain efficient, we can use a single class that contains a type identifier.

Every `BasicState` possesses an ID, for example, a character string to facilitate debugging or a unique number to accelerate the lookup in a map. To allow the interpreter to walk the tree, every `BasicState` possesses a list of pointers to its substates and a pointer to its superstate, which may also be the tree's root. The remaining data in a `BasicState` consists of a list of the outgoing transitions and a list of the attached actions and activities.

Communicating with the Outside World

The rules for interpreting statecharts impose a two-way communication between the interpreter and the rest of the game code.

The interpreter receives events, each of which may cause a transition from one state to another. Events contain a character string describing their type and a pointer to an arbitrary object.

The interpreter passes transition conditions—represented as character strings—to external game code to be evaluated to true or false. This character string could be the name of a Boolean variable, or it could be an expression formulated in a script language, such as Lua or Python.

On taking a transition or on entering or exiting a state, the interpreter may invoke actions in the game. Actions can, for example, be represented by script code, file names, or resource handles to files containing script code, or even a list of function pointers. In our prototype, an action is referred to by an object that specializes the interface IAction, which can be used to implement any of these options.

Activities can be treated similarly to actions. The interpreter can, for example, pass the activity's name and parameters to the game code, which searches through a list of registered services for an appropriate one. On exiting the activity's state, the interpreter must be able to abort the activity using the same means of communication. To prevent ambiguities, the interpreter needs to provide both a StateId and an InstanceId when it launches or terminate an activity.

The programming interface that supports this communication should be as simple as possible to keep the interpreter only minimally connected to the game. Figure 3.10.10 shows a lean and reusable architecture that separates templates from the interpreter code and encapsulates the statechart's communication in an interface. Optimally, both the interpreter and the game can be easily replaced. In particular, the interpreter should be reusable for other projects.

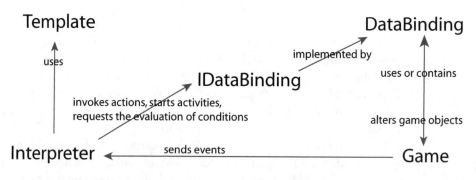

FIGURE 3.10.10   Architecture of the demo implementation.

Four functions suffice for the outgoing communication. The interface employed in our C++ demo is as follows:

```
class IDataBinding
{
public:
    virtual bool EvaluateCondition(
        const std::string &condition,
        void* eventdata,
        InstanceId instance) = 0;
    virtual void ExecuteAction(
        IAction* action,
        void* eventdata,
        InstanceId instance) = 0;
    virtual void InvokeActivity(
        const std::string &src,
        const std::list<Parameter> &parameters,
        const std::string &StateId,
        InstanceId instance) = 0;
    virtual void CancelInvokedActivity(
        const std::string &StateId,
        InstanceId instance) = 0;
};
```

The C# version is a literal translation:

```
public interface IDataBinding
{
    bool EvaluateCondition(
        string condition, object _eventdata,
        InstanceId instance);
    void ExecuteAction(
    IAction action, object _eventdata,
    InstanceId instance);
    void InvokeService(
        string src, List<Parameter> parameters,
        string StateId, InstanceId instance);
    void CancelInvokedService(string StateId,
        InstanceId instance);
}
```

Source Code and Demo

ON THE CD

This article is accompanied by two demonstration statechart interpreters on the CD-ROM. Written in C++ for Microsoft Visual Studio 2005 or Visual C++ Express, the first one is designed for easy integration with existing game code. To use this code, you need to provide a data binding and to construct the statecharts, either in a factory class or by reading them from files or a database. The precise details will depend on your game. To get you started and to illustrate the use of the demo, an example application is provided in which the statechart is explicitly constructed in the code.

The second demo implementation is a comprehensive framework based on .NET, written in C# for Microsoft Visual Studio 2005 or Microsoft Visual C# Express. It can read statecharts from the appropriate XML dialect, called State Chart XML [Barnett07]. The data binding realizes all of the described requirements; in particular, it allows the registration of services that can execute activities.

The C#-based solution employs scripts written in Lua. The data binding for Lua can automatically catch all events issued by a given .NET object. Using reflection, it determines all .NET events that the object can fire, and for each event, it registers a handler function that delegates the event to the statechart interpreter.

The statechart editor/debugger is easily the most complex piece of the .NET implementation. In this tool, the user can create states of all kinds, connect them with transitions, and add conditions, actions, and activities. The execution of statecharts can also be viewed in real time. The interface draws a red outline around each active state. In addition, it briefly flashes the background of every entered state from white to red. Thus, the flow of execution is easily visible even when the view is zoomed out or when the statechart is displayed on a second monitor alongside the game's actual output on the first monitor.

The statechart editor/debugger can be used in other .NET-based projects in two ways. First, you can create a `StateChartWindow` that shows a single `statechart` and allows you to edit and debug it. This is best done in a separate thread because the real-time visualization of a running statechart requires frequent refreshing to highlight every entered state. Second, you can integrate a `StateChartGUIUserControl` on a proprietary form, for example, in a level editor. If the project is not based on Windows Forms, you can still create an object of type `StatechartGUI`, although in this case, the application programmer has to take care of feeding user events into the statechart editor/debugger.

The statechart display employs the standard UML notation. Most of the figures in this article were produced by the same code, rendering to a PDF pseudoprinter. Actually, the rendering is abstracted away from the underlying graphics routines through five functions. The display could use any system ranging from in-game OpenGL to a plotter device at the other end of the world as long as it provides these functions.

An automatic layout routine cleans up the statechart's arrangement, placing states that are connected close to each other, as shown in Figure 3.10.11. This layout is based on an approach inspired by physics: force-directed layout. States that are connected exert strong attractive forces on one other; overlapping states repel each other; states that lie on the same level but are not connected try to stay a set distance from each other. To more easily gain insight into complex hierarchies, the user can hide substates. In addition, every state may be pinned to its current position; the automatic layout then produces a reasonable arrangement without touching the pinned states. This is helpful for "secondary notation," where the user wants to graphically group related states or to force a control flow from bottom to top. This blend of manual and automatic layout can be saved to disk and later restored.

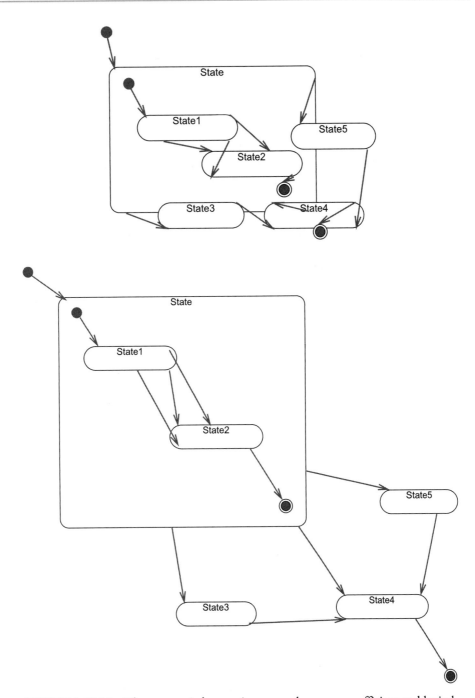

FIGURE 3.10.11 The automatic layout aims to produce a space-efficient and logical arrangement. By default, initial states are placed on the upper left, and final states on the lower right.

Conclusion

A small number of additional features, such as hierarchy and concurrency, dramatically enhances the expressivity of FSMs. We believe that every game developer, looking back to previous projects, will immediately notice places where statecharts would have been much less intricate than the FSMs that were actually used.

The interpreter offers enough flexibility to blend well with most existing projects. Just add a specific data binding and a way to construct statecharts. Employing a standard file format for this will make it even easier to edit statecharts with standard diagramming tools that can be used by any game designer. In this way, the path from design documents to working code becomes fully automated, increasing development speed and leaving less opportunity for errors.

This statechart framework has already been used to script the behavior of items and NPCs in an upcoming commercial adventure game. Game designers find it much easier to read and edit complex behavior if it is presented graphically. In particular, designers with little background in programming easily pick up the framework. The ability to focus on the game's screen, but at the same time watch the graphical statechart representation from the corner of the eye, propels the game's authors to a new level of productivity.

References

[Barnett07] Barnett, Jim, "State Chart XML (SCXML): State Machine Notation for Control Abstraction." Available online at *http://www.w3.org/TR/scxml/*, February 2007.

[Fu04] Fu, Dan, and Houlette, Ryan, "The Ultimate Guide to FSMs in Games." *AI Game Programming Wisdom 2,* Charles River Media, 2004.

[Gamma95] Gamma, Erich, Helm, Richard, and Vlissides, John, *Design Patterns: Elements of Reusable Object-Oriented Software.* Addison-Wesley Publishing Co., 1995.

[Harel87] Harel, David, "Statecharts: A Visual Formalism for Complex Systems." *Science of Computer Programming,* (June 1987): pp. 231–274.

[OMG07] Object Management Group, "Unified Modeling Language: Superstructure." Version 2.1.1. Available online at *http://www.omg.org/docs/formal/07-02-03.pdf,* February 2007.

3.11

Building a Behavior Editor for Abstract State Machines

Igor Borovikov—FrameFree Technologies, Inc.

igor.borovikov@gmail.com

Aleksey Kadukin—Electronic Arts

akadukin@gmail.com

On one of our past game projects, we faced numerous challenges presented by the AI scripting pipeline. In particular, a refactoring of the Behavior Editor, an essential component of the AI tool chain, turned out to be desirable to improve its usability. This article describes the issues analyzed and resolved while building a new version of the Behavior Editor, as well as the enhancements to the scripting introduced during refactoring. The implementation of the Behavior Editor as a standalone application (rather than as a Maya plugin) allowed building an advanced GUI frontend. At the same time, connecting the standalone Behavior Editor with Maya via the Maya Command Port helped keep its tight integration with Maya, which was necessary for streamlined scripting and level building. The backward compatibility of our new XML-based file format allowed a smooth upgrade to the new AI tool chain. With the new extended file format, two object-oriented additions to the scripting language, behavior referencing and template script parameters, have become possible. They were implemented through offline preprocessing of the behavior scripts without changing the runtime code of the underlying abstract state machine (ASM) core of the behavior system.

Abstract State Machines (ASMs)

An *abstract state machine* (ASM) is a powerful theoretical tool for software design that offers a useful framework for modeling game agents' behaviors. Thus, building a behavior system for games with an ASM-like architecture in mind is quite common. This section gives a brief introduction to ASMs. A more formal and much more complete discussion can be found in [Börger03].

An ASM can be viewed as a finite state machine (FSM) with an extended definition of the notion of "state." A regular FSM is based on a number of states and corresponding update functions. When an FSM is in a certain state, it invokes the corresponding update function during each update cycle. Here, a state is just a label, an element of some finite set. A rule in an FSM might look like this:

```
IF state_patrol THEN patrol_region()
```

Here `state_patrol` is a label that denotes the state of an NPC, and `patrol_region()` is the update function corresponding to the patrol state. The FSM will keep calling `patrol_region()` until its state changes.

An ASM extends the notion of states by using dynamic *conditions* instead of static labels:

```
IF condition() THEN update_function()
```

Here `condition()` is a logical function that is evaluated each ASM update cycle. The `update_function()` is executed when the condition returns TRUE. The pair (`condition`, `update_function`) is called a *transition rule*. We will also call a transition rule an *update function* when the context allows. A basic ASM is a finite set of transition rules.

An NPC or, more generally, any agent in the game, can be controlled by a single ASM or by multiple ASMs that work either sequentially or asynchronously. Different AI subsystems can be controlled by different ASMs. It is also possible to dynamically replace ASMs during runtime. Allowing a slight abuse of terminology, we will call an ASM a *behavior* because it represents a smallest meaningful self-contained piece of AI functionality. In addition, we will call a transition rule a *behavior task* or, for short, a *task*. Hence, a behavior is a collection of tasks triggered by conditions.

Note that tasks can have rather complex update functions that actually consist of a number of actions, each encompassing multiple steps. It is also possible for update functions to switch to a different behavior by calling START_BEHAVIOR(new_behavior_name) inside an update function, thus allowing dynamic switching between ASMs.

The execution of a behavior in the game starts by traversing the list of tasks, which has been sorted by priority. When the first task whose condition evaluates to TRUE is found, its transition rule is called. On the next behavior update, we again traverse the list and select a task. Because a task's transition rule may require more than one behavior update cycle to complete, we need to save the state of its execution between behavior updates. If it is reselected on the next behavior update, then we will continue execution where we left off. If a different task is selected, then the previous task transition rule execution state is reset, and we begin execution of the new task's transition rule. The AI engine is responsible for organizing the concurrent functioning of active ASMs and allocating the necessary time slices during each behavior update cycle.

Here is an example of a simple but relatively complete behavior for an NPC guard:

```
BEHAVIOR SimplePatrol

TASK AttackIfPlayerNearby
    IF distance_to_player_less_than(10) THEN
        approach_player(3)
        attack_player()

TASK WalkPatrolPath
    IF TRUE THEN
        walk_path(my_patrol_path)
```

The previous ASM listing can be extended by adding more tasks to the behavior. The execution of this behavior normally starts with WalkPatrolPath task because its condition always evaluates to TRUE. When the distance between the player and the NPC shrinks below 10 units, the behavior activates the AttackIfPlayerNearby task. The update function of this task consists of two actions that are executed sequentially. First, the NPC attempts to come within 3 units of the player, and then the NPC attacks. If the player is defeated or runs away, the condition of this task no longer holds, and the NPC returns to the task of following the patrol path.

Additional task attributes can simplify management of the control flow in the behavior, as follows.

- Remove on completion is a useful task flag that tells the AI to remove the task when it is completed. It is equivalent to execute once and is well suited to a variety of situations, such as immediately after an NPC is spawned.
- Remove on abort is an analogous flag that causes the AI to remove the task when it fails to complete. This flag is useful for preventing the AI from reevaluating tasks that are no longer valid (such as when a path is blocked by a destroyed object).
- The Task must complete flag ensures that control will not be transferred to a different task until the current one is finished.
- The Don't reevaluate task condition(s) flag prevents the AI from passing control to a different task unless the other (higher priority) task's conditions become TRUE. Having this flag set for a task is equivalent to a combined condition

```
IF was_executing_during_previous_behavior_update
   OR my_conditions
THEN …
```

where my_conditions is the original condition of the task.

The actual behaviors controlling NPCs could be much more complex than the SimplePatrol behavior. A behavior set for a real game level with dozens or even hundreds of objects and many behaviors composed of many tasks can become challenging to design, understand, and maintain. In our experience, despite the theoretical convenience and conceptual simplicity of ASMs, they initially proved to be rather hard to use for real-life applications, providing many ways to shoot yourself in the foot. For example, an incorrect flag on a task can break control flow of the behavior in a subtle way. Such a bug could be difficult to localize in a big complex behavior. After some consideration, however, we realized that the problems we were experiencing were partially due to the way in which the behaviors were being built and managed. We therefore decided to create a Behavior Editor that would alleviate these problems.

The Behavior Editor as a Maya Plugin

A game agent behavior extends the pure ASM in a number of ways. In addition to the control flow flags, it has to reference level objects to be useful in the game AI. Typical referenced objects are paths, regions, hotspots, NPCs, effects, and other behaviors. Such references are initially created as symbolic ones and later have to be resolved. This resolution and binding of names happens when the level data is converted into the binary form loadable by the game. Usually, a level-builder application takes care of this by reading, validating, and merging data exported from the level design tool and other tools.

The AI data flow before the refactoring of the Behavior Editor was as follows. An intermediate, (mostly) human-readable form of the AI data was exported from Maya where designers had built the level. The data included descriptions of all the objects that could be referenced by behaviors. These objects were ordered and grouped by type, and their symbolic names replaced by numeric identifiers. A command-line level-builder tool then read these intermediate files and assembled the final binary representation of the level, resolving and replacing references to the symbolic names with numeric identifiers.

Because all of the level data was available in the Maya scene, it seemed self-evident that the Behavior Editor should reside inside Maya as a plugin. This would keep all the level data together, simplifying the design process and the level export, at least during the initial phase of development. The behavior data was embedded into the Maya scene through dummy objects (called "behavior cubes") that held all necessary behavior scripts in their user attributes. Finally, the powerful scripting capabilities of Maya allowed building of an advanced GUI-driven toolset for behavior editing entirely in Maya.

Drawbacks of the Plugin Approach

After we were well into production, it became evident that the "self-evident" approach had a number of serious drawbacks. Behavior data integrated into the Maya binary file was inaccessible outside of Maya. A designer or scripter had to run Maya, open the level scene—which may grow to more than 100 MB—and only after that, he would get access to the behaviors in the scene. Due to problems with file referencing in Maya, it was impossible to separate behaviors from the other data. Thus, the entire level was stored in a single file, and only one designer could work on this file at any given time.

Version control was another concern. Hiding behavior data inside the Maya binary file made version control of the behaviors virtually impossible because binary Maya files were too large for Visual Source Safe. In addition, it is generally inadvisable to merge multiple versions of a binary file. This restriction prevented users from editing multiple copies of the level file and then merging their changes.

Building a Behavior Editor GUI in Maya was yet another problem. Even though Maya's MEL (Maya Embedded Language) scripting opens up many possibilities, it still has some serious limitations. For example, we couldn't easily create a tree control in MEL. Other examples of functionality awkward to implement in MEL are search-and-replace, copy-and-paste, and undo-redo. Of course, undo-redo is supported by Maya itself, but it is intended for editing the 3D scene, not for a MEL-driven GUI. Thus, even though undo was technically there, it was virtually useless in the context of the Behavior Editor plugin. A convenient copy-and-paste was also missing from the plugin-based implementation, which was unfortunate because it would have been useful to be able to script pieces of behavior in smaller mockup scenes and then transfer them to the actual level.

Data and Workflow Decomposition for the Standalone Behavior Editor

Moving the Behavior Editor outside of Maya would solve all of the aforementioned problems, but it would also require some extra effort to keep the behavior script consistent with the level objects that are defined in the Maya scene. In other words, it would still be necessary to access the Maya scene if the designer wanted to pull up the name of an object or assign a behavior to an NPC. In addition, export and data linking would need the same kind of access to ensure the consistency of the behavior with the level objects and the correct resolution of names.

The analysis of the game data formats hinted at a possible way to solve the export and linking problem: a new "dual" format, which would also be backward-compatible. On top of that, Maya Command Port presented a solution to the integration with Maya. Command Port allows sending commands to Maya and receiving responses remotely from a standalone application.

Data Decomposition

We employed an export of the Maya scene minus the behaviors (and minus actual geometry, of course) into a text file containing so-called "mission data." This mission file stores the AI-related data in the scene, in particular, information about all of the objects such as NPCs, regions, paths, and so on. The mission file is mostly human-readable and can be parsed automatically. This allowed us to use it separately from the behavior file and then resolve symbolic names and do the linking at a later stage.

Originally, the mission file used a format shared with few other game data files: a custom line-based format. A line could contain either name of a data section for higher level structuring, or a parameter description belonging to the current data section. A parameter description consisted of a parameter name, its value type and size, the value itself, and an optional comment. Such a custom format was easy to generate, parse, and translate into binary. Reusing the same format for different types of data was convenient because the AI-related scene data could be saved in a single file (complete mission) or in separate files by sections, for example, in-game objects' descriptions, navigation data, behaviors, and so on—each of them in individual files. Another important advantage was in virtually one-to-one correspondence of human-readable format to the binary data loadable into the game. However, such direct correspondence was limiting extensibility: adding metadata that didn't have exact representation in the game was difficult.

The new file format for the behavior file was designed in such a way that, on the one hand, it was compatible with the mission file format, and, on the other hand, it took advantage of the flexibility and convenience of XML, including the wide array of open source libraries for generating and parsing XML files. The behavior file stores each behavior in two formats: a version with symbolic, unresolved object names that uses plain XML, and then a "compiled" version in the format compatible with the mission file. This can be achieved by using a CDATA section in the XML file, which instructs the XML parser to consider the data in that section as an atomic piece.

We had to keep a couple of issues in mind. First, the compiled behavior can't contain the pair of symbols]] because they would be recognized as the end of the CDATA section. Luckily, the compiled behavior data format did not use this pair of symbols. Second, if the XML version of a behavior is modified manually, the behavior file has to be opened and resaved from the Behavior Editor to ensure that the compiled version remains consistent with the canonical XML version. However, it turned out that manual editing was virtually never required, and when it was, resaving was a very quick task.

Another concern was ensuring that the XML version of the behavior was ignored by the existing parser that was used in the level builder. Happily, this already turned out to be the case, but such a simple modification—ignoring all lines with XML tags present—wouldn't be very difficult in any case. As a result, the "dual" XML-based format was easily integrated into the level-building pipeline. The data can be easily linked with mission data, with only a few symbolic name resolutions required. For example, we still need to resolve names of regions, hotspots, game objects, and so on because in the game, they were referred to by their binary ID (usually an index in a list). But this ID was not known at the moment the behavior was created. Thus, an additional name resolution and binding step was still required even with a new format.

The following listing shows a fragment of the combined behavior file for the simple patrol behavior sample. Only one task is shown to avoid clutter.

```
<?xml version="1.0" ?>
<BEHAVIORSET>
<VERSION>1</VERSION>
<DATAFORM>
<![CDATA[
#VERSION=1.0
behaviornames
{
    Behavior_Patrol     # 0
}
behaviorset
{
    behavior
    {
        stringid "Behavior_Patrol"
        behaviorid 0
        task
        {
            stringid     "Task_AttackIfPlayerNearby"
            taskflags     0x00000000 # no flags
            {
                combine    0 # logical operation
                negate     0
                conditiontype 176 #DISTANCE_FROM_OBJECT
                parameter 0x01000003 #%PLAYER
                parameter 3 # LESS_THAN
                parameter 10.0 # 10.0
            }
            action
            {
                actiontype 101 #ATTACK_OBJECT
                parameter 0x01000003 #%PLAYER
            }
        }
    }
...
]]>
</DATAFORM>
  <BEHAVIOR>
  <NAME>Behavior_Patrol</NAME>
  <TASK>
    <NAME>Task_AttackIfPlayerNearby</NAME>
    <CONDITIONS>
      <CONDITION>
        <NAME>DISTANCE_FROM_OBJECT</NAME>
        <COMB>0</COMB>
        <NEG>0</NEG>
        <PARAM>0 # ObjectID # %PLAYER #</PARAM>
        <PARAM>1 # Test # LESS_THAN #</PARAM>
        <PARAM>2 # Value # 10.0 #</PARAM>
      </CONDITION>
    </CONDITIONS>
    <ACTIONS>
      <ACTION>
        <NAME>ATTACK_OBJECT</NAME>
        <PARAM>0 # ObjectName # %PLAYER #</PARAM>
```

```
        <PARAM>1 # TimeOut # 0.0 #</PARAM>
      </ACTION>
    </ACTIONS>
 ...
  </BEHAVIOR>
</BEHAVIORSET>
```

Using the dual format had another very important advantage. Because the changes to the tool chain and level-building data were relatively small, it allowed a smooth transition from the old Behavior Editor to the new one.

Workflow Decomposition

Initially, we feared that moving the Behavior Editor to a standalone application might break integration with the level design tool, Maya. However, Maya Command Port allowed us to establish runtime communication between the standalone Behavior Editor and Maya. Behavior Editor could open communication with Maya Command Port via a TCP/IP socket and then communicate directly with Maya via MEL commands.

The simplest use of this kind of communication was to poll a list of objects of a given type in the scene to ensure that the scripter picks the right object name inside the script. Another, more advanced example was assigning a behavior name to an actor that is represented as an object in Maya. For this task, the Behavior Editor sends a command to the Command Port to set the corresponding attribute of the object inside Maya. As an even more advanced example, the user could start Maya directly from the Behavior Editor, load the correct scene, and manipulate the data in Maya as though the Behavior Editor were a Maya plugin.

Although all of this integration is useful, it also is important that Maya and the Behavior Editor retain the ability to function completely independent of each other if necessary.

Providing a connection between multiple copies of Maya and multiple copies of the Behavior Editor posed another challenge. Fortunately, it is possible to open a Command Port with a unique name for each Maya instance. By keeping track of running Maya instances and maintaining a table with records of open and available command ports, it was possible to arrange concurrent functioning of several instances of Maya and Behavior Editors.

We also used this approach to store the mapping between Maya scene files, exported mission files, and behavior file names. This allowed the Behavior Editor to obtain data directly from the latest exported mission file. Access to the exported scene data allowed the Behavior Editor to be used in "offline" mode without direct access to the Maya scene.

Thus, the Maya Command Port and several custom modules enabled us to turn the Behavior Editor into a standalone application that was still as tightly integrated as a Maya plugin. Figure 3.11.1 shows how the Behavior Editor communicated with Maya.

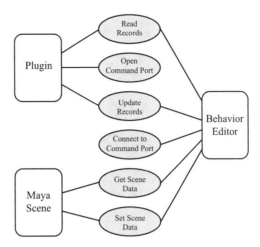

FIGURE 3.11.1   Use-case diagram for the standalone
Behavior Editor communicating with Maya.

GUI for the Standalone Behavior Editor

After decoupling the behavior data from Maya level data and finding a way to enable
runtime communication with Maya, it was possible to develop a completely new
Behavior Editor application outside of Maya.

There were several possible choices for building the new GUI. The choices narrowed down to Python after we found that C# was not immediately available on the
project. Also, Python was already used for several other scripting tasks.

The two most popular GUI toolkits available for Python are wxPython and Tkinter. The choice of wxPython was more logical for several reasons. First, it provided a
native Windows look and feel to its controls. Second, it offered a wider range of standard controls, including a tree control with standard Windows functionality. Third,
wxWidgets, the base library of wxPython, has interfaces reminiscent of MFC, which
simplified development because we had experience with MFC.

In comparison with wxPython, Tkinter has a slight advantage in the way it handles exceptions: Tkinter survives more critical errors than wxPython without causing
the application to crash and close. However, with log reporting, it was not too difficult to ensure that all of the critical bugs were tracked down and fixed, so this advantage was not critical in the long run.

The incredible speed of development offered by wxPython was also a very big
help. The development of the new Behavior Editor had to be done alongside high-priority production and tool tasks. A demo of the basic framework was ready in only
a few days, with a tree control and placeholders for behaviors and tasks, complete
undo-redo, the possibility to open and edit several behavior scripts simultaneously,
and so on. Of course, populating the initial prototype with actual functionality took

much longer than that, but it was still faster than developing an MFC/C++ application by orders of magnitude. It is possible that C#/.NET development would offer similar rapid prototyping benefits to wxPython.

The final task was packaging the editor and distributing it among the team members. An open source py2exe application offered an excellent solution for this. An advantage of wxPython over Tkinter showed itself here as well, as all packaging of wxPython with py2exe was nearly automatic, in contrast to Tkinter with Python Mega Widgets (PMW), which required manual compilation and preparation of a PMW library for distribution.

The resulting editor distribution was an executable file with a number of supporting files, including the Python interpreter. End users thus did not need to install a separate copy of Python to use the Behavior Editor. Figure 3.11.2 shows a screenshot of the Behavior Editor UI.

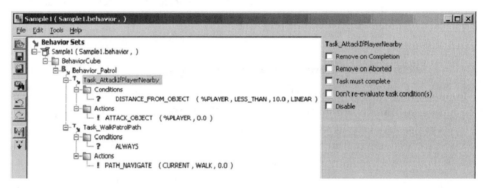

FIGURE 3.11.2   A screenshot of the standalone Behavior Editor UI with a sample behavior.

Extending the ASM Architecture with XML-Based Generic Programming

The flexibility of XML combined with the dual file format for behavior data allowed us to introduce two new features that were highly desirable but virtually impossible when the behavior editing was done inside of Maya. Specifically, we could add parameters to the behaviors, thus making them much more versatile and reusable, and we could support referencing for tasks, behaviors, and behavior groups. Referencing improved the reusability of behavior scripts and introduced an object-oriented flavor to the ASM scripting. The dual format of the behavior data allowed us to expand the new features into explicitly compiled code in a way similar to the preprocessor macros or templates in C++. Thus, a new level of functionality was added to the original ASM implementation without changing its runtime code.

Referencing

Referencing for ASM was inspired by object-oriented class inheritance. Consider a complex behavior where one or two tasks need to be implemented slightly different for certain NPCs. Without referencing, such a modification would require copying the entire behavior and replacing those few tasks. Copying code is not a healthy practice in general, and it is not healthy for ASMs either. When the script programmer changes the original behavior, it is necessary to manually propagate the changes to all similar behaviors. With referencing, it is possible to avoid such copying and manual updates.

The basic rules for inheritance are the following. Each task in the behavior possesses a unique name. When defining behavior B, we can say that it references behavior A. By referencing A from B, we implicitly create a copy of all tasks of A inside B in exactly the same order. Overriding a task definition can be done through a naming convention: If a behavior in B defines a task with the same name as in A, the new task overrides the task from A. This is similar to the way virtual functions work in object-oriented programming (OOP) languages.

Due to its obvious limitations, this referencing scheme falls short of being true inheritance. The most significant limitation is the absence of a mechanism for changing the order of the tasks in the derived behavior. Nevertheless, even as limited as it is, the referencing mechanism adds a good deal of reusability and object-oriented flavor to the ASM design process.

Here is an example of the `SimplePatrol` behavior with the attack task replaced to simulate a coward guard running away from the player instead of attacking:

```
BEHAVIOR CowardGuardPatrol: REFERENCE SimplePatrol

TASK AttackIfPlayerNearby
    IF distance_to_player_less_than(10) THEN
        avoid_player(30)
```

The task of walking the path remains the same as before, whereas the task `Attack IfPlayerNearby` leads to a completely different reaction by the guard. As a result, the guard tries to avoid the player by keeping a distance of at least 30 units at all times.

Extending referencing from the level of behaviors to a higher level of behavior groups is easy. Behavior groups are not part of the original ASM definition but are a convenient mechanism for grouping related behaviors by their purpose or spatial location. For example, the NPCs in one region could have all their behaviors collected into a single group. NPCs in a similar but slightly different region could reference this group to avoid redefining many of the same behaviors.

Parameters

The referencing mechanism would be incomplete and severely limited if it did not support parameterization of the behaviors. In its original definition, an ASM does not expose any parameters. Although we were unable to implement runtime support for this feature, even compile-time parameters turned out to be useful. They were implemented in a way similar to template parameters in C++.

A parameter for a task or behavior is simply a symbolic constant that can be replaced with an actual value during compilation (or export) of the behavior. Consider the following example:

```
BEHAVIOR SimplePatrol(
    detection_distance,
    attack_distance,
    patrol_path)

TASK AttackIfPlayerNearby
    IF
      distance_to_player_less_than(detection_distance)
    THEN
        approach_player(attack_distance)
        attack_player()

TASK WalkPatrolPath
    IF TRUE THEN
        walk_path(patrol_path)
```

Two numeric parameters and one string parameter allow us to modify the patrol behavior to address many useful cases. The parameter patrol_path allows us to specify which path to use, whereas the two numeric parameters set the detection and attack distance for the guard.

Through parameterization, the referencing is enhanced with a new degree of freedom. The referencing behavior can replace some of the symbolic parameters of the referenced behavior. Again, we had the ability to expose parameters on the level of tasks, behaviors, or behavior groups.

Implementation of Referencing and Parameters

On the level of the XML representation, adding referencing is straightforward. Through new tags, you can extend the internal behavior representation in many ways. Exporting or "compiling" a behavior for the level builder unfolds all the references and replaces all parameters with their actual values. Thus, all of the additional mechanisms added to the ASM architecture are only compile-time features.

ON THE CD

Behaviors illustrating these concepts are included on the CD-ROM. The three files included are Sample1.behavior, Sample2.behavior, and Sample3.behavior. Sample1 corresponds to the simple patrol behavior discussed earlier. Sample2 is a parameterized version of the simple patrol. Sample3 shows a parameterized behavior for a coward guard, referencing the behavior from Sample1. Behavior files are human-readable XML documents. The compiled part is located in the CDATA sections and illustrates the way the parameters and references are handled.

ON THE CD

The Behavior Editor, also included on the CD-ROM, is a fully functional albeit slightly stripped-down version of our actual production tool. You can create new tasks, behaviors, and behavior groups (called "behavior cubes"), and experiment with parameters and references.

Compile-Time Versus Runtime

Referencing and parameters, as we introduced them, work similarly to templates in C++: the compiler does all of the work during the export, so no runtime references or parameter resolutions are required. Interesting enough, one of the first commercial implementations of C++ (the Glockenspiel C++ preprocessor) was also built entirely on top of the existing C compiler. Thus, compile-time extensions seem to be a logical first step in developing OOP-flavored scripting systems, especially in situations with a rich legacy.

A rather common argument against C++ templates is that they bloat executable code, which renders them inefficient. In the realm of ASM, however, this extensive template-like approach was still quite practical even though there was some bloat as a result of our implementation of the ASM template and referencing preprocessor. This is because data size was not a big concern for us. Although data cache considerations may come into play at some point in the future, the actual behaviors built for the game were still small enough to ignore such issues.

Probably the biggest advantage of having the new ASM features processed at compile-time was the ability to keep the runtime AI engine code untouched, which ensured backward compatibility with already-built levels. This proved to be highly valuable in light of our tight development schedule.

With that said, there is no doubt that more dramatic improvements to ASMs could be made by moving some features into the runtime system. However, for such an implementation, we would rather consider an existing scripting language, such as Lua, and use its powerful tables to support runtime polymorphism with Lua objects. Of course, such an approach would be a radical departure from the ASM framework.

Conclusion

Extending a behavior scripting system based on ASMs with an advanced Behavior Editor, without interrupting production on our game, turned out to be an educational experience. It was possible to make several significant improvements:

- By using the Maya Command Port feature, we improved the workflow by building a standalone Behavior Editor without compromising integration with the level design tool.
- Maintainability and version control for behavior scripts was improved by moving them to XML-based files.

- Two new features—behavior referencing and template parameters—extended the original ASM framework, providing greater reusability of behaviors and adding an OOP flavor to ASM scripting. By manipulating the behavior data offline in the new Behavior Editor, we were able to do this without changing the runtime AI code at all.

Overall, the ASM proved to be a useful model for behaviors in the game. It also offered a framework for gameplay design that was easy to manipulate and extend.

References

[Börger03] Börger, E., and Stärk, R., *Abstract State Machines: A Method for High-Level System Design and Analysis.* Springer, 2003.

3.12

Multi-Axial Dynamic Threshold Fuzzy Decision Algorithm

Dave Mark—Intrinsic Algorithm LLC

dave@IntrinsicAlgorithm.com

AI designers and programmers commonly need an intuitive, efficient way for their agents to make decisions; in other words, to answer the question, "Given data A, should I perform action B?" The more parameters that comprise data A, the more complex this decision-making process generally becomes. It is therefore imperative that a decision algorithm make it easy to visualize and manipulate the necessary decision parameters.

The Multi-Axial Dynamic Threshold Fuzzy Decision Algorithm (MADTFDA) is one such algorithm. It allows the designer to combine two or more constantly changing values and then compare the result to a defined numerical threshold to make a decision. This algorithm makes it easy for the designer to visualize the interactions of the decision inputs, and it enables the programmer to create quick, robust, parameterized decision calls that accurately reflect the intent of the designer. This article will cover the concept behind MADTFDA, describe its various uses as an AI design tool, and provide an overview of the code that is included on the CD-ROM.

ON THE CD

The Concept

Game developers, whether modern-day programmers or pen and paper gamers from decades past, are all familiar with the idea of a "decision threshold." In the past, you might have rolled a 20-sided die to determine whether you succeeded or failed at a given task. Rolling a number greater than or equal to, say, 14 indicated success, whereas a number less than 14 indicated failure. Game designers, and in particular, AI designers, continue to use much the same concept in their work today, with the venerable 20-sided die replaced by a pseudorandom number generator.

The problem with this approach is that it is one-dimensional; that is, it allows consideration of only a single decision factor, such as the difficulty of hitting a creature. If the designer wants to incorporate a second factor into the decision algorithm, it must be somehow combined with the first factor to arrive at a single value that can be tested against the decision threshold.

One way of combining factors is with weighted sums [Garces06]. In fact, a weighted sum of two factors, each with a coefficient, is simply the equation of a line in two dimensions and is therefore mathematically the same as the MADTFDA threshold line. However, weighted sums can become unwieldy if you need to independently and frequently change the coefficients. Repeated modifications to the sums can become especially cumbersome and even lead to deteriorating accuracy when they involve relative changes, such as applying percentages to the existing numbers, or in nonpredefined ways, such as using the result of another algorithm as a coefficient. For example, increasing a value by 10% is not negated by reducing it by 10%. If this combination of actions were repeated, the base value would drift away from its intended range. Also, weighted sums provide only limited information about the decision outcomes they produce (generally either a flat yes/no or else the simple distance from the decision threshold).

MADTFDA simplifies the process of constructing decision thresholds and extends it in a number of ways. The result is an easy-to-understand, easy-to-use algorithm that the designer and programmer can use to make a wide variety of AI decisions.

Understanding MADTFDA

In its most basic form, a MADTFDA decision model is composed of two axes and a threshold line (see Figure 3.12.1). Each axis represents one input to the decision being modeled. The threshold line determines whether a given point in the decision space yields a positive or negative result. This threshold can have almost any shape (as long as it is a continuous function), but for the sake of simplicity, we will focus most of our discussion on straight lines. The "success zone" (or "result zone") of a given model may be either above or below the threshold. In strictly Boolean terms, if a data point is located in the success zone, it is said to be a "positive" result, or simply "true."

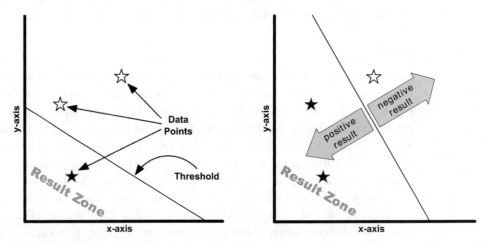

FIGURE 3.12.1   A basic decision model with a linear threshold. In this example, the success zone lies below the threshold.

A Simple Decision Model

Suppose we want to build a decision model that determines when an agent should run away. This model takes as inputs the agent's health (on the *x*-axis) and attack strength (on the *y*-axis). Now suppose that we want a particular agent to run away when a certain combination of low health and low strength is reached. To model this, we draw the threshold as in the left side of Figure 2. In this decision model, anything below and to the left of the threshold is a positive result, in other words, "yes, run away."

Changing the location and slope of the threshold results in different behavior. On the right side of Figure 3.12.2, we have a threshold where attack strength plays a greater part in the decision process. The result is an agent that will tend to run away as attack strength is lowered, even if the agent is in perfect health. On the other hand, if attack strength is near 100%, the agent will be willing to fight to the death without ever retreating.

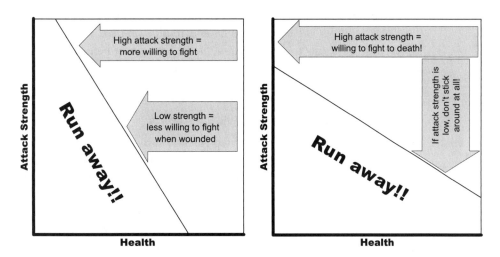

FIGURE 3.12.2   Two thresholds yielding different retreat behaviors.

Dynamic Thresholds

The threshold for an agent's decision model need not be fixed. We can dynamically change the threshold based on a third criterion, say, the proximity of allies, the agent's morale, or the attack strength of the player. This enables a number of interesting capabilities.

Creating Diversity Among Unit Types

A simple use of this method is to provide a common interface for different agents that share similar types of behaviors but exhibit them in different ways. For example, all creatures will run away under certain circumstances. What causes a harmless bunny to bolt, however, will differ dramatically from the circumstances required to panic a tenacious badger or a rabid wolf. Using MADTFDA, the solution is to assign bunnies one threshold formula, badgers another, and rabid wolves yet another. The same codebase can be used to process the "run away" decision for each agent with only a change in the formula for the threshold. In fact, using slight variations in the threshold among similar agents, such as different subtypes of a monster, leads to some interesting results.

Imagine a group of orcs that are attacking the player *en masse*. The game design has the orcs' decision model tracking the strength of the player on one axis and their own group's strength on the other. Because the battle situation changes slightly each time the decision model is checked, slightly different thresholds could be triggered at different times. Perhaps the most poorly armed grunt orcs begin to withdraw first. Then, as some of the more powerful lieutenant orcs begin to pull back, the grunts bolt outright. The captain orcs, who hold steadfast, are left alone and exposed.

In this example, each individual agent received the same perceptions of the battle (the respective sides' attack strengths) but processed them using different threshold formulae (one per orc subtype). The end result was that the three subtypes reacted differently to the exact same situation. Simplifying agent behavior into a single threshold formula allows the designer to quickly and intuitively create, analyze, compare, debug, and tweak the entire set of NPCs.

Creating Diversity Among Individual Agents

Taking the diversity concept one step further, each of the individual agents can have its threshold formula randomized slightly through the addition of parametric noise upon creation. This serves to introduce some behavioral variation among individual agents. As the battle situation changes, these individual agents will flee at different moments. In general, the weakest orcs will still be the first to flee, but each individual grunt orc will do so at a slightly different time. In short, we have created a unique "personality" (at least as far as this single decision type goes) for each orc. Note also that applying parametric noise to the individual agent at creation is much less expensive than applying it to every decision check throughout the combat.

State-Specific Thresholds

Another interesting idea is to provide an agent with a set of thresholds that reflect a range of situations. These thresholds can be linked to a state machine so that as the agent's state changes, a different set of reactions is elicited by the same combination of stimuli. The benefit of this approach is that the thresholds can be hand picked by the designer. Also, a finite set of discrete formulas allows for easier debugging.

Fuzzy Threshold Adjustments

Thresholds can also be specified as an offset from a base threshold. This enables the creation of decision models with thresholds that vary continuously rather than being limited to a set of discrete states. Returning to our previous example, we can move the threshold for a given grunt orc by an amount proportional to some criterion. For example, we can nudge the threshold down (making him less likely to flee) as the distance to his home village decreases. As the orc is pressed nearer to his home village, he will gradually shift from cowardly to downright aggressive. In effect, we have added a third parameter to the initial *x*-axis and *y*-axis in our framework.

Creating Fuzzy Results

So far, the threshold has been used to make only binary determinations. Although this is sufficient for many types of decisions, there are often circumstances when we want to know more about the orientation of a data point in relation to the threshold. That is, we may want to know not just if the data point is in the success zone but how far into the success zone it lays. This is where the "fuzzy" portion of MADTFDA comes into play.

We can measure the distance from a given data point to the threshold in a variety of ways, each of which yields a slightly different perspective. We discuss several methods here.

Absolute Distance

Probably the most common measurement of "decision magnitude" is the absolute linear distance between the data point and the threshold line (which can also be thought of as the length of the line segment that is perpendicular to the threshold line and whose other endpoint is the data point in question). The actual value of this distance is based on the scales of the *x*-axis and *y*-axis. Because a true distance value is used, there is a consistency across the framework. One unit away from the threshold near an axis is the same as one unit away from the threshold in the middle of the grid.

Alternatively, the distance can be measured using a line parallel to the *x*-axis or *y*-axis that intersects the data point and threshold line. Depending on the decision being arrived at, rather than measuring how far away from the threshold the data point is, we may want to measure how far left, right, above, or below it is. We can also define a line with a custom slope to use to measure the distance. Each approach has its own benefits depending on the needs of the AI designer. In fact, given the same instantaneous combination of data point and threshold, it can be useful to use a variety of measurements of distance in different calculations. This allows us to glean multiple outputs at the same time out of a single decision model.

Normalized Distance

Another way of measuring the magnitude of a decision is to determine the distance from the threshold as a percentage of what it could have been. That is, instead of just using the linear distance from the threshold as described previously, we compare that distance to the furthest possible data point, usually in a corner of the decision model.

The decision magnitude is then expressed as a percentage of the maximum possible distance. Thus, a data point right on the threshold would yield a value of 0%. A data point that lies on both axes (such as on the origin) would be as far away from the threshold line as possible, giving a value of 100%. Note that this percentage is independent of the actual distance between the threshold line and the data point.

For example, imagine a decision model with axes that each run 0 to 10 and a threshold line running (0, 10) to (10, 0), that is, diagonally through the middle (see Figure 3.12.3). The maximum decision magnitude is approximately 7.1 units, for the data point (5, 5). If we are evaluating the data point (6, 3), its linear distance from the threshold is 1.4. That distance of 1.4 is 19.7% of the maximum decision magnitude. If the threshold ran from (0, 6) to (6, 0), however, a data point lying at (3, 3), which is again 1.4 units away from the threshold, would yield a value of 33%.

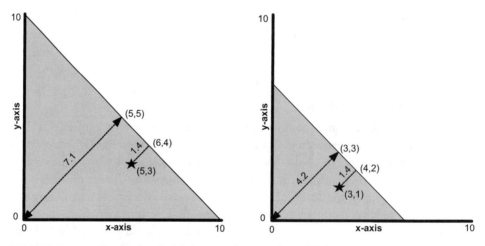

FIGURE 3.12.3   As the threshold changes, the same linear distance may yield different relative distances.

Revisiting our "running away" example, instead of a binary decision of whether or not the orc should run away, we might want to calculate the intensity of the desire to run away. If our design specification for fleeing stated that the potential range of "run away" emotions was expressible on a scale from "mild anxiety" about the situation to a maximum possible value of "abject panic," we could define a continuum with the endpoints being 0% and 100%, respectively. Numerous factors might determine the placement of our threshold line, ranging from the type of orc to some aspects of the current world state, to the orc's current AI state. Our threshold might also have been nudged around by a collection of mathematical parameters (such as proximity to home as described previously) or by adding some randomness to our equations. Regardless of the absolute location of the threshold at any moment, the threshold line itself represents 0% (that is, "mild anxiety"), and the origin represents

100% (that is, "abject panic"). This ensures that all orcs, regardless of type or current situation, will reach a state of "abject panic" just as they are getting to the (0, 0) point in the decision model.

Because the function calls to MADTFDA allow the programmer to specify the type of measurement to return, the programmer can select whether to use the pure absolute distance method or the normalized distance method based on the agent's state. The measurement method itself can thus act as another input type, which allows for greater situational behavior flexibility.

More Advanced MADTFDA

The result from the MADTFDA decision model need not be the end product. Situations often necessitate using the result of one MADTFDA decision model as an input parameter to a second decision model. This allows the designer to "daisy chain" decision models together in interesting ways.

For example, a medic could poll its neighboring allies and triage them using a decision model with the input parameters "health" and "current exposure to enemy fire." The decision magnitude for a given allied agent would represent the urgency of medical care for that agent. This urgency value could then serve as one parameter to a second decision model, with the agent's proximity to the medic being the second parameter. The medic could then sort the results from this second decision model to decide who to tend to first. The possibilities are limitless.

The result of the decision model can be processed further by sending it through other algorithms. For example, the normalized distance (i.e., 0% to 100%) into the success zone of a particular data point could be inserted into an exponential or logarithmic equation to yield a more dramatic increase than is given by the percent result alone. By assigning a custom-contoured continuum to the result set, such as those generated by response curves [Alexander02], the linear or percentage result of the decision model can be sculpted into innumerable shapes to better achieve the designer's desired behavior.

Using Layered Thresholds

Up to this point, we have only used MADTFDA models that utilized a single threshold. A MADTFDA decision model can contain multiple thresholds, which can be used independently or in concert. You could use the same data point applied to any or all of the thresholds to arrive at independent decisions, or the algorithm can use two or more thresholds together. Some of these functions are performed by the MADTFDA code itself, whereas others are left to the programmer to construct using the results from two or more independent calls to the model. We consider both options here.

Independent Thresholds

Any of the thresholds in a decision model can be accessed individually. This is useful when we have multiple discrete decisions that depend on the same input parameters.

For example, we have already created a decision model that determines whether our orc mage wants to run away given the criteria of opposing group strength and own party strength. A second, independent decision might be whether or not to cast a powerful, one-shot spell as the balance of power shifts against his group.

In the left side of Figure 3.12.4, Result Zone A is the "run away" decision, and Result Zone B is the "cast spell" decision. When the situation turns problematic (i.e., the data point moves down and to the left), the orc mage will first decide to cast his spell, and then, as things progress from bad to worse, he will run away. Note that each threshold check is done independently. It is entirely possible for the orc to have established his "run away" state and still decide to cast the spell.

Combining Thresholds

Alternatively, we can combine multiple thresholds using Boolean logic. For example, "Is the data point under threshold A AND under threshold B?" Refer to the right half of Figure 3.12.4. Data point 1 yields a negative result for both thresholds, points 2 and 3 have positive results for thresholds A and B respectively, and data point 4 has a positive result for both thresholds. Data point 4 is thus the only one to return TRUE from the AND statement.

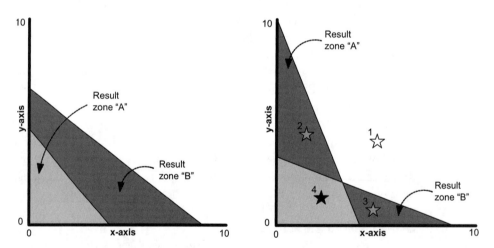

FIGURE 3.12.4   Multiple thresholds can be combined to create more complex decisions.

We are not limited to Boolean operators, of course. We can also use arbitrary mathematical functions to combine the outcomes from two or more thresholds, providing a vast array of subtle results to the designer. For example, we might add the two absolute distances from both results together to yield a third aggregate value, or we might apply the normalized percentage value of one result to the absolute distance value of the second. Because of the wide variety of possibilities in combining results from multiple thresholds, the logical or mathematical combinations are left to the programmer to create. The decision model only provides the shared definition of the model; that is, both of the thresholds are using the same axes to define them.

Hierarchical Thresholds

A slightly more involved way to combine multiple thresholds is to layer them so that one supersedes the other. In this case, we might be most interested in a primary threshold and only process the secondary threshold if the primary threshold returns a negative result. This is often useful in cases where an agent has two similar choices, with one being preferred over the other.

Returning to the example of the orc mage in Figure 3.12.4, if threshold A (running away) was set at a higher priority than threshold B (casting the one-shot spell), then the moment that A returns a positive result, B would no longer be an option. This can be described as the orc mage running away *instead of* casting the spell rather than *in addition to* casting it.

MADTFDA allows the programmer to specify a priority when each threshold is defined. When using the appropriate function calls, MADTFDA would return only the highest-priority threshold that achieved a positive result.

Using the MADTFDA Classes

ON THE CD

The accompanying CD-ROM contains the code for the MADTFDA framework. The framework consists of two classes: a decision model class (CDecisionFramework) and a threshold class (CThreshold). A decision model object holds the definitions and structure for the x-axis and y-axis as well as one or more thresholds. To use it in a project, simply add the two classes and provide the #include statement:

```
#include "DecisionFramework.h"
```

Creating a Decision Model

There are three ways to use a decision model: as a standalone entity that can be shared by many agents, as a member of the agent's class, or as a temporary object in a function. Regardless of the method used to create it, a decision model needs, at a minimum, the maximum values for its x-axis and y-axis. If the decision model is created in code, these can be set at creation time by passing these values into the constructor. Alternatively, if created as a member of a class, these will need to be set at a later time (usually in the agent's constructor) by calling the functions SetMaxX() and SetMaxY().

Adding Thresholds

The threshold's constructor is a private member of the class. To create a new threshold and add it to a decision model, use the AddThreshold() function. This function takes a number of parameters, including the x- and y-intercepts that will define the threshold's line. The optional third parameter defines the threshold's priority. This is only needed if there are multiple hierarchical thresholds in the decision model. You must also define which side of the threshold line represents a positive result and what type of result should be returned. For these parameters and others throughout the classes, you should use the enumerated types provided in the header files.

Putting It All Together

Creating an initial decision model with a single threshold is done as follows. If created locally in a function:

```
CDecisionFramework mDF_Retreat(MAX_HEALTH, MAX_STRENGTH);
unsigned int ThresholdIndex = mDF_Retreat.AddThreshold(
    0, 80, 60, THRESH_RESULT_UNDER, THRESH_GRADE_PERP);
```

If created as a member in the agent's class declaration:

```
class CAgent
{
    private:
    CDecisionFramework mDF_Retreat;
};

CAgent::CAgent()
{
    mDF_Retreat.SetMaxXandY( 100, 100 );

    unsigned int ThresholdIndex =
        mDF_Retreat.AddThreshold( 80, 60, 0,
        THRESH_RESULT_UNDER, THRESH_GRADE_PERP );
};
```

Note that the AddThreshold() function returns the index of the threshold that has been added. This index should be stored so that the specific threshold in the decision model can be called later. If you are only adding a single threshold, its index will always be zero.

Getting Results from MADTFDA

A variety of function calls are available in CDecisionFramework that enable you to set the threshold in different ways. In addition to setting it via the standard x- and y-intercepts, you can pass in the top and/or right-side intercepts as well. This allows for more intuitive setting of the threshold. For example, rather than calculating a y-intercept that is extraordinarily high, you could set the top intercept along with the x-axis. There are set functions for every pair of intercepts. If you ever need these intercept values again, you can use GetThreshYatX() or GetThreshXatY() and pass in the maximum values for the decision model. Thresholds can also be set using any of the four intercept points and a slope value.

At this point, if we want to receive a result back from the decision model, we simply need to insert one of the following calls into our agent's code:

```
bool RunAway = mDF_Retreat.PointInResultZone(
    mAttackStrength, mOwnHealth);
```

```
double Urgency = mDF_Retreat.GetDepth(
    mAttackStrength, mOwnHealth, THRESH_DISTANCE_LINEAR);

double UrgentPercent = mDF_Retreat.GetDepth(
    mAttackStrength, mOwnHealth, THRESH_DISTANCE_PERCENT);
```

ON THE CD

There are more instructions in the code on the CD-ROM that describe individual function calls not addressed here. Additionally, there is an example agent class that shows some of the function calls and uses of MADTFDA in a code environment.

Extensibility of the Code

Although the basic functions described here are available on the CD-ROM version of MADTFDA, this code could be extended and customized in a number of ways. For example, there is no reason that the thresholds must be straight lines. You can easily adjust the code to account for hyperbolic, parabolic, logarithmic, and sigmoid functions. In fact, combining various curves with the fuzzy result capability of MADTFDA provides for some interesting results! Also, by adding a z-axis, the decision model can be extended into three dimensions, making the threshold a plane rather than a line.

Conclusion

As we have shown, MADTFDA replaces and extends the commonly used technique of weighted sums for decision making. MADTFDA provides a simple, easy-to-visualize, customizable interface for making decisions based on a handful of inputs that might change often throughout the course of gameplay. It also allows the designer and programmer to more clearly define sometimes subtle differences between game agents to lend depth to the behavior models. Moreover, it allows the programmer to combine related decisions into a single framework to help manage complex layers of decisions. All in all, MADTFDA can be a quick, powerful addition to your game code.

Resources

[Alexander02] Alexander, Bob, "The Beauty of Response Curves." *AI Game Programming Wisdom*, Charles River Media, 2002.

[Garces06] Garces, Sergio, "Extending Simple Weighted-Sum Systems." *AI Game Programming Wisdom 3*, Charles River Media, 2006.

TACTICS AND PLANNING

4.1

RTS Terrain Analysis: An Image-Processing Approach

Enigma Software Productions

Julio Obelleiro

julio.obelleiro@gmail.com

Raúl Sampedro

rghoul@gmail.com

David Hernández Cerpa

david.hernandez.cerpa@gmail.com

In real-time strategy (RTS) games, high-level AI systems control multiple units, which must be used wisely to defeat the enemy. One prerequisite for accomplishing this is for the AI to have an understanding of the terrain in the area where the battle is taking place (i.e., a terrain analysis). Using this analysis, for example, the AI can decide where to deploy units or find a path to a target that avoids enemy troops. Ideally, the AI precomputes the terrain analysis to minimize the impact on runtime performance.

This article introduces the terrain analysis technique developed for the game *War Leaders: Clash of Nations*. This technique is based on simple image-processing operations, combined with data produced by pathfinding searches that simulate the movement of troops around the map. Mixing data from these two sources results in an analysis that is precise about which points on the map are strategically important.

Background

The first thing to do before implementing a terrain analysis system is to determine what information is needed by the AI [Higgins02]. *War Leaders: Clash of Nations* uses a hierarchical AI with several levels, one of which is devoted to army-level AI. This level is in charge of selecting the tactics to be employed by the army's units. A list of terrain information queries was created to help the AI decide which tactic should be used. Some of these queries include the following:

- Are my troops together in a single logical area of the map?
- Are there enemy forces in the same area as my units?
- Does my area have connections to others?
- When defending an area, how should I place my troops?
- When attacking, how should I approach the enemy?
- Which areas have important strategic value?
- Are there strategically important elements in my area (e.g., bunkers, cities, or bridges)?

To answer these questions, we first need to partition the map into interconnected logical areas. This information should not only include an analysis of the terrain but also of objects. Bridges are good places to put defensive troops, for example, whereas buildings can be used to house infantry. Furthermore, the terrain analysis system should provide information about good attack and defense points for each connection.

These problems are obviously not unique to computer games. As a result, we can turn to solutions that have been devised for real armies [Glinton04, Grindle04, Svenson03]. The two main approaches for terrain analysis are geometric terrain analysis and pathfinding simulation analysis.

Geometric Terrain Analysis Techniques

Geometric terrain analysis techniques analyze the map and build a graph representation using geometric information. *Generalized Voronoi diagrams* [deBerg00] are a common example of these techniques.

A generalized Voronoi diagram is very useful for dividing the map into different areas that can later be classified by other algorithms, such as height processing. However, for our needs, this technique has several drawbacks:

- Voronoi areas are not conceptually the same as game zones (described in the following sections). Voronoi areas might include impassable terrain or subdivide big passable regions.
- Voronoi diagrams provide no connection areas, only simple edges.
- Tactically important vertices (i.e., those shared by several areas) are not well situated. They usually fall in the center of areas and thus are not a good indication of the best tactical position for troop placement.
- Voronoi diagrams give no information about the strategic value of each area.

As a result, although Voronoi diagrams are a good starting point for terrain analysis [Forbus01], they are not a definitive solution. Nevertheless, the ideas behind the Voronoi diagram solution are central to the image-processing portion of our technique.

Pathfinding Simulation Analysis Techniques

Pathfinding simulation analysis techniques try to detect important paths on the map. This is useful to determine paths and avenues of approach (i.e., long, narrow corridors) [Svenson03] that are more likely to be used by troops. ANTS [Dorigo96] is an example of a technique that can find avenues of approach. It employs several agents that move around the map looking for important locations. When one is detected, the agents distribute pheromones along the path they followed so that other agents tend to use it. Avenues of approach are computed as paths with high concentrations of pheromones, based on the assumption that the more paths go over a certain location, the more important that location is. This technique uses interesting concepts but fails to provide all the needed information:

- No information about logical areas
- No information about connections
- No information from the paths about which of their waypoints are strategically important

The Combined Approach

Our research into existing techniques did not find a definitive solution to the problem. It seemed clear that a combination of techniques was most likely to produce good results. Toward that end, we determined to use geometric terrain analysis to detect logical areas and their connections, and pathfinding simulation analysis to determine their importance.

Basic Concepts

Before going into the details of our algorithm, we should define some basic concepts. Many of them come from military terminology that refers to terrain features with high strategic value.

The Passability Map

The *passability map* is a black-and-white image in which each pixel represents 1 square meter on the terrain map. Black pixels represent passable areas (i.e., ones which units can move through), whereas white pixels represent impassable ones. What makes a cell impassable depends on the game, but in our case, a cell was considered to be impassable if a river went through it or if the slope was too steep to traverse.

Objects such as buildings or trees are not included in the passability map. Bridges are the only exception because they make the cells underneath passable. The focus of this step is to detect the big areas of passable terrain that determine the game zones. Objects do not add information on this scale, so we perform this stage of the analysis without them.

Regions, Connections, and Hotspots

Today's strategy games have to handle huge maps that often have very complex terrain features. For this reason, it is critical to precompute a simplified representation of the terrain, so that we can reason about it quickly at runtime [vanderSterren01]. Strategy game maps are typically characterized by relatively large open spaces connected by narrow passages [Dill04]. This information is represented with a graph, with open spaces being the nodes, and passages being the edges. To expand on this slightly, consider the following concepts:

- *Regions* represent areas of passable terrain that are delimited either by impassable terrain or by other regions of a different type. From the image-processing point of view, regions are a set of pixels with the same value (color) surrounded by pixels with a different value. There are two main types of regions:
  - *Game zones* are broad, open, passable areas.
  - *Chokepoints* represent narrow corridors between game zones. There are many kinds of chokepoints, such as avenues of approach and bridges. Chokepoints offer a number of offensive or defensive opportunities. They force armies passing through them to use a narrower formation (greatly decreasing combat power), for example. Therefore, chokepoints are the most strategically significant elements of the map, and the main goal of the analysis should be to find them as accurately as possible.
- *Connections* represent logical links between chokepoints and game zones. This link is not part of the map; instead, it is a data structure used in the system to represent the connection between the chokepoints and adjacent game zones.
- A *hotspot* represents the best position to defend a game zone from attacks coming through a particular chokepoint. Of course, the information given by the hotspot is combined with runtime information to calculate the optimal position.

The Terrain Analysis Algorithm

Processing a map involves several steps, including image-processing transformation, pathfinding, and geometric and numeric data extraction. Figure 4.1.1 gives an overview of the process, providing a clear roadmap of the complete algorithm. Each element of this image is described in detail in the following subsections.

Noise Reduction

The process starts with a passability map, which might have many small islands of impassable terrain, usually near larger impassable areas (such as mountains), producing useless divisions in the map. Noise reduction is the process of removing those areas. We can do this safely because we are not performing pathfinding on the result, we are simply creating a high-level division of the map into regions. To remove the noise, the algorithm selects the zones of impassable terrain and removes those with a small area, filling their pixels with black color. Figure 4.1.2 shows an example section of a map before and after noise reduction.

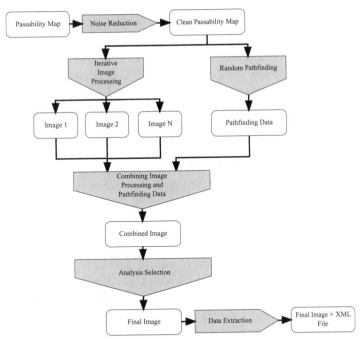

FIGURE 4.1.1   The terrain analysis algorithm. Trapezoid shapes represent the processing performed by the algorithm, whereas rectangular ones denote the data shared between them.

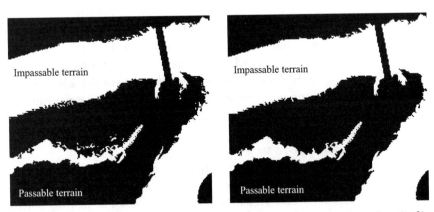

FIGURE 4.1.2   Noise reduction is a very common step in image processing. (Left) Original passability map. (Right) Clean passability map after noise reduction.

After the passability map has been cleaned, the algorithm uses it for two parallel processes: an iterative image-processing step (the core of the algorithm) and a random pathfinding step. The results of these steps will be combined to generate the final image.

Random Pathfinding

Our algorithm takes information from the terrain heightmap and combines it with pathfinding data to infer knowledge about the paths that are most likely to be used by the enemy during the game. This step simply calculates a large number of random paths and stores them. We keep not only the path's waypoints but also the number of paths passing through each cell. These will be used to weight the zone containing those cells in later steps. An example of this step can be seen in Color Plate 4.

Iterative Image Processing

This step divides the map into regions. It takes as input a clean passability map and applies image-processing operations to generate an output image on which each region is clearly marked. Following are the operations performed on the image, shown in Figure 4.1.3:

1. Select all the pixels representing impassable terrain, that is, the white ones. This creates a selection area around each impassable zone.
2. Expand the selection by a given number of pixels (known as the chokepoint detection radius) in all directions. If two impassable areas are close together, the expanded selections will overlap. These overlapping areas are our potential chokepoints, which will be used later in the algorithm.
3. Invert the selection. With this step, broad passable zones are selected. These zones are separated from the impassable ones by a number of pixels determined by the chokepoint detection radius, and they are the center of the game zones into which the map will be divided.
4. Fill the current selection with a new color so that the game zones are marked.
5. Expand the selection by the chokepoint detection radius to move the selection's borders back to the limits of the impassable zones. Note that the potential chokepoints that we discovered in step 2 will not be returned to the selection when we do this. Thus, we now have the game zones completely selected, and the impassable areas and potential chokepoints are unselected.
6. Invert the selection again. The impassable areas and potential chokepoints should now be selected.
7. Deselect pixels representing impassable terrain, that is, white pixels. At this point, only the potential chokepoints should be selected.
8. Fill the current selection with a new color so that the potential chokepoints are marked.
9. Save the result as a potential analysis.

The result is an image where all of the potential chokepoints and the game zones are marked with different colors. This image is just a potential analysis because the whole algorithm is executed several times with different values for the chokepoint detection radius. This parameter determines the distance that must exist between two

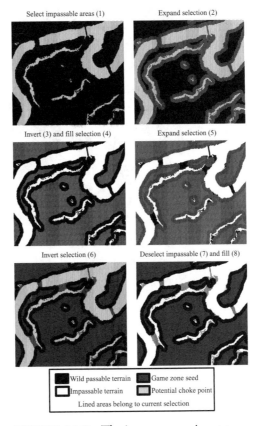

FIGURE 4.1.3   The image-processing step involves several operations. In the title above every image, the number in brackets represents the step the image refers to.

impassable zones to form a potential chokepoint. If, for example, the parameter is set to 5, two impassable zones that are less than 10 pixels away from each other will generate a potential chokepoint between them. As a hint, our game maps use a range of values from 5 to 50 pixels radius. An example of the influence of the chokepoint detection radius in the image analysis is shown in Figure 4.1.4.

Combining Image Processing and Pathfinding Data

Remember that chokepoints are still *potential*, not final. We use the pathfinding data to determine whether each potential chokepoint is relevant. Chokepoints with a small number of paths crossing through them are probably isolated in a corner of the map or have other chokepoints next to them with more paths, so they are discarded. After irrelevant chokepoints have been cleared, the game zones are examined to determine

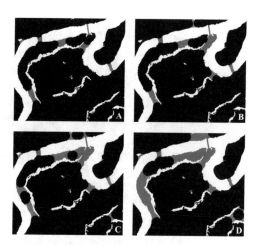

FIGURE 4.1.4   Larger chokepoint detection radii produce bigger potential chokepoints. (A) Potential analysis with 20 px radius. (B) Potential analysis with 23 px radius. (C) Potential analysis with 26 px radius. (D) Potential analysis with 29 px radius.

whether any of them need to be connected because of a cleared false chokepoint between them. Thus, the algorithm continues with a flood fill step through the game zones, joining them where chokepoints no longer exist.

The pathfinding information can also be used to sort the final chokepoints in terms of strategic importance. In our case, after experimenting with several possible metrics, such as the paths per square meter, we determined that the best measure of the relevance of a chokepoint was simply to count the number of paths that crossed it.

Analysis Selection

Now that we have generated a number of possible analyses, with image processing and pathfinding performed on each, we need to choose the best one. Different metrics can be used to make this decision. For our game, it was determined that the number of game zones in the analysis was one of the best metrics, but more research should be done in this respect. When several candidates had the same number of game zones, the one with the shorter chokepoint detection radius was selected. An example of an analysis is shown in Color Plate 5.

Data Extraction

The last step of our terrain analysis is to compute a hotspot for each connection (remember that a *connection* links a chokepoint to a game zone, and a *hotspot* represents the best position to defend a game zone from attacks coming through that chokepoint).

We do this using a simple geometric analysis on the border between the chokepoint and the game zone.

Connections are formed by a concave line of pixels, which represents the boundary between the chokepoint and the game zone. If we draw a straight line between the endpoints of this boundary, the middle point of that line will be the hotspot for the connection. Next, we determine an orientation that will allow defensive units to face in to the chokepoint. We can't simply take the vector to the center of the chokepoint, as an irregularly shaped chokepoint could cause this to face in almost any direction. Instead, we generate a line that is perpendicular to the straight border, passing through the hotspot. Next, we take the two points that are 1 pixel away from the hotspot on this line and calculate the distance from each of them to the midpoint of the curved border. The farther of the two points lies on the correct heading. This calculation can be seen in Figure 4.1.5.

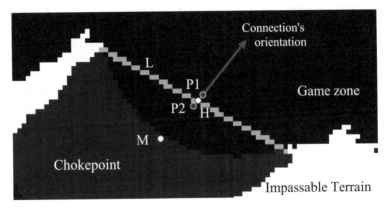

FIGURE 4.1.5   Hotspot computation. An imaginary line (L) joins the chokepoint's edges. The middle point of that line is the hotspot (H). Two points (P1, P2) spawned from the hotspot along the imaginary line's perpendicular vector will be used to calculate the connection's orientation. Note (M) point is the middle point for the chokepoint's real boundary. In this case, as (P1) is farther from (M) than (P2), the connection's direction will be calculated from the hotspot (H) to (P1).

After all the hotspots have been computed, we generate an XML file with the following information for every chokepoint:

- The list of game zones connected by the chokepoint.
- The hotspot for each of the chokepoint's connections.
- The direction from the hotspot to the game zone connected to it.

Use of Terrain Information

Now that we have generated all of this information, the AI system can use its knowledge of game zones, chokepoints, and hotspots to help it defeat the enemy. The questions presented at the beginning of the article can now be answered:

- The image denotes the extent of the different areas, so it is easy to compute which area contains each allied and enemy unit.
- The XML file gives information about connections for a given area and their hotspots. Thus, it is a simple matter to look at where the enemy is and use this knowledge to determine which connections must be attacked or defended. After those connections have been selected, the hotspot and the direction vector pointing away from the chokepoint can be used together to place units at appropriate locations relative to the connection, depending on the situation and the unit types involved.
- Weighting information can be used to decide which areas and connections are most important.

Although the weighting information generated during the terrain analysis is static, we can combine it at runtime with live data about where enemy troops are [vanderSterren01]. For example, the AI looks for enemy troops and makes pathfinding searches from their positions to allied ones to decide which connections must be defended. The resulting paths are then analyzed to find the chokepoints that would be traversed. Those chokepoints will receive a dynamic weighting which, when added to the static one, will allow the AI to perceive their actual importance.

Future Work

Although the algorithm is working properly for all of the maps in our game, it could be improved in several ways.

As previously mentioned, the number of detected game zones and chokepoints depends on the value of the chokepoint detection radius parameter. Additionally, the final analysis is selected with a metric, which, in our case, is the number of game zones detected. The problem is that sometimes there is no single value for this parameter that is best for the entire map. A value that might correctly detect chokepoints on one part of the map might completely miss those in another part. One possible solution to this problem is to subdivide the map into clusters and analyze each cluster separately. Thus, each cluster could have a different value for the detection radius.

Another area for improvement would be to add more tactical data to the algorithm's output. For example, height or slope analysis could easily be added. This information would be part of the zone and chokepoint descriptions and could be useful for detecting positions with height advantage. Our algorithm includes a postanalysis step to add information about strategically important objects on the map, such as bridges or bunkers, which add valuable information to the analysis. The computation of this information and its use is beyond the scope of this article.

Conclusion

An RTS army-level AI must have a good understanding of the terrain over which the battle is taking place. Of course, you could think about generating this knowledge by hand, but the need for good production pipelines in today's video game industry is growing, not to mention the need for automatic understanding of player-generated maps by the AI. In our case, the terrain analysis technique presented here proved to be quite useful, greatly improving the AI's effectiveness.

The technique presented here analyzes two sources of information. First, it processes the image of the terrain passability map to generate information about the game zones and the potential chokepoints. Second, it performs pathfinding simulation analysis to discover the strategic importance of each potential chokepoint detected in the image-processing step. The combination of these steps makes it possible to create robust terrain data.

Finally, the visual nature of the algorithm, which is one of its most interesting features, allows easy debugging and integration with the map creation tool.

References

[deBerg00] de Berg, M., van Kreveld, M., Overmars, M., and Schwarzkopf, O., *Computational Geometry: Algorithms and Applications.* Springer, Berlin, 2000.

[Dill04] Dill, K., and Sramek, A., "Performing Qualitative Terrain Analysis in Master of Orion 3." *AI Game Programming Wisdom 2*, Charles River Media, 2003.

[Dorigo96] Dorigo, M, Maniezzo, V., and Colorni, A., "The ANT System: Optimization by a Colony of Cooperating Agents." *IEEE Transactions on Systems, Man, and Cybernetics Part B: Cybernetics*, Vol. 26, no. 1, (1996): pp. 29–41.

[Forbus01] Forbus, K., Mahoney, J., and Dill, K., "How Qualitative Spatial Reasoning Can Improve Strategy Game AIs: A Preliminary Report." *Proceedings of 15th International Workshop on Qualitative Reasoning*, May, 2001.

[Glinton04] Glinton, R., Grindle, C., Giampapa, J., Lewis, M., Owens, S. R., and Sycara, K., "Terrain-Based Information Fusion and Inference." *Proceedings of the Seventh International Conference on Information Fusion*, Stockholm, Sweden, July, 2004.

[Grindle04] Grindle, C., Lewis, M., Glinton, R., Giampapa, J. A., Owens, S. R., and Sycara, K., "Automating Terrain Analysis: Algorithms for Intelligence Preparation of the Battlefield." *Proceedings of the Human Factors and Ergonomics Society 48th Annual Meeting*, Human Factors and Ergonomics Society, (Sep. 2004): pp. 533–537.

[Higgins02] Higgins, D., "Terrain Analysis in an RTS—The Hidden Giant." *Game Programming Gems 3*, Charles River Media, 2002.

[Svenson03] Svenson, P., and Sidenbladh, H., "Determining Possible Avenues of Approach Using ANTS." *International Conference on Information Fusion*, Cairns, Australia, (2003): pp. 1110–1117.

[vanderSterren01] van der Sterren, W., "Terrain Reasoning for 3D Action Games." *Game Programming Gems 2*, Charles River Media, 2001.

4.2

An Advanced Motivation-Driven Planning Architecture

Enigma Software Productions
David Hernández Cerpa

david.hernandez.cerpa@gmail.com

Julio Obelleiro

julio.obelleiro@gmail.com

Game AI techniques have evolved from simple architectures, such as finite state machines (FSM), to others more complex and powerful, such as goal-oriented action planning (GOAP), hierarchical task networks (HTN), and motivational graphs. However, imperative programming techniques [Wikipedia07], such as FSMs, are still widely used as the main decision-making system because they are simple to implement and do not involve any development risk. Unfortunately, as game AI complexity increases, these techniques become unmanageable, difficult to extend, and present several problems for code maintenance.

The game *War Leaders: Clash of Nations* features two game modes: manager and RTS. Both modes have strong requirements in terms of high-level AI. In manager mode, the AI has to control all of the nonplayer factions, creating complex courses of action (which might require several turns to complete) for each one. In RTS mode, the army-level AI has to select its tactics based on the highly dynamic situation on the battlefield. Clearly, it's desirable to share as much of the AI logic as possible between modes. Toward that end, we have created a new architecture that borrows from STRIPS(STanford Research Institute Problem Solver), GOAP, HTN, and motivational graphs.

Background

A detailed treatment of planning systems is beyond the scope of this article, so we will just briefly cover the background of the technique being presented, as well as the motivation for using a planning system to develop game AI.

Advantages of Planning Systems

In general, planning algorithms are composed of three steps [O'Brien02]. Analyze the world to detect needs and opportunities; create goals based on the previous analysis; and, for each goal, calculate a sequence of actions that leads to the satisfaction of that goal. The advantages of such a system can be summarized as follows:

- Imperative systems, such as FSMs, force the programmer to think of every possible situation that the AI might face during the game. As game complexity increases, these architectures become unmanageable. Within a planning architecture, it's easy to avoid this pitfall because we specify what the AI *can do*, rather than what the AI *has to do*. The planning system selects the actions the AI will actually perform from among this list of possibilities.
- Planning systems can help to create nondeterministic behaviors, facilitating the appearance of emergent behaviors.
- Although it might seem that the creation of a planning architecture is too expensive in terms of development time, the fact that it's much more scalable, reusable, and modular will more than offset these costs in most cases. Planning architectures also adapt better than imperative systems when faced with the continuous changes in game design that are common in our industry.

Related Work

The presented architecture borrows from previous planning systems. One of the earliest planners was *STRIPS* (STanford Research Institute Problem Solver) [Fikes71]. STRIPS operates in a space of world models, where a world model is a representation of the state of the world at a given time, and operators (actions), which function as transitions between world models. Operators are described in terms of preconditions and effects. An operator can be applied if all of its preconditions are true in the current world model, and doing so will cause its effects to become true, thus moving us to a new world model. STRIPS searches this space for a sequence of operators (i.e., a plan), which will place it in a world model in which the current goal is satisfied.

Goal-oriented action planning (GOAP) applies STRIPS to behavior modeling for NPCs [Orkin03, Orkin04]. It handles similar concepts, such as goals, actions, and plans. GOAP defines a plan as a sequence of actions to satisfy a goal. It extends STRIPS by supporting replanning [Orkin05], which allows it to manage situations where a plan becomes obsolete during its execution.

STRIPS and GOAP plan to create a sequence of actions, all at the same level. Other techniques use the concept of hierarchical planning [Wallace03, Gorniak07], which is an important aspect for the architecture being presented. For example, *hierarchical task-network* (HTN) planning plans to create task networks that are hierarchically decomposed into actions [Erol94]. This hierarchical approach has several benefits, such as partial replanning [Knoblock95], which avoids recomputing valid parts of a plan. Additionally, HTN introduces a mix of planning and execution that allows the generation of plans to adapt to changes that have occurred in the game world [Paoloucci00].

Finally, *motivational graphs* introduced the concept of motivations as high-level processes that detect needs. These processes change the agent's state to drive the behavior toward the satisfaction of the needs [Chivas03]. This article presents motivations as processes that detect AI necessities and produce goals to satisfy them.

Architecture

The architecture is composed of two main layers that are completely decoupled. As shown in Figure 4.2.1, one layer is dedicated to the motivations, and the other one is dedicated to the planner. Both will be discussed in detail in the following sections.

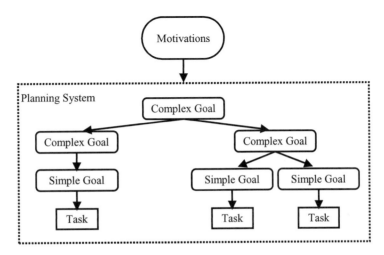

FIGURE 4.2.1   Architecture overview.

Motivations

AI architectures often include the concept of goals as something that an agent tries to achieve. They represent a concrete need or objective that must be satisfied. This concept is used in the architecture, but we introduce a higher level one, which we call the *motivations*. In both game modes, manager and RTS, there are things that must be taken into account that do not, by themselves, represent specific goals. For example, in manager mode, the AI should check that there are no territories in revolt. The result of this check might result in the generation of goals, but it is not a goal itself.

A motivation is a general-purpose, high-level process whose responsibility is to detect needs and create goals that will satisfy them. How these goals are achieved is not determined by the motivation. In our game, motivations are implemented with scripting functions that perform specific tests and create the needed goals. For example, the motivation `DefendFaction` iterates through all of the faction's territories and generates a goal `DefendTerritory` for each territory with an enemy influence greater than the allied one.

Each part of the game has several independent motivations that control different parts of the AI. Examples include researching new technologies, gathering raw materials, and providing military defense. Having independent motivations that do not interfere with one another generates unexpected combinations of goals, which promotes emergent behavior.

The Planner

The function of the planner is to take the goals from the motivation system and find a way to satisfy them. The following sections describe this process in more detail.

Parameters

A *parameter* is a piece of data used by any component in the system. All the elements in the architecture have parameters, whether they function at planning time or at plan execution time.

Most other planning techniques do not use parameters at planning time, which is an important limitation on their ability to generate complex plans. For example, it is not possible to build a good plan for the goal DefendTerritory without knowing which territory should be defended. Some territories might be defended simply by shifting units around, for example, whereas others require new units to be recruited.

Parameters are transferred to subgoals or tasks in the planner, allowing them to be used in lower levels of the plan.

Predicates

Predicates are functions that return a Boolean value. For example, IsTerritoryInRevolt indicates whether or not the population of a given territory is in revolt against its faction. Predicates accept parameters for their evaluation and, as generic functions, can query the game logic using those parameters to compute their values. The function that evaluates a predicate is implemented in a script, which is called when the predicate's current value is needed.

Goals

As discussed earlier, *goals* represent a concrete requirement that must be satisfied. They are the inputs to the planning system. The main purpose of the planner is to find the best sequence of actions that will satisfy any goal that is added to its list of active goals.

As discussed in the section on STRIPS, a goal is defined by a set of preconditions and effects. Preconditions are predicates that must be true to consider a goal for execution. Effects, which are also predicates, represent the changes that might occur in the world if the goal is satisfied. For example, one of the effects of the goal DecreaseTaxes might be TerritoryNotInRevolt. Note that effects only indicate possible outcomes of executing the goal, they are not a guaranteed result. For example, the task MoveArmyToTerritory might fail due to the destruction of the army while moving to the target territory. In this case, although the effects indicate that the army will be at the target territory after the task execution, external circumstances have caused it to fail.

Goals can be satisfied by tasks, which are simple actions, or by subgoals, which produce a hierarchical decomposition of the plan. The idea is to have the ability to interleave simple elements, whose execution will produce an output from the AI system to the game logic, with complex ones, which are broken down into simpler elements. As discussed earlier, other architectures, such as HTN, use a similar approach.

Goals perform some reasoning at planning time. Specifically, they select values for their parameters at planning time, so that those values can be used throughout the rest of the planning process. They also determine information that is used during goal execution to determine whether they need to be replanned. This allows plans to be calculated with up-to-date information from the game logic. Then, as the situation in the world changes, the plan is checked to determine whether it is still valid. If a goal is invalid, then its plan is discarded, and a new one is computed. All of this work is implemented within scripts, which are called from the C++ game engine. Expensive computations needed by these scripts are implemented in C++ and exported to the scripting system.

The planning system can plan and execute multiple goals simultaneously. Goals are assigned a priority, which serves as a heuristic for resolving any conflicts between them. Plans for the main goals (i.e., those added by the motivations) are generated in priority order, and resources are assigned to goals with greater priority in case of conflict. Generating priorities is a hard problem in its own right, and one which other papers discuss in greater detail [Dill06].

Tasks

Tasks are actions that can be executed by the AI to modify the world state. They are associated with goals at planning time and are expected to satisfy their goals when executed. For example, a goal MoveArmyToTerritory does not actually move the army. It will have an associated MoveArmy task that will receive the army and territory parameters and call the appropriate game logic method to move the army. Separating goals and tasks allows decoupling *what* has to be done from *how* it is done. Substituting the set of tasks changes how the system satisfies the same goal set.

Like goals, tasks are described with preconditions and effects that allow the planner to match them to the goals to be satisfied. Tasks compute two important values during planning:

Satisfaction value: In traditional planning architectures, when a task with an effect is found to satisfy a precondition of a goal, the planner supposes that the task will completely satisfy it. Thus, there is a one-to-one correspondence between a precondition and the task that will be used to satisfy it. This schema is insufficient to handle complex situations. Our architecture supports the satisfaction of one precondition through the execution of several tasks. The satisfaction value is an assessment in the range [0..1], which indicates how much the precondition is satisfied by the task. The planner continues to add tasks that can help to accomplish the goal's precondition until a total of 1 is reached.

Application Cost: When the planner has several available tasks, each of which can satisfy some or all of a precondition, it has to decide which of them should be chosen. The application cost is used to sort all the tasks that can satisfy the precondition so that the plan with the lowest cost can be selected.

As with other elements in the architecture, computations relative to game-specific tasks are implemented using functions in scripts.

The Planning Algorithm

The planning process starts when a motivation proposes a goal that the system has to satisfy. The algorithm tries to find the hierarchical sequence of goals and tasks that best satisfies the goal. This process has the following steps:

1. Calculate the top-level goal's data. In this step, we assign values to the goal's parameters and calculate the internal data that will be used during execution to determine if the goal has become invalid. These parameters are passed down to the subgoals and tasks, so that they can determine whether they are sufficient to satisfy the top-level goal and, if so, what their cost will be. For example, in the RTS part of the game, the goal AttackEnemyGroup is in charge of selecting a group of units and using them to attack an enemy group. In this step, the goal computes the position of the enemy group, which is later used to detect whether the goal has to be replanned. The goal will replan if the enemy moves a certain distance from this stored position.
2. Check the top-level goal's preconditions. For every unsatisfied precondition p, follow the remaining steps.
3. Find potential subgoals and tasks that can satisfy p, that is, those that have p as an effect in their descriptions.
4. Run the planner on every potential subgoal task found in the previous step, using the current goal's parameters. We do this by recursively calling the planner with these objects as the top-level goal.
5. Discard those subgoals and tasks for which the planner did not find a plan.
6. Calculate the application cost and satisfaction value for every subgoal or task that remains.
7. Sort the subgoals and tasks by application cost to find the cheapest plan.
8. Select subgoals and tasks to be in the final plan until the precondition is fully satisfied. This means that the total satisfaction value for the selected subgoals and tasks must be greater than or equal to 1.

Although other architectures have opted to use standard graph search algorithms, such as A* [Orkin05, Filion06], we decided to implement specific planning algorithms for simplicity and easier debugging.

Adapting to Change: Replanning

Plans can quickly become invalid in worlds that are in constant change. Thus replanning capabilities are a basic requirement for our system. Plans must be reevaluated in a timely manner and be reconsidered when they become untenable.

Each goal has a generic function named `HasToReplan`, which returns true when the goal needs to be replanned. The implementation of this function is goal specific. In the goal `AttackEnemyGroup`, for example, this function checks whether the enemy group has moved too far away from its initial position. If so, then the goal has to be replanned because there is a new target position where the assigned units must be sent. Furthermore, a different tactic or set of units might be more suitable to attack the target enemy group in its new position.

Periodically, the function `HasToReplan` is called for all the goals of the hierarchical plan. If it returns true for one of them, then that goal (and any subgoals it had) are replanned. Note that if the invalid goal is not the root goal, we do not need to replan the parts of the plan that are still valid.

A Complete Example

Figure 4.2.2 shows an example of the AI update in the manager part of the game. This AI has several motivations, but this example focuses on `ControlRevolts`.

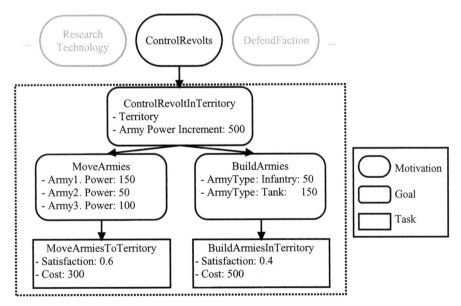

FIGURE 4.2.2   An example of a plan computed to satisfy a goal, which has been generated by a motivation.

During its update, the ControlRevolts motivation detects one territory in revolt, creates a new ControlRevoltInTerritory goal, and adds the territory in question as a parameter to the goal. The aim of this goal is to control the revolt with the presence of allied troops. In support of that, each army has a potential that represents how powerful it is.

The new goal is added to the planning system, which tries to create a plan for it. IncreasedPotential is the only precondition of ControlRevoltInTerritory, and it is an effect of two other goals: MoveArmies and BuildArmies. Thus, the planner calls the function for calculating the amount of potential needed to pacify the territory and then tries to find a plan for each of the aforementioned subgoals.

In the first branch of the plan, the function that calculates the MoveArmies goal's data looks for surrounding armies, which could be moved to the target territory. It finds three armies with the indicated potentials and adds them as parameters. The precondition of MoveArmies is ArmiesInTerritory, which is an effect of the MoveArmiesToTerritory task. This task uses the armies and territory parameters to compute the application cost and the satisfaction value, which are passed back to the upper level.

The planner then analyzes the second branch. The goal BuildArmies computes the types of the armies that must be built and adds them as new parameters. Its precondition ArmiesBuilt is an effect of the task BuildArmiesInTerritory. The task computes the satisfaction and cost values, which are then used in the top level.

After the two branches have been planned, the planner uses the computed satisfaction and cost values to sort and select which goals should be part of the main goal's plan. In this example, both branches are valid and needed to completely satisfy the original ControlRevoltInTerritory goal so they both will be part of the plan.

Building and moving armies take several turns to be completed. For example, while an army is being moved, the enemy could destroy it. In that case, the MoveArmies goal would detect this situation and notify the planner that its part of the plan is no longer valid. Therefore, partial replanning of the branch below the MoveArmies goal would be performed leaving the other branch of the plan unchanged.

Other Uses of the Architecture

This architecture is not only used for the manager AI. While studying the game's requirements, it became clear that the same architecture could be used elsewhere. The first such place, as discussed previously, is the high-level AI in the RTS. Another is the AI for General units. These units have the ability to command troops that have been assigned to them. The player is able to give high-level orders to the Generals, who will use the assigned units to satisfy them.

Generals are somewhat different because they do not have motivations. Instead, they receive orders from superiors (such as the player), which are then transformed into goals to be planned. This introduced the necessity of having pluggable layers in the architecture; that is, the two layers into which the architecture is divided must be independent.

Note that goals and tasks are shared between RTS Army-level AI and the Generals, which promotes code reuse. Sharing the architecture allowed us to reuse goals, tasks, and their code, which reduced the time needed to implement our AI systems.

Future Work

Our algorithm tries to satisfy preconditions by looking for goals and tasks whose effects include them. As shown, the planner keeps searching for new goals and tasks until the total satisfaction value is 1. This value can be exceeded in the current implementation if a goal or task returns a satisfaction value greater than needed. For example, if a part of the plan has already covered 60% of the satisfaction value, and the next goal or task returns a satisfaction of 0.8, then the total satisfaction value will be 1.4. Future implementations will correctly handle this situation by featuring partial task execution, that is, tasks which can be executed to a greater or lesser extent. In the previous example, which only required an additional satisfaction of 0.4, the associated task should be executed just enough to generate that needed satisfaction, rather than the full 0.8 that it is capable of producing. The implementation of this feature would be task dependent. In the case of a MoveArmies goal, for example, it might mean moving only a portion of the available armies.

In this version of the architecture, resources are only distributed between plans that ask for them at the same time. For example, if two plans are being created in the same turn, they can compete for any resource, which will then be divided up. However, plans created in subsequent turns cannot ask for these resources, even when their goals have a higher priority, until the plans that have control of the resources release them. The next step in resource administration is to allow high-priority goals to withdraw resources from previously created plans.

Conclusion

Planning systems represent a great step forward in the development of AI systems for games. The use of imperative techniques to create behaviors could be considered a fast and easy solution, but it entails huge problems as the AI complexity increases. Although planning systems are usually contemplated as a merely academic solution, the presented architecture proved to be very expressive and powerful in a real game environment.

The motivational approach, together with the capability to plan multiple goals in parallel, helped to produce emergent behavior, thus enhancing the game experience. Moreover, the features of the planning part of the architecture helped to create highly adaptable behaviors, which could generate the best plan of action possible in any situation. For example, in the manager part of the game, it is impossible to enumerate every possible combination of situations. The use of different motivations, which generate goals independently, generates sequences of actions that are neither scripted nor expressed in any way in the implementation.

Planning architectures take time to implement because they are much more complex than imperative techniques. On the other hand, the architecture allows high levels of code reusability and modularity and is easily adaptable to game design changes that commonly arise during a project. Furthermore, the use of scripts to implement game-specific AI makes it easy to create new content for the AI. In the long run, the time saved implementing the AI more than makes up for the time spent building the architecture.

References

[Chiva03] Chiva, E., Devade, J., Donnart, J., and Maruéjouls, S., "Motivational Graphs: A New Architecture for Complex Behavior Simulation." *AI Game Programming Wisdom 2*, Charles River Media, 2003.

[Dill06] Dill, K., "Prioritizing Actions in a Goal-Based RTS AI." *AI Game Programming Wisdom 3*, Charles River Media, 2006.

[Erol94] Erol, K., Hendler, J., and Nau, D. S., "HTN Planning: Complexity and Expressivity." *Proceedings of the National Conference on Artificial Intelligence (AAAI)*, 1994.

[Filion06] Filion, D., "A Unified Architecture for Goal Planning and Navigation." *AI Game Programming Wisdom 3*, Charles River Media, 2006.

[Fikes71] Fikes, R. E., and Nilsson, N., "STRIPS: A New Approach to the Application of Theorem Proving to Problem Solving." *Artificial Intelligence*, Vol. 2, no. 3/4, (1971): pp. 189–208.

[Gorniak07] Gorniak, P., and Davis, I., "SquadSmart Hierarchical Planning and Coordinated Plan Execution for Squads of Characters." *Proceedings of AIIDE*, 2007.

[Knoblock95] Knoblock, Craig A., "Planning, Executing, Sensing, and Replanning for Information Gathering." *Proceedings of the Fourteenth International Joint Conference on Artificial Intelligence*, Montreal, Canada, 1995.

[O'Brien02] O'Brien, John, "A Flexible Goal-Based Planning Architecture." *AI Game Programming Wisdom*, Charles River Media, 2002.

[Orkin03] Orkin, Jeff, "Applying Goal-Oriented Action Planning to Games." *AI Game Programming Wisdom 2*, Charles River Media, 2003.

[Orkin04] Orkin, Jeff, "Symbolic Representation of Game World State: Toward Real-Time Planning in Games." *AAAI Challenges in Game AI Workshop Technical Report*, 2004.

[Orkin05] Orkin, Jeff, "Agent Architecture Considerations for Real-Time Planning in Games." *Proceedings of AIIDE*, 2005.

[Paoloucci00] Paoloucci, Massimo, Shehory, Onn, and Sycara, Katia, "Interleaving Planning and Execution in a Multiagent Team Planning Environment." *Technical Report CMU-RI-TR-00-01*, Robotics Institute, Carnegie Mellon University, January, 2000.

[Wallace03] Wallace, Neil, "Hierarchical Planning in Dynamic Worlds." *AI Game Programming Wisdom 2*, Charles River Media, 2003.

[Wikipedia07] "Imperative Programming." Wikipedia. Available online at *http://en.wikipedia.org/wiki/Imperative_programming*, 2007.

4.3

Command Hierarchies Using Goal-Oriented Action Planning

David Pittman—Stormfront Studios, Inc.

david.pittman@gmail.com

Many games feature characters whose behaviors must be coordinated with the actions of other characters to create a believable facsimile of human interaction. For example, tactical squad-based shooters might require the members of a squad to work together to achieve common goals, such as resolving a hostage situation or destroying an enemy blockade. Goal-directed behavior is a practical choice for games with these kinds of scenarios [Atkin05], but how should the individual tasks be coordinated with the common objectives of the team?

This article describes the use of military-style command hierarchies in conjunction with the goal-oriented action planning (GOAP) architecture [Orkin04] to build a flexible framework for coordinated AI behaviors. This method enables the decomposition of high-level orders into atomic tasks and keeps the AI units at each tier of the hierarchy decoupled from the decisions made on other tiers. Individual agents do not implement any group behavior, and high-level units do not apply fine-grained control over low-level units. This also affords each unit a degree of autonomy in its decisions, so the immediate needs of the unit can take precedence over its orders. This architecture produces varied, complex, and believable coordinated AI behaviors.

Goal-Oriented Action Planning

The GOAP architecture is a flexible system for goal-directed behavior. Its primary benefits compared to other goal-based architectures are that its goals are satisfied by sequences of actions (called plans) instead of single actions and that these plans are generated at runtime. These properties increase the potential for complex and varied behaviors without requiring a programmer or designer to explicitly develop anything more than simple actions.

GOAP operates by using a state-space search to formulate ordered sequences of Action objects to satisfy the properties described by Goal objects. For example, a `TakeCover` goal might be satisfied by the Action plan "MoveToCoverNode, then

Crouch." In a typical example of the GOAP architecture, each AI agent has an array of Goals and an array of Actions (called the Goal Set and Action Set, respectively) that indicate the gamut of goals the AI can satisfy and the behaviors it will use to achieve them. Although a full explanation is beyond the scope of this article and available elsewhere [Orkin04], this cursory introduction to GOAP will help explain the concepts used in building a goal-based command hierarchy.

Command Hierarchies

A command hierarchy is a military-style organization of units designed to control the flow of orders and information [Reynolds02]. A command hierarchy has at least two tiers. At the top of the hierarchy is a commanding unit that has some number of subordinates, which might have subordinates of its own. Each unit has a one-to-many relationship with its subordinate units. For example, a squad might contain two fire teams, each of which is composed of four soldiers, but no soldier belongs to both fire teams. Orders are propagated down the tree and subdivided into simpler tasks as needed. In theory, information is propagated back up the tree, but for practical purposes, a high-level unit can have a global view of all the information its subordinates know.

This structure keeps the AI at each level comfortably decoupled from its superior or subordinate AI. A soldier's AI does not need to bother with the reason for its orders any more than his fire team's AI cares how those orders are fulfilled. This lets the AI programmer work on each AI unit in a modular fashion instead of shoehorning group logic code into a soldier's AI. Figure 4.3.1 depicts a four-tier command hierarchy of 32 soldiers collected into 4-person fire teams and their superior squads and platoon. (The right-hand portions of the graph have been collapsed to keep the graph a reasonable size. The hierarchy is assumed to be balanced.)

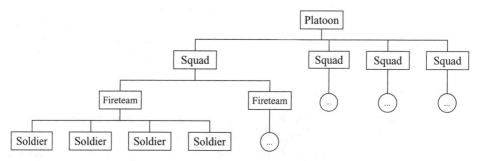

FIGURE 4.3.1   A command hierarchy is a natural fit for a military-themed squad shooter.

This article will refer to the leaf nodes in the hierarchy tree as *atomic units*. These typically exist at the same level in the tree and represent the simplest autonomous AI elements in the hierarchy (e.g., individual soldiers). Nonatomic elements in the hierarchy can also be characters (e.g., a fire team leader) or simply an abstract collection of subordinate units (e.g., a fire team). Either way, a nonatomic unit can be autonomous (i.e., able to make decisions on its own), but an abstract collection only delegates orders and is not concerned with physical Actions.

How Command Hierarchies Use GOAP

With a flexible goal-based architecture and a model for distributed tasks under our belts, we can build an AI system that extends all the benefits of GOAP to the coordination of character behaviors. The fundamental concept of the technique presented here is that the Actions of a superior unit suggest Goals to its subordinates. Figure 4.3.2 illustrates this principle, with a squad's Action suggesting a Goal to one of its fire teams, and the Action to satisfy that Goal suggesting a Goal to one of the fire team's soldiers.

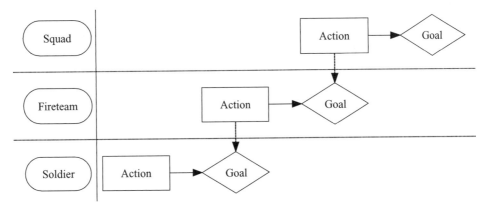

FIGURE 4.3.2   The Actions of superior units suggest Goals for subordinate units.

A subtle consequence of this design is that a superior AI unit only tells its subordinates what to do, not how to do it. Each AI unit formulates its own plan of Actions. This extends the primary benefits of GOAP through the hierarchy and provides more flexibility and variety in how high-level Goals are satisfied.

Giving Orders

A superior class's Actions include properties that indicate which Goals its subordinates should activate to complete the Action. For example, a FireteamClearRoom Action would recommend a MoveToNode Goal for the members of the fire team. When the fire team executes the FireteamClearRoom Action, its members will be alerted that they should evaluate their Goal Sets and activate a new Goal if necessary. Some logic might be performed to determine a point man and find each fire team member a specific movement target in the room.

Subordinate Goals are assigned floating-point values within each superior Action. These values are used as additive modifiers when the subordinate units evaluate their Goals, so a higher value represents a strong order, and a lower value means the order is a loose suggestion and can be ignored with less consequence. By assigning a subordinate Goal a negative modifier, the superior class can effectively prevent its subordinates from activating that Goal. For example, a `FireteamRetreat` Action might apply a −0.5 modifier to the `KillEnemy` Goal to keep the fire team members focused on running instead of fighting back.

Note that in this scheme, a superior Action can only recommend Goals that the subordinate already has in its Goal Set. The superior cannot add new Goals to the subordinate's Goal Set because each unit's Action and Goal Sets might be handcrafted by designers to achieve fine-tuned behavior for individual units. The subordinate unit might not have Actions to support the newly added Goal, or the Goal might simply be one that the designer did not intend for the unit to activate. Of course, new Goals can be added to the subordinate's Goal Set, but the ramifications of that decision should be considered. If new Goals can be added to an AI unit, the designer cannot exclude behaviors by customizing that unit's Goal Set.

Because the completion of the superior Action is dependent on the completion of all its subordinates' Goals (and so on, all the way down the hierarchy), the superior AI unit must wait for reports from its subordinates that their Goals have been fulfilled or invalidated. The Action's success criteria are dependent on the nature of the Action. In practice, the superior unit often needs to reconsider its world state after the subordinate Goals are completed to determine if the Action was actually successful. For example, a fire team's `AssaultEnemy` Action could be successful even if one or more soldiers reported a failure to complete their `KillEnemy` Goal, as long as all the enemy units were defeated by some other means.

Receiving Orders

Whenever an AI unit needs a new plan (because its previous Goal was satisfied or invalidated, or its plan failed in some way), it evaluates each Goal in its Goal Set to determine which one is most relevant in the current world state context. Each Goal performs some logic and returns a floating-point value between 0 and 1 to indicate its relevance relative to the AI unit and its known information. The unit then queries its superior class for the set of Goal modifiers. The highest-rated Goal after this addition is activated.

Table 4.3.1 demonstrates how orders from a superior unit can produce a different outcome than the unit would produce on its own. In this example, a soldier has determined, based on his context, that `TakeCover` is his most relevant Goal. However, his fire team's orders are to charge, which is manifested as a positive modifier on the `KillEnemy` Goal and a negative modifier on the `Retreat` Goal. After the addition, `KillEnemy` is the highest-valued Goal and will be activated.

Table 4.3.1 Based on Contextual Relevance and Active Orders, the `KillEnemy` Goal is Selected

Goal	Relevance	Modifier	Score
KillEnemy	0.6	0.5	1.1
TakeCover	0.8	0.0	0.8
Retreat	0.3	−0.5	−0.2
Patrol	0.0	0.0	0.0

The reason for this system of modifiers is to retain each unit's autonomy. Consider a fire team under orders to scout unexplored terrain ahead of its squad. The fire team is given directed movement Goals by the squad leader, but these need not be rigid orders. If the fire team is ambushed en route to its destination, it is desirable that it would activate a Goal to return fire or take cover. These Goals would be highly relevant in the context and most likely supersede the squad's orders. If the fire team instead chose its Goal based solely on the squad's orders, the information regarding the ambush would need to be propagated back up to the squad before anything useful could be done with it. Furthermore, this would require the squad to reevaluate its own Goal to respond to help the ambushed fire team, and the squad's Goals are probably not designed to handle fine-grained situations for individual subordinates. By this point, things would be looking grim for the fire team. Instead, the fire team is able to override its orders and activate a Goal that makes sense in this context. Allowing each unit to make autonomous decisions using its superior's orders as an influence ensures that information is processed quickly and at the appropriate level of granularity. Table 4.3.2 illustrates the case of the ambushed fire team and how it produces the desirable `TakeCover` Goal despite not having orders to do so.

Table 4.3.2 An Ambushed Fire Team Displays Autonomy by Taking Cover Despite Its Orders

Goal	Relevance	Modifier	Score
Charge	0.4	0.0	0.4
TakeCover	1.0	0.0	1.0
Retreat	0.6	0.0	0.6
Patrol	0.0	0.5	0.5

If an AI unit activates a suggested Goal (one with a positive modifier from its superior), it might need additional information to formulate the plan correctly. For example, a soldier that receives a `KillEnemy` order needs to know which enemy his fire team is ordering him to kill. Existing implementations of GOAP tend to use an agent-centric information scheme in which a unit is responsible for selecting its current targets (such as enemies or movement nodes) [Orkin06]. In this case, instead of querying its targeting subsystem for an enemy target, the soldier will query his fire team. The fire team has its own target selection subsystem and will respond to the soldier's query with its selected enemy target. After the suggested Goal has been finished, either by successful completion or by being invalidated, the AI unit must report this status to its superior so that the superior unit's Action can be completed.

Optimizations

ON THE CD

A game's AI architecture could be implemented primarily in a nonnative scripting language. For example, the *Carnival* demo project on the accompanying CD-ROM was written entirely in UnrealScript. Developing the AI in a scripting language can offer certain benefits in terms of the ease of writing the code or quickly integrating new ideas, but it also has the drawback of being much slower than native code. This might not be a problem for simpler state-based AI, but GOAP requires a state-space A* search to formulate a plan. That cost becomes significant when it is multiplied by a handful of units and their command hierarchies are repeated every time the state of the game changes substantially. Even if the game's AI is written in C++ or hand-tuned assembly, the scale of the game (e.g., an RTS with hundreds of AI units in a multi-tiered command hierarchy) or a modest AI budget might necessitate some optimizations to keep things running smoothly. Two optimizations were considered in the development of *Carnival*. A scheduler was implemented to prevent many units from planning simultaneously and causing a frame rate hiccup, and the state-space search was designed to be performed over a number of frames. Each of these optimizations can be tuned to the needs of a specific game.

Planning Scheduler

AI units using GOAP do not generate plans constantly. Typically, a unit will spend at least a few seconds executing each plan, and units high up in a command hierarchy might idle for minutes at a time while their high-level plans are executed in small increments by their subordinates. If the number of cycles per frame for an AI was graphed over some span of time, it would probably appear as a low line with tall spikes at each frame that the AI unit generated a plan. (This is assuming that the A* to formulate the plan is the most complex part of the AI and ignoring the cost of pathfinding and other intensive algorithms.) As long as these spikes aren't big enough to cause the frame rate to hiccup, everything should be fine—until two or three or a dozen other AI units happen to formulate plans in the same frame, pushing the computation time well over the allotted AI budget. This is the reason for a planning scheduler: to queue up AI units that need plans and allow them to take their turns over subsequent frames, ensuring a smooth frame rate.

In *Carnival*, a simple scheduler was implemented using a FIFO (first in, first out) queue and allowing one AI unit to plan each frame. This required only a minimal change to the architecture. Instead of directly calling its planning function, the AI sends a request to the scheduler, which enqueues a reference to the AI unit. Each frame, the scheduler dequeues the front AI reference and calls its planning function. This simplistic scheme raises some questions about the impact of the scheduler on gameplay. Does using the scheduler cause a perceptible pause before AI units react to information? If two units request to plan in a single frame, which one gets priority? Does that adversely affect the other unit?

In practice, the delay between when an AI receives information and when it finally begins acting on its resulting plan is usually imperceptible. However, it will scale with the number of units scheduled and could become significant in a large RTS skirmish. More important is the question of which units get priority. In *Carnival*, the units are processed in the order they request plans. This seems logical, but when multiple units request plans in the same frame, the order is essentially arbitrary (it is the order in which the units are iterated by the calling code, which has no relevance to the gameplay). This could result in all the enemy units getting their plans before any of the player's allies get theirs, and the split-second difference between when each unit begins attacking could tip the scales in a fight. A reasonable solution is to use a priority queue and prioritize the units based on some heuristic. For example, friendly units might be given priority over the equivalent enemy units. Highly visible units could be processed before less visible ones, such as the abstract squad type units higher in the command hierarchy. Noncombative characters could be given low priority if their actions would not substantially affect gameplay.

Finally, an ideal scheduler should be tunable to allow the maximum number of units per frame to plan without causing frame hitches. This could be a constant number set by an engineer or designer, or it could be computed at runtime based on the performance of the player's computer. In this latter scenario, the AI would be changed in subtle but potentially significant ways by the performance of the platform, which could, in the worst case, manifest as a quantum bug. Proceed with caution.

Interruptible A*

Another simple but useful optimization to this architecture is the addition of an interruptible search in the planning function. If the search takes too long, it will be paused and resumed on a subsequent frame. Another way to think of it is that the search is performed asynchronously over a number of frames. The venerable A* algorithm is actually very simple to make interruptible—given the source and destination nodes, its open and closed lists completely describe the state of the search.

Some heuristic value is used to determine when a search is running too long for a single frame. This might be the number of iterations completed or the total time in cycles or milliseconds spent in the search. After the heuristic is exceeded, the open and closed lists are saved to a persistent location, and the search function exits with a flag to indicate that it is incomplete. On a subsequent frame, the planning function is called with a flag to remind it that a search was in progress, and the open and closed lists are restored. The search continues from exactly where it was before and can be interrupted as many times as necessary until it completes.

Interrupting a Scheduled Search

A final consideration in using these optimizations is how to reschedule units whose planning searches are interrupted. The unit should not just continue to search on every frame because the scheduler might be ordering other units to plan in those same frames. The two systems must be coordinated. In *Carnival*, a unit with an in-progress search will simply submit another request to the scheduler and wait its turn in the FIFO queue as many times as needed. This can cause interrupted searches to take many more frames to complete. An alternative, if using a priority queue for the scheduler, is to submit follow-up requests with an increased priority. This ensures that units still take their fair turns, but units that have already begun to plan do not get stalled by the scheduler.

To prevent units from just idling during this process, planning can be started while the previous plan is still being executed. For this purpose, the planner can either assume the success of the previous plan or simply use the current world state. If the AI budget has cycles to spare, both plans could be generated and the appropriate one chosen when the plan is needed. When the previous plan is completed, the unit will already have a new plan ready to go and will not have to waste even a moment idling. If the world state changes substantially before the new plan is executed, the plan could be invalidated, so it is advantageous to begin planning as near to the end of the previous plan as possible while still allowing time to formulate the plan—for example, just after the last Action in the previous plan is activated.

Demo on the CD-ROM

ON THE CD

The full source code for the *Carnival* project referenced in this article is included on the CD-ROM. The project is written in UnrealScript and requires *Unreal Tournament 2004* [Epic04] to compile and run. For complete instructions, refer to the readme.txt file included with the project.

Conclusion

Command hierarchies are a practical choice for coordinating AI behavior. They are an effective model of the flow of orders and information in a military-style chain of command, and the tiered structure keeps the AI at each level decoupled from its superior and subordinate AI. The method presented here for integrating command hierarchies with a GOAP-based agent architecture extends the benefits of the GOAP architecture throughout the hierarchy. Specifically, it affords structure and reusability in the code and the potential for complex and varied behavior from each unit in the hierarchy.

This architecture is built upon the fundamental concept that a superior unit's Actions suggest Goals for the subordinate unit. These suggestions are applied as additive modifiers on the subordinate unit's relevance scores for its Goals. This allows the subordinate unit a degree of autonomy in the event that its orders do not correlate well with its current context. A generic method of information sharing is not directly addressed by this architecture, but the *ad hoc* solution of requesting Action targets from a superior unit covers the primary need for information sharing.

The suggested optimizations help the technique perform efficiently and open its use up to a range of potential scenarios, including script-based planning AI or larger-scale RTS games. The planning scheduler in particular can be tuned to fit the precise needs of any game design, and the interruption heuristic on the A* search provides a simple way to scale back the per-frame cost of one of the most expensive parts of the planning process.

Consider using this technique as a basis for coordinated behavior in your game, especially if you are already using or are considering using a goal-based agent architecture. The command hierarchy paradigm is simple and effective, and coupled with the GOAP architecture, its potential for exciting team-based AI is endless.

References

[Atkin05] Atkin, Marc, and Abercrombie, John, "Using a Goal/Action Architecture to Integrate Modularity and Long-Term Memory into AI Behaviors." *Game Developers Conference Proceedings*, 2005.

[Epic04] *Unreal Tournament 2004*. Epic Games/Digital Extremes/Atari, 2004.

[Orkin04] Orkin, Jeff, "Applying Goal-Oriented Action Planning to Games." *AI Game Programming Wisdom 2*, Charles River Media, 2004.

[Orkin06] Orkin, Jeff, "3 States and a Plan: The AI of F.E.A.R." *Game Developers Conference Proceedings*, 2006.

[Reynolds02] Reynolds, John, "Tactical Team AI Using a Command Hierarchy." *AI Game Programming Wisdom*, Charles River Media, 2002.

4.4

Practical Logic-Based Planning

Daniel Wilhelm—California Institute of Technology

dan@dkwilhelm.net

This article presents an easy-to-implement planner based on the principles of logic programming. Although not as expressive as other planners for game AI [Cheng05, Munoz-Avila06, Orkin99], it uses familiar IF/THEN structures and constructs plans efficiently. Strategies, such as dynamic rule modification, for encoding rich environments are also discussed.

We show by example that planners do not have to be complex or require months of work to implement. The simple planner developed here is not only efficient, but it can be easily extended to accommodate more feature-rich environments. The ideas presented here should encourage you to explore what planning has to offer game AI.

Why Planning?

Given a description of the initial environment, planners generate an ordered list of actions required to achieve a goal. Planners can provide many benefits to game AI:

Strategies are dynamically reevaluated: A real-time planner can respond quickly to environmental changes by automatically drafting new plans. No additional coding is necessary to draft plans for new environment configurations.

Scripters can use high-level abstractions: By writing goal-oriented scripts for a planner rather than traditional action-oriented scripts, scripters can focus on strategy. The coordination of low-level actions is left to the planner.

Generated plans are flexible: As shown in this article, planners can often be tweaked to satisfy game mechanics. Planners also can generate multiple strategies to achieve a single goal, allowing the AI to appear less predictable.

A Simple Example

Suppose that the AI for a real-time strategy (RTS) game is instructed to build a barracks. First, it gathers facts about the environment—a worker is present (W), and a town center is present (T).

Besides the environment facts, three implicit production rules are known that can be described using IF/THEN statements. IF a worker and town center are present, THEN gold can be produced (G). IF a worker and town center are present, THEN lumber can be produced (L). IF a worker is present, and gold and lumber can be produced, THEN a barracks can be produced (B).

Each parenthesized symbol denotes a proposition—a statement that is either true or false. We can summarize the previous facts and rules using propositional logic, where $A \rightarrow B$ denotes "IF A THEN B" (or alternatively, "A IMPLIES B"), and $\wedge$ denotes "AND":

W	Environment fact
T	Environment fact
$W \wedge T \rightarrow G$	Production rule
$W \wedge T \rightarrow L$	Production rule
$W \wedge G \wedge L \rightarrow B$	Production rule

Note that each production rule also implies an action. For the previous rules, the actions may be mining gold, harvesting lumber, and building a barracks, respectively. Hence, the desired plan is a sequential list of actions that corresponds to the production rules invoked to "prove" that a barracks can be produced:

G (from $W \wedge T \rightarrow G$)	"Assign the worker to mine gold."
L (from $W \wedge T \rightarrow L$)	"Assign the worker to harvest lumber."
B (from $W \wedge G \wedge L \rightarrow B$)	"Assign the worker to build a barracks."

When a production rule is used, it generates a new fact about the environment. For the sixth line, a worker is present (W), and a town center is present (T), so gold can be produced (G). Hence, G is now a fact that can be used later in the proof (line 8). In mathematical logic, proofs can be even more detailed, but this procedure is enough for our purposes. Of course, a second plan is also valid—harvesting lumber first, then mining gold, and then building the barracks.

You may have noticed that several important features are ignored in this simple example. For example, rules may require access to continuous values rather than true/false propositions; propositions may need to be negated to indicate the lack of something; and in many scenarios, certain rules should not be present until other actions allow their inclusion. Strategies for handling these issues will be presented later.

Planners

As in the previous example, a planner requires knowledge of environment facts, production rules, and a goal state. Environment facts are single propositions that describe the game world. Production rules are IF/THEN statements that describe the preconditions (the IF clause or *antecedent*) and the postconditions (the THEN clause or *consequent*) of actions. The goal state is a fact that represents the desired final state of the game world.

In this planner, each production rule is mapped to an action. For example, the rule "IF a worker and a town center are present, THEN gold can be produced" may be mapped to the action "Assign the worker to mine gold." Inside the planner, a theorem prover attempts to show that a sequence of rules exists that transforms the initial facts into the goal state. The immediate output of the prover is a list of production rules that achieves the goal state when its rules are applied in succession. After translating each production rule used in the proof into an action, a plan is produced that can be parsed by the game engine. See Figure 4.4.1 for a flowchart of the relationship between the planner and the game engine.

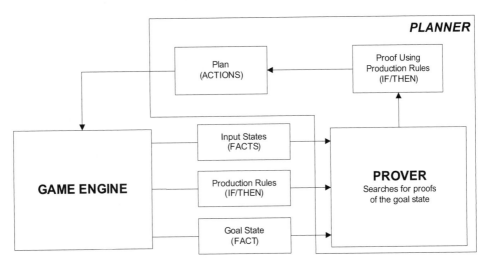

FIGURE 4.4.1 The planner receives input states, production rules, and a goal state from the game engine. If possible, the theorem prover constructs a proof that the goal state can be reached. The planner then translates each line of the proof into an action, returning this final plan to the game engine for execution.

General theorem provers for first-order logic are often too inefficient for practical applications. To counteract this, specialized planners have been written for games [Orkin99]. Specialized planners typically use heuristic search, Graphplan, or satisfiability algorithms to search the space of possible plans [Cheng05]. This article introduces the use of a propositional satisfiability planner for game AI. Satisfiability planners construct a Boolean formula describing the environment and goal and then try to find an assignment of truth values that satisfies it.

By only allowing facts and IF/THEN production rules called *Horn clauses*, an efficient, easy-to-implement satisfiability planner can be written. IF/THEN structures, such as rule-based systems [Christian02], have been used extensively in game AI and are well understood. Hence, they provide a natural starting point for our adventure.

Inside a Logic-Based Planner

Now that we know the inputs and outputs of the planner and how it interacts with the game engine, we are ready to dive into its inner workings. Here, we will discuss the implementation of a simple planner and then investigate optimization strategies.

Modus Tollens

Our IF/THEN planner relies on a classical rule of logic called *modus tollens*. We know that IF a dog is here, THEN a mammal is here. Suppose that a mammal is not here. Then, we can conclude that a dog is not here. In general, for any propositions A and B, each a statement that is either true or false, modus tollens states that if $A \rightarrow B$, and we know that B is false, then we can conclude that A is false.

With our planner, we will begin with a single goal; suppose that we want to produce gold. We will represent this goal state using the proposition from the earlier example: G—"Gold can be produced." The central idea for a logic-based planner is to use a proof technique called *contradiction* to show that a proposition is true. Using contradiction, we suppose that our goal cannot be attained ($\overline{G}$—"Gold cannot be produced," where the overhead bar denotes negation). Now, we try to derive an impossibility, for example, that a proposition is both true and false. If successful, then our initial assumption $\overline{G}$ must be incorrect because it was used to deduce an impossible scenario! Hence, because any proposition is either true or false, then G must be true. The production rules used to prove it constitute the proof.

We will use modus tollens to make our first deduction. We suppose $\overline{G}$, and we know that $W \wedge T \rightarrow G$ from the prior example. Using modus tollens, we can deduce $\overline{W \wedge T}$. So, if gold cannot be produced, then a worker and a town hall cannot both be present. This makes sense! We now treat $\overline{W \wedge T}$ as a new negated goal because we showed that it must be true if the original negated goal $\overline{G}$ is true.

We will continue applying similar deductions until we deduce a contradiction. However, our new negated goal $\overline{W \wedge T}$ is now a conjunction of several propositions, and so modus tollens can no longer be used for inferences. Hence, we need a more powerful inference rule.

The Resolution Inference Rule

We will now continue our quest for G. From $\overline{W \wedge T}$, we know that either a worker is not present, a town hall is not present, or both are not present. From the environment facts, we know that a worker is present (W). Hence, a town hall must not be present. We will write this deduction as follows, with a dashed line representing "Given the statements above the line, we can deduce the statements below the line":

$$W$$
$$\overline{\overline{W \wedge T}}$$
$$\text{- - - - - - - -}$$
$$\overline{T}$$

We deduced that the town hall cannot be present, but we know from the environment facts in the first example that the town hall *is* present. We have reached a contradiction! Hence, our initial assumption, that gold cannot be produced, must be false; by supposing it, we deduced an impossible scenario. The single production rule $W \wedge T \rightarrow G$ was used, which we map to the action "Assign the worker to mine gold." Because we reached a contradiction without using any additional production rules, this constitutes the plan. By executing it, we obtain gold as desired.

The previous deduction is still inadequate—often single facts do not directly apply to our negated goal. Using a similar proof, we can generalize further and derive a general inference rule called *resolution*. Given a production rule $A_1 \wedge A_2 \wedge \ldots \wedge A_n \rightarrow B_1$ and a negated goal $\overline{B_1 \wedge B_2 \wedge \ldots \wedge B_m}$, we can deduce a new negated goal that lacks B_1:

$$A_1 \wedge A_2 \wedge \ldots \wedge A_n \rightarrow B_1$$
$$\overline{B_1 \wedge B_2 \wedge \ldots \wedge B_m}$$
$$- - - - - - - - - - - - - - - - - - -$$
$$\overline{A_1 \wedge A_2 \wedge \ldots \wedge A_n \wedge B_2 \wedge \ldots \wedge B_m}$$

As an example application of this rule, suppose that our goal is to construct a barracks. We use modus tollens on $W \wedge G \wedge L \rightarrow B$ and $\overline{B}$ to produce $\overline{W \wedge G \wedge L}$. (Modus tollens is actually a special instance of resolution.) Now, we notice that one of the possible production rules implies L. Hence, using the resolution rule, we can eliminate L from the negated goal as follows:

$$W \wedge T \rightarrow L$$
$$\overline{W \wedge G \wedge L}$$
$$- - - - - - - - - - - -$$
$$\overline{W \wedge T \wedge W \wedge G}$$

For any proposition W, note that $W \wedge W$ is true if, and only if, W is true; hence, any duplicate propositions in the goal can be removed. Because of this, $\overline{W \wedge T \wedge W \wedge G}$ can be simplified to $\overline{W \wedge T \wedge G}$, and this becomes our new negated goal.

Backward Chaining

In the first example, a proof was found by moving *forward*—beginning with the environment states W and T, and then continually using production rules until the goal B was reached. Because environment facts describing units and resources likely are used in many production rules, moving forward may not be an efficient proof strategy. Hence, as in the previous section, we will move *backward*, beginning with the negated goal state and determining which rules and environment facts are necessary to achieve it. To summarize the complete backward inference of B as begun in the previous section, see Figure 4.4.2. Note that if multiple production rules have a consequent in the negated goal, then the depicted tree will branch.

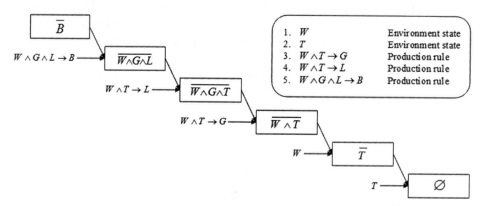

FIGURE 4.4.2   Using backward chaining, a proof of B is given based on the rules and facts from the first example. At each double arrow head, resolution is performed. The proof queue contains the sequential production rules at the left of each stage. Note that two of the production rules could resolve with $\overline{W \wedge G \wedge L}$, creating two possible paths down the tree although only one is depicted.

The following is a formal algorithm for a simple prover using backward chaining:

```
function ruleQueue = BACK-CHAIN(ruleList R, negatedGoal g):
   1. If g is empty, then return empty queue.
   2. For each rule and fact r in R:
          a. If the consequent of r is a proposition in g:
                  i. Let newGoal = RESOLUTION(r, g).
                 ii. If (Q = BACK-CHAIN(R, newGoal)) != NULL:
                          1. Enqueue r in Q.
                          2. Return Q.
   3. Return NULL.
```

As each recursion step that contributes to finding the goal state terminates, we enqueue the production rule used. Recall that the resulting queue of production rules constitutes a plan because each production rule maps directly to an action.

Several quick extensions can be made to this algorithm. First, if one proposition is required to derive several rules, then its generating rule may be repeated multiple times in the proof. A single pass through the proof can remove these repeats if desired.

Second, we can find the shortest proof by performing an iterative deepening search of the proof tree. Here, all n-rule proofs are attempted, incrementing n by one until a proof is found. (See the accompanying code on the CD-ROM for an implementation.) For more information on inference techniques, planning, and extensions to this implementation, see [Russell02].

Optimizations

We will store each production rule and the antecedent of each goal as bit vectors, where each bit indicates the presence of a unique proposition. For example, if the third bit position represents the proposition W, and the second represents T, then the binary value 110 represents the conjunction $W \wedge T$. Negated goals will also be represented as bit vectors, but the negation will be implicit.

By assuming that each consequent is a single proposition, the backward chaining algorithm can be executed very efficiently. In the following, we assume that there are, at mos,t 32 possible propositions, so they can be stored in a single 32-bit variable:

```
struct Rule
{
    ULONG antecedent; // Bit vector (max 32 propositions)
    ULONG consequent; // Index of a single proposition
};
```

Use this method to represent production rules; optimizations follow that are implemented in the accompanying source code for an arbitrary number of propositions:

Use bitwise operators: If an n-bit bit vector is used to represent, at most, n propositions as earlier described, then resolution becomes a simple bitwise operation.

We have seen that after resolution, propositions listed multiple times in the new negated goal are redundant. Hence, if either the goal or the antecedent of the production rule contains a certain proposition, then the resulting goal will contain a single instance of that proposition. This is a logical OR statement.

After this, the single proposition present in both the consequent and the negated goal must be removed:

```
// Resolution
resolution  = negatedGoal | rule.antecedent;
resolution &= ~mask; // Remove the repeated proposition
```

Store facts as IF/THEN rules: Note that resolution can also be applied to facts. Facts are a special type of IF/THEN statement. For example, the fact W can be represented as $\varnothing \to W$, where $\varnothing$ is the empty set (or empty bit vector), indicating that nothing is required to conclude that W is true; hence, it is always true. With this representation, facts can be treated as production rules and used in resolution:

```
// Representation of the fact "W" (bit position 2)
rule.antecedent = 0;     // No propositions in IF
rule.consequent = 0x02;  // Only "W" in THEN
```

Order rules by consequent: For each proposition in the negated goal, we search for all production rules for which the proposition is the consequent. Hence, we can store rules with the same consequent together in a list. Then, an array indexed by consequent can point directly to the relevant list of rules. Instead of searching through every rule, now a list of relevant rules is supplied immediately. The following is an implementation of steps 1 and 1a in the backward chaining algorithm using this optimization:

```
// Loop through all possible propositions
ULONG mask = 1;
for (int bitNum = 0; bitNum < bitsPerULONG; bitNum++)
{
  // Is proposition 'bitNum' in the goal?
  if (negatedGoal & mask)
  {
    // Try all rules that imply proposition 'bitNum'
    std::list<Rule>::const_iterator ruleIter;
    for (ruleIter = rulesByConsequent[bitNum]->begin();
        ruleIter != rulesByConsequent[bitNum]->end();
        ruleIter++)
    {
      // Resolution, recursion
      ...
    }
  }

  mask << 1;
}
```

Representing Rich Environments

ON THE CD

In this section, extensions to the planner that allow for the description of rich game environments will be discussed. Each technique is demonstrated in the source code on the accompanying CD-ROM.

Dynamic Rule Insertion and Removal

Production rules were previously available for use at any step of a proof. Now, to better model the real world, at every step only a subset of the rules will be available. When used in a proof, each production rule can now insert and/or remove a fixed set of other rules. Here, we will show how to achieve this using backward chaining.

As we work backward from the negated goal, the availability of the production rule used at each step is unknown because we are working backward. Hence, we will now examine the conditions under which a rule we add will be valid, that is, added only when it is available. See the four example proofs in Figure 4.4.3 for reference.

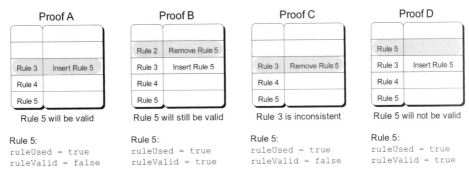

FIGURE 4.4.3 In each of these proofs, the right column indicates the insertions and deletions associated with using each production rule in the left column. Here, we are constructing the proof backward from Rule 5, and we are considering whether to add the shaded rule. In Proof C, adding Rule 3 would be inconsistent, and so we will not add it. In Proof D, we must set `ruleValid` to `false` when we use Rule 5 again because we no longer know whether Rule 5 is valid.

Suppose that we decide to use a rule R, and we place it in the proof. If no rule before it modifies its availability, then R is valid if, and only if, it is initially available. Instead, suppose that multiple rules before R modify its availability (Proof B). Then, the validity of R is only affected by the modification rule immediately before it. If the rule inserts R, then R is valid. If the rule removes R, then R is not valid.

Using this logic, we can associate two flags with each rule: `ruleUsed`, set to `true` when the rule is used in the proof, and `ruleValid`, set to `true` only if we are certain that the rule is valid. Constructing the proof backward from the goal, at each step we will consider rules from the entire set of rules because their validity is unknown.

If a rule is used below the rule that inserts it, and no rules removing it are in-between, then the inserted rule is valid (Proof A). Now suppose that a rule we will use removes a rule below it (Proof C). Then, if `ruleValid` is `false` for the rule that will be removed, indicating that another rule did not insert it in-between, and then using the rule in the proof would make the proof inconsistent. Hence, we cannot use the rule requiring the removal.

Using this method will ensure internal consistency—the use of each rule is consistent with the other rules' insertions and deletions. However, it does not ensure external consistency—that each rule used is initially available. Hence, the validity of each constructed proof must be verified. This is easy and efficient—each rule is valid only if ruleValid is true and/or the rule is initially present. This is not obvious, so we will examine a tricky case. Suppose that a rule is initially present, but that it is removed and not reinserted below the removal (Proof C). Then, the proof would not be valid. However, because our logic does not allow internal inconsistencies to occur, this case will never arise.

This leads to the following algorithm for dynamic rule insertion and removal. Note that in the previous algorithm, we constructed the proof only when we found a solution. Because we must now test the validity of each proof, we must construct the proof as we explore the solution space so that we will have the proof ready when we find a solution:

```
function PROVER(ruleList R, negatedGoal g, proofStack P):
  1. If G empty:
        a. If ValidateProof(P), then return Success.
  2. For each rule and fact r in R:
        b. If the consequent of r is a proposition in G:
              i. Let newGoal = RESOLUTION(r, g).
             ii. Let oldValid = ruleValid[r].
            iii. Let addNewRule = true.
             iv. For each rule u inserted by r:
                   1. If ruleUsed[u], then ruleValid[u] = true.
              v. For each rule u removed by r:
                   1. If ruleUsed[u] and !ruleValid[u],
                      then addNewRule = false.
             vi. If addNewRule is true:
                   1. Push the current rule onto P.
                   2. Let ruleUsed[r] = true.
                   3. Let ruleValid[r] = false.
                   4. If PROVER(R, newGoal, P) succeeds:
                         a. Return Success.
                   5. Otherwise revert the changes:
                         a. Pop a rule from P.
                         b. Let ruleUsed[r] = false.
                         c. Let ruleValid[r] = oldValid.
  3. Return Failure.
```

This algorithm always avoids inconsistent removal rules. It also finds all proofs that require insertion rules but only when those rules are logically required, that is, those that imply a proposition in the current goal. Hence, a proof will not be found if a rule must be applied only to insert a necessary logical rule. This can be alleviated at each stage by trying all rules that are either logically required or that add a rule that has already been used below it in the proof. However, this is not as efficient.

Negated Propositions

Rule insertion and removal can be used to implement negated propositions, for example, *W* ("A worker is present.") and *notW* ("A worker is not present."). The trick is to assign two propositions to represent one statement as just shown; however, both cannot be asserted at once, or a contradiction will occur. When scripting, the dual propositions are easy to enter—simply establish a convention that a negated proposition begins with a "not." Then, it will automatically be treated as a unique proposition by the parser because it is typographically distinct.

Suppose we are given that a worker is present, a town center is not present, and the rule "A town center can be built if a worker is present, and a town center is not present":

$$W \qquad\qquad\qquad \text{Environment fact}$$

$$notT \qquad\qquad\qquad \text{Environment fact}$$

$$W \wedge notT \rightarrow T \qquad \text{Production rule}$$

From these rules, $T \wedge notT$ can be derived, which is a seeming contradiction. However, if we use the techniques from the last section to remove $notT$ after T is derived, then both cannot exist simultaneously, and no contradiction can occur.

Be careful, however, because the previous example is really a matter of semantics. The English sentence actually would translate so that T indicates that "a town center can be produced [in the future]," and $notT$ indicates the same negated but "in the present." Hence, T and $notT$ are not truly opposites. However, because we still do not want both to be true simultaneously, this notation is still desirable.

It is also important to avoid cyclic states. $P \rightarrow P$ will cycle endlessly, as will the pair $S \rightarrow notS$ and $notS \rightarrow S$. These conflicts can be removed as shown previously; if one rule is used, we can remove the other. Even more wisely, cycles should be avoided altogether.

Value Functions for Representing Time and Quantity

Each production rule can have a change in value associated with its use. These value changes are most useful for representing continuous values, such as quantity or time. They are also useful if the value can be continuously incremented or decremented given that certain preconditions are met, for instance, mining gold continuously if a worker is present. Note that in many games, costs tend to be associated with goals rather than plans. Building a barracks, for example, has a fixed cost.

First, the planner determines how a resource, such as gold, can be continuously obtained, for example, by training a worker. Next, it constructs a plan for the desired goal, beginning with the amount of gold the player has and then incrementing or decrementing the total when each production rule is used. Each line of the developing plan has a cost associated with it indicating the cost of the plan so far. This cost can then be used by the planner to accept or reject plans at any stage. For example, if a plan requires the player's gold to dip below zero, then the plan should likely be rejected at an early stage.

The Next Step

More expressive planners may provide additional benefits. For example, an extension to this one used in PROLOG allows variables in addition to objects [Russell02]. Variables allow production rules to apply to certain classes of objects. For example, instead of writing a separate statement for each unit type mentioning that it can rally at the town center, a single statement can be written with variable x:

$$IsUnit(x) \rightarrow CanRallyAt(x, TownCenter)$$

Conclusion

An easy-to-implement, efficient satisfiability planner was described in addition to methods for representing a rich game environment in logic statements. Several easy extensions to the planner, such as adding iterative deepening search to find the shortest plan, adding negations, inserting and removing rules dynamically, and supporting continuous values, were discussed. If more expressive planners are found necessary, the references point to accessible resources on more advanced topics.

References

[Cheng05] Cheng, Jamie, and Finnegan, Southey, "Implementing Practical Planning for Game AI." *Game Programming Gems 5*, Charles River Media, 2005.

[Christian02] Christian, Mike, "A Simple Inference Engine for a Rule-Based Architecture." *AI Game Programming Wisdom*, Charles River Media, 2002.

[Munoz-Avila06] Munoz-Avila, Hector, and Hoang, Hai, "Coordinating Teams of Bots with Hierarchical Task Network Planning." *AI Game Programming Wisdom 3*, Charles River Media, 2006.

[Orkin99] Orkin, Jeff, "Symbolic Representation of Game World State: Toward Real-Time Planning in Games." *AAAI Challenges in Game AI Workshop Technical Report*. Available online at *http://www.jorkin.com/WS404OrkinJ.pdf*, 1999.

[Russell02] Russell, Stuart, and Norvig, Peter, *Artificial Intelligence: A Modern Approach*, Prentice-Hall, 2002.

Abstract

An efficient, easy-to-implement planner is presented based on the principles of logic programming. The planner relies on familiar IF/THEN structures and constructs plans efficiently, but it is not as expressive as other planners. Many easy extensions to the planner are discussed, such as inserting and removing rules dynamically, supporting continuous values, adding negations, and finding the shortest plan. The accompanying source code provides easy-to-follow implementations of the planner and the proposed extensions.

4.5

Simulation-Based Planning in RTS Games

University of Alberta
Frantisek Sailer

sailer@cs.ualberta.ca

Marc Lanctot

lanctot@cs.ualberta.ca

Michael Buro

mburo@cs.ualberta.ca

RTS game developers face the problem of creating AI systems capable of playing well in a team and against a large variety of opponents. The common approach is to script behaviors with the goal of covering the most important strategies used by human players. Creating scripts that perform well for RTS games, however, is hard—it resembles writing good chess programs based solely on static rules without a way of evaluating future developments. To offset the lack of such planning capabilities, game designers often resort to giving AI systems unfair advantages, such as complete information, faster build times, or more resources. Although this approach may be sufficient to create challenging single-player campaigns for novices, it cannot replace the planning, reasoning, and opponent modeling required when playing at a more advanced level. To increase game AI competence in future game titles, more CPU-intensive methods need to be considered. The advent of multiprocessor hardware platforms helps to make this possible.

In this article, we present RTSplan, a practical planning framework for RTS games that addresses this issue by simulating scripts and computing best-response strategies based on opponent modeling in real time. From an RTS game design perspective, RTSplan offers several interesting features:

- It makes use of scripted policies that AI programmers are familiar with.
- During a game, it frequently selects a script to follow next from the set of scripted policies with the goal of defeating each fixed individual script, provided no script is dominant.
- It monitors the opponent and adapts its strategy selection accordingly.
- The CPU load generated by RTSplan is adjustable. More frequent replanning will lead to better performance, but simulations can also be spread over multiple frames if necessary.

ON THE CD

In the remainder of the article, we first set the stage for RTSplan by describing the RTS game environment our planning algorithm is tested in. Next we present RTS-plan, its opponent modeling extension, and implementation details. Third, we discuss our experimental results, and then we conclude with a brief description of the RTS-plan software on the accompanying CD-ROM.

Game Environment

We study the effectiveness of RTSplan by applying it to an army deployment problem: how to coordinate multiple units to defeat the opponents' forces. The approach taken extends to other aspects of RTS games quite naturally, so we chose the most interesting aspect of the game and cover it in detail. We begin this section by describing the dynamics of the game environment in which we tested RTSplan.

The game environment is a simplified, abstract version of an RTS game. The only objects present are groups (of units) and bases, and the only actions available are movement and combat. The objective is to destroy all of the opponent's bases before he destroys all of ours. An example of what our environment looks like and how a typical game progresses is shown in Figure 4.5.1.

In this example, the two opposing players are executing different strategies, with one player choosing to spread out and attack the enemy bases, while the other first gathers all forces into a large army that will be used to wipe out the enemy forces afterward.

Game Cycle

RTS games must execute in real time. A low frame rate, unexpected choppiness, and lag are unacceptable. Because planning is computationally intensive, calculations may have to be spread out over multiple game cycles to ensure a minimal frame rate. The game cycle can conceptually be described as follows:

```
while (game not finished) {
    if (planning finished)
        select new current strategy
    else
        continue planning
    continue executing current strategy
    apply actions
    graphics and network activities
}
```

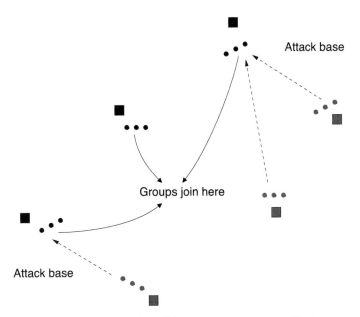

FIGURE 4.5.1   A snapshot of the game environment. Circles are tanks, and squares are bases.

Planning is dynamic: if there is CPU time available, then RTSplan can take advantage of it by continuing the planning process. Otherwise, it executes the last strategy chosen by the planner. When the planning process is complete, the current strategy is updated, and the system starts executing it as seen in Figure 4.5.2. In modern multicore architectures, the cycle can be executed in multiple threads.

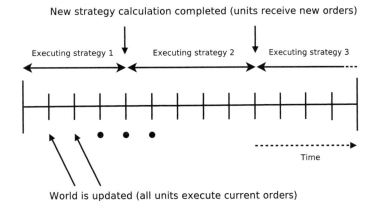

FIGURE 4.5.2   Simulation timeline showing interleaving of planning and execution.

Simulation-Based Planning

Traditional two-player games, such as tic-tac-toe and chess, have *perfect information*: both players can see the full state of the game (e.g., the set of board positions of all pieces) and can reconstruct any state given an initial state and sequence of moves made by the players. Minimax search (and its improvement alpha-beta) is the technique of choice for perfect information games [Russel95]. In its simplest form, this algorithm assesses the quality of each possible move, maximizing the potential gain and minimizing the opponent's potential gain in the worst case by searching the set of valid states a fixed number of moves into the future. It is tempting to use minimax search in RTS games to lessen the burden of creating rule sets able to cope with a large variety of situations in favor of an algorithmic approach that takes the game dynamics into account. However, given hundreds of units under player control and games that last thousands of game cycles, alpha-beta search is infeasible when applied to the raw RTS game state representation, which consists of unit and structure locations, health points, list of discovered regions, and so on. Moreover, RTS games require fast decisions and do not provide players with perfect information. In what follows, we will present a planning technique that addresses most of these problems by means of state and action space abstraction and simulation.

Reducing the Search Space via Abstraction

To look ahead in such complex decision domains requires us to simplify the problem. A common approach is to abstract the state representation and the available actions. For RTSplan, we did this by greatly reducing the number of possible actions. Rather than assessing each individual unit's action, we restrict the AI's choice to selecting scripted policies that implement high-level strategies, such as joining forces and attacking bases. Such strategies are composed of lower-level actions that are determined by the policy's high-level goals. Here are some sample policies that we implemented to test RTSplan:

Null: All groups stop what they are doing and do not move. They do, however, still attack any groups or bases within range.

Join Up and Defend Nearest Base: This policy gathers all the groups into one army, with groups joining at their combined center of mass to speed up joining time, and then moves the army to defend the base that is closest to an enemy group.

Mass Attack: All groups form one army in the same manner as in the Join policy, and then the army goes to attack the nearest enemy base until no enemy bases remain.

Spread Attack: All groups attack the nearest enemy base, and this repeats until all enemy bases are destroyed.

Half Base Defense Mass Attack: Groups are divided into two armies. One defends nearby bases, while the other executes the Mass Attack policy.

Hunter: Groups join with their nearest allied groups and then attack the nearest enemy group.

Attack Least Defended Base: This policy first creates one army like the Join policy, and then sends it to attack the least defended enemy base, which is the base that is farthest away from its friendly forces. The least defended base is reconsidered periodically, in case the opponent moves forces to defend the target base.

Harass: This policy harasses the enemy but never engages in direct combat if it can be helped. Several groups of armies are formed, and each is sent at the nearest enemy base. However, if an enemy army gets near any of our harassing armies, our armies retreat in the direction of one of our bases. When they are sufficiently far enough from the enemy, however, they proceed to attack the nearest base once again.

Choosing Strategies

By selecting scripts rather than individual units' actions, the number of choices is drastically reduced. Given this action abstraction, how can we select strategies? Borrowing again from the minimax idea, we look ahead to gauge the merit of our move decisions. Here, moves consist of selecting a strategy and following it for a certain period of time. In the simplest case—minimax search at depth 2—we could select one of our available strategies at a time and loop through all opponent strategies executing the strategy pairs until the end of the respective game is reached. This way we select strategies that maximize our chance of winning against the strongest counterstrategy. However, a problem arises from limiting each player's selection to only one strategy without the prospect of reconsidering later: by alternating the strategy selection, the second player will be able to choose the right counter-measure every time. A good analogy is rock-paper-scissors (RPS): if one player announces his move (say, Rock), the other player can win all the time (by playing Paper in this case). To counter this effect, we will require our RTS game players to choose their strategies simultaneously, just like in rock-paper-scissors.

Acting Optimally in Simultaneous Move Games

Game theory tells us that in RPS we need to randomize our move selection. If we were to play one move with probability greater than $\frac{1}{3}$ repeatedly and stick to our (randomized) strategy, our opponent can win against us in the long run by playing the respective countermove all the time.

Game theory also provides us with a method for finding optimal strategies for zero-sum simultaneous move games. These games can be described by a payoff matrix in which we note the payoff for player 1 for each pair of move decisions. Player 2 receives the corresponding negative amounts. The payoff matrix for RPS is shown in Figure 4.5.3.

	R	P	S
R	0	+1	−1
P	−1	0	+1
S	+1	−1	0

FIGURE 4.5.3 Payoff matrix
for rock-paper-scissors.

For fixed player strategies x and y and payoff matrix R, the expected payoff for the first player is the matrix product $y'Rx$. There exist strategies x and y with

$$\max_x \min_y y'Rx = \min_y \max_x y'Rx$$

for which both players receive their optimal payoff when facing the strongest opposition [Neumann28]. In the case of RPS, the minimax strategies are given by probability distribution $x = y = (\frac{1}{3}, \frac{1}{3}, \frac{1}{3})$, which selects each move with probability $\frac{1}{3}$. x and y can be found by solving a linear program (LP) of the following form:

Find the maximum value for Z such that:

$$x_1, x_2, x_3, \ldots, x_n \geq 0$$

$$x_1 + x_2 + \ldots + x_n = 1$$

$$x_1 R[1][1] + x_2 R[1][2] + \ldots + x_n R[1][n] \geq Z$$

$$x_1 R[2][1] + x_2 R[2][2] + \ldots + x_n R[2][n] \geq Z$$

$$\ldots$$

$$x_1 R[m][1] + x_2 R[m][2] + \ldots + x_n R[m][n] \geq Z$$

where n, m are the number of moves for player 1 and 2, and Z is the maximal payoff player 1 can expect to receive. Note that x is a probability distribution, and the intermediate equations ensure that x performs well against each single opponent move. An analogous LP exists for y. As an example, consider the LP for RPS:

Find the maximum value for Z such that

$$x_{rock}, x_{paper}, x_{scissors} \geq 0$$

$$x_{rock} + x_{paper} + x_{scissors} = 1$$

$$x_{paper} - x_{scissors} \geq Z$$

$$x_{scissors} - x_{rock} \geq Z$$

$$x_{rock} - x_{paper} \geq Z$$

which has solution $Z = 0$ (on average no gain, no loss) and $x_{rock} = x_{paper} = x_{scissors} = \frac{1}{3}$. Efficient software exists to solve these systems; one example is the GNU Linear Programming Kit [GLPK].

The RTSplan Algorithm

We are now in the position to formulate the RTSplan algorithm. The moves RTSplan considers are scripted policies. Each row of the payoff matrix corresponds to a script that player 1 (the AI) chooses, and each column represents a policy of player 2 (the opponent). Entry $R[i][j]$ of the payoff matrix then is the expected result when pitting strategy j of player 1 against strategy i of player 2. RTSplan computes each entry by executing the corresponding strategies until the game is finished. If the strategies themselves are randomized, or there are other chance events in the game, each strategy pair should be simulated multiple times to better estimate the expected payoffs. After establishing all matrix entries, RTSplan computes the mixed minimax strategy x for the first player and selects the strategy to follow next by sampling from distribution x. For example, for $x = (\frac{1}{2}, \frac{1}{3}, \frac{1}{6})$, we would pick policy 1 with probability $\frac{1}{2}$, 2 with $\frac{1}{3}$, and 3 with probability $\frac{1}{6}$.

The following code summarizes the simulation approach to selecting an appropriate policy from a given set of policies:

```
int RTSplan(ourPolicies, theirPolicies, curState) {
    int n = ourPolicies.size;
    int m = theirPolicies.size;
    int R[m][n];

    for (i=0; i < m; i++) {
        for (j=0; j < n; j++) {
            R[i][j] = ourScore(curState,
                               ourPolicies[j],
                               theirPolicies[i]);
        }
    }
    return ourPolicies[sample(SolveLP(R))];
}
```

`SolveLP()` returns a probability distribution over policy indexes, from which an element gets sampled by `sample()`.

Opponent Modeling

Playing the minimax strategy maximizes the gains against strong players. However, it does not exploit their weaknesses. Consider a RPS player who always chooses Rock. Against it, the minimax strategy $(\frac{1}{3}, \frac{1}{3}, \frac{1}{3})$ only achieves an even score, whereas the Paper player would win all the time. So, rather than playing the minimax strategy, we want to model the opponent and play a best-response strategy that maximally exploits the opponent's weaknesses.

In the RTSplan framework, a straightforward way to determine what the opponent is doing is to observe the opponent's actions for some time period and to see how the state changes from the first point of observation to the last point of observation. We can then go back to the beginning of the observation period repeatedly to observe the results of our own policy playing against every opponent policy. If a produced end-state is exactly the same as the state at the last point of observation that the opponent is in, then it is very likely that the opponent is following the chosen strategy.

To generalize this concept, a distance metric can be used to gauge how similar two states are. If two identical states are passed to the distance function, then zero should be returned, whereas the distance between two completely different states should be high. Such distance measures are application specific.

In our army deployment problem, we track object positions and compute their total pair-wise distance. If the number of objects in the two states are different (due to combat), the distance is set to a high value indicating that the states are "very" different from each other. An example of the technique is visualized in Figure 4.5.4.

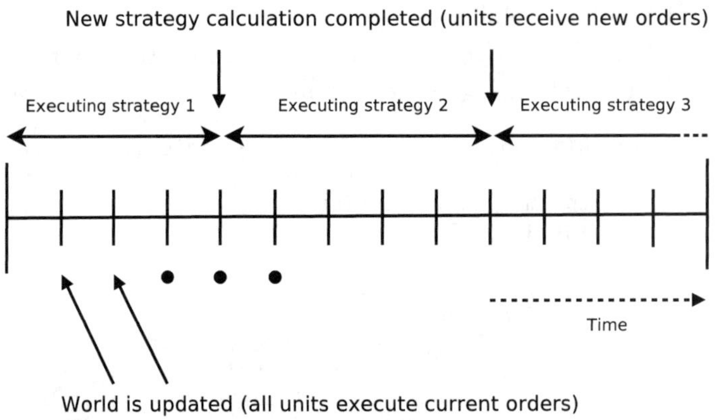

FIGURE 4.5.4   An example of an observed behavior, described by the trajectory between initial state (Si) and end state (Se), and simulated end states using four different strategies (SS_1, SS_2, SS_3, and SS_4). The opponent is using a strategy that most resembles the third strategy because the distance between Se and SS_3 is the smallest.

Opponent Modeling Algorithm

Following is the algorithm for opponent modeling:

1. Starting with the state at the beginning of the observation period, compute $SS_1 \dots SS_n$, that is, the states that result from following some opponent strategy while replaying our policy.

2. Compute policy distances $d_i = dist(Se, SS_i)$, where Se is the state reached at the end of the observation period.
3. Set threshold $h = average(d_i) \cdot f$, where f is a constant (we chose $f = 0.5$).
4. Collect all active opponent strategies i with $d_i \leq h$. If this set is empty, consider all opponent strategies active.

Active strategies are those that most closely match the observed behavior. In Figure 4.5.4, SS_3 would almost certainly be an active strategy, SS_2 and SS_4 might be depending on the value of f, and SS_1 would almost certainly not be active. After certain opponent strategies have been ruled out, the corresponding rows can be removed from the payoff matrix. The effect is a reduced computation time because the payoff matrix is smaller and a strategy subset that allows RTSplan to detect opponents who keep using the same strategy and select proper counterstrategies that maximally exploit their weaknesses.

Implementation Issues

There are a few implementation considerations when using RTSplan. Most importantly, we need a mechanism to speed up forward simulations because they need to be significantly faster than the actual game to be useful. We also need ways to deal with combat and pathfinding.

Simulation Process

When RTSplan with opponent modeling is implemented, the main loop of our simulator looks like this:

```
currTime = 0;

while (!isGameOver()) {
    for (int i=0; i < players.size(); ++i) {
        Strategy bestStr = calcBestStrategy(policies,
            curState, players[i]);
        players[i].updateOrders(bestStr);
    }

    currTime += timeIncrement;

    if (isTimeToUpdateActiveStrategies())
        recalculateActiveStrategies();

    updateWorld(currTime);
}
```

The function `calcBestStrategy()` uses RTSplan to compute the result matrix and return the new best strategy. Regardless of whether a strategy was changed, the world advances forward in time by the specified time increment in `updateWorld()`.

The given time increment could be a constant value (for running experiments) or the actual time elapsed between subsequent calls to this function (when run in a real-world situation). The function isTimeToUpdateActiveStrategies() is only used for opponent modeling and calculates the size of the opponent's strategy set.

Fast-Forwarding Strategies

Each of our forward simulations runs a game all the way to the end or to some point in the far future. Therefore, it is crucial to compute successor states quickly. However, such simulations can be expensive, especially if we were to simulate every single time step. To reduce this cost, we instead calculate the next "interesting" point in time and advance there directly. This time point is derived in such a way that there is no need to simulate any time step in between our start time and the derived time because nothing interesting will happen during that time interval. We call this method *fast-forwarding*. In our RTS game simulation environment, the next interesting point in time is the minimum of the return values of the following four functions:

- nextCollideTime() is calculated by solving a quadratic equation with the input being the direction vectors of the two groups in question. The quadratic equation may not be solvable (no collision), or it my produce a time of collision. Two groups are considered to be colliding if either one of them is within attack range of the other. The collision time is computable this way because all units travel in straight lines.
- getNextOrderDoneTime() is a simple calculation. Divide the distance to the goal for a group by its maximum velocity. We do this for every group and return the time at which the first group reaches its goal.
- getNextShootingTime() applies to groups that are already within range of an enemy group and are recharging their weapons. This function returns the next time at which one of these groups can fire again.
- getNextStrategyTimeoutTime() function returns the next time that any one of the strategies in question is allowed to reevaluate the game state to give out new orders if necessary. Thus, this is the only time when units could change their direction of travel, for example.

Fast-forwarding allows us to safely skip all simulation steps during which nothing of importance happens. It can also be applied to settings with more complex maps, as long as the pathfinder provides a series of waypoints as orders to our groups. For more complex abstract models than we use here, it may become more difficult to find the next time of interest, and it is likely that the times of interest will be closer to each other, thus reducing the effectiveness of fast-forwarding. Thus, to best use fast-forwarding, the model should be kept as abstract as possible.

Combat Simulation

Because we are creating an AI for the high-level commander who deals with army deployment, we abstract individual units into groups. A human player usually sends out groups of units and deals with individual units only in combat situations. Our combat simulation method does not deal with combat tactics; instead, we have a simple combat model that generally favors numerical advantage.

Pathfinding

None of our scenarios contain obstacles. Pathfinding is irrelevant in this particular application, and, therefore, no sophisticated pathfinding algorithm is included in the simulator. However, the subject of pathfinding is not ignored. Our algorithm is meant to work in conjunction with any type of pathfinder. In a full RTS game environment, a pathfinder would examine the terrain and find a path composed of waypoints. These waypoints would then be passed to our abstract model as orders to be executed sequentially by the groups.

Experiments

The ultimate test of game AI systems is to compare their performance with that of human players. While using our GUI for playing, we have gathered some anecdotal evidence that the RTSplan players are indeed stronger than the individual strategies. To test the effectiveness of RTSplan more rigorously, we ran tournaments to compare RTSplan with and without opponent modeling against single fixed strategies. We also gathered some execution time information.

To make the experimental results independent of specific hardware configurations, the simulator used an internal clock. Thus, processor speed did not affect our experimental results. To do this, we had to slightly modify our main execution loop because we could no longer use an execution time limit for interleaving world execution and planning. We instead calculated a specified number of entries (eight for these experiments) in the payoff matrix before allowing the world to move forward, which leads to real-time performance of 2–40 world ticks a second on average running on common computing hardware (see Table 4.5.3 later in this article).

Results of Experiments Without Opponent Modeling

First, we tested how well RTSplan does against the single strategies. The results shown in Table 4.5.1 indicate that RTSplan wins easily against most opponents. RTSplan struggles against the more aggressive strategies, however, because they manage to inflict losses on it before it has computed its first strategy. One way of mitigating this effect would be to pick a random strategy to start with.

Table 4.5.1   RTSplan Versus Fixed Policy, with Opponent Modeling Disabled and Enabled

Fixed Policy	Opp. Mod. Disabled			Opp. Mod. Enabled		
	Wins	Losses	Ties	Wins	Losses	Ties
Null	100	0	0	100	0	0
Join Defense	98	2	0	97	1	2
Mass Attack (base)	98	2	0	99	1	0
Mass Attack (units)	98	2	0	99	1	0
Spread Attack (base)	51	49	0	92	8	0
Spread Attack (units)	51	49	0	92	8	0
Half Defense-Mass Attack	98	2	0	99	1	0
Hunter	31	69	0	95	4	1
Attack Least Defended Base				100	0	0
Harass				93	8	9

Results of Experiments with Opponent Modeling

Next, we enabled opponent modeling for RTSplan, set its parameters to $t = 2.0$ and $f = 0.5$, and repeated the first experiment. As shown in Table 4.5.1 the addition of opponent modeling allows for RTSplan to clearly defeat the single strategies, even the ones it had trouble with earlier. This is not surprising because the opponents never deviate from their strategies. After we correctly detect what strategy they are using, we can execute a proper counterstrategy.

RTSplan Against Unknown Strategies

In real game scenarios, it is unlikely that the opponent will be following a strategy we have in our strategy set. To test how RTSplan copes with "unknown" strategies, we designed an experiment in which we removed the policy the opponent was using from the active policy set. This meant that is was impossible for the AI to detect their opponent's strategy. The results shown in Table 4.5.2 indicate that RTSplan plays well, even against opponents that are doing something completely unexpected. There is an additional disadvantage for RTSplan in this setting compared to a real-world situation: we blindfolded it to major strategic options that players would employ.

Table 4.5.2   RTSplan with Opponent Modeling Versus Fixed Unknown Policy

Unknown Policy	Wins	Losses	Ties
Null	95	5	0
Join Defense	97	3	0
Mass Attack (base)	98	2	0
Mass Attack (units)	98	2	0
Spread Attack (base)	61	39	0

$\rightarrow$

Unknown Policy	Wins	Losses	Ties
Spread Attack (units)	61	39	0
Half Defense-Mass Attack	100	0	0
Hunter	41	59	0
Attack Least Defended Base	100	0	0
Harass	45	53	2

Execution Times

For our algorithm to be useful in a real RTS game setting, computations must be able to finish in a reasonable amount of time. Table 4.5.3 shows the execution time percentiles for computing a single forward simulation. Different scenarios, sizes, numbers of policies, and the effects of opponent modeling are shown. All runs were executed on a dual-processor Athlon MP CPU (2 GHz), of which only one CPU was used. Even though some slight spikes in performance are exhibited, as can be seen in the max value, generally the execution time of a single simulation is low. Even in the worst of our test cases, the simulation took less time than it takes a human to blink (350 ms).

Table 4.5.3   Execution Time Percentiles (Milliseconds)

Map Size (# of policies)	10th	25th	Median	75th	90th	Max
3 bases (8)	1.13	2.08	3.34	5.42	9.16	71.39
5 bases (8)	2.26	4.72	7.83	21.93	38.92	194.85
4 bases (10)	18.62	38.3	67.01	102.12	132.22	225.57
4 bases (10) (modeling)	5.19	11.5	28.21	50.15	95.4	220.3

These results show that even while computing several forward simulations every frame, we can still run at a real-time speed, with the number of simulations run per frame determined by available CPU time. These numbers are mainly dependent on the simulation timeout parameter. Lowering this parameter will result in faster execution times, at the cost of lower playing strength. If the execution times are unacceptably high, it is possible to simulate a shorter time into the future by decreasing the simulation length parameter. Currently, we simulate the entire game. Lowering this threshold will decrease execution time significantly.

Conclusion

Our simulation-based planning approach RTSplan takes a set of scripted AI policies, repeatedly determines which one is currently optimal based on some simplifying assumptions, and follows this policy for a certain period of time before replanning. RTSplan interleaves adversarial planning with plan execution, and its CPU demand is adjustable, making it well suited for RTS games and other real-time games. Furthermore, adding simple opponent modeling makes RTSplan-based AI even stronger and faster.

RTSplan is easy to implement, suggesting that the algorithm would be a valuable addition to an RTS game AI. It is an important first step toward RTS game AI systems that are capable of judging the merit of actions, as opposed to executing simple rule-based policies.

Future Work

RTSplan is an original planning framework. Presented in the article are initial implementations and results that show the usefulness of the concept. Several aspects of the algorithm can be improved. For example:

- There is room for performance optimizations, mainly in the forward simulation section. The collision-detection algorithm that is currently used runs in quadratic time and therefore does not scale well.
- The algorithm also needs to be tested in a full RTS game setting. This requires all the other parts of the AI system to be completed. This includes a working scout AI, base management AI, pathfinder, and so on. These were not available at the time of writing, but we plan to integrate RTSplan into our RTS game engine [ORTS].
- Although our current set of strategies captures many of the common strategies used in RTS games, it is by no means complete. Adding more complex strategies will improve the performance of RTSplan-based players.

Source Code and Documentation

ON THE CD

The accompanying CD-ROM contains software for our game environment, RTSplan, and a graphical interface that allows human players to play against RTSplan in a variety of scenarios. Our program compiles under Linux and Cygwin. The README.txt file describes the installation process and how to run the application. We also included the master's thesis this article is based on.

References

[GLPK] The GNU Linear Programming Kit. Available online at *http://www.gnu.org/software/glpk/*.

[Neumann28] von Neumann, J., "Zur Theorie der Gesellschaftsspiele." Math. Ann. 100, (1928): pp. 295–320.

[ORTS] A free software RTS game engine. Available online at *http://www.cs.ualberta.ca/~mburo/orts*.

[Russell95] Russell, S., and Norvig, P., *Artificial Intelligence: A Modern Approach.* Prentice Hall Series in Artificial Intelligence, 1995.

Particle Filters and Simulacra for More Realistic Opponent Tracking

Christian J. Darken—The MOVES Institute

cjdarken@nps.edu

Bradley G. Anderegg—Alion Science and Technology Corporation

bradanderegg@gmail.com

The AIs for games such as the *Halo* and *Thief* series feature searching for the player as a prominent and entertaining behavior. Hiding from the player is also a common AI feature. We believe that for some games, realistic searching and hiding might make for more interesting gameplay than cheating (i.e., approaches based on letting the AI know where the player is). A realistic way for the AI to decide where to search or where to hide is by having a representation of where its opponent might be (i.e., by tracking the possible location of the opponent). Predicting an opponent's location is a limited form of mental simulation, one of the ways human decision makers solve problems [Kunde06].

Space-based techniques for opponent tracking compute the likelihood that the target player or agent is in each region of space [Tozour04, Isla06]. A logical alternative is to represent a sampling of precise coordinates where the target might be. The basic technique for doing this is called the particle filter. Particle filters have computation and memory costs that can be quite different from occupancy maps and, therefore, are a less expensive alternative in some applications. We describe the basic particle filter technique, and then consider adding some intelligence to the particles, resulting in *simulacra* that more accurately imitate the behavior of the agents or players they represent.

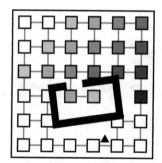 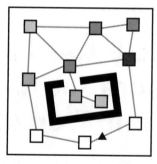 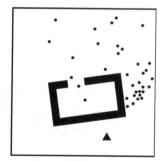

FIGURE 4.6.1   The agent is the black triangle. His target has recently moved out of sight around the eastern edge of a building, outlined in black. These diagrams are snapshots of various possible models that the agent could have of the target. (Left) An occupancy map on a rectangular graph of nodes (Isla model). (Center) An occupancy map on a more sparse navigation graph. (Right) A small particle filter. Each dot represents one possible location of the target.

Occupancy Maps

We first summarize a space-based opponent tracking approach, the occupancy map, for easy comparison to particle filters, which we introduce next.

Data

Let's assume that the game level is represented by a directed graph of the same type as that used for navigation. Each node of the graph has specific coordinates but can also be taken to represent the part of the level closer to that node than to any other (i.e., the node's Voronoi region). An edge between two nodes means that it is possible to move from the first node to the second. Each node A stores a value p_A, a "weight" that is proportional to the probability of the target being at the corresponding place on the level. The sum of the p_A is also stored. Let's call the sum p. Then the expected probability of the opponent being at node A is just p_A/p. Each pair of nodes is assigned a parameter, λ_{AB}, which is the probability of moving directly from node A to node B in one update of the occupancy map. If there is no edge from A to B, λ_{AB} is zero. Obviously, for each node A, $\sum_B \lambda_{AB} \leq 1$.

Initialization

In the instant that a visible target moves out of sight, its position is known. The model can be initialized to track this target by setting p_A to one at the known location and zero everywhere else. A more uncertain awareness of target, for example, from hearing a noise, might be modeled by making p_A nonzero over the entire range of locations where the noise could have originated.

Update

The occupancy map must be periodically updated via a move-cull process.

Move

If we define $p_A(n)$ to be the value of p_A after the nth update, then

$$p_A(n+1) = p_A(n) - \sum_B \lambda_{AB} p_A(n) + \sum_C \lambda_{CA} p_C(n).$$

Roughly speaking, because p_A is only proportional to the probability and not the probability itself, the probability that the target is at A is reduced by the amount of probability that moves to adjoining locations and is increased by the amount of probability coming in from adjoining locations.

Cull

If at any time it is observed that the target is not at location A, we subtract p_A from p, and set p_A to zero. The exact nature of this test involves a key design decision, namely whether to consider a visibility test of a single point sufficient (i.e., testing the node coordinates) or whether checking multiple points or even a volumetric approach is necessary.

The Isla Model

The model we have presented is a more general version of Isla's [Isla02]. This model reduces to his if each node has four neighbors (because the places the nodes represent are centers of a rectangular grid, for example, as in Figure 4.6.1 left). Furthermore, if all of the probabilities of motion are identical (i.e., for all adjacent nodes A and B) $\lambda_{AB} = \lambda$, then this model becomes identical to Isla's.

Analysis

Occupancy maps have several weaknesses. Each update, some probability always bleeds from each node to each connected node, independent of whether enough time has elapsed for the target to move between those nodes or not. The "wavefront" of where the probability values are greater than zero moves independent of, and is possibly much different from, the maximum speed of the target. This results not only in quantitative error in the probability values but also in the serious qualitative error of assigning nonzero probability to places where the target could not possibly be or zero probability to places the target might be. Spacing location nodes uniformly and synching the map update rate to the speed of the target can eliminate this problem, but neither is necessarily convenient in a game context.

If the AI cannot observe locations A or B, but it can observe the only route between them, probability should not move between A and B; however, it might in the model, especially if the cheapest approach to culling (visibility testing the node coordinates only) is used. This causes the target to seem to teleport directly between the two points.

The memory and computation requirements are proportional to the number of nodes in the graph, which might be arbitrarily large.

In the Isla model, it is considered equally likely that the target will move in any direction, which might not be correct for many targets. In comparison, simulacra (described later) allow us to apply different movement behaviors depending on the context.

Particle Filters

Particle filters represent the location of the target as a finite set of possibilities called *particles* [Arulampalam02, Bererton04].

Data

Each particle has a "weight," a value proportional to its probability, which indicates how likely that possibility is. Typically, each particle consists of a single position that could be the target's current location. We will use N to represent the current number of particles, x_n to represent the vector position of the nth particle, and p_n for its weight. We use p to represent the sum of p_n, so the probability that the target is at x_n is taken to be p_n/p.

Initialization

When a visible target moves out of sight, the model is initialized by placing some desired number of particles at an extrapolated position for the target that is not visible. If the target is detected via a sensory modality that has significant positional error (such as sound, sonar, etc.), the particles are placed by sampling the position uncertainty distribution, if known, or by uniformly sampling the approximate region of uncertainty.

Update

As with occupancy maps, particle filters are periodically updated via a move-cull cycle.

Move

Each particle is updated by independently selecting a direction of motion by uniformly sampling [(0, 360) degrees and then attempting to move the particle the distance it could have moved at maximum velocity since the last update. If obstacles exist that might interfere with motion, which there usually are for random direction movement in game levels, each particle's movement must be collision tested, and the particle's motion adjusted if a collision occurs.

Cull

After each particle is moved, a visibility check to the owning agent is performed. If the agent can see particle n, it is removed from the filter, and p is reduced by p_n.

Analysis

Particle filters avoid many of the problems of occupancy maps:

*   The particles move at the exact maximum velocity of the target.
*   Particles can be spotted while in motion (i.e., no teleportation).
*   The memory requirements of a particle are completely independent of the size of the level or the number of nodes in its navigation graph.

Particle filters also have several weaknesses:

*   The random choice of movement direction does not match the behavior of many targets, as was our complaint of the Isla model. Movement choices depending upon context are not possible.
*   The filters need to test during update to make sure the particles are not moving through walls, up impassably steep cliffs, and so on.
*   The computational expense of particle filters is directly proportional to the number of particles. If the particle set is too small for the region in which the target could be, the particle set will no longer represent the target's possible position well (i.e., the sampling error, associated with representing a continuum of possible locations with the finite set of particles, becomes large). Although methods to "regularize" or repopulate the particle set after it has been created have been suggested [Arulampalam02], the existing methods run the risk of creating particles where no particle could possibly be, given previous culls.
*   Tracking multiple enemies requires multiple sets of particles.

Simulacra

For us, a *simulacrum* is one agent's (NPC's) behavior model *for another agent or the player.* That is, simulacra represent how *an agent* believes another agent or the player will act. Simulacra can solve, partially or completely, many of the problems of particle filters described earlier. The behavior of a simulacrum must be simpler than that of the agent it represents for several reasons:

*   To maintain realism, the simulacrum should not have access to the environmental information that is driving the behavior of the actual agent. For example, a simulacrum could have a rule that triggers a behavior that would occur when it sees an object whose position is known to the agent but not when it sees an object whose position the agent is not aware of.
*   Also, for maintaining realism, the simulacrum might not have an accurate idea of the intentions or behavior models of the actual agent. For example, a simulacrum might only be capable of an aggressive fighting behavior, where the agent it models is also capable of a "hide and heal up" behavior.
*   To keep simulacra computationally tractable, each must use only a small fraction of the computation time of an actual agent because each agent might need to maintain simulacra for multiple targets.

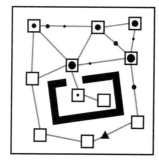 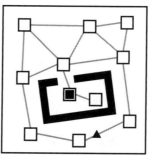 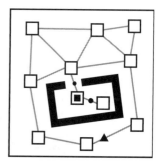

FIGURE 4.6.2   The same scenario as in Figure 4.6.1 but with different target location models. (Left) Simulacra that wander constrained to the navigation graph. Size is used to represent the weight (relative probability) of each simulacrum. (Center) A hider simulacrum that moves directly to the nearest location inside a building. (Right) Simulacra that all hide, and then switch to a wander behavior with some transition probability. Hider simulacra are represented as the square particle, and wander simulacra as the circular ones. The wander simulacra will soon occupy most of the graph, including sharing the node occupied by the hiders.

The occupancy map and particle filter techniques previously described both make implicit use of a simulacrum. In fact, both use the same simulacrum. Both techniques implicitly assume that the target is performing the wandering behavior referred to in the mathematical literature as a "random walk." The most probable location for a target that moves out of sight, according to a random walk model, is immediately adjacent to its last known location, as is clearly visible in Figure 4.6.1. This is a highly inappropriate model for many targets in a game context. Often, the most unlikely behavior would be for the target to stop just out of sight. We contend that we will get more realistic hiding and searching behavior with better simulacra. If we know that the opponent will hide in a building, for example, searching based on a hiding simulacrum (see Figure 4.6.2 center) is bound to be more realistic than searching based on a wandering simulacrum (see Figure 4.6.2 left).

Simulacra are simple to implement because they are just lightweight, nonrendered agents, and the agent infrastructure of a game can generally be easily repurposed to support simulacra.

Data

Simulacra are particles, so they have a position x_n and weight p_n. Additionally, simulacra have a behavior state variable b_n, which might be a structure storing arbitrary amounts of data. For the simplest simulacra, no behavior state is needed. Because it is necessary for reasons previously described to keep the simulacra simple, generally the behavior state should be small. As for particles, we store the sum of the p_n in a variable p. N stores the current number of simulacra, and N^* stores the desired number.

Update

Before moving, if $N < N^*$, simulacra might be split. The simplest approach to splitting is to select a random simulacrum using p_n/p as the probability of selection. The selected simulacrum is then split into two identical simulacra each with weight $p_n/2$, and N is incremented. This procedure can be repeated until N reaches N^*. The weakness of this simple approach to stabilizing the size of the simulacrum set is that it is really only helpful if the "move" part of the update assigns different movements to the newly split twin simulacra. A more sophisticated approach to splitting could enforce this by taking place during "move" and only allowing the split when the twins will move differently. This approach could also capitalize on knowledge of how likely different movement choices are according to the movement logic. For example, if there is a 75% chance of going left and 25% of going right, one twin could be chosen to go left and its weight changed to $0.75p_n$ with the other going right and assigned weight $0.25p_n$.

Move

Simulacra can be assigned arbitrary movement logic that depends on their behavior state, b_n. Although they might be made to move like particles, rather than moving in a random direction, they could alternatively be made to move only to adjacent nodes in a navigation graph. They might even choose target destinations based on their state and plan paths to them, storing the paths in their b_n. We give some examples in a later section.

Cull

Simulacra are culled exactly like particles (i.e., for each simulacrum, a visibility check to the owning agent is performed). If the agent can see simulacrum n, it is deleted, and p is reduced by p_n.

Analysis

How do simulacra solve the problems of basic particle filters? The main difference is that the movements simulacra make are not necessarily those of a random walk. Compare Figure 4.6.2 left with Figure 4.6.2 center for an extreme example of tighter localization of the target based on knowledge of its behavior. Examples of alternative movement policies are described in a later section. Consider the problem of needing to check the particle's motion for collisions, and so on. If the simulacrum is designed to move only on a carefully constructed navigation graph in the same manner as a rendered agent, this need disappears. The two simulacrum splitting approaches mentioned solve the problem of repopulating heavily culled simulacra sets so that all simulacra are guaranteed to be consistent with all previous culls. Problems of needing large numbers of simulacra under some circumstances and of requiring multiple simulacra sets to represent multiple targets are inherited from particle filters. As Figure 4.6.2 illustrates, however, one simulacrum with the right behavior can be worth a large cloud of wanderers. For this reason, generating just a few simulacra with more expensive behavior (e.g., including path planning) should be considered in applications where the opponent's behavior is relatively predictable.

Examples

The following are a few examples of types of simulacra that might be used to model the behavior of different agents.

The Wanderer

As previously mentioned, the particles of the basic particle filter technique perform an unconstrained wandering behavior (refer to Figure 4.6.1). To avoid collision checking, wanderer simulacra can have their motion constrained to a navigation graph (refer to Figure 4.6.2 left). This is implemented by having simulacra arriving at a node of the graph and selecting a random neighbor node to move to.

The Hider

Consider a simulacrum of an agent that is the hider in a game of hide-and-seek. A simple model might be that the simulacrum chooses one out of a set of known good positions to hide in. When the seeker starts the countdown, the hider proceeds to his chosen location via the shortest path. Each simulacrum would store the path to its hiding place, which would not change after initialization, in its behavior state variable.

Likewise, a simulacrum can be built for a ship that is attempting to evade the agent. When the agent turns on radar to detect the ship but fails, it is possible that the ship detects the radar and will use this information to run away, as shown in Figure 51 of Borovies [Borovies07]. Each simulacrum requires a Boolean behavior state variable describing whether the ship is in the flee state. The simulacrum move logic would contain a conditional so that movement choices are consistent with the mode.

The Hunter

Similarly, consider a simulacrum of a ship that is attempting to find the agent. When the agent turns on radar to detect the ship but fails, it is possible that the ship detects the radar and will use this information to set a course toward the agent, as shown in Figure 52 of Borovies [Borovies07]. As with the hider, each simulacrum requires a Boolean variable to change to capture mode.

The Capture the Flag Player

A simulacrum could be used specifically to represent the possible locations of an opposing Capture the Flag player who has just taken the agent's flag. Obviously, the initial location of the target is known (he's at the flag), as is his destination (his own base). One simulacrum could be used to trace each route back. The cull logic could be changed slightly to allow all members of the agent's team to collaborate in eliminating simulacra. If the agent's team takes a flag as well, this could trigger the simulacra to change to a "hide" behavior.

Source Code and Demo

ON THE CD

The CD-ROM includes simulacrum demos in the context of simple games in 3D urban-style environments.

Conclusion

Tracking the possible location of an opponent is a potentially important game AI capability for enabling intelligent hiding from, or searching for, the opponent. This article provides an introduction to particle filters for this purpose. Particle filters have a very different performance profile from occupancy maps and thus represent an interesting alternative. We also show how adding a small amount of intelligence to the particles, transforming them to simulacra, can improve the quality of tracking. Finally, we note that there is vast potential for hybrid approaches integrating the best features of simulacra and occupancy maps.

References

[Arulampalam02] Arulampalam, S., Maskell, S., Gordon, N., and Clapp, T., "A Tutorial on Particle Filters for On-line Non-Linear/Non-Gaussian Bayesian Tracking." *IEEE Transactions on Signal Processing*, Vol. 50, no. 2, (2002): pp. 174–188.

[Bererton04] Bererton, C., "State Estimation for Game AI Using Particle Filters." *Proceedings of the AAAI Workshop on Challenges in Game AI*, Technical Report WS–04–04, AAAI Press, 2004.

[Borovies07] Borovies, D., "Particle Filter Based Tracking in a Detection Sparse Discrete Event Simulation Environment." Master's Thesis, Naval Postgraduate School, Monterey, California. Available online at *http://www.nps.edu/Library/index.html*, 2007.

[Isla06] Isla, D., "Probabilistic Target Tracking and Search Using Occupancy Maps." *AI Game Programming Wisdom 3*, Charles River Media, 2006.

[Kunde06] Kunde, D., and Darken, C., "A Mental Simulation-Based Decision-Making Architecture Applied to Ground Combat." *Proceedings of BRIMS*, 2006.

[Tozour04] Tozour, P., "Using a Spatial Database for Runtime Spatial Analysis." *AI Game Programming Wisdom 2*, Charles River Media, 2004.

4.7

Using Bayesian Networks to Reason About Uncertainty

Devin Hyde

devinhyde@gmail.com

The goal of this article is to help you understand the fundamentals of Bayesian networks. The article shows how a Bayesian network can be created to model a problem description that could fit into a video game. By the end of the article, you should know how to form and solve similar problems on your own. This article presents Bayesian network information through examples that step through the process of designing the layout of the presented Bayesian network solutions. Implementations of the examples are provided on the accompanying CD-ROM. These working models require the use of the free demo version of *Netica* (available at *www.norsys.com*) and are useful for showing how beliefs are updated based on observations. Unfortunately, it is beyond the scope of this article to explain all the math required to implement the Bayesian networks shown in this article.

ON THE CD

Bayesian Network Introduction

Bayesian networks may also be referred to as Bayes nets, Bayes networks, and belief networks. To illustrate Bayesian networks and how to build one, we'll work through an example based on a question in Russell and Norvig's textbook on AI [Russell03]. This example shows a Bayesian network acting as a diagnostic system. Later examples will show that these same principals can be applied more directly to video game situations.

A Bayesian network has a graphical part and a numerical part. The graphical part is a *directed acyclic graph* (DAG). The nodes represent random variables, which can have discrete or continuous domains. For simplicity's sake, this article uses discrete domains. The directed arcs between nodes show a causal relationship between those two variables. The node at the tail of the arc is called the parent of the node at the head of the arc [Russell03]. The arrangement of nodes in the graph shows conditional independence. Each node also contains probability information.

Russell and Norvig's question involves building a Bayesian network to act as a diagnostics system for a car. If you were having problems with your car, some things you could check include whether the car starts, if the radio works, if the gas tank is empty, if the ignition creates a spark, and if the battery is dead. We will represent these five checks with five Boolean values: Starts, Radio, Gasoline, Ignition, and Battery. More complicated examples could use variables with larger domains. For this example, it's sufficient to say that if the car starts, then Starts = true; if the battery is charged, then Battery = true; if the gas tank contains fuel, then Gasoline = true; and so on.

Now that the variables have been defined, we could jump right to defining probabilities for them. Your first thought might be to define a probability for each combination that the five variables could have. This would allow us to look up the probability of any of the 32 combinations of values that our 5 variables could possess. Although this might seem viable, the number of combinations will continue to grow as we add variables. This problem is made worse if the variables' domains contain more than two values. Luckily, we can define smaller *conditional probability tables* (CPTs) based on the relationships between variables expressed in the graph. A CPT defines the probability of a variable, given the value of its parent variable(s). After we have finished defining probabilities using CPTs, we'll have 20 values. This may seem like a modest savings, but its impact will increase as the size of the examples increase.

As mentioned before, a directed acyclic graph, or DAG, is the structure used for a Bayesian network. Figure 4.7.1 shows the DAG for the car diagnostic system example. The nodes of the graph represent the five variables we defined earlier. Connection arcs between the variables are directed and often show a causal relationship between those variables. The variable at the arrowhead of the arc is affected by the variable at the tail of the arc. Variables connected by arcs have a cause-and-effect relationship. Our Bayesian network is a model that we'll use to approximate the world. We want to show when a given part is dependent on one or more of the other parts in the vehicle. In our example, the battery needs to work for the radio and ignition to work. The ignition needs to spark, and we need gasoline in the car for the engine to start. These relationships between variables define how we will draw the graph for this problem.

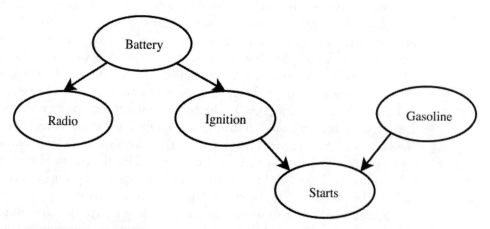

FIGURE 4.7.1   The DAG for a car diagnostic system.

We can now return to the probability section of this Bayesian network. The preferable way to assign probabilities is with the help of an expert in that area or by using statistical data. The car's owner may suffice as an expert for this example. A more complicated system could require a trained mechanic and/or information from various parts manufacturers. Probabilities are assigned to each possible value of the variable, given each possible combination of values that the parent(s) of this variable can take on.

For each variable in our DAG, we'll create a CPT. Variables with no parents in the DAG may be a good place to start assigning probabilities. In our example, Battery and Gas have no parents. We need to decide the probability that the battery has a charge, denoted P(Battery = true). P(Battery = false) = 1 - P(Battery = true), which is to say that probability tables must sum to 1.

Variables with one or more parent have more complicated CPTs. These tables assign probabilities to the variable, given each combination of values that the parent variables can be assigned. From Figure 4.7.1, we can see the need to define P(Radio | Battery), P(Ignition | Battery), and P(Starts | Ignition, Gasoline). The CPT for P(Starts | Ignition, Gasoline) could be defined with the data in Table 4.7.1.

Table 4.7.1 Conditional Probability Table for P(Starts | Ignition, Gasoline)

Ignition	Gasoline	Starts = true	Starts = false
True	True	0.94	0.06
True	False	0.03	0.97
False	True	0.02	0.98
False	False	0.01	0.99

A Bayesian network's graph structure directly shows dependence between nodes. Through active and blocked paths, the graph also shows conditional independence. Conditional independence means that the value of one variable has no effect on the value of another. More formally, the probability of variables A and B given C is the same as the probability of A given C times the probability of B given C [Russell03]. When a Bayesian network has been completed, the value assigned to each node will be updated based upon active and blocked paths in the DAG.

To elaborate on the independence and dependence shown in a DAG, we'll look at three types of paths that can be formed by groups of three nodes. We'll call the three nodes X, Y, and O. In each case, we want to look at the path from node X to node Y, going through node O. In the three types of paths, when nodes X and Y are independent, the path between them is blocked. If X and Y are dependent, the path between them is active.

A *linear*, or serial, path has an arc from node X to node O and an arc from node O to node Y. Reversing both these arcs also forms a linear path. If we have not observed the state of node O, then, in a linear path, the knowledge that we have about node X influences the value of node Y, and vice versa. This is because the child node (Y) is dependent on its parent (0), which is dependent on its parent (X). Observing the center node breaks the dependence that the last node has on the first. An example of a linear path can be seen on the left side of Figure 4.7.2. In the car example, the path from Battery to Ignition to Starts is a linear path. If we have only observed the value of Starts, it influences the value of Battery, and we have an active path between these two variables. In other words, if the car doesn't start, then we might not have ignition, which could mean that the battery is dead. If we then observe the value of Ignition (e.g., by discovering that the ignition works), then our knowledge of Starts no longer influences the value of battery—we know the battery is likely to be good even though the car is not starting. In this case, the path between Starts and Battery is blocked.

A *diverging* path is one where node 0 is a parent of both node X and node Y. If we have not observed node 0, then once again we have an active path between nodes X and Y. If we have not observed the parent node, then the knowledge about one child node influences the value of a sibling node. An example of a diverging path can be seen in the center of Figure 4.7.2. Returning to Figure 4.7.1, the Battery's arcs to Radio and Ignition form a diverging path. If we have not observed the value of the Battery, then observing the value of Radio will influence the value of Ignition—if the radio works, then the battery is probably good, which means that the ignition should work, too. Observing the value of Battery stops the observation of one child node from influencing the value of a sibling node. Again, the path from one sibling to the other is blocked.

A *converging* path is when nodes X and Y share a common child, node 0. Nodes X and Y are independent, unless the child node is observed. If node 0 is observed, then the path between X and Y is activated, and observations about the state of one node affect our belief in the state of the other. An example of a converging path can be seen on the right side of Figure 4.7.2. In the car example, Ignition and Gasoline share a common child, Starts. Observing the value of Ignition only influences the value of Gasoline if we have observed the value of Starts. For example, if we know that the car doesn't start, but it has ignition, this will increase the probability that we are out of gasoline. If we have not checked whether the car starts but know that the ignition works, this does not change the probability that the car has gas.

Our CPTs provide probabilities for many connections, both direct and indirect, but they will not cover every possibility. When we don't have a probability in our table, we need to use Bayes' theorem. An in-depth explanation of Bayes' theorem is beyond the scope of this article. The examples presented here do not require that you understand the theorem, but it will be helpful when translating Bayesian networks into code. Robert Cowell has written an article that offers three problems involving Bayes' rule to work through [Cowell99]. The first one is fairly straightforward. The other two may require additional explanation if you are unfamiliar with Bayesian networks. Eugene Charniak offers a good starting place for further reading on Bayesian networks [Charniak91]. Judea Pearl offers a great deal of information about how beliefs are passed around a Bayesian network [Pearl86].

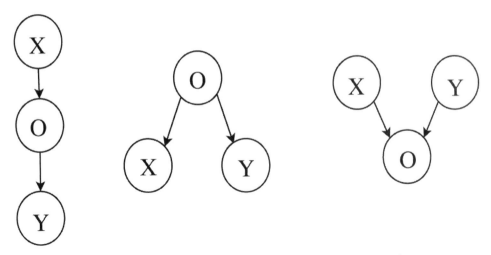

FIGURE 4.7.2 Linear, diverging, and converging paths in Bayesian networks.

Solutions

This section of the article presents detailed solutions for two problems. These problems have been created to help motivate the use of Bayesian networks in video games. The solutions are written to help you understand the steps taken and allow you to form and solve similar problems. These examples start with a story that could fit into a video game. The Bayesian networks created are models that approximate the world created in the story.

Thief Bayesian Network

The following example is inspired by the Bayesian network example presented in the first *AI Game Programming Wisdom* volume [Tozour02]. The situation we will be modeling involves an NPC guard who is stationed outside of a building, protecting it from thieves. The player controls a thief, and one of the thief's objectives is to get inside this building without being detected. While on patrol, the guard might hear a muffled noise, see a subtle movement in the dark, or discover a footprint. The building is in a rundown part of town, so either rats or a thief could have caused the movement and noise. Footprints would obviously not be caused by a rat but could be caused by a thief. These factors will be treated as uncertain evidence. We'll build a Bayesian network to model this part of the world, and the guard's actions will be drawn from this model. This is done as an alternative to scripting the guard's actions.

Tozour's original thief example uses a DAG consisting of four parent nodes and one child node. The parents are Saw Something, Noises, Dead Body, and Hit By an Arrow. Each of these nodes contains one arc from it to a node labeled Conclusion = {Thief, Rats}.

Most Bayesian networks are used to model the world—gasoline and ignition cause a car to start, or an earthquake causes a house's alarm system to sound. After observed evidence has updated the probabilities of the rest of the nodes in the model, the user (perhaps an NPC or a person using a diagnostic system) draws conclusions from the Bayesian network. Note that the parent in each case is something about the state of the world that we might want to infer (the cause), whereas the child is something that we might observe (the effect). Thus the network is a model of how the world works. It allows us to generate expectations about the state of the world (expressed as probabilities) based on our observations.

The solution presented in this section allows a separate probability to be assigned to the presence of both thieves and rats, whereas Tozour's Bayesian network generates a single probability that one or the other is present. In Tozour's DAG, a converging path is created from one parent node, to the conclusion node, to another parent node. Given that we do not observe the conclusion node, the parent nodes (which represent the observable evidence) are independent. This is counterintuitive because seeing something and hearing noises are not independent events. When two variables should be dependent but are arranged so all the paths between them are blocked, then the model might give unintuitive results.

The first step in building the Bayesian network is to decide on our variables and their graph structure. The three pieces of evidence the guard can observe are noise, movement, and footprints, so we will create corresponding nodes. These nodes will each have a value of true if the guard observes this piece of evidence, and false if the guard does not. Our world only provides two possible sources for these pieces of evidence: rats or a thief. Thus, we will create a Rats node and a Thief node. People reason from observations to conclusion, but as we explained earlier, we do not want to model this explicitly. Instead, we will model from cause to effect. In this case, only a thief will leave footprints, whereas either rats or a thief can cause noise or movement. Correspondingly, arcs should be drawn from Rats to Noise, from Rats to Movement, from Thief to Noise, from Thief to Movement, and from Thief to Footprints. The final graph structure can be seen in Figure 4.7.3.

Before this Bayesian network is ready to use, we need to populate the CPTs. We can start with the parentless nodes in the graph.

This building is not in a very well kept area, so it's likely that there are rats nearby. The presence of rats is not a part of the original specification, so an assumption about their presence will be made—there is a 60% chance of rats being nearby (and a 40% chance of them being absent).

The building holds important corporate secrets, which makes it a likely target for thieves. In the past year, there have been 30 attempts at robbing the building. We do not have any data on why the thieves chose those days. We might then decide that any day is equally likely for a thief to attempt to break in. The 30 attempts divided by 365 days gives us approximately an 8% chance of a thief being on the premises on any given day.

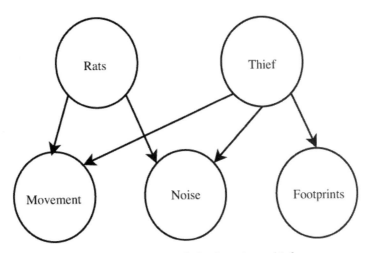

FIGURE 4.7.3   Bayesian network for detecting a thief.

The next step is to determine the conditional probabilities of Movement, Noise, and Footprint. For the movement node, we need to determine P(Movement | Rats, Thief). This means we need to come up with probabilities that there will be some noticeable movement given that rats are or are not present and that a thief is or is not present. We determine that if both rats and a thief are present, the guard has a 60% chance of catching some movement out of the corner of his eye. This value may be refined later, of course, after we investigate some actual occurrences of movement and find out what caused them. Similarly, if just rats are present, then the guard has a 55% chance of seeing movement. If just a thief is present, then he has a 10% chance of seeing movement. Finally, if neither rats nor a thief is present, then there is still a 5% chance of the guard seeing something—perhaps the wind blowing some leaves around, for example. These values are summarized in Table 4.7.2. Note that the total probability for each line on the table has to add up to 100%.

When looking through the *Netica* implementation of this example, it's more important to see changes in P(Rats) and P(Thief) given the observed evidence, than to worry about the exact probabilities of child nodes, given the values of their parents.

Table 4.7.2   CPT for P(Movement | Rats, Thief)

Rats	Thief	Movement = True	Movement = False
True	True	0.60	0.40
True	False	0.55	0.45
False	True	0.10	0.90
False	False	0.05	0.95

Table 4.7.3 is similarly constructed for P(Noise | Rats, Thief). The numbers are weighted based on the assumption that rats are likely to make some noise, while thieves generally remain very quiet. If both rats and a thief are present, then they would each cause the other to make more noise than if they were alone.

Table 4.7.3   CPT for P(Noise | Rats, Thief)

Rats	Thief	Noise = True	Noise = False
True	True	0.90	0.10
True	False	0.55	0.45
False	True	0.33	0.67
False	False	0.15	0.85

P(Footprint | Thief), given in Table 4.7.4, is constructed with the belief that a thief will probably leave behind some evidence of where he has traveled. This assumption could be changed for different environments. For example, a thief is more likely to leave footprints in mud. In a rainstorm, evidence left behind by a thief will be quickly washed away. A further revision might be to add a weather node and a surface node, both of which would influence the Footprint node.

Table 4.7.4   CPT for P(Footprint | Thief)

Thief	Footprint = True	Footprint = False
True	0.60	0.40
False	0.01	0.99

After the graph and the CPTs are complete, rules could be designed to use the Bayesian network because it only calculates probabilities. Observed evidence will be noted on the Bayesian network. For example, the guard has seen movement and heard a noise but has not found any footprints. This information is passed though the network, and the probabilities of Rats and Thief are updated. A simple rule to use is that if the probability of a thief being present, given the observed evidence, exceeds a certain threshold, then the guard should sound an alarm or call for backup. This probability does not have to be as large as 90%—the building owner might want his guards to err on the side of caution if they think a thief is on the premises. More intricate rule systems could take different actions for different beliefs that a thief is present. P(Thief) = 0.20 might result in the guard being more alert, for example, whereas P(Thief) = 0.30 would cause the guard to report his suspicion to his boss, and P(Thief) = 0.40 would cause him to call for backup.

Baseball Manager Bayesian Network

Our next example is based on another article from the first volume in this book series, which proposes software to help a baseball manager [Laramée02]. The manager needs to make a series of decisions related to his pitcher. If the pitcher is nervous, then the manager could send the pitching coach in to talk to him. If he is tired, then the manager could put in a relief pitcher. The manager's observations on pitch speed, whether the pitch is hit, who is at bat, and the presence of runners on base can affect his conclusion.

Laramée's article states that this problem has too many variables and too many interdependencies for Bayesian networks to be used successfully [Laramée02]. The purpose of this section is to show that a Bayesian network can be created to serve approximately the same purpose as Laramée's solution. Much larger Bayesian networks have been created for medical diagnosis and genealogy applications. The examples presented in this article are tractable. Models do not have to represent every interaction that takes place in the real world to be useful. The Bayesian network is modeling the video game's constructed world, which will not model every interaction that exists in the real world either.

Laramée also objected to the use of Bayesian networks because the values for conditional probabilities are too difficult to define. Not being able to use Bayesian networks because the required probability distributions are not, or cannot, be known is a reasonable concern. This concern is less reasonable when creating models in a computer game because the world is fully constructed by humans. In a scientific application, you may not know if a certain environmental factor causes cancer or how to define the CPT that expresses that. As a developer, you know if the world was created with that factor contributing to cancer. Knowing that the cause-and-effect relationship is true does not mean that the AI has to cheat by modeling the exact interactions in the game's world, but it does greatly simplify the task of building a Bayesian network for its decision making.

The first two variables we will look at are Tired and Nervous. The pitcher could be one, the other, both, or neither. We want this Bayesian network to determine a probability that the pitcher is nervous and/or tired based on factors that we can observe. The nodes Tired and Nervous can each have a value of true or false.

The manager can observe the speed of the pitch. The speed can be affected by whether or not the pitcher is tired or nervous. True and false are obviously not very useful values for the speed of a pitch. Further, the speed of a nonfastball pitch (such as a curve ball) is not a good indicator of whether the pitcher is tired or nervous. Thus, we assign a number of possible values for different speeds of a fastball, plus a value for pitches other than fastballs. The original article suggested four ranges for fastball speed, so we will use that as well. Specifically, we separate pitches into fastballs above 93 mph, fastballs between 87 and 92 mph, fastballs below 87 mph, and pitches that are not fastballs. These ranges could be changed for faster or slower pitchers. Ranges are used because continuous variables are computationally more difficult to deal with than discrete values. In the diagram, an arc will be drawn from the Tired node to the Speed node, and from the Nervous node to the Speed node.

Next, our manager can observe the outcome of the pitch—a ball, a strike, a hit, or an out (from a hit). The outcome of the pitch may depend on other factors as well. Whether or not a runner is on base might affect the batter's strategy and therefore would affect the outcome of the pitch. Who is at bat would also have an effect. We will now talk briefly about these two variables.

Onbase's value can be set to true or false. The assumption is that a runner on base might cause the pitcher and batter to take a different approach than if the bases were empty. Later revisions could account for the number of runners on base and what bases they are on. For now, we will stick to a Boolean and draw an arc from Onbase to Outcome.

The current batter also has an effect on the outcome of the pitch. Three values were decided on for this node: good, average, and poor. They are based on an explanation of Major League batting averages available in Wikipedia's "Batting Average" article. A batting average of over .300 is considered good, .250-.300 is average, and below .250 is poor. Note that averages below .200 are generally considered to be unacceptable, whereas averages above .400 are nearly impossible [Wikipedia06]. An arc is drawn from Batter to Outcome. The current batter also influences whether the pitcher is nervous. A batter with a high batting average could make a pitcher nervous, so an arc is drawn from Batter to Nervous.

Other factors, such as the current score of the game, could also contribute to the batter's nervousness. These factors will be left out of the model at this time, although we could add them later if we were unhappy with the results of our current model.

A given batter will typically receive anywhere from one to six pitches while at the plate or even more if the batter hits a number of foul balls. Rather than dealing with all the possible combinations of strikes, balls, and fouls, and changing probabilities accordingly, we will assume that each pitch for a batter is independent. Again, we can always account for this factor later if we find that it is significant.

Figure 4.7.4 shows the graph structure for one pitch. You could expand this graph further by creating additional copies of the Outcome, Speed, Onbase, and Batter nodes. Looking at the last several pitches will provide a better evaluation of whether the pitcher is nervous or tired. In addition, if we use information from multiple pitches, then the DAG could be used to predict the outcome of the next pitch.

When declaring probabilities for Tired and Nervous, we will use values that make sense for our particular pitcher. These values can be changed each inning and will be different for each individual pitcher. For example, a rookie pitcher might be more likely to be nervous, regardless of who is at bat. A veteran pitcher may have a higher P(Tired = true) value if he is not as physically fit as a younger pitcher.

A CPT has to be created for P(Speed | Tired, Nervous). The probabilities given in Table 4.7.5 suggest that if the pitcher is tired, then he is most likely to throw a pitch below 86 mph and will only very rarely throw one above 93 mph. Similarly, if he is nervous, according to these values, it is more likely that he will pitch between 87 and 92 mph. These values could be improved by studying actual pitchers.

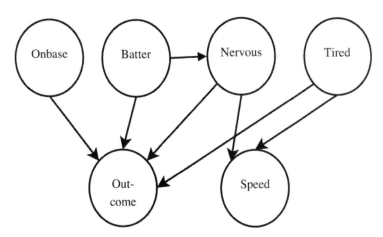

FIGURE 4.7.4 One pitch Bayesian network for determining the state of a pitcher.

Table 4.7.5 CPT for P(Speed | Tried, Nervous)

Tired	Nervous	Fastball 93+	Fastball 87-92	Fastball 86-	Not a fastball
True	True	0.05	0.20	0.55	0.20
True	False	0.05	0.25	0.50	0.20
False	True	0.10	0.35	0.30	0.25
False	False	0.50	0.22	0.10	0.18

The probability that there is a runner on base was arbitrarily set to 33%. This value is not that important because we will always be able to observe whether or not someone is on base.

The probability of Batter = average is set to 0.60. The probability of Batter = good is set to 0.10. The probability of Batter = poor is set to 0.30. We could populate a better CPT by examining the batting averages of all the players on the opposing team or by looking at all batters in the league. Once again, the manager will always be able to observe the player who is at bat. Prior to the game, the team should be able to access each player's batting average, making it easy to classify the batter as good, average, or poor.

The CPT for Outcome is a larger table. Its values are based on the corresponding batting average of the given batter. Table 4.7.6 shows a section of the completed CPT (which is available in its entirety on the CD-ROM). If Nervous and/or Tired are true, then the probability of a base hit is greater than the corresponding batting average. If Nervous and Tired are false, then the probability of a base hit is less than the corresponding batting average of a given batter. This table could be further improved if statistics were gathered on the average number of strikes and balls a pitcher throws, as well as the number of hits that are caught for an out.

Table 4.7.6 CPT for P(Outcome | Tired, Nervous, Onbase, Batter)

Tired	Nervous	Onbase	Batter	Strike	Base hit	Out from hit	Ball
True	True	True	Good	0.15	0.35	0.10	0.40
True	True	True	Average	0.15	0.30	0.15	0.40
True	True	True	Poor	0.15	0.25	0.20	0.40
True	True	False	Good	0.18	0.35	0.10	0.37
True	True	False	Average	0.18	0.30	0.15	0.37
True	True	False	Poor	0.18	0.25	0.20	0.37

If the model is extended, we could observe evidence for the last n pitches. More observed evidence might give us a better overall picture about the actual values for Tired and Nervous, which we could use to reduce the effect of lucky hits and unlucky pitches. Because Tired and Nervous are never actually observed, if we observe $n-1$ sets of Outcome, Speed, Onbase, and Batter, there will be an active path from them to the nth set of Outcome and Speed. This active path means that the observed values influence the value of the nth pitch. This value can serve as a prediction about the next pitch. Rules could be developed to send in the pitching coach or pull the pitcher if the manager is not happy with the prediction. If P(Nervous = true), given the observed evidence, is greater than P(Tired = true), given the observed evidence, then the manager should send in the pitching coach to try to calm down the batter. If P(Tired = true) is above some threshold, such as 40%, then the manager should warm up the relief pitcher. Finally, if P(Tired = true) is above 60%, then the manager should put the relief pitcher in.

Conclusion

This article has offered an introduction to Bayesian networks, as well as suggesting several articles for further reading. The examples provided will help you formulate similar problems and complete Bayesian network solutions. The next step is to turn the Bayesian networks into code that can be used in a video game. One approach to that problem is to use existing software, such as *Netica*, a software application that offers APIs for working with Bayesian networks in C and Java. Alternately, a good reference on implementing Bayesian networks using a minimal amount of space can be found in [Grant05].

References

[Charniak91] Charniak, E., "Bayesian Networks Without Tears: Making Bayesian Networks More Accessible to the Probabilistically Unsophisticated." *AI Magazine*, Vol. 12, no. 4, (1991): pp. 50–63.

[Cowell99] Cowell, R., "Introduction to Inference for Bayesian Networks." *Learning in Graphical Models,* Jordan, M. I. Editor, The MIT Press, (1999): pp. 9–26.

[Grant05] Grant, K., and Horsch, M., "Practical Structures for Inference in Bayesian Networks." Available online at *http://www.cs.usask.ca/research/techreports/2005/TR-2005-04.pdf,* 2005.

[Laramée02] Laramée F., "A Rule-Based Architecture Using the Dempster-Shafer Theory." *AI Game Programming Wisdom*, Charles River Media, 2002.

[Pearl86] Pearl, J., "Fusion, Propagation, and Structuring in Belief Networks." *Artificial Intelligence,* Vol. 29, No. 3, (1986): pp. 241–288.

[Russell03] Russell, S. J., and Norvig, P., *Artificial Intelligence: A Modern Approach.* Second Edition. Prentice-Hall, 2003.

[Tozour02] Tozour, P., "Introduction to Bayesian Networks and Reasoning Under Uncertainty." *AI Game Programming Wisdom*, Charles River Media, 2002.

[Wikipedia06] Wikipedia. "Batting Average." Available online at *http://en.wikipedia.org/wiki/Batting average#Baseball,* 2006.

4.8

The Engagement Decision

Baylor Wetzel—Brown College

baylorw@yahoo.com

You have 3 tanks, 2 fighters, and 5 infantry. Close by is the enemy's army of 1 tank and 18 infantry. Should you attack? That is the engagement decision.

Whether or not to engage in battle—there are numerous ways to answer this question, each with its own advantages and disadvantages. In this article, we look at some of the ways to make this decision.

Deciding at Random

We should never discuss video game AI without mentioning random numbers. If we are faced with an opponent, it is certainly possible to decide whether or not to attack based on the flip of a coin or roll of a die.

Random numbers have many positive attributes, such as being easy to design, easy to implement, and quick to execute at runtime. On this, most people agree. But the goal of a video game AI technique is not merely to be efficient (although that is important, too) but to produce behavior our player is happy with, and on this, many people feel random numbers are the worst possible option, which in certain circumstances is true. There are, however, a number of common situations where random numbers produce perfectly acceptable behavior. For the past three quarters, my AI students were required to play a simple turn-based strategy game against 14 different AI opponents we've created. Students are given one week to play each opponent as many times as they choose and document which target selection strategy they believe the AI is using. They must also rate how fun and human-like each AI opponent is. One of those opponents, Moe, makes every decision completely at random. Before the assignment, students seem in agreement that a random decision strategy would be easily spotted and not very much fun. Despite this, Moe is consistently ranked as being human-like and a lot of fun. This AI is currently the second highest rated opponent (the top opponent, Allen, chooses his opponents in alphabetical order).

So, under the right circumstances, a strategy of making decisions completely at random can produce acceptable results. One of those circumstances is that there cannot be any options that are glaringly, obviously wrong. If an AI must decide between casting a fireball or an ice bolt (assuming the target takes equal damage from either) or between attacking a weak target or a strong one, there is no obviously incorrect option. There will certainly be those who vehemently argue that it is better to attack the strongest targets first and then the weak ones, but there are just as many people who will passionately argue the opposite. When there is uncertainty, people dream up those details necessary to make almost any option seem plausible. And when an AI acts in a way the person does not understand, more often than not, the person simply assumes the AI has a different, but perfectly valid, strategy. For example, in the target selection exercise described earlier, many students have documented that one of the AI opponents, George, always attacks bandits, dwarves, and other units before black dragons, bone dragons, and dragon golems. They have explained this away through a complex back-story that involves George being afraid of dragons; in reality, George attacks opponents based on the lengths of their names.

In most games, the previous condition does not apply for engagement decisions. Quite often, a battle is so lopsided that it is suicide for one side to attack. If the enemy's army contained 10 black dragons, 100 vampires, and 1,000 dwarves, and my army consisted only of a small, half-dead gerbil, it would make no sense for me to attack the enemy and only slightly less sense for the enemy to not attack me. Yet with a purely random approach, such things can happen.

So a completely random strategy is unlikely to be a good option. This does not mean that randomness does not have its place. We will come back to random numbers when we discuss some of the more advanced techniques.

The Simple Strategy

When we discuss simple strategies, we are referring only to those strategies so simple that they involve no (or almost no) calculation. An "attack anyone" strategy falls into this category as does "run away from anyone." You could also have the strategies "attack anyone who gets within a certain distance," "attack when our side outnumber theirs," "attack if they're all human-sized or smaller," "attack unless they have people who look magical," "attack anyone who looks wounded," "attack anyone carrying food," "attack females," and "attack anyone wearing white."

Perhaps the most obvious simple strategy is the berserker strategy—always attack. This strategy is extremely common in arcade, FPS, RPG, and action games, where every guard, cave rat, robot, and alien slave charges at the player the minute he walks into view. Games where the actor attacks regardless of outcome are probably more common than the alternative. However, even in games where the controller (AI or human) must make a discrete decision to attack, there are times when certain units will always attack. For example, while guards might consider alternatives to attacking, such as retreating, taking up defensive positions, or surrendering, guard dogs and automated turrets would likely always attack.

Using a simple strategy has the advantage of being easy and quick to design, implement, and execute. For many games, where the player is a normal-looking human wandering through an enemy base containing carefully placed enemy guards, this strategy makes perfect sense. It also makes sense for certain types of creatures—

even in a strategy game, one expects bees, zombies, and trained guard dogs to attack, even when there is no chance of winning.

Power Calculation

In many games, the decision of whether or not to start a fight depends on whether or not you think you can win that fight, which, in turn, depends on how powerful you believe each side to be.

To answer this question, we need some way of calculating the power of a given side. Techniques for doing this range from very simple to quite complicated, but, ultimately, they depend on the design of your game.

Basic Formulas

Suppose we have a game in which combat is done by rolling a 6-sided die for each piece, and, if the number is less than or equal to that piece's attack score, it kills an enemy. Infantry have an attack score of 1, fighters and tanks a 3, and bombers a 4. There are no other statistics for these pieces other than the cost to build them. In this situation, the most obvious way to calculate the combat value of the army is to add the attack scores of all the pieces together. So if we had 10 infantry, 2 tanks, and a bomber, the combat value of the army would be $(10 \cdot 1) + (2 \cdot 3) + (1 \cdot 4) = 20$.

Now let's assume a more complicated game where each piece has a level, attack score, defense score, health points, speed, movement, damage range, and cost. As with the previous example, we can calculate the combat value of each piece using a single attribute, such as level. For example, if we had 10 first-level skeletons, 2 third-level vampires, and a fourth-level bone dragon, the combat value of the army would be $(10 \cdot 1) + (2 \cdot 3) + (1 \cdot 4) = 20$.

The previous calculation, of course, assumes that a single level-two unit is worth the same as two level-one units. In many games, that's not the case. Suppose a unit at a given level is worth four units of the next lower level. In this case, there is exponential growth, so the formula to determine the combat value of a single unit would be $4^{level-1}$ and the combat value of our army would be $(10 \cdot 4^0) + (2 \cdot 4^2) + (1 \cdot 4^3) = (10 \cdot 1) + (2 \cdot 16) + (1 \cdot 164) = 106$.

In the previous formula, we use a single attribute, in this case, *level*. We could certainly use a more involved formula. For example, we could use the formula shown in Equation 4.8.1.

$$value = (10 \cdot 4^{level-1}) + (2 \cdot defense) + (2 \cdot attack) + health \qquad (4.8.1)$$

So for a level-three vampire with a defense score of 30, an attack score of 30, and health of 75, the combat value of the unit would be $(10 \cdot 4^2) + (2 \cdot 30) + (2 \cdot 30) + 75 = 355$, and the combat value of a level-one bandit with a defense of 10, attack of 10, and health of 10 would be $(10 \cdot 4^0) + (2 \cdot 10) + (2 \cdot 10) + 10 = 60$.

Creating the Formula

Equation 4.8.1 uses quite a bit more data and, unsurprisingly, took significantly more time to create. The computer can execute the formula quickly enough, but it still takes the human a fair amount of time to think up the formula, test it, and then tune it. And the result isn't great—a level-three vampire is now worth roughly as much as six level-one bandits, which, based on our earlier discussion about the exponential growth of power, probably isn't quite right.

So how do you come up with the formula?

One option is to build a formula—any formula—and then play test and revise until it feels right. This, obviously, takes time, along with requiring a decent amount of skill at the game.

A second option is to find someone who has done this before. A considerable amount of knowledge exists in board games and military schools, and a large amount of this knowledge is available online, including both background information and actual formulas you can bring directly into your game (a good overview is given in [Sidran04]; a game-oriented explanation of Lanchester's Square Law is presented in [Adams04], inspired by [Paulos03]).

A third option is to simply do away with complex formulas, at least ones similar to Equation 4.8.1. Simple formulas can often be as good as or better than complicated ones, at least in the real world because attributes of the same object tend to be linked. A unit with a high level often has a lot of health and a high attack power, whereas a low-level unit has low health and low attack power. As an example, lions tend to be both stronger and harder to kill than house cats, which in turn are both stronger and harder to kill than mice. So a formula that determines the power of a unit by combining the various attributes of the unit will likely get the same relative ranking and spread as a formula that used a single attribute.

This is often more true of video game worlds than the real world. If a game has been professionally play-balanced, each unit (or option) at a given level or cost will be roughly as valuable as the other units at the same level or cost (although, given the rock-paper-scissors approach used in many games, a unit might be weak against another unit of equivalent power; we'll discuss this in more detail in the "Context-Dependent Values" section). For example, in the game we use in my class (which is based on an award-winning commercial strategy game), students are adamant that some units are simply better, more powerful units than others (on average, I hear five claims of this in each class, always on five different units). We hold tournaments in class where each student is given $20,000 in gold to purchase their armies and, despite student predictions to the contrary, so far no army configuration has produced noticeably better performance than any other.

Note that because all the attributes tend to signify the same thing (the relative combat value of the unit), you can often pick one of the attributes at random and get the same result as picking either a combination of attributes or the "best" attribute (usually level or cost because these are essentially summaries of the other attributes).

We've tested this in the AI course, where students play a turn-based strategy game against multiple AI opponents, some of which use complicated formulas and several of which base their decisions on a single attribute of the opponent (level, cost, attack, health, etc.). The students are unable to tell the difference (the sole exception is the attribute speed, which in our game determines the order of attack and is unrelated to the overall power of the unit).

Unit-Specific Formulas

In the previous discussion, we assumed that we had a relatively small number of units with a set amount of "power." This isn't true of all games. For example, in many RPGs, mages are weak at a low level, compared to fighters, and extremely powerful at high levels. The fighter's power grows linearly, whereas the mage's grows exponentially. Because of this, we might use different power calculations based on the class of the character. For a fighter, the combat value might simply be the fighter's level (or, more realistically, his level times a health multiplier so that a wounded fighter with one health point remaining is not treated the same as an unwounded one). For the mage, we might use the formula $value = 2^{(level-2)*0.3}$. Using this formula, a level-one fighter is worth 1.0, and a level-one mage is worth 0.8. At level six, the fighter is worth 6.0 and the mage 2.3. At level 15, both are worth 15. At level 20, the fighter is worth 20, and the mage is now worth 42, twice as much as the fighter (the formula in your game, obviously, would depend on your game).

Summing Variables

There are limits to what you can put in a single formula and still have it be manageable, both to write and understand. Suppose we're working on an RPG where characters level up, learn spells, and have different types of weapons and armor. In this instance, a level 10 fighter with leather armor and a short sword should not be seen as equally challenging as a level 10 fighter with 100% magic resistance, +10 brimstone armor, and a +10 dancing vorpal sword.

At this point, things get a little complicated. Putting all of the possible options into a predefined formula would be fairly difficult, especially if we are dealing with collections (e.g., the unit might have in their inventory an arbitrary number of magic items that affect their combat value). We need to break the problem down into pieces, so we turn to summing variables. We'll give the unit a base combat value and then modify it for each significant feature of the unit. Suppose we have decided that the base combat value of a unit is its level (in this case, 10), the combat value of weapons and armor is half of their modification values (10 for both the leather armor and short sword), the combat value of being brimstone (which we'll say offers fire resistance) is two, dancing four, vorpal five, and magic resistance a tenth of its strength (which here is 100%). So the combat value of our 10th level, fully magic resistant fighter with +20 brimstone armor and a +5 dancing vorpal sword is:

```
//—- The unit's base value is 10
int value = unit.level;
//—- 100% magic resistance = +10 value
//—- The unit's value is now 20
value += unit.getMagicResistance() / 10;
//—- +10 armor = +5 value
//—- The unit's value is now 25
value += unit.getArmor().getValue() * 0.5;
//—- brimstone armor = +5, total is now 30
value += unit.getArmor().getModifiers().getValue();
//—- +10 sword = +5 value, total is now 35
value += unit.getWeapon().getValue() * 0.5;
//—- dancing + vorpal = +9, total is now 44
value += unit.getWeapon().getModifiers().getValue();
```

So the combat value of this fighter is 44, roughly twice the combat value of a 10th level fighter with no armor, weapon, or special ability.

Context-Dependent Values

In the previous example, the combat value of each feature is fixed. We've decided that 100% magic resistance is worth 10 points. But suppose we are deciding whether to attack a given team, and we don't have any magic users? Then the fact that that team has magic resistance means nothing to us. Likewise, if we have nothing but magic users, the fact that they're completely resistant to magic is probably much more important than how we're valuing it here.

If both our army and the opponent's army have a single type of unit, say magic-wielding genies for us, magic-resistant dragons for theirs, we can use a valuation formula specific to our unit type. Thus, our genies would have a genie-specific formula for valuing the opposing army, and the opposing dragons would have a dragon-specific power calculation used to value our army. Unfortunately, in these types of games, the armies are rarely made up of a single unit type. To solve this problem, we could perhaps have every unit in our army calculate the combat value of the opposing army and then take the average, but as you can see, this situation quickly becomes complicated. And complicated means it's hard to hold everything in the designer's head at one time, error-prone to code, and time-consuming to test and tune.

Adapting to the Player

So far, we have discussed the creation of formulas that will, at runtime, calculate the combat value of a given unit and set of units. After play testing, these formulas will hopefully result in an AI that plays well against the game's designers. This does not, however, guarantee that it will play well against all game players.

Players can be unpredictable, so it is helpful to be able to adapt the AI to the player. In terms of determining a unit's combat value, one option is to add a historical bias factor. The combat value formula allows you to predict how well one set of units will do against another. If the actual outcome is significantly different from the predicted outcome, this information can be stored and used in future calculations. A good example of this is seen in [Dill06].

Power Lookup

With power calculation, we look at the traits of a unit and decide its combat value at runtime. With power lookup, the designer determines the combat value of the unit at design time, and the AI loads this value at runtime. For example, rather than using a formula based on level, health, attack power, and so on to determine that a vampire is worth 355 "points" and a bandit is worth 60, the designer simply says it is true, and the AI believes it.

This approach has many advantages. One is that the designer has complete control over the relative combat values of the pieces. The second is that the designer is not required to come up with a formula—he may simply feel that dragons are worth 64 times as much as orcs and that is the end of it. The caveat is that the designer might have guessed wrong—the values still need to be play tested and tuned. Of course, tuning hard-coded combat values is probably a bit easier than tuning a formula.

The disadvantage to the power calculation approach is that it is not particularly mod-friendly. If an expansion pack comes out, someone must spend time determining the combat value of the new pieces relative to the old ones (although you might be able to automate this process using reinforcement learning or a similar technique), and if the AI designer on the expansion pack is different from the original designer (or if the original designer simply no longer remembers), time must be spent asking why, exactly, are dragons worth 60 points? After this, the new values must be play tested and tuned, which can be a fair amount of work. Compared to the power calculation method, then, the power lookup method requires less upfront work but potentially more long-term work.

The previous analysis assumes that you have access to the original source code or data files and the ability to modify them. This is often not the case with user mods.

We said in the previous section that the power calculation method works well when the types of pieces are clearly defined but has a harder time when pieces are configurable or relatively unique, such as a fighter carrying magic armor or a battle mech that can be configured with flame throwers, machine guns, or rocket launchers. We also said the power calculation method had problems dealing with abilities, such as magic resistance, and special abilities that are important in some contexts and not others. In this respect, power lookup and power calculation are the same.

Monte Carlo

In the previous techniques, we used intelligence and reasoning to determine the combat value of various units and attempted to predict how a battle might turn out. The Monte Carlo method does none of these things. The Monte Carlo method is an empirical method—it tries a given action multiple times and then tells you how it turned out.

Suppose we have 5 tanks, 2 fighters, and 8 infantry, and the enemy has 1 tank and 18 infantry. Rather than use reason to guess about whether we'll win, we attack and make a note of whether we won or lost. We do this 50 times and note that, overall, we won 6 times and lost 44 times. We now know that the chance that we'll win this battle is roughly 12% (a note about performance: for the particular game this was tested on, the Monte Carlo method can both run 80,000 tests and display the results in roughly 1 second on a 1.86 GHz Pentium M).

Obviously, you would not actually attack the player in the game. This method assumes that the game has exposed the combat engine to the AI and allows the AI to simulate potential battles.

The Monte Carlo approach allows us to predict with reasonable accuracy how likely a given result is if we behave one way, and the other person behaves a certain way. Obviously, this depends on our ability to predict how the other person will act. In some games, the player simply doesn't have that many good options. In other games, the player has quite a few, although they might be qualitatively the same. Assume that we have a game where the pieces can either attack or cast buffing spells and where they can determine, to an extent, the order of their attack. The pieces might choose to attack the first chance they get; they might choose to cast spells that increase their speed, health, or attack by 25%, or they might choose to cast spells to protect them from fire, evil, chaos, or other such properties. When they choose to attack, the weaker pieces might go on their turn, or they might wait for the stronger pieces to soften the opponent up. In this situation, you would need to simulate each of these possible strategies and then gauge the success of each.

This is worth a little more discussion. Suppose that we had a band of vampires and that vampires have the ability Life Drain, which allows them to heal themselves and resurrect any vampire in their group that has been slain. Suppose further that this army contained a variety of other units but that none of them were as strong as the vampires. The player might choose a strategy in which he only attacks with vampires and never with the other units. In this way, the weaker units never get hurt and the vampires are always able to heal themselves. This is not a strategy someone is likely to predict (although with play testing it might become obvious to the designer of the game).

How does this affect our Monte Carlo solution? Not as much as you might think. In normal battles, regardless of which pieces attack or who they choose as their target, the combat value of the vampires and the effect of their healing powers will impact the outcome, causing both a general and a vampire-specific battle to have roughly the same outcome when both sides are of roughly equal power. When the vampire side is much stronger than the other side, both the player and Monte Carlo simulation of the player using a non-vampire-specific strategy will still win. When the other side is much stronger than the vampires, the player, with his intimate knowledge of vampire tactics, might lose by fewer pieces than the Monte Carlo method might predict, but he will still lose. Because vampires can only heal from living units, if the vampires face an army of equal combat value composed of nonliving creatures (gold golems, skeletons, catapults, etc.), the vampires will lose, as both the player and the Monte Carlo method will learn. Where Monte Carlo's predictions and the actual outcome diverge will be only on those borderline cases where both sides are relatively balanced, and even then, Monte Carlo will not say that the player will lose, it will merely say, perhaps, that the player has a 45% chance of victory when, in fact, the actual number is really 55%. Although this is a difference between a win and a loss, the probability is close enough that the AI can (and should) accommodate it in other portions of the system.

The Monte Carlo method does not technically tell us whether we won or lost a battle. Instead, it tells us the state of the world after some set of actions. Although we can simplify this to "if I still have units left, I won," we can also use it to evaluate the quality of the win. For example, if the end result is that we would win the battle but lose half our army in the process, we might decide that this leaves us too weak to hold off the enemy's next attack, and, therefore, engaging in this battle is a bad idea. Of course, we might not have a better option—if we lose this battle or retreat, perhaps the enemy takes the capitol, and the game is over. Determining the outcome of a battle and making a decision based on that data are two separate issues. So far, we have only covered how to predict an outcome. We cover the actual decision making in the next section.

Making the Decision

The previous techniques have told us how strong a given army is and what the chances are of us winning a given battle, but they have not told us whether we should or should not engage in battle. We still need to make a decision.

Rules and Intelligent Randomness

Based on the information we have, there are a number of ways to decide whether to engage the enemy in combat. The most obvious is to start a fight with anyone you are stronger than or (if you use the Monte Carlo) where the chances of you winning are greater than 50%. If you want a defensive AI, you might only attack when you are twice as strong as the enemy. If you want a bold AI, you might attack anyone up to twice as strong as you.

There are more sophisticated ways of making the engagement decision. Consider this excerpt from an AI design document.

1. The predicted outcome is based on the ratio of the armies' combat values.

Category	Ratio
Significant Win	> 200%
Likely to Win	121% – 200%
Evenly Matched	80% – 120%
Likely to Lose	50% – 79%
Significant Loss	< 50%

2. Whether the computer-controlled player attacks depends on the AI difficulty level.

Difficulty Level	Attack When
Easy	Likely to Lose: 50% chance
	Likely to Win: 25%
	Significant Win: 90%
	Other categories: do not attack
Medium	>= Significant win
Hard	>= Likely to win

The first rule takes the ratio of the combat value of the two armies and binds them into one of five Predicted Outcome Categories. If my army's combat value is 10, and the other person's is 21, we categorize it as a Predicted Significant Loss. We convert the raw numbers into an easier-to-use form to make our other rules easier to write.

The second rule looks at the Predicted Outcome Category and the game's current difficulty level and uses that to decide the probability that we will attack. On the normal difficulty level, the AI plays defensively and thus only attacks when it is sure of a significant win. On hard, the AI is aggressive and attacks when it believes it will win.

Now let's discuss how decisions are made. On the easy difficulty level, the AI has a 50% chance of attacking when it is likely to lose, but a 0% chance when it believes it will be a significant loss. A Predicted Outcome Category of Likely To Lose means that, done enough times, the army will lose more often than it will win, but it still has a chance of winning. Thus, attacking at this point does not seem suicidal, merely optimistic. On the easy level, we want the player to win the majority of the battles, but we do not want him to think that we are purposely throwing the game. For this reason, we never attack when the Predicted Outcome Category is Significant Loss because it is obvious to everyone that the AI will not win. If the AI were to attack under those conditions, the player would either feel insulted or consider the AI to be extremely poor. With a Predicted Outcome Category of Likely To Lose, the outcome is far more in doubt, and the AI's actions begin to look plausible (especially because this game's combat system is heavily based on random numbers, the AI will win from time to time).

The AI has a 25% chance when it believes it can win and a 90% chance of attacking when it is convinced of a significant victory. The first condition is to prevent the AI from pressing its advantage (although, as with Likely To Lose, it does stand a chance of losing) without making the player think that the AI is afraid or throwing the game. Humans have a remarkable ability to perceive in-depth strategy in areas where there is none, and attacking 25% of the time is random enough to make most players believe the AI has an ulterior motive other than making it easier for the player.

The AI almost always attacks when the Predicted Outcome Category is Significant Win because to not do so would insult the player and cheapen those battles that the player had already won (the player would be left wondering, "Did I only win because the AI is throwing the game?" which upsets most players even more than actually beating them).

Personality Statistics

Whether or not a particular AI agent engages in combat can (and in most cases probably should) be based on the agent's personality. For example, consider the case of a squad-based shooter where a four-person SWAT team has arrived to find a group of terrorists holed up in an abandoned building playing kick the puppy. Using one of the techniques discussed earlier, the AI has decided that there is only a 50% chance of surviving a rescue attempt. The player, as team captain, decides not to engage.

Whether his AI-controlled squad mates engage the enemy could depend on their personality. Suppose Bob had a Self-Preservation score of 0, Discipline of 100, Emotional Stability of 0, and a Love of Furry Animals of 90. Bob would be happy to charge in to rescue the puppy but because he was given a direct order by the player, would simply stand there and complain. Carl, with a Self-Preservation score of 30, Discipline of 60, Emotional Stability of 70, and a Love of Furry Animals of 100 would likely disobey the player's order and charge in. And Don, with a Self-Preservation score of 100, Discipline of 10, Emotional Stability of 10, and a Love of Furry Animals of 50 would feel bad for the puppy but would still run off to hide in a closet.

Alternatives and Best Options

The previous examples have assumed that the AI only has two options—attack or do nothing. In many games, you'll often have other options. These include both combat options (wait for reinforcements, take defensive position, etc.) and noncombat options (collect resources, build, explore, etc.). Choosing between these options is beyond the scope of this article.

Conclusion

Ultimately, the proper technique to use for the engagement decision will depend on the game you're working on. What types of battles you have, the number of attributes for each piece, the uniqueness of your units, the number of qualitatively different strategies you have in your game, the skill level of your designers, the time you have for play testing, whether your customers will be able to create new units, and many other factors will determine which technique is right for you. After reading this article, you should better understand what options you have and the pros and cons of each.

References

[Adams04] Adams, E., "Kicking Butt by the Numbers: Lanchester's Laws." Available online at *http://www.gamasutra.com/features/20040806/adams_01.shtml*, August 4, 2004.

[Dill06] Dill, K., "Prioritizing Actions in a Goal-Based RTS AI." *AI Game Programming Wisdom 3*, Charles River Media, 2006.

[Paulos03] Paulos, J. A., "Lanchester's Law: Too Few American Soldiers?" Available online at *http://abcnews.go.com/Technology/WhosCounting/story?id=97277&page=1*, March 30, 2003.

[Sidran04] Sidran, D. E., "A Calculated Strategy: Readings Directed Towards the Creation of a Strategic Artificial Intelligence." Available online at *http://www.cs.uiowa.edu/~dsidran/ReadingsForResearch2.pdf*, Spring 2004.

GENRE SPECIFIC

5.1

A Goal Stack-Based Architecture for RTS AI

David Hernández Cerpa—
Enigma Software Productions

david.hernandez.cerpa@gmail.com

In a real-time strategy (RTS) game, the AI needs to make decisions at different levels of abstraction, from high-level issues, such as which city should be attacked, to low-level ones, such as moving a single unit to a certain location. To make this feasible, the usual approach is to create different decision-making modules, one for each level in the chain of command.

The AI for the RTS part of the game *War Leaders: Clash of Nations* is divided into three levels. This article is focused on the architecture developed for the lower two of these levels, that is, the AI levels for units, groups, and formations. This architecture is based on the concept of a goal stack as a mechanism to drive the agent behavior. The end result is an AI system that has loose coupling with the game logic engine.

The Need for AI Levels

Having a hundred units under your control and figuring out what has to be done with each of them to defeat your enemy is a daunting task. The key to success in the management of large groups of individuals is to introduce levels of abstraction, making it easier for higher levels to command all of the elements that are below them. Military chains of command constitute an example of how an AI system might be divided to tackle the problem [Kent03, Ramsey03].

The characteristics of the game determine what levels the AI system should have. Questions that help an AI engineer delimit the needed levels and their responsibilities include the following:

- Can units satisfy orders individually, or can they only be satisfied by groups?
- Can they join together to create groups or formations?
- Are they able to behave autonomously?
- Are they part of an army that must act as a whole?

Following an analysis of our game, we felt it necessary to create three levels of AI: one for units, one for groups and formations, and one to control the entire army. The army-level AI selects high-level tactics for defeating its enemies. This level is beyond the scope of this article.

Although units, groups, and formations might seem different in terms of their AI needs, similarities between them are apparent:

- They must respond to orders from their superiors.
- They are able to act autonomously in certain situations.
- They might temporarily suspend their current actions to execute others of higher priority.
- They should be notified by the game logic about events that happen in the world.

With this analysis at hand, a unique architecture was developed that can be shared by both levels.

The Architecture

In addition to the requirements described in the analysis earlier, there was a desire to keep the AI system loosely coupled to the rest of the game engine. To satisfy this constraint, AI system classes were isolated so that they communicate with the rest of the engine through a very simple interface. The architecture's main components are goals, the goal stack, orders, events, and behaviors. These are shown in Figure 5.1.1 and introduced in the following sections.

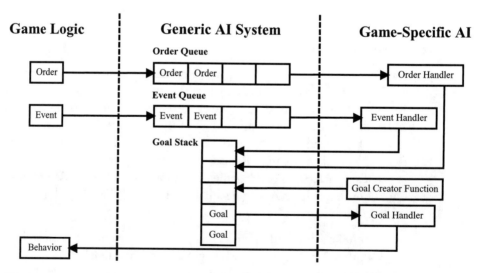

FIGURE 5.1.1 Architecture overview showing the main components.

Goals

Goals are the architecture's foundation. They represent the objective that a unit, group, or formation (referred to as an agent from this point on) is trying to achieve. An agent can't do anything without a matching goal. A goal's description includes its type and a variety of information describing how it can be satisfied. That information is specific to the type of goal and could include, for example, a target position or a target entity.

Goal Stack

Just as a military unit in the real world is not limited to a single objective, agents are not limited to a single goal. The goal stack contains all of the goals that the agent is pursuing at any given time. Only the goal at the top is active and accessible by the rest of the AI system. The agent will always try to satisfy this goal while the others goals remain dormant.

On each decision-making step, goals might be pushed onto the stack or popped from it in response to orders or game events. For example, a unit that receives a GoToPos order, indicating that a movement to a target position must be performed, might satisfy it by pushing a GoToPos goal onto the stack. Suppose that, while the unit is moving, it detects that a grenade is going to explode close to its position. The unit might decide to push an AvoidExplosion goal to avoid the grenade. In this case, the GoToPos goal becomes inactive and the AvoidExplosion goal becomes the one that must be satisfied. There is no limit to the size of the goal stack, so it's perfectly possible for this goal to be interrupted in turn. After the goal at the top of the stack is completed, it is popped. In our example, if the AvoidExplosion goal is satisfied, then it will be popped from the stack, the previous GoToPos goal will become active again, and the unit will continue with its movement after avoiding the grenade.

The resulting behavior is similar to a subsumption architecture [Yiskis03], where low-priority behaviors are executed until a high-priority one becomes active. After that happens, the low-priority behaviors are inhibited until the high-level ones are completed. There are several important differences from the subsumption scheme, however. First, behaviors are not always active and processing the inputs from the game logic. Second, the hierarchy is not fixed; that is, it does not have to be determined at design time, which promotes emergent behavior [Wotton06]. This allows easy addition of new goals to the system as new actions become available to the agents. Finally, priorities have not been defined. This architecture does not make use of an explicit concept of priority, although there is an implicit ordering in the goal stack.

Behaviors

Goals are satisfied by executing their corresponding behaviors. Whenever the goal on the top of the stack must be satisfied, a goal handler is called. This handler will decide which behavior to execute based on the goal type and will pass the goal's associated data to that behavior.

Behaviors are not part of the AI system. They link the AI with the game logic and are used to produce an effect over the agents when a decision has been made. This decouples the AI system from the implementation of the concrete actions that still reside in game logic classes.

Using the previous example, if a GoToPos goal is at the top of an agent's goal stack, the goal handler will be called with the goal as a parameter. The handler detects the goal type and calls the corresponding method on the unit's class, passing the available data for that goal. This method will effectively move the unit to the target position.

Orders

Superiors do not directly push goals on to their agents' goal stacks. Instead, they send orders to be accomplished. Orders have an associated handler whose responsibility is to interpret them and produce the appropriate changes in the goal stack. Usually this means that new goals are pushed onto the stack. When a goal from an order is pushed, any previous goals the agent might have been pursuing are removed. Clearing the goal stack prevents the agent from inappropriately returning to previous actions when it satisfies these new orders.

As in real chains of commands, orders represent the wishes of a superior that must be satisfied in one way or another. Orders decouple what *has* to be done from *how* it is accomplished, so that different agents can pursue the same goal in different ways. For example, suppose the player has two infantry units selected, one of which is standing, while the other is kneeling on the ground. They both receive a GoToPos order to reach a target position. This order is simple for the standing unit because it only needs to push a GoToPos goal. The kneeling unit, on the other hand, pushes both a GoToPos and a StandUp goal. As the top goal is the active one, this unit will stand up, pop that goal, and then start to move.

An order is not directly processed when it is received. An agent's AI state has a queue where orders are stored. They will be processed later during the decision-making process. Order queuing is a common technique used in RTS games [Rabin01]. Having an order queue allows higher-level AIs to send a chain of commands to their subordinates with the certainty that they will satisfy all of them one after another. Thus, the higher-level AIs can associate a sequence of orders to a complex concept, such as a "flank attack."

When a goal is popped, the AI system checks to see if the goal came from an order. If so, and if the goal is the last one on the goal stack, then the current order is removed. There are no longer any goals associated with that order, so it must be complete.

Events

For performance reasons, the AI does not poll the game logic to know whether an executing goal has been completed. Instead, the behavior sends an event up to the AI when it finishes. Events are used any time the game logic detects a situation that the AI might need to know about. For example, when a unit arrives at its destination, it sends an AtDest event to the AI. Note that the game logic does not know which goal is on the top of the stack. It sends the AtDest event whether or not the AI is pursuing a related goal. It is the AI's responsibility to interpret the meaning of the event. As with orders, events are not handled when received. Instead, they are stored in a queue for later processing.

The AI system has event handlers that are responsible for producing the appropriate operations on the goal stack. In many cases, this means that the event handlers pop the topmost goal from the stack because most events indicate that some behavior has finished. Continuing with the earlier example, when the handler receives the AtDest event, it pops the GoToPos goal. Note that the AtDest event handler just pops the top goal from the goal stack, which in this case is the GoToPos goal. However, the top goal could just as easily be another that implies movement, such as ApproachEnemy.

In other cases, the event handler might push goals onto the stack. This happens with events informing the AI about situations that have arisen in the game. For example, the game logic sends an EnemyOutOfRange event when an enemy goes out of the range of the weapon being used to attack it. In this case, the event handler might push an ApproachEnemy goal to try to get the enemy in weapon range again.

The Decision-Making Process

The decision-making process examines each agent's current state, along with the order and event queues, and determines what the agent should do next. The algorithm is composed of the following steps:

1. **Process received events.** This step iterates through the event queue and calls the event handler for each one. This might update the goal stack by popping or pushing goals. It is important to do this first because it synchronizes the AI with the game logic.

2. **Process the current order.** If there is an unsatisfied order, then the handler is called for it. This can also produce changes in the goal stack.

3. **Call the Goal Creator Function.** If after processing the events and orders the goal stack is empty, a special "Goal Creator Function" might be called if the agent can perform actions autonomously (see the "Improvements" section). For example, medical units use this function to detect if there are units around them that need their help. For performance reasons, this function is not called every frame. A configuration parameter determines how often it is invoked.

4. **Satisfy the top goal.** After every possible change to the goal stack has been applied, the algorithm checks whether the goal on top of the stack is already being satisfied. If it isn't, the goal handler is called for it, which in turn calls the behavior associated with the goal type.

After these four steps have been applied, the AI state has been updated, the agent has decided what to do, and appropriate methods to start doing it have been called.

Improvements

The architecture presented so far constitutes the basic version of our AI. As more requirements were added, the architecture was expanded with several improvements. Some of them are introduced in the following sections.

Chained Goals

Some situations require knowing that several goals in the stack belong to the same conceptual group. For example, if a tank receives an AttackEnemy order, it will push an AttackEnemy goal. Later, the enemy goes out of range, and the tank receives an Enemy-OutOfRange event informing it of this situation. In response to this event, the handler pushes an ApproachEnemy goal whose associated behavior will move it toward the enemy. Suppose that, while moving, the tank receives an EnemyDeath event indicating that the assigned enemy has died due to fire from another allied unit. In this case, the event handler should pop both goals from the stack, not just the ApproachEnemy goal. Although, conceptually, the tank is attacking an enemy, it had to push more goals to satisfy the order.

To handle these situations, the concept of chained goals was introduced. Chained goals are conceptually connected to others that are below them in the stack. Continuing with the example, ApproachEnemy is a chained goal because it is in the stack to help to satisfy the AttackEnemy goal. With this addition, the event handler for the Enemy-Death event pops the chained goals together with the AttackEnemy goal. A chained goal is pushed on the stack as a normal one but with a control flag indicating its condition. Thus, ApproachEnemy doesn't always have to be a chained goal. We know that it is in this case because the handler flagged it as such when it was pushed.

Delayed Goals

Orders can be sent to a group of agents. For example, the player might have selected several units or formations and ordered all of them to move. In the naïve approach, every unit would try to satisfy the order in the next decision-making process. This would cause all the units to start their movements at the same time, which is an unnatural-looking behavior.

To solve this problem, a maximum possible delay for being satisfied was added to orders and goals. When an order is sent to a set of agents, it has a maximum delay that depends on the number of elements in the set. This delay affects the goals, not the order. In other words, the order is immediately processed in the next decision-making step. However, the goals are assigned a random delay between zero and the order's maximum delay. When a delayed goal is going to be pushed, it is pushed onto a separate stack (not the main goal stack). Goals on this stack remain dormant until their delays have elapsed. When that occurs, they replace the ones that are on the main stack as if they have been pushed from an order handler.

Other approaches are also valid to reach the same effect of delayed responses to orders. For example, it would be possible to have delayed orders instead of immediate orders and the delayed goal stack. The current implementation was determined by some restrictions from the game logic and produced several bugs in the correspondence between orders and the goals they generate. This issue will be addressed in the future, after the restrictions have disappeared.

Parallel Goals

With the architecture described so far, agents are only able to do one thing at a time. It is possible to do more than one thing at the same time by creating goals that represent a combined action. For example, it would be possible to create a MoveAndAttack goal that would enable units to attack an enemy while moving. However, this is a very restrictive approach. It requires the creation of a separate goal and its corresponding behavior for every desired combination. In addition, there are problems presented by units such as tanks or airplanes. These units have several weapons. It should be possible to assign an enemy to each weapon so that multiple enemies can be attacked at once. To support this, a vector of goals was added to the AI state. They were called parallel goals because they are satisfied in parallel to the ones in the main goal stack.

Note that a vector of goal stacks is not needed. Parallel goals are simple goals that should not interfere with the main ones while executing. If an order or event results in pushing more than one goal, those goals represent complex actions that must be performed in sequence, not in parallel, so that all of the goals go on the main goal stack. As an example, suppose that a tank is satisfying a GoToPos order and has a GoToPos goal in its stack. While moving, it detects a new enemy that could be attacked with one of the weapons in its turret. In this case, the AttackEnemy goal is pushed on a parallel free slot, and the enemy is attacked while it is in range. If it goes out of range, the AttackEnemy goal is just popped. If an ApproachEnemy goal were pushed instead, both the GoToPos and ApproachEnemy goals would try to take control of the unit. This would be undesirable because the parallel goal would have interfered with the main goal stack. The unit should not stop its movement while trying to satisfy other independent goals.

Autonomy

As has already been mentioned, agents are sometimes able to push goals autonomously. Of course, we need to put limits on the permissible actions in some cases. For example, the player's units will not start a movement on their own because this would produce a bad game experience. It is useful for AI-controlled units to be able to do so, however, because this frees the higher-level AIs from having to control every unit in detail.

To solve this problem, an autonomous flag was added to the AI. When the autonomous flag is activated, agents have more available actions and can initiate them without waiting for an order. For example, consider a healing unit. Autonomous medics would heal injured units around them without the need to receive an explicit order. This approach helps to avoid the need to micromanage the entire army by giving units the ability to decide different courses of action on their own.

Using the Architecture in Higher-Level AIs

This architecture is not limited to unit-level AI. Groups and formations receive orders, generate goals to satisfy them, and are informed about situations in the world through events in the same way as units. The only difference is the way that they implement their behaviors.

For example, when a group receives a GoToPos order, the order handler pushes a GoToPos goal on the goal stack as if it were a unit. The difference is that when a behavior is called for this goal, it gets the data from the goal and sends an order to each of the units that compose the group, rather than performing actions on an individual unit. The behavior takes care of things, such as offsets between units in the group, so each of them receives a GoToPos order with a different target position. Additionally, the orders contain a maximum delay depending on the number of units in the group as explained previously.

As the units reach their target positions, events arrive from the game logic and are sent to the group that is able to keep track of how many units are still moving. When all the units have reached their destinations, the goal is finished and can be popped, which in turn removes the order from the group's order queue.

Implementation Details

Following the general guidance of having a loosely coupled AI system, the core was implemented in a set of C++ classes, while game-specific code was implemented using Lua scripts. Goals, orders, and events are simple structures with a type and any necessary data. In addition to data, there are some control attributes. For containers such as stacks, queues, and vectors, the STL was used. The following code listing shows the Goal struct.

```
struct Goal
{
    enum GoalType {
        NO_GOAL,        // No goal
        GOTO_POS,       // Go to the target position
        ATTACK_OBJECT,  // Attack to the target object
        HEAL_OBJECT,    // Heal target object
                        // ... Many more goal types
    };

    GoalType type;      // Goal type
    Vector3 pos3D;      // Target position in 3D
    CObject *object;    // Target object
    dword   delay;      // Delay in execution
    float   number;     // Numerical data
    bool    boolean,    // Boolean data
            fromOrder,  // True if comes from an order
            parallel,   // True if parallel
            chained,    // True if chained
            satisfying; // True if is being satisfied
}
```

The decision-making process is a C++ method in an `AIModel` class. This method connects with the scripts when a handler is called for an event, order, or goal. In these cases, the element to be processed is exported as a global variable, and the corresponding handler is called. There is a generic function that just gets the element type and calls the appropriate handler. To make this association, there are tables that map from a type to a function. The following code listing shows an example of a table and two handlers:

```
InfantryUnitTable.OrderToGoalTable = {
    [Order.GET_ON_TRANSPORT] =
      InfantryUnitTable.GetOnTransportOrder,
}

function InfantryUnitTable.GetOnTransportOrder()
    PushGoal(Goal.GET_ON_TRANSPORT, order.maxDelay,
      true,  — fromOrder?
      false, — chained?
      false) —- parallel?

    — Copy data attributes
    pushedGoal.object = order.object
end

function InfantryUnitTable.OnTransport()
    PopGoal()
end
```

Future Work

As discussed earlier, the introduction of the delayed goal stack produced many bugs in the correspondence between orders and their generated goals because they could be in two possible stacks. A better approach would be to remove the delayed goal stack, adding the concept of a delayed order, which will not be satisfied until its delay has elapsed. This problem will be addressed in the future, simplifying the handling of delays.

Apart from the autonomous flag, other flags have been considered as possible additions to the architecture. The idea is to have a fine-grained control over the available actions for agents. For example, an "aggressive flag" could activate behaviors that would lead to more automatically offensive agents. This set of flags has to be carefully considered because it has to fit within the game design and could cause a classification of behaviors that could make them incompatible, resulting in strange and unrealistic behavior from the agent.

Conclusion

The architecture presented here is flexible, scalable, and powerful enough to handle the different types of units, groups, and formations in a typical RTS game. It is easy to add new behaviors to an agent without changing existing ones. Because the game-specific AI is in scripts, designers can modify current handlers or create new ones without assistance. Being able to reuse the same architecture for different AI levels is very convenient from an engineering point of view. It allows us to share a lot of code and to be familiar with only one technique, cutting down development times.

It is impossible to predict all the possible situations that an agent could face during a battle. For that reason, emergent behavior is an important aspect of this AI system. This architecture promotes emergent behavior by allowing the different components to reason and act independently.

The concepts of orders, goals, and events are intuitive in an RTS game, but it should be possible to use this architecture in other types of games. For example, each bot in a squad-based FPS might behave as a unit in an RTS: receiving orders, pushing goals to satisfy them, and reacting autonomously to changes in the world.

References

[Kent03] Kent, Tom, "Multi-Tiered AI Layers and Terrain Analysis for RTS Games." *Game AI Programming Wisdom 2*, Charles River Media, 2003.

[Rabin01] Rabin, Steve, "An Architecture for RTS Command Queuing." *Game Programming Gems 2*, Charles River Media, 2001.

[Ramsey03] Ramsey, Michael, "Designing a Multi-Tiered AI Framework." *Game AI Programming Wisdom 2*, Charles River Media, 2003.

[Wotton06] Wootton, Benjamin, "Designing for Emergence." *Game AI Programming Wisdom 3*, Charles River Media, 2006.

[Yiskis03] Yiskis, Eric, "A Subsumption Architecture for Character-Based Games." *Game AI Programming Wisdom 2*, Charles River Media, 2003.

5.2

A Versatile Constraint-Based Camera System

Julien Hamaide—10Tacle Studios Belgium/Elsewhere Entertainment

julien.hamaide@gmail.com

The camera has always been a central actor in the player's experience; it's the window on our virtual world. Camera glitches often frustrate the player because they harm the continuity of play. This article tries to ease the camera-development process by leveraging the power of a constraint-based system. Game designers are free to combine a set of behaviors. From fixed-point to free cameras, the presented system provides a versatile environment for camera development.

Constraint-Based Camera System

Our system is built on a constraint-based system [Bourne06a] that evaluates the suitability of a set of potential camera positions and then places the camera at the best one. The suitability value of a position, $S(Position)$, is given by the weighted sum of suitability functions $s_i(Position)$, which are the constraints.

$$S(Position) = \sum_i w_i s_i(Position)$$

The suitability function $s_i(Position)$ maps a position in 3D space to a suitability value, the smaller the better. A typical camera might have three constraints:

- A distance constraint, which gives maximum value when the potential position is at the desired distance
- A height constraint, which gives maximum value when the potential position is at the desired height
- An orientation constraint, which gives maximum value when the vector from the character to the potential position is aligned with the character's forward vector

In an ideal world, the set of potential positions would encompass the entire world. Obviously, this is impractical, so we limit the search to a set of points around the current camera position. This region is called the search space. In Bourne's implementation, the search space is expressed as a box iterated with a sliding octree. This box is situated at the current camera position and extends to a specified size. Its orientation is aligned to the z-axis of the camera. The sliding octree algorithm cuts the box into eight smaller boxes. The suitability function is evaluated at the center of each box. The center of the box is then moved to the best-evaluated position. The algorithm stops after a given number of iterations and the best-evaluated position is used as the new camera position. Figure 5.2.1 shows a typical setup from a top-down view.

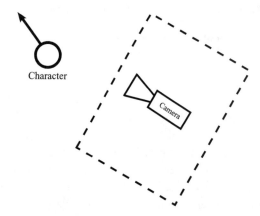

FIGURE 5.2.1   Top-down view from a typical setup.

We have revised the concepts presented in Bourne's system based on problems we encountered during the development of a 3D platform game, although we think that our improvements could be used in other genres.

Constraint Responsibility

In a constraint-based system, each constraint is given responsibility for evaluating one of the many factors that could contribute to determining the optimal behavior. A constraint could try to keep the camera at a given distance behind or above the player, for example.

After experimenting with this for awhile, however, we found that the weights were difficult to tune even in simple cases, resulting in unexpected (and undesirable) behavior. Our goal was to implement a camera that tries to stay at a given height and a given 3D distance. When the character approaches a wall, the camera should rise up the wall to stay at the given distance. Thus, we lowered the weight of the height constraint to allow the distance constraint to overcome its influence in this case. When we did this, the camera started to dip down when the character was running. The system was finding a better solution at that position because the distance constraint suitability value was higher and also had a greater weight than the height constraint.

One solution would have been to use a learning approach to find the ideal weights for the constraints [Bourne06b]. We had no resources available to create training trajectories, however, so this was unsuitable. Moreover, a learning solution would still be a compromise between the two behaviors, albeit a better balanced one.

We decided to approach constraints differently. A complete camera behavior can easily be expressed as a suitability function. Equation 5.2.2 shows a simple way to create a constraint from an existing algorithm, given P_{ideal} as the desired position. The system is now composed of a main constraint, trying to achieve a complex behavior (i.e., being behind the player at height x with distance y), and a set of specialized constraints (e.g., collision and visibility handling). The goal of the other constraints is to influence this behavior. Collision detection and player visibility are examples of constraints that only influence the currently desired position. A center of interest constraint allows the camera to show enemies and interesting objects with a better view than usual.

$$s_i(Position) = \left| Position - P_{ideal} \right| \tag{5.2.2}$$

This approach allows development of the behavior embedded in the main constraint as if the world was completely empty with no collisions, no visibility problems, and no other objects. The camera system and modules are more loosely coupled, as most behavior only needs to be implemented once (e.g., collision management). Moreover, it allows finer and more precise control over the desired position, while influence constraints adapt it to more complex situations.

Constraint Properties Ensure Stability

The solver is a weighted sum optimization system. If we want the system to be fair (i.e., a constraint does not exert more influence than you expected), constraints must respect certain properties [Garces06]. The smoothness of the camera trajectory is ensured by this set of properties.

Range of the Constraint

The expected output range of a constraint is 1, extending from 0 to 1. The range of a constraint inside a search space, as defined in Equation 5.2.3, is the difference between its maximum and minimum values inside that search space. If the constraint's range is less than 1, its weight to the final suitability value will be less than expected.

To illustrate this point, consider the following example. A camera is set up with the distance and height constraints presented earlier. The distance constraint is considered more important and is assigned a weight of 2, whereas the height constraint is assigned a weight of 1. The worst position for the distance constraint has a suitability value of 50% (0.5), whereas the best position's value is 80% (0.8). The height constraint has minimum and maximum values of 0% and 100%, respectively. The worst overall point has a suitability value of $(1 \cdot 0.0) + (2 \cdot 0.5) = 1$, and the best point has a value of $(1 \cdot 1.0) + (2 \cdot 0.8) = 2.6$. The range of the global suitability is 1.6. The contribution of the height constraint is 1.0, whereas the contribution of the distance constraint is only 0.6. Thus, the distance constraint will have less impact on the camera position than desired.

To compensate for this effect, the effective weight of a constraint is equal to the assigned weight multiplied by its range.

$$range(s_i, SearchSpace) = max\ s_i(SearchSpace) - min\ s_i(SearchSpace) \qquad (5.2.3)$$

The normalized version of Equation 5.2.2 is shown in Equation 5.2.4, where d_{min} and d_{max} are the minimum and maximum distances from any potential position in the search space to the ideal position. The constraints now have a range of 1.

$$s_i\left(Position\right) = \frac{\left|Position\text{-}P_{ideal}\right|\text{-}d_{min}}{d_{max}\text{-}d_{min}} \qquad (5.2.4)$$

Continuity of the Constraint

The suitability function must be continuous in both time and space. This property prevents jumps in camera movement. We should also ensure that the constraint suitability value does not oscillate between two values, often resulting in oscillation of the camera position. A smoothing function can provide a solution to this problem but may result in delay in the movement of the camera.

Uniqueness of Solution

Ideally, there should be a single best position for the entire search space. If several positions are equally good, they should be contiguous. If not, slight changes in other constraints' suitability functions can cause oscillation between those positions.

Exceptions: Collision and Visibility Constraints

Constraints, such as collision avoidance and visibility, are special cases. If nothing is in the way, these constraints have no influence on the position. In this case, the range can be small, thus lowering the influence of the constraint. We built our collision and visibility constraints with the following set of rules:

- The suitability function should be zero if the camera is beyond a threshold distance from the closest collision, or the main character is entirely visible (remember that we prefer small values).
- The suitability function should be one if the camera is just colliding, or the main character is less than half-visible.
- The values in-between are linearly interpolated.
- The suitability function is independent of the search space position. This means that the suitability value of a position is constant in time (i.e., it doesn't ever change). For the visibility constraint, this is only true if the main character is not moving.

We first implemented both constraints using ray and shape casts, but the discrete aspect of this approach produced shaking near obstacles. We decided to use a continuous approach, in which a simple representation of the world is created, composed of primitive shapes such as planes, boxes, spheres, and cylinders. The shortest distance from the camera to a shape in the world is used to compute the suitability value of the constraint using Equation 5.2.5. The constraint's suitability function has a range of 0 if all points in the search space are farther from an obstacle than the threshold distance, thus having no influence at all on the solution. The same idea is used for visibility, but we use the distance from the line-of-sight of the evaluated camera position (the line that goes from the camera to the character's position) as shown in Figure 5.2.2.

$$s\left(Position\right) = \begin{cases} 0 & d_{Position} > d_{thresh} \\ 1 - d_{Position}/d_{thresh} & d_{Position} \leq d_{thresh} \end{cases} \qquad (5.2.5)$$

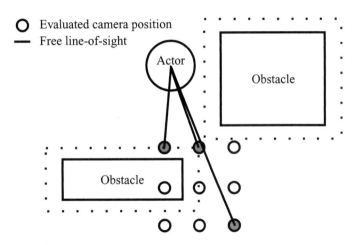

FIGURE 5.2.2 Line-of-sight used to compute visibility constraint.

Profile-Based Architecture

A camera should be able to adapt to special situations, such as locomotion/wall-climbing, in a third-person game or a cockpit/outside view in a driving game. Tuning the same camera to behave adequately in all situations is not trivial. To limit the problem, we decided to create a specific camera for each problem. The scope of the camera's work is then smaller and easier to tune. A profile-based architecture allows us to dynamically change the behavior of the camera. In Bourne's implementation, profiles could make changes in constraints' weights, but they could not alter the number or type of constraints. The new constraint concept, with a main constraint specialized for each behavior, is not compatible with this architecture.

In our system, a profile is composed of a set of constraints and their weights. When the profile is active, the solver evaluates its constraint list. The logic used to switch between profiles is game-specific and camera-specific. For example, a fall camera can be activated when the character is falling but only if there is no specific environment camera. When switching between profiles, one of several transitions can be activated to ensure continuity between camera behaviors:

- If the two profiles are already expected to be continuous, no special action need be taken, so the new profile is applied directly.
- The solver can compute the suitability function of both profiles and interpolate from one to the other. The disadvantage of this approach is that both profiles must be evaluated, increasing the CPU requirements.
- If neither of the preceding approaches will provide a good result, we can simply cut to the new profile's best position. In this case, a bigger search space should be used, so that we can be sure of finding the true best solution.

Suitability Value Transformations

One way to improve camera control is to give the game designers access to a set of suitability value transformations. Value transformations are functions that can be applied to the suitability value of a constraint. They are used to change the output value of a constraint.

Transformations should map the input value to the range [0, 1]. Equation 5.2.6 shows the adapted suitability function of the system. A transformation is assigned to each constraint and stored in the profile.

$$S(Position) = \sum_i w_i t_i (S_i(Position)) \tag{5.2.6}$$

Some common transformations include the following:

- We can apply a constant exponent (either greater or smaller than 1), as shown in Equation 5.2.7.
- Ease-in ease-out transformations can be applied with a sigmoid, as shown in Equation 5.2.8. α adjusts the slope of the curve.
- We can take the inverse of the constraint (so that a position attractor becomes a repulsor, and vice versa), as shown in Equation 5.2.9.

$$t(x) = x^\alpha \tag{5.2.7}$$

$$t(x) = \frac{1}{1 + \exp(\alpha(2x - 1))} \tag{5.2.8}$$

$$t(x) = 1 - x \tag{5.2.9}$$

Figure 5.2.3 shows the effect of these transformations.

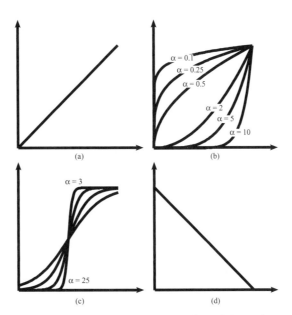

FIGURE 5.2.3 Transformation of suitability value:
(a) none, (b) exponent, (c) sigmoid, (d) inverse.

For example, the collision constraint outputs a value that is proportional to the distance of the nearest wall. If you apply an exponential transformation (Equation 5.2.7) with $\alpha = 0.1$, the suitability value quickly approaches 1, forcing the camera to stay away from the wall.

Search Space Improvements

The original solver algorithm uses a box as the search space [Bourne06a]. In the next section, problems inherent to this search space are exposed, and solutions are proposed. Other kinds of search spaces are also presented.

Search Space Size

The box size gives the maximum displacement of the camera in one frame. So, if the game runs at 60 fps, a frame lasts around 16 ms, and the search space extent is 1 meter, the maximum camera speed is 60 m/s or 216 km/h. Therefore, the search space size should be chosen carefully, limiting unneeded computation. To allow independent maximum speeds, a search space resized using the time step was tested, but the variability of the size accumulated a rounding error that introduced shaking in the camera. Because we use an octree to iterate over the box, it is also important to ensure that the bigger the box, the bigger the approximation made by the octree.

Sliding Octree Improvements

When using a sliding octree to iterate over the region, we found that the current point, at the center of the box, could not be reached. As previously explained, the sliding octree algorithm cuts the box into eight smaller boxes. The suitability function is evaluated at the center of each box. The center of the box is then moved to the best-evaluated position. The current center of the box is not tested at all, preventing the search space from staying at its current position. The simple solution is to test the center with the eight other points and move the box accordingly.

Other Search Spaces

Although the box search space allows complete freedom of movement, there are times when you want to limit the camera to a specific path or region. Planes or splines can be used to achieve this.

The search algorithm must be adapted to the search space. The algorithm is therefore moved to the search space class. Every search space class must be derived from an abstract class that provides the interface with the following functionality:

- The search algorithm to be used by the solver
- A function for computing the minimum distance from a given point to the search space
- A function for computing the maximum distance from a given point to the search space
- Point projection or clamping used to remain inside the search space

The last three functions allow constraints to be implemented without any knowledge of the search space. Figure 5.2.4a shows a setup where a torus can be used to encircle an arena, and Figure 5.2.4b shows a setup using a spline.

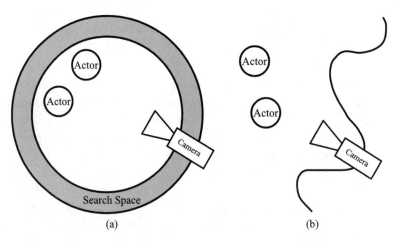

(a)   (b)

FIGURE 5.2.4   (a) Torus as a search space. (b) Spline as a search space.

Debugging the System

When the camera exhibits weird behavior, finding the fault can be difficult. Is one constraint not behaving as intended? Are the weights incorrectly balanced? To answer these questions, a visual debugging system is needed. Every search space has the ability to implement debug rendering. Evaluated points are displayed as colored points, with the color representing the suitability of this point. Each constraint or the weighted sum can be displayed independently. Our current implementation, when paused, switches to a detached camera that can be moved around the scene. Then we can use a set of command keys to iterate and study the different constraints independently. Figure 5.2.5 shows a screenshot of the debugger in action for a box search space, and a full-color version can be found in Color Plate 6.

FIGURE 5.2.5   Debugging system for visualizing evaluated points of a box search space (also shown in Color Plate 6).

Source Code and Demo

ON THE CD

A demo with the source code is provided on the CD-ROM. The demo covers most of the topics presented here. Collision and visibility constraints are not included due to dependency on other systems not provided here.

Further Work

We still need to address better techniques for smoothing camera movement. We originally thought that it would be a good idea to use constraints to limit the camera's speed and acceleration. Our first attempt was to try a 3D velocity constraint, but that did not behave as expected. The problem was that the solver, following the minimum cost path, was always trying to reduce the traveled distance. Figure 5.2.6 shows the actual and expected paths to get from one point to another.

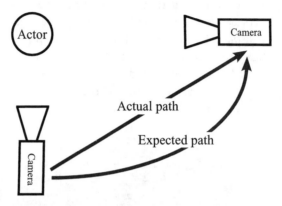

FIGURE 5.2.6   Path followed when using 3D velocity constraint versus expected path.

Our next attempt was to develop a speed limiter constraint in a spherical coordinate system. Although this system was better, tuning was difficult, and a central point was needed to convert to the spherical coordinate system to world space.

A third solution consists simply of clamping the output position. Clamping has been implemented in several speed coordinate systems: Euclidean, radial, and spherical.

Each solution has its own advantages and disadvantages, however, none are universal. You should try each one to find the one that best suits your needs.

If you don't always want the camera to look at your main character, you might want to use a constraint system to control its orientation. The suitability function should map an orientation to a value. To express the orientation, Euler angles can be used. The source code is designed (with the help of a template) to adapt easily to use vectors of Euler angles. Search spaces must be adapted, and the warped nature of Euler vectors should be handled with care. It might also be a good idea to use a separate set of constraints for selecting the camera's position and its orientation, so that the orientation constraints do not influence the position.

Conclusion

This article presents a versatile camera system that uses a constraint-based solver. The camera is defined by a set of profiles, with only one profile active at a time. The ability of the camera to switch between profiles allows the camera to adapt to different situations.

A profile is composed of a main constraint, defining the base behavior, and influencing constraints, such as collision and center of interest visibility. A suitability function is created by computing a weighted sum of the constraints' suitability functions. The position with the best suitability value is chosen as the solution.

The search space defines the region where the system searches for a solution. New search spaces have been presented, extending the use to limited space and path cameras.

Several possible extensions were proposed, including constraints to adjust camera velocity, acceleration, and orientation.

References

[Bourne06a] Bourne, Owen, and Sattar, Abdul, "Autonomous Camera Control with Constraint Satisfaction Method." *AI Game Programming Wisdom 3*, Charles River Media, 2006: pp. 174–187.

[Bourne06b] Bourne, Owen, and Sattar, Abdul, "Evolving Behaviours for a Real-Time Autonomous Camera. *AI Game Programming Wisdom 3 CD Bonus Material*, Charles River Media, 2006.

[Garces06] Garces, Sergio, "Extending Simple Weighted-Sum Systems." *AI Game Programming Wisdom 3*, Charles River Media, 2006: pp. 331–339.

5.3

Seeing in 1D: Projecting the World onto a Line

Andrew Slasinski

ExtraStanlo@gmail.com

In game AI, vision can be simulated using line-of-sight testing. Line-of-sight checks are often implemented by ray casts from an agent to a target. This has several disadvantages, however. Depending on the number of potential objects a ray can hit, the tests can be very expensive. The obvious solution is to reduce the number of ray casts, or even restrict yourself to a single one, but this technique can result in false negatives. If only a few ray casts are made from one object to another, all of them might fail to reach the target even though it is clearly visible, as shown in Figure 5.3.1.

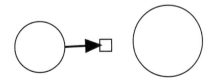

FIGURE 5.3.1 A failed line-of-sight check to an object that should be visible.

This article proposes an alternate solution for 2D games and 3D games with 2D gameplay. By using the graphics processing unit (GPU), the world can be projected onto a 1D line across an agent's field of view. Intelligent decisions can then be made using the data collected. Additionally, source code and a demo for this article are provided on the CD-ROM.

ON THE CD

Overview

Using the GPU for simulated agent vision is straightforward. Here's a quick summary of the algorithm:

1. Draw objects in the scene as simplified bounding areas to a row of pixels in a texture.

2. Draw interesting targets for an agent into the same area using a different color.
3. Read back the pixels of the texture.
4. Iterate over the pixels, and search for any colors matching that of the targets.
5. Make a decision based on the number of targets seen.

Drawing the World

To offload work from the CPU, a line representing the world is drawn onto an off-screen surface using a graphics API, such as DirectX or OpenGL. The accompanying demo uses DirectX, but the techniques can be implemented using OpenGL just as easily.

Object Representations

For this technique to work, it must be possible to represent everything that an agent can see as 2D geometric primitives, such as lines. In the case of a 3D game in which agents are only able to interact on a 2D plane, a bounding visibility area must wrap around the agent. In 3D, this might look like an inner tube around a character's waist, as shown in Figure 5.3.2. In memory, it would be represented as a 2D polyline. This polyline is used as a proxy for the agent's 3D geometry; therefore, it should maintain a tight fit around the agent to prevent false positive results.

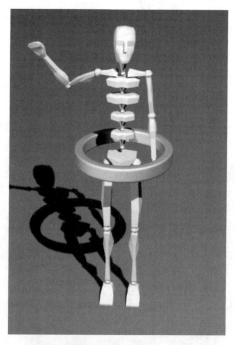

FIGURE 5.3.2   A 3D model and what its
bounding visibility area should logically look like.

In the case of a 2D sprite-based game, the bounding visibility area would be a contour around the sprite. This concept is similar to generating bounding areas for collision used by the physics engine in a game.

Projecting 2D to 1D

To draw in 1D, a view and projection transform are required just like normal 3D rendering. Because most video cards only support square render targets, the viewport of the 2D agent can take up a row of pixels on a square texture.

The view matrix transforms points in the world to a reference frame local to the 2D agent. A normal 3D camera can be used for this. If the 2D world were drawn on a chalkboard, the 3D camera would be placed up against the chalkboard looking in the same direction as the 2D agent. For the accompanying demo, the camera is oriented so that the "up" direction for the camera points out of the chalkboard.

The projection matrix is determined by the way the 2D agent sees. It can either see along a long column as an orthographic projection or a trapezoidal area as a perspective projection, as shown in Figure 5.3.3.

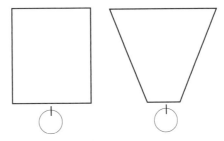

FIGURE 5.3.3 An orthographic projection on the left, and a perspective projection on the right.

Component Labeling

Colors for the objects in the 2D scene must be selected to differentiate between scenery and targets. In the demo, scene objects are labeled cyan, and targets are labeled dark blue.

Multiple Viewers

To support views for multiple agents, rather than fetching data from a render target after every view has been drawn, it is easier to render the views of multiple agents all to the same render target. To keep them separate, simply adjust the viewport to render each view on a different row of the texture.

Interpreting the Data

Now that a scene has been projected onto a 1D line, the data can be processed to get information about the scene. Each pixel of the line can be thought to represent a ray cast from the agent. For example, rendering 32 pixels to a render target is the same as casting 32 rays and recording data about the first nearest intersection for each of them. An example is shown in Figure 5.3.4.

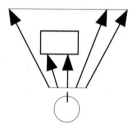

FIGURE 5.3.4   A 2D view frustum with rays that represent the meaning behind pixels drawn to a render target. In this example, the rectangle will cause two pixels to be drawn.

To check whether a specific target is visible to an agent, perform a search for that target's color in the agent's row. The number of pixels matching the target's color is related to how well an agent can see the target. Fewer matching pixels will be present if the target is far away, partially behind something, or out of the agent's field of view.

Additional data can also be found from the scene. For example, the distance to the viewer can be stored in each pixel when rendering the scene. This may be useful for an agent that uses ray casting to steer itself around the environment. If an agent is quickly approaching a wall or an obstacle, the agent can steer away or brake to prevent a collision.

Querying as an Alternative

Rather than reading back the pixels of the render target from the GPU, occlusion querying can be used instead. Occlusion querying works by submitting a fake draw call to the GPU. The GPU returns a list of pixels that would have been drawn had it been a real draw call. To use this feature, draw the 2D scene into a 1D line, and then use occlusion querying with the targets in the scene. If no pixels would have been drawn, the target would not appear in the scene. This may be faster than reading back texture data, but it is less flexible because custom information cannot be saved to the texture.

Potential Issues

The most obvious issue is that by using this technique, game AI has become dependent on the player's video card. If the game is targeted toward a specific console, this may be a nonissue. PC graphics cards that are shader model 1–compliant should be decent candidates for this technique due to the general performance of the cards released at the time. If shader model 2 cards are targeted, however, much more work can be potentially offloaded onto the GPU due to the large pixel shader instruction set. Some easy-to-implement ideas are presented in the next section.

Rendering the scenes must also be done in an intelligent manner. As few draw calls as possible should be made to keep performance high. Visibility determination techniques, such as frustum culling, can be adapted to reduce the amount of draw calls made to the GPU.

Finally, the quality of the 1D scene is also important to the agent. A lower resolution render target means that fewer virtual rays are being cast, and there is a higher chance to miss targets.

Extensions

A nice feature of this technique is that it provides a measure of how well a target can be seen. Targets off in the distance take up fewer pixels using a perspective projection, and partially occluded targets take up fewer pixels regardless of projection. Different actions can be taken if a target is very visible, mostly visible, or barely visible.

Rather than reading back all the data into system memory, the GPU can process the scene a bit first. For example, with some clever work, the GPU could count the number of labeled pixels in a scene with a shader. This means less data needs to be sent back to the CPU to process, offering better performance. The GPU could even count the number of differently labeled targets in view, or even compute a direction that an agent should steer toward, all in hardware using special pixel shaders.

Camouflaged targets can be simulated with this technique by testing pixels surrounding a target. If the surrounding pixels are too similar in color, the agent may not be able to see the target.

Drawing reflections in mirrors is nothing new to 3D graphics, and this technique can support agents that see targets reflected in mirrors. They can even see targets reflected by multiple mirrors! This would be quite difficult to implement using ray casts.

Source Code and Demo

ON THE CD

Included on the CD-ROM is source code and a demo showing the concepts from this article. In the demo, an agent rotates clockwise in a top-down 2D world. The resulting 1D vision information is then displayed in the top-left corner with white pixels representing no visible object, cyan representing occluders (scene objects), and dark blue representing targets (the star-shaped object). The 1D vision is stretched vertically to make it easier to see. When a target is seen, the borders of the screen turn red. An image from the demo can be seen in Color Plate 7.

Conclusion

With a little bit of cleverness, the GPU can be coerced into performing non-graphics-related operations for you with great results. Visibility determination is one of the few components of AI that can take advantage of the massively parallel nature of new GPU hardware. Although rendering a 3D scene onto a 1D line loses a great deal of information that rendering to a 2D plane may not miss, the complexity of searching a 2D texture for targets is exponentially larger. This technique is also simple enough that smaller, 2D sprite-based games might take advantage of it for some new game-play ideas using searchlights, security guards, or dynamic levels used by the player to stay out of sight.

5.4

Reaction Time with Fitts' Law

Baylor Wetzel—Brown College

baylorw@yahoo.com

The player walks into a bot's line-of-sight. How long should it take for the bot to fire at the player? It's an easy problem to solve—you could just make up a number—but it's not an easy problem to solve well. If the bot reacts too slowly, it's not as exciting as playing against a human opponent. If the bot reacts too quickly, the player will accuse your AI of cheating. Moreover, if you simply plug in a number without taking into account variables such as how far away the player is, your AI will seem both unintelligent and like it's cheating.

If we want our bots to behave like humans, it's helpful to know how humans behave. In this article, we discuss *Fitts' Law*, a model of human reaction time, and how we can use it to simulate human-like reaction time in games.

Fitts' Law

The player runs into your field of view. How long will it take for you to point your weapon at him and pull the trigger? The answer depends on a few things. How long does it take for you to notice that the player has appeared? How long does it take for your brain to tell your hand to move? How far must you move your hand to point at the target? How large is the target?

Fitts' Law is named after Paul Fitts, a World War II–era psychologist who studied equipment design and human factors engineering. As part of this work, he studied how long it took people to move their hands to an object based on the object's size and how far the hand had to move. Based on this analysis, he created a formula that could predict a person's movement time. This model was based heavily on Claude Shannon's writings on information theory. Information theory deals with things such as signal-to-noise ratios and encoding data in bits using binary logs, and as such can be a little difficult to understand by nonengineers. So before we discuss the specifics of Fitts' Law, let's talk about how to use it.

In the next section, we'll discuss the formula as it is traditionally written. For now, here is how we choose to write it:

$$indexOfDifficulty = \log_2\left(\frac{distance}{width}+1\right)$$

$$movementTime = reactionTime + (timePerBit \cdot indexOfDifficulty)$$

Let's try a quick example. Suppose an agent becomes aware of the player. The center of the player is 32 units to the left of where we are currently aiming our weapon, and the player appears to be 2 units wide. It doesn't matter what the units are (meters, inches, pixels, etc.) because we'll be taking the ratio of the two. In our case, the index of difficulty would be the following:

$$indexOfDifficulty = \log_2\left(\frac{32}{2}+1\right) = \log_2(17) = 4.09 \text{ bits of "difficulty"}$$

If the player was further away (say, 64 units rather than 32), or the target was smaller (say, 1 unit wide rather than 2), then the index of difficulty would be higher. Likewise, the larger the target or the closer it is, the less difficult it is.

To determine how long it will take for the agent to aim at the player, we need to know both the reaction time and the time per bit. For now let's use the numbers 304 ms and 125 ms. Later in the article, we'll explain how to determine these numbers.

$$movementTime = 304 + 125 \cdot 4.09 \approx 304 + 511 \approx 815 \text{ ms}$$

Let's do a few more examples to show how this works. Suppose the agent aims for the player's head, which is only one unit wide. Then the time to aim would be the following:

$$movementTime = 304 + 125 \cdot \log_2\left(\frac{32}{1}+1\right) \approx 934 \text{ ms}$$

Because he is aiming at a smaller target, it takes him longer to properly aim at the target.

To make the shot easier, the agent uses a sniper rifle with a zoom that makes the player's head 4 units wide. To keep the example simple, assume that the player is still only 32 units away.

$$movementTime = 304 + 125 \cdot \log_2\left(\frac{32}{4}+1\right) \approx 700 \text{ ms}$$

A larger target means the player can aim at the target faster.

You might have noticed that all of the previous examples are subsecond response times. Included on the CD-ROM is a program that allows you to measure your own response time. My response times varied from 322 ms to 929 ms (depending on the

ON THE CD

index of difficulty), which is in line with measurements taken from other groups [Cuijpers07].

Here's one last example. Assume the agent is aiming his weapon in a given direction when the player just pops up directly in his crosshairs. Assume that the width of the player is one. The time it would take for the agent to aim and pull the trigger would be the following:

$$movementTime = 304 + 125 \cdot \log_2 \left(\frac{0}{1} + 1 \right) = 304 + 0 = 304 \text{ ms}$$

Even given a perfect shot, the shot is not instantaneous. The brain still needs time to recognize the situation and give the command.

How It Works

Fitts' Law has been modified (slightly) several times. The version we'll discuss here is called the Shannon formulation. This version is named after Claude Shannon, whose work on information theory is the basis of Fitts' original formula.

The Shannon formulation of Fitts' Law is given here:

$$ID = \log_2 \left(\frac{A}{W} + 1 \right)$$

$$MT = a + (b \cdot ID)$$

ID stands for index of difficulty and represents, for our purposes, how hard it is to click the mouse button on the target. To calculate ID, take the distance from the mouse to the center of the target (A for amplitude; if the name seems funny, it's because Fitts' Law was derived from signal processing theory), and divide it by the effective width of the target (W). Because Fitts' Law measures data in bits, you'll need to take the base 2 log of this number. If the distance is less than the width, the resulting number is less than one, and the log of a number less than one is negative, meaning the problem has a negative difficulty rating. Because this is an odd situation to be in, the Shannon formulation adds one to the number to prevent it from becoming negative.

MT stands for movement time, which is the time it takes to move the mouse to the target and click the fire button.

The variables a and b are more difficult to explain. Suppose you had someone playing your game, and each time someone shot a target, you recorded his movement time and the target's index of difficulty. If you plotted those on a graph and then used linear regression to run a line through the center of that data, a would be the x-intercept (where the line runs through the x-axis), and b would be the slope of the line. There isn't an accepted definition for what those represent in the real world, but consider that for a target of difficulty zero (meaning your mouse is already on the target, all you have to do is push the button), movement time (technically, the time to move and fire) will be the same as intercept *a*. You might consider the intercept to be the time it takes the actor to notice the event and react to it. If the intercept is the startup time, then slope *b* is the amount of time it takes for each unit of difficulty. In reality, the meaning of intercept and slope are probably a bit more complex than this, but these are useful approximations.

Gathering the Data

The previous formula uses the constants *a* and *b*. Because they represent the base reaction time and how quickly you can aim at targets of various difficulties, they will be different for each person. That leads to the question, how do you get these numbers?

ON THE CD

The constants *a* and *b* are obtained empirically, meaning that before we can predict how fast someone will be, we must first have the person aim at a few targets and measure how quickly he reacts. Included on the CD-ROM is a program to do this. The player aims at a number of objects, measures all the relevant variables (how large the target is, how quick the player was, etc.), and saves them to a comma-delimited file.

After you have this information, you determine *a* and *b* through linear regression. An easy way to do this is to import the data file into Excel and use Excel's `slope` and `intercept` functions. If you stored the movement time in column A and the index of difficulty in column B, you would get the constant *a* (the intercept) with the formula:

$$=\text{INTERCEPT(A:A, B:B)}$$

and the constant *b* (the slope) with the formula:

$$=\text{SLOPE(A:A, B:B)}$$

ON THE CD

An example is included on the CD-ROM.

To give you an idea of what range of numbers you should expect to get, my personal values are 304 ms (a, the intercept) and 125 ms (b, the slope). The average for my 11-year-old daughter Amber was 498 ms (a) and 121 ms (b). The average for the Fittsbits project, which analyzed data from more than a thousand subjects (and which used a slightly different formulation), was 460 ms and 130 ms for experienced computer users and 480 ms/140 ms for novice users [Cuijpers07].

Details Worth Knowing

Fitts' original goal was to be able to predict the average amount of time it would take someone to make a quick but precise move in a single dimension to a stationary target. This has a couple of implications.

First, the movement time predicted by this formula is an average movement time. Obviously, people do not always move at an average rate. Using my own performance as an example (see Figure 5.4.1), over the course of 60 trials, I was within 10% of my predicted time on roughly half the trials and within 20% on more than three-quarters of the trials. I was more than 40% off on 7% of the trials (in each of these cases, I was slow to notice the target; time spent moving was normal). The numbers for my 11-year-old daughter Amber were similar. For this set of trials, predicted times ranged from 322 to 929 ms.

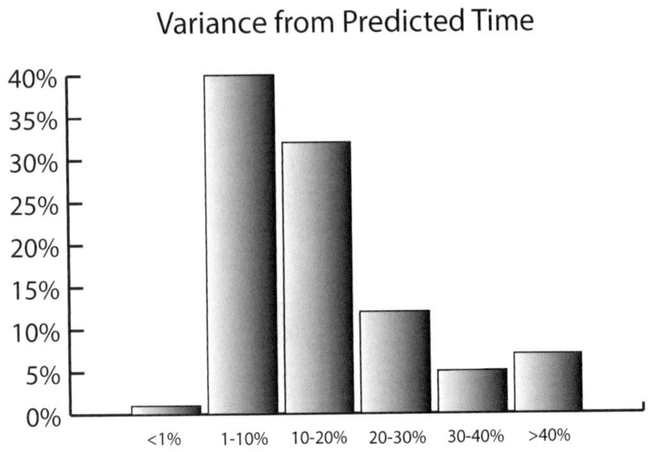

FIGURE 5.4.1 Fitts' Law rarely predicted my movement time to the precise millisecond, but it was often very close (in this graph, 10% variance ranged from 32 ms to 93 ms, depending on the trial).

Second, the assumption is that the user is aware that he is about to be aiming at a target. This is a realistic assumption if your AI-controlled agent is in the middle of a firefight or actively searching for the player, but it isn't true for a guard sitting as his post expecting a quiet night.

Third, the assumption is that the user is able to make this movement with relatively few mistakes. Specifically, the user is expected to have an error rate of 4% (this number doubles to 8% when approaching a target at a diagonal [MacKenzie92]), with more of those errors being undershooting than overshooting [Oliveira05]. There is a tradeoff between speed and accuracy. To click on the target the first time every time, the user must move slower, whereas a user that moves faster will miss more often.

Fourth, the original work was designed for single-dimension movement. As a result, the size of the target was always assumed to be its width. Later studies found that Fitts' Law holds up in two dimensions, but the size of the target needs to be calculated somewhat differently. The method typically recommended and the one used in my own work is to look at the object's width and height and use whichever is smaller (known in the literature as the SMALLER-OF model). Although it might sound overly simple, studies have found it to give extremely good results [MacKenzie91].

Fifth, Fitts' Law assumes that the target is stationary. The program included on the CD-ROM allows you to analyze data for both moving and stationary targets. My own tests showed that Fitts' Law applies equally well to both moving and stationary targets (see Figure 5.4.2), although the error rate with moving targets is higher. Specifically, across 60 trials, the distribution of response times was roughly the same as when aiming at stationary targets (45% of trials within 10% of predicted time, 68% within 20%, 7% greater than 40%), but 17% of the trials resulted in more than one press of the mouse button, representing a miss on the first shot (13% involved two clicks, one trial resulted in three clicks, one trial contained four). In three of the 60 trials, the subject failed to hit the target before it left the screen.

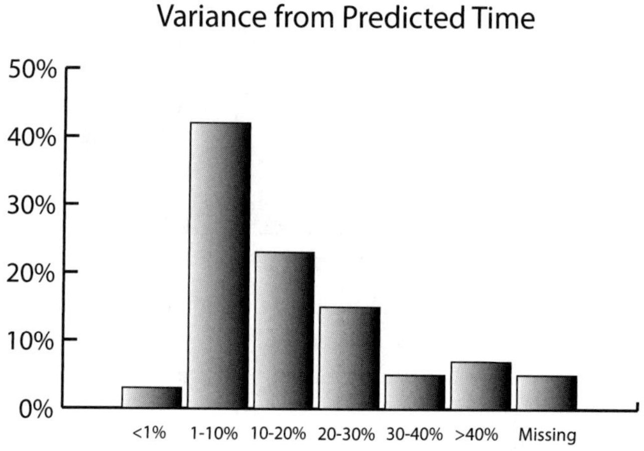

Variance from Predicted Time

FIGURE 5.4.2   When Fitts' Law is used to predict movement time to click on a moving target, accuracy remains qualitatively the same.

There are two things to note about moving targets. First, in the author's experience, there was substantially more panic when trying to intercept a moving target and a firmly held belief that small, quick targets were much harder to catch than large or slow ones. The data, however, seems to indicate that performance was roughly the same.

Second, in these trials, the object moved at random angles and random speeds. In a traditional FPS, objects are more likely to be moving along the horizontal plane, and all objects of a certain class (soldier, rocket, tank, etc.) are likely to move at the same speed in a predictable manner. Therefore, this test should represent a worst-case scenario, with the exception that objects in this test moved in a straight line rather than circle-strafing, randomly walking, or randomly jumping.

Future Work

This paper describes how quickly an AI-controlled agent will react but does not describe what the movements will look like, which might be important to a game where the player can view the world from the bot's eyes. One possibility is to look into the Accot-Zhai steering law, derived from Fitts' Law, which handles the case of a user trying to move a mouse through a 2D tunnel.

Conclusion

Reaction time is an important part of many games, so getting it right is a task worth undertaking. With Fitts' Law, you get a good model of human reaction time that's both widely accepted and extensively documented. Because it is an empirical method, different AI agents can be based on different people, allowing you to customize the reaction time of your AI-controlled agents. Requiring only two pieces of readily available data at runtime, Fitts' Law is easy to add to your game. And, because it only requires a few simple calculations per target, it's fast. The code only needs to be written once—to change reaction time, you change the input data, not the code. Fitts' Law won't solve every AI problem your game will have but it does a good job for reaction time, meaning one less problem you have to worry about.

References

[Cuijpers07] Cuijpers, L., and Vervuurt, W., "Fittsbits: A Game Investigating Fitts' Law." Available online at *http://www.rodo.nl/fittsbits/*, April 17, 2007.

[MacKenzie91] MacKenzie, I. S. *Fitts' Law as a Performance Model in Human-Computer Interaction*. Doctoral dissertation, University of Toronto, 1991.

[MacKenzie92] MacKenzie, I. S., and Buxton, W., "Extending Fitts' Law to Two Dimensional Tasks." *Proceedings of the CHI '92 Conference on Human Factors in Computing Systems*, 1992.

[Oliveira05] Oliveira, F. T. P., Elliott, D., and Goodman, D. "Energy-Minimization Bias: Compensating for Intrinsic Influence of Energy-Minimization Mechanisms." *Motor Control*, (2005): pp. 101–114.

Enabling Actions of Opportunity with a Light-Weight Subsumption Architecture

Habib Loew—ArenaNet

habibloew@gmail.com

Chad Hinkle—Nintendo of America Inc.

hinks85@gmail.com

With the ever-increasing physical and graphical fidelity in games, players are beginning to demand similar increases in the performance of unit AI. Unfortunately, unit AI is still most often based on simple finite state machines (FSMs) or, occasionally, rule-based systems. Although these methods allow for relatively easy development and behavioral tuning, their structure imposes inherent limitations on the versatility of the units they control. In this article, we propose an alternate methodology that allows units to effectively pursue multiple simultaneous goals. Although our method isn't a panacea by any means, it has the potential to lead to far more flexible, "realistic" unit AI.

A Brief Review of Subsumption

To give our unit AI the ability to pursue multiple simultaneous goals, we use a simple subsumption architecture [Brooks86, Yiskis04]. Subsumption is a layered approach in which each layer represents a behavior or action. Lower priority layers operate within the context set by the higher priority layers. If necessary, higher priority layers can completely override lower priority layers, ensuring that the overall behavior of the system always encompasses (or subsumes) the goals of the highest priority layers. Subsumption has a number of advantages, including robustness and flexibility. The principle of subsumption is fairly simple, but in practice, subsumption architectures have a tendency to become convoluted due to a lack of independence between the layers. We have appropriated the layered approach from subsumption while greatly simplifying our architecture by requiring a uniform interface to and between the layers. This was done at the expense of some flexibility, but we believe the gains in maintainability and layer portability are well worth the costs.

An Example Scenario

We will use a simple RTS as our example scenario. Suppose that we have a single air unit that can be used as a scout but that also possesses moderate offensive capabilities. The player has the ability to give our air unit orders to move, patrol, and attack. Additionally, our world contains a number of enemy tanks and a power-up that our air unit can collect.

In our example, the player has given the air unit an order to patrol the unknown territory to the north. Unbeknownst to the player, this patrol path will bring the air unit into contact with enemy tanks and near to a desirable power-up. If an actual pilot were controlling the air unit, we would expect them to alter their course slightly to collect the power-up, or to briefly engage with the enemy, as long as those actions do not conflict with their basic orders. Of course, there are many other possible actions for the pilot to take here, including exploring new territory, avoiding enemies, seeking out friendly units, and so on. For the sake of simplicity, we will only consider the first two opportunistic actions mentioned (engaging the enemy and seeking a power-up).

If the air unit used a simple FSM, it would likely be in a patrol state after receiving the player's order and would be unable to take advantage of the opportunities presented by its path. Certainly an FSM could be constructed to allow the unit some flexibility while patrolling; however, such an FSM would quickly become difficult to maintain as each state would be linked to every other state. Furthermore, a complex system would be required to ensure that the correct state was reentered after an opportunistic action was completed. Our problem, then, is to construct an easily maintainable system that will allow our air unit maximum flexibility to take advantage of opportunities while still following the player's orders effectively.

Light-Weight Subsumption

To solve our example problem, we have created a simple subsumption-inspired system with three layers. Each of our layers is self-contained and enables a particular sort of action or response. Our three layers (from lowest to highest priority) are the following:

Power-up Layer: Attempts to collide with power-ups.

Attack Layer: Attempts to engage enemy units by adjusting course and issuing firing orders.

Command Execution Layer: Executes commands given by the player. In our example, the patrol command is executed by this layer.

Each layer uses a standardized interface to manipulate the unit and interoperate with the other layers. All of our units implement a common command interface that allows us to mix and match layers between units with ease. Additionally, we can specify the layer ordering for individual units, allowing us to give a semblance of personality to units essentially for free.

Note that our layers are organized with the highest priority layer on the bottom to conform to the standard convention used when describing subsumption architectures.

Layer Execution

To arrive at the final behavior of our air unit, we will execute each layer in order of priority. As each layer executes, we evaluate its output to determine if it can be effectively combined with the layers that have already executed and, if so, combine the output of the current layer into the cumulative output of the subsumption system. Deciding if a given layer is compatible with its predecessors and combining the output of multiple layers intelligently are the most difficult issues when implementing a system like this.

Unfortunately, there are no universal solutions to these problems. Evaluation of when it is appropriate to execute a given layer is heavily application dependent and layer dependent. Lower priority layers should be prevented from causing higher priority layers to fail, but this can be difficult to enforce if the layers operate in significantly different ways. This is the main motivation for our standardized layer and command interface.

In our example scenario, all of our units effectively operate in 2D, so our command system is built around manipulating their headings. We use bounds on the headings to evaluate the appropriateness of a given layer as well as to combine the output of the layers as they execute. As execution of a layer begins, it is provided with a set of bounds on the possible headings it can choose by the higher priority layer(s) below it. We will call these the layer bounds. The executing layer then calculates the optimal heading that the unit should assume to achieve the layer's goal. Next, the executing layer uses this optimal heading to calculate bounds that indicate the maximum allowable deviation from the optimal heading, which will still allow the goal of the layer to be achieved. We call these the current bounds. This calculation should be as simple as possible because it will be done for every layer for every unit in the system. As long as any heading inside the current bounds will still allow the unit to achieve the goal of the executing layer (via steering corrections in later updates), the bounds are sufficiently correct. After the current and layer bounds have been calculated, we compute their intersection. We call these the working bounds.

If we arrive at this point in the process, and there are no working bounds (i.e., the intersection of bounds was the empty set), then the currently executing layer is ignored. No heading currently exists that will allow the unit to pursue the current layer's goal while preserving the goals of higher priority layers. Execution then moves on to the next layer with no changes made to the layer bounds.

If, however, the optimal heading lies within the working bounds, then the layer is considered to have executed effectively. The unit's target heading is then set to the optimal heading, any instantaneous orders (such as firing) are issued, the working bounds are passed to the next layer as the layer bounds, and the entire process repeats. When the final layer has either executed or been ignored, the heading of the unit will satisfy the maximum number of layers, with higher priority layers winning out over lower priority layers.

ON THE CD
        The demo included on the CD-ROM contains a full example of the layer execution process with all of the changing bounds illustrated.

Pitfalls and Misconceptions

The system we have presented here is highly simplified to make the layer interactions as clear as possible. Specifically, we only consider the unit heading when evaluating the layer interactions. A more robust implementation would have to take into account all aspects of layer behavior when evaluating and combining layers. For example, firing would be subjected to constraints other than unit heading, such as stealth, resource management, and so on. The more complex the interactions between the layers, the harder they are to codify. Even within our simple system, there are subtleties that should not be overlooked.

One very important fact to keep in mind is that while the layers represent a prioritized set of actions, most of the time, no single action will be chosen to the exclusion of all others. Instead, the system attempts to engage in as many simultaneous actions as possible. This can lead to situations in which lower priority actions end up completing successfully while higher priority actions fail. As long as the bounds provided by the highest priority layer are valid, in no case will the highest priority action fail while lower priority actions succeed. The danger is only to the middle priority layers. We have an explicit example of this behavior in the included demo.

After all the setup we went through to keep higher priority actions from getting overrun by lower priority actions, how did we end up in this situation? Simplifying assumptions in the calculation of the current bounds can be the source of problems like this, but even without those assumptions, the danger remains. Each layer encompasses an action that the system will attempt to simultaneously pursue. Eventually, adjustments made to accomplish very low priority actions "on the way" to completing higher priority actions can cause some of the middle priority layers to be temporarily excluded as the highest priority actions take precedence.

A specific example of this issue occurs in our demo. We set up the air unit with the following layers (remember, the highest priority is on the bottom):

- Attack Layer
- Power-up Layer
- Command Execution Layer

Additionally, the air unit is given a player command to patrol a location directly north of its starting position. About half way to the patrol point and just west of the patrol path is an enemy tank, and west of the tank is a power-up. Without the Attack Layer, the air unit would head directly for the power-up and then resume its path to the patrol point. However, because the Attack Layer is the last to execute, the air unit will always point at the tank as long as that path doesn't violate any higher priority layers. The air unit reaches a critical point when the power-up falls outside the bounds set by the Command Execution Layer. This causes the Power-up Layer to be ignored. The final behavior of the air unit is to attack the enemy tank on the way to the patrol point without making any apparent effort to pick up the power-up, even though the Power-up Layer is a higher priority than the Attack Layer. This situation can be difficult to visualize, so we encourage you to examine the included demo to get a better sense of how things might go wrong.

Conclusion

The method we have presented allows for semiautonomous agents to take advantage of unexpected opportunities and generally behave in a more flexible, believable fashion. By standardizing the layer and command interfaces, complex unit behavior groups can be created simply by mixing and matching layers that are in use by existing units. Control over the ordering of the layers can be given to players to increase their sense of customization of, and ownership over, their units. Giving individual units the ability to take more actions of opportunity, and doing so in a way that meshes with the player's own approach to the game, can increase the realism and immersion of the battlefield dramatically and at relatively little cost!

References

[Brooks86] Brooks, Rodney A., "How to Build Complete Creatures Rather than Isolated Cognitive Simulators." Available online at *http://people.csail.mit.edu/brooks/papers/how-to-build.pdf*, December 1, 2006.

[Yiskis04] Yiskis, Eric, "A Subsumption Architecture for Character-Based Games." *AI Game Programming Wisdom 2*, Charles River Media, 2004.

5.6

Toward More Humanlike NPCs for First-/Third-Person Shooter Games

National University of Ireland Galway
Darren Doherty

darren.doherty@nuigalway.ie

Colm O'Riordan

colm.oriordan@nuigalway.ie

In recent years, much effort has been put into increasing the believability of the actions of nonplayer characters (NPCs) in first-/third-person shooter (FTPS) games. Currently, NPCs in FTPS games generally use a common set of logic for reasoning, which can result in very monotonous and predictable behavior. If the agents in the gaming environment act and appear like real human players and are given a greater sense of individuality, then the experience will be more immersive for the player. NPCs in FTPS games typically have a limited ability to interpret and react to both changes in their environment and the actions of other characters.

Humans have personalities, display emotions, are unpredictable, and are influenced by physiological stressors. They define goals they want to achieve and develop plans to attain these goals. Humans have a memory enabling them to remember past events from which they can learn. They have the ability to sense their environment through sight, sound, touch, taste, and smell, and can communicate and coordinate their behavior with others. Humans can reason about their environment, have definite reaction times, and have a specific set of actions that they can perform. In addition, not all humans possess the same skills or the same level of expertise in skills they do possess. Rather than discuss briefly each of these human capabilities, we select a sampling of these capabilities and discuss in detail how they can be used to make NPCs more individual and humanlike.

Class-Based AI Systems

The emergence of squad-based FTPS games in recent years has given rise to more complex behavioral systems being developed. Some developers have begun to incorporate class-based AI systems into their FTPS games to allow for the development of different classes of NPCs, each with its own attributes, features, and modes of behavior, (e.g., *Battlefield 2* [BFII05]). Teams can then be comprised of agents from different classes; for example, a team could consist of an engineer, a sniper, a medic, and a rifleman, each with its own specific role on the team. NPCs in a particular class are instilled with specific abilities or attributes common to their class, but an individual NPC within a class is still indistinguishable from other NPCs in the same class.

The human behavioral capabilities discussed in this article can be applied to an existing AI architecture, such as a class-based AI system, to create more humanlike and individual NPCs. For example, all snipers may have common attributes, such as good aim, but one sniper might be more patient than another, so he may choose to camp at one location for long periods of time, whereas the other sniper might change his location often.

Human Sensing

To make an NPC humanlike, our first challenge is to make its perceptual abilities humanlike. NPCs should have limited sensory regions within which they can sense information; they should not have superhuman sensing abilities or perfect knowledge of the map. The sensory region is relative to the individual, and its size and shape differs for each sense. The perceptual systems inherent in FTPS AI engines deal mainly with the tactile, visual, and aural sensing of an agent. However, depending on the design parameters of the game, the senses of smell and taste could also be added.

Tactile Sensing

In modern games, tactile sensing is usually achieved through the use of a collision detection system and smart terrain. An NPC's tactile sensing region is the area immediately surrounding it on all sides. If the NPC touches something, or something touches the NPC, the collision detection system will detect a collision between the NPC and another game object. Smart terrain can then be used to tell the NPC about the properties of the game object it has just collided with, allowing the NPC to "feel" the object. For example, if an NPC touches a wall, then the wall can send a message to the NPC informing the NPC that the object it has touched is a wall, what type of material the wall is made from, if the wall is traversable, or if the NPC can break through the wall. Similarly, if something touches the NPC—whether it is a bullet piercing its flesh or a falling obstacle hitting it on the head, a message can be sent from the game object to the NPC telling the type of object that hit the NPC; its weight, material, and velocity; how much damage should be incurred, and so on.

Visual Sensing

To instill humanlike vision into an NPC, we need to model its visual system on that of a human. An agent's sensing region for sight should be cone-shaped and extend to a limited distance in front of the agent to simulate a binocular field of view and viewing distance [WauGra01]. With humans, the brain classifies any known objects that are sensed visually. For FTPS games, game objects are tested to see which ones lie unobstructed within the NPC's viewing range based on the field of view and viewing distance. Those that do are recorded as being sensed. The field of view and viewing distance can be altered for different NPCs to give a greater sense of individuality, such as short-sightedness or 20/20 vision.

Another idea is to allow NPCs to use binoculars, scopes, or even glasses. If an NPC is equipped with a pair of binoculars or a scope, its viewing distance should be magnified and its field of view narrowed accordingly. Likewise, if an NPC wears glasses, then its viewing distance with the glasses should be better than without. In addition, an agent who is blind in one eye should have monocular vision [WauGra01]. Its field of view should be biased to the side its eye is on, and it should have difficulty judging the distance and speed of objects. The agent's ability to classify objects could also be relative to how far away from the agent the object is, as vision generally deteriorates with distance. For example, an agent might sense another agent from a distance but might not be able to tell if that agent is a friend or foe until it comes closer.

Lighting conditions can also affect an NPC's ability to see. Flash-bang grenades or bright lights shone directly into an NPC's eyes could temporally blind it, rendering its visual sensing abilities inoperable for a time. Furthermore, an NPC walking around in a darkened environment should find it more difficult to visually sense other game objects than if the environment were fully lit. Players could take advantage of this by hiding in shadowed areas or by turning off the lights in a room when equipped with night-vision goggles. It would also give the NPCs incentive to use flashlights, wear night-vision goggles themselves, or search for a light switch in a darkened room, making their behavior more akin to a human player. This has already been done to an extent in some games, such as *Splinter Cell* [SpltrCell07]. However, if a light suddenly goes out in a room, and the NPCs do not have flashlights or night-vision goggles, it should generally cause panic among the NPCs and cause them to bump into objects when trying to navigate around the darkened room. Also, a cautious NPC may be reluctant to use flashlights because the light beam can give away the NPC's position and make it an easier target for the player.

Auditory Sensing

Sound waves have a pitch, timbre, and volume. The pitch is the frequency of the sound waves, the timbre is the nature of the sound (combination of different frequencies), and the volume is the loudness of the sound [MalBir98]. The volume of a sound attenuates with distance and attenuates in different ways depending on the types of media it passes through along the way. To reflect this effect, an NPC's auditory ability should also degrade with distance. For example, if an explosion occurs close to an NPC, it should be heard much more clearly than if it occurred far away. Hence, the NPC should become more alert and anxious if it hears a loud noise in close proximity than if it barely senses one far off in the distance. The pitch of a sound should affect human NPCs the same way it affects humans; very high pitched sounds might hurt an NPC's ears and cause it to cringe. In addition, some animals (such as dogs, cats, and mice) can hear frequencies outside of the human hearing range, so animal NPCs should be able to do the same.

An NPC's auditory sensing region should be spherical in shape, as sounds can be heard from any direction. Because the pinnae, or outer ears, of humans point forward, it is slightly easier to hear sounds coming from the front. Some mammals, such as dogs and cats, have movable pinnae that allow them to focus their hearing in a particular direction [EEIIME07]. This could allow for more interesting animal or beast NPCs. Their auditory sensing region could be distorted according to the direction their pinnae are pointing. The player could be made aware of this by displaying the NPC's auditory sensing region on the player's radar, similar to the way the player is made aware of an NPC's visual sensing region in many FTPS games, for example, *Metal Gear Solid 3: Snake Eater* [MGS305].

A human NPC should be able to hear all the sounds that a human player in the same situation can hear. This includes any gunfire, explosions, or loud noises within earshot of the NPC; any detectable enemy agents trying to sneak up from behind (e.g., if the enemy steps on a twig or knocks something over); an ally's cry for help; an order from a commander; and background noises, such as radios, TVs, wind blowing, chatter of allies, and so on.

Background noises could be used to influence an NPC's fear or alertness levels. If the background noises suggest a spooky atmosphere, an NPC might become afraid, or if an NPC hears a TV or radio that was earlier turned off, it may become alerted and investigate. Furthermore, the way humans perceive sound depends on ear shape, age, and psychological state; not all humans perceive sound in the same way [Menshikov03]. This idea could be incorporated to make some NPCs better able to distinguish one sound from another or to make older NPCs hard of hearing, giving the NPCs a greater sense of individuality.

Because some sounds are more significant than others, sounds in the game world could be tagged with an importance level to indicate how relevant the sound is to the NPC. This idea and suitable examples are provided by Tozour [Tozour02]. The auditory sensing region of an NPC may grow or shrink depending on the state of an agent. This means large, nearby explosions might temporarily deafen the agent, thus reducing the region; or seemingly quiet environments might peak the agent's alertness, thus increasing its sensory region. NPCs should be able to use this concept to their advantage. For example, snipers might wait for artillery fire in the background to mask the sound of their gunshot, so that enemies are not aware of their presence. In the same way, if a player is sneaking up behind an NPC, and there is a noisy wind blowing, the NPC should not be able to sense the sound of the player's footsteps over the sound of the wind.

Olfactory Sensing

Olfactory sensing refers to the sensing of information from the environment via the sense of smell. The sense of smell has not been used to the same extent as that of touch, vision, or hearing in FTPS games because design parameters do not normally require it. Including olfactory sensing would make NPCs more humanlike and the game more interesting to play as a whole. An agent's olfactory sensing region would be similar in shape to its auditory sensing region but generally not as large because the sense of smell is not usually as far-reaching as that of hearing. The human sense of smell is less sensitive than in animals [WauGra01]. The olfactory region for a dog NPC, for example, should be made much larger than that of a human NPC.

The smell coming from a game object could be emitted out across some smell radius whose length depends on the strength of the smell. If the object emitting the smell moves from one area to another, a trail of the smell could be left behind similar to the pheromone trail of an ant. This smell left by the trail should deteriorate over time as it disperses through the air. *Half Life 2* [HLife06] uses a sort of smell sensing using antlions and pheropods. When the player throws a pheropod and the pheropod bursts, the antlions will "smell" the exposed contents and swarm on the location of the burst pod.

Some smells can also get stronger or weaker over time, causing their smell radius to grow or shrink, respectively. For example, the smell of an NPC's corpse that the player has killed and hidden away should get stronger as the corpse decays, making it more likely to be found by another NPC. It should also be possible for the player to use the environment to keep smells concealed to certain areas. For example, the smell coming from a corpse hidden in a locker would not be as prominent as it would be if the corpse were outside of the locker. Similarly, smells confined to enclosed spaces should be a lot stronger than those that are out in the open. An agent might smell an object more easily if it were in a small room than if it were outside.

Smells can be masked by other stronger smells. For example, the player could mask its own smell with the smell of a strong-smelling plant or spray, or the player could wear clothing belonging to an enemy NPC to lead dogs or other beasts off its scent by disguising its smell as an ally rather than an enemy. Smells can also be used to influence NPC behavior. In a sewer setting, an NPC might feel sick from the smell and not be as effective in combat. In *Gears of War* [GOW07], the Berserker creatures in the game are blind and can only sense the player through sound and smell.

Furthermore, there are the issues of anosmia and adaptation with respect to olfactory sensing. *Anosmia* is an inflammation of the nasal mucosa that prevents odors from reaching the olfactory nerves in the nose, essentially causing a loss of smell [WauGra01]. For example, an NPC who has contracted a cold virus (a common cause of anosmia) would be prevented from smelling objects in the game while the cold is active. *Adaptation* is the way in which the perception of an odor decreases (and eventually ceases) the longer an individual is exposed to it [WauGra01]. This could be an interesting concept to bring into FTPS games. For example, a security guard NPC might be stationed in a room where the player has just hidden a dead body. Over time, the smell would be getting worse, but the NPC would also be adapting to it and so might not sense it, whereas if another NPC entered the room, he would smell it right away.

Gustatory Sensing

Gustatory sensing is the sensing of objects through taste. For FTPS games, taste is of little importance because the amount of information that NPCs in a FTPS game can sense through taste is very limited. However, gustatory sensing could bring many interesting factors to an FTPS game. Beasts or monsters in the game could become more aggressive when they get a taste for blood or raw meat. Thus, if an agent is bleeding from an open wound, it's in the agent's interest to stop the bleeding as soon as possible and to keep dead prey out of the path of the beasts.

Gustatory sensing could also be used to bring a fun element to the game by allowing the player to play tricks on guards. For example, a guard might leave its lunch unattended while it goes off to investigate a diversionary sound the player has made. The player could then tamper with the unattended lunch and put something foul tasting into it. When the guard comes back, he would be none the wiser and begin eating, causing him to wretch at the taste, much to the amusement of the player.

Konami's *Metal Gear Solid 3: Snake Eater* [MGS305] integrated a type of gustatory sensing for the main character of the game. In the game, the player can kill and eat snakes and other prey to replenish his health. However, each prey eaten has a different taste, and the amount of health recovered is determined by how tasty the prey is. The player can also get sick from eating rotten food. If dead prey is stored for too long in the player's inventory, it can become stale and taste worse than it would if eaten when it was freshly caught.

Summary of Human Sensing

FTPS games of the past have needed very little (if any) olfactory or gustatory sensing because tactile, visual, and auditory sensing have been sufficient to create rudimentary AI for NPCs that act in a somewhat rational manner. However, in recent years, gamers are demanding more immersive experiences from their games and that means making the NPCs more interesting, humanlike, and distinctive. Broadening the ways in which NPCs can sense information from their environment is an essential element for achieving this.

Senses can also be combined to allow NPCs to more accurately sense information from their environment. For example, if an NPC sees another agent in the distance, it might not be sure if the other agent is an ally or an enemy. However, if the NPC also hears the agent commanding an attack on the NPC's position, it would be more certain that the sensed agent is an enemy and not an ally.

Memory

Three different kinds of memory exist: sensory memory, short-term memory, and long-term memory [Gross01]. Each sense has a sensory memory associated with it that filters significant information from the environment to the short-term memory. The short-term memory of a human is like a temporary store of significant information that it has just perceived. Short-term memory has limited capacity and deteriorates quickly. After about 30 seconds, information is either forgotten or passed to long-term memory. Long-term memory has a much larger capacity and duration than short-term memory [MalBir98]. Memory and learning go hand in hand because humans need to be able to remember in order to learn [Gross01].

The sensory systems of an NPC can be viewed as their sensory memory because information from the game environment is fed into the NPC's short-term memory via their senses. The NPC's short-term memory should have a limited memory span and capacity. This means that an NPC should forget its oldest or least-significant memories after a specified time of being perceived or when the capacity of its short-term memory has been overloaded.

The memories of an NPC could be tagged with a timestamp and importance level when perceived to facilitate this process. The importance level could be determined by the NPC's current state and the type of information perceived. For example, an enemy's location is of higher importance to an NPC with full health than a health pack's location.

In a realistic setting, more important information should be sent to an NPC's long-term memory rather than being forgotten. Long-term memory stores are generally not included in the NPCs of most FTPS games because the NPC's lifespan is too short to make good use of long-term memory. However, FTPS games are moving away from the old school style of cannon fodder NPCs, and games are becoming more immersive. As a result, NPCs are becoming more intelligent and humanlike. The longer they live, the better they can exhibit the sophistication of their AI.

Sandbox-style FTPS games are beginning to emerge, where the player is given goals to complete, and the game is played in a nonlinear fashion. NPCs tend to live for much longer in a sandbox-style game than in a conventional FTPS game, enabling them to make good use of long-term memory. If a long-term memory were in place, the NPC could remember the details of the environment and the enemies it encounters. This could enable the NPC to learn or to make more informed decisions. NPCs might remember such things as the fighting patterns of human players, the locations of good sniping and cover positions, or the locations of weapon and ammunition stores.

Memory spans could be altered to affect game design. Both the short-term memory and long-term memory stores of individual NPCs or classes of NPCs could be varied to account for different remembering abilities of agents. For example, a team leader might have a larger long-term memory store than a rifleman because a team leader must plan and make informed tactical decisions for his team, and as such, he must know as much about the map and the enemy as possible. On the other hand, if we want to make an inexperienced, rookie NPC (who is prone to making mistakes), we could simply give him a high rate of forgetfulness to simulate the level of panic he would be experiencing on the battlefield. In addition, an NPC's ability to determine the importance of memories could vary. Thus, some NPCs might forget important game information because they have not tagged it as being important, giving NPCs a greater sense of individuality.

Personality

One popular model used to describe personality is known as "The Big Five," which states that personality is comprised of five factors: extraversion, agreeableness, conscientiousness, neuroticism, and openness [Gross01]. Extraversion identifies the degree to which a person is outgoing and sociable. The agreeableness of a person is the degree to which they are friendly and appeasing as opposed to aggressive and domineering. Conscientiousness describes the reliability and orderliness of a person. Neuroticism defines whether a person is more pessimistic or optimistic. Lastly, openness defines how open to new ideas and change a person is.

A simple method of adding personality to NPCs in games that use desirability algorithms to decide on their course of action is to add a bias to the algorithms depending on the NPC's personality. For example, if an NPC is aggressive, you could simply bias its desirability algorithm for its "attack enemy" action. This is a very simple method of giving NPCs a personality element and is not ideal. Instead, "The Big Five" personality traits could be encoded into an NPC's behavior by defining a fuzzy variable for each of the five traits and a set of fuzzy rules that decide how they combine to influence a given NPC's behavior. For example, if an NPC has a very high extraversion level and very low levels of neuroticism and agreeableness, then the agent might like to aggressively explore the map for enemies with little fear of getting hurt. In addition, an agent who has high levels of conscientiousness and agreeableness and a low level of openness might follow an order he is given exactly, whereas an agent with low levels of conscientiousness and agreeableness and a high level of openness might not follow an order at all or decide to change his course of action halfway through fulfilling the order because another opportunity presented itself.

Personality can have a number of very interesting applications to the FTPS genre of games because every behavior of an individual NPC can be affected by its personality. Whether an NPC is passive or aggressive can determine how (and indeed if) it fires its weapon. An aggressive agent would naturally be more trigger-happy, whereas a passive agent would want to confirm that the enemy is actually an enemy and that there is a clear shot before attempting to shoot it. Whether the agent is spontaneous and laid back or reliable and routine-orientated could determine an NPC's patrol patterns or how effectively an NPC follows orders. The list of possibilities for using personality traits to influence NPC behaviors is vast and gives them a uniqueness needed to make them truly humanlike.

Emotions

Emotion is a very subjective experience, and as such, it is difficult to define precisely what an emotion is. Over the years, a number of conflicting theories of emotion have emerged that endeavor to define and categorize emotions and what causes us to experience them. Plutchik proposes an emotional model that defines eight primary emotions. They are arranged in a circle so that adjacent emotions combine to form more complex emotions, and opposites on the circle describe contrary emotions [Plutchik80]. The eight primary emotions identified are joy, acceptance, fear, surprise, sadness, disgust, anger, and anticipation. Adjacent pairs of these can be combined to form more complex emotions, such as optimism (anticipation and joy), love (joy and acceptance), and disappointment (surprise and sadness). Some researchers argue that emotions have behaviors associated with them and cause physiological changes to occur over which we have little control [Gross01]. Emotions such as fear, joy, and anticipation can cause physiological changes, such as alterations in blood pressure and increased heart rate [WauGra01]. Furthermore, the associated behavior might be crying or hiding for fear, smiling or laughing for joy, and restlessness or fidgeting for anticipation.

Most commercial games do not have any infusion of emotions into their agents, which can leave the agents appearing lifeless and thus not humanlike. Although there is no absolute model to say how emotions impact human behavior, its incorporation into games would make NPCs more humanlike [Laird00]. For example, a human player might kill an NPC's teammate; the NPC might initially be sad and shocked at the sight of his teammate's body but then be overwhelmed with anger toward the human player. As a result, it would aggressively seek out and attack the player with less regard for his own health and safety than before. An NPC might also feel fear if it's in unfamiliar and intimidating surroundings. For example, walking down a bombed out street with explosions going off in the distance might cause the NPC to become more afraid (and correspondingly more alert). At the other extreme, joy or happiness could also be expressed by NPCs to make them more humanlike. For example, two guards at the entrance to a military compound could be joking and laughing with one another, not paying full attention to their duties, which could make them easier for the player to dispatch.

In the past, some developers have attempted to add emotions to the NPCs of their games (e.g., *The Sims* [TheSims00], *Fable* [Fable04]), but the behaviors associated with the emotions appear very scripted and unhumanlike. Perhaps, if the personality of the NPC is combined with the emotions it can experience, it may lead to more humanlike behavior. For example, conscientious, pessimistic NPCs might not excite as easily as spontaneous, optimistic NPCs, or passive NPCs might not anger as easily as aggressive NPCs. As well as the influence an NPC's emotions might have on its behaviors, the expression of the NPC's emotions displayed by the animation and sound systems of the game engine would give the NPC a more human feel.

Physiological Stressors

Physiological stressors include any factors (whether real or anticipated) that cause a significant change in the human body to occur [Gould06]. Stressors include such things as muscle fatigue, pain, health levels, anxiety or fear, exposure to cold or hot temperatures, chemicals, and hunger. The physiological changes that occur in the body can often influence human behavior. For example, when we get tired, we tend to be less alert than usual. Or, if we are in a stuffy room, we might have trouble breathing, prompting us to open a window. Physiological stressors could also be applied to the NPCs of FTPS games to give them more humanlike qualities.

Fatigue is a physiological stressor that is already prominent in a number of titles, such as *Pro Evolution Soccer 6* [PES06]. Fatigue negatively impacts the reaction time and error rate of individuals. The more fatigued an NPC is, the slower he would be to react and the more prone he would be to making mistakes, such as missing a ball or misfiring a weapon.

Fear and anxiety are both a physiological stressor and an emotional construct, and as such have been talked about already in the preceding section.

Health is a physiological stressor that some developers have incorporated into their games to affect their characters' behaviors. If an NPC has low health, he should appear wounded, move slower, and actively search for a health pack or medic rather than continuing to engage his enemy.

If an NPC is in a room with a very high temperature, such as a boiler room, he should be perspiring. He may feel drowsy or tired, and his vision may be blurred with the heat coming off the surfaces in the room. Likewise, if an agent is in an extremely cold environment, he should be shivering, making it more difficult to aim and fire his weapon. Furthermore, remaining in hot or cold conditions for long periods of time could lead to death (as was seen in the game *The Thing* [Thing02]).

The handling of chemicals could cause an allergic reaction or burns to NPCs, causing them to scratch the affected area or even reduce their health. This could cause NPCs to go looking for some sort of ointment to relieve the pain or itch. Some types of NPC may be more prone to being affected by chemicals than others, such as those that generally do not wear gloves or are not used to handling chemical substances. In *S.T.A.L.K.E.R.* [Stalker07], players can become affected by radiation poisoning, which in turn causes their health to diminish. To halt the effects of the radiation, players can use med-packs, anti-radiation injections, or drink vodka.

Hunger is another physiological stressor that could be incorporated into FTPS games. Agents could have a hunger level that gradually depletes over time. When NPCs get hungry, it could affect their fatigue and energy levels, causing them to have trouble concentrating and eventually leading to their death. In *S.T.A.L.K.E.R.* [Stalker07], the player must satisfy his hunger by eating food to avoid fainting.

The human player could use these physiological stressors to his advantage against the NPCs. Examples of this might include locking NPCs out in the cold, hiding food that the NPCs may have stored, or turning off the air conditioning. Incorporating physiological stressors into computer games and allowing them to affect NPC behavior could lead to a very immersive gameplaying experience for the player because it gives the NPCs more human abilities and allows the player the freedom to come up with innovative ways of disposing of opponents beyond simply shooting them.

As a final note, it's possible for people to perceive stressors differently, and some people might be better able to cope with certain stressors than others [Gould06]. What might cause one person great excitement might not interest another, for example. Similarly, one individual might have an innate ability to endure pain, whereas another might succumb easily. Thus, physiological stressors have great potential to give NPCs more individuality within FTPS games.

Weapon Proficiency and Skills

Not all humans are trained in the use of firearms, and of those that are, not all are equally competent in using them. Some soldiers are more proficient at using certain types of weapons than others. A marksman, for example, is an expert with a sniper rifle because his hand is steady and his aim precise. Heavy weaponry, such as rail-cannons and rocket-launchers, might be better suited to larger and stronger soldiers. Just as humans have different proficiency levels for handling different types of weapons, so too should the NPCs of FTPS games. Sniper NPCs could have high proficiency in using rifles and sniper rifles but might be less skilful with an AK-47 or a grenade-launcher. Similarly, riflemen may be highly competent in using assault rifles but not very skilled in using sniper rifles.

In addition, there could be different levels of skill based on the NPC's level of experience. Both a rookie sniper and an expert sniper would be specialized in using sniper rifles, but the expert would still be more proficient than the rookie. In a sand-box-style FTPS game, where the NPCs would tend to live longer, you might allow the rookie's weapon proficiency to increase with time and experience.

This idea of NPC proficiency is not limited to weapons. NPCs could also have a proficiency level for using tools, chemicals, and other game objects. For example, engineers might be very proficient in using tools, or scientists might be expert in handling chemicals, but neither might be very good at firing weapons. Drivers could be good at navigating vehicles, whereas commanders might be good at reading maps. Some types of NPCs might even be better at target selection than others when attacking the enemy. For example, snipers tend to take out officers first as it causes confusion and panic among the rest of the soldiers. Likewise, commanders might be able to pick out strategic enemy positions to destroy with a rocket launcher, whereas a rookie might not use the rocket ammunition as effectively. All in all, varying the skills and proficiency levels of NPCs would give them more humanlike qualities and a greater sense of individuality.

Conclusion

Giving NPCs more humanlike qualities and a greater sense of individuality will create more immersive gameplaying experiences that capture and hold the player's attention and interest. In this article, we discussed providing NPCs with realistic human sensing and memory systems, as well as personality and emotions. We discussed the impact that physiological stressors might have on NPCs' behaviors, the different weapon-handling skills of NPCs, and how these factors can all contribute to making the NPCs of FTPS games more individual and humanlike.

Most sensory systems of FTPS games only include tactile, visual, and auditory sensing, and memory-management systems rarely contain a long-term memory element for their NPCs. Emotions, personality, physiological stressors, and weapon-handling skills are rarely handled to any degree in FTPS games, but they have great potential to make NPCs more humanlike and distinctive. Creating these NPCs to be more individual and humanlike will provide a more immersive environment for the player, which is the ultimate goal for any developer.

References

[BFII05] Digital Illusions, "Battlefield 2." Available online at *http://www.ea.com/official/battlefield/battlefield2/us/*.

[EEIIME07] Ear Encyclopedia II, "The Mammalian Ear." Available online at *http://www.experiencefestival.com/a/The_mammalian_ear/id/593677*.

[Fable04] Lionhead Studios, "Fable." Available online at *http://fable.lionhead.com/*.

[GOW07] Epic Games, "Gears of War." Available online at *http://gearsofwar.com/*.

[Gould06] Gould, Barbara E., *Pathophysiology for the Health Professions*. 3rd ed. Saunders, 2006.

[Gross01] Gross, Richard, *Psychology: The Science of Mind and Behaviour*. 4th ed. Hodder and Stoughton, GB, 2001.

[HLife06] Valve Corporation, "Half Life 2." Available online at *http://half-life2.com/*.

[Laird00] Laird, John, et al., "Design Goals for Autonomous Synthetic Characters." Available online at *http://ai.eecs.umich.edu/people/laird/papers/AAAI-SS00.pdf*.

[MalBir98] Malim, Tony, and Birch, Ann, *Introductory Psychology*. Palgrave Ltd., 1998.

[Menshikov03] Menshikov, Aleksei, "Modern Audio Technologies in Games." Available online at *http://www.digit-life.com/articles2/sound-technology/index.html*.

[MGS305] Konami Computer Entertainment Japan, "Metal Gear Solid 3: Snake Eater." Available online at *http://www.konami.jp/gs/game/mgs3/english/index.html*.

[PES06] Konami, "PES 6." Available online at *http://uk.games.konami-europe.com/game.do?idGame=118*.

[Plutchik80] Plutchik, R., *Emotion: A Psychobioevolutionary Synthesis*. Harper & Row.

[SpltrCell07] Ubisoft, "Tom Clancy's Splinter Cell." Available online at *http://splintercell.uk.ubi.com/*.

[Stalker07] GSC GameWorld, "S.T.A.L.K.E.R." Available online at *http://www.stalker-game.com/*.

[TheSims00] Maxis, "The Sims." Available online at *http://thesims.ea.com/*.

[Thing02] Computer Artworks, "The Thing." Available online at *http://www.thethinggames.com/*.

[Tozour02] Tozour, Paul, "First Person Shooter AI Architecture." *AI Game Programming Wisdom*, Charles River Media, 2002.

[WauGra01] Waugh, Anne, and Grant, Allison, *Anatomy and Physiology in Health and Illness*. Churchill Livingstone, London, 2001.

5.7

Stop Getting Side-Tracked by Side-Quests

University of Alberta

Curtis Onuczko

onuczko@cs.ualberta.ca

Duane Szafron

duane@cs.ualberta.ca

Jonathan Schaeffer

jonathan@cs.ualberta.ca

Computer role-playing games (CRPGs) are story-driven games in which the player character (PC) is the protagonist in an interactive story. Most CRPGs contain a complex main storyline and a series of smaller optional independent stories called side-quests. *Side-quests* serve four principal purposes:

- Create an open-world feeling because they provide the PC with choices about how to independently explore the world, rather than just following a predetermined storyline.
- Provide opportunities for the PC to gain rewards and experience in a variety of different ways, instead of simply performing monotonous predictable tasks, such as repeatedly fighting hostile nonplayer characters (NPCs). Without a believable mechanism to gain rewards and experience, the PC's capabilities would vary through such a narrow range during the story that it would be difficult to create an appropriate story arc (rising tension) through escalating challenges.
- Add optional texture to a story without complicating the main storyline. For example, you can use optional side-quests to allow the player to discover/create aspects of a back-story, to develop the personality of the PC and NPCs, and to provide motivation and optional clues for pursuing the main storyline.

- Reward exploration with interesting content, such as custom locations, novel creatures, and unusual game objects.

Increasing the number of high-quality side-quests in a game will result in a richer player experience, but it also increases the amount of content that must be created. Side-quests are a useful complement for the game, but they should not detract from the time and resources invested to create the main story. How do you find time to create entertaining side-quests, without adversely affecting the main story?

This article describes a Side-QUEst GEnerator tool (SQUEGE) that reduces the time and effort required to add side-quests to a game story. SQUEGE generates a rich diversity of side-quests for you to choose from, each guaranteed to have at least one path that is playable to completion. It provides a detailed outline for each side-quest, which you fill out by writing the character dialog and the scripts that control each side-quest. Alternatively, a game-dependent script generator can be constructed to automatically translate outlines to game scripts without the need for programmer support. For example, we are currently connecting SQUEGE to ScriptEase [McNaughton04] so that scripts can be automatically generated for BioWare's *Neverwinter Nights*.

Patterns for Side-Quests

A side-quest is a small adventure that is independent from the main story. A side-quest is often short, simple, and optional. However, you can combine several side-quests into a themed mini-story.

Consider the following example. The PC wants to obtain a map from an old man. The old man asks the PC to slay a dragon that has been terrorizing the surrounding area in exchange for the map. The PC travels to the dragon's lair, kills the beast, and then reports back to the old man that the dragon is dead. For successfully accomplishing this quest, the old man relinquishes the map, and the PC is awarded 500 experience points (XP).

Many side-quests share similarities. For example, here is a second side-quest. As the final step in the process of becoming a knight, the queen commands the PC to evict an evil black knight from her kingdom. The PC travels to the black knight, and the confrontation turns into a battle. The PC kills the black knight, and reports his death to the queen. The queen rewards the PC by granting knighthood and awarding 1000 XP.

Both quests involve the same set of actions: Obtain the quest from the quest giver, travel to the antagonist, kill the antagonist, and report back to the quest giver to receive a reward. Note that the player might think that there are different quest-resolution actions available in the second side-quest. The player is only instructed to convince the black knight to leave the area, not to kill him. The black knight's dialog tree might be constructed so that he refuses to leave, however, forcing the player to fight him. Thus two quests that appear different to the player can be different flavors of the same quest "pattern." There is variety in the presentation, while the underlying structure is the same.

By recognizing these structural similarities, we have abstracted quests into common groups that we call patterns. This process is similar to using design patterns in software engineering [Gamma95]. Selecting a pattern and then adapting it to the specifics of your game can create a side-quest. For example, our two quest examples are instances of a quest pattern called *assassinate antagonist*. This pattern has a structure consisting of three stages: *talk to quest giver, kill antagonist,* and *report antagonist dead.*

ON THE CD

The CD-ROM provides code for eight quest patterns. These patterns do not generate all imaginable side-quests, but they show how a small set of simple patterns can effectively generate a large number of different quests. The eight patterns are as follows:

Talk chain: The PC talks with a chain of one or more NPCs. If the last NPC dies, then the quest fails. This pattern can create chains of arbitrary length.

Acquire item: The PC finds the location of an item and then acquires the item.

Deliver item: The PC acquires an item and then delivers the item to an NPC.

Kill antagonist: The PC finds the location of an NPC and then kills the NPC.

Assassinate antagonist: The PC kills an NPC and then reports the assassination to another NPC.

One of many tasks: The PC is presented with several tasks and must complete one of them. The tasks are generated using one or more of the other patterns. The implementation on the CD-ROM supports only two tasks, but this pattern can be easily adapted to support an arbitrary number.

All of many tasks: This pattern is similar to the *one of many tasks* quest, except that the PC must complete all of the tasks specified. After all the tasks are completed, the PC must report to an NPC to finish the quest. Again, the version on the CD supports only two tasks.

Chain quest: The PC completes a chain of quests, one after another. This pattern creates quest chains of arbitrary length.

The last three quests are actually meta-quests that can be used to combine simple quests into more complex adventures.

Other patterns can be added to the pattern catalog. For example, *escort NPC, locate object, defend NPC,* and *defend location* quests could be added. Sometimes, what appears to be a new pattern can be treated as an existing pattern or a combination of existing patterns. For example, a *discover a secret* quest can be expressed as an instance of *one of many tasks*, where there are two tasks: *acquire item* (a book) or *talk chain* (where an NPC reveals the secret). Similarly, an *assemble an item* quest can be expressed as an instance of an *all of many tasks*, where there are several *acquire item* tasks. Although these quests can be constructed from existing quests, it is useful to include them so their intent is clear. Adding patterns to SQUEGE is discussed later.

To manually create a simple side-quest instance (without SQUEGE), you can select a pattern, create an instance of it, and then adapt the instance by selecting options by hand. To create an *assassinate antagonist* side-quest, for example, you first select the pattern to create an instance of it. Next, adapt it by setting its options: a node in a conversation tree where the PC receives the quest from the quest giver, the antagonist to kill, a conversation node where the PC reports success, and the rewards that are given to the PC. Although SQUEGE automates this process by selecting pattern instances and options for you, the concept of a quest pattern is independent of this tool, and options and other adaptations can be done manually.

More radical adaptations to a quest instance, beyond just setting its options, are available. You can add or remove quest points (the stages of a quest), change the nature of a quest point, and even insert a whole pattern in place of a quest point to create a subquest inside of a quest. As an example, you could add a new quest point called *acquire magic sword* before the *kill antagonist* quest point in the *assassinate antagonist* quest pattern instance for the dragon side-quest. We will explain these adaptations in more detail later.

Using SQUEGE

Figure 5.7.1 gives a summary of the side-quest generation process. First SQUEGE uses its pattern catalog and the lists of NPCs, items, and containers to generate an outline of a side-quest instance. You can also supply other settings as input to SQUEGE (e.g., the number of side-quests to generate). After accepting an outline, you can adapt it, add story content by placing items and writing dialog, and finally give the outline to a programmer or generative script system to create the required scripts to control the side-quest. There is a random element to how SQUEGE selects which pattern a side-quest will be generated from and which game objects are associated with it. If the process is repeated, you will obtain a different side-quest, likely using a different pattern and different NPCs, containers, and items in the same setting.

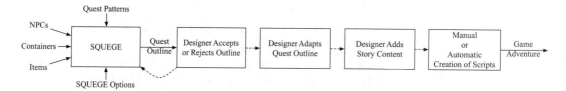

FIGURE 5.7.1   The process SQUEGE uses for generating side-quests.

Here is a simple example of how to use SQUEGE to generate the outline for one simple side-quest. Later we'll show how SQUEGE can be used to generate multiple side-quests of arbitrary complexity within the same CRPG story.

First, you create a setting for the game story. For example, you might use a city setting with several buildings that the PC can enter. Next, populate the setting by creating game objects in three categories: NPCs, containers (that can hold items), and items (that can be stored and carried). Note that each game object must have a label that can be used to uniquely identify it. Place the NPCs and containers at various locations inside and outside the buildings, but do not place the items yet. Their locations will be determined later through the side-quest generation process.

ON THE CD

The version of SQUEGE that is provided with the CD-ROM is independent of any specific CRPG. As a result, you will need to provide SQUEGE with lists of the labels of all the NPCs, containers, and items that can be used in the generated side-quests. Any game object that you do not want to be used in a side-quest should not be included in these lists. For example, if an NPC is important to the main story, you might not want that NPC to be the antagonist in an *assassinate antagonist* side-quest. However, excluding this NPC from the lists prevents SQUEGE from using the NPC in any other side-quest role. This might make the side-quests feel too independent from the main story. Therefore, you might want to exercise finer control by including at least some of the story NPCs in SQUEGE's lists. If necessary, some story NPCs in the generated side-quests can be replaced by other NPCs on those occasions where the generated roles are contrary to your main story.

This version of SQUEGE has only three different types of game objects listed: NPCs, containers, and items. Other types of game objects can be created to use in the patterns. For example, the NPC list could be split into protagonist and antagonist lists. This allows specific NPCs to be specified as protagonists and antagonists so that in the *assassinate antagonist* quest, only antagonist NPCs are selected to be assassinated, and protagonist NPCs are selected to give the quest. Furthermore, instead of providing separate lists of objects, each object provided as input can be given a set of tags. In the previous example, only objects with an antagonist tag are selected as antagonists.

SQUEGE also requires a catalog of the quest patterns to be used in your story. For each side-quest to be generated, SQUEGE selects a quest pattern from its catalog at random. The various options of the quest pattern are then instantiated from the lists of objects provided. SQUEGE does not create game objects; it only selects them from its lists. However, if you want to simulate the creation of game objects, fictitious labels can be included in the object lists (e.g., NPC-1, NPC-2, ... NPC-N). SQUEGE may generate side-quests that include some of these labels.

SQUEGE produces a graphical outline for each side-quest that it generates. This outline contains all the information needed to implement the side-quest. Four tasks must be performed to implement a side-quest. First, place any item referenced in the outline in an appropriate location. For example, the outline might require that a specific item be placed in a specific container so that the PC can retrieve it. Second, write any dialog that is necessary for the side-quest, including motivation and, optionally, any connection to the main storyline. For example, the outline might specify that the PC must talk to a quest giver to obtain the quest. If a conversation for the quest giver has already been written, then an additional conversation node must be added to enable the quest giver to assign the quest. Otherwise, an entire conversation for the quest giver must be written, including the conversation node that assigns the quest. Third, provide additional actions that will occur in response to the PC reaching specific points in the quest. For example, in the *assassinate antagonist* quest, when the PC reports the antagonist's death, some additional actions might make the quest giver jump up and down in jubilation over the antagonist's death. Fourth, write the game-dependent scripts necessary to control the quest points in the quest.

The placement of the items and creation of the conversations use game-specific tools. Although a game-dependent version of SQUEGE could place the items, you must also use the outline to write the scripts. Fortunately, the outline is specific enough that all of the information necessary to convey the structure of the side-quest is contained in it. The controlled and limited vocabulary of the outlines should prevent errors resulting from a difference between the intent of the quest structure and the programmer's implementation of the scripts. Naturally, outlines cannot prevent programming blunders that are unrelated to structural intent. Ideally, a visual scripting system, such as that found in McNaughton et al. ([McNaughton06]), would be implemented to work with SQUEGE to allow any changes made to the side-quest outline to be immediately realized in the scripts.

Figure 5.7.2 shows a graphical outline generated by SQUEGE. This *deliver an item* side-quest instance has three main actions for the PC to perform. First, the side-quest is started when the PC reaches a conversation node while talking to Robbie. Second, the PC locates and acquires the Magic Boots. Third, the PC gives the Magic Boots to Sifton to complete the quest. However, locating and acquiring the Magic Boots is a subquest, where the PC talks to a chain of NPCs to discover the location of the boots and then acquires them by removing them from Alana's Armoire. In fact, talking to a chain of NPCs is another subquest, but for brevity, it is collapsed in Figure 5.7.2 to hide its details. In addition, talking to the chain of NPCs is optional, so the PC could just discover the location of the Magic Boots by accident.

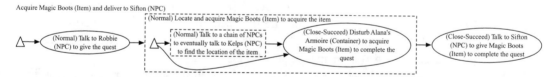

FIGURE 5.7.2   The outline for a *deliver an item* side-quest generated by SQUEGE.

You can decide whether to use the side-quest as generated by SQUEGE, to adapt it manually, or to reject it and generate a new one. There are many reasons for manually adapting or rejecting side-quests. First, the side-quest might have an adverse affect on a game object that is critical to the main story (as described earlier). Second, there might be too many similar side-quests already in the story. A particular game object might appear repeatedly in the side-quests so that the story becomes too interconnected or too repetitious, for example. Third, a set of side-quests might take the PC to an area too often or never take the PC to an important area.

Another common reason for adapting or rejecting a side-quest is that it is either too simple or too complex. For example, the side-quest in Figure 5.7.2 is hierarchical with two levels of subquests in the main quest. This might not be the required level of complexity for your needs. Fortunately, SQUEGE has some internal parameters that can be adjusted to increase or decrease the complexity of the side-quests by specifying the probability that a quest point will become a subquest. These parameters can be adjusted to control the complexity of the side-quests generated.

Because SQUEGE does not automatically implement its side-quests in your game, you retain complete freedom to adapt them as needed or to generate a multitude of options and reject the ones you don't like. For example, you might want to adapt the side-quest in Figure 5.7.2 to allow the PC to choose to keep the Magic Boots instead of delivering them to Sifton. The side-quest could be adapted to support this by adding an alternate ending in which the PC returns to Robbie and lies, telling him that the boots could not be found. This adaptation is simple because it only requires one more quest point to be added to the outline. The new point must be connected to the *locate and acquire* subquest to show that lying about the boots follows locating and acquiring them. This change can be made at a high level, rather than thinking about it at the level of individual scripts. You can also adjust SQUEGE's output by editing the game object lists to prevent certain objects from being selected in future side-quests or simply to increase the chances that the remaining game objects will be selected.

Quest Patterns and Instance Details

A quest pattern represents a commonly occurring story scenario at a high level, focusing on the actions that the PC can take to directly affect the quest. It abstracts the low-level details, such as how the quest is scripted, so that you do not have to be concerned about them. To use a quest pattern, simply create an instance of it and then adapt that instance to suit your story. The simplest form of adaptation is setting the options for the quest pattern instance.

A fully adapted quest pattern instance should completely determine which actions are available to the PC at any point in the quest. By looking at an instance, you should be able to understand its structure and all of the ways that the quest might unfold in your story. A programmer can examine a quest instance and clearly understand what scripts are needed to control it. We now provide a structure for quest patterns that satisfies these properties.

Each quest pattern consists of a set of quest points. A quest point corresponds to an important encounter that the PC experiences during the quest (a stage in the quest's mini-story). The *assassinate antagonist* quest described earlier has three quest points: *talk to quest giver*, *kill antagonist*, and *report antagonist dead*. Each quest point can be in one of three states: *disabled*, *enabled*, or *reached*.

At the beginning of the *assassinate antagonist* quest the PC is told about the antagonist by the quest giver. Although this pattern only specifies a single quest giver, the pattern can be adapted so that there are multiple quest givers. The *talk to quest giver* point is enabled, whereas the other points are disabled. When the PC actually talks to the quest giver, the point changes from enabled to reached. Reaching a point can cause other points to become enabled or disabled. In this example, when the *talk to quest giver* point is reached, the *kill antagonist* point becomes enabled. When the PC kills the antagonist, this quest point becomes reached, and the final quest point, *report antagonist dead*, is enabled. This is an example of a linear quest. Not all quests are linear. We give an example of a branching (nonlinear) quest later.

Contents of Quest Points

Each quest point includes a label, a type, a list of quest point *enablers,* and a list of possible encounters (actions). When any of the quest point *enablers* is reached, that quest point becomes enabled. You can also use the enablers list to specify that a quest point is enabled at the start of the quest. As soon as one of the encounters for a quest point has occurred, and the quest point becomes enabled, the quest point changes its state to reached.

These two conditions can happen in either order. Normally, a quest point is enabled before its encounter occurs. For example, the PC would first speak with the quest giver to reach the *talk to quest giver* point, which would enable the *kill antagonist* point. Then the PC would have an encounter that kills the antagonist. At this point, the *kill antagonist* quest point would be reached. However, the conditions can also happen in the reverse order. The PC can stumble upon the antagonist and kill it in an encounter. Because the *kill antagonist* quest point is not enabled, it does not immediately become reached. Later, when the PC speaks with the quest giver to reach the *talk to quest giver* point, this causes the *kill antagonist* point to be enabled. Because the encounter has already occurred, this quest point is immediately reached. This is the desired semantics in most CRPGs (*Neverwinter Nights, Oblivion, Fable, Star Wars: Knights of the Old Republic,* etc.). In essence, if the encounters for the quest have already occurred, the author would like to credit the PC for the quest as soon as the quest is assigned. To support this common practice, the SQUEGE model and outlines differentiate between the encounter occurring and the quest point being reached. State is maintained at the quest point to record whether it is enabled or reached, independent of the occurrence of the encounter.

When SQUEGE creates a quest instance from a pattern, it uses one of the possible encounters listed for a quest point as its only encounter. This allows encounters to differ between quests. For example, when acquiring an item in a quest, the item might be acquired through a conversation with an NPC or by removing it from a container. The specifics behind how the encounter is selected are discussed later.

Types of Quest Points

The three different types of quest points are *normal, optional,* and *close.*

When a PC reaches a *normal* quest point, all points in the quest become disabled except for those that have this point in their enablers list. This means that if there are two quest branches and each contains normal quest points, then as soon as one of these points is reached on either branch, the PC cannot progress on the other branch. For example, consider a quest that can be accomplished either by killing an antagonist or by sneaking past the antagonist. Assume each of these is represented by a normal quest point, *kill antagonist* and *sneak past antagonist,* respectively, and that both are enabled when a *talk to quest giver* point is reached. We have a branching quest. If the PC sneaks past the antagonist, then the *sneak past antagonist* quest point will be reached (it is already enabled). If specified, a journal entry will be displayed indicating that the PC has sneaked past the antagonist. The *kill antagonist* quest point will be disabled because it is now irrelevant. This does not prevent the PC from going back and killing the antagonist. However, this encounter will no longer cause the *kill antagonist* quest point to be reached because it is now disabled. No journal entry will appear, which is appropriate because the PC has already advanced this quest on another branch.

An *optional* quest point is a point that does not need to be reached during a quest. Previously enabled quest points are not eliminated when an optional point is reached. Optional quest points provide a way for the PC to proceed on two different quest branches simultaneously. For example, an instance of the *assassinate antagonist* (dragon) quest discussed at the beginning of this article could be adapted by adding two branches that each contain an optional quest point to help give the PC an edge in fighting the dragon. The first, *acquire sword*, might involve acquiring an enchanted sword from a nearby sorcerer, whereas the second, *acquire potion*, might involve acquiring a potion of strength from an alchemist. The player would have the option of doing one, both, or neither of these quest points before killing the dragon, depending on how easy the player thinks the dragon will be to defeat.

A *close* quest point completes a quest. When a close point is reached, all points for the quest become disabled and no new points can become enabled. If the game journal is segregated into active and completed quests, the journal entry or entries for that quest are moved to the completed section when the quest is closed. Note that there are actually two flavors of the close point: *close-succeed* and *close-fail.* You use a close-fail quest point to indicate that the quest has failed. For example, in a *talk chain*, if one of the NPCs dies, a close-fail point is reached. The distinction between close-succeed and close-fail is particularly important in subquests (discussed later).

Quest Graphs

Quest patterns and instances of quest patterns can be represented as graphs, giving a visualization of the quest. Each quest point has a corresponding graph node that is labeled with a description. Appearing in parentheses at the beginning of the description is the type of quest point (normal, optional, close-succeed, or close-fail). Each graph has a starting point (represented as a triangle) that serves to describe which quest points are initially enabled. Arcs connect related points where the quest point at the head of the arc is enabled when the quest point at the tail is reached.

Quest pattern graphs are a high-level visualization of the quest. They do not display the journal entries, experience awarded, conversations, and additional actions associated with each quest point. The quest point labels are often enough information to remind the author what extra information occurs at each point. Figure 5.7.3 shows the graph for the *assassinate antagonist* quest where the player is asked to kill a dragon.

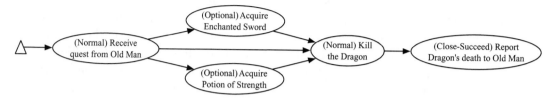

FIGURE 5.7.3   Graph of the example quest where the PC kills a dragon.

Side-Quest Generation

With quest patterns, generating a quest is simple. Each quest pattern describes a different type of quest. Producing a new side-quest can be done by simply specifying the NPCs and/or objects that interact with the PC. For example, you might have a quest pattern where the PC acquires an item from a container. Selecting the item acquired (Magic Boots) and the container (Alana's Armoire) fully specifies the quest instance.

ON THE CD

When generating a side-quest instance, SQUEGE first randomly selects a pattern from its catalog of quest patterns. The implementation of SQUEGE on the CD-ROM comes with an initial catalog of eight patterns. For example, SQUEGE might choose a *deliver an item* quest pattern. This pattern contains three quest points: *talk to a quest giver*, *acquire item*, and *deliver item*. Figure 5.7.4 shows the outline for this quest pattern.

FIGURE 5.7.4   The outline for the *deliver an item* quest pattern used by SQUEGE.

Next, SQUEGE selects encounters. Each quest point in the pattern includes a set of possible encounters. Each encounter has a weight associated with it. SQUEGE selects one of the encounters based on their weights. An encounter with a higher weight has a greater chance of being selected. The encounter SQUEGE selects becomes associated with its quest point in the quest instance. For example, the *acquire item* quest point in Figure 5.7.4 has two possible encounters: *talk to an NPC to acquire an item* and *remove an item from a container*. Both of these encounters have a weight of one, meaning that they are equally likely to be selected. If the first encounter had a weight of two, and the second encounter had a weight of one, then the first encounter would be twice as likely to be selected over the second. In this example, SQUEGE selects the *talk to an NPC to acquire an item* encounter to be used in the quest instance.

Finally, each encounter has a number of options associated with it. The *talk to an NPC to acquire an item* encounter has two options: an NPC and an item. SQUEGE selects both options from the lists of NPCs and items provided as input. After all of the options for each encounter are specified, the side-quest instance is generated. SQUEGE outputs an outline for the side-quest in graph form.

Subquest Generation

Figure 5.7.2 showed a side-quest where one of the encounters is a subquest to locate and acquire a pair of Magic Boots. This subquest contains a quest point that is really another subquest where the PC talks to a chain of NPCs to discover the item's location. SQUEGE facilitates the generation of subquests by allowing them to appear in the list of possible encounters associated with each quest point. When SQUEGE selects an encounter that represents a subquest, a new quest instance is generated and inserted as the encounter. SQUEGE then recursively generates the contents for this instance. By modifying the weights of the encounter random variables, you can determine how often subquests are generated relative to normal encounters.

Two types of subquests can be listed as possible encounters. The first type is a normal quest, which implies that the PC is beginning a new mini-story. All journal entries for the subquest will appear under a new heading in the PC's journal, and the PC is made aware of the subquest.

You don't always want the PC to begin a new mini-story. Sometimes a subquest should behave as an extra set of encounters within the original quest. This type of subquest is called a quasi-quest, and it allows the PC to proceed along a subquest without the player recognizing it as a subquest. The quest and all of its quasi-quests share the same quest heading for their journal entries.

Using subquests allows arbitrarily complex side-quests to be generated. The *deliver an item* pattern shown in Figure 5.7.4 has an *acquire item* quest point. This quest point can use an *acquire item* quasi-quest as its encounter. The *acquire item* quest pattern has two encounters, *talk to discover item location* and *acquire item*. Figure 5.7.5 shows the quest outline of the *deliver an item* pattern that contains an *acquire item* quasi-quest. The quasi-quest is displayed as a rectangle with a dashed line. If this subquest were a normal quest, then the rectangle would be displayed with a solid line.

The difference between close-succeed and close-fail is important for subquests. If a subquest ends in a close-succeed, then it enables its next quest point. However, if a subquest ends in a close-fail, then the next quest point in its enclosing quest is not enabled.

FIGURE 5.7.5   *Deliver an item* outline that contains an *acquire item* quasi-quest.

Specifying Patterns in SQUEGE

ON THE CD

Designing patterns is a one-time investment. The contents of a library of patterns can be used and reused many times within the current game or across multiple games. Thus, time should be invested in pattern design to ensure that the patterns have desirable properties (e.g., generally useful, not too specific, not too general, etc.). The CD-ROM provides eight patterns that are useful across many CPRG games to get you started, as described earlier in the article. Expect to add and delete patterns, based on your experience and the genre of your game.

To create new patterns for SQUEGE, you need to specify the quest points and possible encounters for each quest point. A new quest pattern specification can be easily created by starting off with a copy of an existing pattern specification and then extending/adapting it as needed.

The patterns on the CD-ROM are designed to show how quests can be generated without making the description of SQUEGE complicated. However, more complexity can be added to the patterns so that the generated side-quests become more intricate. Current patterns only use three encounters for talking to an NPC: *talk to an NPC, talk to an NPC to acquire an item*, and *talk to an NPC to give an item*. New encounters that add requirements to reach a quest point can be created. For example, the *persuade NPC* encounter can be added, in which a persuade skill check that is higher than a threshold is required. Similarly, three new encounters can be added for acquiring an item from an NPC: *persuade NPC acquire item* (requires a persuasion skill check), *steal item from NPC* (requires a pickpocket skill check), and *kill NPC take item*.

As an example of how quest patterns are specified, here is the entry for the *deliver an item* quest pattern in SQUEGE's pattern catalog. It has been edited for brevity.

```
QUEST_PATTERN:
  NAME: Deliver item
  OPTIONS: <QuestGiver>, <Item>, <ItemOwner>
  DESCRIPTION: Deliver <Item> to <ItemOwner>
  QUEST_POINTS:
    QUEST_POINT:
      LABEL: GiveQuest
      TYPE: Normal
      DESCRIPTION: to give the quest
      ENABLERS: initially_enabled
      POSSIBLE_ENCOUNTERS:
        ENCOUNTER:
          WEIGHT: 1
          NAME: Talk to
          OPTIONS: <QuestGiver>
        NOTHING:
          WEIGHT: 1
    QUEST_POINT:
      LABEL: AcquireItem
      TYPE: Normal
      DESCRIPTION: to acquire the item
      ENABLERS: GiveQuest
```

```
        POSSIBLE_ENCOUNTERS:
          QUASI_QUEST:
            WEIGHT: 1
            NAME: Acquire item
            OPTIONS: <_>, <Item>
    QUEST_POINT:
      LABEL: DeliverItem
      TYPE: Close
      DESCRIPTION: to complete the quest
      ENABLERS: AcquireItem
      POSSIBLE_ENCOUNTERS:
        ENCOUNTER:
          WEIGHT: 1
          NAME: Talk to NPC to give item
          OPTIONS: <ItemOwner>, <Item>
```

This quest pattern specification has three options: the NPC that the PC converses with to begin the quest, the item that the NPC must acquire and deliver, and the NPC that the PC must deliver the item to. These three options are referenced in the pattern specification using the variable names <QuestGiver>, <Item>, and <ItemOwner>, respectively. Quest options allow quest points to share the same values for their encounter option variables. For example, the AcquireItem and DeliverItem quest points both use the <Item> quest option. This ensures that the corresponding encounter option variables for these two quest points are set to the same value. When generating a side-quest, SQUEGE will not select the same option twice unless it has been specified using quest options.

In the preceding pattern specification, the GiveQuest quest point has two possible encounters. The first encounter is for the PC to talk to the quest giver NPC (as referenced by the <QuestGiver> option). The second encounter is a special construct with the heading NOTHING. If SQUEGE selects this encounter, the quest point will not exist in the generated quest instance. This allows the PC to initially acquire the item and deliver it without ever having to talk to a quest giver. The AcquireItem quest point uses the *acquire item* quasi-quest as its only possible encounter. This quasi-quest takes two options: the NPC the item is acquired from and the item itself. The former is specified using <_>, meaning that a new creature object, which is different from the other creature objects specified in the pattern, should be used for this option. The DeliverItem quest point has one possible encounter where the PC must talk to the item owner to give the item. Both the item owner and item are specified using the quest options <ItemOwner> and <Item>, respectively.

Changing the pattern specification causes SQUEGE to generate different side-quest instances. For example, you might remove the <ItemOwner> option from the pattern. In the final quest point, you would use the <QuestGiver> instead of the <ItemOwner> option. This would result in the item being delivered to the same NPC that gives the PC the side-quest. Other adaptations, such as adding a new quest point or changing the weights of the possible encounters, can be easily made as well.

SQUEGE Implementation

ON THE CD

The implementation of SQUEGE included on the CD-ROM uses a Prolog program to generate side-quests. Default input files for SQUEGE are provided on the CD-ROM. You can change any of the input files, adding your own patterns, for example, as you see fit.

SQUEGE outputs quest outlines in an XML file format. An external Quest Viewer program (included on the CD-ROM) is used to render the XML output as a graph (e.g., refer to Figure 5.7.2). It allows you to view the side-quest graphs, rearrange the visual layout of the side-quests, and produce an image file of the side-quests.

Conclusion

In this article, we presented SQUEGE, a tool that uses commonly occurring story scenarios (quest patterns) to generate side-quest outlines. You must write the character dialog and scripts that control each side-quest. However, writing good dialog is something that most game developers enjoy and do very well. SQUEGE's side-quest outlines are detailed enough that a programmer can quickly produce the scripts needed, or a game-dependent script generator can be built to automate this process. The emphasis in this approach is on allowing the game author to have the final say as to what is included in the game. This ensures that the side-quests are of the same high quality that you would normally create. The difference is that the side-quests take less time and effort to produce.

A trial was conducted to determine if SQUEGE could save an author's time and generate high-quality side-quests. A detailed description of this trial is beyond the scope of this article (see [Onuczko07]). Briefly, three side-quests were removed from a *Neverwinter Nights* community story and replaced by three SQUEGE-generated side-quests, using the NPCs, containers, and items in the original story. An author read the SQUEGE outlines, added the conversations manually, and used a prototype version of ScriptEase to add the quest patterns to the story module. The quest-controlling scripts were then generated by ScriptEase. The time required was much less than the time required to write the scripts manually. The side-quests in the original story and the side-quests generated by SQUEGE were then demonstrated to a group of university students. Students evaluated the original side-quests and SQUEGE side-quests without knowing which were computer generated. The results showed an interleaving of the ratings of the side-quests in this order: original, SQUEGE, original, SQUEGE, SQUEGE, and original. This provides preliminary evidence that SQUEGE is capable of producing quality side-quests. This trial showed that SQUEGE saves time when used in conjunction with a script generator and that it generates quality side-quests. If you use SQUEGE, we are very interested in receiving feedback.

References

[Gamma95] Gamma, Erich, et al., *Design Patterns: Elements of Reusable Object-Orientated Software*. Addison Wesley Professional, 1995.

[McNaughton04] McNaughton, Matthew, et al., "ScriptEase: Generative Design Patterns for Computer Role-Playing Games." *Proceedings of 19th IEEE International Conference on Automated Software Engineering (ASE)*, (September 2004): pp. 88–99.

[McNaughton06] McNaughton, Matthew, and Roy, Thomas, "Creating a Visual Scripting System." *AI Game Programming Wisdom 3*, Charles River Media, 2006: pp. 567–581.

[Onuczko07] Onuczko, Curtis, *Quest Patterns in Computer Role-Playing Games*. M.Sc. Thesis, University of Alberta, 2007.

6

SCRIPTING AND DIALOGUE

6.1

Spoken Dialogue Systems

University of Sheffield

Hugo Pinto

hugo@hugopinto.net

Roberta Catizone

R.Catizone@dcs.shef.ac.uk

Since the 1970s, game developers have pursued the goal of allowing the user to interact and communicate with the game using natural language. From *Adventure* [Montfort03] to *Neverwinter Nights* [Infogrames02], language interaction has often been present, even if discreetly.

Spoken language provides one of the most natural ways to interact with a character. Voice recognition programs, such as Voice Buddy, Microsoft Sidewinder, and VR Commander, try to address part of the issue by providing ways for the player to issue simple commands to the game. However, for more complex interactions, full dialogue processing is necessary. In an adventure game setting, the character might need to ask the player to clarify his request, and then interpret the player's explanation according to the dialogue history. The adventure game *Lifeline* [Sony04] is an example of a game that tried to deliver such capability while providing a full speech-based interface. Non-player characters (NPCs) in RPGs, adventures, and social simulation games are obvious examples of applications that could benefit from state of the art speech-based dialogue systems.

Unfortunately, despite the huge progress in graphics and general game AI, spoken dialogue technology has not kept the same pace in games. However, academia, telecommunications, and transport industries have been pursuing research in the field aggressively in the past 15 years and offer interesting insights and suggestions for game development. Among the applications already delivered are speech-controlled cars, houses, and personal information management assistants. There are helpdesk systems that engage in complex dialogue with the user and even a couple of less-known games.

This article provides an overview of modern spoken dialogue systems. We start by presenting the issues of voice recognition, language processing, dialogue management, language generation, and speech synthesis. Next, we analyze two robust speech-based interactive systems, examining how they solved each of the issues involved in spoken dialogue. Finally, we examine the particulars of the game domain and provide suggestions on how to approach them, with illustrations from the presented systems.

Spoken Dialogue Concepts and Particularities

Before embarking on the analysis of speech-based dialogue systems, let's clarify some terms. What exactly do we mean by dialogue? How do our conceptualizations of dialogue impact the engineering of the dialogue system? What are the particular characteristics of spoken dialogue language?

There are three main views of dialogue, each complementary to the other: dialogue as discourse, dialogue as purposeful activity, and dialogue as collaborative activity [McTear04].

When we view dialogue as discourse, we focus on how words, phrases, and utterances are interpreted considering a related group of sentences. Usually, a discourse is segmented into different contexts, each of which usually has a topic and salient entities. A dialogue participant needs to be able to interpret each discourse element in relation to the current context and know how the entities are related across contexts.

When we approach dialogue as purposeful activity, we will be mostly interested in why a dialogue participant said something in a certain way. That is, our focus will be on the effects of the utterances in a certain context, which might go beyond the meanings of the words used. Consider the meaning of "I am hungry." We could envision at least four functions for this utterance:

- A neutral statement about your inner body status, as in response to a physician's question
- A confirmation that you want food, after a food offer
- A request for money or help, coming from a beggar
- A demand for food, from a two-year-old to his dad

This view of an utterance as an action is the basis of the idea of speech acts, further explained in the "Dialogue Management" section later in this article.

A dialogue involves at least two participants, and they are expected to collaborate at least to let each other have a turn at speaking (turn-taking) and to confirm that what they said has been understood (called *grounding* in dialogue systems terms). These two issues form the skeleton of the view of dialogue as a collaborative activity.

We should mention some properties of spoken dialogue. The utterances in spoken dialogue are usually simpler than in written language, and spoken dialogue is filled with disfluencies. *Disfluencies* include false starts as in, "Do do do you wanna dance?"; hesitation markers such as "uh," "oh," and "err"; and fillers such as "[…]you know. . . ." Silence is not just the absence of speech; it may act as a communicative act itself or indicate some problem.

The next section presents the standard components of spoken dialogue systems and illustrates the concepts of this section.

Standard Components of Speech-Based Dialogue Systems

Five components form the core of most spoken language dialogue systems: speech recognizer, language understanding module, dialogue manager (DM), language generator, and text-to-speech module. The speech recognizer is responsible for transforming sequences of sounds into words and expressions. The language understanding module is responsible for interpreting a sequence of words into a definite meaning. The DM decides what to say at each time step based on what the user said, the system's goals, and the dialogue history. The language generator transforms a decision from the manager into an actual phrase or sequence of phrases. Finally, the text-to-speech module converts the phrases of the generator into an appropriate sequence of sounds.

Speech Recognition

Recognizing a word from a sequence of sound units (phonemes) is a daunting task. The recognizer must be able to choose between different words that sound almost the same, such as "right," "write," and "rite" or the pair "mist" and "missed." The recognizer must also recognize different sequences of sounds that represent the same word, for example, a Yorkshire Englishman and a Texan American ordering a "bottle of water." Even the same individual can sound different when he wakes up compared to in the middle of his workday.

The first problem is usually addressed by exploiting the context and biasing or constraining the options of what will be reasonably recognizable at each point in a conversation. For example, when talking about the weather, it's reasonable to associate a higher probability to "mist" instead of "missed" whenever the sound sequence associated with them appears. If the word before "mist" or "missed" was already recognized as Thomas, then "missed" would usually make more sense, unless a proper name had previously qualified the noun "mist" in that context. When talking about hurricanes, for example, a qualifying proper name would not be unusual.

The set of mappings of phoneme sequences to recognizable words and their associated probabilities is called *the acoustic-language model*. The most common way of building this model is by collecting a series of dialogues using a simulated system and real users. The system is simulated by a human, without the users being aware of it. This technique is known as *Wizard of Oz*. The spoken dialogues are then manually annotated with information, such as word boundaries and word transcriptions, and then probabilities and rules are derived using automatic methods. Often, the system is bootstrapped with domain knowledge by a speech recognition expert, and the automatically generated results are again pruned and extended manually.

In many speech-recognition toolkits, the acoustic-language model is actually separated into two parts: the acoustic model and the language model. The acoustic model deals just with the mapping of phonemes to words, and the language model deals with the valid words that will be recognized in an application, together with their probabilities, if any.

As you might have inferred, the usual output of an automatic speech recognition (ASR) system is a ranked list of words/expressions. The language interpretation module or the DM can use domain knowledge and other kinds of information to select among them.

Developers will probably use a third-party ASR toolkit instead of developing a system from scratch. The work will basically be tuning the acoustic and language models, including new words, pronunciation examples, and rules, and then retraining the system. There are literally dozens of ASR solutions, both commercial and public [Sphinx07, Julius07]. In the commercial toolkits, you can expect to have acoustic models for the most common words of English and language models for some scenarios. Often, present are programs to extend and modify those models.

Natural Language Understanding

Consider a bulletproof ASR system or a typed text scenario. All that is left to deal with is the interpretation of the sequence of words into a definite meaning. There are several challenges from the outset:

- How to group the words into phrases?
- How to check if a given sentence makes any sense?
- How to discover the possible meanings of a sentence?
- How to select the right meaning?

Sentence splitting is the computational linguistics name for this grouping of words into phrases. Sometimes this is done partially or totally in the ASR module; more often, it will be the job of the natural language understanding (NLU) module. When dealing with speech, quite often there will be incomplete and elliptical phrases, such as "brown," or "the other," especially in response to a question. There are two approaches to deal with this—tune the NLU module to treat it, or just accept the incomplete sentence and send it for further interpretation in the DM.

The process of checking if a sentence is valid is called *parsing* or *syntactic analysis*. There are several different parsing paradigms, and for each, many available parsers. The most suitable parsers for a spoken language system are those that can output partial analysis and deal with incomplete sentences. Popular parsers are the dependency-based ones, such as Connexor's Machinese Syntax and CMU's Link Parser. When a sentence does not make any sense, the parser rejects it.

However, just knowing if the sentence makes any sense is not enough. The system needs to select the right interpretation of the sentence. In some cases, this is a matter of just selecting among the several available parses. Consider the sentence "Mike saw the man with the telescope." Did Mike see the man by means of a telescope, or did Mike see a man who was holding a telescope? The only way for the system to guess is by exploiting the context and background knowledge. For example, if the system knows that Mike has a telescope, it would interpret it in the first way. The system could also select the first if it had encountered many examples and determined that the first interpretation was correct. However, in a dialogue system, it is often preferable to keep the two possibilities open with a measure of confidence for each and let the DM decide—after all, the system can just ask the user a clarifying question to come to a conclusion!

Returning to the NLU problem, the cases where all the system has to do is select the right parse are few and rare. Often, the system needs to know what pronouns and words refer to, what classes words belong to, and what particular meanings words have. For instance, consider "Mike said to Jane that he does not love her." To properly interpret this, we need to know that Mike and Jane are people and that Mike is male and Jane is female. The process of discovering the categories to which a noun belongs is usually called *named entity recognition*. The process of attaching pronouns and nouns to other nouns or definite entities is called *reference resolution*.

Let's consider yet another phrase, "John ate the bass." To properly interpret this sentence, we need to know that bass is a fish, not a musical instrument. We could know this by at least three means: exploiting background knowledge that the verb eat usually requires an argument of type *food*; using statistical information that would show that in most cases when *bass* appears near *eat*, it is in the food sense; or if available, through pronunciation information because bass (the fish) and bass (the instrument) are pronounced in quite different ways.

You can expect to use sentence splitters and parsers just as they come off-the-shelf, without any significant customization. Named entity recognizers are usually the components that have to be tuned, either by providing annotated examples and training a model or by modifying the entity-detection rules, if you are not lucky enough to find a recognizer that totally matches your needs. Three toolkits that have components for most NLU tasks and that are easy to customize are GATE [GATE07], NLTK [NLTK07], and OpenNLPTools [OpenNLP07].

The results of this phase—the phrase(s) discovered, the syntactic analysis (parse), the entity types, and the referents—are fed into to the DM. The DM, using higher level information and the dialogue history, will be able to complement, extend, and correct these results, and based on them, decide what to do in the next step.

Dialogue Management

The DM is responsible for deciding what to say at each time step based on the information from NLU and ASR, what has been said so far, its knowledge, and its goals. A good background in agents or robotics helps; a DM is very similar to the control structure of an agent or robot. If you substitute the agent actions for speech acts and the agent perceptions for the inputs from NLU and ASR, you get a DM!

A DM's output is basically a speech act coupled with information on how to perform it. Speech acts [Searle69] are based on the view that saying something is performing an action—commanding, requesting, clarifying, complaining, and so on. In cognitive terms, it can be viewed as the intention of the person when saying something and the intention the person ascribes to something someone says when the person hears it. A good way to catch what speech acts are really about is seeing some examples—Table 6.1.1 provides utterances tagged with Human Communication Research Centre Map Task tags [Carletta97].

Table 6.1.1   Dialogue Acts with Their Descriptions and Examples

Dialogue Act	Example	Description
Instruct	Could you bring me a cup of tea, please?	Speaker tells hearer to do something.
Explain	I am Pinto, Caio Pinto.	Speaker says something without being asked by hearer.
Query-w	Who is John Galt?	A "who" or "what" question.
Reply-w	John is a character of Ayn Rand.	Reply to a Query-w question.
Acknowledge	I see…	Acknowledges the understanding of the previous utterance.
Query-yn	Do you want another piece of cake?	A question to which the answer is equivalent to yes/no.
Reply-y	Sure thing!	Reply to a query that is equivalent to yes/no.

One of the most common operations in a DM is recovering from or preventing misunderstandings. Let's get back to the sentence "Mike saw the man with the telescope." Suppose the DM gets these two interpretations as input:

- {[Mike- > saw, saw->man, saw ->with telescope], 0.51}
- {[Mike- > saw, saw->man, man ->with telescope], 0.49}

As both have very close probabilities/confidences, the system might decide to ask the user which one he means. It could ask "Did the man have the telescope?" using the speech act *confirm(man->with telescope)*. By using clarification questions or explicitly asking for more information, the DM can overcome or resolve many of the problems that the ASR and NLU modules might face. The caveat is that care must be taken not to turn the dialogue into a painful experience for the user, where the system keeps confirming and clarifying every utterance it encounters. The TRIPS system, presented in the second case study, usually opts for the risk of a wrong guess instead of confirming.

The DM is probably the component that will need the most attention because it determines in greater part the interaction with the character and its perceived personality. The DM is likely to exploit every cognitive capability of the character to bring about its functionalities in a way that will probably be defined closely with the game designer. A more complete handling of DMs is given in Article 6.5 *Dialogue Managers* [Pinto08] in this volume. The rest of this section details how the speech act will be transformed into an actual spoken phrase.

Natural Language Generation

If language understanding takes a phrase and assigns to it a definite meaning, natural language generation (NLG) does the reverse—it starts from a definite piece of knowledge and turns it into a textual passage. Here too can be many possibilities—the order of the facts or pieces of information to convey, the type of language to be used, the mood desired to impart, the level of politeness, and the cognitive aspects of the character, all might play a role on the generated language. However, in most commercially deployed spoken language systems, language generation is quite simplistic—canned or template based.

Canned NLG is the kind of language used in *Warcraft II*, *The Secret of Monkey Island*, *Ultima VIII*, and most games. It consists of predefined, immutable phrases that will be output depending on certain conditions. It is quite popular in various industries, and the most popular solution in the telecom sector. Canned language can be used by retrieving what has to be said from some database—flight booking systems and telecom systems that try to provide instructions are the archetypical examples of canned-language in dialogue systems.

Template-based NLG is the most popular paradigm in current commercially deployed systems. In this scenario, the system selects a template and fills in the details according to the semantic content—the information the system has is used not just to select a text passage, but also to fill in its details or slots. Template-based NLG works well when presenting the same set of messages with slight variations.

Template-based generation can be used to implement simple interactions and characters, for example, a shopkeeper or a soldier that just follows orders and reports simple facts. If a more complex interaction is needed, such as a bar fellow that chats about the local past and future events at the local tavern with the players, then the developers might need to delve into proper language generation and address the questions presented in the beginning of the section. These include what information to present, the order in which to present it, and how to present it. In this scenario, NLG is also an area where special attention needs to be devoted because it also determines in great part the personality of the character and the style of the interaction. The difficulty of implementing such an NLG module depends on the kind of DM being used. If the DM is already linked to a cognitive model and keeps track of emotions and moods, then the work is made simpler because this information can just be included in the DM output and exploited when making decisions. However, if the developers are using a simple DM, they probably need to use additional information from external modules or include them in the NLG component. Additional information to consider might be whether to use simple or pompous language, be polite or blunt, and so on.

Unlike other components, it's unlikely that developers will find an off-the-shelf NLG module. GATE (General Architecture for Text Engineering) [GATE07] has a prototypical NLG component that can be customized. Most projects in spoken dialogue systems start with canned language, evolve to template-based approaches, and only then proceed to more sophisticated NLG. This usually ties in well with a spoken dialogue system development lifecycle because in the initial stages, the team is probably tuning the ASR and NLU modules, which greatly constrain the design of the DM. The development of the NLG, like the DM, requires close involvement of the game designers to properly deliver its results.

After generating textual output, the output is made into actual speech.

Text-To-Speech

Text-to-speech (TTS) is seldom developed in-house or even customized. The majority of spoken dialogue implementers use an off-the-shelf solution. Most ASR providers also have TTS solutions, giving many choices once again. Current TTS technology has improved significantly in past years, and current systems often display good performance regarding the similarity of the generated sounds to human speech.

The main problem with TTS is that most solutions have few voices to choose from (usually just a couple), presenting a problem for developers who need different voices for different characters. If the game has several speaking characters, or if some character needs a special kind of voice, the developers might need to get involved in speech synthesis. Up to a certain point, they could just use sound effects on a given voice to try to achieve different pitches and contours—the sound effects specialist could play a key role in this!

A brief review of the issues involved in a TTS system will create an appreciation of the work inside a TTS module and an understanding of the technical language of the solution vendors. Usually the speech synthesis is divided into two phases: text analysis and speech generation.

The text analysis starts in a way similar to NLU—there is segmentation of the text into phrases and syntactic analysis, followed by normalization, and then the modeling of continuous speech. Normalization involves basically putting abbreviations, currencies, measures, and times into a form suitable to be spoken. The modeling of continuous speech must deal with the variations in speech that happen when two or more words are spoken together. Consider the "of" in "I want a bottle of water" and in "I can't recall a girlfriend I am not still fond of" for the different sounds. Sometimes, by the text analysis, we may be able to infer prosodic information—information about intonation, pitch contour, intensity, and so on. At other times, we can provide it externally—in our case, it would be the output of NLG.

The results of the text analysis and prosody information are passed on to a speech generator. There are three main paradigms for speech synthesis: articulatory, formant, and concatenative. The first is based on the modeling of the speech articulators, the second in the properties of the sound signal, and the third aims to smoothly join prerecorded units of speech.

If the game has a relatively small set of utterances to be spoken, and they are known in advance, then the game will probably be better off with recorded speech from professional actors. Nonetheless, TTS might be useful to get a feel of the game during prototyping and production [Kirby98]. *Operation Flashpoint* used this approach until shortly before the game release, when voice actors were called in to record the characters' utterances [Codemasters01].

The following two case studies show how it all fits together in deployed systems.

Case Studies

In this section, we will examine two robust dialogue systems: The Rochester Interactive Planning System (TRIPS) [Allen07] and the NICE Game system [NICE07]. Both have demonstration videos on their Web sites.

The NICE game system was done as part of a three-year European Union project that involved five partners from academia and industry, including the game company Liquid Media. It not only demonstrates key issues in the design of a dialogue system but also features solutions dear to game developers, such as a domain-independent kernel coupled to domain-dependent scripts to control the agent's behavior.

The TRIPS system actually stands for a big family of different implementations and has been in development for almost 10 years. The brief discussion here focuses on a small part of the family. TRIPS shows a different approach to solve the issues of a spoken dialogue system, although there are noticeable commonalities with NICE—both systems, at the lowest level, use a hub-and-spoke architecture. One feature that will be dear to game developers is the strong separation of domain and generic knowledge in the system—the parser, the generator, and the planner have domain-independent cores, allowing a great deal of reuse.

The NICE Game System

The NICE game system was built to investigate the interaction of adults and children with game characters using dialogue and mouse clicks [Gustafson05]. Although a commercial game company was involved in its creation, NICE was mainly a research project. Interesting issues addressed in the game demo are the speech recognition of children and adults, the interaction of ASR and NLU, how to make up for ASR errors, how to exploit the game scenario and game plot for dialogue management, and how to tune the speech to match the desired personalities of the various characters.

The game world is a typical 3D adventure setting—there are several objects, each with certain properties, and the user must do a series of tasks using them for the story to unfold. What is not so typical is that the user interacts with the game characters via mouse clicks and speech for them to carry out the actions necessary for game progression; the user does not directly manipulate anything in the game world. This indirection in task performance was part of the game design, to bring interaction with the characters to the forefront of the game.

The game plot is very simple—the player must operate a machine, explore the world, and traverse a bridge. It has two main scenes—in the first, the user has to operate a "story machine," where he needs to guide his faithful assistant, Cloddy Hans, to put the right objects into the proper places in the machine for it to function. This first scene is designed to make the player familiar with the game controls. In the second scene, the player needs to help Cloddy Hans traverse a bridge. For this, the player and Hans have to convince another character, Karen, to lower the bridge so they are able to pass. Karen will only lower the bridge after bargaining for some item that is in the opposite end of the gap. Cloddy Hans does more than carry out user commands and answer player questions; he can also talk directly to Karen and provide the player with tips on what she might want.

Hans and Karen had the requirements to have distinct personalities. Hans is a dunce and slow to understand but is honest, friendly, polite, and eager to help. Karen is intelligent, frivolous, confident, unfriendly, touchy, and anxious. These different roles and personalities will bring about different requirements in their DMs, generators, and TTS systems, not to mention their animations. For example, Cloddy Hans displays small, slow, and deliberate body gestures, whereas Karen uses large and fast body movements.

Architecture

The system uses a hub-based, event-driven, asynchronous architecture to mediate communication between the various components. Communication is through message passing over TCP/IP. The central hub, called Message Dispatcher, timestamps every message and coordinates input and output by means of a set of rules that determines what to do for each message type. This allows simple reactive responses when receiving a message. This central hub also issues timeouts to enable the system to keep track of the passage of time. The various modules of the system could (and actually did) exist in different machines, and it was possible to render different scenes on different machines.

Automatic Speech Recognition (ASR)

The ASR module was made by training a statistical language model over 5,600 utterances of 57 children aged 9 to 15. Those dialogues were collected over a 5-month period, in 4 different sections, using a method similar to the Wizard of Oz. This data was used not only to do the ASR module but also to drive the building of this system's parser. The results of the ASR were not very good—only about 38.6% of the words were properly recognized. One of the reasons was that children's speech was less consistent than adults' [Gustafson04]. However, as shown in the following section, the NLU system was able to compensate for part of this.

Natural Language Understanding (NLU)

The NLU module consists of a parser that combines pattern matching and limited inference to output a simple semantic representation of the ASR output. The input is the best hypothesis of the speech recognizer, and the output is a dialogue act represented as a typed tree. The parser is implemented using two phases: a domain-dependent pattern-matching phase and a domain-independent rule-rewriting phase.

The pattern matching, based on a set of syntactic rules, is done left-to-right and results in a list of semantic constraints. The most common kind of constraint is the stipulation of the existence of an object or action. For example, if the parser finds the noun "nail," it would put the constraint nail_*thing,* meaning that there is a "nail" of type "thing." If the parser encountered the verb "drop," it would put the conjunction drop(x,y)_*action* ∧ x_*character* ∧ y_*thing,* which means there is a drop action where "x" is a character and "y" is a thing. Other types of semantic constraints are inequality and equality constraints. The rules are specified using a definite clause grammar. An example of a rule set able to interpret a command to pick up a banana or an apple follows:

```
PickUpHints([pickUp(X,Y)_action, X_character, Y_character| MoreHints
],Tail) -> [take,the], thingHints( [Y_character | moreHints], Tail).
PickUpHints([pickup(X,Y)_action, X_character,
Y_character|Tail],Tail) -> [take].
ThingHints([banana_thing|Tail],Tail) -> [banana].
ThingHints([apple_thing|Tail],Tail)->[apple].
```

The algorithm tries to match the right side of a rule with an initial segment of input. If the match is successful, the semantic constraints in the left side are added to the output list, and the input segment matched is discarded. If no match on any rule is possible, then the initial segment is discarded, and the process starts over. The rules are matched in the order that they appear in the rule base, so it is important to put the rules that match longer inputs first, enabling the parser to match smaller parts of the input if the longer match fails.

Another source of constraint in the parsing process is the particular mouse input. If the user says "pick up this" and clicks on the hammer, it will add a constraint hammer_*thing.* This is a nice example of how natural language processing might fit into an adventure game—instead of wholly substituting the point-and-click interaction, it can be used to extend and complement it, as well as being enriched by it.

The rule-rewriting phase uses the constraints parsed to build a dialogue act suggestion for the DM. It unifies the proposed objects with concrete instances, expands the set with the constraints that can be inferred from the current ones, merges actions and objects, filters out trivially true facts, and, finally, binds all free variables into a dialogue act. Some examples of parsed utterances are shown in Table 6.1.2.

Table 6.1.2   Sentences and Corresponding NICE Dialogue Acts

Sentence	Dialogue Act
User: I will give you the ruby.	Offer(user,Karen, ruby)
User: I am 14 years old.	Tell(user, Cloddy, 14[user.age=14])

The particularly good result of the parser is that it partially compensates for the bad speech recognition. If the concepts expressed are considered instead of just the words, the parser achieved a 53.2% accuracy [Boye06].

Dialogue Management

The DM in this system not only processes the dialogue acts coming out of the NLU module but also acts as the whole brain of the character, deciding what to do in response to events in the environment and changes in the characters' goals. It is implemented as a kernel, which provides common functionality, coupled with scripting code, which deals with the game-specific and scene-specific events.

The kernel issues timed events in response to changes in the environment, results from ASR and NLU, and its internal state. The scripting code can react to events by using callbacks. Among the events accepted as input are ParserEvent (NLU has produced a dialogue act), PerformedEvent (animation has completed), RecognitionFailureEvent (ASR failed to recognize utterance), WorldEvent (an event happened in the world), AlreadySatisfiedEvent (the goal added to the agenda has already been satisfied), CannotSolveEvent (an insolvable goal has been put in the character's agenda), and TimeoutEvent (a timeout has expired). The scripting code can access the kernel to bring about the actual dialogue behavior via the following operations: interpret an utterance, convey a dialogue act, perform an action, add a goal to the character's agenda, remove a goal from the character's agenda, and pursue the next goal in the agenda.

The agenda keeps track of the character's actions, goals, and the relations between them in a tree-like structure. It is the main driving force of the dialogue behavior—the character does its actions, including utterances, to fulfill its goals. In addition to the agenda, the DM keeps a discourse history, composed basically of a list of dialogue acts in reverse chronological order and a domain model. The dialogue history is used mainly for reference resolution, whereas the domain model is used to constrain the possible choices of actions; that is, picking up a hammer would be allowed but picking up a house would not.

Finally, the outputs of the dialogue system as a whole are *convey<dialog_act>*, which will transform the dialogue act into words by the NLG module, and *perform<action>*, which sends a command to the animation system for performance of the action.

Spoken Language Generation

Language generation in the system picks the dialogue act output by the DM and converts it into a text string using a 200-rule definite clause grammar.

The TTS module was implemented with the Snack toolkit [Snack07] using a concatenative approach, as mentioned in the "Text-to-Speech" section. The authors report that all they had to do was provide the system with a set of speech recordings and the matching orthographic transcription files to get a basic voice. One aim in the making of the TTS system was to have symmetric analysis and synthesis components to hopefully have better performance. The voice actors were told to read the utterances made for training in a way that matched the desired personalities of the characters. As a result, Karen's voice had a higher pitch and speaking rate than Cloddy Han's. To further accentuate this difference, the utterances were resampled changing speaking rate and voice pitch, making Karen sound younger and Hans sounding larger.

TRIPS—The Rochester Interactive Planning System

TRIPS is well described by its subtitle, The Rochester Interactive Planning System, because its main goal is building and executing a plan iteratively with the user to accomplish a concrete task. The system has many versions, which were deployed in several different scenarios, including crisis management (Pacifica and TRIPS-911), multi-robot exploration (Underwater survey), and a medical advisor. Our exposition will focus on the crisis management scenarios and will be based on the project Web site [Allen07] and on the expositions of [McTear04] and [Allen00, Allen01a, Allen01b].

TRIPS is composed of a set of loosely coupled components divided in three basic clusters: interpretation, behavior, and generation. Each cluster has one central component and shares one or more mediating components. Logical communication happens between the central components directly and from them to the mediating components. The language used for communication is a variation of the Knowledge Query Manipulation Language (KQML). Physically, all components are connected to a central hub that routes the messages between the components and coordinates initialization and shutdown of the whole system. Figure 6.1.1 depicts a functional representation of the architecture. It shows the central components (the interpretation manager (IM), the behavioral agent, and the generation manager), and the discourse context, reference, and task manager mediating the interaction between the clusters.

What follows is a principled analysis of the system, similar to what was done with NICE.

Speech Recognition

Speech recognition is based on the Sphinx-II system from Carnegie Mellon University. Sphinx-II is a general-purpose, user-independent system. TRIPS developers used the Sphinx-II's acoustic models to create their own language models based on the task they were implementing. One problem they faced that might afflict a game developer developing a new game was the lack of utterance examples in their domain to create new language models. They used two techniques to ameliorate this problem: creating an artificial corpus and adapting corpora from other domains. In the first, they invented a few hundred sentences, derived a context-free grammar (CFG) from it, and then used the grammar to generate a bigger corpus. In the second, they tagged the words in the corpora using generic concepts, derived a language model based just on the concepts, and then expanded these concepts using words of the target model. They reported good results using these techniques, both in combination and by themselves [Galescu98].

Natural Language Understanding (NLU)

NLU is centralized in the interpretation manager (IM). It communicates with the parser, the reference manager, the discourse context, the task manager, and the behavioral agent to form an interpretation of what was said taking into account the current task and context.

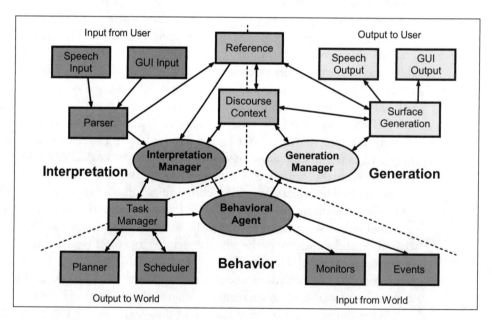

FIGURE 6.1.1   TRIPS architecture.

The parser receives as input the ranked list of the speech recognizer and the mouse clicks from the GUI. It also requests information from the reference manager and updates it with new information. The parser is speech-act based, instead of sentence-based. It searches for speech acts anywhere in the utterance and chooses the shortest sequence of acts that cover as much of the input as possible. This way, the parser is able to deal with ungrammatical sentences, which are common in spoken language. The parser is implemented as a best-first bottom-up chart parser using a feature-augmented CFG with semantic restrictions. The grammar has a generic part and an application-dependent part. The generic part represents the core meanings of conversational English. The application-specific part has domain-specific words and semantic categories, as well as mappings between the general categories of the original grammar and the specific ones in the application. The parser's output is a list of speech acts, which are realized with predicates from both grammars.

The task manager abstracts away the domain-specific task knowledge from the other parts of the system. It has information about particular goals and subgoals, what particular actions can be used as part of solutions for the objectives, what domain-specific resources are used by the actions, and so on. The central service it provides to the IM is discovering what a speech-act means in that problem-solving context—mapping a speech-act into a problem-solving act. The mapped problem-solving act is returned to the IM with two scores: the recognition score and the answer score. The recognition score is the confidence of the task manager about the mapping, and the answer score is an estimate of the viability of the problem-solving act given the current problem-solving context.

The discourse manager manages the knowledge about the discourse, keeping a speech-act history, whose turn it is to speak, the obligations of the participants, and a model of the salient entities of the dialogue. The reference manager queries it about salient entities and updates its entities' entries. The IM uses information about the obligations of the participants and whose turn it is to speak to decide how to interpret a given speech-act.

Dialogue Management

The behavior agent (BA) is responsible for deciding what to do at each step, based on the system's goals and obligations, the current problem-solving act, the external events, and the task being carried out. BA implements a general problem-solving model that encompasses concepts such as objectives (goals and restrictions on goals), solutions (plans that fulfill a goal), resources (objects used in solutions), and situations (the state of the world). An utterance here is interpreted as a manipulation of one of these concepts—the creation or deletion of a goal, a description of a solution, and so on.

The BA queries the task manager to interpret the problem-solving act that comes from the IM and to carry out actions specific to the domain. In this way, domain-specific and generic problem-solving knowledge is separated, which is a good approach to a game with several different subplots and scenes.

Event notification modules and monitors might be linked to the behavioral manager, which would be able to decide whether to inform the user about what happened and the implication for the current problem-solving task.

The BA, upon coming to a decision, sends a request to the generation manager to issue the corresponding utterance.

Natural Language Generation (NLG) and Speech Synthesis

The generation manager will decide what to actually output to the user based on the messages from the BA and the discourse context. It has some degree of autonomy in that it can plan a response before receiving a message from the behavioral agent based just on a change in the discourse context. Whenever the generation manager actually sends a response for surface generation, it updates the discourse context. The messages to surface generation are still in logical form. The surface generator realizes the output as text and objects in the GUI. The actual text generation was done using templates and simple CFGs for noun phrases [Stent99].

Speech synthesis was done with the TrueTalk generation engine from Entropics, Inc. [Allen07]. Because, in this system, the voice was used just to convey information, there was no need to further develop the TTS system.

Discussion

We saw the main characteristics and issues of spoken dialogues, proceeded to an analysis of the standard components of speech-based dialogue systems, and finally studied two robust systems. This section reflects on what has been touched on so far and on how the particulars of the game domain affect the design of dialogue systems.

One of the most interesting particularities of games is that designers can lower the performance requirements of the system by exploiting the game design and plot. In NICE, Cloddy was presented as a dunce that was slow to understand. This fitted in well with the flaws of the speech-recognition system and with the relatively long processing time it took until he started acting on a user request. Karen, on the other hand, was presented and perceived by the players as more intelligent, even though she used the same underlying technology. The key to hide a lack of intelligence that was as big as Cloddy's was to present her as stubborn and with her own goals. This allowed her DM to have faster responses and to make sensible utterances more often than Cloddy's, contributing to the perception of her superior intelligence.

Another way to simplify the system considers the character's role in the game. To simplify the language model of a bartender, the bartender could be made to say that he was very busy or not interested in what the player said whenever the player strayed from bar service vocabulary. A similar principle applies to the generation module—a shy or secondary character could have few possible phrases, all with the same emotional tone.

A similar, but more risky possibility, is retroactively introducing elements to the game that would explain the character's limitations. For example, if there is no problem for the story and setting to have the user interact with a key character that is very old, ASR problems can be attributed to the character being hard of hearing. The same goes for limitations in the other components—having "the dumb assistant" instead of just "the assistant" covers for a limited DM. A messenger can be very shy to compensate for his limited language generation. Here, the integration with the animation to convey these personality traits is key for believability.

Games provide particular challenges for ASR. The system must be able to recognize voices from many different users, each with its particular accents and inflections, because a game is targeted at hundreds of thousands of players. Shouting, laughing, and screaming usually present problems to current systems, and these are quite common in a game setting. In RPGs and adventure games, they might be less common than in FPSs. Adaptation for game genres where these phenomena are common should be expected. The language model, however, can be made manageable by tuning it for a given context or scene. Contrary to systems deployed in the real world, game developers know in advance what utterances are sensible in a given scene and context, making the language model building task far easier.

We have seen three approaches to parsing: the archetypical, standard approach described in the introduction; the logic-based, domain-dependent approach of NICE; and the dialogue act-based one from TRIPS. NICE made the parser domain-dependent and tightly coupled to overcome the complexity of the language, even though its rewriting phase is generic. TRIPS, on the other hand, encapsulates all task- and domain-dependent information in the task manager. The NICE approach might be easier to implement and test, but the more modular approach of TRIPS might lead to greater reuse.

Both TRIPS and NICE used a goal-oriented action planner as the core of their DMs. This is good news for game developers because this subject is certainly more advanced in the games community than in the dialogue world. Starting a DM from a planner, such as the one described in [Orkin06], might be a sensible approach.

The voices of the game character have a far greater impact than in other applications, such as an airline flight reservation system. The text output must not only have correct pronunciation, rhythm, and intonation but also must be appropriate to the character. Professional actors might have to be used to record the voices that will be the basis of the game's TTS. Quite often, sound processing of the TTS output might be needed to enhance some aspect of the voice. For less demanding situations, applying simple sound transformation on the TTS output might be enough to provide the needed characteristics.

Conclusion

We have seen that spoken dialogue technology has reached a level where it is feasible to build characters that engage in spoken conversation with the player. By carefully considering the game plot and scenes, game developers are able to simplify the building of their systems. Games also provide the opportunity to turn some of the system's limitations into harmless features, if they can be justified as plausible character traits.

Goal-oriented action planning is in the core of the dialogue systems examined here, providing a familiar ground for game developers to start implementing their dialogue systems.

References

[Allen00] Allen, James, et al., "An Architecture for a Generic Dialogue Shell." *Journal of Natural Language Engineering, special issue on Best Practices in Spoken Language Dialogue Systems Engineering*, Vol. 6, no. 3, (December, 2000): pp. 1–16.

[Allen01a] Allen, James, et al., "Towards Conversational Human-Computer Interaction." *AI Magazine*, (2001).

[Allen01b] Allen, James, et al., "An Architecture for More Realistic Conversational Systems." *Proceedings of Intelligent User Interfaces 2001 (IUI-01)*, Santa Fe, NM, (January 14–17, 2001).

[Allen07] Allen, James, et al., "The Rochester Interactive Planning System." Available online at *http://www.cs.rochester.edu/research/cisd/projects/trips/*, June 14, 2007.

[Boye06] Boye, Johan, et al., "Robust Spoken Language Understanding in a Computer Game." *Speech Communication*, Vol. 48, (2006): pp. 335–353.

[Carletta97] Carletta, Jean, et al., "The Reliability of a Dialogue Structure Coding Scheme." *Computational Linguistics*, Vol. 23, no. 1, (1997): pp. 13–32.

[Codemasters01] *Operation Flashpoint*. Codemasters, UK, MS Windows, PC platform, 2001.

[Galescu98] Galescu, Lucian, et al., "Rapid Language Model Development for New Task Domains." *Proceedings of the ELRA First International Conference on Language Resources and Evaluation (LREC)*, Granada, Spain, (May 1998).

[GATE07] General Architecture for Text Engineering. Available online at *http://gate.ac.uk*, June 15, 2007.

[Gustafson04] Gustafson, Joakim, and Sjoelander, K., "Voice Creation for Conversational Fairy-Tale Characters." *Proceedings of the 5th ISCA Speech Synthesis Workshop*, Carnegie Mellon University 14–16, (June 2004).

[Gustafson05] Gustafson, Joakim, et al., "Providing Computer Game Characters with Conversational Abilities." *Proceedings of Intelligent Virtual Agents, 5th International Working Conference, IVA 2005*, Kos, Greece, (September 12–14, 2005).

[Infogrames02] *Neverwinter Nights*, published by Infogrames, USA, PC platform, 2002.

[Julius07] Open-Source Large Vocabulary CSR Engine Julius. Available online at *http://julius.sourceforge.jp/en_index.php?q=en/index.html*, June 15, 2007.

[Kirby98] Kirby, Neil, "Lies, Damn Lies, and ASR Statistics." *Proceedings of Computer Game Developers Conference*, (1998).

[McTear04] McTear, Michael F., *Spoken Dialogue Technology: Toward the Conversational User Interface*. Springer Verlag, London. 2004.

[Montfort03] Montfort, Nick. *Twisty Little Passages: An Approach To Interactive Fiction*. The MIT Press, 2003.

[NICE07] Nice Project. Available online at *http://www.niceproject.com*, June 9, 2007.

[NLTK07] Natural Language Toolkit. Available online at *http://nltk.sourceforge.net*, June 15, 2007.

[OpenNLP07] Open NLP Tools. Available online at *http://opennlp.sourceforge.net*, June 15, 2007.

[Orkin06] Orkin, Jeff, "3 States & a Plan: The AI of F.E.A.R." *Proceedings of Game Developers Conference,* (2006).

[Pinto08] Pinto, Hugo, "Dialogue Managers." *AI Game Programming Wisdom 4.* Charles River Media, 2008.

[Snack07] Snack Sound Toolkit. Available online at *http://www.speech.kth.se/snack/*, June 15, 2007.

[Sony04] *Lifelines*, published by Sony Computer Entertainment and Konami, USA, Playstation 2 platform, 2004.

[Sphinx07] CMU Sphinx. Available online at *http://sourceforge.net/projects/cmusphinx*, June 15, 2007.

[Stent99] Stent, A., "Content Planning and Generation in Continuous-Speech Spoken Dialog Systems." *Proceedings of the KI-99 Workshop May I Speak Freely?* (1999).

6.2

Implementing Story-Driven Games with the Aid of Dynamical Policy Models

Fabio Zambetta—School of Computer Science & IT, RMIT University

fabio@cs.rmit.edu.au

Although strategy games have often integrated policy as a key gameplay element, RPGs have generally lacked in this area. You need only consider games such as *Balance of Power*, the *Civilization* franchise, or *Rome Total War* to realize how political components can be successfully integrated in the gameplay to provide fun and interesting experiences for players. RPG designers, on the other hand, are not totally oblivious to the basic building blocks needed to recreate political scenarios, but they have failed so far in tying all the elements into a coherent picture. For example, games such as *Diablo, Neverwinter Nights, Planescape Torment*, or *Oblivion* provide a gameplay experience relying on epic and intricate storylines.

At the same time, most of these titles provide *factions*, which are defined in politics as *"a group of persons forming a cohesive, usually contentious minority within a larger group."* Factions provide a mechanism that groups PCs and NPCs of an RPG game based on the homogeneity of their behavior by specifying how members of a faction feel about the reputation of a member of another faction. Unfortunately, reputation is seldom modified in-game, and even worse, it is only rarely used throughout the plot arc to influence the game's story and the player experience. Our approach attempts to address both limitations by means of a dynamical policy model based on Richardson's Arms Race model [Goulet83]. First, we reshaped the original model semantics to fit the RPG games context, and second, we extended Richardson's model by means of a scaling operator so that the new model can manage interactive scenarios.

Although interactive scenarios tend to be stochastic in nature, the original model generated deterministic solutions. Therefore, our improved model can be regarded as an HCP (Hybrid Control Process) [Branicky94] because it exhibits both continuous and discrete dynamic behavior: The former is usually modeled via a system of ODE (Ordinary Differential Equations) [Boyce04], whereas the latter is represented by FSMs (finite state machines).

The remainder of this article is organized as follows: We analyze Richardson's model in the first section, and then we proceed to clarify the rationale and the details of our improved model in the second section. The third section details possible applicative scenarios of our model, and the fourth section details some experimental results obtained so far. Finally, the fifth section wraps up the article by introducing our future work: *Two Families: A Tale of New Florence*, and an *NWN2* (*Neverwinter Nights 2*) mod currently in development in our labs.

Richardson's Arms Race Model

A dynamical system is a mathematical abstraction (or model) of a real-world system whose behavior can be described by a fixed rule governing the change in its state (a real valued vector). The rule of the dynamical system is deterministic, and it is usually modeled by differential equations. One such system comes from Lewis Fry Richardson, a renowned English mathematician and psychologist. Richardson is deemed to have started the scientific analysis of conflict, an interdisciplinary field devoted to systematic investigation of the causes of war and peace. His model of an arms race was devised to predict whether armament build-up between two alliances was a prelude to a conflict [Goulet83].

The model consists of a system of two linear ODEs, but it can be easily generalized to a multidimensional case [Goulet83].

Richardson's assumptions about the system he modeled are given here:

- Arms accumulate because of mutual fear.
- A society will internally be opposed to a constant increase in arms expenditures.
- There are factors independent of expenditures that are conducive to the proliferation of arms.

The equations describing the intended behavior are given here:

$$\dot{x} = ky - ax + g$$
$$\dot{y} = lx - by + h$$

Rewriting the equations in matrix form yields:

$$\dot{z} = Az + r$$

$$A = \begin{pmatrix} -a & k \\ l & -b \end{pmatrix}$$

$$z = \begin{pmatrix} x \\ y \end{pmatrix}$$

$$r = \begin{pmatrix} g \\ h \end{pmatrix}$$

The solutions of the system [Boyce04] will mainly depend on the relative magnitude of the values involved and on the signs of g and h. The constants k and l are the *fear constants* (induced by mutual fear), a and b are the *restraint constants* (internal opposition against arms expenditures), and g and h are the *grievance terms* (independent factors, which can be interpreted as grievance against rivals). Only g and h are allowed to assume negative values. To analyze the equilibrium of the model, you need to take into account the optimal lines where the first derivatives of x and y equal 0; the equilibrium point $P^* = (x^*, y^*)$ where the optimal lines intersect; and the dividing line L^* for cases where the equilibrium depends on the starting point. System trajectories heading toward positive infinity are said to be going toward a *runaway arms race*, whereas the ones going toward negative infinity are said to be going toward *disarmament*.

Two cases can occur in practice, in the general assumption that $det(A) \neq 0$:

- All trajectories approach an equilibrium point (stable equilibrium, see Figure 6.2.1, left). An equilibrium point is considered stable (for the sake of simplicity, we will consider *asymptotic stability* only) if the system always returns to it after small disturbances.
- Trajectories depend on the initial point, and they can either drift toward positive/negative infinity after small disturbances or approach a stable point if they start on the dividing line (unstable equilibrium, see Figure 6.2.1, right).

It can be proven that if $ab > kl$, we will reach stable *equilibrium*, whereas if $ab < kl$, we will obtain *unstable equilibrium*.

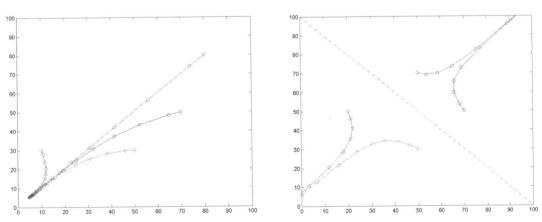

FIGURE 6.2.1 System trajectories showing stable and unstable equilibrium.

An Improved Arms Race Model

The bulk of our work has been aimed so far at refining Richardson's model for use in an RPG and has involved three main steps:

1. Reinterpret the model semantics to fit an RPG game context.
2. Improve the model to produce a satisfactory representation of faction interaction.
3. Feed a classic RPG faction system (in our scenario, the *Neverwinter Nights 2* faction system) with the model output.

Our improved version of the model can produce alternating phases of stability and instability as required in a computer RPG scenario. It yields variable results that give rise to a rich simulation of faction dynamics because alliances can be repeatedly broken leading to war, or conflicts can be halted temporarily.

Reinterpreting the Model Semantics

We will start our analysis by naming two factions **X** and **Y**, and by reinterpreting *x* and *y* as the (greater than or equal to zero) level of *cooperation* of faction **X** and **Y**, respectively. The parameters of the model will assume new semantics as highlighted in Table 6.2.1. In our version of the model, increasing values will signify increasing *cooperation* instead of increasing *conflict*. It should be noted that having both a *belligerence* and a *pacifism* factor allows for a fine-grain modeling of a faction. In fact, it isn't necessarily true that each push toward belligerence will cause an equal reaction toward pacifism or vice versa. On the other hand, *friendliness* accounts for the innate predisposition of a faction toward another, or in other words, it factors in all the history of conflict or cooperation between them.

The level of cooperation of each faction will lead the system either to a stable equilibrium point P^* or to an unstable equilibrium that will drive the system toward increasing levels of competition or cooperation (where decreasing cooperation indicates increasing competition). We will restrict to the case of unstable equilibrium because we are interested in obtaining a behavior that mimics the interactive and changeable scenarios provided by video games.

Table 6.2.1 The Parameters and Semantics Have Been Reinterpreted in Our Model

Parameters	Semantics
K	Faction X belligerence factor
L	Faction Y belligerence factor
A	Faction X pacifism factor
B	Faction Y pacifism factor
G	Friendliness of X toward Y
H	Friendliness of Y toward X

A Satisfactory Representation of Faction Interaction

The formulation of Richardson's model in an unstable equilibrium case implies that the final state of the system will be determined by its initial conditions. The initial condition of the system will give rise to one of three possible outcomes:

- If P lies in the half-plane above the dividing line L^*, then the system will be driven toward infinite *cooperation*.
- If P lies in the half-plane below the dividing line L^*, then the system will be driven toward infinite *competition*.
- If P lies on the dividing line L^*, then the system will be driven toward a stable condition of *neutrality*.

Even though Richardson's model seems to posses the main ingredients to formalize conflict, it still lacks in two respects: first and foremost, it does not cater for interactivity, and second, it is deterministic. An ODE solver [Boyce04] would start to approximate its solution, leading always to the same outcome in any given run (any of the three listed previously, depending on the initial position of P). Video game scenarios, on the other hand, will involve stochastic PC and NPC actions interacting with each other and the game world. Therefore we developed a *stop-and-go* version of Richardson's model where the ODE solver initially computes the solution of the system until an external event is generated in-game.

When such an event occurs, the parameters of the model listed in Table 6.2.1 are conveniently recomputed, and the dividing line L^* is moved. This alters the direction of motion of the current system trajectory, possibly leading to a change in equilibrium. We will recalculate the parameters by scaling the matrix of the model so that:

$$A_{new} = \lambda A_{old}$$

How will the scaling of A influence the equilibrium of the system? To appreciate that, let's first compute the equation of L^*, which is the locus of points where both the derivatives in our system will go to zero.

The equation of L^* is:

$$\dot{x} + \dot{y} = (ky - ax + g) + (lx - by + h) = (l - a)x + (k - b)y + (g + h) = 0$$

Scaling A will yield:

$$\dot{x} + \dot{y} = \lambda(l - a)x + \lambda(k - b)y + (g + h) = 0$$

Thus, we will have in the end:

$$\left(1 - a\right)x + \left(k - b\right)y + \frac{\left(g + h\right)}{\lambda} = 0$$

Hence, three cases may occur:

$0 < \lambda < 1$: L^* is moved in its original upper half-plane, giving rise to a possible decrease in cooperation.

$\lambda = 1$: The scale factor does not change A.

$\lambda > 1$: L^* is moved in its original lower half-plane, giving rise to a possible increase in cooperation.

To verify these claims, you need only look at Figure 6.2.2 (the scale is exaggerated for illustration purposes), where the case $0 < \lambda < 1$ is depicted. The dividing line is initially L_1, and the point describing the trajectory of the system is P: the ODE solver generates increasing values of cooperation until P_1 is reached, when an external event occurs. Now, A is scaled, and as a result of that, L_2 becomes the new dividing line. The new dividing line brings P_1 in the lower half-plane, leading to decreasing values of cooperation (increasing competition). Generalizing from this example, suppose that initially $L_1 \cdot P_1 > 0$ (increasing cooperation) and that $0 < \lambda < 1$. Then we will have three alternatives when an external event occurs:

$L_2 \cdot P_1 > 0$: The level of cooperation keeps on increasing.

$L_2 \cdot P_1 < 0$: The level of cooperation starts to decrease.

$L_2 \cdot P_1 = 0$: The level of cooperation moves toward a stable value.

Clearly, if $L_1 \cdot P > 0$ and $\lambda > 1$, then $L_2 \cdot P_1 > 0$. Similar conclusions can be drawn when $L_1 \cdot P < 0$.

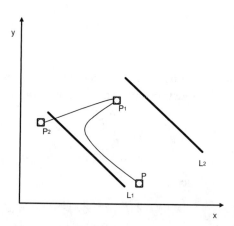

FIGURE 6.2.2   The effect of scaling A on the system.

Any application using our model will need to provide a set (or a hierarchy) of events, along with a relevance level $\lambda_j, j \in \{1 \dots M\}$ that could be either precomputed in a lookup table or generated at runtime. Obviously, all the events having $\lambda_j > 1$ will correspond to events that increase cooperation, whereas events having $0 < \lambda_j < 1$ will exacerbate competition. The effect of the λ-scaling is to change partitioning of the first quadrant, giving rise from time to time to a bigger semi-plane either for cooperation or for competition. This improved version of Richardson's model can be characterized in terms of an HCP [Branicky94], a system involving both continuous dynamics (usually modeled via an ODE) and controls (generally incorporated into an FSM). The system possesses memory affecting the vector field, which changes discontinuously in response to external control commands.

Converting to the *Neverwinter Nights 2* Faction System

Converting the to the *NWN2* faction system is straightforward after the proper values of cooperation have been computed. A few function calls are available in *NWN* script [Lexicon06] to adjust the reputation of NPCs (e.g., AdjustReputation, ga_faction_rep, etc.). In *NWN2* faction standings, assume a value in the [0, 100] range per each faction: values in [0, 10] indicate competition (in *NWN* hostility), whereas values in [90, 100] represent cooperation (in *NWN* friendship).

The most straightforward conversion possible would simply use x and y as the faction standings for each faction: x would indicate the way NPCs in faction **X** would feel about people in faction **Y** and vice versa. Another approach would introduce a scaling factor that could represent the relative importance of each NPC in a faction: It is often reasonable to expect that more hostility or friendship would be aroused by people in command positions. Hence, splitting a faction (say, **X** for explanatory purposes) in N different ranks, and setting some coefficients ε_i, with $i \in \{1 \dots N\}$, we will have:

$$x_{NWN} = x\varepsilon_i$$

Converting to other games' faction systems may entail different types of linear transformations, but the essence of the approach will remain unchanged.

Applicative Scenarios

The interactions underpinning our conceptual model imply that the level of cooperation or competition is influenced by the player actions, but in turn, the model alters the game world perceived by the player in a feedback loop. First, we present some ideas related to the generation of random encounters in an RPG, such as *Neverwinter Nights 2*. Second, we concentrate our attention on possible ways to integrate our model in a piece of nonlinear game narrative, the main motivator of our research. Other applications are also possible, as detailed in [Zambetta06].

Generating Random Encounters in an RPG

Random encounters are commonly used in RPGs, for example, to attenuate the monotony of traversing very large game areas. However, expert players will not suspend their disbelief if creatures are spawned without any apparent rationale. Values of cooperation/competition generated by our model can be used as cues for the application to drive the random encounters generation process and to provide some context.

In a scenario where players joined faction **X**, their actions cause specific in-game events that can influence the equilibrium of the system. The game AI could deliberate that the higher the level of competition of **X** toward **Y**, the harder and the more frequent the encounters will be. Also, players could encounter NPCs willing to negotiate truces or alliances if the level of cooperation is sufficiently high to render the interaction more believable and immersive. This improved process for random encounter generation can be designed by using fuzzy rules [Zadeh73] describing which class of encounters should be candidates for spawning creatures based on the level of competition/cooperation.

For example, possible rules will resemble this form:

```
R1: IF cooperationX IS LOW THEN ENCOUNTER
R2: IF cooperationX IS HIGH THEN NEGOTIATION_ENCOUNTER
```

Note that *NWN2* already provides five classes of standard encounters (very easy, easy, normal, hard, very hard), but they all assume players can only take part in hostile encounters. Ultimately, our goal becomes to extend the existing set of encounters with another five classes of encounters aimed at negotiation. The defuzzification process could use some of the parameters included in the encounter classes, first to decide whether a standard or a negotiation encounter takes place, and second to calibrate the level of difficulty of such an encounter. Going back to the rules R_1 and R_2 with levels of membership r_1 and r_2, our defuzzification operator will compute:

$$K = \max(r_1, r_2)$$

$$C = \text{round}(NK)$$

Here N represents the number of encounter classes, and C is the class candidate to spawning creatures. It makes sense to order the classes for a hostile encounter from *very low* to *very high* and to do the reverse with negotiation encounters. Such a mechanism could be refined using some of the parameters included in the classes (e.g., number of monsters spawned, monsters challenge rating, etc.).

Navigating Nonlinear Game Narrative

Consider a game with narrative content that is arranged as a nonlinear story. We will visualize its structure as a collection of game scenes (see Figure 6.2.3). Each circle marked with a bold label represents a scene of the game where multiple paths are allowed, whereas the other circles represent ordinary scenes that will make the storyline progress linearly. Striped circles indicate start or end scenes. Attaching scripting logic to each of the selection nodes, alternative paths can be taken based on the current level of competition. Thus, if our players replayed the game multiple times, they could visit different subplots as a result of the strategies adopted in any specific game session.

We will adopt fuzzy logic to express selection conditions and their formal proper-ties. Because of the quasi-natural linguistic variables, fuzzy logic can be better under-stood by game designers. Fuzzy logic is also renowned for providing robust solutions to control problems.

For example, plausible fuzzy rules would resemble:

```
R: IF cooperation IS HOSTILE THEN State3.2
```

or

```
R': IF cooperation IS NEUTRAL THEN State3.1
```

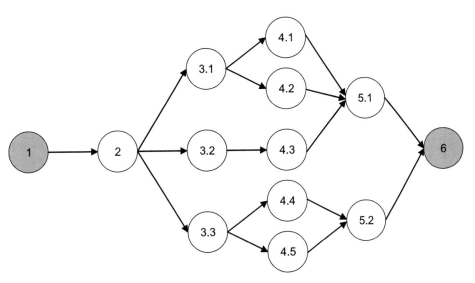

FIGURE 6.2.3   The depiction of a game narrative based on a nonlinear plot.

For example, the fuzzy predicate *cooperation* will use fuzzy membership functions as depicted in Figure 6.2.4. In practice, scene transitions will likely be triggered by conditions that contain both fuzzy predicates and crisp conditions relating to com-mon in-game events such as quests completion, items retrieval, and so on. A game structure will be needed to preserve nonlinear design without leading to exponential resource consumption. In literature, this is referred to as a *convexity* [Rabin05].

Ultimately, in this approach, role-playing and real-time strategy (RTS) are blended so that the story-driven approach familiar to RPG players can contain strategic ele-ments influencing the gameplay experience.

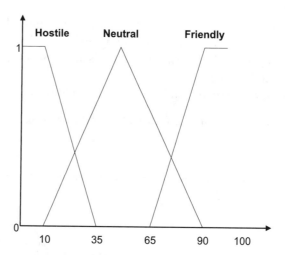

FIGURE 6.2.4   Membership functions chosen to model fuzzy cooperation predicates.

Experimental Results

To conduct a functional test of the model, we have implemented a prototype that will be integrated in our main scenario dubbed *Two Families*, an *NWN2* module currently in development in our labs.

The ODE solver necessary for the task has been based on the midpoint method (or Runge-Kutta order two) [Vetterling02], a good compromise between accuracy and efficiency in our specific situation. The scripts solving the ODE can be hooked up as an event handler in *NWN2*, in our case, the module's OnHeartbeat, which is invoked by the game engine every six seconds of real time.

The following code implements the ODE solver:

```
void main()
{
    if(GetGlobalInt("first")==0)
    {
        SetGlobalInt("first",1);
    }
    else
    {
        // Get objects and globals
        object oPC=GetObjectByTag("city");
        object oKal=GetObjectByTag("kalkarin");

        float x=GetGlobalFloat("x");
        float y=GetGlobalFloat("y");
        float dt=GetGlobalFloat("dt");
        float a=GetGlobalFloat("A");
        float b=GetGlobalFloat("B");
        float g=GetGlobalFloat("G");
```

```
float h=GetGlobalFloat("H");
float k=GetGlobalFloat("K");
float l=GetGlobalFloat("L");

// first evaluation of the derivative
float dx1=dt*(-a*x+k*y+g);
float dy1=dt*(l*x-b*y+h);

// second evaluation
float dx2=dt*(-a*(x+0.5*dx1)+k*(y+0.5*dy1)+g);
float dy2=dt*(l*(x+0.5*dx1)-b*(y+0.5*dy1)+h);

// ODE update
x+=dx2;
y+=dy2;
SetGlobalFloat("x",x);
SetGlobalFloat("y",y);
// adjust reputation now
SetFactionReputation(oPC,oKal,FloatToInt(x));
SetFactionReputation(oKal,oPC,FloatToInt(y));
AssignCommand(oKal, DetermineCombatRound());
AssignCommand(oPC, DetermineCombatRound());
        }
    }
```

First and foremost, the first if...else clause is used to delay the execution of the ODE solver by a few seconds: Apparently, there seems to be a delay between the end of the loading phase of a module and its execution (due to unpacking and other initialization).

The first instructions will retrieve two creatures representing their factions, and then all the parameters values will be copied to temporary variables: *NWN2* has global variables that can be retrieved via GetGlobalType statements, where Type is the type of the variable (Float in the previous example). Later on, two evaluations of the derivative are computed, and the final update is written to the global variables x and y. The last portion of code updates the reputation of the two factions' members, and a command is executed to determine whether hostilities will start. The SetFaction-Reputation function is not standard in *NWN2*, hence its code is listed here:

```
void SetFactionReputation(object oPC, object oSource, int nReputation)
{
    int nCurrentReputation =
        GetReputation(oPC, oSource);
    int nDelta = nReputation - nCurrentReputation;
    AdjustReputation(oPC, oSource, nDelta);
}
```

Even though we have not yet built an entire module integrating all the features of our model, we are going to present some relevant results obtained simulating in-game external events (in the sense explained in the section "An Improved Arms Race Model"). We maintain that being able to analyze in advance how the parameters affect the model's long-term behavior is a clear advantage. The model is random in nature, and the sources of external events can be either the players or the decision-making component of the game AI; we will draw no distinction between them to obtain more robust and general results.

However, before illustrating our results, here is some clarifications on the experimental data. First of all, we used a portion of the first quadrant (the subset $I = [0,100] \times [0,100]$) to constrain the trajectories of the system: This is a natural choice because we want to obtain positive values for both x and y. Besides, *NWN2* accepts reputation values in the range $[0,100]$ with lower values indicating a tendency to conflict.

Second, we assumed that if the value of competition for any faction falls outside the prescribed range, first it will be clamped, and after a certain amount of time, reset to a random coordinate indicating *neutrality*. This can be implemented by providing a constant that counts the number of times the system trajectory has been "banging" on the border of I. This assumption makes sense because we do not want to keep the system in a deadlock for too long.

The formulas currently used for resetting the system trajectory are:

$$x = 50 + 25 \cdot (0.5 - r)$$
$$y = 50 + 25 \cdot (0.5 - r)$$

Here r is a random number in the $[0,1]$ range, which means that after resetting the point, each coordinate will lie in $[37.5, 62.5]$. Clearly, other formulas could be used to bounce P, but this seems to produce interesting and robust results.

Finally, the examples provided here sample the state of the system over 5,000 iterations: Assuming our ODE solver is hooked to our module's `OnHeartbeat`, this will result in a time span of around 8.3 hours (a good-sized game session). Under these assumptions, we will inspect the qualitative effect of using different parameter sets and how this can be related to game scenarios. Let's examine the following cases:

Changing Richardson's model parameters set (a, b, k, l, g, h)

- Selecting different starting points
- Altering the probability distribution of the external events set
- Altering the λ–values

Changing the Original Parameters Set

The values of the parameters used in this first set of experiments are listed in Table 6.2.2.

Table 6.2.2 The Value of the Parameters Used in Our First Experiments

Parameter	Exp. 1	Exp. 2	Exp. 3	Exp. 4
a	10	100	1000	1
b	10	100	1000	1
k	20	200	2000	15

$\rightarrow$

Parameter	Exp. 1	Exp. 2	Exp. 3	Exp. 4
l	20	200	2000	15
g	−400	−4000	−40000	−400
h	−600	−6000	−60000	−600
Starting point	(30,50)	(30,50)	(30,50)	(30,50)
Prob. distribution	{0.5,2}	{0.5,2}	{0.5,2}	{0.5,2}

The effect of changing the fundamental parameters of the model is portrayed in Figures 6.2.5 and 6.2.6. Increasing the magnitude of the parameters has the effect of causing the system trajectory to bounce off the borders more often, being randomly reset to a new position as a result. Hence, the smaller the coefficients, the more deterministic the system is going to be. Because the number of possible paths is small, after some time, the same path will be taken again. In practice, game designers could fine-tune these values to tie in different types of political scenarios with their storylines and predict the average behavior of the system.

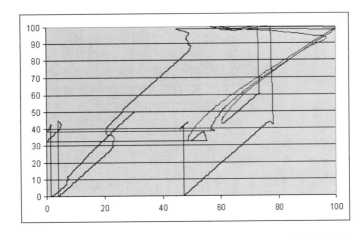

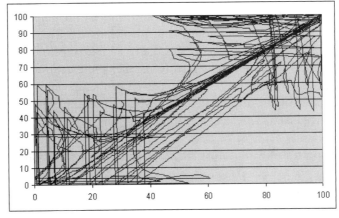

FIGURE 6.2.5 A simple trajectory and the recurrent double arrow shape.

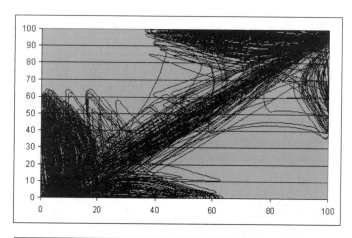

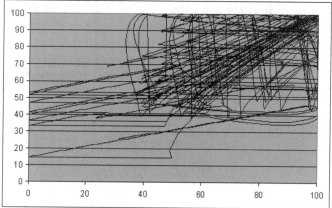

FIGURE 6.2.6   A thicker recurrent double arrow and an unusual arrow.

Selecting Different Starting Points

The moderate impact of selecting different starting points on the long-term behavior of the system did not come as a surprise. Given the random nature of the system (induced by external events and the reset mechanism), the starting point becomes a small factor in the whole picture. Clearly the magnitude of the original parameters plays a much bigger role as evidenced in the previous subsection. Nevertheless, we report in Figure 6.2.7 examples of different starting points in the hypothesis of having the original parameters set as in the previous section (Experiment 1).

Altering the Probability Distribution of the External Events Set

A very important role for the overall behavior of the system is played by the probability distribution of external events. Recalling that external events are in our current definition both induced by players and by the game AI, we proceed to present an interesting experiment.

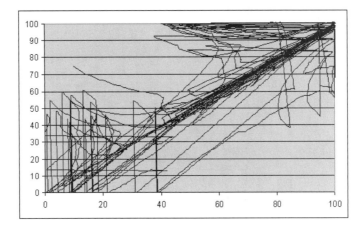

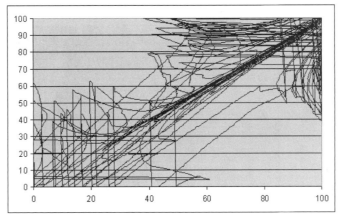

FIGURE 6.2.7 Starting from (10,75) and (50,50).

Let's examine a case where only two possible events are allowed: one intensifies the cooperation level, and the other weakens it. The effect of different probability distributions is provided in Figure 6.2.8. If we increase the probability of one event over the other, then we will witness either the system trajectories gathering around the origin (uttermost competition) or the opposite corner (total cooperation).

We want to stress that this conclusion is true in a probabilistic sense: If the system is more likely to be in a cooperative state, it does not mean it will never enter a phase of competition. This is in accordance with the examples provided earlier where the system gathered around the two points (0,0) and (100,100), giving rise to a peculiar double-arrowed shape. By adjusting the probability distribution, a game designer can steer a scenario more toward cooperation or competition.

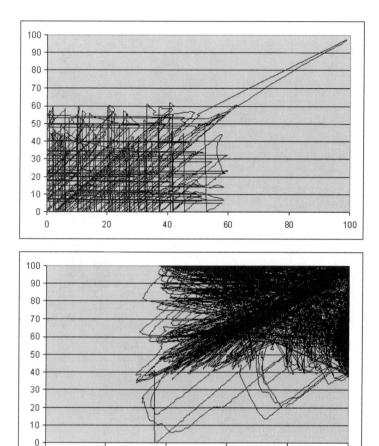

FIGURE 6.2.8   Using a {0.05,0.25} and a {0.5,0.25} distribution for external events.

Altering the λ-Values

The values of λ for each coefficient play a role similar to that of the probability distribution (see Figure 6.2.9). It is intuitive to think of the probability distribution as a set of weights for the λ-values, but a formal proof will need to be provided in the future.

Some simple results are given in Figure 6.2.9 that show how different values of λ influence the system trajectories. The same remarks on competition/cooperation given previously apply in this case as well.

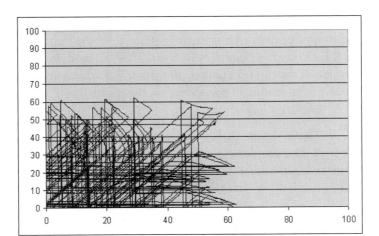

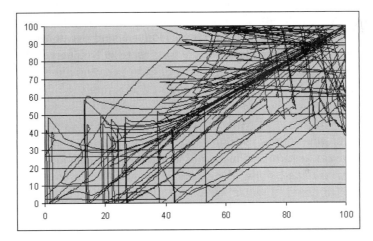

FIGURE 6.2.9 $\lambda=\{0.25,4\}$ and $\lambda=\{0.025,1.05\}$.

Future Work

We plan to analyze our model in more depth. It is not entirely clear if increasing the number of classes of events will cause the solution generated by the model to vary considerably. More classes of events clearly require more λ-values and more complex probability distributions, and a step in this direction will only be justified by a remarkable gain. Also, we will focus on clarifying the interaction between the manipulations of different parameters: For example, what would happen if λ-values and probability distributions were changed at the same time? Subsequently, the interaction between our model and the fuzzy rules presented here will be tested and incrementally refined.

Considerable resources will also be put into creating a narrative apparatus that can showcase, and at the same time, profit from the technical infrastructure provided here. Finally, while building a nonlinear *NWN2* module, the need will likely arise for a plugin of the Electron toolset [Electron07] that can preview the result of selecting a specific combination of parameters on the system.

Conclusion

We have introduced our stop-and-go variant of Richardson's model that can provide game designers with a tool to integrate political scenarios in their story-driven games and game mods. We have discussed the formal properties of the model, its advantages over existing approaches, and its current limitations.

The models and techniques introduced here will support *Two Families: A Tale of New Florence*, our *NWN2* module featuring a nonlinear plot. In *Two Families*, the player will take the side of one of two influential families in the fight for supremacy in a fictional recreation of medieval Florence, and decide whether to further their faction's political agenda or to act as a maverick. Treachery, political schemes, and plotting will be the main ingredients of our upcoming piece of interactive drama whose development is involving staff and students from the School of Computer Science & IT, and the School of Creative Media at RMIT University.

Our model provides for a complete way to modulate political balance in games, but it must not be necessarily limited to that. As long as a fundamental gameplay feature can be identified in a game, and an HCP can be built that abstracts its interaction with the game world, the game's AI programmers will be able to support the game's design team.

We hope that the discussion provided here will further developments in the area of formal methodologies for game design, game AI, and interactive storytelling, but even more, that game developers will find imaginative new ways to incorporate these ideas in their work.

References

[Boyce04] Boyce, W., and DiPrima, R., *Elementary Differential Equations and Boundary Value Problems*. John Wiley & Sons, 2004.

[Branicky94] Branicky, M., et al., "A Unified Framework for Hybrid Control." *Proceedings of the 33rd IEEE Conference on Decision and Control*, Vol. 4, (1994): pp. 4228–4234.

[Electron07] The Electron Toolset. Available online at *http://en.wikipedia.org/wiki/Electron_toolset*, May 31, 2007.

[Goulet83] Goulet, J., "Richardson's Arms Model and Arms Control." *Proceedings of the SIAM Conference on Discrete Math and Its Application*, 1983.

[Lexicon07] The NWN Lexicon. Available online at *http://www.nwnlexicon.com/*, May 31, 2007.

[Rabin05] Rabin, S. (ed.), *Introduction to Game Development.* Charles River Media, 2005.

[Vetterling02] Vetterling, W. T., and Flannery B. P., *Numerical Recipes in C++: The Art of Scientific Computing.* Cambridge University Press, 2002.

[Zadeh73] Zadeh, L. A., "Outline of a New Approach to the Analysis of Complex Systems." *IEEE Transactions on Man, Systems, and Cybernetics,* Vol. 3 (1973): pp. 28–44.

[Zambetta06] Zambetta, F., "Shaping Interactive Stories by Means of Dynamical Policy Models." *Proceedings of the GDTW2006 Conference,* 2006.

6.3

Individualized NPC Attitudes with Social Networks

Christian J. Darken—The MOVES Institute

cjdarken@nps.edu

John D. Kelly—U.S. Navy

wackonian@aol.com

Making the player feel that his actions are meaningful is a primary consideration in game design. To capture the social consequences of player actions, faction systems are a common choice. In a simple faction system, each NPC (nonplayer character, i.e. computer-controlled character) is assigned membership in a single faction. The faction's attitude toward the player is captured by a single number. When the attitude number is at one extreme, the faction hates the player. At the other extreme, the faction loves the player. Each possible player action is manually tagged with the numeric change in attitude that will occur for each faction if the action occurs.

Even a simple faction system adds significance to the player's choice of actions. First, the attitude number captures the history of the player's interaction with the faction, so the player's actions have long-term social consequences. Second, the grouping of NPCs into factions broadens the social implications of the player's actions; that is, if he offends one member of a faction, not only the one NPC, but also all of the other members of his faction will be hostile.

Despite these positives, this simple faction system has a frustrating limitation. Each NPC belonging to a given faction will have exactly the same attitude toward the player. This is simply not realistic enough for some applications. Real people participate in many faction-like relationships. Their loyalties are often in conflict. It is not uncommon for different members of the same faction to have wildly different attitudes toward a single issue or individual. In principle, this problem can be solved by considering each individual to be his own faction. In practice, this solution breaks down for even moderate numbers of NPCs and actions because specifying attitude changes for each action and NPC combination is too onerous. This article attempts to solve this problem through a technique that largely automates the computation of attitude changes.

In the next section, we describe how our mathematical attitude model is derived from the relationships among NPCs. We then describe an efficient implementation of the model and provide advice on content generation for it. We conclude with a brief discussion of how we tested the model.

The Attitude Model

In this section, we incrementally build up the attitude model, starting from our basic assumptions on how attitude and interpersonal relationships will be modeled, and proceeding through two candidate models before arriving at the model we think is best.

Let's assume that an NPC's attitude toward the player is described by a single floating-point number, where zero is a neutral attitude, and more positive means a more favorable attitude. Our primary goal is to compute an attitude change toward the player given his latest action. The attitude change can then be added to the NPC's previous attitude, possibly limiting the result to lie within a desired interval, such as [−1, +1], where −1 is hatred, and +1 is love.

Social Networks

Social networks represent the social relationships among a group of individuals as a mathematical graph. Individual people are the nodes of the graph, and the directed edges represent the relationships that exist between the connected individuals. Directed edges let us model asymmetric situations, such as that of a false friend or a father who keeps his eye on a son who is not aware of his existence. The edge direction convention we will use is that the "to" node of an edge perceives that he has the indicated relationship with the "from" node. The study of behavior as it is influenced by social networks is called social network analysis and is an active area of behavioral science research [Wasserman95].

Given the social network in Figure 6.3.1, we expect that actions that are good for Bill are also welcomed by Art, although to a lesser extent than an equally helpful action done directly for Art. Similarly, actions that are good for Cal are bad for Bill as Cal's enemy and thus somewhat bad for Art as well.

Social Networks as Dynamical Systems

We will now reconceptualize the social network as a dynamical system, that is, a set of mathematical equations that precisely defines the changes in attitude that result from any single player action. One pass through the equations reflects each NPC reacting only to those NPCs that it cares about. The equations can then be applied repeatedly to model higher-order effects, for example, the reaction of one NPC to another NPC's reaction to a third NPC. The state of the system will be a vector containing each NPC's attitude change toward the player resulting from the action. Let's assume that the attitude change that each action precipitates in each NPC if there were no other people in the world is known. We call these change numbers the "direct effect"

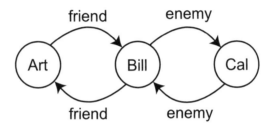

FIGURE 6.3.1 A simple social network.

of the action. If each NPC did not care about any NPC other than himself, the result of a player action simply adds the direct effect of the action to the NPC's attitude toward the player.

NPC-to-NPC Affinity

We now add to our model a notion of affinity. Each NPC X has an affinity of zero with all NPCs Y with which he has no relationship, that is, all NPCs Y such that there is no edge from Y to X (note the direction) in the social network. For all NPCs with which X has one or more relationships, we summarize that relationship as a single number. A positive affinity means that X's attitude toward the player will improve (increase) if the player helps Y. A negative affinity means that X's attitude toward the player will deteriorate (decrease) if the player helps Y. The larger the magnitude of affinity, the greater this effect will be for any given action. For completeness, we will also include a self-affinity value that moderates how sensitive an NPC is to direct effects versus effects on the other NPCs that it cares about.

First Approach: Linear Model

Consider the following approach to completing our model. When a player takes an action, we initialize the value at each node (NPC) to be the direct effect of the action on that NPC times his self-affinity. Now we want these values to propagate around the system to get effects as described in Figure 6.3.1. For each NPC X's node, we could simultaneously update X's attitude change to be the direct effect on X times his self-affinity, plus the sum of the product of the other NPC's attitude changes with X's affinity for the NPC. This already represents changes in the attitude of NPC X due to actions that have no (zero) direct effect on him but do affect other NPCs with which he has either positive or negative affinity. To add in higher-order effects, such as Art's reaction to a player action with a direct effect only on Carl, we can repeat the update multiple times.

Let's try to put some numbers to this example. Consider an action that only directly affects Carl and with magnitude +1.0; that is, Carl likes it. The direct effects on Art, Bill, and Carl, respectively, can therefore be represented as the vector $(0.0 \ 0.0 \ 1.0)^T$. Art's affinities for Bill and Carl can be represented as the vector $(0.0 \ 0.5 \ 0.0)$. Note that the first position in the vector represents his affinity for himself, which is represented elsewhere as we choose to construct the model. He has a positive affinity for Bill and none for Carl. Bill's affinities might be (0.4 0.0 –0.3); that is, he likes Art, but a little less than Art likes him, and he dislikes Carl. Carl's affinities are (0.0 –0.3 0.0); that is, he returns Bill's dislike. We can put the affinities together in the form of a matrix:

$\begin{pmatrix} 0.0 & 0.5 & 0.0 \\ 0.4 & 0.0 & -0.3 \\ 0.0 & -0.3 & 0.0 \end{pmatrix}$. Letting the self-affinities all be 1.0 and putting them on the diagonal

of a matrix gives us a self-affinity matrix of $\begin{pmatrix} 1.0 & 0.0 & 0.0 \\ 0.0 & 1.0 & 0.0 \\ 0.0 & 0.0 & 1.0 \end{pmatrix}$. This matrix modifies the

direct effects by multiplying them, which does nothing with this choice of self-affinity values. Initializing the attitude change vector to be the self-affinity matrix times the direct effect vector yields $\mathbf{x}(0) = (0.0\ 0.0\ 1.0)^T$. Carl is happy, and the other two guys do not care. But Carl's happiness is bound to make Bill unhappy. To reflect this, we should update the attitude changes as follows:

$$\mathbf{x}(1) = \begin{pmatrix} 0.0 & 0.5 & 0.0 \\ 0.4 & 0.0 & -0.3 \\ 0.0 & -0.3 & 0.0 \end{pmatrix} \mathbf{x}(0) + \begin{pmatrix} 0.0 \\ 0.0 \\ 1.0 \end{pmatrix} = \begin{pmatrix} 0.0 \\ -0.3 \\ 1.0 \end{pmatrix}.$$

Now Bill is unhappy, but to see any effect on Art, we need to update again:

$$\mathbf{x}(2) = \begin{pmatrix} 0.0 & 0.5 & 0.0 \\ 0.4 & 0.0 & -0.3 \\ 0.0 & -0.3 & 0.0 \end{pmatrix} \mathbf{x}(1) + \begin{pmatrix} 0.0 \\ 0.0 \\ 1.0 \end{pmatrix} = \begin{pmatrix} -0.15 \\ -0.3 \\ 1.09 \end{pmatrix}.$$

Notice that Carl is now even happier than before because his enemy has become unhappy. Note that the additive term, which is simply the self-affinity matrix multiplied by the vector of direct effects, remains the same in each iteration.

But with multiple updates, some ugly questions arise. Clearly the attitude change values will be altered with each update, so how many times should the update be repeated? And will the NPC attitude change converge to stable values, oscillate, or maybe even blow up? The answer is that any of these behaviors are possible. Fortunately, the linear model can be enhanced to avoid this problem.

Second Approach: Recurrent Neural Network Model
To keep the attitude change value bounded, we might then pass the attitude through a saturating sigmoidal function, such as tanh (hyperbolic tangent), which is never larger than +1 or less than –1. The result is a classic recurrent neural network. We mention this fact merely as a point of interest for those of you who may be interested

in the application of neural networks. Recurrent neural networks are able to produce an incredibly broad range of behavior. This type of model might be interesting for applications that require a complicated response to a single player action unfolding over time, but it is overkill for our immediate problem.

Recommended Approach: Constrained Linear Model

The main model we want to study is a linear model that is subject to constraints on the affinity values to ensure that the model converges nicely. Let's assume that for each NPC, the sum of the magnitudes of all its affinities to other NPCs is strictly less than one.

Our system can then be mathematically described as follows:

- **A**: Matrix of affinities.
- $A_{i,j}$: The affinity of NPC i for NPC j. $A_{i,j} = 0$ for all i as we handle self-affinity below.
- **B**: Diagonal matrix of self-affinities
- $B_{i,j}$: The self-affinity of NPC i. $B_{i,j} = 1$ if $i = j$, and zero otherwise.
- **u**: The vector of direct effects.
- $\mathbf{x}(n)$: The attitude change after n updates.

Our constraints are that for all i, $B_{i,j} > 0$ and $\sum_j \left| A_{i,j} \right| < 1$.

The matrix update equation is simply: $\mathbf{x}(n + 1) = \mathbf{Ax}(n) + \mathbf{Bu}$, where $\mathbf{x}(0) = \mathbf{Bu}$.

Convergence of the Constrained Linear Model

The most important property of the constrained linear model is that the attitude change vector always converges; that is, it never oscillates forever or blows up. The point of the following discussion is to show that the model does have this property. This section may be skipped if desired.

If $\mathbf{x}(n)$ converged to a constant vector, what would that vector be? If $\mathbf{x}(n)$ converged, then we would have $\mathbf{x}(n + 1) = \mathbf{x}(n)$. In this case, let's name this value $\bar{\mathbf{x}}$. If $\bar{\mathbf{x}}$ is the converged value, it must satisfy the so-called fixed point equation, $\bar{\mathbf{x}} = \mathbf{A}\bar{\mathbf{x}} + \mathbf{Bu}$. Let's define $\mathbf{y}(n) = \mathbf{x}(n) - \bar{\mathbf{x}}$. If $\mathbf{x}(n)$ converges to $\bar{\mathbf{x}}$, then clearly $\mathbf{y}(n)$ converges to zero and vice versa.

We will now show that $\mathbf{y}(n)$ does converge to zero. $\mathbf{y}(n + 1) = \mathbf{x}(n + 1) - \bar{\mathbf{x}}$, so by the matrix update equation:

$$\mathbf{y}(n + 1) = \mathbf{Ax}(n) + \mathbf{Bu} - \bar{\mathbf{x}} = \mathbf{Ax}(n) + \mathbf{Bu} - \bar{\mathbf{x}} + (\mathbf{A}\bar{\mathbf{x}} - \mathbf{A}\bar{\mathbf{x}}) = \mathbf{Ay}(n) + \mathbf{Bu} - \bar{\mathbf{x}} + \mathbf{A}\bar{\mathbf{x}} + \mathbf{Ay}(n)$$

The first and last expressions from the extended equality constitute an update equation for $\mathbf{y}$, namely $\mathbf{y}(n + 1) = \mathbf{Ay}(n)$. We know from the constraints, that the magnitudes in each row of $\mathbf{A}$ sum to less than 1. Let $\alpha < 1$ be the largest sum of magnitudes from any row, and $y_{\max}$ be the magnitude of the largest element of $\mathbf{y}(n)$. Thus, the largest element in $\mathbf{y}(n + 1)$ can be no larger than αy_{max}. We see that the largest element in $\mathbf{y}(n)$ is shrinking at least as fast as α^n, and because α^n converges to zero, so does $\mathbf{y}(n)$, and thus $\mathbf{x}(n)$ converges to $\bar{\mathbf{x}}$.

Implementation

In this section, we provide advice on implementing the model and also on content creation for it, that is, the practical aspects of defining the parameters of the model. We will show that iterating the dynamical system we defined in the previous section is not necessary; the solution can be directly computed. We suggest a "divide and conquer" approach to the development of affinity matrices for games with large numbers of NPCs. Finally, we discuss one specific potential problem—NPCs with very different numbers of relationships—and how it can be managed.

Solving for Attitude Change Without Iteration

Although the previous analysis shows that the constrained linear model converges at an exponential rate, it also indicates that iterating the model until it converges is not strictly necessary. $\mathbf{x}(n)$ converges to $\bar{\mathbf{x}}$, and we know that $\bar{\mathbf{x}} = \mathbf{A}\bar{\mathbf{x}} + \mathbf{B}\mathbf{u}$. This equation can be directly solved to yield $\bar{\mathbf{x}} = (I - \mathbf{A})^{-1}\mathbf{B}\mathbf{u}$. So if we are willing to pay the roughly $O(n^3)$ cost of inverting the appropriate matrix, we can compute the attitude change vector corresponding to a vector of direct effects by a simple matrix multiplication. Note that if the NPC affinities do not change at runtime, this matrix inversion can be precomputed. If affinities do change at runtime, it may be more efficient to use techniques that directly solve for $\bar{\mathbf{x}}$ without matrix inversion [Press07].

Construction of Affinity Matrices

Constructing affinity matrices is a challenging aspect of this technique when the number of NPCs and types of relationship become large. To better manage large examples, several matrices, one per relationship type, can be created separately. We used three matrices in our large example: family, work, and friends/foes. We then combined the matrices by summing them and then normalizing the total magnitude to satisfy the constraint. For even larger systems, we suggest constructing a rule-based system that turns each relationship into an increment or decrement of one of the affinity values in a generic way; for example, "coworkers get a +0.1 increment." The values resulting from running the rules can then be tweaked to enhance NPC individuality and represent special circumstances before being magnitude-normalized.

For very large numbers of NPCs, such as required for a massively multiplayer game, we further suggest a hierarchical approach to determining attitude changes. Each faction or other group can be conceptualized as an "abstract individual" that participates in relationships with the other factions and groups. As a preliminary step, the mechanics previously described can determine an "official group attitude change" vector **v**. Group membership for individual NPCs can be represented as having positive affinities toward the "abstract individuals" represented in an additional matrix **C**. Individuals that are proximate to one another and strongly interacting can then be modeled separately with the update equation $\mathbf{x}(n + 1) = \mathbf{Ax}(n) + \mathbf{Bu} + \mathbf{Cv}$, having fixed point solution $\bar{\mathbf{x}} = (I - \mathbf{A})^{-1}(\mathbf{Bu} + \mathbf{Cv})$. We have thus decomposed what would otherwise be a massive matrix equation into a hierarchy of much smaller ones.

Modeling Individuals with Vastly Different Numbers of Relationships

Modeling individuals with vastly different numbers of relationships represents a special challenge. For example, when we were developing our test scenarios, we created an event where a child's life was saved, but we only had a direct effect on the child herself. Because the child's friends had very few relationships, and the child's parents had many, this resulted in the child's friends having a larger positive change in affinity than the parents of the child. This problem can be solved either by modeling the action as having a positive direct effect on the parents or by simply scaling the child friendship affinities down relative to the parents and adjusting the magnitude of the direct effect on the child appropriately.

Testing

We have shown that the constrained linear model is well behaved: it always converges to a single value that is in a known range. But how realistic are the attitude changes it predicts? This is a daunting question that cannot be dealt with authoritatively. However, we can create some extreme scenarios where we have a clear intuition as to the "correct" attitude change, and see how the model compares. We modeled both a tiny scenario of 5 NPCs and a larger, more complicated, social network with 27 NPCs and put them through testing [Kelly07]. Because the test set includes more than 70 cases, we refrain from a detailed discussion here. In each case, we found the model was capable, with proper tuning, of matching our qualitative expectations of behavior change. The most problematic case involved NPCs with very different numbers of relationships, and we resolved it as discussed in the previous section. The spreadsheet containing the test examples and results is provided on the CD-ROM.

ON THE CD

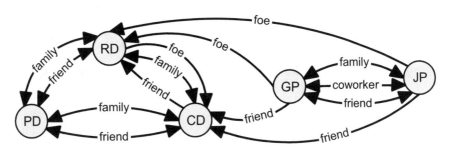

FIGURE 6.3.2 Detail of 5 NPCs from a social network of 27 NPCs.

Source Code and Demo

ON THE CD

The CD-ROM includes a spreadsheet containing 5-person and 27-person test cases and an implementation of the constrained linear model written in Python, either of which may be useful for testing other sample cases.

Related Work

This article has focused on a single aspect of building a system to track and exploit NPC attitudes. Two previous articles give a better big-picture system view, as well as offering interesting mechanisms of their own, such as specific event knowledge tracking [Alt02] and a multidimensional approach to modeling attitude [Russell06].

Conclusion

This article introduced a method for largely automating NPC changes in attitude due to a player action. The method resolves the conflicting loyalties of the NPCs to produce a single number per NPC that can be used to update the NPC's feelings toward the player and drive future player-NPC interactions. This simple model could be further developed in a straightforward way by allowing NPC affinities to vary at runtime. A more difficult but extremely interesting improvement might involve modeling the time delay required for information to propagate through the social network. Our tests of more than 70 cases involving scenarios of 5 and 27 NPCs support our belief in the utility of the model.

References

[Alt02] Alt, Greg, and King, Kristin, "A Dynamic Reputation System Based on Event Knowledge." *AI Game Programming Wisdom,* Charles River Media, 2002: pp. 426–435.

[Kelly07] Kelly, John, "Automated Run-Time Mission and Dialog Generation." Master's thesis, Naval Postgraduate School 2007. Available online at *http://www.nps. edu/Library/index.html.*

[Press07] Press, William, Teukolsky, Saul, Vetterling, William, and Flannery, Brian, *Numerical Recipes: The Art of Scientific Computing,* 3rd ed.. Cambridge University Press, 2007.

[Russell06] Russell, Adam, "Opinion Systems." *AI Game Programming Wisdom 3,* Charles River Media, 2006: pp. 531–554.

[Wasserman95] Wasserman, Stanley, and Faust, Katherine, *Social Network Analysis: Methods and Applications.* Cambridge University Press, 1995.

6.4

Scripting Your Way to Advanced AI

Alistair Doulin—Auran Games

alistair@doolwind.com

In the past, AI has primarily been created by programmers to meet the needs of game designers. This article discusses the advantages of using scripting to empower game designers to create advanced AI themselves. By tightly linking each level's script with its AI, designers create the AI as the level is being prototyped. This allows natural AI creation because each level has its own specialized behaviors created by the designers.

To highlight the benefit of AI scripting, an example is given of how the designer on *Battlestar Galactica* (*BSG*) [Auran07] for Xbox Live Arcade used script to create the single-player AI. Through a good mix of native code and script, advanced AI can be created, taking advantage of the flexibility of script while leveraging the performance of native code.

This article opens with an introduction to GameMonkey Script (GM) along with a discussion on the types of functions that should be bound. Next, the reasons for using script for AI instead of relying solely on programmer-created AI are discussed. Following this are details on the implementation used in *BSG* and the common pitfalls of using script for AI. The article concludes with a discussion on the future opportunities for script use.

An Introduction to GameMonkey (GM) Script

This article is relevant to any scripting language. However, due to first-hand experience and knowledge, GM will be the focus. GM is an embedded scripting language designed specifically for games. It has concepts similar to Lua and has a C-style syntax, which makes it easily accessible to game programmers. GM natively supports multithreading and the concept of states for use in finite state machines (FSMs). It is free for any use, and its C++ code base is easily modified.

The following is a short example of a GM script used to make a unit kill an enemy:

```
KillEnemy = function( a_enemy )
{
    MoveTo( a_enemy.GetPosition() );
    result = FireOnEnemy( a_enemy );
    if( result.status == SUCCESS )
    {
        // Insert code to kill other enemies
    }
};
```

Most of this script should be familiar to C/C++ programmers with the main exception being the function declaration itself. In GM, functions are treated as variables and therefore have a slightly different syntax than C++. Because GM is loosely typed, the single parameter to the KillEnemy function does not need its type specified.

The first line of KillEnemy calls the MoveTo function, passing in the enemy's position, and will block/wait until the entity has reached it. FireOnEnemy will also block until either the player or the enemy is killed and returns SUCCESS if it was successful.

As a full introduction to GM is beyond the scope of this article, refer to the GM script reference [Douglas05] or other online tutorials [Wilkinson06] for more information.

Binding Functions to GM

ON THE CD

The key to using GM is binding C++ functions to script, making them accessible to designers within their script files. The online tutorials and source code included with this article have details for achieving this.

The following code shows an example of a bound C++ function:

```
int GM_CDECL GameSys_GetImageWidth(gmThread * a_thread)
{
    GM_CHECK_NUM_PARAMS(1);
    GM_CHECK_INT_PARAM( a_imageID, 0);

    int width = GetWidth( a_imageID );

    a_thread->PushInt( width );

    return GM_OK;
}
```

All bound functions take a gmThread as their only parameter, which is used to interact with the script system. The first two lines of the function contain two macros built in to GM that check for one parameter and then read the first parameter into the variable a_imageID. The next line is general game code that finds the width of an image given an ID. The PushInt function is used to return a value back to the GM system, allowing it to be read by the script that calls this function. GM_OK is returned to the GM system to inform it that the function completed successfully.

The following code shows an example of calling the previous C++ function from within script:

```
width = gameSys.GetImageWidth( imageID );
```

A single parameter is passed in, with a single return value being stored in `width`. *BSG* used helper functions to automate binding, making it relatively seamless and painless. The following is an example of the syntax used:

```
Bind( "GetImageWidth", &GetWidth, "i", 'i' );
```

This code automates the process of binding the script's `GetImageWidth` function to the native `GetWidth` function. The third and fourth parameters specify that the bound function takes and returns an `int` parameter, respectively. This single line removes the need for the `GameSys_GetImageWidth` function, simplifying the task of binding C++ functions to script.

Game Data in GM

Another feature of GM is its data structure support. GM allows game data to be stored in a convenient and flexible format. It has advantages over simple XML data structures due to its human-readable syntax, simple commenting, and expression evaluation. The simplest AI scripts can be nothing more than data structures that are edited by designers and loaded in by the C++ code at runtime. Although this usage will not take full advantage of GM, it's a good way of introducing GM to designers to demonstrate the flexibility they can achieve. The following is an example of how game data can be stored in a GM script:

```
print("Parsing Level Data");
global config =
{
    levelDisplayName = "Level1\nFirst Level",
    levelFilename = `\levels\level1.lvl`,
    localizedName = LanguageString("STR_Level1"),
    numLives = 3,

    // difficulty: 0 = easy, 1 = medium, 2 = hard
    difficulty = GameSys.GetDifficulty(),
    difficultyFactors = { 0.75, 1.0, 1.25 },
    enemyHealth = 500 * difficultyFactors[difficulty],
};
// On hard, one less life
if( config.difficulty == 2 )
{
    config.numLives-=1;
}
```

This example shows a number of GM features that support game data structures, some of which are listed here:

- Printing debug information for the user
- Different data types, including strings, integers, and floating-point numbers
- C++-style commenting
- Arrays
- Function calls to query or calculate values
- Conditionals

Choosing Functions to Bind

Function choice is an integral part of empowering designers for scripting AI. With the right selection of functions, designers can access the functionality they require without worrying about the implementation details of different techniques.

When binding these functions, the AI programmer must determine how low level or high level the functions should be. Low-level functions allow access to the inner workings of game objects and tend to be better suited to technical designers or programmers. High-level functions are better suited to more complex operations, such as navigation. Should the core workings of game objects be bound, or should more high-level functions be created that do a lot of work to help the designer? The core user of the functions will be the level designers, so their skill and preferences will help determine the type of bound functions.

Advantages and Disadvantages of Low-Level and High-Level Bindings

The following is a list of each style's advantages and disadvantages:

Low-level advantages include the following:

- Designers have complete freedom to create any behaviors they choose.
- Each function maps directly to a single action, making them easily understandable.
- They are quick and easy for programmers to implement.
- No design specification is needed because programmers simply bind the properties of game objects that are required.

Low-level disadvantages include the following:

- It can be confusing for nontechnical designers to deal with raw object interactions.
- AI becomes script-heavy, and performance must be monitored.
- Experimentation by other team members can be reduced because they must explicitly code every behavior.
- There is less abstraction from straight C++ code. Any major changes to C++ code can require entire rewrites of script.

High-level advantages include the following:

- AI is executed quickly because the AI functionality is primarily written in native code.
- Complex solutions can be hidden and abstracted into a single function.
- It is easier to use for nontechnical designers.
- Programmers still have control over the core workings of AI.
- Complexity of scripts is reduced.

High-level disadvantages include the following:

- Designers have less flexibility.
- A large investment of programmer time is required.
- A good design specification must be set out before programmers can begin creating functions.

Often, the best solution is to use a mix of low-level and high-level functions. For clarity, it is good practice to keep different types of functions separated into groups when documenting. This separation makes the types clear to the designers and allows them to focus on the style they prefer while having the option to experiment.

Low-level functions must be explained to nontechnical designers because they will generally be overwhelmed by the complexity of the functions. Experience has shown that giving examples of a function's use is the best way to bridge the gap for most designers. When designers see the flexibility that can be achieved, they will take the time to understand how the functions work and experiment with them. Tables 6.4.1 and 6.4.2 show a comparison of functions used in the AITest example source code. The functions are called on the player's ship to access its properties and invoke its actions.

Table 6.4.1 Low-Level Functions from Example Source Code

Function	Parameters	Description
Turn	Float	Turn the craft left or right. Input ranges from −1.0f to +1.0f.
Fire	Boolean	Turn bullet firing on or off.
GetX	None	Returns the x position on screen of this ship.
GetVX	None	Returns the velocity in the x direction of this ship.

Input ranges from −1.0f to +1.0f. Fire Boolean Turn bullet firing on or off. `GetX` None Returns the x position on screen of this ship. `GetVX` None Returns the velocity in the x direction of this ship.

Table 6.4.2 High-Level Functions from Example Source Code

Function	Parameters	Description
MoveTo	Float, Float	Move this ship to a position.
AttackPlayer	Table	Make this ship attack the enemy ship. The parameter is a table representing the enemy ship.
EvadeSun	None	Stop this ship from running into the sun.

Binding Other Objects

There are two other types of objects that require bound functions along with the game objects. The first is the game system object, which includes functions such as returning the world size and returning the game's last frame time. This object exposes functions allowing designers to interact with the game engine. The second includes any helper objects that are used within the script. These can include different data types, such as a vector or math library.

Although these objects do not relate directly to the game objects that designers will be interacting with to add AI, they are an integral part of creating the AI scripts. The functionality for these objects should be created as early as possible and should be well documented so that designers can take full advantage of them.

Rapid Prototyping

One of the key advantages of using GM to write AI code is its support for rapid prototyping. Due to language features, such as simple threading and data manipulation, GM makes many tasks faster to develop than C++.

Scripts can be changed and reloaded at runtime, reducing the time to fix and retest problems. When an error occurs, the entire game is not broken, instead the problem is kept within a level or even a single game object. This saves time because designers will make many mistakes as they begin creating AI scripts. GM allows a designer to change a few lines of code and retest immediately rather than waiting for recompilation of their code.

Because game-level scripting and AI are tightly linked, the AI can be prototyped along with the level. Rather than creating a full level and its gameplay before the AI code is added, the designer has control over the AI throughout all stages of level development. This also helps to find problems in the level's design that the AI might not support early in its development. It can also feed back into the level-creation process if the AI is particularly intelligent in areas that can be expanded.

An example of this tight linking is the creation of a level boss. If the boss's AI is particularly strong when fighting in close quarters, then the designer can create large sections of the map that require close-quarters combat. If the boss has a particular weakness when trying to navigate up stairs, the designer can make sure to keep stairs to a minimum in the level. Level design then becomes more natural for the designer because he interacts with the AI during its creation. Designers build the level around the AI rather than creating a level that the AI must fit into.

Another advantage of rapid prototyping is that designers, or any other team members, are able to take a build and experiment with the AI without interrupting programmers or requiring an intricate knowledge of the game systems. This experimentation can be invaluable as ideas that might usually be overlooked due to time constraints can be prototyped by any team member in a short period of time. On *BSG*, all team members from QA to management have been interested enough to experiment and bring new ideas to the designer.

Specialization FSM Example

GM also allows rapid prototyping through the use of specialization. Rather than creating new classes for each behavior, specialized functions are created. The following is an example of how specialization can be used to create powerful scripts specific to each level of the game. The first code sample shows a generic FSM that would be executed in all AI entities:

```
// CurrentState is a variable of type function
entity.CurrentState = function() { yield(); };

while( true )
{
    // Call the function represented by CurrentState
    result = entity.CurrentState();
}
```

Throughout its lifetime, the entity calls the function represented by its current state. CurrentState is a variable holding a function. Any function within the script can be assigned to this variable.

Within each particular game level, specialized code can then be written and is assigned to the CurrentState variable. The following is an example of a function that searches for an enemy:

```
InitLevel = function()
{
    playerAlly = GetPlayerAlly();
    playerAlly.CurrentState = SearchForEnemy();
};

SearchForEnemy = function()
{
    enemy = FindClosestEnemy();

    while( !IsFacing( enemy ) )
    {
        TurnTowards( enemy.GetDirection() );
        yield();
    }

    entity.CurrentState = AttackEnemy();
};
```

In this example, the InitLevel function is called at the start of the level and assigns the SearchForEnemy function to the ally's current state. The generic AI FSM will then call this specialized function. Also notice that when the entity is facing the enemy, it changes its own state to AttackEnemy, another specialized function. Through this specialization, powerful AI behaviors are created that can be shared between missions or written specifically for level entities.

Nontechnical Designers

The term nontechnical is used to describe designers who have little to no scripting or coding experience. These designers must be taught the basics of programming followed by an introduction to GM. We spent a number of days teaching the designer these basics followed by weeks of sitting with him and creating his first AI scripts. The following is an overview of the lessons learned from this, with tips on how to best help designers learn the complex task of AI scripting.

Nontechnical designers will generally use one of the following techniques for their development while they are learning to script [Poiker02]:

- Copying and pasting code from other examples, and changing values and small pieces of code.
- Trial and error by spending countless hours testing and retesting different code. Because GM scripts can be reloaded at runtime, this process was far shorter than performing it in C++.
- Searching through the GM and bound script function documentation.
- One-on-one time spent with programmers asking them for advice on solving complex problems or learning different techniques of development.

An important problem when nontechnical designers create AI scripts is the performance overhead. Because they do not have a thorough knowledge of software development, they will often create solutions that are suboptimal. Care must be taken to continually review their scripts to make sure no major bottlenecks are being created. Designers will often create endless loops rather than using a more event-based system. Both styles can be used for convenience in prototyping gameplay; however, care must be taken when game performance begins to suffer.

To aid the nontechnical designer, a template style of development was implemented. Programmers create the core script with most of the levels' functionality, allowing the designer to simply change the existing code. Because the AI is a strong part of the level, it evolves in the same way. The basic steps are as follows:

1. The programmer creates the script.
2. The programmer sits with the designer and explains each part of the script.
3. The designer spends time tweaking the code that is there and takes code from other levels if necessary.
4. When the designer is happy with the basic functionality, he goes through their modifications with the programmer to make sure there are no major problems.
5. The designer polishes the level until it is complete.

This template system was a great help to the designer while he created his first levels and became accustomed to writing AI script. He created a number of boss-type characters, which exhibited some excellent AI that surprised both him and the programming team. After the designers are capable of creating levels on their own, the programmer's job becomes one of simple maintenance and support, allowing them to move on to other areas.

GM's ease of use for nontechnical designers was proven by the designer's ability to create moderately advanced AI within one month of learning to write script. This AI included different unit behaviors, bosses, and intelligent teammate design. The designer then went on to create an entire single-player game with only 40 bound script functions relating to AI.

Common Pitfalls

AI scripting will not solve all problems, and trying to make it do so will result in an underperforming and bloated script. The weaknesses of script must be taken into account when trying to solve a problem. Some games are simply too complex to allow designers to create the AI. The following is a list of the core weaknesses of script with information on how to overcome them.

Performance

GM is 10 to 100 times slower than native C++ code. Small simple tasks can be completed in script, however, anything complex should be moved into native code and bound to script. A good example of this is navigation. All of the complexities of navigation—navigation mesh generation, A* calculations, and so on—are kept in native code while a simple function MoveTo() is bound to script. This function is difficult to abuse because it is a simple function that sets the destination for a game object. In the object's next native code update loop, it can then do all the work necessary to path to the destination, without the designer knowing anything of its implementation.

Performance was never a problem with any of the scripts the designer created for *BSG*. This was made easier by the fact that the designer had never programmed before and therefore had not picked up any bad habits in the past. A proactive attitude was taken when dealing with performance issues to make sure they were caught and fixed before they became problems.

Limited Debugger Support

Unfortunately, there is little debugging support in GM at the moment. This encourages keeping scripts short and robust, with an emphasis on making them event-driven. It is important that designers are aware of the common programming techniques for debugging without a full IDE. Simple techniques, such as Print() statements and onscreen debug text, should be shown to designers as well as techniques for using these to find and solve problems. Although it's fun for experienced programmers to try and write infallible scripts, it is a nightmare for designers and will be another barrier for experimentation for the rest of the team.

ON THE CD

In the source code included on the CD-ROM with this article, all debugging errors are printed to the console window. In *BSG*, the designer knew that whenever a problem occurred, he should check the console for any errors to help solve the problem. He was then able to fix the problem, reload the script, and continue testing immediately without the need for recompilation or restarting the game.

The GME command-line executable is included with GM. It can compile script outside of the game. It provides limited compile-time error checking that allows basic syntax-style errors to be caught. Use gme.exe, located in the bin directory of the GM source, to compile scripts as shown in the following example:

```
gme.exe player2AI.gm —d
```

This will compile the script in player2AI.gm. The —d switch will compile it in debug mode so that if any problems are encountered, the exact line will be displayed.

Complexity

The two main areas of complexity that grow as AI and levels become more advanced are bound functions and level files. The AI programmer must continually check these issues and fix them before they become a problem.

Bound function issues include the following:

- Each piece of functionality exposed to designers adds another function they must learn about and remember.
- When the list grows over 100 functions, designers can become overwhelmed because they waste time searching for functions.
- Related functions should be grouped together, and AI functions should be completely separated from the other bound functions.
- If there are multiple AI programmers, functions might be duplicated, which leads to confusion for the designers.

Level file issues include the following:

- Level files can become quite complex during their development.
- AI code might only take up 30% of a level file, however, because it is mixed in with the rest of the level files' code, it is more difficult to maintain.
- Level files can grow into the thousands of lines making them difficult for designers to keep track of.
- Designers should be encouraged to clean up their code as it is developed. *BSG* experienced problems where a level was rewritten several times, and the script increased in size each time, leaving a lot of wasted code. When the designer was forced to clean up the level file, over 50% of the code was removed, making it easier to maintain.

Part of the programmer's job is to help the designer keep these two areas of complexity under control. As the designer's reliance on the programmer decreases, the programmer should begin cleaning up the work that has already been completed. Nearly all problems of complexity can be removed by keeping documentation up to date, cleaning out unused parts of script, and rewriting any functions that become bloated.

Source Code

ON THE CD

Included on the CD-ROM is the source code for a *Space Wars* [Cinematronics77] clone. All of the AI for this game has been written in GM. The game itself is also written in GM with the C++ executable simply loading and rendering images. This was done to show the power of GM and give more reference to its uses. In the real world, a full game would not be programmed entirely in GM. The game uses SDL for rendering and input. The art was created by Shaun Campbell at *www.squidtank.com*.

Experimentation with the code is encouraged as well as creating completely new script files. Both high-level and low-level functions have been bound to show examples of their usage.

Future Work

There is great opportunity to use AI scripting for game development in the future. The following is a discussion about two areas that will greatly benefit from moving AI into script.

Mod Creators

Developing AI through script lends itself well to being modified by the community. Mod creators who create their own levels will have access to the same tools for AI creation as the designers. Because the AI is bound to script (rather than being simple configuration files), mod creators have greater flexibility when creating AI. After mod creators have learned the skills required to create regular level modifications, it is a small step for them to start modifying the AI.

Player Creation

Another exciting area that AI script can move into in the future is empowering players to create scripts. Players will have the ability to create the scripts for their teammates or the units under their control. As games become more complex, and units have more complex AI, the player has less control over them. By allowing players to write their own scripts, they are able to tailor their units to their own play style.

As games like *Spore* [Maxis07] move toward more player-created content, should not AI do the same? Instead of only having players compete against each other, they can create their own AI and have the AI compete. This adds a new level of gameplay only seen in games such as *Robot Battle* [Schick02]. Features like this make excellent selling points.

To keep complexity and performance acceptable, most bound functions should be high level. An example of this is exposing the "Commander's" AI in an RTS game rather than individual units. This involves allowing the player to decide which units should attack which areas, rather than how each individual unit will react to a given situation.

Another method for achieving simplicity for players is having a GUI for them to modify their scripts. This could be achieved in-game, allowing players to feel like they are still playing the game rather than programming. Games could begin with simple options that most games have today (such as pursuit range and damage tolerance) and move toward more advanced options. Players could drag and drop behaviors for their units, creating seemingly complex behaviors while simply changing data values within script files. As research into this develops, the scripts themselves could possibly be generated on the fly.

Many hurdles must be overcome before players will want to get involved in creating their own AI; however, this as an exciting possibility for the future. If care is taken to simplify interactions between players and the AI script, the barrier for entry will be reduced substantially.

Conclusion

In this article, the use of scripting to write advanced AI in games was discussed. With a focus on GameMonkey Script, the language basics were shown with source code supplied for further study. Using script for AI has many advantages over straight C++ code with the following core benefits:

- Rapid prototyping allows faster development of AI as well as experimentation by both designers and other team members.
- Nontechnical designers can quickly pick up GM and begin writing AI scripts after only a few weeks.
- Game data structures can be stored in GM scripts.
- Mod creators will have access to the same tools as designers when creating AI.
- In the future, players might customize their teammate or unit AI by writing their own simple scripts.

For these reasons, AI should start moving into script. As discussed, the *Battlestar Galactica*'s designer, with no programming experience, used script to create an entire single-player game with all of its AI in only a few months. By empowering designers with the tools required for creating advanced AI, games will show more natural and specialized AI behaviors.

References

[Auran07] Auran/Sierra Entertainment, Inc., *Battlestar Galactica*. Available online at *http://www.bsgarcade.com/*, 2007.

[Cinematronics77] *Space Wars*. Cinematronics Inc., 1977.

[Douglas05] Douglas, Greg, et al., "Game Monkey Script Reference." Available online at *http://www.somedude.net/gamemonkey/GameMonkeyScriptReference.pdf*, January 23, 2007.

[Maxis07] Maxis/Electronic Arts Inc., *Spore*. Available online at *http://www.spore.com/*, 2007.

[Poiker02] Poiker, Falko, "Creating Scripting Languages for Nonprogrammers." AI Game Programming Wisdom, 2002: pp. 524–525.

[Schick02] Schick/GarageGames Inc., *Robot Battle. Available online at http://www.robotbattle.com/*, 2002.

[Wilkinson06] Wilkinson, Oli, "Introduction to GameMonkey Script Part 1." Available online at *http://www.gamedev.net/reference/programming/features/gmscript1/*, 2006.

6.5

Dialogue Managers

Hugo Pinto—University of Sheffield

hugo@hugopinto.net

Since the 1970s, with *Colossal Cave Adventure*, game developers have pursued the goal of allowing the user to interact with the game using natural language. Progress in the area has been slow but steady, as shown by *Neverwinter Nights* and *Lifeline*. These games pushed the boundaries of text-based and speech-based interaction in games.

At the center of every interactive language system, be it speech or text-based, lies the dialogue manager (DM). This component is responsible for determining what will be said at any time, based on what has already been talked about, the goals of the character, and its possible actions.

In this article, we present the main techniques and paradigms of dialogue management, with references to games, industrial applications, and academic research. We cover DMs based on stacks, finite state machines (FSMs), frames, inference-engines, and planners. For each technique, we point out its strengths, applicability, and issues when integrating into a broader dialogue system in a game setting.

Introduction

First, let's clarify what exactly the term *dialogue management* means because historically it has been used with several distinct meanings. We approach dialogue management as the process of deciding what a character is to say at each time step. This is based on what has just been spoken to the character, the character's goals, the character's knowledge, and what has been said so far. This is very similar to a goal-oriented control structure of a game bot that chooses its actions based on its knowledge and perceptions of the environment. Substituting utterances from the dialogue participants for the bot's perceptions and possible speech acts of the character for the bot's actions yields a dialogue manager!

To fully appreciate the issues of dialogue management and the advantages of each approach, you need to know how the DM fits into a full dialogue system and what are the distinctive properties and views of dialogue. These are discussed in the first two sections of the article "Spoken Dialogue Systems," in this volume [Pinto08]. Although the discussion in that article is focused on speech-based systems, it applies to text-based systems as well. The main difference is that text-based systems do not worry about speech recognition or speech synthesis.

Historically, discussion of dialogue management has been centered on initiative: whether a DM favored system-initiative, user-initiative, or mixed-initiative. Although we will mention whether an approach favors the user, the system, or both to lead the conversation, the focus here will be on the core engineering characteristics of each approach and how they can be applied to the solution of dialogue management issues in a game.

Approaches to Dialogue Management

This section presents five fundamental dialogue management techniques: FSMs, frames, stacks, inference engines, and planners. Each is first demonstrated in a problem that it tackles naturally and then in a harder problem that it is not suited to tackle. The harder problem will be comfortably solved by the next technique presented. This shows models capable of dealing with progressively more complex dialogues.

Finite State Machines (FSMs)

FSMs are probably the most popular dialogue management paradigm and implementation technique of commercial spoken dialogue systems. They are extensively used in industry and constitute the backbone of several dialogue description languages, including VoiceXML [Oshry07]. This is good news for game developers because FSMs are pervasive in the games industry [Houlette03], with several caveats and tips for design [Carlisle02] and implementation [Alexander03] in a game setting.

FSMs have a distinctive advantage when dealing with spoken language: we can use a specially tuned acoustic-language model for each dialogue state because we know what utterances to expect, making the automatic speech recognition task much easier. They are specially suited for situations when the system has most of the dialogue initiative, and the dialogue states and the dependencies between them are well defined and not many. A simple example is a coffee-shop assistant dealing with a user request for his breakfast beverage (Figure 6.5.1 shows an FSM that would support this dialogue):

```
Bartender: Hello, would you like some coffee, tea, or cake?
User: Coffee, please.
Bartender: Brazilian, South African, or Italian?
User: Brazilian.
Bartender: What about sugar?
User: No.
Bartender: Would you like it with milk?
User: Yes.
Bartender: Enjoy your Brazilian Latte! Thank you!
```

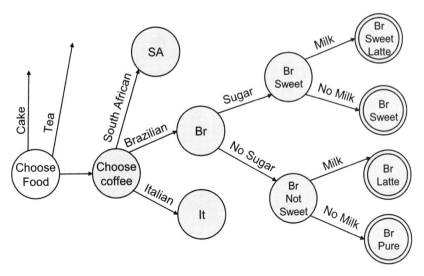

FIGURE 6.5.1 Partial coffee-shop bartender FSM.

FSMs provide a straightforward way to go from a task breakdown to the DM implementation. It is also easy to check for uncovered conditions, shortest paths, cycles, and so on. The problem is that FSMs become very difficult to manage as the possible paths in the dialogue grow. Some workarounds, such as appropriate graphical tools [Carlisle02] or scripting languages [Yiskis03] can alleviate the problem. This path-escalation problem makes FSMs a difficult solution in the face of user interruptions to the system-directed dialogue with a request of their own. These can be handled by extensions, such as augmenting the DM with stacks, as will be shown in the "Stacks" section. The standard approach in this case is ignoring the request and steering the user back to the dialogue. Considering the coffee-making bartender, we could just answer the user with a "Please let me finish your <beverage/food>, first." and present the question again, as in the following excerpt:

```
Bartender: Hello, would you like some coffee, tea, or cake?
(…)
Bartender: Would you like it with milk?
User: Yes.
Bartender: What about sugar?
User: I want some cake, too.
Bartender: Please, let me finish your coffee first. Do you want some
sugar?
User: No.
Bartender: Enjoy your Brazilian Latte! Thank you!
```

In a game setting, FSMs would be a good choice for very simple, informative characters, or to implement task-oriented subdialogues. Being simple and quite familiar to game developers, they could be a good starting point when implementing characters with dialogue capabilities. However, some of their limitations could be quite annoying, particularly the need for all the data in a particular task to adhere to specific ordering constraints and any information not expected in a state to be discarded. For an example, consider the following coffee-ordering dialogue:

```
Bartender: Hello, would you like coffee, tea, or cake?
User: I would like a Brazilian coffee, with milk and sugar.
Bartender: Brazilian, South African, or Italian?
User: Uh? Brazilian!
Bartender: Would you like it with milk?
User: Yes, milk and sugar!
Bartender: What about sugar?
User: YES, YOU IDIOT! I WANT SUGAR IN MY COFFEE!
Bartender: Here you go. Thank you!
```

The user was not very satisfied in the previous dialogue, and you might wonder how long it would take to ask for two differently prepared coffees, a tea, and a cake. Frame-based systems were created to properly deal with this kind of situation.

Frames

Frame-based systems are probably the second most popular dialogue-modeling technique, being a foundational paradigm of VoiceXML [Oshry07] and widely used in many commercial dialogue systems. Most of these systems use a dialogue to fill a form and populate and/or query a database. Typical applications are getting transport timetable information and call routing [Chu-Carroll99].

Frame-based dialogue systems (FBDS) do not directly translate into a particular architecture but rather get this name from the way information is usually gathered from the user. A frame can be viewed as an object in the object-oriented paradigm that has no methods defined in it. What is common among most systems is a frame that keeps track of the wanted information, and an algorithm that will determine what to do to fill the missing items. Usually, the system starts by prompting an initial question, fills as many slots as possible with the user's current utterance, and then asks questions to clarify existing information or fill the remaining slots. A frame-based system for the coffee-making bartender would be able to handle the following interaction:

```
Bartender: Hello, would you like coffee, tea, or cake?
User: I would like a Brazilian coffee, with sugar and milk.
Bartender: Here you go. Thank you.
```

To keep track of the information and spawn clarification questions, some systems keep a confirmation flag and a confidence value associated with each slot. Slots filled with high confidence are marked automatically as confirmed, whereas slots filled with low confidence are candidates for a clarification question. Note that this issue of clarification in form filling is stronger in the case of spoken dialogue systems, due to the potential errors in automatic speech-recognition, but we might also have to clarify information due to ambiguity in the sentence or other interpretation problems, which happen in text-based systems as well. In the following example, the DM checks with the user to see if "with sugar and milk" applies just to the tea or to both the tea and coffee.

```
Bartender: Hello, would you like a coffee, tea, or cake?
User: I would like a Brazilian coffee and an Earl Grey tea, with
sugar and milk.
Bartender: Ok, the Brazilian coffee with sugar and milk too?
User: Yes.
Bartender: Here you go. Thank you.
```

Frame-based systems allow a more efficient and natural interaction with the user because the system is able to use information that was not explicitly asked for but still relevant to the frame. They also ease the burden on the software engineer because we are allowed to specify the dialogue rules for each frame declaratively, and the management algorithm generates the appropriate dialogue moves dynamically.

These advantages over FSM-based systems do not come without a price: to use a frame-based DM in a spoken dialogue system, any automatic speech recognition component must be far more robust. It needs to be able to deal with the utterances used to describe all of the items in a given frame. The same goes for the natural language understanding module, which might be faced with long coordinated phrases, negations, and embedded clarifications.

FBDSs are unable to deal with information that falls out of the current frame but that still might be relevant and supported by the system. This forces the use of recourses similar to the ones employed in FSMs to deal with unexpected utterances. Consider the following dialogue, where the bartender can now also make table reservations in the coffee shop:

```
Bartender: Hello, how may I help you?
User: I would like a Brazilian coffee with sugar.
Bartender: Ok, would you like some milk too?
User: Ah, I want to reserve a table for two, for nine p.m., is it
possible?
Bartender: Please, let me finish your coffee. Ok, would you like some
milk too?
User: Uh, ok…yes.
Bartender: Here you go. Anything else?
User: Nevermind…
```

To ask the user if he wanted something else after postponing his table reservation was clearly inappropriate for a polite bartender. The system should have caught up with the user and resumed the table-booking conversation upon completion of the coffee talk or, conversely, dealt with the table reservation before finishing the gathering of the information of the client's coffee. Stacks provide just such a capability.

Stacks

Besides being a fundamental computer science data structure, stacks provide a natural way to change the topic of a conversation and then resume the halted conversation from where the speaker left off. Any new conversation is pushed over the old ones, and when it is over, the stack is popped to continue with the previous conversation. Remarkably, the basic idea is very similar to using stacks and FSMs to allow the stopping and resuming of game bots behaviors [Tozour03, Yiskis03].

Stacks can be a complement to both FSMs and FBDSs. They can be either the data structure used to implement a hierarchy of FSMs or frames, or an independent data structure where we put FSMs or frames for later revisiting.

The COMIC [Catizone03] system used a stack and augmented finite state machines (AFSM) as the basis of its DM. These AFSMs were called Dialogue Action Forms (DAF) and had as main differences from ordinary FSMs the abilities to execute an arbitrary action in a state transition, to wait for arbitrary and external information in a given state, and to have indexing terms, such as keywords, associated to it. Like in hierarchical FSMs [Champandard03], each state of a DAF could stand for a whole DAF, allowing cascaded calls to more specific DAFs to solve a problem.

The really novel information from a game programming perspective is how the DAF creation, indexing, and selection were made. For a DM, this is how it changes topics. When each DAF was built, the designer associated with it some properties: verbs, nouns, entities, and restrictions on world properties (such as *time > 18:00*). A combination of these formed a key, with which the DAF was put into an index. When the system received a user utterance, it would make such a key from extracted bits of information from the sentence (verbs, nouns, and entities) and the application (world properties). It would then select the DAF that most closely matched this key. This selected DAF would be put on top of the current one, and the dialogue would proceed according to it. When it was finished, it would be popped, and the previous one would be resumed from where the user left off.

Augmenting a frame-based system with a stack in the vein of the COMIC project, we could now deal with the dialogue of the preceding section in an appropriate way:

```
Bartender: Hello, how may I help you?
User: I would like a Brazilian coffee with sugar.
Bartender: Ok, would you like some milk too?
User: Ah, I want to reserve a table for two, for nine p.m., is it
possible?
Bartender: Sure. In the smoking or non-smoking area? (Started the
reservation DAF)
User: In the smoking.
Bartender: Ok, your reservation is complete. (Pops reservation and
resumes coffee DAF)
```

```
Bartender: Do you still want the coffee?
User: Yes.
Bartender: I remember it is a Brazilian coffee with sugar. Do you
want it with milk?
User: Yes, that would be great.
Bartender: Here you go. Anything else?
```

The combination of stacks with frames or FSMs gives more power, as dialogue systems are now able to change a topic and come back to it later, or pursue subdialogues necessary for a broader conversation. Again there is no free lunch; any ASR (automatic speech recognition) system needs to have at least one general layer capable of identifying all utterances that might lead to a topic or task shift in the dialogue. The natural language understanding module needs to be able to spot keywords, dependencies, and entities that signal a topic shift. Some dialogue systems go as far as using an additional specialized module for the detection of these shifts. Finally, tuning the indexing and retrieval mechanism can be a challenging task in itself, depending on the nuances of the tasks being pursued. Moreover, it should be noted that a system with task-resuming capabilities also needs a more sophisticated language generation module that is capable of summarizing what was said before and introducing appropriate cues and introductions to resume the previous conversation.

Despite its augmented capabilities, there are still plenty of situations that will be difficult to solve with stacks and FSMs or FBDSs, unless augmented with explicit checks and tricks. Consider the following situation, again with the now tired coffee-shop bartender:

```
Bartender: Hello, how may I help you?
User: I would like a Brazilian coffee with sugar.
Bartender: Ok, would you like some milk too?
User: Actually I want a tea instead of coffee.
```

What now? The proper action should be to pop the current task and its associated conversation and initiate the tea-making task with its associated chat. A COMIC-like system would need to have a special module to detect when a topic or task should be dropped on user request because there is no innate support for that. In COMIC specifically, task dropping is implemented as a special DAF that is matched by several "topic dropping" words, and that DAF then performs a hard-coded dialogue to confirm which DAF to drop. It then inspects the stack and marks the dropped DAF as "ignorable." When an ignored DAF is reached, the system will just pop again, without reinstating any ignored DAFs as the current topic. The COMIC stack then is effectively a list where normal insertions and deletions are from a single side, but particular conditions might call for inspection and removal of elements from any place in the list. This violates a pure stack behavior. An inference-engine coupled with some declarative rules could be a better tool for this job.

Inference-Based Systems

Inference-based dialogue systems (IBDS) try to satisfy a proposed axiom by firing a series of rules from a knowledge base. Despite their power and flexibility, inference-based systems are not very widespread in the dialogue systems community except in academia. One reason is that most commercial systems do well enough without such capabilities, although for computer games, its advantages might be needed.

An inference-based DM will have basically four components: knowledge base, inference engine, working memory, and facts selector.

The knowledge base is usually composed of a set of declarative rules in a standard logical formalism, such as propositional logic (PL) or first-order logic (FOL). Some of the rules (at least the terminal ones) will have actions associated with them. FOL and its approximations offer existential quantification (entering facts such as "there exists K" and "all X are K"), but the inference engines usually support these operations only in a limited way.

The inference engine is responsible for finding a valid proof for a given fact, or conversely, to find and fire the appropriate rules given some fact. When a rule is matched, a new fact is entered into the working memory. The most common operations an inference engine supports are unification—finding predicates that can be filled with the selected values/facts from the working memory—and forward-chaining and backward-chaining. Backward-chaining starts with a given goal and fires rules in a sequence that terminates into a set of facts known to be true. Forward-chaining starts from a set of facts known to be true and uses them to derive as many other facts as necessary to satisfy a desired goal.

The working memory is where the facts of current interest are kept. The facts selector is the algorithm that chooses and combines the facts of interest before feeding them into the inference system. Usually a planner is used as part of the facts selector to add new facts and choose among existing ones.

The NICE game system is an example of a hybrid of IBDS and a plan-based system used in a game domain. It uses a formalism that lies between PL and FOL to represent its knowledge and a simplified form of unification and forward-chaining in its parser. NICE uses a planner as its facts selector. See "Spoken Dialogue Systems," in this volume for a review of the system and further references. Without going into a step-by-step demonstration of an inference-based cycle in the NICE system, we will revisit the dialogue of the last section to show how an IBDS might handle it gracefully:

```
Bartender: Hello, how may I help you?
User: I would like a Brazilian coffee with sugar.
Bartender: Ok, would you like some milk too?
User: Actually I want a tea instead of coffee.
Bartender: Ok, and how to you want your tea?
User: An Earl Grey with sugar and milk.
Bartender: Here you go. Enjoy!
```

Here, after the second user utterance, the system would exploit the following rule to discover that it should drop the old topic and start the new one:

```
InsteadOf(x,y) -> drop(y)^execute(x)
```

It is very difficult to use tuned automatic speech recognition models for different dialogue parts with an IBDS. Such systems really need to have a system capable of recognizing all user utterances supported. Also, the language-understanding module needs to provide enough information to populate the working memory with all relevant facts of the current utterance, which in some cases might involve complicated language processing operations. An upside is that having a knowledge base in place for the DM often improves the language-understanding module by using the knowledge-base information to guide the interpretation of the utterances.

Plan-Based Systems

Planners are an integral part of most research and cutting-edge commercial dialogue management systems. Even systems based on inference engines usually employ planners to select the facts of interest. The basic structure of a planner is a set of operators and a procedure to find a sequence of operators that achieve one or more goals. The operators are usually specified in terms of preconditions and effects. A planner can actually be seen as an inference system and vice versa—the conditions and effects of the operator correspond to the facts and goals of the knowledge base, in this order. The inference engine can be used in this way to draw a plan that corresponds to the set of steps in the inference process. Conversely, a planner can be used to do inference—the last step of the plan will be the conclusion arrived at. Usually the knowledge base of a hybrid system is used to store the task-independent knowledge, and the planner is used to store the task-dependent one.

There are basically two common uses of a planner in a dialogue system: encoding the speech-acts/DM output directly into the operators' actions and using the planner to select the facts of interest to be fed into the inference system.

The main benefit of a planner comes when the user and the system have to build a solution to a task together. Consider the following situation:

```
Bartender: Hello, how may I help you?
User: I want to organize a dinner with a few friends.
Bartender: Ok. How many of them will be coming?
User: Nine or Ten.
Bartender: Excellent, we will need a large table. We have one in the
balcony and two in the upper part.
User: Can't I take that one in the ground floor?
Bartender: Sorry, that one is already reserved.
User: I want one in the upper floor then.
```

```
Bartender: Perfect. Do any of the guests have special needs?
User: Ah, yes, Mike uses a wheelchair.
Bartender: In this case I suggest you take the table in the balcony
because the upper ones are not wheelchair-accessible.
User: Ah, ok then.
```

There is an ordering between the actions to organize a dinner: we need to know how many people will come and then consider where the group will sit. Also, as we know new facts, we might need to revise our plan—in the example, knowing that a member was in a wheelchair triggered the search for a table that was wheelchair-accessible. Just querying the user for a long list of facts and keeping track of all the dependencies would be too cumbersome and difficult to manage without a planner, even with a frame-based system.

A plan-based system offers the same complications for automatic speech recognition and natural language understanding (NLU) as an inference-based system. Luckily, developers can exploit its structure to inform the NLU and natural language generation (NLG) systems. For example, the path computed in the planning process can be an input to the NLG, and the dependencies between the phases can be used as information for NLU. In the previous example dialogue, the last utterance from the bartender clearly illustrates the exploitation of this information in a causative sentence. In most cutting-edge research systems, such as TRIPS[Allen07], this is exactly what happens—the task-dependent part of its planner is used to inform both the generation and understanding processes.

Conclusion

We have seen five dialogue management techniques, each capable of dealing naturally with ever more complex dialogue phenomena. This increase in power does not come without a price; the systems interacting with the DM usually have to be made more complex for it to exert its full power. Fortunately, the structure and operation of the more advanced DMs can be exploited to inform the other components of the system, particularly the NLU and NLG modules. Stacks and FSMs have been used in game development for over a decade, and planning systems are becoming ever more popular, as the articles on the AI of *F.E.A.R.* [Orkin06] and *Full Spectrum Command* [Dybsand03] illustrate. Perhaps the time for dialogue-enabled characters is arriving?

References

[Allen07] Allen, J. et al., "The Rochester Interactive Planning System." Available online at *http://www.cs.rochester.edu/research/cisd/projects/trips/*, June 14, 2007.

[Alexander03] Alexander, Thor, "Parallel-State Machines for Believable Characters." *Massively Multiplayer Game Development*, Thor Alexander(Ed.), 2003.

[Carlisle02] Carlisle, P., "Designing a GUI Tool to Aid in the Development of Finite State Machines." *AI Game Programming Wisdom*, Charles River Media, 2002.

[Catizone03] Catizone, R., Setzer, A., and Wilks, Y., "Multimodal Dialogue Management in the COMIC Project." *Workshop on Dialogue Systems: interaction, adaptation and styles of management*, (EACL)Budapest, Hungary, 2003.

[Champandard03] Champandard, A., *AI Game Development.* New Riders Publishing, 2003.

[Chu-Carroll99] Chu-Carroll, Jennifer, "Form-Based Reasoning for Mixed-Initiative Dialogue Management in Information-Query Systems." *Proceedings of the European Conference on Speech Communication and Technology*, Vol. 4, (1999): pp. 1519–1522.

[Dybsand03] Dybsand, E., "Goal-Directed Behavior Using Composite Tasks." *AI Game Programming Wisdom 2*, Charles River Media, 2003.

[Houlette03] Houlette, R., and Fu, D., "The Ultimate Guide to FSMs in Games." *AI Game Programming Wisdom 2*, Charles River Media, 2003.

[Orkin06] Orkin, J., "3 States and a Plan: The AI of F.E.A.R." *Proceedings of the Game Developers Conference*, 2006.

[Oshry07] Oshry, M. et al., "Voice Extensible Markup Language 2.1." Available online at *http://www.w3.org/TR/voicexml21/*, August 4, 2007.

[Pinto08] Pinto, Hugo, "Spoken Dialogue Systems." *AI Game Programming Wisdom 4*, Charles River Media, 2008.

[Tozour03] Tozour, Paul, "Stack-Based Finite-State Machines." *AI Game Programming Wisdom 2*, Charles River Media, 2003.

[Yiskis03] Yiskis, Eric, "Finite-State Machine Scripting Language for Designers." *AI Game Programming Wisdom 2*, Charles River Media, 2003.

LEARNING AND ADAPTATION

7.1

Learning Winning Policies in Team-Based First-Person Shooter Games

Lehigh University

Stephen Lee-Urban

sml3@lehigh.edu

Megan Smith

mev2@lehigh.edu

Héctor Muñoz-Avila

hem4@lehigh.edu

Imagine designing challenging and flexible AI team behavior for a first-person shooter (FPS) game. Among the decisions that must be made are whether to use static or dynamic strategies, whether or not these strategies should be represented symbolically, whether the AI should be able to learn, and, finally, the extent to which the actions that are taken by individual team members will be controlled by the team strategies.

This article presents an approach, called RETALIATE, which addresses these questions using an online reinforcement learning (RL) algorithm. In a case study performed using the *Unreal Tournament* (UT) game engine, we found that RETALIATE can quickly develop winning strategies against opponents of various levels of sophistication. Furthermore, the approach taken in RETALIATE is easy to implement because it frees the developer from having to create complex planning and communication systems for team coordination and automatically learns effective strategies and adapts them to changes that occur at runtime.

Coordinating Bots in Domination Games

UT is a typical FPS game in which the immediate objective for a player is to shoot and kill an opponent. An interesting feature of *UT* is that it offers the choice of several different game variants, one of which is called a domination game. In a domination game, teams of players compete to control or "own" domination locations. A domination location is considered to be owned by the team of the last player that touched it, and *UT* scores teams by assigning one point every four seconds to the team that controls each location. A domination game ends when one team scores a predetermined number of points and is declared the winner. Because there are typically multiple domination locations on each map, proper coordination of team behavior is important to win a domination game.

Reinforcement Learning (RL)

RL is a form of machine learning that can be used in a game to allow an agent or team of agents to learn a *policy*—what action to select in every perceived state of the game world—in a potentially stochastic environment online and in real time. The goal in RL is to arrive at an optimal policy, which maximizes the rewards that are received, through a process of trial and error. For an overview of RL in general, see [Manslow03]. Unlike some other learning algorithms, RL requires neither annotated training examples to learn nor an expert to provide feedback.

In RL, interaction with the world is the only way an agent gains information: the agent (1) senses the state of the environment, (2) chooses an action, (3) performs the action, and (4) receives a reward or punishment [Sutton98]. For the developer of game AI, the use of RL means that little or no time is spent in the design, coding, and debugging of strategies nor is time spent "teaching" the AI how to behave. With RL, time is instead spent creating the representation of the game state, called the "problem model"—that is, how the various complexities of actual game states are abstracted into a simpler form that RL can use. This is typically significantly easier than manually designing and coding individual and team behavior in symbolic representations, such as scripts.

RETALIATE is an implementation of RL that is designed specifically for controlling teams of bots in domination games.

Reinforcement Learning for Coordinating Bots

RETALIATE focuses on controlling which domination locations team members are sent to, so the low-level behavior of the bots in a team can be controlled by a standard finite state machine (FSM). RETALIATE makes no *a priori* assumptions about what that behavior is, which allows bots to be used as plugins. In principle, this allows the design decisions for the team AI to be made independent of the design decisions relating to the control of individual bot behavior. Similarly, by using bots as plugins, the game developer can swap different bot types in and out of the game and even use bots developed for single-player nonteam game modes in multiplayer games.

Problem Model: Definition of States and Actions

When deciding upon the problem model to use in RL, you must consider the crucial features of the problem being addressed. For example, while the amount of ammunition remaining might be important for an individual team member, the overall team's strategy might safely ignore this detail. A problem model that takes into consideration too many features of the game state can lead to a learning problem that is very difficult to solve in a reasonable amount of time. Similarly, an overly simplified problem model leads to a system that does not play very well and can only learn the most basic of strategies.

In RETALIATE, game states are represented in the problem model as a tuple indicating the owner O_i of domination location i. For instance, if there are three domination locations, the state (E,F,F) describes the state where the first domination location is owned by the enemy, and the other two domination locations are owned by our friendly team. Neutral ownership of a domination location is also considered and is represented by an N in the relevant location in the tuple. For 3 domination locations and 2 teams, there are 27 unique states to the game, taking into account that domination locations are initially not owned by either team.

The addition of other features to this representation, such as the ammo of each bot on a team, was considered, but their effect was to reduce the speed of learning without producing an increase in the complexity of the strategies that were learned. In contrast, not only did the simple representation produce much more rapid learning, but, as our results show, it also contained sufficient information to develop a winning policy. Features, such as a bot's ammo, form part of the conditions in the FSM that controls individual bot behavior, and the separation of parameters—those used to define team tactics versus those used for individual bot behavior—is one of the central qualities of RETALIATE. This separation is reminiscent of hierarchical RL but with the difference that there is no commitment to using RL at all levels in the AI hierarchy.

In RETALIATE, states are associated with a set of team actions that tell the team what to do. A team action is defined as a tuple indicating the individual action A_i that bot i should take—for a team of 3 bots, a team action tuple consists of 3 individual actions. An individual action specifies to which domination location a bot should move. For example, in the team action (Loc1, Loc2, Loc3), the 3 individual actions send bot1 to domination location 1, bot2 to domination location 2, and bot3 to domination location 3, whereas in (Loc1, Loc1, Loc1), the individual actions send all 3 bots to domination location 1. If a bot is already in a location that it is told to move to, the action is interpreted as instructing the bot to stay where it is. Individual bot actions are executed in parallel and, for a game with 3 domination locations and three bots, there are 27 unique team actions because each bot can be sent to 3 different locations.

Despite the simplicity in the representation of our problem model, it not only proves to be effective, but it actually mimics how human teams play domination games. The most common mistake that is made by novice players is to fight opponents in locations other than the domination ones; these fights should be avoided because they generally do not contribute to victories in these kinds of games. Part of the reason is that if a player is killed away from a domination location, it will not directly affect ownership and will not affect the score. Consequently, it is common for human teams to focus on coordinating to which domination points each team member should go, which is precisely the kind of behavior that our problem model represents.

The RETALIATE Algorithm

Figure 7.1.1 shows a flow diagram of RETALIATE. RETALIATE is designed to run across multiple game instances so that the policy, and therefore the RETALIATE-controlled team, can adapt continuously to changes in the environment while keeping track of what was learned in previous games. Such changes might be changes in RETALIATE's own team (e.g., wielding new weapons), changes in the opponent team (e.g., changes in tactics), or changes in the game world (e.g., a new map).

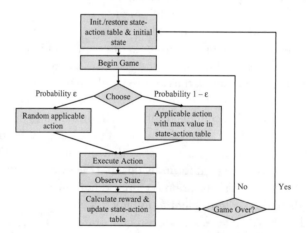

FIGURE 7.1.1   A flow diagram of the RETALIATE algorithm.

RETALIATE is controlled by two parameters: ε, and α. ε is known as the epsilon-greedy parameter and controls the tradeoff between exploration and exploitation by setting the rate at which the algorithm selects a random action rather than the one that is expected to perform best. α is referred to as the step size parameter and influences the rate of learning. For our case study, we found that setting ε to 0.1 and α to 0.2 worked well.

The particular form of RL that is used in RETALIATE uses a Q-table that maps pairs of states s and actions a to a value $Q(s,a)$, which represents the expected reward that will be received for taking action *a* in state *s*. RETALIATE starts by either initializing all entries in the *Q*-table with a default value, which was 0.5 in our case study, or by restoring the *Q*-table from a previous game. A new game is then started, and the game state representation *s* is initialized to each domination location having neutral ownership (N,N,N).

The following computations are iterated through until the game is over. First, the next team action to execute, *a*, is selected using the epsilon-greedy parameter; this means that a random team action is chosen with probability ε, or the team action with the maximum value in the *Q*-table for state *s* is selected with probability $1 - \varepsilon$. By stochastically selecting actions, we ensure that there is a chance of trying new actions or trying actions whose values are less than the current maximum in the *Q*-table. This is important to ensure that RL experiments with a wide range of behaviors before deciding which is optimal.

The selected action *a* is then executed, and the resulting state *s'* is observed. Each bot can either succeed in accomplishing its individual action or fail (e.g., the bot is killed before it could reach its destination). Either way, executing a team action takes only a few seconds because the individual actions are executed in parallel. Updates to the *Q*-table occur when either all individual actions have completed (whether successfully or unsuccessfully), or domination location ownership changes because of the actions of the opposing team.

Next, the reward for the new state *s'* is computed as the difference between the utilities in the new state and the previous state *s*. Specifically, the utility of a state *s* is defined by the function $U(s) = F(s) - E(s)$, where $F(s)$ is the number of friendly domination locations, and $E(s)$ is the number that are controlled by the enemy. This has the effect that, relative to team A, a state in which team A owns two domination locations and team B owns one has a higher utility than a state in which team A owns only one domination location and team B owns two. The reward function, which determines the scale of the reward, is computed as $R = U(s') - U(s)$.

The calculated value of the reward *R* is used to perform an update on the *Q*-table entry *Q(s,a)* for the previous state *s* in which the last set of actions *a* were ordered. This calculation is performed according to the following formula, which is standard for computing the entries in a *Q*-table in temporal difference learning [Sutton98]:

$$Q(s, a) \leftarrow Q(s, a) + \alpha(R + \gamma \max_{a'} Q(s', a') - Q(s, a))$$

In this computation, the entry in the *Q*-table for the action *a* that was just taken in state *s*, *Q(s,a)*, is updated. The function $\max_{a'}$ returns the value from the *Q*-table of the best team action that can be performed in the new state *s'*, which is simply the highest value associated with *s'* in the table for any *a'*.

The value of γ, which is called the discount factor parameter, adjusts the relative influences of current and future rewards in the decision-making process. RETALIATE diverges from the traditional discounting of rewards by setting γ equal to 1 so that possible future rewards are as important in selecting the current action as rewards that are available immediately. Initially, we set $\gamma < 1$ to place more emphasis on immediate rewards but found that the rate of adaptation of RETALIATE was slower than when γ was set to 1. In general, however, care should be taken when setting γ to 1 as doing so can prevent RL from converging.

Case Study

We performed a series of experiments that were designed to assess the effectiveness of RETALIATE in controlling a team of *UT* bots in a domination game. Our methodology, and the results that we were able to obtain, are described in the following sections.

Overall System Architecture

To experiment with RETALIATE, we integrated with *UT* using the approach shown in Figure 7.1.2. The RETALIATE-controlled team's and an opposing team's decision systems interfaced with the *UT* game engine through the GameBots API. GameBots serves as middleware between the decision systems and the *UT* game engine [Gamebot07] and allows *UT* to be controlled over a network. GameBots connects to a *UT* server, which sends it information about the game state. The decision systems process this information to decide what actions the bots should take, and GameBots sends the corresponding instructions back to the *UT* server. Both of the decision systems, the one controlling the RETALIATE team and the one controlling the opposing team, are built independent of the AI controlling the behavior of the individual bots, which therefore work as "plugins" that can easily be changed.

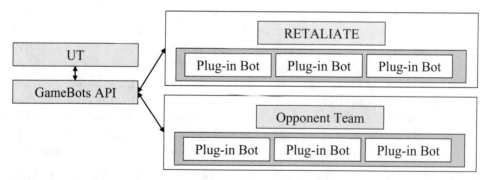

FIGURE 7.1.2   The data flow between the systems used in the experiments.

To ensure fairness in the experiments, both RETALIATE and its opposing teams used bots with the same FSM. This guaranteed that any performance differences that were observed were the result of the team strategies rather than of individual bot behavior. We took as our starting point for the experiments the bots that were readily available in the GameBots distribution and made some enhancements to them. The behavior encoded in the FSMs of these enhanced bots had the following basic functionality:

- At any point in time, a bot is performing a single task (e.g., going to location X).
- If, while performing the task, the bot encounters items that it needs, it will pick them up.
- If the bot encounters an opponent, it will engage them and continue with its original task when they have been eliminated.

Note that the these behaviors are independent of team strategies, allowing for modular design of the AI.

The Opponents

The teams that competed against RETALIATE in the experiments that we performed were controlled according to the following strategies:

Opportunistic Control: Did not coordinate team members whatsoever and moved bots randomly from one domination location to another. If a location was under the control of the opposing team when a bot arrived, it captured it.

Possessive Control: Assigned a different location to each bot. The bots attempted to capture their respective locations and hold them for the whole game.

Greedy Control: Attempted to recapture any location that was taken by the opponent. If more than one location needed to be recaptured, bots were assigned to them randomly.

HTN control: Used the *HTN team* environment described by Hoang [Hoang05], which makes use of a hierarchical task network (HTN) planning techniques. HTN control kept track of the state of a game, and when it changed dramatically, HTN planning techniques were used to (dynamically) generate a new strategy.

HTN control was able to consistently defeat the other three control strategies and hence was expected to be the most difficult for RETALIATE to beat.

Performance Results

We ran several domination game experiments, pitting a single RETALIATE team against a single opposing team. Games were played until one team had accumulated 50 points. Their durations varied but averaged around five minutes, and the number of updates to the Q-table per game was typically in the region of 150. Five tournaments of three games each were played against each opponent. At the beginning of each tournament, RETALIATE started untrained (i.e., all entries in the Q-table were initialized to the same value of 0.5), but the values of the entries in the Q-table were retained between games within each tournament so that learning would continue from one game to the next.

Against the opportunistic, possessive, and greedy control strategies, RETALIATE won all three games in each tournament. Furthermore, within the first half of the first game, RETALIATE developed a *competitive* strategy. This was observed by computing the slope of the curve that represents the difference in scores between the RETALIATE team and the opposing team. When the slope was near zero, both teams were accumulating points at approximately the same rate, and the performance of the RETALIATE team was competitive with that of the opposing team. Because a winning strategy was developed in the first game, and the opposing teams have no dynamic behavior, RETALIATE led the second and third games from the outset.

As expected, the competition against the HTN-controlled team was very close. RETALIATE was sometimes able to develop a competitive strategy within the first game of a tournament, although it also sometimes lost the first game. The RETALIATE team usually won the second and third games, however, and a winning strategy that the HTN team could not successfully counter was usually discovered roughly one-quarter to one-half of the way through the second game. The results of a typical pair of games against the HTN team are shown in Figure 7.1.3. The first game, which is shown in the first graph in the figure, was very close, and the difference in the final scores was only 2 points. In the second game, which is shown in the second graph, around the first quarter of the game, RETALIATE started winning, and by the end of the game, RETALIATE had more than a 10-point advantage over the HTN team.

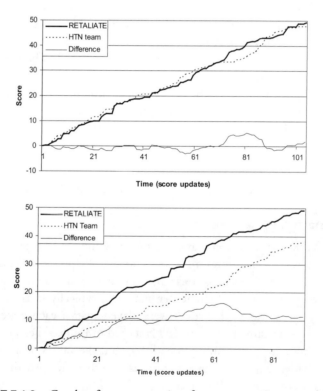

FIGURE 7.1.3   Graphs of score versus time for two successive games between the RETALIATE and HTN teams. The first game, which is shown in the first graph, is very close, as shown by the difference between scores hovering around zero. RETALIATE discovers a winning strategy roughly a quarter of the way through the second game, which is shown in the second graph.

To see how RETALIATE would cope with changing opponent strategies, we ran a study of 5 tournaments of 10 games. As before, the entries in the Q-table were reinitialized at the start of each tournament but retained between the individual games within them. During each tournament, games were successively played against the opportunistic, possessive, and greedy opponents. Table 7.1.1 shows the average number of points by which RETALIATE beat each opponent during the tournaments and shows that it was able to perform well even when the opposing strategy was continually changing.

Table 7.1.1   The Average Difference in the Final
Scores of RETALIATE and Its Opposing Teams
Across 5 Tournaments of 10 Games Apiece.

Team	Difference in Final Score
Opportunistic	13
Possessive	20
Greedy	25

In each game of each tournament, the opposing team was selected by round-robin selection over the opportunistic, possessive, and greedy teams. Each game was played to a maximum of 50 points.

The competitiveness of the HTN team in our experiments shows that such dynamic, symbolic, nonlearning AI can be effective. However, RETALIATE was still eventually able to learn a winning strategy, which shows the importance of using online learning techniques to provide maximum adaptability. Furthermore, RETALIATE was able to learn winning strategies against a new opponent, even when it had previously learned to play against a completely different one. This suggests that a game could be shipped with a RETALIATE-style AI that had already learned to play against the most common strategies and could still adapt to new strategies that it encountered after release.

Sample Learned Strategy

Regardless of which team RETALIATE was playing against, it always converged toward a strategy that aimed to maintain control of two of the three domination locations that were closest to each other. There were several variations on how this strategy was enacted depending upon the opposing team, but RETALIATE typically assigned bots to the two domination locations that were closest together and made the third bot patrol between them.

We speculate that this strategy was, in part, caused by the behavior of the FSM that was controlling the bots. Specifically, the FSM made the bots fight whenever they encountered an enemy, and because domination games are more about geographic control than frags, the only times this aggressive behavior was useful was when the enemy was between two friendly dominated locations or when an enemy approached a location that was controlled by the RETALIATE team. RETALIATE therefore learned a strategy that maximized the utility of the fixed behavior of the FSMs.

Demo on CD-ROM

ON THE CD

Included on the CD-ROM are two video demos that show the early and late stages of a domination game, before and after RETALITATE learned a winning strategy. The field of view of members of the RETALIATE team are represented by red cones, and those of members of the opposing team are represented by blue cones. The three domination locations on the map are represented by solid points of either red or blue depending upon whether they are controlled by RETALIATE or the opposing team. The first video shows that, early in the game, RETALIATE simply clustered its bots around a single domination location, whereas the second shows that it later learned to control the two that were closest to each other. The full source code of RETALIATE is available at *www.cse.lehigh.edu/~munoz/projects/RETALIATE/*.

Conclusion

In this article, we have described an adaptive domination game team AI called RETAL-IATE. From our work with RETALIATE, we learned that it is beneficial to separate individual bot behavior from team behavior because doing so dramatically simplifies the learning problem, producing more rapid and reliable adaptation and offering greater flexibility through the use of individual bot AI as plugins. We also learned that it is important to develop a simple problem model to produce a system that can learn quickly, and we have shown that such a model exists that can facilitate rapid real-time learning of effective team strategies in *UT* domination games.

Acknowledgements

This research was in part supported by the National Science Foundation (NSF 0642882) and the Defense Advanced Research Projects Agency (DARPA).

References

[Gamebot07] Gamebot. Available online at *http://www.planetunreal.com/gamebots/*, June 14, 2007.

[Hoang05] Hoang, H., Lee-Urban, S., and Munoz-Avila, H., "Hierarchical Plan Representations for Encoding Strategic Game AI." *Proceedings of Artificial Intelligence and Interactive Digital Entertainment Conference* (AIIDE-05), AAAI Press, 2005.

[Manslow03] Maslow, J., "Using Reinforcement Learning to Solve AI Control Problems." *AI Game Programming Wisdom*, Vol. 2, Charles River Media, 2003.

[Sutton98] Sutton, S., and Barto, A. *Reinforcement Learning: An Introduction.* MIT Press, 1998.

7.2

Adaptive Computer Games: Easing the Authorial Burden

Georgia Institute of Technology

Manish Mehta

mehtama1@cc.gatech.edu

Santi Ontañón

santi@cc.gatech.edu

Ashwin Ram

ashwin@cc.gatech.edu

Game designers usually create AI behaviors by writing scripts that describe the reactions of game agents to all imaginable circumstances that can occur within the confines of the game world. The *AI Game Programming Wisdom* series of books [Rabin02, Rabin04] provides a good overview of the scripting techniques that are currently used in the games industry. Despite its popularity, scripting is difficult, and the behaviors it generates are often repetitive or fail to achieve their desired purpose.

Behavior creation for AI game agents typically involves generating behaviors and then debugging and adapting them through experimentation. This is typically a complex and time-consuming process that requires many iterations to achieve the desired effects. In this article, we present techniques that provide assistance with, and improve the efficiency of, this manual process by allowing behaviors to be learned from demonstrations and then automatically adapted if they are found wanting at runtime.

Overview

Figure 7.2.1 provides an overview of the architecture that we have developed for assisting in the development, and facilitating the adaptation of, game AI. The architecture contains two core functional components that perform behavior learning and behavior adaptation.

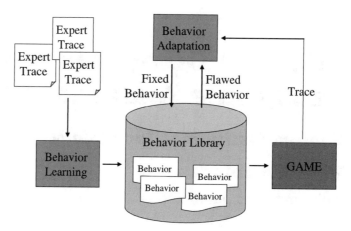

FIGURE 7.2.1   Overview of an automatic behavior learning and adaptation architecture.

In the behavior learning process, developers specify the required AI behaviors by demonstrating them instead of explicitly coding them. The system observes these demonstrations, automatically learns behaviors from them, and stores them in the behavior library. At runtime, the system retrieves appropriate behaviors and revises them according to the current game state.

In the behavior adaptation process, the system monitors the performance of behaviors that are executed at runtime. It keeps track of the status of the executing behaviors, infers from their execution trace what, if anything, might be wrong with them, and adapts them after the game is over. This approach allows the AI to reflect on potential problems in the learned behaviors and revise them in response to things that went wrong during the game.

These techniques allow non-AI experts to define behaviors by demonstration that can automatically be adapted to different situations, thereby reducing the development effort that is required to address all contingencies that might occur in a complex game.

The following sections describe the behavior learning and adaptation processes in more detail and present the design of a behavior representation language that can support the automated reasoning required within the system. We will also show how the techniques can be applied in the domain of the real-time strategy game *Wargus*, which is an open source version of *Warcraft II*.

Behavior Representation Language

The fundamental constituent of any behavior language is the *behavior*. To support automatic reasoning, a behavior must have two main parts: a *declarative* part that tells the AI what the behavior does, and a *procedural* part that contains the executable code of the behavior. Let's present a particular definition of a language called the Behavior Representation and Reasoning Language (BRL). BRL allows the developer to define three kinds of declarative information: goals, context, and alive conditions.

- A *goal* is a representation of the intended aim of a behavior, and, for each domain, an ontology of possible goals is defined. For example, a behavior might have the goal of "building a tower." The goal is the only declarative information that is mandatory for the techniques presented in this article.
- *Context* is information that encodes the circumstances under which the behavior makes sense. In BRL, two kinds of context information can be defined:

  Preconditions: Conditions that must be true to execute the behavior. For example, an "attack" behavior might have as its preconditions the existence of an army and an enemy.

  Game state: A more general definition of context that specifies a particular game state in which the behavior is appropriate; if the current game state is dissimilar to the specified game state, then the behavior is likely to be less applicable.
- A set of *alive conditions* is a representation of the conditions that must be satisfied during the execution of a behavior for it to succeed. If these alive conditions are not met, the behavior is stopped because it will not achieve its intended goal. For example, the peasant in charge of building a farm must remain alive for the entire time it takes for the farm to be built; if he is killed, the farm will not be built.

BRL does not require the developer to define all of these pieces of information, but the more information that is provided, the better the AI will understand the behaviors that are available to it. The procedural part of a behavior consists of executable script, and, as with any script in game AI, it is necessary to define two additional elements:

- *Sensors* are the variables that are used to represent the game state. For example, we might define a sensor called `path(x,y)` that allows a script to verify whether there is a path between locations `x` and `y`.
- *Actions* are the actions that our scripts can perform in the game world. In our implementation, we use all the possible actions available to a human player of *Wargus*, so we have actions such as `build(unit,x,y,building-type)` and `move(unit,x,y)`.

Our current implementation uses a common way to define sensors, preconditions, and alive conditions because all our sensors are Boolean (although our approach can be easily extended to non-Boolean sensors). At the implementation level, global classes called `Condition` and `Sensor` are defined that contain `test` functions that check whether the condition is satisfied or whether a sensor has fired based on the current game state. By extending the classes for each different condition or sensor, different types of conditions and sensors can be defined. For *Wargus*, we defined a variety of subclasses:

```
BuildingComplete(unitID)
Gold(minGold)
UnitExists(UnitID)
And(condition1, condition2)
Not(condition)
```

A goal is a particular task that can be achieved in a given domain. For example, in the *Wargus* domain, possible goals are win the game, build a base, gather resources, and so on. To represent such goals, we need to define a *goal ontology*, which is nothing more than a collection of possible goals. If there are relationships between goals, the ontology might also describe them so that the system can reason about them, but, for the purposes of this exposition, we will consider the goal ontology to be a plain list of goal names. Goals might have parameters associated with them so that, for example, we can define the goal `BuildBuilding(type)`, which requires the type of building to be constructed to be specified. For our *Wargus* implementation, we used the following goal ontology:

```
WinWargus(playerToWin)
DefeatPlayer(playerToDefeat)
BuildUnits(player,unitType,number,x,y)
GetResources(player,gold,wood,oil)
KillUnit(player,unitID)
KillUnitType(player,enemyPlayer,unitType)
Research(player,researchType)
ResourceInfrastructure(player,nFarms,nPeasants)
```

In addition to the names and parameters of each goal, the AI needs a way to verify if a particular goal has been achieved. Thus, a simple way to implement goals is by defining a `Goal` class, extending that class for each different goal type that we want to define, and implementing a function called `generateTest` that returns a `Condition` (built using the `Condition` or `Sensor` classes that were described earlier) that is capable of testing whether the goal has been achieved. Behaviors can also contain subgoals that must be completed by executing some other behavior. When a behavior containing a subgoal is executed, the AI will identify the behavior best suited to satisfying the subgoal based on the nature of the subgoal and the context of any other behaviors that are also being executed. This process is explained in detail later. The source code on the companion CD-ROM includes a demo and the definition of our goal ontology.

ON THE CD

Behavior Learning from Human Demonstrations

Automatic behavior learning can be performed by analyzing human demonstrations. The techniques presented in this section differ from the approaches of classical machine learning, which require lots of training examples, because these techniques can learn behaviors from a single demonstration using a process of manual *annotation*. Annotation involves a human expert providing the AI with information regarding the goal being pursued for every action that is performed during a demonstration. Annotated demonstrations contain much more information than ones without annotation and allow our system to automatically extract behaviors.

Let's examine the annotation and behavior learning processes in more detail. The output of a human demonstration is an *execution trace*, which is a list of the actions that the human performed during the demonstration. The annotation process simply involves labeling each action in the trace with the goals that the player was pursuing when the player performed the action. This process might seem tedious but can be automated in several ways. For example, the approach we used was to develop a tool that loads the demonstration and allows an expert to associate groups of actions with goals. An alternative and better approach is to develop a tool that runs alongside the game that allows the player to select the goals he is pursuing in real time, thereby providing an annotated trace at the end of the game.

To learn behavior, the system analyzes an annotated trace to determine the temporal relations between the individual goals that appear in the trace. The left side of Figure 7.2.2 shows a sample annotated trace that shows the relationships among goals, such as "the goal *g2* was attempted *before* the goal *g3*" or "the goal *g3* was attempted *in parallel* with the goal *g4*." The analysis that is needed to detect the temporal ordering is based on a simplified version of the temporal reasoning framework presented by Allen [Allen83], where 13 different basic temporal relations among events were identified. For our purposes, temporal reasoning helps to figure out if two goals are being pursued in sequence, in parallel, or if one is a subgoal of the other.

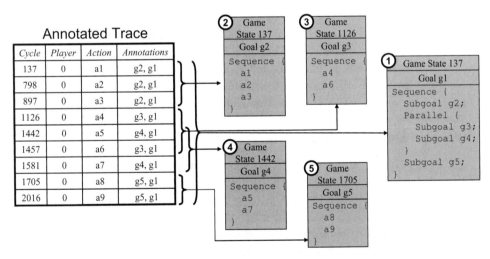

FIGURE 7.2.2   Illustration of five behaviors being extracted from a sample annotated trace.

For example, we assume that if the temporal relation between a particular goal *g* and another goal *g'* is that *g* happens *during g'*, then *g* is a subgoal of *g'*. For example, in Figure 7.2.2, *g2, g3, g4,* and *g5* happen *during g1*; thus they are considered to be subgoals of *g1*. In this example, we could imagine that *g1* means "Win Wargus," and *g2* to *g5* are individual steps that are required to win the game, such as "build a base," and so on. Notice that each action can be annotated with more than one goal, and that, in principle, all the actions should be annotated at least with the top-level goal, which is "WinWargus" in the *Wargus* domain.

From the temporal analysis, procedural descriptions of the behavior of the expert can be extracted. Figure 7.2.2 shows that five behaviors were extracted from the example trace. Each of these behaviors consists of three parts: the game state, a goal, and the behavior itself. For example, behavior number 1 can be extracted, specifying that to achieve goal *g1* in the game state at game cycle 137, the expert first tried to achieve goal *g2*, then attempted *g3* and *g4* in parallel, and pursued *g5* after that. Then, a similar analysis is performed for each one of the subgoals, leading to four more behaviors. For example, behavior 3 states that to achieve goal *g2* in that particular game state, basic actions *a4* and *a6* should be executed sequentially. Notice that preconditions or alive conditions cannot easily be extracted from the annotated trace, so we simply leave them blank.

In our system, we do not attempt any kind of generalization of the expert's actions; if a particular action is `Build(5,"farm",4,22)`, it is stored in exactly that form without any modifications. When the learned behavior is used to play a new scenario in *Wargus*, it is likely that the particular values of the parameters in the action are not the most appropriate (the coordinates 4, 22 might correspond to a water location, for example). There are two possible ways to solve this problem. The first is to generalize behaviors and simply store, for example, that a farm has to be built and then handcraft code to select the best location for it. The second, and the one we used, is to apply a simple *revision* process based on the Case-Based Reasoning (CBR) paradigm. CBR is a technique [Aamodt94] that is based on reusing previously found solutions to solve new problems. Following that approach, the system stores the actions without any modifications and, at runtime, when the behaviors have to be executed, they are revised as necessary. The following section explains this process in detail.

Learned Behavior Execution

A BRL that supports automatic behavior learning and adaptation is much more powerful than a standard behavior language; subroutine calls are replaced with subgoals, and a behavior revision process is used at runtime. Let's look at these two factors, which change the execution of behaviors, in more detail. Initially, the system is started by defining an initial goal, which, in the *Wargus* domain, is simply "WinWargus." The system retrieves a behavior for this initial goal from the behavior library; the behavior library provides a behavior that has a similar goal and a similar context to the current game state. The selected behavior is associated with the initial goal. If the selected behavior has any subgoals, the system recursively performs the same process of retrieving appropriate behaviors for them but only when the subgoals need to be executed and hence dynamically expands the plan at runtime. Each time an action is ready to be executed, it is sent to the revision subsystem to adapt it for the current game state.

The following sections consider the processes of behavior retrieval, plan expansion, and behavior revision in more detail.

Behavior Retrieval

When the system needs to find a behavior for a particular goal in a particular game state, it performs a two-step process. First, the system selects all the behaviors whose preconditions are satisfied and then looks for the behavior with the most similar goal and game state. To do so, similarity metrics among goals and among game states need to be defined. To assess the similarity between game states, a set of features that represent the essential characteristics of the game state must be computed. These features should capture the key elements in the game that a player would consider to decide which actions to perform next. In the *Wargus* domain, we have defined 35 features that represent the terrain, the number and composition of each player's military force, the buildings they have constructed, and the resources that are available to them. To compute the similarity between 2 game states, we compute the values of their 35 features and measure the Euclidean distance between them.

Assessing similarity between goals is a bit trickier. A simple approach would be to assess the similarity between goals of different types to be zero and calculate similarity between goals of the same type using the Euclidean distance between the parameters of the goals. This simple similarity computation can be enhanced by making use of the ontology by defining a base distance between goal types that represents their difference and combining that with the distance that is computed based on their parameters. For example, we might decide that the goal "DefeatPlayer" is more similar to "WinWargus" than to "GatherResources." After the game state and goal distances have been computed, they are simply averaged, and the behavior with the highest average similarity is retrieved as the most appropriate. The underlying assumption behind the similarity calculation is that the retrieved behavior should be the one with the most similar goal that was learned in the most similar game state.

Plan Expansion

The plan expansion module is in charge of maintaining the current plan, which consists of the current goals and the behaviors that are associated with them. Our current implementation is based on the execution module of the A Behavior Language (ABL) [Mateas2002], with which BRL shares some ideas. The current plan is represented as a *partial goal/behavior tree*, which we simply refer to as the *plan*. The plan is a tree composed of two types of nodes: goals and behaviors. Initially, the plan consists of the single goal "WinWargus." The plan expansion module requests a behavior for that goal form the behavior library. The resulting behavior might have several subgoals, for which the plan expansion module will recursively request behaviors at runtime. For example, the right side of Figure 7.2.3 shows a plan where the top goal is to "Win-Wargus." The behavior assigned to the "WinWargus" goal has three subgoals, namely "build base," "build army," and "attack." The "build base" goal has a behavior assigned to it and contains no further subgoals. The rest of the subgoals still don't have a behavior assigned to them and hence are described as being *open*.

Open goals can either be *ready* or *waiting*. An open goal is waiting unless all the behaviors that had to be executed before it have succeeded, in which case, it is ready. For example, in Figure 7.2.3, "behavior 0" is a sequential behavior, and therefore, the goal "build army" is ready because the "build base" goal has already succeeded and thus "build army" can be started. However, the goal "attack" is waiting because "attack" can only be executed after "build army" has succeeded.

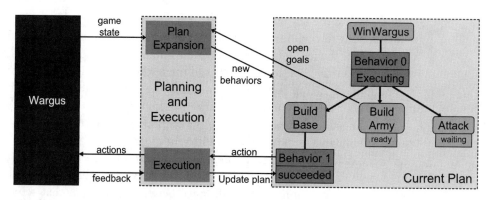

FIGURE 7.2.3   Illustration of how the plan expansion module maintains the current plan.

As mentioned earlier, behaviors might contain *basic actions* that represent the actions that can be performed in the game. When a behavior needs to execute a basic action, the action is first sent to the *Revision Module*, which will revise its parameters to make them better suited to the current game state. After the action is revised, it is sent to the game engine for execution.

The plan expansion module also monitors the execution of behaviors. If a behavior has *alive conditions*, it checks them periodically, and the behavior is cancelled if its alive conditions are not satisfied because it has no further chance of succeeding. Moreover, because the plan expansion module knows the goal that is associated with a particular behavior, the goal is checked after the behavior completes to verify that the behavior succeeded. Notice that knowing the goal that a particular behavior is trying to achieve allows the AI to properly assess whether the behavior was successful or not. A classical scripting language does not allow for the definition of the goals of behaviors, so a classically scripted AI will not know whether a behavior has succeeded and has no basis on which to adapt its behaviors.

If a behavior fails, the subgoal that is associated with it will be considered *open*, and the plan expansion module will attempt to find another behavior to satisfy it. To prevent the system from indefinitely trying to satisfy a subgoal, we limited the number of different behaviors it can try to three. If this maximum number of retries is reached, and the goal has not been satisfied, then the subgoal is considered to have failed, and the failure is propagated one level up so that the behavior of which the subgoal was a part is also considered to have failed. An additional consideration when implementing such plan expansion systems is that if we allow parallel behaviors (behaviors that can spawn subgoals in parallel or that can execute basic actions in parallel), we might have two parallel subtrees in the plan that can potentially interfere with each other. One way of handling this problem is to ignore it and assume that the expert who generated the demonstrations used two behaviors in parallel because they can always be executed in parallel without interference. This approach has the disadvantage that it makes an assumption that might not always be correct.

An alternative approach is to make the plan expansion module responsible for maintaining the consistency of the plan. Each behavior uses a set of resources, which takes the form of spatial resources on the map (such as squares occupied by individual troops), simulated resources (such as gold and oil), and in-game objects (such as individual buildings or troops). The plan expansion module has to make sure that no two behaviors that are executing in parallel use the same resource. In our *Wargus* implementation, we have created a simple version of this that only considers troops as resources and does not consider more complex resource conflicts, such as where two behaviors try to use the same map space. This issue should be addressed to make the system more robust; however, we found that in our implementation this was not necessary for the system to play at an acceptable level.

Behavior Revision

The behavior revision process is implemented as a series of rules that are applied to each one of the basic actions that comprise a behavior so that they can be performed in the current game state. Specifically, we have used two revision rules in our system:

Unit revision: Each basic action sends a particular command to a particular unit, but when a behavior is applied to a different map, the particular unit that the behavior refers to might not correspond to an appropriate unit or such a unit might not even exist. Thus, the unit revision rule tries to find the most similar unit to the one that is specified in the action. To do this, each unit is characterized by a set of five features: owner, type, position, hit points, and status. Status indicates whether it is idle, moving, and so on. The most similar unit, as measured by the Euclidean distance between the unit's feature vector and the feature vector of the required unit, is assigned the required action.

Coordinate revision: Some basic actions, such as move and build commands, make reference to particular coordinates on a map. To revise such coordinates, the revision module gets (from the context information of the behavior) a 5 × 5 window of the map centered on where the action was performed. It then looks at the current map for a similar spot and uses those coordinates for the action. To assess the similarity of two windows, we can simply compare how many of the cells within them are identical. We found that assigning more weight to cells closer to the center (e.g., a weight of 32 to the center cell, a weight of 3 to its neighbors, and weights of 1 to the outermost cells) also produced good results.

After a basic action has been revised using the processes that have just been described, it is sent to the game engine for execution. The process that has been described so far is static in the sense that the same game state will always produce the same behavior. Our system can also adapt behaviors, however, and the means for doing so will be described in the following section.

Automatic Behavior Adaptation

Everything that has been described so far is sufficient to produce a system that can play *Wargus*. However, the system as it has been described is static and suffers from the same types of problems as if it had been hand-crafted. Even the behavior library might not contain enough behaviors to respond intelligently to every event that might occur in the game world, and when a behavior fails, the system has no way of adapting. To overcome these problems, our system incorporates a reasoning layer that can analyze failed behaviors and adapt them. One of the essential requirements for a reasoning system that is responsible for behavior adaptation is that it must be able to detect when adaptation should occur. BRL provides this by associating goals with behaviors; if a behavior completes and its goal has not been achieved, the reasoning layer knows that the current behavior library is not able to achieve its objectives and should be modified. In addition to specifying goals, it is also possible to specify constraint conditions that should be satisfied during the game. For example, one of the conditions that we defined for *Wargus* was that a peasant should not be idle for a significant amount of time.

The reasoning layer consists of two components, the first of which identifies whether behaviors have achieved their specified goals and whether constraint conditions have been violated. If a behavior fails to achieve its goal or a constraint is violated, the system uses an execution trace to perform blame assignment, which aims to identify one or more behaviors that contributed to the failure [Cox99] and need to be changed. The execution trace records the events that occurred during the game, such as which behaviors were started, when they were started, what the game state was, whether they succeeded or failed, the delay between the behavior entering the ready state and starting, and so on. To simplify the problem of reasoning about the execution trace, various data are extracted from it to produce an abstracted execution trace, including data relating to the various units in the game (their hit points, location, statuses), combat data (when units attacked, were attacked, killed, or were killed), how many resources each player had gathered, and so on. Crucially, whenever a behavior fails, the reason for the failure is recorded.

After failed behaviors have been identified, they are passed to the second component in the reasoning layer where they are modified using a set of modification operators (called *modops*), which are described in the next section.

Detecting Failures from the Abstracted Trace

A modop consists of a failure pattern that is used to match a modop to the type of failure that occurred and rules that describe how a behavior should be changed to prevent the failure from happening in the future. After a modop has been applied to a behavior, a new behavior is produced that consists of the same goal as the original failed behavior, the game state for which the behavior was adapted, and the adapted behavior itself. The new behavior can either be included in the behavior library alongside the original or used as a replacement for it depending on the type and severity of the original failure. The following are four examples of failure conditions and the modops that are associated with them:

- *Peasant idle failure* detects if a peasant has been idle for a certain number of cycles, which indicates that he is not being properly used by the existing behavior set in the behavior library. The modops that are associated with this failure aim to use the peasant to gather more resources or to create a building that could be needed later on. Figure 7.2.4 shows how these modops can change the `BuildBase` behavior.
- *Building idle failure* detects whether a particular building has been idle for a certain number of cycles even though there were sufficient resources available to make use of it. The modops that are associated with this failure aim to make use of the free building. For example, a barracks could be used for creating footmen if sufficient resources were available.
- *Peasant attacked military units idle failure* detects whether military units were idle while peasants or buildings were under attack. One of the modops for this failure type takes the form of inserting a basic action that issues an attack command to offensive units.
- *Basic operator failures* detect when behaviors are failing due to the "preconditions," "alive conditions," or "success conditions" not being met at runtime. For example, the preconditions for a behavior that builds a farm or barracks could fail due to a lack of resources or a peasant being unavailable to carry out the plan. Basic operator failures can be fixed by modops that add a basic action that addresses the cause of the failure. For example, if the behavior failed due to a lack of resources, a basic action is added to gather the required resources.

In our *Wargus* implementation, we currently have the four failure patterns listed here and nine fixes. However, this could easily be expanded if necessary.

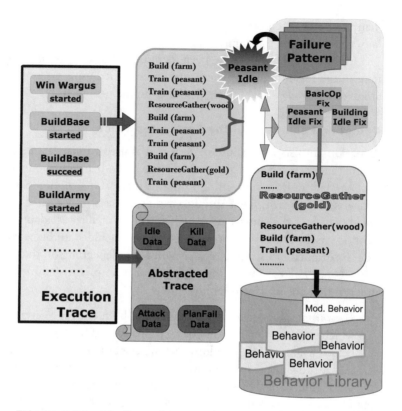

FIGURE 7.2.4   The figure shows an adaptation to the "build base" behavior that is made by inserting a ResourceGather(gold) basic operator. The adaptation is carried out in response to the failure "peasant idle."

Resulting AI Performance

To evaluate the potential of our system for creating effective AI, we performed experiments on two player versions of the map "Nowhere to Run, Nowhere to Hide." This map separates the two players by a wall of trees down the center of the map. The different versions placed the town halls and goldmines in radically different locations as well as changing the shape of the wall of trees so that, on one particular map, it was thin enough to be tunneled through quite quickly. We recorded demonstration traces for two variations of the map and used quite different strategies in each. In the first, we used ballistae to fire over the trees, and in the second, we built towers to prevent the enemy from chopping wood from them. Each of these traces contained about 50 to 60 actions and about 6 to 8 behaviors.

One interesting result of our experiments is how quickly we could produce new AI. Specifically, to record a trace, an expert has to play a complete game (which took about 10 to 15 minutes in the maps that we used) and then annotate it (which took about 5 minutes per trace). Therefore, in 15 to 20 minutes it was possible to train our architecture to play a set of *Wargus* maps similar to the one where the trace was recorded. In contrast, one of our team members took several weeks to hand-code a strategy to play *Wargus* at the same level of play as our system. Moreover, our system is able to combine several traces and select behaviors from whichever is most appropriate, so an expert trace does not have to be created for each individual map.

To assess the performance of our system, we used it to play 27 games against the game's built-in AI. In the first experiment, our system played without the behavior adaptation module and won 17 of 27 games. Moreover, we noticed that when the system used the behavior libraries generated from both expert traces, its performance increased significantly; from the 9 games the system played using both expert traces, it won 8 of them and never lost a game, tying only once. When we ran experiments with the behavior adaptation module, we found that the system used resources more effectively because the peasant idle fixes helped the AI collect resources more quickly.

Some of the other fixes ran into problems, however, due to weak AI decision making at the lower levels. For example, one of the fixes was to add an attack behavior for military units in situations where military units are idle for a significant time when peasants or buildings are under attack. This fix tended to cause problems because the low-level AI would move attacking ballistae too close to the enemy so that they were quickly destroyed. This problem can be solved in two ways. First, the low-level decision systems that are responsible for positioning the ballistae could be improved, and we are working on adding an FSM-based tactical layer to the system for this purpose. Second, it might be possible to create a learning component at the lower level that automatically learns the appropriate parameters from the successes and failures of lower level actions.

Discussion

The techniques that we have presented in this article have several advantages and, of course, certain limitations. The main advantages are that they provide an easy way to define behaviors by demonstration and a way in which behaviors can automatically be adapted. The behavior adaptation system offers a clean way to specify domain knowledge; by defining failure patterns with associated modops, the system can automatically adapt any behavior. This system is also easily expandable because by adding new failure patterns, the system is automatically able to detect them and modify any behavior that might suffer from them. One of the difficulties with our approach is that the features that are used to characterize the game states should reflect all the important details in the game state because, if it fails to do so, the system might retrieve suboptimal behaviors. For example, if maps are characterized only as the percentages of them that are covered by land and water, the system could not use different strategies on two maps that have the same proportions of land and water even if the player and the AI share a single island on one, but have their own islands on the other.

Another problem arises from the fact that it is not always feasible for a player to demonstrate what the AI should do to produce a behavior library. For example, in a game where characters must adjust their facial expressions and body language, it would be difficult for an expert to control every aspect of movement and gesture to show the AI what to do. One solution to this problem could be to provide a high-level abstracted action set to make it easier for the expert to provide a demonstration. For example, instead of providing individual controls for all the muscles in a character's face and body, the expert could be provided high-level controls for mood and emotion, and the underlying system would take care of the corresponding body and facial movements. Finally, if the demonstration execution traces are long, the annotation process could become tedious. In our experiments, annotation was easy but traces for some other kinds of games might be more complex to annotate.

The work that has been described in this article can be taken in various directions. First, the expert demonstrator currently has to play a complete game to provide game traces from which the system can build a behavior library. A possible extension to this process could be to provide the demonstrator with the ability to demonstrate only sub-portions of the game by allowing the expert to see a performance of the learned behavior library and to modify the learned behaviors by intervening at any point. The subportions that need to be modified could be identified by the expert or suggested by the behavior adaptation subsystem. The new demonstration could then be used as replacements for existing behaviors or as new additions to the behavior library.

The BRL still doesn't provide the capability to create daemons (behaviors that are continually waiting for some condition to be true to start executing). Part of the reason for this is that it's difficult to automatically identify daemons from expert demonstrations. One solution to this problem could be to define adaptation rules in the behavior adaptation system that write daemons as part of fixing existing behaviors. For example, instead of fixing the behavior library at the end of a game each time a peasant idle failure is detected, the behavior adaptation system could create a daemon that is always active at runtime and that detects the peasant idle condition and modifies the behavior library by inserting a proper fix in the executing behavior set.

Conclusion

AI behaviors in games are typically implemented using static, hand-crafted scripts. This causes two problems: First, it creates an excessive authorial burden where the script author has to hand-craft behaviors for all circumstances that are likely to occur in the game world. Second, it results in AI that is brittle to changes in the dynamics of the game world. In this article, we have presented an approach that addresses these issues using techniques that can dramatically reduce the burden of writing behaviors and increase the adaptability of the AI's behavior. We have described a behavior learning system that can learn game AI from human demonstrations and automatically adapt behaviors at runtime when they are not achieving their intended purpose.

References

[Aamodt94] Aamodt, Agnar, and Plaza, Enric, "Case-Based Reasoning: Foundational Issues, Methodological Variations, and System Approaches." *Artificial Intelligence Communications*, Vol. 7 no. 1(1994): pp. 39–59.

[Allen83] Allen, James, "Maintaining Knowledge About Temporal Intervals." *Communications of the ACM,* Vol. 26, No. 11 (1983): pp. 832–843.

[Cox99] Cox, Michael, and Ram, Ashwin, "Introspective Multistrategy Learning: On the Construction of Learning Strategies." *Artificial Intelligence*, Vol. 112, (1999): pp. 1–55.

[Mateas2002] Mateas, Michael, and Stern, Andrew, "A Behavior Language for Story-Based Believable Agents." *IEEE Intelligent Systems,* Vol. 17, No. 4 (2002): pp. 39–47.

[Rabin02] Rabin, Steve, *AI Game Programming Wisdom,* Charles River Media, 2002.

[Rabin03] Rabin, Steve, *AI Game Programming Wisdom 2*, Charles River Media, 2003.

7.3

Player Modeling for Interactive Storytelling: A Practical Approach

University of Alberta

David Thue

davidthue@gmail.com

Vadim Bulitko

bulitko@ualberta.ca

Marcia Spetch

mspetch@ualberta.ca

As computer graphics becomes less of a differentiator in the video game market, many developers are turning to AI and storytelling to ensure that their title stands out from the rest. To date, these have been approached as separate, incompatible tasks; AI engineers feel shackled by the constraints imposed by a story, and the story's authors fear the day that an AI character grabs their leading actor and throws him off a bridge.

In this article, we attempt to set aside these differences, bringing AI engineers together with authors through a key intermediary: a player model. Following an overview of the present state of storytelling in commercial games, we present PaSSAGE (Player-Specific Stories via Automatically Generated Events), a storytelling AI that both learns and uses a player model to dynamically adapt a game's story. By combining the knowledge and expertise of authors with a learned player model, PaSSAGE automatically creates engaging and personalized stories that are adapted to appeal to each individual player.

Storytelling in Games: The Usual Suspects

To date, the vast majority of storytelling strategies in commercial video games have used linear, branching, or player-created stories, or some combination of all three. In this section, we discuss the advantages and disadvantages of each of these strategies and motivate a new paradigm for both selecting and authoring story events.

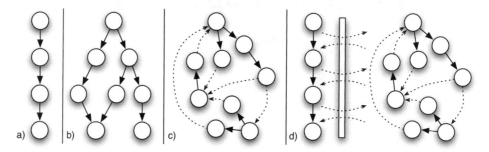

FIGURE 7.3.1   Four common storytelling strategies: Linear (a), Branching (b), Player-created (c), and Layered (d). Nodes represent events, solid arrows show predefined connections to subsequent events, and dashed arrows show potential player-created connections.

Linear Stories

Often favored by games in the first-person shooter (FPS) and action genres, *linear* stories present a highly expressive medium for game story authors (as can be seen in games such as *Half-Life* and *Halo*). When player choices are limited to selecting which side of a hallway to run along or which enemy to shoot first, authors can carefully plan the precise sequence of events that the player will experience, knowing with certainty that no story-relevant alternatives can occur. This type of linear story structure is shown in Figure 7.3.1a.

Unfortunately, this lack of alternatives severely restricts the replay value of such games; although AI-controlled enemies might present different challenges during subsequent plays, the novelty of experiencing a new, interesting story is lost after the first play. Fans of FPS and action games might now raise the point that experiencing a compelling story sits rather low among their concerns when choosing which games to play and argue that compelling stories in such games are unnecessary. In fact, this argument highlights an opportunity for FPS and action games to expand their appeal to a wider audience; by allowing players to make story-relevant decisions while they play, players who appreciate more compelling stories could be drawn into these genres.

The typical tactic for appealing to a wider audience in linear stories relies on including events that, although appealing to some players, might greatly displease others (such as adding puzzles to FPS games, or combat to adventure games). Given that no alternative events exist in these stories, every player is forced to experience every event, regardless of what they might prefer. In this article, we present a method for authoring alternative story events that incorporates the author's knowledge of how they might be preferred by different types of players. By combining this knowledge with a model of a player's type, stories can be constructed that avoid potentially unappealing events, and, given a large enough library of alternatives, improve the replay value of the game when multiple event alternatives are well-suited to the player's current type.

Branching Stories

Found most often in games in the adventure and role-playing genres (such as *Star Wars: Knights of the Old Republic*), *branching* stories introduce a set of story-relevant choices that allow the player to experience different sequences of events (as shown in Figure 7.3.1b). Like linear stories, branching stories allow for highly expressive story-telling, as each alternative sequence of events is created in a similar way to each linear story.

Unfortunately, the number of choices that are presented to a player is typically very small due to the cost of creating at least one alternative event (and usually many more) for every choice that the player can make. Given this cost, the benefit of creating each alternative event (in terms of added player choices) is small, and creating a large number of player choices is prohibitively expensive as a result. In addition, most branching stories tend to implement a form of "foldback" scheme, wherein different sequences of events all lead to the same event, diminishing the perceived impact of the player's decisions.

In this article, we propose to solve these problems by creating story events that are *generic*: the details of where, when, and for whom they occur remain largely undecided until runtime. By varying these details, multiple player choices can be presented using a single generic event, greatly improving the returns gained for the work involved in creating each event.

Player-Created Stories

In games from the simulation genre (such as *Sim City* and *Spore*), the stories that players perceive are created directly by the actions that they take and the events that they experience. Short, self-contained sequences of game events are driven by sets of predefined rules (represented by solid arrows in Figure 7.3.1c), and any two of these sequences are related only by their proximity in the timeline of the player's experience (as shown by dashed arrows in Figure 7.3.1c); the occurrences of the events within them are entirely independent of the events in other sequences. Although this strategy affords a great deal of player choice, the stories that emerge rarely achieve the quality of the stories that are created using the linear or branching techniques because the rules that govern a simulation are typically insufficient to specify how events should be sequenced to produce an entertaining story.

In this article, we present a strategy for authoring and sequencing story events that chooses events from a sequence of libraries, each of which contains a set of events written for a particular part of a story. By selecting events from these libraries that are well-suited to the current player's preferred style of play, entertaining stories can emerge from a simulation-styled game.

Layered Stories

A more recent trend for games from the RPG genre has been to combine the three previous strategies in a *layered* approach; a linear or branching story is set in a simulation-based world (as in games such as *Fable* and *Oblivion*). In between the events of the main story, the player is free to roam the world, engaging in one of many optional side-quests (as represented by dashed arrows between linear and player-created stories in Figure 7.3.1d).

Although having the freedom to experience the substories offered by side-quests gives players some sense of control, often the results of these side-quests have no significant bearing on the course of the main story aside from making the player's avatar strong, fast, and smart enough to live to see the ending.

In this article, we attempt to improve upon the layered story approach by allowing the player's choices in *every* event to have an influence in adapting the story. By learning a model of the player at runtime and using it to adapt the story, we aim to make game stories *player-specific*.

Player-Specific Stories

In this section, we discuss techniques for both learning and using a representation of the behavior, personality, or preferences of a player of a video game, in the context of interactive storytelling. We refer to this representation as a *player model*, and the associated learning problem as *player modeling*. Alongside descriptions of previous work, we present our approach as a set of four techniques: (1) learning a player model, (2) using a player model, (3) authoring generic events, and (4) telling a structured story.

Learning a Player Model

Before a game's story can be adapted to its player, knowledge about that player must be obtained. Although it would certainly be possible to ask each player to fill out a questionnaire before starting to play (an approach called *offline player modeling*), we prefer the less intrusive and more immersive approach of *online player modeling*, which involves learning about players *while* they play by automatically observing their in-game reactions to the events that occur. Although some player-modeling strategies combine both offline and online modeling (e.g., [Sharma07]), we restrict the following discussion to techniques that require only an online component, leaving offline modeling as an optional addition.

Previous Work

In *Mirage* [SeifElNasr07], both player behavior and personality are modeled online; mouse movements are tracked to gauge the player's decisiveness, and the player's actions are used to adjust a vector of values representing tendencies toward various traits such as reluctant hero, violent, self-interested, coward, and truth-seeker. Barber and Kudenko have created an interactive soap opera generator [Barber07] that learns the personality of its players by applying predefined increments or decrements to a vector of personality traits such as honesty, selfishness, and so on, in response to the players' choices.

Learning Styles of Play

The approach that we present in this article is similar to those described for *Mirage* and in Barber and Kudenko's work in that it maintains a vector of values, but we concern ourselves with learning player preferences rather than behavior or personality. More specifically, we chose five of Laws' player types for pen-and-paper role-playing games [Laws01], each of which represents a different style of play. We then model a player's preferences toward playing in each of those styles; this choice is similar to Peinado and Gervás' work on applying game mastering rules to interactive storytelling [Peinado04], although their method of player modeling was strictly offline. The player types that we chose were fighter, storyteller, method actor, tactician, and power gamer. For each type, a numeric value tracks the degree to which players prefer to play in that style. Table 7.3.1 describes each type in more detail. Whereas Peinado and Gervás assume that each player fits a single player type, we aim to model a single player as a mixture of five player types, based on our intuition that the types are not mutually exclusive; some primarily tactical players also enjoy combat, and others like complex plots.

Table 7.3.1   Player Types Used for Player Modeling

Player Type	Player Preferences
Fighter	Engaging in combat
Storyteller	Following complex plots
Method Actor	Performing dramatic actions
Tactician	Solving puzzles
Power Gamer	Gaining special items and skills

To learn about a player's preferences, our PaSSAGE system leverages the expertise and experience of game authors by incorporating their knowledge of how different types of players might enjoy reacting to their story's events. We refer to each potential player reaction as a *branch* of the event in question because each reaction represents a different player choice similar to those that are available in branching stories. For example, consider the following story event:

Name:	Murder
Initial Situation:	Fred has been murdered in the park.
	Clare is near Fred's body, screaming for help.
	The killer (Jim) is hiding in the basement of a mansion nearby.
Initial Action:	Clare approaches the player and asks for help in catching the killer.

Upon discovering the killer's hideout, a player might react in one of several ways; he might rush in headlong in a frontal assault, search around the mansion for a more subtle solution, or make contact with the killer to hear his side of the story. By monitoring the different ways of performing each of these actions (such as attack initiations, container inspections, or conversation initiations), the player's choices can be captured and used to adjust the player model. Many game scripting languages include facilities for running code in response to player actions; in the following example, the murderer's OnAttacked script is used to increase the assessment of the player's inclination toward the Fighter style of play, in addition to providing the usual response to being attacked:

```
void OnAttacked(object oAttacker)
{
    // increase the player's inclination
    // toward the fighter type by a lot

    pmUpdateType(PM_FIGHT, PM_ADJUST_HIGH);

    SpeakString("Die!");   // shout "Die!"
    ActionAttack(oAttacker)); // attack the player
}
```

As mentioned earlier, the player model is maintained as a vector of numbers, each representing the player's inclination toward playing in one of the five chosen styles of play. Positive updates to a type's value indicate that the player prefers that type; negative updates show that the player is less inclined to play in that style. This scheme results in the following simple code for pmUpdateType; we simply add the update's value to the appropriate field of the player model's type vector:

```
enum PM_Type{ PM_FIGHT, PM_STORY, PM_METHOD,
             PM_TACT, PM_POWER          };

const int PM_ADJUST_HIGH = 100; // large adjustment
const int PM_ADJUST_LOW = 40;  // small adjustment

void pmUpdateType(PM_Type type, int value)
{
    // add the adjustment to the proper type's value
    playerModel[type] += value;
}
```

Using a Player Model

After a model of the player's personality, behavior, or preferences has been obtained, it can be used to adapt the content of the story being told.

Previous Work

In *Mirage* [SeifElNasr07], the selection priority of each story event is adjusted based on rules that monitor both the personality defined in the player model and the set of previous story events. For example, a rule might say that if event #4 is available to be run, event #1 has already occurred, and the player has shown the "reluctant hero" trait, then the priority of event #5 should be increased by 20 points. When several story events are applicable in a given situation, the one with the highest priority is chosen, thereby allowing the player model to influence the story.

The system described by Barber and Kudenko [Barber07] uses its model of the player's personality to predict his choices in a sequence of dilemmas that make up the events of an interactive soap opera. By combining predefined measures of the "interestingness" of each dilemma's choices (which are independent of personality type) together with the likelihood of each choice being made by the player as calculated using their modeled personality type, the system presents the dilemma that has the highest expected interestingness.

A recent version of Magerko's Interactive Drama Architecture (IDA) [Magerko06] uses a predefined model of player behavior to predict when player actions will fall outside the scope of what the story's author intended. If such actions can be predicted far enough in advance, IDA can employ subtle techniques to steer the player toward an intended course of action; this is a welcome alternative to attempting to recover after a story-invalidating action has occurred.

Unlike the work that has been described so far, Peinado and Gervás' system [Peinado04] was designed for more than one player. After having each player indicate his preference toward one of Laws' player types [Laws01], the system uses two similarity metrics to select four events that are, respectively, the most obvious, most surprising, most pleasing, and most challenging. It then chooses one of the four at random, ensures that it satisfies a set of predefined rules, and then adapts its content to the current set of players by adding elements that appeal to each of their types (such as surprise monster attacks during a journey to appeal to fighter-style players).

Leveraging Author Experience

Similar to Peinado and Gervás' system, PaSSAGE aims to please its players by selecting story events that are well-suited to their preferred styles of play. As mentioned earlier, PaSSAGE leverages the authors' knowledge of how different types of players might prefer to react to the events that they create. For every branch of an event, a vector of values is maintained that indicates that branch's suitability for each of the five player types. In the example of the murder event that was given earlier, we identified three potential player reactions; Table 7.3.2 shows how they might be annotated by the author of the event. In the table, ticks indicate preferences toward a branch held by the given player type, and crosses represent aversions. The number of symbols shows the strength of the expected preference or aversion. Dashes show when players of the given type are expected to be indifferent to a branch.

Table 7.3.2　Annotations on Three Branches of the Murder Event.

Description	Fighter	Storyteller	Method Actor	Tactician	Power Gamer
1. Headlong assault	✓✓✓	–	–	✓	–
2. Subtle approach	–	–	✗	✓✓✓	✓
3. Converse with killer	✗ ✗	✓✓✓	✓✓✓	–	–

For example, the third branch, "Converse with killer," has been annotated to indicate that while it will likely be preferred by storytellers and strongly preferred by method actors, tacticians and power gamers will be indifferent to that approach, and fighters will be averse to it.

Selecting Story Events

Given a library of story events where each event has one or more preference-annotated branches, PaSSAGE chooses events based on a calculated measure of suitability. This calculation is performed as follows:

$$Event\ Suitability = \overset{max}{branches}\left(\frac{author}{annotation} \bullet clamp\left(\frac{player}{model}, [0, \infty) \right) \right)$$

To understand our reason for clamping negative values in the model to zero, consider the following example in Table 7.3.3, where each branch's suitability is calculated via an inner product between the author annotations on each branch and the (unclamped) player model values.

Table 7.3.3　Branch Suitability Calculated via an Inner Product Between the Author Annotations on Each Branch and the Unclamped Player Model Values

Player Type	Player Model	Branch 1	Branch 2	Branch 3
Fighter	1	4	0	–2
Storyteller	101	0	0	3
Method Actor	–41	0	–1	4
Tactician	41	1	4	0
Power Gamer	1	0	1	0
Branch Suitability:		45	206	137

In this case, the model is fairly certain that the player is *not* a Method Actor, but as a result, the simple inner product leads PaSSAGE to believe that Branch 2 is the best choice. The error occurs in two places: for players who are not Method Actors, whether or not branches are well-suited (Branch 3) or poorly suited (Branch 2) to Method Actors is irrelevant; the other types should be considered exclusively instead.

By clamping negative values in the model to zero, we achieve a better result, as shown in Table 7.3.4.

Table 7.3.4 Branch Suitability Calculated via an Inner Product Between the Author Annotations on Each Branch and the *Negative Player Model Values Clamped to Zero*

Player Type	Player Model	Branch 1	Branch 2	Branch 3
Fighter	1	4	0	−2
Storyteller	101	0	0	3
Method Actor	0	0	−1	4
Tactician	41	1	4	0
Power Gamer	1	0	1	0
Branch Suitability:		45	165	301

Steering the Player

A serious problem of game design in general lies in ensuring that players experience all of the content that the designers intend for them to see. The usual storytelling strategies solve this problem by either constraining players to a particular sequence of content and events or relying on players being persistent enough to find the content that they enjoy (consider side-quests in layered stories, for example). While implementing PaSSAGE, we discovered that we had the potential for a more flexible approach. Given that we were already calculating which of a chosen event's branches (i.e., ways of reacting) the player would prefer, we realized that we could use that information to direct the player to play along that particular branch: fighters could be given the pretext to fight, and power gamers could be tempted by the offer of a reward.

One means of achieving this sort of direction is to make the other branches of the event impossible to experience; however, this is problematic if our model of the player is poor because forcing the player to behave in an unnatural manner is precisely one of the flaws of linear stories that PaSSAGE attempts to avoid. Even worse, if only one way of behaving were available to the player, PaSSAGE would be unable to refine its knowledge of the player's preferred style of play. Given that players' styles of play might change while they play, continual learning in PaSSAGE is essential. To direct the player while still retaining both the player's perception of freedom and PaSSAGE's ability to learn the player's style of play, we devised a strategy called *hinting*, which is similar to previous work by Sharma *et al.* [Sharma07]. In hinting, each *hint* is encoded as a slight, optional modification of the action of each story event that is designed to subtly nudge the player toward playing out the branch that PaSSAGE thinks is best. Continuing further with the murder example, Table 7.3.5 shows potential hints for each of the event's three branches. By gently steering a player toward what is hopefully his preferred style of play, PaSSAGE capitalizes on the author's experience through the annotations on each event.

Table 7.3.5   Potential Hints for Each Branch of the Murder Event

Branch	Hint
1. Headlong assault	Instead of waiting for the player to attack, the killer attacks the player on sight; however, the player can still choose to start a conversation instead of fighting back.
2. Subtle approach	Clare (the witness) notices that the killer drops a key as he runs away, and she gives it to the player. The key fits the door to the basement that the murderer is hiding in; the key can usually be found by searching the mansion's main floor.
3. Converse with killer	As the player approaches, the killer initiates a conversation; however, the player can still choose to attack the killer or search the mansion instead.

Making Decisions in General

Although selecting story events and steering the player toward expected enjoyable behavior are two particular ways to use a player model, the potential exists to use the player model to make story-related decisions in general. In the following section, we present a method that takes advantage of the fact that, as we delay more and more of the author's decision processes to runtime, the number of decision-making opportunities for player modeling will increase as well.

Expanding the Decision Space: Generic Events and Behaviors

In a previous publication, we described PaSSAGE as having three phases of decision making when considering an event (Selection, Specification, and Refinement) [Thue07], each designed to answer subsets of the questions "Who? What? When? Where? Why? How?" The answers to these questions (as they pertain to a story's events) are typically fixed by authors long before a game is released, leading to the disadvantages of linear and branching stories that were discussed earlier in this article. With PaSSAGE, we aim to make the events that authors create reusable by delaying the answering of all six of these questions to runtime. To do so, we ask authors to create story events that are, as much as possible, independent of when, where, and for whom they occur, leaving these details to be decided by PaSSAGE *while* the game is played, based on the player model and a set of author-designed rules. For example, instead of defining our murder event as given previously, we can abstract away its details of place and actor identity (time has already been abstracted to enable anytime event selection):

Name:	Generic Murder
Initial Situation:	Someone has been murdered. *Who? Where?*
	A witness stands near the body. *Who is the witness?*
	The killer is hiding nearby. *Who is the killer? Where is he/she?*
Initial Action:	The witness approaches the player for help in catching the killer.

Along with this specification, the event's author describes a set of conditions (called *trigger conditions*) governing which of the storyworld's characters can be selected to play each role (victim, witness, or killer) in the event, considering their attributes, location, and so on. Table 7.3.6 shows a set of conditions that might be desired for each of the murder event's roles. In this case, the author has specified that the victim must be greater than 50 feet away from the player, the witness must be within 20 feet of the victim, and the killer must be within 5 feet of the victim. Additionally, neither the victim nor the killer can be a child. After the murder event has been selected to occur, PaSSAGE waits for characters in the storyworld to satisfy the event's conditions; as soon as they are satisfied, *role passing* is used to begin the event.

Table 7.3.6 Potential Trigger Conditions for Each Role of the Murder Event

Role	Condition
Victim	distanceFrom(Player) > 50ft & not(child)
Witness	distanceFrom(Victim) < 10ft
Killer	distanceFrom(Victim) < 5ft & not(child)

Role Passing

Originally proposed by Horswill and Zubek [Horswill99] and later extended by Mac-Namee *et al.* [MacNamee03], *role passing* refers to the practice of dynamically assigning behaviors to intelligent agents based on their current situation. In PaSSAGE, storyworld characters that simultaneously satisfy the trigger conditions of a selected event are assigned roles corresponding to the conditions that they satisfy; that is, they assume the behavior and dialogue that was authored for their role. For example, consider the arrangements of storyworld characters in relation to the player in Figure 7.3.2a. No set of characters currently satisfies the murder event's trigger conditions, so nothing happens. As soon as the highlighted character moves to the given location, however, the trigger conditions are satisfied, and the three satisfying characters each take on their roles.

Telling a Story: Joseph Campbell's Monomyth

To give stronger global structure to the sequence of events that it chooses, PaSSAGE uses Joseph Campbell's Monomyth to inform its decisions [Campbell49]. Although originally intended as a tool for analyzing myths, the Monomyth has been used prescriptively to create a number of blockbuster films (including the *Star Wars* and *Matrix* trilogies) and helped to motivate our approach. The Monomyth describes a heroic journey as a cycle of general phases, such as "Call to Adventure," "Crossing the Threshold," and "Ordeal." After dividing its library of events into groups corresponding to each phase, PaSSAGE moves through the cycle, choosing only among the events that are appropriate for the current phase. For a walkthrough of this process set

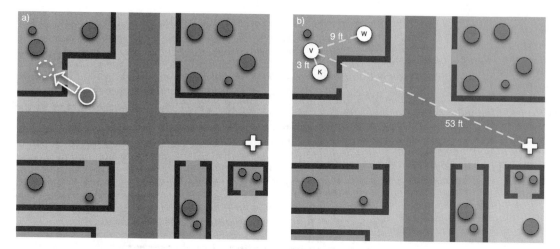

FIGURE 7.3.2   The murder event's trigger conditions are satisfied (in b) when the highlighted character moves to the location shown in (a). Storyworld characters are circles (children are small), and the player is the plus sign. V = Victim, K = Killer, and W = Witness.

in a storyworld based on the *Little Red Riding Hood* fairy tale, the reader is directed to our previous publication [Thue07]. You might be worried that this approach is rather wasteful: if only one of several possible events is chosen at each phase, the time spent creating all of the other events seems to be wasted. You must realize, however, that the Monomyth can be used as a cycle; when multiple (and perhaps coincidental) heroic stories are told, events that are skipped in earlier iterations can occur later on.

Human User Study

To gain a better understanding of the value of using PaSSAGE to create player-specific stories, we conducted a user study wherein 90 university students played through a short adventure based on the *Little Red Riding Hood* fairy tale, implemented in BioWare Corp's *Aurora Neverwinter Toolset* [BioWare07]. We compared PaSSAGE's stories to two prewritten plots through a postgame survey, where players gave ratings of both "fun" (their enjoyment of the game) and "agency" (their sense of having influence over the story). We found that for female players who rated the game as being "easy to follow," with 86% confidence, player-specific stories had better agency, and with 93% confidence, player-specific stories were more fun [Thue07]. Although our study also included players who were male and players who found the game difficult to follow, our results across all players, although encouraging, were not statistically significant. By considering only female players who found the game easy to follow (59 out of 90 participants), we aimed to establish that this particular segment of the market should be well-targeted by our player-specific approach. For further details, the reader is encouraged to consult our previous work [Thue07].

Limitations and Future Work

In this section, we discuss the current limitations of our approach and suggest areas of future work that lie along the path to achieving high-quality storytelling AI with the help of a player model. The primary limitations of our approach rest in the practical construction and effective use of PaSSAGE's library of story events.

Building a Library of Events

For PaSSAGE to succeed in telling multiple successive stories, it must have a large library of story events to draw on; otherwise, players might begin to find that an event in one story is too similar to one that occurred in a story before. Although making events generic by specifying roles, trigger conditions, and hints helps to alleviate this problem with relatively small overhead, the burden of creating the events themselves could make creating a large library impractical. To help solve this problem, we suggest a model wherein *players* are given the opportunity to create the story events (using a tool such as the *Aurora Neverwinter Toolset*). Although some might question the usefulness of this solution for creating content for a game's initial release, there is some precedent in the industry for releasing development tools to the community months *before* a game is released (*Neverwinter Nights 2* is a notable example). By collecting player-created events in a professionally reviewed repository, new experiences could be distributed to the community at little cost to the developer.

Running Out of High-Suitability Events

Although PaSSAGE's generic events encourage reuse, care must be taken in reusing any single event too frequently; the variations available for each event will eventually run out. Unfortunately, restricting the reuse of events results in fewer and fewer high-suitability events being available for selection as the story proceeds. The implementation of PaSSAGE presented in this article will exhaust the highest-suitability events first, leaving only lower-suitability events remaining to continue the story. An alternative to this method is to include an element of pacing: intersperse lower-suitability events with the chosen high-suitability events, extending the useful lifetime of the library of events. Including this pacing also has the benefit of prompting PaSSAGE's player-modeling process to explore in its learning and adapt to changing player styles.

Conclusion

In this article, we presented PaSSAGE, a storytelling AI designed to help overcome the limitations of existing storytelling techniques by basing its decisions on a model of the player's preferred style of play. We expanded the set of available storytelling decisions through generic events and role passing, and suggested the Monomyth as a viable way of achieving global story structure. Finally, we presented the current limitations of PaSSAGE and suggested potential solutions, offering our vision of how future work might proceed to achieve an ideal storytelling AI.

References

[Barber07] Barber, Heather, and Kudenko, Daniel, "A User Model for the Generation of Dilemma-Based Interactive Narratives." *Technical Report, AIIDE 2007 Workshop on Optimizing Player Satisfaction*, Palo Alto, California, AAAI Press, 2007.

[BioWare07] BioWare Corp., "Aurora Neverwinter Toolset." Available online at *http://nwn.bioware.com*, 2007.

[Campbell49] Campbell, Joseph, *The Hero with a Thousand Faces*. Princeton University Press, 1949.

[Horswill99] Horswill, Ian D., and Zubek, Robert, "Robot Architectures for Believable Game Agents." *Proceedings of the 1999 AAAI Spring Symposium on Artificial Intelligence and Computer Games*, AAAI Technical Report SS-99-02, 1999.

[Laws01] Laws, Robin, "Robin's Laws of Good Game Mastering." *Steve Jackson Games*, 2001.

[MacNamee03] MacNamee, Brian et al., "Simulating Virtual Humans Across Diverse Situations." *Technical Report,* Computer Science Department, University of Dublin, Trinity College, Dublin, Ireland, 2003.

[Magerko06] Magerko, Brian, "Intelligent Story Direction in the Interactive Drama Architecture." *AI Game Programming Wisdom 3*, Charles River Media, 2006.

[Peinado04] Peinado, Federico, and Gervás, Pablo, "Transferring Game Mastering Laws to Interactive Digital Storytelling." *Proceedings of the 2nd International Conference on Technologies for Interactive Digital Storytelling and Entertainment* (TIDSE 2004), Darmstadt, Germany: Springer, (2004): pp. 1–12.

[SeifElNasr07] Seif El-Nasr, Magy, "Interaction, Narrative, and Drama Creating an Adaptive Interactive Narrative Using Performance Arts Theories." *Interaction Studies*, Vol. 8, No. 2, 2007.

[Sharma07] Sharma, Manu et al., "Player Modeling Evaluation for Interactive Fiction." *Technical Report,* AIIDE 2007 Workshop on Optimizing Player Satisfaction, Palo Alto, California, AAAI Press, 2007.

[Thue07] Thue, David et al., "Interactive Storytelling: A Player Modelling Approach." *Proceedings of the 3rd Artificial Intelligence and Interactive Digital Entertainment Conference* (AIIDE), Palo Alto, California, AAAI Press, (2007): pp. 43–48.

7.4

Automatically Generating Score Functions for Strategy Games

Universiteit Maastricht

Sander Bakkes

s.bakkes@micc.unimaas.nl

Pieter Spronck

p.spronck@micc.unimaas.nl

Modern video games present complex environments in which their AI is expected to behave realistically, or in a "human-like" manner. One feature of human behavior is the ability to assess the desirability of the current strategic situation. This type of assessment can be modeled in game AI using a *score function*. A good score function not only drives the decision making of the AI but also provides feedback on the effectiveness of the playing style of human players. Furthermore, score functions that change during gameplay can be used to implement adaptive strategies.

This article discusses our work on a means for automatically generating a score function for strategy games. Due to the complex nature of modern strategy games, the determination of a good score function can be difficult. This difficulty arises in particular from the fact that score functions usually operate in an imperfect information environment. In this article, we show that machine learning techniques can produce a score function that gives good results despite this lack of information.

Approach

Score functions can be used to rate the desirability of game states for the AI and have a variety of applications. Such ratings can, for example, be used for the implementation of effective adaptive game AI, which has been explored with some success in previous research [Demasi02, Graepel04, Spronck04]. However, due to the complex nature of modern video games, generating a good score function is often difficult.

This article discusses our work on automatically generating a score function for strategy games. Our approach uses a machine learning algorithm to derive a score function from a central data store of samples of gameplay experiences and is therefore well suited to games that can access the Internet to upload gameplay experiences to a central server [Spronck05], which allows the AI to be updated and for new versions to be downloaded automatically by game clients.

In our research, we use *Spring*, which is a typical state-of-the-art, open source RTS game. In *Spring*, as in most RTS games, a player needs to gather resources for the construction of units and buildings. The aim of the game is to defeat an enemy army in a real-time battle. A *Spring* game is won by the player who first destroys the opponent's "Commander" unit (the gameplay mechanic and term "Commander" originated with the commercial RTS game *Total Annihilation* and its unofficial sequel *Supreme Commander*).

In the following sections, we first discuss how to collect and represent the domain knowledge about a strategy game in a data store and then show how to automatically generate a score function, based on the collected data. We give a short introduction to TD-learning (Temporal Difference learning), the machine learning technique that we used to learn the effectiveness of different types of units in the game. We then discuss how information on the phase of the game can be incorporated into a score function. The results of an experimental evaluation of the performance of the generated score function are then presented, and we describe how a score function can practically be used in a game. We finish by providing conclusions and describing future work.

Data Store of Gameplay Experiences

We define a gameplay experience as a list of values that represent a set of observable features of the game environment at a certain point in time. To create a data store of gameplay experiences for *Spring*, we start by defining a basic set of features that play an essential role in the game. For our experiments, we decided to use the following five features:

- Number of units observed of each unit type
- Number of enemy units within a 2,000 radius of the Commander
- Number of enemy units within a 1,000 radius of the Commander
- Number of enemy units within a 500 radius of the Commander
- Percentage of the environment visible

Spring implements a line-of-sight visibility mechanism for each unit. This means that the AI only has access to feature data for those parts of the environment that are visible to its own units. When the information that is available to a game's AI is restricted to what its own units can observe, we call this an *imperfect-information environment*. When we allow the AI to access all information, regardless of whether it is visible to its own units or not, we call this a *perfect-information environment*. It seems reasonable to assume that the reliability of a score function will be highest when it has access to perfect information. We therefore assume that the quality of the scores obtained using a score function that is generated with perfect information sets an upper limit on the quality of the scores that might be expected from using a score function that is based on imperfect information.

For our experiments, we generated a data store consisting of three different data sets: the first contained training data collected in a perfect-information environment, the second contained test data collected in a perfect-information environment, and the third contained test data collected in an imperfect-information environment.

Score Function for Strategy Games

The five aforementioned features were selected as the basis of a score function. To allow the score function to deal with the imperfect information that is inherent in the *Spring* environment, we attempted to map the imperfect feature data to a prediction in the perfect feature data. Our straightforward implementation of this mapping is to linearly extrapolate the number of observed enemy units to the unobserved region of the environment. If the opponent's units are homogeneously distributed over the environment, the score function applied to an imperfect-information environment will produce results close to those of the score function in a perfect-information environment. Obviously, such a homogeneous distribution is not realistic, but when a reasonably large part of the battlefield is observed, the straightforward mapping seems to give good results.

Our score function consists of two terms, and is given by

$$v(p) = w_p v_1 + (1 - w_p) v_2$$

where w_p is a free parameter that is used to determine the weight of each term v_i of the score function, which are explained in detail later, and $p \in N$ is a parameter that represents the current phase of the game.

Material Strength

The term v_1 in our score function represents material strength. It uses data from feature numbers 1 and 5 in the data store and is calculated using

$$v_1 = \sum_u w_u \left(C_{u_0} - \frac{O_{u_1}}{R} \right)$$

where w_u is the experimentally determined weight of unit type u, C_{u_0} is the number of the AI's units of type u, O_{u_1} is the observed number of the opponent's units of type u, and $R \in [0,1]$ is the fraction of the environment that is visible to the AI. The values w_u are determined by TD-learning, as described later.

Positional Safety

The term v_2 in our score function represents the safety of the current tactical position and is designed to assess the threat to the Commander unit. In *Spring*, the Commander is a strong and very useful unit, which the player must make good use of to win the game. However, if the player allows the enemy to destroy it, he will lose the game.

Positional safety is computed using data from features 2, 3, 4, and 5 in the data store as

$$v_2 = \sum_{r \in D} w_r \left(\frac{O_{r_1}}{R_{r_1}} - \frac{O_{r_0}}{R_{r_0}} \right)$$

where w_r is the weight of the radius r, O_{r_1} is the number of units belonging to the AI that are observed by the opponent within a radius r of the opponent's Commander, $R_{r_i} \in [0,1]$ is the fraction of the environment within radius r that is visible to the opponent, O_{r_0} is the observed number of opposing units within a radius r of the AI's Commander, $D = \{500, 1000, 2000\}$, and $R_{r_0} \in [0,1]$ is the fraction of the environment within radius r that is visible to the AI. The values of w_r are experimentally determined, as described later in this article.

TD-learning

Temporal Difference learning (TD-learning) [Sutton88] is a form of reinforcement learning that can be used to create estimates of the utility values of game states, such as our $v(p)$. To achieve this, it estimates the long-term value of visiting a state by updating the estimate of its value to make it more similar to the value of its successor state when a state transition occurs. By repeating this procedure many times, the information about the rewards or punishments that are associated with winning and losing game states gradually propagate backward through the game to states that occur much earlier.

The origins of TD-learning lie in animal learning psychology and, in particular, in the notion of secondary reinforcers. A secondary reinforcer is a stimulus that has been paired with a primary reinforcer, such as food or pain, and, as a result, has come to take on similar reinforcing properties [Jonker07]. A famous example of the application of TD-learning to game AI is the work of Tesauro on Backgammon [Tesauro92]. Tesauro's program, *TD-Gammon*, was programmed with little knowledge of how to play Backgammon and yet learned to play extremely well, near the level of the world's strongest grandmasters.

We used TD-learning to establish appropriate values w_u for all unit types u (the MatLab code that we used to do this is available on the CD-ROM), which is similar to the work of Beal and Smith [Beal97] for determining piece values in chess.

ON THE CD

Phase of the Game

Modern RTS games typically progress through several distinct phases as players perform research and create new buildings that provide them with new capabilities. The phase of a game can be straightforwardly derived from the observed traversal through the game's tech tree. Traversing the tech tree is (almost) always advantageous, yet there is a cost for doing so in time and game resources. In *Spring*, three levels of technology are available. At the start of the game, a player can only construct Level 1 structures and Level 1 units. Later in the game, after the player has performed the required research, advanced structures and units of Level 2 and Level 3 become available.

Previous research performed in the *Spring* environment has shown that the accuracy of win-lose outcome predictions is closely related to the phase of the game in which they are made [Bakkes07]. To distinguish game phases in the *Spring* game, we map tech levels to game phases and distinguish between when tech levels are "new," and when they are "mature," as indicated by the presence of units with a long construction time. This leads us to define the following five game phases:

Phase 1: Level 1 structures observed.
Phase 2: Level 1 units observed that have a build time $\geq 2,500$.
Phase 3: Level 2 structures observed.
Phase 4: Level 2 units observed that have a build time $\geq 15,000$.
Phase 5: Level 3 units or Level 3 structures observed.

Experiments

To test our approach, we gathered data by pitting two game AIs against each other and collected feature data for each player. Games were played in the mod *Absolute Annihilation v2.23*. Multiple *Spring* game AIs are available online. We found one that was open source, which we labeled AAI, and enhanced it with the ability to collect feature data in a data store and the ability to disregard radar visibility so that perfect information was available. As opposing AIs, we used AAI itself, as well as three others, namely TSI, CSAI, and RAI. The following descriptions are based on information provided by "neddiedrow" and "tow_dragon:"

- *AAI* is a configuration file-based skirmish AI developed by "Submarine," also known as Alexander Seizinger. It features powerful group handling, streamlined economy management, and the ability to learn and adjust its behavior on the basis of gameplay experiences. It can interpret zones of conflict, and the configuration files allow game makers to tweak rates of expansion and production.
- *TSI* is a configuration file-based skirmish AI that was developed by Mateusz Baran and Michal Urbańczyk and uses an extensive pathfinding system that is good at finding and exploiting chokepoints on the map.

- CSAI was developed by Hugh Perkins as a proof of concept for a C#-based skirmish AI and implements an aggressive rapid "rush" strategy.
- RAI is a generalized skirmish AI developed by "Reth." RAI features effective unit handling of individuals and groups, rapid construction, and the ability to erect secondary bases of operation.

Table 7.4.1 lists the numbers of games from which we built the data store. During each game, feature data was collected every 127 game cycles, which corresponds to the update frequency of AAI. With 30 game cycles per second, this resulted in feature data being collected every 4.2 seconds. The games were played on a map called "SmallDivide," which is a symmetrical map without water areas. All games were played under identical starting conditions.

Table 7.4.1   The Number of *Spring* Games Collected in the Data Store

Friendly Team	Enemy Team	#Games in Training Set (Collected with Perfect Information)	#Games in Test Set (Collected with Perfect Information)	#Games in Test Set (Collected with Imperfect Information)
AAI	AAI (self-play)	500	200	200
AAI	TSI	100	200	200
AAI	CSAI	100	200	200
AAI	RAI	–	200	200

ON THE CD

We used a MatLab implementation of TD-learning (which is available on the CD-ROM) to learn the unit type weights wu, which are used by the term v_1 of the score function. Unit type weights were learned from feature data collected with perfect information from the 700 games stored in the training set. We did not include feature data collected in games where AAI was pitted against RAI because we wanted to use RAI to test the generalization ability of the learned score function.

The values of the parameters that controlled TD-learning were chosen in accordance with the research of Beal and Smith [Beal97]. The unit type weights were initialized to 1.0 before learning started, and the weights of the radii defined in the set D were chosen by the experimenter to be 0.75, 0.20, and 0.05 for radii of 500, 1,000, and 2,000, respectively, which reflected the experimenter's prior belief about their relative importance.

A gradient descent optimization algorithm [Snyman05] was applied to optimize the term weights w_p for all phases. A step value of 0.01 was used initially to allow the algorithm to explore the state space using random jumps. Slowly, the step value was decreased to 0.001, to encourage the algorithm to perform local optimization. The term weights for each phase were initialized to 0.5 before learning started.

Performance Evaluation

To evaluate the performance of the learned score function, we determined to what extent it was capable of predicting the actual outcome of a *Spring* game. The prediction was interpreted as being for a win if the output of the score function was positive and for a loss otherwise. To assess the accuracy of these predictions, we defined the measure "final prediction accuracy" as the percentage of games for which the outcome is correctly predicted at the end of the game. It might seem easy to achieve a final prediction accuracy of 100% but, in practice, there are several reasons why that is not the case, which will be discussed later. For a score function to be useful, it is also important that it has some ability to predict the eventual outcome of a game some time before it finishes. To assess this ability, the predictions made by the score function were recorded throughout a game and compared to its eventual outcome.

We determined performance using two test sets, one of which contained feature data collected in a perfect information environment and the other contained feature data collected in an imperfect information environment. Feature data, listed in Table 7.4.1, was collected from 800 games.

Results

In this section, we will discuss the unit type weights that were obtained with the TD-learning mechanism first and then present the prediction accuracy results that were obtained, which illustrate the effectiveness of our approach.

Learned Unit-Type Weights

The *Spring* environment supports more than 200 different unit types. During feature data collection, we found that 89 different unit types were used (some were not used due to the AIs' preferences for different unit types and the characteristics of the map on which the data was collected). The TD-learning algorithm learned weights for these 89 unit types, a summary of which is given in Table 7.4.2.

Table 7.4.2 Summary of Learned Unit-Type Weights

Unit Type	Weight
Advanced Metal Extractor *(Building)*	5.91
Thunder Bomber *(Aircraft)*	5.57
Metal Storage *(Building)*	4.28
Freedom Fighter *(Aircraft)*	4.23
Medium Assault Tank *(GroundUnit)*	4.18
...	...
Minelayer/Minesweeper with Anti-Mine Rocket *(GroundUnit)*	−1.10
Arm Advanced Solar Collector *(Building)*	−1.28
Light Amphibious Tank *(GroundUnit)*	−1.52
Energy Storage *(Building)*	−1.70
Defender Anti-Air Tower *(Building)*	−2.82

It is interesting to observe that the highest weight has been assigned to the Advanced Metal Extractor. At first glance, this seems surprising because this unit type is not directly involved in combat. However, when the AI destroys an Advanced Metal Extractor, not only is the opponent's ability to gather resources reduced but also the AI has likely already penetrated its opponent's defenses because this unit is typically well protected and resides close to the Commander. This implies that, when the AI destroys an Advanced Metal Extractor, it is a good indicator that the AI is likely to win the game.

It is also interesting to observe that some unit types obtained weights less than zero. This indicates that these unit types are of little use to the AI and are actually a waste of resources. For instance, the Light Amphibious Tank is predictably of limited use because our test map contained no water. The weights of the unit types that are directly involved in combat show that the Medium Assault Tank, Thunder Bomber, and Freedom Fighter are the most valuable.

Prediction Accuracy

Table 7.4.3 lists the final prediction accuracies for the trials where AAI was pitted against each of its four opponent AIs. For the score function in a perfect information environment, the final prediction accuracy is 97% on average. For the score function in an imperfect information environment, the final prediction accuracy is 90% on average. From these results, we may conclude that the established score function is effective in evaluating a game's status at the end of the game and thus might form an effective basis for a score function that can be used in all phases of the game (i.e., a game-spanning score function).

We should point out here that a human player would probably score 100% on correctly predicting the outcome of a game, when the game is at its very end. The fact that the score function does not achieve human performance is not an indication that it is badly designed, for two reasons. First, the score function is tuned to make predictions that are good during a large part of the game, not only at the end, and hence it will trade prediction accuracy at the end of the game for higher prediction accuracy earlier in the game.

Second, if the goal of the game was to destroy all the opponent's units, a correct prediction would be easy to make at the end. However, the goal is to destroy the opponent's Commander, and we found that it sometimes happens that a player who is behind in military strength can win, often because the opponent's Commander makes a high-risk move, such as attacking strong enemy units on its own. A score function that is based on a comparison of military force and positional safety cannot take such moves into account other than allowing for their general statistical likelihood.

Table 7.4.3 Final Prediction Accuracy Results

Trial	Final Prediction Accuracy Perfect Information Environment	Final Prediction Accuracy Imperfect Information Environment
AAI-AAI	99%	92%
AAI-TSI	96%	88%
AAI-CSAI	98%	93%
AAI-RAI	95%	87%

Figure 7.4.1 shows the percentage of game outcomes that were correctly predicted as a function of how far through the game the predictions were made. The figure compares the predictions of the score function in a perfect information environment with the predictions of the score function in an imperfect information environment. The results reveal that these predictions are comparable, which suggests that our approach to extrapolating to unobserved areas of the map did not limit the performance of the score function in an imperfect information environment. Additionally, we observe that later in a game, when the AI has more units and thus can observe a larger area of the map, the reliability of the score function increases.

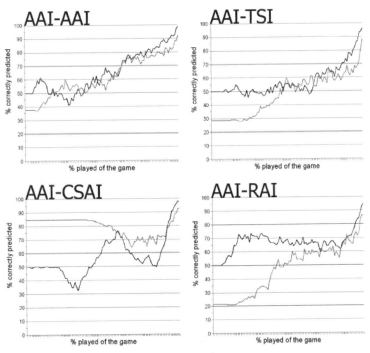

FIGURE 7.4.1 Comparison of outcomes correctly predicted as a function over time. The black line represents the prediction performance of the score function in a perfect information environment, and the gray line represents the prediction performance of the score function in an imperfect information environment.

The results that were obtained in the AAI-AAI trial are pleasing, considering that reasonable predictions in this self-play trial were obtained relatively early in each game. Similar results were obtained in the AAI-TSI trial, although the predictions became accurate later in each game. The results that were achieved in the AAI-RAI trial are also satisfactory considering that no AAI-RAI games were included in the training set; the fact that the score function achieves greater than 50% accuracy demonstrates its ability to generalize. The reason that the score function can more accurately predict the outcome in self-play might be that the score function was overfitted to the training data from the AAI-AAI games.

Games between AAI and CSAI were very short because CSAI employed a successful rush strategy. The fluctuations in the prediction accuracy results for these games is therefore less significant than it would at first appear. We note, however, that at the beginning of the game, the score function in an imperfect-information environment can predict the outcome more accurately than it can in a perfect-information environment. This phenomenon can be explained as follows: early in the game, CSAI will rapidly send a large number of tanks to the base of AAI while AAI is still in the process of constructing its base and can only see a small part of the map. Observing the tanks, AAI will assume that many more tanks are stationed in the remaining large part of the map that it cannot see. Thus, in this scenario, the score function overestimates the strength of the CSAI opponent. Because CSAI employs a successful strategy that will ultimately win the game, however, the overestimation of the score function actually causes it to accurately predict the outcome of the game.

Discussion

Our experimental results show that our approach made it possible to automatically generate an effective score function for the *Spring* game. However, game developers should note that the effectiveness of the score function will largely depend on the training data provided to the TD-learning algorithm. For example, our results showed some signs of overfitting, which might have resulted from the fact that most of the feature data was collected from AAI-AAI games. To avoid overfitting, we recommend gathering data from training games played against a relatively large number of different types of opponents on different types of maps.

Additionally, developers who wish to incorporate our approach in a game should note the following. In the AAI-AAI trial we observed a somewhat variable prediction performance in the first phase of the game. A straightforward explanation of this phenomenon is that it results from optimizing the term weights for each phase of the game. For each phase, the optimization process is focused on obtaining the highest *overall* prediction accuracy in that particular phase. This optimized result might well overfit part of the data, as we observe in the first phase of the AAI-AAI game, where a large peak is followed by a small valley. It is also important to remember that even with optimized term weights, outcome predictions that are made in the early phases of the game will always be unreliable because the future of the game will always be unclear at that time.

How to Use a Generated Score Function

An automatically generated score function can be incorporated immediately into a game to provide feedback to a player on the effectiveness of their play. Because the value returned by the score function reflects the chance of winning, it can provide the player with a useful indication of their performance relative to other players or to the AI. Additionally, because score functions are typically composed of several components, they can be used to provide feedback on the different strengths and weaknesses of a player. For example, the score function that we have described consists of separate terms for military advantage and positional safety. If the value of the latter is unusually low or negative, then it might indicate that the player should focus on improving the safety of their Commander rather than increasing their military strength.

In games with relatively large action spaces, such as RTS games, you would typically implement a score function for the purpose of allowing the AI to establish high-level game plans in predefined moments of the game. Adaptation of such game plans can occur online, after receiving feedback, or offline when the game is finished, but adaptive game AI always needs a score function to rate newly generated behaviors. An automatically generated score function is more objective than a function that has been created manually and can therefore produce better results. For example, in previous research, we compared the results of learning with a manually designed score function with the results of learning with an automatically generated score function, and found that the resulting AI was learned more quickly, and performed more effectively, with the latter approach [Ponsen05].

Using the techniques that we have described for automatically generating score functions, it is also possible to cheaply generate map-dependent AI. Weights can be learned for each different map, allowing the score function to rate effectiveness while taking into account the specific characteristics of a map. For example, our experiments were performed on a map without water, and hence the amphibious tank was rated as having little value by the score function. Finally, an automatically generated score function can provide insight into the balance of a game and thus help in testing and debugging it. For instance, it might reveal that certain unit types are simply inferior in all of the tested circumstances and thus might need a boost in attributes to ensure that there is an incentive for players to build them.

Conclusions and Future Work

In this article, we discussed an approach for automatically generating a score function for game AI in RTS games. The score function was developed within a framework that contained a mechanism to take account of the phase of the game and two terms to evaluate a game's state; a term based on material strength, and a term based on positional safety. Our experimental results with the *Spring* game show that, just before the game's end, the score function was able to correctly predict the outcome of the game with an accuracy that approached 100% and could make fairly accurate predictions before half of the game was played. From these results, we conclude that the score function effectively predicts the outcome of a *Spring* game and that the proposed approach is suitable for generating score functions for highly complex games, such as RTS games.

For future work, we will extend the score function with more features and incorporate our findings on evaluating a game's state into the design of an adaptation mechanism for RTS games. We will also extend our work to other game genres.

References

[Bakkes07] Bakkes, Sander, Kerbusch, Philip, Spronck, Pieter, and van den Herik, Jaap, "Automatically Evaluating the Status of an RTS Game." *Proceedings of the Belgian-Dutch Benelearn Conference 2007*, (2007).

[Beal97] Beal, Don F., and Smith, Malcolm C., "Learning Piece Values Using Temporal Differences." *International Computer Chess Association (ICCA) Journal*, Vol. 20, no. 3, (1997): pp. 147–151.

[Demasi02] Demasi, Pedro, and de O. Cruz, Adriano J., "Online Coevolution for Action Games." *International Journal of Intelligent Games and Simulation*, Vol. 2, No. 3, (2002): pp. 80–88.

[Graepel04] Graepel, Thore, Herbrich, Ralf, and Gold, Julian, "Learning to Fight." *Proceedings of Computer Games: Artificial Intelligence, Design and Education (CGAIDE)*, (2004).

[Jonker07] Jonker, Catholijn, "Learning Aspect in Analysis and Modelling of Cognitive Processes." Delft University of Technology, lecture notes of the SIKS Learning and Reasoning course.

[Ponsen05] Ponsen, Marc J. V., Muñoz-Avila, Héctor, Spronck, Pieter, and Aha, David W. "Automatically Acquiring Adaptive Real-Time Strategy Game Opponents Using Evolutionary Learning." *Proceedings of the Twentieth National Conference on Artificial Intelligence and the Seventeenth Innovative Applications of Artificial Intelligence Conference (IAAI-05)*, (2005).

[Snyman05] Snyman, Jan, *Practical Mathematical Optimization: An Introduction to Basic Optimization Theory and Classical and New Gradient-Based Algorithms*. Springer Publishing, 2005. ISBN 0-387-24348-8.

[Spronck04] Spronck, Pieter H. M., Sprinkhuizen-Kuyper, Ida G., and Postma, Eric O., "Online Adaptation of Game Opponent AI with Dynamic Scripting." *International Journal of Intelligent Games and Simulation*, Vol. 3, No. 1, (2004): pp. 45–53.

[Spronck05] Spronck, Pieter, "A Model for Reliable Adaptive Game Intelligence." *Proceedings of the IJCAI-05 Workshop on Reasoning, Representation, and Learning in Computer Games*, (2005): pp. 95–100.

[Sutton88] Sutton, Richard S., "Learning to Predict by the Methods of Temporal Differences." *Machine Learning*, Vol. 3, (1988): pp. 9–44.

[Tesauro92] Tesauro, Gerald, "Practical Issues in Temporal Difference Learning." *Machine Learning*, Vol. 8, (1992): pp. 257–277.

7.5

Automatic Generation of Strategies

Maastricht University, The Netherlands

Pieter Spronck

p.spronck@micc.unimaas.nl

Marc Ponsen

m.ponsen@micc.unimaas.nl

Real-time strategy (RTS) games are highly complex. They have extremely large decision spaces that cover military and economic research and development, civilization building, exploration, and sometimes diplomacy. They are also highly chaotic, and the outcomes of actions are often uncertain. This makes designing the AI for an RTS game extremely challenging and time consuming.

In this article, we discuss how a genetic algorithm can be used to help AI developers create effective RTS AI by automatically generating strong strategies. We concentrate on the representation of a strategy in the form of a chromosome, the design of genetic operators to manipulate such chromosomes, the design of a fitness function for the evaluation of the effectiveness of the strategies, and the evolutionary process itself. The techniques and their results are demonstrated in the game of *Wargus*, which is an open source clone of *WarCraft II*.

Genetic Algorithms

In a genetic algorithm, a solution to a problem is encoded as a string of genes, called a chromosome. The genes in a chromosome represent a parameterization of the solution that is encoded within it. A collection of chromosomes, called a population, is processed by means of genetic operators that take one or more chromosomes, combine them, and make small changes to them to generate new chromosomes that form a new population. Each chromosome has a fitness value associated with it that represents the relative quality of the solution that it encodes. The higher the fitness value, the higher the chance that the chromosome will be selected by a genetic operator to contribute genes to the production of new chromosomes.

The goal of any genetic algorithm is to generate a chromosome with a fitness that is sufficiently high that the solution it encodes is good enough to be practically useful in its intended application. Because genetic algorithms are, in essence, performing a directed random search through a solution space, they are not *guaranteed* to come up with a good solution—not even a mediocre one. However, with careful design of the encoding used in the chromosomes, the genetic operators, and fitness function, genetic algorithms are known to be able to produce good solutions to highly complex problems in an efficient manner.

This article will not cover the basics of genetic algorithms, which have been described in detail in previous volumes of the *AI Game Programming Wisdom* series [Laramée02, Buckland04, Sweetser04, Thomas06] and many other excellent books on the subject [Goldberg89, Michalewicz92]. Instead, we will tackle the advanced subject of how genetic algorithms can be applied to automatically generate complete battle plans for RTS games, which are arguably among the most complex types of games available today.

Strategic Decisions for RTS Games

In a typical RTS game, a player controls an army of units of which there are typically several types, each with their own properties. Some units might be "workers" that have the ability to gather resources and erect new buildings; others might be "fighters," whose purpose it is to fight enemy units and destroy enemy buildings. Typically, not all unit types are available in the initial phases of a game; players must research new technologies, or construct buildings, to be able to create more advanced unit types. The goal of an RTS game is usually to annihilate all opposing forces.

Several levels of decisions can be distinguished in an RTS game. At the lowest, or "operational" level, the actions of single units are defined. For example, individual units are moved across the map or assault an enemy unit or building. At a somewhat higher, or "tactical" level, a short sequence of actions is executed to achieve a specific goal. For example, a small team of units might be commanded to perform a tactical task, such as taking over an enemy city or guarding some territory. At the highest, or "strategic" level, a plan for the whole game is formed, which will incorporate constructing buildings, training units, conducting research, and planning battles. Strategic decisions might involve choosing between an offensive or defensive strategy, one that relies on a full-scale ground offensive or one that uses small-scale tactical assaults.

In this article, we focus on evolving a plan that consists of decisions at a strategic level only. We assume that the execution of a strategic plan at a tactical or operational level is handled adequately by other parts of the game code. Thus, a part of the strategic plan might specify that an attacking team must be constructed and that is must consist of five foot soldiers and two knights, but it will not give tactical specifications, such as where the team will move and what exactly it will attack. Similarly, the plan might specify that a certain building must be constructed, but it will not specify at what location. This approach reduces the complexity of the problem faced by the genetic algorithm and increases the likelihood that highly effective strategic decision-making systems will evolve. Note, however, that you can also employ the techniques described in this article to evolve tactical or operational plans.

Wargus

To demonstrate the techniques that we have developed, we use the game *Wargus*, which is a clone of *WarCraft II* built on the open source engine *Stratagus* [Stratagus05]. The goal of a game of *Wargus* is to defeat the opponent or opponents by obliterating all of their units. Four types of strategic decisions must be made in *Wargus* that relate to the four main areas of gameplay:

- *Construction* decisions need to be made because buildings are required to produce certain unit types, to perform research into more advanced types, and to make it possible to construct more advanced buildings. In our *Wargus* setup, 10 different types of buildings were available. A player never needs more than one of some building types, whereas multiple instances of others might be useful.
- *Combat*-related decisions need to be made when constructing a team of fighting units. They consist of specifying the number of each unit type that is in the team and whether the team is meant for offensive or defensive purposes. In our *Wargus* setup, six different types of fighting units were available, and each unit type comes in several different versions, of which the more advanced become available only after they have been researched.
- *Economic* decisions center around the gathering of resources. In *Wargus*, the number of worker units available determines the rate at which resources can be gathered.
- *Research*-oriented decisions are important because research can produce advancements such as better weaponry and armor. In our *Wargus* setup, nine different advancements were available for research, some of which required other research to have been performed first.

The preceding list summarizes the key areas where a strategic RTS AI needs to make decisions. A strategy consists of a set of such decisions.

Chromosome Encoding

To use a genetic algorithm to evolve strategies for playing *Wargus*, it is necessary to encode a strategy as a chromosome, that is, to translate the sequence of actions that form the strategy to a string by using some kind of mapping. For *Wargus*, we used the following encoding procedure:

Construction: A construction action is translated to **B***x*, where *x* is the identifier of the type of building that is constructed.

Combat: A combat action is translated to **C***sxyz*, where *s* is the state number (which will be explained later), *x* is the identifier of the team that is constructed, *y* is a list of numbers representing how many of each of the unit types there should be in the team, and z is either a character **o** for offensive or **d** for defensive, which indicates whether the team should be used in offensive or defensive actions.

Economy: An economic action is translated to **E**x, where x is the number of worker units that are trained.

Research: A research action is translated to **R**x, where x is the identifier of the advancement that is researched.

Any valid strategy can be represented as a string of these encoded actions. But there is a snag. You can also encode invalid strategies this way, even when all the individual variables are restricted to legal values. For example, a construction action might specify the construction of a building that can only be created in the presence of more basic buildings that do not yet exist. If the evolutionary process is allowed to create such invalid strategies, the population gets tainted by useless chromosomes that should not be used for further procreation because their descendants are very likely to be useless too. These chromosomes effectively reduce the size and diversity of the population and thus reduce both the effectiveness and the efficiency of the evolutionary process. We therefore had to ensure that the genetic algorithm did not generate invalid strategies, and the best way to do that was to enhance the encoding mechanism so that it simply did not allow for invalid strategies to be represented.

For *Wargus*, we realized that the available buildings determine which actions are legal. Figure 7.5.1 represents the *Wargus* building state lattice, starting in state 1 at the top, where only a Townhall and Barracks are available (which all players in our simulations started a game with), and ending in state 20 at the bottom, where all buildings are available. State transitions are effected by the construction of a new building. In a *Wargus* game, players traverse this lattice from top to bottom, visiting a maximum of 9 of the 20 states.

By storing state information in the chromosome, genetic operators can be created that take into account which actions are legal and which are not for particular states. The chromosome architecture that we settled upon, with part of an example chromosome, is depicted in Figure 7.5.2. The chromosome consists of a sequence of states, and each state consists of a state marker and state number, followed by a sequence of actions. Except for the final state, the last of the actions in a state is always a construction action that causes a state transition. The next state is thus always determined by the construction action that ended the previous state.

The actions are encoded as described earlier and consist of a marker with a value **B**, **C**$_s$, **E**, or **R**, followed by one or more parameters. The **B**, **E**, and **R** markers and their parameters are a straightforward translation of the actions that were defined at the start of this section. The **C**$_s$ marker and its parameters define a combat action, where the state s determines the number and interpretation of the parameters. As explained earlier, the first of the parameters is always a team identifier, and the last is an indicator as to whether the team should be used for offensive or defensive purposes. In between, there is a set of one or more parameters that give the number of each of the unit types that are available in state s that will be in the team. For example,

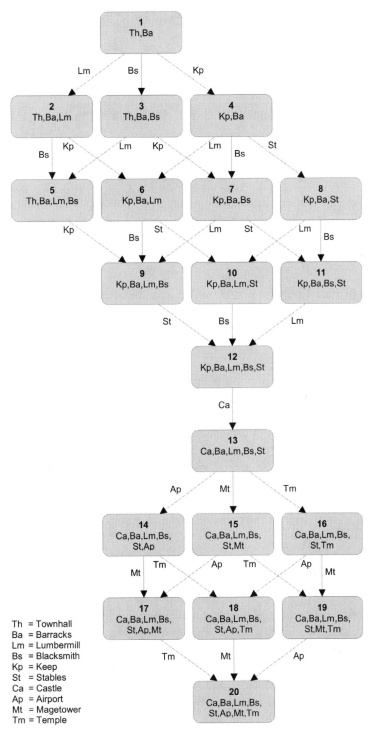

FIGURE 7.5.1 The *Wargus* building state lattice.

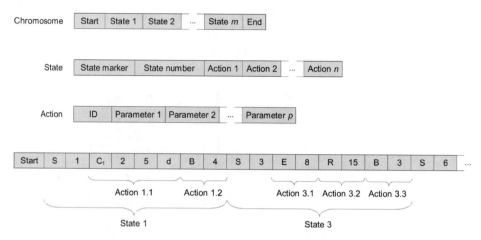

FIGURE 7.5.2   Chromosome design, with part of an example chromosome.

in state 1 only "foot soldiers" are available, and the set therefore consists of one parameter that indicates the number of foot soldiers in the team. In state 11, both foot soldiers and knights are available, but no other units. Thus, in state 11, the set consists of two parameters, the first indicating the number of foot soldiers, and the second the number of knights.

For the initial population, a random set of chromosomes was produced using the following algorithm. First, the state marker for state 1 was placed at the start of the chromosome. Then, random legal actions for state 1 were generated, encoded, and appended to the chromosome. When a construction action that would cause a state transition was generated, the state marker for the next state was appended, and from that point on, the process was repeated for each new state. Since state 20 is the last state, a fixed number of actions were produced in that state (a total of 20 in our implementation), after which a constant attack loop was written to the chromosome to finish it. In our experience, however, games in which state 20 were actually reached were rare.

Genetic Operators

Genetic operators are used in the process of creating new chromosomes and generally fall into two categories. *Mutation operators* take a single chromosome and make small changes to it; *crossover operators* combine two or more parent chromosomes and produce one or more child chromosomes. Regular genetic operators, such as one-point crossover and uniform crossover are not suitable for our chromosomes because they are likely to produce invalid strategies. We therefore designed four new genetic operators that are guaranteed to produce valid strategies when their inputs consist of chromosomes that also represent valid strategies.

State Crossover: State Crossover is illustrated in Figure 7.5.3. This genetic operator takes two parent chromosomes and produces one child chromosome by copying complete states with their corresponding actions from one or the other parent chromosome to the child chromosome. The operator is controlled by matching states, which are states that exist in both parent chromosomes. As Figure 7.5.1 showed earlier, in *Wargus,* there are at least four matching states for any pair of chromosomes, namely states 1, 12, 13, and 20. Using matching states, a child chromosome is created as follows. States are copied to the child sequentially from one parent, starting with state 1. When there is a transition to a state that is also present in the other parent chromosome, there is a chance (in our implementation 50%) that from that point, the states are copied from the other parent. Such a switch can occur at all matching states. This process continues until the last state has been copied into the child chromosome. In Figure 7.5.3, parent switches occur at states 9 and 18.

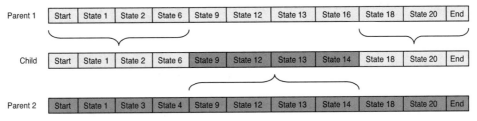

FIGURE 7.5.3 Example of the State Crossover genetic operator.

Action Replacement Mutation: With the Action Replacement Mutation operator, one parent chromosome is copied to a new child chromosome and, for each action in the child chromosome, there is a chance (in our implementation 25%) that the action will be replaced by a randomly generated action. Combat, Economy, and Research actions can all be replaced and can all act as replacements. However, Construction actions are excluded from this process, both for and as replacements to avoid the introduction of new state transitions, which might produce an invalid chromosome.

Action Biased Mutation: With the Action Biased Mutation operator, one parent chromosome is copied to a new child chromosome, and for each combat and research action in the child chromosome, there is a chance (in our implementation 50%) that the parameters that determine the number of desired units are changed by adding a random value (which was in the range [−5,5] in our implementation). Only positive values for the parameters are allowed because it is impossible to train a negative number of units, so if the operator produced a negative number it was set to zero.

Randomization: With the Randomization operator, a completely random new chromosome is generated using the same process that was used to create the chromosomes in the initial population.

In our implementation, the Randomization operator was used to generate 10% of the child chromosomes and the other three 30% each of the child chromosomes. Although our mutation rates might be considered high, they allow for a fast exploration of the enormous space of possible *Wargus* strategies.

Fitness Determination

To evolve chromosomes that represent effective strategies, it was necessary to develop a fitness measure that was correlated with the relative effectiveness of the strategy encoded by a chromosome. Because the aim of the strategies is to win a game, pitting them all against the same set of opponents allows us to assess their relative effectiveness. It is not sufficient to measure only whether a strategy will win or lose, however. Knowing the magnitude of the victory or defeat is important to rank the strategies effectively. Therefore, we defined the fitness value $F \in [0,1]$ as follows:

$$
F = \begin{cases}
\min\left(\dfrac{C_t}{C_{\max}} \cdot \dfrac{M_c}{M_c + M_o}, b \right) & \{defeat\} \\[2em]
\max\left(b, \dfrac{M_c}{M_c + M_o} \right) & \{victory\}
\end{cases}
$$

In this equation, M_c and M_o represent the "military points" scored by the evolved strategy c and the opponent strategy o, respectively. Military points are an indication of how well a strategy was able to build military units and destroy the military units of its opponent. In *Wargus*, military points are a reasonably good way of measuring the success of a strategy; for other games, a different measure might need to be designed.

The value b is supposed to be the fitness of a strategy that is about as equally powerful as its opponent. Therefore, if the evolved strategy achieves a victory, it should get at least a fitness b. However, if it is defeated, b is the maximum fitness it can achieve. For our implementation, we chose $b = 0.5$. Finally, C_t is the time step at which a game finished, whereas $C_{\max}$ is the maximum time step to which games are allowed to continue. The factor $C_t/C_{\max}$ ensures that losing strategies that manage to survive for a long time are awarded a higher fitness than losing strategies that are defeated quickly.

If the fitness is assessed against multiple opponents or on multiple maps, simply averaging the fitnesses achieved against each of the opponents on each of the maps is sufficient to produce a measure of overall fitness.

Evolutionary Process

The goal of the evolutionary process is to generate a chromosome that represents a strategy that is able to consistently defeat its opponents. Clearly, from the way we designed our fitness function, a fitness value of 1.0 is, in practice, unattainable, except against an opponent that never builds any military units. However, we found that, in *Wargus*, a fitness of 0.75 on large maps, or 0.7 on small maps, was sufficient to ensure that the evolved strategy would consistently defeat the opponent strategies that it was evolved against.

We used size-3 tournament selection to determine the parent chromosomes for the genetic operators, which means that each time a parent was required, three chromosomes were selected randomly from the population, and the one with the highest fitness was used as the parent. However, other selection mechanisms, such as straightforward roulette wheel selection, are likely to work just as well. After a child chromosome is generated and its fitness determined, it is inserted into the population, replacing an existing chromosome. For this we used size-3 crowding, which is similar to tournament selection, except that the selected chromosome with the lowest fitness is replaced.

It is common when using genetic algorithms to set a limit on the number of children that can be generated before an experiment is aborted. Thus, an experiment ends when either the target fitness is achieved or the maximum number of children has been generated. In our experiments, we had a population size of 50 and set the maximum number of children to 250. For those who are familiar with genetic algorithms, that number might seem uncomfortably low. However, we found that, more often than not, the target fitness was reached within this limit.

Experimental Results

We used two different opponents against which to evolve strategies, one was used on a small map, and the other was used on a large map. Both opponents implemented "rush" strategies. On the small map, the rush strategy was based on low-level soldier units that are available in the very first state of the game, so we called this opponent the "soldier rush." On the large map, the rush tactic was based on medium-level knight units that are available in state 12, so we called this opponent the "knight rush."

We evolved a strategy against each of these opponents and repeated the experiment 10 times. Against both opponents, strong strategies with high fitness scores were evolved in a relatively short time, almost always within the limit of 250 children. The few that did not reach the target fitness within that limit were typically very close to it.

We observed that, against the soldier rush, the only successful strategy was another slightly more effective soldier rush. The typical pattern of behavior of the evolved strategies was to start by building a Blacksmith, causing a transition to state 3, and then build a steady line of defenses. The strategies would then research better weapons and armor for soldier units, before finally creating large numbers of them. In a few cases, the research was skipped, and the enemy was simply overwhelmed by sheer numbers.

Several of the counterstrategies for the knight rush made a beeline to state 12, by quickly building a Blacksmith, a Lumber mill, a Keep, and Stables, usually in that precise order. State 12 is special because it is the first state where knights are available, and knights are arguably the most powerful unit in the game. The evolved strategies used mainly knights for offensive purposes, and, in virtually all the evolved strategies, their economies were boosted by building additional resource sites (including associated defenses) and training large numbers of workers. Also, many of the evolved strategies developed and built units that were capable of stemming a knight rush, in particular large numbers of catapults, before starting to use a knight rush themselves. All were viable strategies.

The preference for catapults is remarkable because domain experts often view these units as inferior because catapults have a high cost and are also highly vulnerable. However, their impressive damaging abilities and large range make them effective for both defensive and offensive purposes. They work particularly well against tightly packed armies, such as large groups of knights, which are encountered when playing against the knight rush opponent.

Applications

We have described a procedure for automatically evolving strong strategies for RTS games (which might work well in other game types too). But what are the applications of the procedure that we have developed?

- **Testing and debugging:** When a programmer has implemented a strategy in a game's AI, a genetic algorithm can be used to test it for weaknesses; if there are weaknesses, they are likely to be discovered by the evolutionary process. Game balancing issues will also come to light: if an undefeatable strategy exists, the evolutionary process will probably find it.

- **Generation of map-specific strategies:** It is difficult for AI developers to build a general strategy that takes into account the features of particular maps, and it can be resource intensive to manually create map-specific strategies in a game that might ship with dozens of maps. Although the evolutionary process will probably not produce a generally applicable strategy unless fitness values are averaged over a wide range of different kinds of maps, it is easy to evolve a different strategy for each map individually.

- **Generation of strategies for different difficulty levels:** Starting with a fairly weak, manually designed opponent, a strategy can be evolved that regularly defeats this opponent. This strategy could be used for the lowest difficulty level (although the evolutionary process should be aborted as soon as a reasonably good strategy is constructed; otherwise, it might become too effective to be used at the lowest difficulty level). The evolved strategy is then used as the opponent to evolve a strategy for the next difficulty level. After that, we evolve an opponent for the next higher difficulty level by evolving it against both of the previously created opponents. By repeating this process, strategies can be evolved for all desired difficulty levels. Combining this with the previous application makes it possible to create map-specific strategies at a range of difficulty levels, which is impractical to do manually; if a game has 5 difficulty levels and 50 maps, 250 different strategies would be needed.

- **Automatic creation of knowledge bases for adaptive game AI techniques:** We applied dynamic scripting (described in volume 3 of *AI Game Programming Wisdom* [Spronck06]) to *Wargus* and automatically populated the dynamic scripting knowledge bases with tactics discovered by the genetic algorithm that is described in this article. This very efficiently produced strong game AI against a large variety of opponent strategies [Ponsen06].

Caveats

Some caveats have to be taken into account when using the techniques described here:

- The evolutionary process generates strategies that are rated purely according to their ability to defeat an opponent. This does not mean that the generated strategies are interesting or entertaining to play against. Using them directly as game AI might not be opportune. There are two remarks we want to make in this respect. First, we did find in our experiments that interesting strategies were actually generated, in the sense that unexpected but quite strong tactics were part of them (e.g., the use of catapults against the knight rush). Second, the evolved strategies consist of readable code, which can, if necessary, be manually tweaked to make them more interesting.
- An evolved strategy is not necessarily able to defeat strategies other than the ones it has been evolved against. In our experiments, strategies were evolved only against the soldier rush and the knight rush. Because these are very strong strategies, the evolved counterstrategies are likely to work well against most other strategies too, and we found that that was the case. However, to evolve more generalized strategies, the opponents should consist of a number of different strategies, and fitness evaluations should be performed on a number of different maps. Some preliminary work has already been performed in this area [Ponsen06].
- The evolutionary process necessarily concentrates on the early game states because the game is often finished before the later game states are encountered. An evolved strategy might therefore fail when a game lasts longer than most of the games that were played during its evolution. To overcome this problem, maps of different sizes can be used. Bigger maps usually make games last longer, giving the evolutionary process the opportunity to optimize the strategy in later game states. Another solution to this problem is to assign high fitness values to chromosomes that participate in longer lasting games, thus driving the evolutionary process toward chromosomes with more elaborate strategies.
- The techniques described here generate static strategies that cannot adapt during gameplay and are therefore unable to take the behavior of their opponent into account; they construct buildings when the strategy says it is time to construct buildings and attack when the strategy says it is time to attack, regardless of what

their opponent is doing. This problem can be overcome by evolving shorter scripts for separate game states, which might include dependencies on opponent behavior rather than a single script for the entire game, or to use adaptive techniques, such as dynamic scripting [Spronck06].

Conclusion

In this article, we described how complete strategies for RTS games can be automatically generated using an evolutionary process. We described how a chromosome can represent a strategy, how genetic operators can be designed to ensure that child chromosomes always represent valid strategies, and how a fitness function can be designed to rank strategies according to their quality. Our experiments with the techniques in the RTS game *Wargus* showed that the evolutionary process can finish quickly, and that the resulting strategies are usually strong.

Evolved strategies can be used for testing and debugging purposes and also for automatically generating map-specific strategies for different difficulty levels, which would be far too time consuming to build by hand. Furthermore, we found that the evolutionary process that we developed is particularly well suited to generating strong knowledge bases that can be used by some forms of online adaptive game AI, such as dynamic scripting.

References

[Buckland04] Buckland, Matt, "Building Better Genetic Algorithms." *AI Game Programming Wisdom 2*, Charles River Media, 2004: pp. 649–660.

[Goldberg89] Goldberg, David E., *Genetic Algorithms in Search, Optimization & Machine Learning*. Addison-Wesley Publishing Company Inc., 1989.

[Laramée02] Laramée, François Dominic, "Genetic Algorithms: Evolving the Perfect Troll." *AI Game Programming Wisdom*, Charles River Media, 2002: pp. 629–639.

[Michalewicz92] Michalewicz, Zbigniev, *Genetic Algorithms + Data Structures = Evolution Programs*. Springer-Verlag, Berlin, 1992.

[Ponsen06] Ponsen, Marc, Muñoz-Avila, Héctor, Spronck, Pieter, and Aha, David W., "Automatically Generating Game Tactics with Evolutionary Learning." *AI Magazine*, Vol. 27, no. 3, (Fall 2006): pp. 75–84.

[Spronck06] Spronck, Pieter, "Dynamic Scripting." *AI Game Programming Wisdom 3*, Charles River Media, 2006: pp. 661–675.

[Stratagus05] Stratagus Team, "Stratagus–A Real-Time Strategy Game Engine." Available online at *http://www.stratagus.org*.

[Sweetser04] Sweetser, Penny, "How to Build Evolutionary Algorithms for Games." *AI Game Programming Wisdom 2*, Charles River Media, 2004: pp. 627–637.

[Thomas06] Thomas, Dale, "Encoding Schemes and Fitness Functions for Genetic Algorithms." *AI Game Programming Wisdom 3*, Charles River Media, 2006: pp. 677–686.

7.6

A Practical Guide to Reinforcement Learning in First-Person Shooters

Michelle McPartland— University of Queensland

michelle@itee.uq.edu.au

The notion that bots could learn how to play a game, particularly one with the complexities of a modern first-person shooter (FPS), might appear to be wishful thinking, but it can actually be achieved using a class of algorithms known as reinforcement learning (RL). FPS bots are generally rule based and look at the information available to them about their environment and internal state to decide what actions they should take. As such, most FPS bots fall into the action-selection paradigm; that is, they select an action to perform from a predetermined list.

RL provides an action-selection model that is well suited to controlling FPS bots because it manages the conflicting requirements of short-term reactivity and long-term goal-driven behavior. For example, a bot's long-term goal could be to traverse the map to a particular power up, but it will also need to react if it is attacked on the way. RL can also save time in developing effective FPS bots because it can automatically learn effective behaviors, thereby avoiding the need to design and code elaborate sets of rules and tune parameters through play testing.

In this article, we present an overview of a form of RL called Sarsa and show how it can be used to allow FPS bots to learn some of the behaviors that are necessary to compete in a multiplayer-style FPS game.

Overview of Reinforcement Learning (RL)

RL provides a class of algorithms that allows an agent to learn by interacting with its environment. A bot that is equipped with RL is therefore able to learn how to play a game by playing against other RL-controlled bots, rule-based bots, human players, or a combination of opponents. An RL-based bot does not have to be programmed or taught in the same way as those that are based on rules or some other learning technologies, such as neural networks. The following section provides a brief overview of

RL and describes some of the design decisions that must be made when creating an implementation.

RL Basics

In general, RL algorithms observe the state s of their environment and react to it by selecting an action a. The environment might respond by producing a reward r and might transition to a new state s'. The mapping that RL performs from states to actions is referred to as the policy, and, by visiting each state many times and performing different actions, RL is able to learn an optimal policy that tells it which actions to perform in which states to maximize its reward. If rewards are provided in response to desirable outcomes, RL is able to learn the sequences of actions and hence the behaviors that lead to those outcomes.

There are a wide range of different types of RL algorithms that vary in the ways they represent the information they gather about the rewards in their environments, how they update that information, and how they use it to select actions. For example, the RL algorithm TD-lambda associates rewards with states and relies on some extrinsic action-selection process to select an action that will cause a transition to a state where a high-value reward can be obtained. The requirement for an extrinsic action-selection process is fine for games, such as chess, that have very simple and well-defined dynamics but extremely problematic for FPS games, so TD-lambda will not be discussed further in this article.

Other RL algorithms, such as Q-learning [Watkins92] and Sarsa [Sutton98], associate rewards with selecting specific actions in specific states, which are known as state-action pairs and denoted (s,a). This means that they can select an action in any state simply by choosing the one that is expected to produce the greatest reward. The advantage of this approach is that action selection is intrinsic to the learning algorithm, which learns the dynamics of the state space at the same time as it learns its reward structure, thereby avoiding the need for an external action-selection process. This major advantage does come at the cost of slower learning, however, which results from the fact that the size of the space of state-action pairs is typically much larger than the space of states and hence takes longer to explore.

Because Q-learning and Sarsa associate rewards with taking specific actions in specific states, they need some representation of a mapping from each state-action pair to the reward that is associated with it. This mapping is usually denoted by $Q(s,a)$ and is typically implemented as a lookup table or using a function approximator. A lookup table simply has an entry for every possible combination of states and actions, so it suffers from the disadvantage that it can only be used with discrete state and action representations and can be extremely large if there are many states where many actions can be performed. However, lookup tables are very popular because they offer the advantages of fast learning, computational efficiency, numerical stability, as well as being human readable.

Function approximators can also be used to implement $Q(s,a)$, and they have the advantage of being able to generalize in a way that simple lookup tables cannot. An agent using a function approximator-based RL implementation can make an intelligent guess about how to act in a novel state based on its similarity to familiar states, whereas one that uses a lookup table can only act randomly. Function approximators typically suffer from problems such as slow learning, computational complexity, and numerical instability when used in conjunction with RL, so the experiments that are described in this article used a lookup table to represent $Q(s,a)$.

When using a lookup table, selecting the best action a to perform in a state s is simply a matter of searching the row or column of a lookup table $Q(s,a)$ that corresponds to state s for the action a that maximizes $Q(s,a)$. Most of the time Q-learning and Sarsa will exploit what has been learned and perform the best action. Occasionally, however, they will explore some other action in case the reward estimates in the lookup table are inaccurate and to give them the opportunity to learn something new. There are a variety of different ways to manage this tradeoff between exploration and exploitation [Sutton98], but the approach we take in this article is to use ε-greedy selection, which is one of the simplest and most common and relies on selecting the best action with probability ε and some other action with probability $1 - \varepsilon$ where ε is a parameter that must be set by the user.

Sarsa

Sarsa works by selecting an action in a state and then updating its estimate of the value of its selection based on the reward it receives and the estimated value of the action it selects in the next state. This basic algorithm is called Sarsa(0) and can be a little slow to learn because when a state is visited, information about how good it is only propagates back to its immediate predecessor state. For example, the first time that a large reward is encountered in a state, information about its existence will propagate to the state's immediate predecessor state; the next time that predecessor state is encountered, information about the location of the reward is only propagated to its immediate successor, and so on. In a large state space with sparse rewards, it therefore takes a very long time for information about the locations of the rewards to spread throughout the state space.

An enhancement to the basic Sarsa(0) algorithm is Sarsa(λ), which uses a technique called eligibility tracing to accelerate learning. Eligibility tracing enhances the basic Sarsa algorithm by recording a history of the states that have been visited and the actions that have been taken within them so that information can be propagated much farther than one state back each time the algorithm is applied. Thus, if a reward is encountered in a state, information about its existence can immediately be propagated many states back rather than just to the state's immediate predecessor, greatly accelerating the speed with which sequences of actions can be learned.

Table 7.6.1 gives the update algorithm for Sarsa. The algorithm begins on line 1 by initializing the policy $Q(s,a)$ and eligibility trace $e(s,a)$. The values inside the lookup table $Q(s,a)$, which define the policy, are usually initialized to zero or random values close to zero, such as lie in the range $[-0.1,+0.1]$. Line 2 indicates that learning can occur over multiple games. In deathmatch games, only a single game needs to be played because bots can respawn after being killed. On line 4, the value of s', which represents the state of the game world, is set up to represent the current game state. This process will be discussed in greater detail later. On lines 5 and 6, an action a' is selected based on the current state s', a transition occurs to a new state, and a reward r is received.

Table 7.6.1   Sarsa Algorithm with an Eligibility Trace

1	Initialize $Q(s,a)$ arbitrarily, set $e(s,a)=0$ for all s, a
2	Repeat for each training game.
3	Repeat for each update step t in the game.
4	Set s' to the current state.
5	Select an action a'.
6	Take action a'; observe reward r.
7	$\delta \leftarrow r + \gamma Q(s',a') - Q(s,a)$
8	$e(s,a) \leftarrow e(s,a) + 1$
9	For all s, a:
10	$Q(s,a) \leftarrow Q(s,a) + \alpha\delta e(s,a)$
11	$e(s,a) \leftarrow \gamma\lambda e(s,a)$
12	$s \leftarrow s'$, $a \leftarrow a'$
13	Until end game condition is met.

Line 7 calculates the difference between the discounted estimated value of the current state-action pair $\gamma Q(s',a')$ plus the reward r, and the estimated value of the previous state-action pair $Q(s,a)$, where s and a correspond to the action a that was selected in the previous state s. Note that the first time the algorithm is run, the previous state-action pair is not defined, so steps 7 to 11 are omitted. The discount factor parameter γ is used to control the extent to which RL will forgo small rewards that might be immediately available for much larger rewards that might take much longer to reach. The role of this and other parameters will be discussed later.

Line 8 updates the eligibility trace $e(s,a)$ for the previous state-action pair by incrementing its value. Line 10 updates estimates of the values of all the state-action pairs using the learning parameter α, the difference that was calculated on line 7, and the eligibility trace. Finally, line 11 decays all eligibility trace values by the trace factor λ and the discount factor γ, and line 12 records the current state and the action that was selected into variables representing the previous state and action ready for the next pass of the algorithm. This process is repeated until an end game condition is met, such as a time limit is reached or a maximum number of deaths is exceeded. Refer to Update() in SarsaTabular.cpp on the CD-ROM for an implementation in code.

The requirement to repeat lines 10 and 11 for every combination of states and actions might seem unreasonable for all but the most trivial games, but, in practice, the values of $e(s,a)$ will be so small for all but the most recently visited state-action pairs that the updates given in lines 10 and 11 only need to be performed on a small number of state-action pairs that can easily be identified by a first-in first-out list of those that have recently been visited. For example, $e(s,a)$ for the nth most recent state-action pair will typically be no greater than the order of γ^n where $\gamma < 1$.

Designing the State Representation

The game state information on which an RL algorithm must base its decisions and the set of actions that it can take in the game world need to be carefully designed for each specific application. The game state representation s typically consists of many variables that describe features of the game world that are likely to be relevant to the decisions that the RL algorithm will have to make. If too few variables are chosen or they do not contain relevant information, RL will perform poorly and will only learn simple and relatively ineffective behaviors. If too many variables are chosen, the lookup table that is required to store every combination of their values against every possible action will become large, and RL will learn very slowly because it will have to play many games to explore even a small part of the state-action space.

Some of the variables that need to be included in the state representation will be discrete, such as whether the bot is holding a weapon of a specific type, whereas others will be continuous, such as the level of the bot's health. Because we are using a tabular approach to store estimates of the values of state-action pairs, $Q(s,a)$, we must discretize continuous variables by breaking them up into a series of discrete ranges. For example, a bot's health could be broken up into three ranges of values: low, medium, and high. Ranges should be defined to provide as much relevant information as possible in as few ranges as possible because each additional range affects the size of the lookup table in the same way, and the learning performance of RL as one extra variable.

Designing a good state representation is important for the success of RL, but there is little practical advice for guiding the process other than to include as much relevant information as possible in as few variables as possible and not to include two variables that provide similar information. Some amount of trial and error might be necessary to arrive at a good state representation, and analyzing the lookup table of the estimated values of state-action pairs after a period of learning can also provide clues as to how the representation can be improved. For example, if multiple states differ only by the values of one variable but have very similar values for all actions, then the differing variable is probably irrelevant and can be removed.

Experimental Setup and Results

To investigate the potential of RL for the creation of FPS bots, we performed two experiments that were designed to assess the ability with which RL was able to control the navigation of a bot around its environment and to control it during combat. The details of the state representations that were used in each of these experiments are given later along with a description of the results that were obtained. At the start of the experiments, the entries in the table $Q(s,a)$ were initialized to 0.5. It was expected that the values of most actions in most states would be lower than this, and hence this form of initialization was expected to encourage exploration and ensure that the state-action space was thoroughly investigated.

Navigation Controller

The aim of the first experiment was to create a bot that could navigate around its environment. Although there are far more efficient techniques than RL that can be used for pathfinding, this experiment provided a simple test bed for our RL implementation that was useful for debugging it. First of all, we needed to decide how to represent the relevant features of the game state, the actions the bot should be able to take, when it should be presented with rewards, and how large they should be. The main aim in designing the representation of the game state is to include the minimum amount of information that is required to learn the task.

For the navigation task, we equipped the bot with two sets of sensors that indicate the presence of obstacles and power-ups to the left of, in front of, and to the right of the bot, and allowed them to indicate whether an obstacle or power-up was near (within 5 meters) or far. For example, if there was a wall near and to the left of the bot, and there was a power-up far to the front of the bot, the values of the sensors would be {1 0 0 0 2 0}, where the first three values represent the left, front, and right obstacle sensors, and the next three represent the left, front, and right power-up item sensors.

Next, we needed to decide what actions the bot could perform. Actions can be defined as high-level composite actions, such as moving to a particular location on a map, or low-level primitive actions, such as shoot. For simplicity, we decided to use only primitive actions in our first experiment and to perform the selected action only for a single time step. One problem with this approach is that the bot cannot perform more than one action at a time, so it can move forward or turn but not turn while moving forward. For this experiment, the bot was able to move forward, turn left, and turn right.

RL uses two types of rewards to reinforce good behavior and punish bad behavior: goal and guide [Manslow04]. Goal rewards are given infrequently when a major event occurs and tend to be quite large. Guide rewards are used to encourage behaviors that will lead to a goal reward. They occur more frequently and should therefore be kept very small to not overshadow the goal reward when it occurs. For a bot to navigate its environment competently, we want to encourage it to avoid obstacles, move around rather than staying in one place, and pick up items along the way. Table 7.6.2 shows the rewards that were used in the navigation experiment to encourage these behaviors.

Table 7.6.2 Goals and Rewards for the Navigation Experiment

Goal	Reward
Runs into wall	−1.0
Picks up item	+1.0
Takes a step forward	+0.00002

The four main parameters to tune in the tabular Sarsa algorithm with eligibility traces are the decay rate (γ), the discount factor (λ), the learning rate (α), and the ε-greedy parameter (ε). Hand-tuning is one option for finding the best values for these parameters, but it is a long and tedious process. A second option is to automate the process by loading a range of parameters from a file or writing an external program that runs repeated experiments with different sets of parameters. Among the advantages of automating the process is that it makes it easier to experiment with the state representation, the action set, and when rewards are provided.

We performed a set of experiments using an automated process to evaluate all combinations of the parameters listed in Table 7.6.3. This came to a total of 240 experiments. The parameters were spread so far apart to examine a wide range of combinations while keeping processing time down, to understand what values affect the learning performance of RL, and to find combinations that should be explored further. Experiments were run over 7,000 frames, and the Sarsa update procedure was applied once per frame. A single experiment took approximately 5 minutes on an AMD 3500+ CPU with rendering disabled.

Table 7.6.3 List of Parameters and Values Tested for the Navigation Experiment

Parameter	Values
Random Seed	101, 102, 103
Discount Factor (γ)	0.0, 0.4, 0.8
Eligibility Trace (λ)	0.0, 0.4, 0.8
Learning Rate (α)	0.0, 0.4, 0.8
ε-Greedy (ε)	0.1, 0.5, 0.9

A subset of the best and worst results obtained from these experiments is displayed in Figure 7.6.1. To assess the performances of the bots, we counted the number of power-ups that they collected and measured the distance they moved during a trial replay period of 1,000 frames with ε and α set to zero, so that they always selected the best action and did not learn. The number of power-ups collected and the distance traveled by each bot is shown on the left y-axis scale, whereas the number of collisions with obstacles is shown on the right y-axis scale. The aim of the experiment was for RL to learn to minimize the number of collisions with obstacles, maximize the number of power-ups collected, and maximize the distance traveled.

The first experiment in Figure 7.6.1 was performed with the parameters $\gamma = 0.0$, $\lambda = 0.0$, $\alpha = 0.0$, and $\varepsilon = 0.1$, meaning that the bot did not learn, and its behavior was based on the initial unlearned policy. We see here that the number of collisions is very high (169), the number of power-ups collected is low (3), and the distance traveled is medium (22 m).

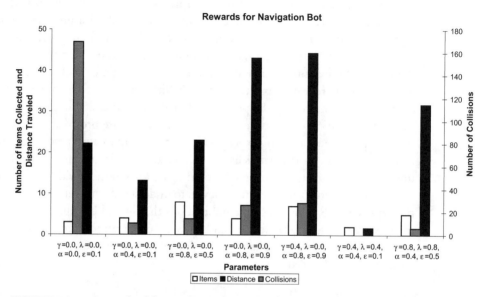

FIGURE 7.6.1   Rewards of the navigation bot with different parameters and random seed 103.

The overall best-performing bot was learned with parameters $\gamma = 0.0$, $\lambda = 0.0$, $\alpha = 0.8$, and $\varepsilon = 0.5$. This bot was able to travel a reasonable distance while picking up the items in its path and avoiding obstacles. This, and most of the best-performing bots, had an eligibility trace parameter and discount factor of zero. This seems a little surprising because a nonzero discount factor is important for learning sequences of actions. Such a sequence would be useful when a bot identifies a power-up far in front of it, for example, when a sequence of move forward actions would allow the power-up to be collected. Because a power-up that is far away is at least 5 m away and will take 25 frames to reach, the effective reward for moving toward it is only, at most, $0.8^{25} \approx 0.004$ using the largest tested value of the discount factor, which might have been too small to have had any practical affect. This problem could be overcome by experimenting with larger discount factors, such as 0.9 or 0.95; updating RL less often than once per frame; or using a more detailed state representation of the distance to an object.

One of the overall worst-performing bots used the parameters $\gamma = 0.4$, $\lambda = 0.4$, $\alpha = 0.4$, and $\varepsilon = 0.1$. This bot did not collide with any obstacles but did not travel very far or collect any items because the bot spent all of its time alternatively turning left and then right, so it never collided with anything but never moved anywhere either. This behavior is likely to have been the result of the replay trial starting in a little-visited state where action selection was based essentially on the initial policy values, which caused a transition to another state that had the same problem, which caused a transition back to the first. This problem could be overcome by initializing the values in $Q(s,a)$ to 0 rather than 0.5, by running the learning experiments for many more frames, or by using a function approximator for $Q(s,a)$ rather than a lookup table so that RL can make smarter guesses about what to do in unfamiliar states.

The last experiment displayed in Figure 7.6.1, with parameters $\gamma = 0.8$, $\lambda = 0.8$, $\alpha = 0.4$, and $\varepsilon = 0.5$, was able to learn an overall good result in all three rewards; the number of collisions that it experienced were very low, and the distance it traveled and the number of power-ups it collected were both close to the maximum recorded results. Overall, the results that were achieved with different combinations of parameters were varied, with some performing well, while others were not able to learn the desired behaviors. A good proportion of bots were able to perform well, however, in terms of collecting power-ups, avoiding collisions, and moving around the environment.

Figure 7.6.2 shows how the estimated values $Q(s,a)$ of three state-action pairs changed over time during the experiment with parameters $\gamma = 0.8$, $\lambda = 0.8$, $\alpha = 0.4$, and $\varepsilon = 0.5$. For the navigation setup, there were a total of 2,187 state-action pairs (3^6 state combinations × 3 actions). Although this is a lot of data to be presented on one graph, it does give an idea of when the policy values have converged. In the case of the navigation task, for example, most policy values remained stable after 4,000 time steps; however, as can be seen in Figure 7.6.2, some were still changing quite significantly up until the end of the experiment, which indicates that the bot's behavior was still adapting and that its performance might have improved further if the experiment had been extended.

We can also see from the graph, that two state-action pairs were not visited until after the 3,400[th] time step. Many other state-action pairs were not visited at all, so their values did not change from their starting values of 0.5, which is one of the problems with the tabular representation—those values tell the bot nothing about how it should behave. To work around this problem, the training environment needs to be set up so that all state-action pairs that the bot will need to use in a real game will be encountered many times. To achieve this, it will be necessary to include all combinations of weapons, opponent types, room geometries, and so on, and to ensure that sufficient training time is provided for them to be thoroughly experienced. Function approximators could also be used for $Q(s,a)$, instead of a lookup table, to allow RL to generalize more intelligently to novel states although it would still be necessary to provide a rich learning environment to achieve good results.

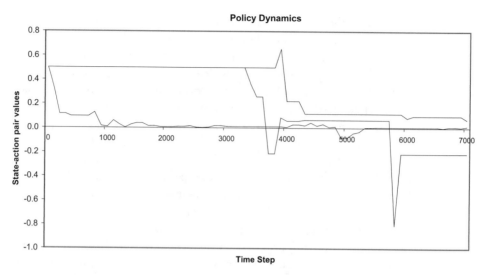

FIGURE 7.6.2 Sampled values of three state-action pairs.

Combat Controller

The second experiment that we performed was to use RL to learn a combat controller so that the bot could fight against other bots. In this example, the RL bot was fighting against one rule-based bot, and two bots that moved around the environment but could not shoot. The purpose of including bots that could not fight back was to give the RL bot a chance to experience combat without the risk of being killed straight away during the early phases of the learning process. The bot was given three sensors that were similar to those used in the navigation experiment and defined regions to its left, front, and right. Each sensor indicated whether or not there was a bot in sight, and, if there was, how far away it was. A fourth sensor was provided that classified the bot's health as low or high.

So that multiple actions could occur at the same time, we defined actions for the combat controller by interpreting the actions as initiations; for example, move forward was interpreted as meaning start moving forward. The actions of the combat controller included all of those that were available to the navigation controller with the addition of being able to move backward, strafe left and right, shoot, stop moving, and stop turning. During combat, the ultimate goal is to survive the fight and kill the enemy. Guide rewards were therefore used to encourage these behaviors by rewarding accurate shots and punishing being hit. Table 7.6.4 provides a list of the goals and rewards that were chosen for the combat experiment.

Table 7.6.4 Goals and Rewards for Combat Task

Goal	Reward
Killing another bot	+1.0
Killed by another bot	−1.0
Shot an enemy	+0.0002
Shot by an enemy	−0.000002

Multiple experiments were automatically run with the same combinations of parameters as were used in the navigation experiment, but each game was run for 5,000 frames. These frames were only counted when combat was actually in progress, so the total length of the combat controller experiments was longer than the navigation controller experiments even though the number of iterations that were experienced by the learning algorithm was smaller. To further mitigate this effect, a small open map was used for the combat experiment to maximize the amount of time that combat was in progress. Rewards from the training games were recorded, and a subset of the best and worst cases is displayed in Figure 7.6.3. The first three columns in the figure represent the performance that was achieved without any learning, when behavior was determined by the initial policy.

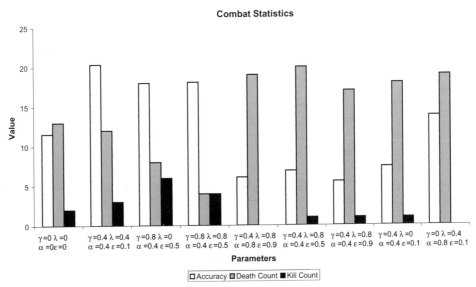

FIGURE 7.6.3 Rewards of trained combat bots with different parameters and random seed 100.

The parameter values $\gamma = 0.8$, $\lambda = 0.0$, $\alpha = 0.4$, and $\varepsilon = 0.5$ produced the highest kill rate, whereas the values $\gamma = 0.8$, $\lambda = 0.8$, $\alpha = 0.4$, and $\varepsilon = 0.5$ produced good accuracy while also being able to avoid being shot by the enemy, as evidenced by the low death count. Both of these parameter sets have nonzero discount factors, and the latter adds an eligibility trace to accelerate the learning of sequences of actions. This suggests that the ability to learn sequences of actions might be useful in achieving high accuracy and a reasonable kill rate.

The experiment with parameters $\gamma = 0.4$, $\lambda = 0.4$, $\alpha = 0.4$, and $\varepsilon = 0.1$ produced the highest hit accuracy, medium death count, and medium kill count. As seen in Figure 7.6.3, the worst RL bots performed worse than when no learning had occurred. It is not immediately obvious why this should have happened, but it is likely that 5,000 iterations were insufficient for the bots to learn effective behaviors. Examining the policy dynamics supported this idea by revealing that the values of many state-action pairs were still changing significantly at the end of the experiments. Running the combat controller experiments for significantly longer might therefore produce better results.

Although we decided to allow the bot to perform multiple actions simultaneously by interpreting them as action initiations, this might have complicated the learning process because the bot had no way of knowing what it was doing when deciding what to do next because that information was not included in the state representation. Furthermore, the bot also had no access to information about its proximity to obstacles and hence could easily become trapped. Although the bots in this setup struggled to compete with the bots that could fire back, they were able to learn some key aspects of combat, such as turning toward the enemy and shooting, and strafing haphazardly when under fire.

Conclusion

This article has shown how RL can be used to learn low-level behaviors for deathmatch-style FPS bots. The advantage of using RL is that the bots are able to learn how to play through their own experience. Our example experiments have shown bots learning by playing against other bots, and this demonstrates one of RL's most appealing features: that it should, theoretically, require less of a developer's time to create and balance bot behaviors with the help of RL, as well as make it possible for sophisticated emergent behaviors to arise that had not been anticipated by the developers.

RL isn't without its drawbacks, however. The developer must design a state representation rich enough for the bot to learn complex behaviors but simple enough that they can be learned quickly; a set of rewards must be designed that encourages desirable behaviors and punishes those that must be avoided; and the many parameters that control the learning process need to be set so that learning proceeds smoothly and converges on useful behaviors. Each of these might require multiple experiments and significant amounts of computer time. Despite these problems, RL has great potential in the field of FPS bot AI, and this article has demonstrated some of what can be achieved.

References

[Manslow04] Manslow, John, "Using Reinforcement Learning to Solve AI Control Problems." *AI Game Programming Wisdom 2*, Charles River Media, 2004.

[Sutton98] Sutton, Richard S., et al., *Reinforcement Learning: An Introduction*. The MIT Press, 1998.

[Watkins92] Watkins, Christopher J., et al., "Q-learning." *Machine Learning*, Vol. 8, (1992): pp. 279–292.

About the CD-ROM

This book's CD-ROM contains source code and demos that demonstrate the techniques described in the book. Every attempt has been made to ensure that the source code is bug-free and that it will compile easily. Please refer to the Web site *www.aiwisdom.com* for errata and updates.

Contents

The source code and demos included on this CD-ROM are contained in a hierarchy of subdirectories based on section name and article number. Source code and listings from the book are included. At each author's discretion, a complete demo or video is sometimes included. Demos were compiled using Microsoft Visual C++ 2005. Executables for each demo are also included.

Related Web sites

There are many Web resources for game developers. Here are a few of the best:

AIWisdom: The home of this book is also a great place to research published game AI techniques. AIWisdom.com features the only online listing of game AI articles and techniques written for books, magazines, conferences, and the Web. Article titles and their abstracts can be searched by topic, genre, or resource. The Web site is at *www.aiwisdom.com*.

IntroGameDev: IntroGameDev.com is a more comprehensive version of AIWisdom.com that lists over 1000 articles addressing all topics within game development, such as graphics, physics, architecture, artificial intelligence, game design, production, and asset creation. The Web site is at *www.introgamedev.com*.

GameAI: GameAI.com is a great place to go for tons of info and links on game AI. The Web site is at *www.gameai.com*.

Game/AI: Game/AI is a blog co-written by six game-industry veterans. The Web site is at *www.ai-blog.net*.

AIGameDev: AIGameDev.com has interesting articles and opinions on the state of game AI. The Web site is at *www.aigamedev.com*.

AI-Depot: AI-Depot.com fosters its own AI community by providing articles, news, and message boards. The Web site is at *www.ai-depot.com*.

AI-Junkie: AI-Junkie.com contains interesting AI articles by Mat Buckland. The Web site is at *www.ai-junkie.com*.

Generation5: Generation 5 covers interesting developments and news stories from the field of AI. It also has sections covering interviews, books, programs, software, and competitions. Of particular value are the AI solutions page, the discussion boards, and the great AI glossary section. The Web site is at *www.generation5.org*.

GDConf: The Game Developers Conference is currently held every year in San Jose, California (USA). Their Web site is at *www.gdconf.com*.

GDMag: *Game Developer Magazine* is an asset to the game development industry and includes advice for all aspects of game development, including AI. It is published monthly, and you might be able to subscribe for free in the U.S. if you're a professional developer. Source code from their articles can be found on their Web site at *www.gdmag.com*.

Gamasutra: Gamasutra is the Web equivalent of GDMag. It publishes some of the articles from *Game Developer Magazine* as well as articles written specifically for the Web site. Gamasutra also includes industry news, community chat areas, job listings, and a variety of other useful services. Find Gamasutra at *www.gamasutra.com*.

GameDev: GameDev features news, discussions, contests, tutorials, and links for game developers. Find GameDev at *www.gamedev.net*.

International Game Developers Association: The IGDA is a non-profit association dedicated to linking together game developers around the globe and encouraging the sharing of information among them. Their Web site is *www.igda.org*.

Next Generation: Next Generation is a daily news site for the games industry, based on the former magazine of the same name. Find Next Generation at *www.next-gen.biz*.

Games Industry: GamesIndustry.biz is a Web site specializing in press releases and news stories from the games industry. Find their Web site at *www.gamesindustry.biz*.

Blue's News: Blue's News features daily PC game news, no matter how obscure. Not necessarily for game developers, but it gives insight into what game developers are working on. Find Blue's News at *www.bluesnews.com*.

Penny Arcade: Penny Arcade features comics and commentary on the games industry, with dead-on accuracy. Find Penny Arcade at *www.penny-arcade.com*.

INDEX

License Agreement/Notice of Limited Warranty

By opening the sealed disc container in this book, you agree to the following terms and conditions. If, upon reading the following license agreement and notice of limited warranty, you cannot agree to the terms and conditions set forth, return the unused book with unopened disc to the place where you purchased it for a refund.

License:

The enclosed software is copyrighted by the copyright holder(s) indicated on the software disc. You are licensed to copy the software onto a single computer for use by a single user and to a backup disc. You may not reproduce, make copies, or distribute copies or rent or lease the software in whole or in part, except with written permission of the copyright holder(s). You may transfer the enclosed disc only together with this license, and only if you destroy all other copies of the software and the transferee agrees to the terms of the license. You may not decompile, reverse assemble, or reverse engineer the software.

Notice of Limited Warranty:

The enclosed disc is warranted by Course Technology to be free of physical defects in materials and workmanship for a period of sixty (60) days from end user's purchase of the book/disc combination. During the sixty-day term of the limited warranty, Course Technology will provide a replacement disc upon the return of a defective disc.

Limited Liability:

THE SOLE REMEDY FOR BREACH OF THIS LIMITED WARRANTY SHALL CONSIST ENTIRELY OF REPLACEMENT OF THE DEFECTIVE DISC. IN NO EVENT SHALL COURSE TECHNOLOGY OR THE AUTHOR BE LIABLE FOR ANY OTHER DAMAGES, INCLUDING LOSS OR CORRUPTION OF DATA, CHANGES IN THE FUNCTIONAL CHARACTERISTICS OF THE HARDWARE OR OPERATING SYSTEM, DELETERIOUS INTERACTION WITH OTHER SOFTWARE, OR ANY OTHER SPECIAL, INCIDENTAL, OR CONSEQUENTIAL DAMAGES THAT MAY ARISE, EVEN IF COURSE TECHNOLOGY AND/OR THE AUTHOR HAS PREVIOUSLY BEEN NOTIFIED THAT THE POSSIBILITY OF SUCH DAMAGES EXISTS.

Disclaimer of Warranties:

COURSE TECHNOLOGY AND THE AUTHOR SPECIFICALLY DISCLAIM ANY AND ALL OTHER WARRANTIES, EITHER EXPRESS OR IMPLIED, INCLUDING WARRANTIES OF MERCHANTABILITY, SUITABILITY TO A PARTICULAR TASK OR PURPOSE, OR FREEDOM FROM ERRORS. SOME STATES DO NOT ALLOW FOR EXCLUSION OF IMPLIED WARRANTIES OR LIMITATION OF INCIDENTAL OR CONSEQUENTIAL DAMAGES, SO THESE LIMITATIONS MIGHT NOT APPLY TO YOU.

Other:

This Agreement is governed by the laws of the State of Massachusetts without regard to choice of law principles. The United Convention of Contracts for the International Sale of Goods is specifically disclaimed. This Agreement constitutes the entire agreement between you and Course Technology regarding use of the software.